Tragedy: Texts and Commentary

TRAGEDY

❧ Texts and Commentary ❧

Edited, with an introduction and comments, by

MORRIS FREEDMAN

UNIVERSITY OF MARYLAND

CHARLES SCRIBNER'S SONS

New York

CONTENTS

CONTENTS

INTRODUCTION

 Tragedy has been a challenge to the great writers and philosophers of the western world from the time of the ancient Greeks to the present. "Men in highest dignity," Milton remarked in his preface to *Samson Agonistes,* "have labour'd not a little to be thought able to compose a Tragedy." And Aristotle was only the first, although still the foremost, in a long line of critic-philosophers to attempt a definition of the character and effect of tragedy. Tragedy, as Milton put it, "hath been ever held the gravest, moralest, and most profitable of all other Poems." It has quite properly captured the creative and critical imagination of western man. Tragedy has not only always been thought to please in some way, it has also been thought, at its best, to teach, deeply and firmly.

Earlier critics discussed tragedy in large part in terms of form, effect, persons, and tone, but not necessarily including each of these or giving each equal emphasis. Thus, Aristotle, who inspired so much later commentary, offered the following descriptions of tragedy, based principally on the works of Sophocles: the time is limited to a day; tragedy records an "imitation" of a serious action of some magnitude; the action has a beginning, middle, and end, properly proportioned; plot is more important than characterization (although the hero is usually the victim of *hamartia,* sin, or of *hubris,* an excess of pride or of both); it includes (1.) "peripety," a reversal of fortune, (2.) "discovery," a significant new realization, (3.) "suffering," and (4.) a descent from happiness to misery. The effect of tragedy is to rouse pity and fear with an accompanying purgation, or catharsis. The persons of tragedy have to be good, consistent, and superior. It is sometimes forgotten or obscured that Aristotle's discussion in his *Poetics* was *descriptive,* that is, limited to what the Greek tragedians did, rather than *prescriptive,* laying down rules for future writers. (The Aristotelian material is obviously much simplified in this paragraph.)

Later critics and writers of tragedies, especially during the Renaissance, codified the rules of tragedy making them into laws, and applied them strictly. Professor Joel Spingarn, in his *A History of Literary Criticism in the Renaissance,* Second edition (New York, 1930); pages 66-67, for example, summarized the differences that had emerged between comedy and tragedy. These indicate how crystallized the criticism of tragedy had become, a crystallization that over the years emerged, more or less, as the traditional description which later critics accepted as their point of departure, implicitly or explicitly:

"i. The characters in tragedy are kings, princes, or great leaders; those in comedy are humble persons and private citizens.

"ii. Tragedy deals with great and terrible actions; comedy with familiar and domestic actions.

"iii. Tragedy begins happily and ends terribly; comedy begins rather turbulently and ends joyfully.

"iv. The style and diction of tragedy are elevated and sublime; while those of comedy are humble and colloquial.

"v. The subjects of tragedy are generally historical; those of comedy are always invented by the poet.

"vi. Comedy deals largely with love and seduction; tragedy with exile and bloodshed."

To complete this list of rules, we may add the injunction against mixing comic and tragic elements as well as the one on observing the unities. Milton, for example, wrote (1671) of "the Poet's error of intermixing Comic stuff with Tragic sadness and gravity; of introducing trivial and vulgar persons, which by all judicious hath been counted absurd; and brought in without discretion, corruptly to gratify the people." And Crites, a character in John Dryden's *Essay of Dramatic Poesy* (1668), spoke approvingly and succinctly of "The Three Unities, which ought to be observed in every regular play: namely of Time, Place, and Action."

"The Unity of Time," Crites went on, the French writers "comprehend in twenty-four hours, the compass of a natural day, or as near as it can be contrived; and the reason of it is obvious to every one,—that the time of the feigned action, or fable of the play, should be proportioned as near as can be to the direction of that time in which it is represented. . . .

"For the second Unity, which is that of Place, the Ancients meant by it, that the scene ought to be continued through the play, in the same place where it was laid in the beginning: for, the stage on which it is represented being but one and the same place, it is unnatural to conceive it many,—and those far distant from one another. . . .

"As for the third Unity, which is that of Action, the Ancients meant no other by it than [that] the poet is to aim at one great and complete action, to the carrying on of which all things in his play, even the very obstacles, are to be subservient. . . . For two actions, equally laboured and driven on by the writer, would destroy the unity of the poem; it would be no longer one play, but two. . . ."

In the last century or so, the consideration of tragedy has become much more general, esthetic, philosophical, psychological, and anthropological. Even the Aristotelian approach has been much modulated and expanded, especially in the sophisticated applications and analyses of

William Arrowsmith and Gerald F. Else. Nietzsche in *The Birth of Tragedy,* suggested that tragedy blended the "Apollonian," the intellectual, with the "Dionysiac," the emotional; Frye, that, archetypally, tragedy is a "mimesis of sacrifice." Steiner, in *The Death of Tragedy,* traced the transformation of tragedy, in form and substance, from the Greek world to the present. Scheler and Jaspers, in different ways, spoke of the tragic hero becoming "guilty" while doing something in itself "guiltless." Auden distinguished between Greek tragedy as the "tragedy of necessity" and Christian tragedy as that of "possibility." Martz considered the problem of the saint as tragic hero. Miller proposed a tragedy of the "common man." Langer described what she called a "tragic rhythm." Krutch, in "The Tragic Fallacy," contended that "every real tragedy . . . is an affirmation of faith in life." Sewall emphasized the element of primitive "un-reason" in the tragic vision. Abel argued that tragedy should conceptually be defined by comparison with what he described as "meta-theatre," a work in which man tries to shape his destiny rather than live out a destiny shaped for him by someone or something. All of these positions, and many others, have in recent years become part of the voluminously expanding library of available comment on tragedy.

It is best to begin—and to conclude—the study of tragedy by way of the texts themselves, through the very sources which critics have used as evidence for their theories. In the history of literature, the attempt to apply narrow definitions of form or determinants of value to a work of art has led to a mechanical reading, to what Arrowsmith, a modern translator of Euripides and a leading critic of Greek tragedy, has called a "crude or vulgar Aristotelianism." We must look at the words first before we determine the laws.

Toward the end of James Joyce's *The Portrait of the Artist as a Young Man,* Stephen Dedalus, the hero, engages in a long disquisition comparing the lyrical, the epical, and the dramatic in literature. He concludes that the dramatic is the highest form, for in the dramatic, "the personality of the artist, at first a cry or a cadence or a mood and then a fluid and lambent narrative, finally refines itself out of existence, impersonalises itself, so to speak. . . . The artist, like the God of the creation, remains within or beyond or above his handiwork, invisible, refined out of existence, indifferent, paring his fingernails." In short, drama is superior to lyric or epic because it is least subjective; the intention of the author is never made explicit; the action speaks for itself.

Certainly one of the great attractions of tragedy, even on the stage, is that the action does live itself out, apparently without the manipulation or intercession of author or any other intermediary. Joyce was emphasizing the objectivity of drama. There is no author in drama to comment on action or character, as in the epic or novel; what the people say or do is not what the author himself might say or do, as in a lyric. A play with all of its people and events has an existence quite independent from that of the author. Sometimes, the author—let alone a critic or a philosopher—is the last person to consult about the intention of the play. The play speaks for itself, and may not always say precisely what the author wanted it to. "What I have said, I have said," Ibsen is supposed to have replied to persistent questions about what he meant with one of his plays.

Perhaps all this is so plain that it need scarcely be said, much less labored. Yet a produced play cannot ever be as objective, as free of control, as Joyce said drama in the abstract is. If the author is not always present in the theater next to one's elbow, whispering in one's ear, turning one's head this way or that, then certainly everyone else connected with a play is, from the composer of the incidental music to the director of lighting. For a produced play is more than the reading and acting out of the text; it is a spectacle of which all the elements speak to us. Surely one of the elements that made so memorable one performance by Orson Welles of Dr. Faustus was the genuine agony he projected, presumably because of his fear of eternal damnation; he was actually playing the last scenes with a broken ankle.

Nor should we forget that when we go to the theater, we engage in a communal ritual; we submit ourselves to becoming part of an audience; we respond as a member of a group. Drama, as we know, has its origin in religious rite. Both in pagan and medieval times, productions of drama were consciously intended to develop a community response, to evoke awe and piety, to "purge" or instruct the viewers, or otherwise to transform or affect them.

A produced play always invites a collaboration between the audience and the business on the stage. We never suspend our disbelief in the theater in quite the same way or so thoroughly as when *reading* a novel or poem or play. Very well aware of this, Pirandello has used this continuum between play and audience to construct some of his most meaningful works, exploring not only the areas where reality and appearance blend, but, more significantly, the interaction between reality and appearance, the effect of a play and the players on the audience, and of the audience on the play and players. Indeed, *Henry IV* is an examination of the dangers inherent in excessive role playing, in extending and prolonging the theatrical mode as a means of coping with a difficult reality.

A dramatic performance is a conspiracy, then, to affect the members of an audience in every way possible. If the spoken words alone and the movements will not communicate sufficiently or with just the right modulation of intention, then music may be added, or lighting, or details in setting. An enormous tree, O'Neill tells us, broods maternally and heavily over the house in *Desire Under the Elms*. The bleak, harsh extremes of Strindberg's *The Father* would undoubtedly be emphasized by extreme blacks and whites.

Yet while we may be pleased and instructed in various ways by the performance of a play, it remains for us to read the text to understand it and to enjoy it fully as a work of literature. No matter how many

times we see *Othello,* we always go back to the text, often indeed provoked by a performance to do so, to look at the words again, to linger
over a phrase, a sentence, a speech, a scene. "I have never found an
acquaintance with a dramatist founded on the theatre alone," Shaw
wrote, "a really intimate and accurate one." This is surely obvious to
anyone who has seen, say, Laurence Olivier's *Oedipus* and *then* read
Sophocles, or his *Othello* and *then* read Shakespeare. We are tremendously moved by Olivier's passion, but for understanding Sophocles, for
understanding Shakespeare, in order to add the response of the mind
to that of our senses, we must go to the bare bones of the text. This is
especially so when we see a verse drama or listen to poetry. We may let
ourselves be carried away in the theater or lecture hall, but it is to the
library, to the text, that we finally go to find the intellectual source for
our response.

If a play belongs in any sense to the domain of literature, of writing,
it is elementary that it does so because of the words on the page. The
history of dramatic production is replete with instances of plays that
went through hundreds of performances and are now largely forgotten
except for their antiquarian interest. The history of dramatic performance is not identical with that of dramatic literature. One needs to *read*
drama to understand, appreciate, evaluate fully and meaningfully. This
is perhaps an academic reason for reading drama. We don't always
read simply to understand, appreciate, and evaluate; we read for
pleasure. We read for an edification not too different in its effect from
that we expect when exposing ourselves to a performance of a drama.
What does reading drama offer in and of itself, without regard to a
performance?

If a poor play can appear to be better than it is, the converse is also
true: a play when read cannot ever be spoiled in the same way as it can
be when performed poorly. A performance must by its very nature be
a specific critical comment: it limits (or enlarges) interpretation of
character and event and relationship according to the particular notions
of actor and director; it substitutes immediate response for thoughtful
rumination since it must move on relentlessly; while it may open new
horizons in the text for us, it must also constrict them since it must
always choose: Oedipus or Othello can never be in a single performance all the many things they are to us, simultaneously and legitimately,
in the text. Lorca on the page is poetry; on stage, at best, ballet.

In a sense a play, before it is a work of art, is a document. It is a
record in dialogue of the confrontation between certain types of persons in certain situations. No doubt what fascinates us in reading the
transcript of a trial or of a Congressional hearing or of any exchange
that takes place in the formal, social, public working out of our daily
affairs is the same thing that holds our attention in reading a play: we
are present when people talk out their relationships, reveal their characters in their words alone. It is this documentary aspect of drama
which is of the essence of that objectivity of which Joyce spoke.

Ibsen's *Ghosts*, Strindberg's *The Father*, Chekhov's *Three Sisters*, Betti's *Corruption in the Palace of Justice*, each has an adequate documentary validity to make it serve as evidence of a sociological and historical situation: the changing role of woman in nineteenth century Europe; the decay of Russian aristocratic society preceding the revolution; the moral confusions in modern politics. The challenge to the artist, his peculiar problem in shaping this material, is to make of what appears to be mere document—a record of actuality with all of its whimsy, accident, inevitability, and hardness—a shaped work of art. A play must simultaneously and unmistakably appear to be both the piece of marble found in the quarry and also the work of art the sculptor fashioned.

And where else but in the unadorned document, that is, in the text of the play which we read and examine by ourselves, can we find the purity of the art-document? The playwright works with the poetry inherent in sheer statement, in sheer colloquy, and even when he works in verse, it is not so much in the language that we find the poetry (although, of course, we may extract the poetry from the dramatic moment), it is still in the declaration in its environment. However, affecting Othello's final speech may be in isolation, we are far more responsive to its import in the dramatic context, as a revelation of his feeling and thought at a particular time in the progress of events. We respond completely, I would say, only to the documentary revelation of the speech, that is to say, to its total *literary* impact.

If tragedy, then, may be argued to be a greater literary form than lyric or epic, it can only be so in terms of the text, for whatever is added to a text through a performance may be just what is present in lyric and epic: the personal and subjective, the individual and transient. And the reading of a play need not only precede seeing it; it should follow as well; seeing drama should be an aid to reading drama. Reading is the final and complete way for apprehending tragedy.

Drama which has met some of the expectations of tragedy has varied enormously over the centuries, in form, effect, persons, and tone. A continuing critical problem has simply been distinguishing among sorts of tragedy. The adjectives classifying tragedy are manifold: heroic, bourgeois, classical, Senecan, Christian, Shakespearean, social, domestic, tragicomic; critics have attempted to separate melodrama, black comedy, and morality, among other forms, from tragedy. Some recent writers have extended the territory of study to include non-dramatic works, the novels of Dostoyevsky and of Faulkner, for example. An important group has studied tragedy as a problem in theology or in existence.

We do not have and are not likely ever to get any single formula, a fixed check-list, a collection of definitions, that would reduce the problems to compact dimensions of what is or is not tragedy, of what is or is not a "great" or even a "good" tragedy, or even of what kind of tragedy a particular work may be, if it is indeed a tragedy at all. The critics, the philosophers, and, above all, the dramatists themselves continue to enlarge and refine our sense of what tragedy has been and of what it might be. It is futile to hope to settle the issue except in a tentative and qualified way, and sometimes only for a particular work, or group of works, at a particular time and in a particular place. We shall, of course, continue to settle and resettle and unsettle the question of tragedy as part of conscious, examined living, as part of carrying on a civilized dialogue about serious matters. The continuing study of tragedy is not less than the informed study of mortal life.

This volume ranges from the Greek world to the present in its gathering of plays that in some meaningful way may be thought of as tragedy. The individual introductions relate the texts to one another and suggest other reading for illumination. A select bibliography lists readily available critical material and several collections of plays and essays.

Since this is an introductory volume ranging across periods and languages, it seemed particularly important to offer texts that provided the least difficulties and the greatest pleasures in reading, texts which would at the same time be faithful to the original in word and spirit. The texts written originally in English are based on authoritative modern editions that reflect both recent and traditional scholarship. Textual footnotes, so important to the examination of a play as part of an author's total work or as reflecting a period, are here dispensed with as not significantly necessary in the reading of tragedy as a genre.

Translation as a discipline and art has made significant advances in recent years, including the production of two collections of critical essays examining the peculiar problems. (*The Craft and Context of Translation,* ed. William Arrowsmith and Roger Shattuck [New York, 1964]; *On Translation,* ed. Reuben A. Brower, [Oxford, 1966]). The translations in this volume were selected on the basis of their fidelity to the spirit of tragedy in the original work as well as their intrinsic worth as literature. Mere contemporaneity of language, idiom, and form was not the main guide. Thus, William Archer's solid, no-nonsense, and respectful translation of Ibsen's *Ghosts,* which introduced that play to the English speaking world, seemed to be more faithful, in small turns of speech and in the larger texture, to its original Victorian atmosphere than later versions, in which some phrases are more naturally "modern," easier for actors to speak today, but not so faithful in nuance to the original, or versions in which the text is the result of a careful scholarly collation of all early copies and editions. On the other hand, Robert Lowell's very recent rendition of Racine's *Phaedra* seemed to offer the best blending of intelligent contemporary poetry with the French Neo-Classical virtues. Serious students may wish to undertake the analytical comparison of translations of a particular work as a means of determining its essential character; see Brower's "Seven Agamemnons" in his book cited above.

A collection of this kind is long in conception. I want to thank my teachers, colleagues, and students who have contributed to this project, in one way or another, over the years. Particular gratitude is owed to Miss Bess Earp, formerly of the University of New Mexico, for her meticulous and extensive editorial collaboration; to Professor Joseph Wood Krutch, then at Columbia University, who first taught me some of the complexities and pleasures to be found in the serious reading of drama; to Professors Edith Buchanan and Katherine Simons, of the University of New Mexico, who favored me with their gracious learning; to Professors Hoyt Trowbridge, Franklin Dickey, and Dudley Wynn, who introduced and supported courses in tragedy at the University of New Mexico, both on the undergraduate and graduate levels; to my students in English 675 at the University of New Mexico and in English 244 at the University of Maryland; to my colleagues Mrs. Carolyn Banks, Miss Mary Slayton, and Professor Denzell Smith of the University of Maryland; and to Mrs. Carolyn Tranum for her patience and fortitude with my manuscript. I am alone responsible for all shortcomings.

MORRIS FREEDMAN

University of Maryland
College Park, Maryland

Agamemnon

AESCHYLUS

COMMENTARY

 Aeschylus (525-456 B. C.), an Athenian aristocrat, fought at Maramon and probably at Salamis, where the Greeks defeated the Persians both times. Around 500 B. C., he began his career as a writer of tragedy; before he died, he wrote over eighty plays, of which seven have survived: *The Suppliants, The Persians, Prometheus Bound, Seven Against Thebes,* and the *Oresteia* trilogy: *Agamemnon, The Libation-Bearers,* and *The Eumenides.* All were probably written between 490 and 458 B. C.

Writing about *Agamemnon* in "The Criticism of Greek Tragedy" (in *Tragedy: Vision and Form,* ed. Robert W. Corrigan, originally in *Tulane Drama Review,* III, 3 [March 1959], 31-57), William Arrowsmith emphasizes its moral complexity. He speaks of the play as "a nightmare of justice." Agamemnon, who sacrificed his own daughter Iphigeneia to the gods, himself becomes a victim on his return from victory. Agamemnon's fate seems determined as much by the morally disordered world in which he lives as by his own pride. Not Agamemnon, not Clytemnestra, commit any act worse than the gods themselves commit.

The tragedy in Aeschylus, then, has roots not only in the nature of the principal characters but in the nature of their world. That world would seem to have a different order from the worlds of Sophocles and Euripides, and the nature of the tragedy, consequently, would also differ. Clytemnestra ought to be compared with Medea, Agamemnon with Oedipus, in any attempt to define the differences in the tragic tone, the tragic import, of the three Greek dramatists. Agamemnon in his relations to Clytemnestra and his family might also be considered in the company of Strindberg's captain in *The Father* in any effort to examine tragic climates separated by centuries.

How might you stage the play to bring out your particular reading? Would masks emphasizing character, for example, be helpful in making a point or harmful? Would a "concert reading," actors sitting on stools, dressed in modern clothes, and reading from scripts, do the text justice?

Aeschylus

AGAMEMNON

Translated by Louis MacNeice

INTRODUCTION

(i) The Family Tree

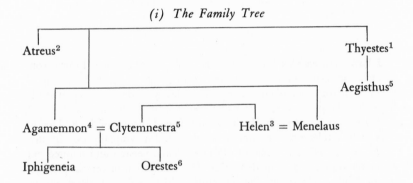

(ii) The Chain of Crimes

Two brothers, Agamemnon and Menelaus, were kings of Argos. They married two sisters, Clytemnestra and Helen; each married to his cost. On the Greek view Helen and Clytemnestra were not just bad women; they were agents rather than creators of evil. Nobody on this view is either simply a protagonist of evil or simply a victim of circumstance. The family is physically, and therefore morally, a unit: the same blood runs in all, and through it descends an inherited responsibility which limits, without wholly destroying, the power of choice in each. The sins of the fathers are visited on the children, so the children are victims of circumstance. But the children, because they are of the same blood, are tempted to sin in their turn. If a man holds such a view he will

Aeschylus, *Agamemnon,* trans. Louis MacNeice. By permission of Faber and Faber, Ltd., London, and Harcourt, Brace & World, Inc., New York.

tend simultaneously to vindicate the ways of God and kick against the pricks of chance. It is this paradox that gives tension to a play like the Agamemnon. Here we have a chain of crimes, one leading on to another from generation to generation by a logic immanent in the blood and working through it. But the cause of the crimes, not only of the first link, the first crime, but present in every one of them, is the principle of Evil which logic cannot comprehend.

The chain of crimes in this play is as follows (see Family Tree above):

Past

(1) Thyestes seduced Atreus' wife.

(2) Atreus killed Thyestes' young children and gave him them as meat.

(3 Helen forsook her husband and went to Troy with Paris.

(4) Agamemnon, to promote the Trojan War, sacrificed his daughter Iphigeneia.

Present

(5) Aegisthus and Clytemnestra murder Agamemnon.

Future

(6) Orestes will kill Aegisthus and his mother Clytemnestra.

(iii)

I have written this translation primarily for the stage. I have consciously sacrificed certain things in the original—notably the liturgical flavor of the diction and the metrical complexity of the choruses. It is my hope that the play emerges as a play and not as a museum piece.

My thanks are very much due to my friend, Professor E. R. Dodds, who, with a tolerance rare among scholars and a sympathy rare in anyone, read through the whole of my unacademic version and pointed out to me its more culpable inadequacies. The translation of certain passages is our joint product; but for the faults which remain I alone am responsible.

                                                    LOUIS MACNEICE

CHARACTERS

WATCHMAN
CHORUS *of old men of the city of Argos*
CLYTEMNESTRA, *wife of Agamemnon*
HERALD
AGAMEMNON, *king of Argos*
CASSANDRA, *a prophetess, daughter of King Priam of Troy*
AEGISTHUS, *the paramour or lover of Clytemnestra*

SCENE. *A space in front of the palace of Agamemnon in Argos.
Night. A* WATCHMAN *on the roof of the palace.*

WATCHMAN: The gods it is I ask to release me from this watch
A year's length now, spending my nights like a dog,
Watching on my elbow on the roof of the sons of Atreus
So that I have come to know the assembly of the nightly stars
Those which bring storm and those which bring summer to men,
The shining Masters riveted in the sky—
I know the decline and rising of those stars.
And now I am waiting for the sign of the beacon,
The flame of fire that will carry the report from Troy,
News of her taking. Which task has been assigned me
By a woman of sanguine heart but a man's mind.
Yet when I take my restless rest in the soaking dew,
My night not visited with dreams—
For fear stands by me in the place of sleep
That I cannot firmly close my eyes in sleep—
Whenever I think to sing or hum to myself
As an antidote to sleep, then every time I groan
And fall to weeping for the fortunes of this house
Where not as before are things well ordered now.
But now may a good chance fall, escape from pain,
The good news visible in the midnight fire.

(*Pause. A light appears, gradually increasing, the light of the beacon.*)

Ha! I salute you, torch of the night whose light
Is like the day, an earnest of many dances
In the city of Argos, celebration of Peace.
I call to Agamemnon's wife; quickly to rise
Out of her bed and in the house to raise
Clamor of joy in answer to this torch
For the city of Troy is taken—
Such is the evident message of the beckoning flame.
And I myself will dance my solo first
For I shall count my master's fortune mine
Now that this beacon has thrown me a lucky throw.
And may it be when he comes, the master of this house,
That I grasp his hand in my hand.
As to the rest, I am silent. A great ox, as they say,
Stands on my tongue. The house itself, if it took voice,
Could tell the case most clearly. But I will only speak
To those who know. For the others I remember nothing.

(*Enter* CHORUS *of old men. During the
following chorus the day begins to dawn.*)

CHORUS: The tenth year it is since
      Priam's high
Adversary, Menelaus the king
And Agamemnon, the double-throned and
      sceptred
Yoke of the sons of Atreus
Ruling in fee from God,
From this land gathered an Argive army
On a mission of war a thousand ships,
Their hearts howling in boundless blood-
      lust
In eagles' fashion who in lonely
Grief for nestlings above their homes hang
Turning in cycles
Beating the air with the oars of their
      wings,
      Now to no purpose
      Their love and task of attention.
But above there is One,
Maybe Pan, maybe Zeus or Apollo,
Who hears the harsh cries of the birds
Guests in his kingdom,
Wherefore, though late, in requital
He sends the Avenger.
Thus Zeus our master
Guardian of guest and of host
Sent against Paris the sons of Atreus
For a woman of many men
Many the dog-tired wrestlings
Limbs and knees in the dust pressed—
      For both the Greeks and Trojans
      An overture of breaking spears.

Things are where they are, will finish
In the manner fated and neither
Fire beneath nor oil above can soothe
The stubborn anger of the unburnt offer-
      ing.
As for us, our bodies are bankrupt,
The expedition left us behind
And we wait supporting on sticks
Our strength—the strength of a child;
For the marrow that leaps in a boy's body
Is no better than that of the old
For the War God is not in his body;

While the man who is very old
And his leaf withering away
Goes on the three-foot way
No better than a boy, and wanders
A dream in the middle of the day.

But you, daughter of Tyndareus,
Queen Clytemnestra,
What is the news, what is the truth, what
      have you learnt,
On the strength of whose word have you
      thus
Sent orders for sacrifice round?
All the gods, the gods of the town,
Of the worlds of Below and Above,
By the door, in the square,
Have their altars ablaze with your gifts,
From here, from there, all sides, all cor-
      ners.
Sky-high leap the flame-jets fed
By gentle and undeceiving
Persuasion of sacred unguent,
Oil from the royal stores.
Of these things tell
That which you can, that which you may,
Be healer of this our trouble
Which at times torments with evil
Though at times by propitiations
A shining hope repels
The insatiable thought upon grief
Which is eating away our hearts.
Of the omen which powerfully speeded
That voyage of strong men, by God's
      grace even I
Can tell, my age can still
Be galvanized to breathe the strength of
      song,
To tell how the kings of all the youth of
      Greece
Two-throned by one in mind
Were launched with pike and punitive
      hand
Against the Trojan shore by angry birds.
Kings of the birds to our kings came,
One with a white rump, the other black,
Appearing near the palace on the spear-
      arm side

Where all could see them,
Tearing a pregnant hare with the unborn
      young
Foiled of their courses.
      Cry, cry upon Death; but may the good
      prevail.

But the diligent prophet of the army see-
      ing the sons
Of Atreus twin in temper knew
That the hare-killing birds were the two
Generals, explained it thus—
"In time this expedition sacks the town
Of Troy before whose towers
By Fate's force the public
Wealth will be wasted.
Only let not some spite from the gods
      benight the bulky battalions,
The bridle of Troy, nor strike them un-
      timely;
For the goddess feels pity, is angry
With the winged dogs of her father
Who killed the cowering hare with her
      unborn young;
Artemis hates the eagles' feast."
      Cry, cry upon Death; but may the good
      prevail.

"But though you are so kind, goddess,
To the little cubs of lions
And to all the suckling young of roving
      beasts
In whom your heart delights,
Fulfil us the signs of these things,
The signs which are good but open to
      blame,
And I call on Apollo the Healer
That his sister raise not against the Greeks
Unremitting gales to baulk their ships,
Hurrying on another kind of sacrifice,
      with no feasting,
Barbarous building of hates and disloyal-
      ties
Grown on the family. For anger grimly
      returns
Cunningly haunting the house, avenging
      the death

Of a child, never forgetting its due."
So cried the prophet—evil and good to-
      gether,
Fate that the birds foretold to the king's
      house.
In tune with this
      Cry, cry upon Death; but may the good
      prevail.
Zeus, whoever He is, if this
Be a name acceptable,
By this name I will call him.
There is no one comparable
When I reckon all of the case
Excepting Zeus, if ever I am to jettison
The barren care which clogs my heart.

Not He who formerly was great*
With brawling pride and mad for broils
Will even be said to have been.
And He who was next has met†
His match and is seen no more,
But Zeus is the name to cry in your
      triumph-song
And win the prize for wisdom.

Who setting us on the road
Made this a valid law—
      "That men must learn by suffering."
Drop by drop in sleep upon the heart
Falls the laborious memory of pain,
Against one's will comes wisdom;
The grace of the gods is forced on us
      Throned inviolably.

So at that time the elder
Chief of the Greek ships
Would not blame any prophet
Nor face the flail of fortune;
For unable to sail, the people
Of Greece were heavy with famine
Waiting in Aulis where the tides
      Flow back, opposite Chalcis.

But the winds that blew from the Stry-
      mon,
Bringing delay, hunger, evil harborage,

* Ouranos.   † Cronos.

Crazing men, rotting ships and cables,
By drawing out the time
Were shredding into nothing the flower
    of Argos,
When the prophet screamed a new
Cure for that bitter tempest
And heavier still for the chiefs,
Pleading the anger of Artemis so that the
    sons of Atreus
Beat the ground with their sceptres and
    shed tears.
Then the elder king found voice and an-
    swered:
"Heavy is my fate, not obeying,
And heavy it is if I kill my child, the
    delight of my house,
And with a virgin's blood upon the altar
Make foul her father's hands.
Either alternative is evil.
How can I betray the fleet
And fail the allied army?
It is right they should passionately cry for
    the winds to be lulled
By the blood of a girl. So be it. May it be
    well."

But when he had put on the halter of
    Necessity
Breathing in his heart a veering wind of
    evil
Unsanctioned, unholy, from that moment
    forward
He changed his counsel, would stop at
    nothing.
For the heart of man is hardened by in-
    fatuation,
A faulty adviser, the first link of sorrow.
Whatever the cause, he brought himself
    to slay
His daughter, an offering to promote the
    voyage
To a war for a runaway wife.

Her prayers and her cries of father,
Her life of a maiden,
Counted for nothing with those militarists;
But her father, having duly prayed, told
    the attendants

To lift her, like a goat, above the altar
With her robes falling about her,
To lift her boldly, her spirit fainting,
And hold back with a gag upon her lovely
    mouth
By the dumb force of a bridle
The cry which would curse the house.
Then dropping on the ground her saffron
    dress,
Glancing at each of her appointed
Sacrificers a shaft of pity,
Plain as in a picture she wished
To speak to them by name, for often
At her father's table where men feasted
She had sung in celebration for her father
With a pure voice, affectionately, virgin-
    ally,
The hymn for happiness at the third
    libation.
The sequel to this I saw not and tell not
But the crafts of Calchas gained their ob-
    ject.
To learn by suffering is the equation of
    Justice; the Future
Is known when it comes, let it go till then.
To know in advance is to sorrow in ad-
    vance.
The facts will appear with the shining of
    the dawn.

(*Enter* CLYTEMNESTRA)
But may good, at the least, follow after
As the queen here wishes, who stands
Nearest the throne, the only
    Defence of the land of Argos.
    LEADER OF THE CHORUS: I have come,
    Clytemnestra, reverencing your au-
    thority.
For it is right to honor our master's wife
When the man's own throne is empty.
But you, if you have heard good news for
    certain, or if
You sacrifice on the strength of flattering
    hopes,
I would gladly hear. Though I cannot
    cavil at silence.
    CLYTEMNESTRA: Bearing good news, as
    the proverb says, may Dawn

Spring from her mother Night.
You will hear something now that was
    beyond your hopes.
The men of Argos have taken Priam's city.

    LEADER: What! I cannot believe it. It
    escapes me.

    CLYTEMNESTRA: Troy in the hands of
    the Greeks. Do I speak plain?

    LEADER: Joy creeps over me, calling out
    my tears.

    CLYTEMNESTRA: Yes. Your eyes pro-
    claim your loyalty.

    LEADER: But what are your grounds?
    Have you a proof of it?

    CLYTEMNESTRA: There is proof indeed—
    unless God has cheated us.

    LEADER: Perhaps you believe the in-
    veigling shapes of dreams?

    CLYTEMNESTRA: I would not be credited
    with a dozing brain!

    LEADER: Or are you puffed up by
    Rumor, the wingless flyer?

    CLYTEMNESTRA: You mock my common
    sense as if I were a child.

    LEADER: But at what time was the city
    given to sack?

    CLYTEMNESTRA: In this very night that
    gave birth to this day.

    LEADER: What messenger could come so
    fast?

    CLYTEMNESTRA: Hephaestus, launching
    a fine flame from Ida,
Beacon forwarding beacon, despatch-
    riders of fire,
Ida relayed to Hermes' cliff in Lemnos
And the great glow from the island was
    taken over third
By the height of Athos that belongs to
    Zeus,
And towering then to straddle over the sea
The might of the running torch joyfully
    tossed
The gold gleam forward like another sun,
Herald of light to the heights of Mount
    Macistus,

And he without delay, nor carelessly by
    sleep
Encumbered, did not shirk his interme-
    diary role,
His farflung ray reached the Euripus' tides
And told Messapion's watchers, who in
    turn
Sent on the message further
Setting a stack of dried-up heather on fire.
And the strapping flame, not yet enfee-
    bled, leapt
Over the plain of Asopus like a blazing
    moon
And woke on the crags of Cithaeron
Another relay in the chain of fire.
The light that was sent from far was not
    declined
By the look-out men, who raised a fiercer
    yet,
A light which jumped the water of Gor-
    gopis
And to Mount Aegiplanctus duly come
Urged the reveille of the punctual fire.
So then they kindle it squanderingly and
    launch
A beard of flame big enough to pass
The headland that looks down upon the
    Saronic gulf,
Blazing and bounding till it reached at
    length
The Arachnaean steep, our neighbouring
    heights;
And leaps in the latter end on the roof of
    the sons of Atreus
Issue and image of the fire on Ida.
Such was the assignment of my torch-
    racers,
The task of each fulfilled by his successor,
And victor is he who ran both first and last.
Such is the proof I offer you, the sign
My husband sent me out of Troy.

    LEADER: To the gods, queen, I shall
    give thanks presently.
But I would like to hear this story further,
To wonder at it in detail from your lips.

    CLYTEMNESTRA: The Greeks hold Troy
    upon this day.

The cries in the town I fancy do not
mingle.
Pour oil and vinegar into the same jar,
You would say they stand apart unlov-
ingly;
Of those who are captured and those who
have conquered
Distinct are the sounds of their diverse
fortunes,
For *these* having flung themselves about
the bodies
Of husbands and brothers, or sons upon
the bodies
Of aged fathers from a throat no longer
Free, lament the fate of their most loved.
But *those* a night's marauding after battle
Sets hungry to what breakfast the town
offers
Not billeted duly in any barracks order
But as each man has drawn his lot of luck.
So in the captive homes of Troy already
They take their lodging, free of the frosts
And dews of the open. Like happy men
They will sleep all night without sentry.
But if they respect duly the city's gods,
Those of the captured land and the sanc-
tuaries of the gods,
They need not, having conquered, fear re-
conquest.
But let no lust fall first upon the troops
To plunder what is not right, subdued by
gain,
For they must still, in order to come home
safe,
Get round the second lap of the doubled
course.
So if they return without offence to the
gods
The grievance of the slain may learn at
last
A friendly talk—unless some fresh wrong
falls.
Such are the thoughts you hear from me a
woman.
But may the good prevail for all to see.
We have much good. I only ask to enjoy
it.

LEADER: Woman, you speak with sense
like a prudent man.
I, who have heard your valid proofs, prepare
To give the glory to God.
Fair recompense is brought us for our
troubles.

(CLYTEMNESTRA *goes back into the palace.*)

CHORUS: O Zeus our king and Night
our friend
Donor of glories,
Night who cast on the towers of Troy
A close-clinging net so that neither the
grown
Nor any of the children can pass
The enslaving and huge
Trap of all-taking destruction.
Great Zeus, guardian of host and guest,
I honor who has done his work and taken
A leisured aim at Paris so that neither
Too short nor yet over the stars
He might shoot to no purpose.

From Zeus is the blow they can tell of,
This at least can be established,
They have fared according to his ruling.
For some
Deny that the gods deign to consider those
among men
Who trample on the grace of inviolate
things;
It is the impious man says this,
For Ruin is revealed the child
Of not to be attempted actions
When men are puffed up unduly
And their houses are stuffed with riches.
Measure is the best. Let danger be distant,
This should suffice a man
With a proper part of wisdom.
For a man has no protection
Against the drunkenness of riches
Once he has spurned from his sight
The high altar of Justice.

Sombre Persuasion compels him,
Intolerable child of calculating Doom;

All cure is vain, there is no glozing it over,
But the mischief shines forth with a deadly
     light
And like bad coinage
By rubbings and frictions
He stands discolored and black
Under the test—like a boy
Who chases a winged bird
He has branded his city for ever.
His prayers are heard by no god;
Who makes such things his practice
The gods destroy him.
     This way came Paris
     To the house of the sons of Atreus
     And outraged the table of friendship
     Stealing the wife of his host.
Leaving to her countrymen clanging of
Shields and of spears and
Launching of warships
And bringing instead of a dowry destruc-
     tion to Troy
Lightly she was gone through the gates
     daring
Things undared. Many the groans
Of the palace spokesmen on this theme—
"O the house, the house, and its princes,
O the bed and the imprint of her limbs;
One can see him crouching in silence
Dishonored and unreviling."
Through desire for her who is overseas, a
     ghost
Will seem to rule the household.
     And now her husband hates
     The grace of shapely statues;
     In the emptiness of their eyes
     All their appeal is departed.

But appearing in dreams persuasive
Images come bringing a joy that is vain,
Vain for when in fancy he looks to touch
     her—
Slipping through his hands the vision
Rapidly is gone
Following on wings the walks of sleep.
Such as these and worse than these,
But everywhere through the land of Greece
     which men have left

Are mourning women with enduring hearts
To be seen in all houses; many
Are the thoughts which stab their hearts;
     For those they sent to war
     They know, but in place of men
     That which comes home to them
     Is merely an urn and ashes.

But the money-changer War, changer of
     bodies,
Holding his balance in the battle
Home from Troy refined by fire
Sends back to friends the dust
That is heavy with tears, stowing
A man's worth of ashes
In an easily handled jar.
And they wail speaking well of the men
     how that one
Was expert in battle, and one fell well in
     the carnage—
But for another man's wife.
Muffled and muttered words;
And resentful grief creeps up against the
     sons
Of Atreus and their cause.
     But others there by the wall
     Entombed in Trojan ground
     Lie, handsome of limb,
     Holding and hidden in enemy soil.

Heavy is the murmur of an angry people
Performing the purpose of a public curse;
There is something cowled in the night
That I anxiously wait to hear.
For the gods are not blind to the
Murderers of many and the black
Furies in time
When a man prospers in sin
By erosion of life reduce him to darkness,
Who, once among the lost, can no more
Be helped. Over-great glory
Is a sore burden. The high peak
Is blasted by the eyes of Zeus.
     I prefer an unenvied fortune,
     Not to be a sacker of cities
     Nor to find myself living at another's
     Ruling, myself a captive.

AN OLD MAN: From the good news'
beacon a swift
Rumor is gone through the town.
Who knows if it be true
Or some deceit of the gods?

ANOTHER OLD MAN: Who is so childish
or broken in wit
To kindle his heart at a new-fangled mes-
sage of flame
And then be downcast
At a change of report?

ANOTHER OLD MAN: It fits the temper of
a woman
To give her assent to a story before it is
proved.

ANOTHER OLD MAN: The over-credulous
passion of women expands
In swift conflagration but swiftly declining is gone
The news that a woman announced.

LEADER OF THE CHORUS: Soon we shall
know about the illuminant torches,
The beacons and the fiery relays,
Whether they were true or whether like
dreams
That pleasant light came here and hoaxed
our wits.
Look: I see, coming from the beach, a
herald
Shadowed with olive shoots; the dust upon
him,
Mud's thirsty sister and colleague, is my
witness
That he will not give dumb news nor
news by lighting
A flame of fire with the smoke of mountain timber;
In words he will either corroborate our
joy—
But the opposite version I reject with
horror.
To the good appeared so far may good
be added.

ANOTHER SPEAKER : Whoever makes
other prayers for this our city,

May he reap himself the fruits of his
wicked heart.

(*Enter the* HERALD, *who kisses the ground
before speaking.*)

HERALD: Earth of my fathers, O the
earth of Argos,
In the light of the tenth year I reach you
thus
After many shattered hopes achieving one,
For never did I dare to think that here in
Argive land
I should win a grave in the dearest soil of
home;
But now hail, land, and hail, light of the
sun,
And Zeus high above the country and the
Pythian king—
May he no longer shoot his arrows at us
(Implacable long enough beside Scaman-
der)
But now be savior to us and be healer,
King Apollo. And all the Assembly's gods
I call upon, and him my patron, Hermes,
The dear herald whom all heralds adore,
And the Heroes who sped our voyage,
again with favor
Take back the army that has escaped the
spear.
O cherished dwelling, palace of royalty,
O august thrones and gods facing the
sun,
If ever before, now with your bright eyes
Gladly receive your king after much time,
Who comes bringing light to you in the
night time,
And to all these as well—King Agamem-
non.
Give him a good welcome as he deserves,
Who with the axe of judgment-awarding
God
Has smashed Troy and levelled the Tro-
jan land;
The altars are destroyed, the seats of the
gods,
And the seed of all the land is perished
from it.

Having cast this halter round the neck of
Troy
The King, the elder son of Atreus, a
blessed man,
Comes, the most worthy to have honor of
all
Men that are now. Paris nor his guilty city
Can boast that the crime was greater than
the atonement.
Convicted in a suit for rape and robbery
He has lost his stolen goods and with con-
summate ruin
Mowed down the whole country and his
father's house.
The sons of Priam have paid their account
with interest.

LEADER OF THE CHORUS: Hail and be
glad, herald of the Greek army.

HERALD: Yes. Glad indeed! So glad that
at the gods' demand
I should no longer hesitate to die.

LEADER: Were you so harrowed by desire for home?

HERALD: Yes. The tears come to my eyes
for joy.

LEADER: Sweet then is the fever which
afflicts you.

HERALD: What do you mean? Let me
learn your drift.

LEADER: Longing for those whose love
came back in echo.

HERALD: Meaning the land was home-
sick for the army?

LEADER: Yes. I would often groan from
a darkened heart.

HERALD: This sullen hatred—how did
it fasten on you?

LEADER: I cannot say. Silence is my
stock prescription.

HERALD: What? In your masters' absence were there some you feared?

LEADER: Yes. In your phrase, death
would now be a gratification.

HERALD: Yes, for success is ours. These
things have taken time.
Some of them we could say have fallen
well,
While some we blame. Yet who except
the gods
Is free from pain the whole duration of
life?
If I were to tell of our labors, our hard
lodging,
The sleeping on crowded decks, the scanty
blankets,
Tossing and groaning, rations that never
reached us—
And the land too gave matter for more
disgust,
For our beds lay under the enemy's walls.
Continuous drizzle from the sky, dews
from the marshes,
Rotting our clothes, filling our hair with
lice.
And if one were to tell of the bird-destroy-
ing winter
Intolerable from the snows of Ida
Or of the heat when the sea slackens at
noon
Waveless and dozing in a depressed calm—
But why make these complaints? The
weariness is over;
Over indeed for some who never again
Need even trouble to rise.
Why make a computation of the lost?
Why need the living sorrow for the spites
of fortune?
I wish to say a long goodbye to disasters.
For us, the remnant of the troops of Argos,
The advantage remains, the pain cannot
outweigh it;
So we can make our boast to this sun's
light,
Flying on words above the land and sea:
"Having taken Troy the Argive expedition
Has nailed up throughout Greece in every
temple
These spoils, these ancient trophies."
Those who hear such things must praise
the city

And the generals. And the grace of God
be honored
Which brought these things about. You
have the whole story.

LEADER: I confess myself convinced by
your report.
Old men are always young enough to
learn.

(*Enter* CLYTEMNESTRA *from the palace.*)

This news belongs by right first to the
house
And Clytemnestra—though I am enriched
also.

CLYTEMNESTRA: Long before this I
shouted at joy's command
At the coming of the first night-messenger
of fire
Announcing the taking and capsizing of
Troy.
And people reproached me saying, "Do
mere beacons
Persuade you to think that Troy is already
down?
Indeed a woman's heart is easily exalted."
Such comments made me seem to be wan-
dering but yet
I began my sacrifices and in the women's
fashion
Throughout the town they raised trium-
phant cries
And in the gods' enclosures
Lulling the fragrant, incense-eating flame.
And now what need is there for you to
tell me more?
From the King himself I shall learn the
whole story.
But how the best to welcome my honored
lord
I shall take pains when he comes back—
For what
Is a kinder light for a woman to see than
this,
To open the gates to her man come back
from war
When God has saved him? Tell this to
my husband,
To come with all speed, the city's darling;

May he returning find a wife as loyal
As when he left her, watchdog of the
house,
Good to *him* but fierce to the ill-inten-
tioned,
And in all other things as ever, having
destroyed
No seal or pledge at all in the length of
time.
I know no pleasure with another man, no
scandal,
More than I know how to dye metal red.
Such is my boast, bearing a load of truth,
A boast that need not disgrace a noble
wife.

(*Exit.*)

LEADER: Thus has she spoken; if you
take her meaning,
Only a specious tale to shrewd interpreters.
But do you, herald, tell me; I ask after
Menelaus
Whether he will, returning safe preserved,
Come back with you, our land's loved
master.

HERALD: I am not able to speak the
lovely falsehood
To profit you, my friends, for any stretch
of time.

LEADER: But if only the true tidings
could be also good!
It is hard to hide a division of good and
true.

HERALD: The prince is vanished out of
the Greek fleet,
Himself and ship. I speak no lie.

LEADER: Did he put forth first in the
sight of all from Troy,
Or a storm that troubled all sweep him
apart?

HERALD: You have hit the target like a
master archer,
Told succinctly a long tale of sorrow.

LEADER: Did the rumors current among
the remaining ships
Represent him as alive or dead?

HERALD: No one knows so as to tell for
sure
Except the sun who nurses the breeds of
earth.

LEADER: Tell me how the storm came
on the host of ships
Through the divine anger, and how it
ended.

HERALD: Day of good news should not
be fouled by tongue
That tells ill news. To each god his season.
When, despair in his face, a messenger
brings to a town
The hated news of a fallen army—
One general wound to the city and many
men
Outcast, outcursed, from many homes
By the double whip which War is fond of,
Doom with a bloody spear in either hand,
One carrying such a pack of grief could
well
Recite this hymn of the Furies at your
asking.
But when our cause is saved and a mes-
senger of good
Comes to a city glad with festivity,
How am I to mix good news with bad,
recounting
The storm that meant God's anger on the
Greeks?
For they swore together, those inveterate
enemies,
Fire and sea, and proved their alliance,
destroying
The unhappy troops of Argos.
In night arose ill-waved evil,
Ships on each other the blasts from Thrace
Crashed colliding, which butting with
horns in the violence
Of big wind and rattle of rain were gone
To nothing, whirled all ways by a wicked
shepherd.
But when there came up the shining light
of the sun
We saw the Aegean sea flowering with
corpses
Of Greek men and their ships' wreckage.

But for us, our ship was not damaged,
Whether someone snatched it away or
begged it off,
Some god, not a man, handling the tiller;
And Saving Fortune was willing to sit
upon our ship
So that neither at anchor we took the tilt
of waves
Nor ran to splinters on the crag-bound
coast.
But then having thus escaped death on the
sea,
In the white day, not trusting our fortune,
We pastured this new trouble upon our
thoughts,
The fleet being battered, the sailors weary,
And now if any of *them* still draw breath,
They are thinking no doubt of us as being
lost
And we are thinking of them as being
lost.
May the best happen. As for Menelaus
The first guess and most likely is a dis-
aster.
But still—if any ray of sun detects him
Alive, with living eyes, by the plan of Zeus
Not yet resolved to annul the race com-
pletely,
There is some hope then that he will re-
turn home.
So much you have heard. Know that it is
the truth.

(*Exit.*)

CHORUS: Who was it named her thus
In all ways appositely
Unless it was Someone whom we do not
see,
Fore-knowing fate
And plying an accurate tongue?
Helen, bride of spears and conflict's
Focus, who as was befitting
Proved a hell to ships and men,
Hell to her country, sailing
Away from delicately-sumptuous curtains,
Away on the wind of a giant Zephyr,
And shielded hunters mustered many
On the vanished track of the oars.

Oars beached on the leafy
Banks of a Trojan river
For the sake of bloody war.

But on Troy was thrust a marring mar-
    riage
By the Wrath that working to an end
    exacts
In time a price from guests
Who dishonored their host
And dishonored Zeus of the Hearth,
From those noisy celebrants
Of the wedding hymn which fell
To the brothers of Paris
To sing upon that day.
But learning this, unlearning that,
Priam's ancestral city now
Continually mourns, reviling
Paris the fatal bridegroom.
The city has had much sorrow,
Much desolation in life,
From the pitiful loss of her people.

So in his house a man might rear
A lion's cub caught from the dam
In need of suckling,
In the prelude of its life
Mild, gentle with children,
For old men a playmate,
Often held in the arms
Like a new-born child,
Wheedling the hand,
Fawning at belly's bidding.

But matured by time he showed
The temper of his stock and paid
Thanks for his fostering
With disaster of slaughter of sheep
Making an unbidden banquet
And now the house is a shambles,
Irremediable grief to its people,
Calamitous carnage;
For the pet they had fostered was sent
By God as a priest of Ruin.

So I would say there came
To the city of Troy

A notion of windless calm,
Delicate adornment of riches,
Soft shooting of the eyes and flower
Of desire that stings the fancy.
But swerving aside she achieved
A bitter end to her marriage,
Ill guest and ill companion,
Hurled upon Priam's sons, convoyed
By Zeus, patron of guest and host,
Dark angel dowered with tears.

Long current among men an old saying
Runs that a man's prosperity
When grown to greatness
Comes to the birth, does not die childless—
His good luck breeds for his house
Distress that shall not be appeased.
I only, apart from the others,
Hold that the unrighteous action
Breeds true to its kind,
Leaves its own children behind it.
But the lot of a righteous house
Is a fair offspring always.

Ancient self-glory is accustomed
To bear to light in the evil sort of men
A new self-glory and madness,
Which sometime or sometime finds
The appointed hour for its birth,
And born therewith is the Spirit, intracta-
    ble, unholy, irresistible.
The reckless lust that brings black Doom
    upon the house,
A child that is like its parents.

But Honest Dealing is clear
Shining in smoky homes,
Honors the god-fearing life.
Mansions gilded by filth of hands she
    leaves,
Turns her eyes elsewhere, visits the inno-
    cent house,
Not respecting the power
Of wealth mis-stamped with approval,
But guides all to the goal.

(*Enter* AGAMEMNON *and* CASSANDRA *on
                    chariots.*)

CHORUS: Come then my King, stormer of Troy,
Offspring of Atreus,
How shall I hail you, how give you honor
Neither overshooting nor falling short
 Of the measure of homage?
There are many who honor appearance too much
Passing the bounds that are right.
To condole with the unfortunate man
Each one is ready but the bite of the grief
 Never goes through to the heart.
And they join in rejoicing, affecting to share it,
Forcing their face to a smile.
But he who is shrewd to shepherd his sheep
Will fail not to notice the eyes of a man
Which seem to be loyal but lie,
 Fawning with watery friendship.
Even you, in my thought, when you marshalled the troops
For Helen's sake, I will not hide it,
Made a harsh and ugly picture,
Holding badly the tiller of reason,
Paying with the death of men
 Ransom for a willing whore.
But now, not unfriendly, not superficially,
I offer my service, well-doers' welcome.
In time you will learn by inquiry
Who has done rightly, who transgressed
 In the work of watching the city.

AGAMEMNON: First to Argos and the country's gods
My fitting salutations, who have aided me
To return and in the justice which I exacted
From Priam's city. Hearing the unspoken case
The gods unanimously had cast their vote
Into the bloody urn for the massacre of Troy;
But to the opposite urn ʹ
Hope came, dangled her hand, but did no more.
Smoke marks even now the city's capture.
Whirlwinds of doom are alive, the dying ashes

Spread on the air the fat savor of wealth.
For these things we must pay some memorable return
To Heaven, having exacted enormous vengeance
For wife-rape; for a woman
The Argive monster ground a city to powder,
Sprung from a wooden horse, shield-wielding folk,
Launching a leap at the setting of the Pleiads,
Jumping the ramparts, a ravening lion,
Lapped its fill of the kingly blood.
To the gods I have drawn out this overture
But as for your concerns, I bear them in my mind
And say the same, you have me in agreement.
To few of men does it belong by nature
To congratulate their friends unenviously,
For a sullen poison fastens on the heart,
Doubling the pain of a man with this disease;
He feels the weight of his own griefs and when
He sees another's prosperity he groans.
I speak with knowledge, being well acquainted
With the mirror of comradeship—ghost of a shadow
Were those who seemed to be so loyal to me.
Only Odysseus, who sailed against his will,
Proved, when yoked with me, a ready tracehorse;
I speak of him not knowing if he is alive.
But for what concerns the city and the gods
Appointing public debates in full assembly
We shall consult. That which is well already
We shall take steps to ensure it remain well.
But where there is need of medical remedies.

By applying benevolent cautery or surgery
We shall try to deflect the dangers of disease.
But now, entering the halls where stands my hearth,
First I shall make salutation to the gods
Who sent me a far journey and have brought me back.
And may my victory not leave my side.

(*Enter* CLYTEMNESTRA, *followed by women slaves carrying purple tapestries.*)

CLYTEMNESTRA: Men of the city, you the aged of Argos,
I shall feel no shame to describe to you my love
Towards my husband. Shyness in all of us
Wears thin with time. Here are the facts first hand.
I will tell you of my own unbearable life
I led so long as this man was at Troy.
For first that the woman separate from her man
Should sit alone at home is extreme cruelty,
Hearing so many malignant rumors—First
Comes one, and another comes after, bad news to worse,
Clamor of grief to the house. If Agamemnon
Had had so many wounds as those reported
Which poured home through the pipes of hearsay, then—
Then he would be gashed fuller than a net has holes!
And if only he had died . . . as often as rumor told us,
He would be like the giant in the legend,
Three-bodied. Dying once for every body
He should have by now three blankets of earth above him—
All that above him; I care not how deep the mattress under!
Such are the malignant rumors thanks to which
They have often seized me against my will and undone

The loop of a rope from my neck.
And this is why our son is not standing here,
The guarantee of your pledges and mine,
As he should be, Orestes. Do not wonder;
He is being brought up by a friendly ally and host,
Strophius the Phocian, who warned me in advance
Of dubious troubles, both your risks at Troy
And the anarchy of shouting mobs that might
Overturn policy, for it is born in men
To kick the man who is down.
This is not a disingenuous excuse.
For me the outrushing wells of weeping are dried up,
There is no drop left in them.
My eyes are sore from sitting late at nights
Weeping for you and for the baffled beacons,
Never lit up. And, when I slept, in dreams
I have been waked by the thin whizz of a buzzing
Gnat, seeing more horrors fasten on you
Than could take place in the mere time of my dream.
Having endured all this, now, with unsorrowed heart
I would hail this man as the watchdog of the farm,
Forestay that saves the ship, pillar that props
The lofty roof, appearance of an only son
To a father or of land to sailors past their hope,
The loveliest day to see after the storm,
Gush of well-water for the thirsty traveller.
Such are the metaphors I think befit him,
But envy be absent. Many misfortunes already
We have endured. But now, dear head, come down
Out of that car, not placing upon the ground

Your foot, O King, the foot that trampled
Troy.
Why are you waiting, slaves, to whom the
task is assigned
To spread the pavement of his path with
tapestries?
At once, at once let his way be strewn
with purple
That Justice lead him toward his unex-
pected home.
The rest a mind, not overcome by sleep,
Will arrange rightly, with God's help, as
destined.

AGAMEMNON: Daughter of Leda, guard-
ian of my house,
You have spoken in proportion to my
absence.
You have drawn your speech out long.
Duly to praise me,
That is a duty to be performed by others.
And further—do not by women's methods
make me
Effeminate nor in barbarian fashion
Gape ground-grovelling acclamations at
me
Nor strewing my path with cloths make
it invidious.
It is the gods should be honored in this
way.
But being mortal to tread embroidered
beauty
For me is no way without fear.
I tell you to honor me as a man, not god.
Footcloths are very well; embroidered
stuffs
Are stuff for gossip. And not to think
unwisely
Is the greatest gift of God. Call happy
only him
Who has ended his life in sweet pros-
perity.
I have spoken. This thing I could not do
with confidence.

CLYTEMNESTRA: Tell me now, according
to your judgment.

AGAMEMNON: I tell you you shall not
override my judgment.

CLYTEMNESTRA: Supposing you had
feared something. . . .
Could you have vowed to God to do this
thing?

AGAMEMNON: Yes. If an expert had prescribed that vow.

CLYTEMNESTRA: And how would Priam
have acted in your place?

AGAMEMNON: He would have trod the
cloths, I think, for certain.

CLYTEMNESTRA: Then do not flinch before the blame of men.

AGAMEMNON: The voice of the multitude is very strong.

CLYTEMNESTRA: But the man none envy
is not enviable.

AGAMEMNON: It is not a woman's part
to love disputing.

CLYTEMNESTRA: But it is a conqueror's
part to yield upon occasion.

AGAMEMNON: You think such victory
worth fighting for?

CLYTEMNESTRA: Give way. Consent to
let me have the mastery.

AGAMEMNON: Well, if such is your wish,
let someone quickly loose
My vassal sandals, underlings of my feet,
And stepping on these sea-purples may
no god
Shoot me from far with the envy of his
eye.
Great shame it is to ruin my house and
spoil
The wealth of costly weavings with my
feet.
But of this matter enough. This stranger
woman here
Take in with kindness. The man who is
a gentle master
God looks on from far off complacently.
For no one of his will bears the slave's
yoke.

This woman, of many riches being the chosen
Flower, gift of the soldiers, has come with me.
But since I have been prevailed on by your words
I will go to my palace home, treading on purples.

(*He dismounts from the chariot and begins to walk up the tapestried path. During the following speech he enters the palace.*)

CLYTEMNESTRA: There is the sea and who shall drain it dry? It breeds
Its wealth in silver of plenty of purple gushing
And ever-renewed, the dyeings of our garments.
The house has its store of these by God's grace, King.
This house is ignorant of poverty
And I would have vowed a pavement of many garments
Had the palace oracle enjoined that vow
Thereby to contrive a ransom for his life.
For while there is root, foliage comes to the house
Spreading a tent of shade against the Dog Star.
So now that you have reached your hearth and home
You prove a miracle—advent of warmth in winter;
And further this—even in the time of heat
When God is fermenting wine from the bitter grape,
Even then it is cool in the house if only
Its master walk at home, a grown man, ripe.
O Zeus the Ripener, ripen these my prayers;
Your part it is to make the ripe fruit fall.

(*She enters the palace.*)

CHORUS: Why, why at the doors
Of my fore-seeing heart

Does this terror keep beating its wings?
And my song play the prophet
Unbidden, unhired—
Which I cannot spit out
Like the enigmas of dreams
Nor plausible confidence
Sit on the throne of my mind?
It is long time since
The cables let down from the stern
Were chafed by the sand when the seafaring army started for Troy.

And I learn with my eyes
And witness myself their return;
But the hymn without lyre goes up,
The dirge of the Avenging Fiend,
In the depths of my self-taught heart
Which has lost its dear
Possession of the strength of hope.
But my guts and my heart
Are not idle which seethe with the waves
Of trouble nearing its hour.
But I pray that these thoughts
May fall out not as I think
And not be fulfilled in the end.

Truly when health grows much
It respects not limit; for disease,
Its neighbor in the next door room,
Presses upon it.
A man's life, crowding sail,
Strikes on the blind reef:
But if caution in advance
Jettison part of the cargo
With the derrick of due proportion,
The whole house does not sink,
Though crammed with a weight of woe
The hull does not go under.
The abundant bounty of God
And his gifts from the year's furrows
Drive the famine back.

But when upon the ground there has fallen once
The black blood of a man's death,
Who shall summon it back by incantations?

Even Asclepius who had the art
To fetch the dead to life, even to him
Zeus put a provident end.
But, if of the heaven-sent fates
One did not check the other,
Cancel the other's advantage,
My heart would outrun my tongue
In pouring out these fears.
But now it mutters in the dark,
Embittered, no way hoping
To unravel a scheme in time
   From a burning mind.

(CLYTEMNESTRA *appears in the door of the palace.*)

CLYTEMNESTRA: Go in too, you; I speak to you, Cassandra,
Since God in his clemency has put you in this house
To share our holy water, standing with many slaves
Beside the altar that protects the house,
Step down from the car there, do not be overproud.
Heracles himself they say was once
Sold, and endured to eat the bread of slavery.
But should such a chance inexorably fall,
There is much advantage in masters who have long been rich.
Those who have reaped a crop they never expected
Are in all things hard on their slaves and overstep the line.
From us you will have the treatment of tradition.

LEADER OF CHORUS: You, it is you she has addressed, and clearly.
Caught as you are in these predestined toils
Obey her if you can. But should you disobey . . .

CLYTEMNESTRA: If she has more than the gibberish of the swallow,
As unintelligible barbaric speech,
I hope to read her mind, persuade her reason.

LEADER: As things now stand for you, she says the best.
Obey her; leave that car and follow her.

CLYTEMNESTRA: I have no leisure to waste out here, outside the door.
Before the hearth in the middle of my house
The victims stand already, wait the knife.
You, if you will obey me, waste no time.
But if you cannot understand my language—

(*to* CHORUS LEADER)

You make it plain to her with the brute and voiceless hand.

LEADER: The stranger seems to need a clear interpreter.
She bears herself like a wild beast newly captured.

CLYTEMNESTRA: The fact is she is mad, she listens to evil thoughts,
Who has come here leaving a city newly captured
Without experience how to bear the bridle
So as not to waste her strength in foam and blood.
I will not spend more words to be ignored.

(*She re-enters the palace.*)

CHORUS: But I, for I pity her, will not be angry.
Obey, unhappy woman. Leave this car.
Yield to your fate. Put on the untried yoke.

CASSANDRA: Apollo! Apollo!

CHORUS: Why do you cry like this upon Apollo?
He is not the kind of god that calls for dirges.

CASSANDRA: Apollo! Apollo!

CHORUS: Once more her funereal cries invoke the god
Who has no place at the scene of lamentation.

CASSANDRA: Apollo! Apollo!
God of the Ways! My destroyer!
Destroyed again—and this time utterly!

CHORUS: She seems about to predict her own misfortunes.
The gift of the god endures, even in a slave's mind.

CASSANDRA: Apollo! Apollo!
God of the Ways! My destroyer!
Where? To what house? Where, where have you brought me?

CHORUS: To the house of the sons of Atreus. If you do not know it,
I will tell you so. You will not find it false.

CASSANDRA: No, no, but to a god-hated, but to an accomplice
In much kin-killing, murdering nooses,
Man-shambles, a floor asperged with blood.

CHORUS: The stranger seems like a hound with a keen scent,
Is picking up a trail that leads to murder.

CASSANDRA: Clues! I have clues! Look! They are these.
These wailing, these children, butchery of children;
Roasted flesh, a father sitting to dinner.

CHORUS: Of your prophetic fame we have heard before
But in this matter prophets are not required.

CASSANDRA: What is she doing? What is she planning?
What is this new great sorrow?
Great crime . . . within here . . . planning
Unendurable to his folk, impossible
Ever to be cured. For help
Stands far distant.

CHORUS: This reference I cannot catch. But the children
I recognized; that refrain is hackneyed.

CASSANDRA: Damned, damned, bringing this work to completion—
Your husband who shared your bed
To bathe him, to cleanse him, and then—
How shall I tell of the end?
The end comes hand over hand
Grasping in greed.

CHORUS: Not yet do I understand. After her former riddles
Now I am baffled by these dim pronouncements.

CASSANDRA: Ah God, the vision! God, God, the vision!
A net, is it? Net of Hell!
But herself is the net; shared bed; shares murder.
O let the pack ever-hungering after the family
Howl for the unholy ritual, howl for the victim.

CHORUS: What black Spirit is this you call upon the house—
To raise aloft her cries? Your speech does not lighten me.
Into my heart runs back the blood
Yellow as when for men by the spear fallen
The blood ebbs out with the rays of the setting life
And death strides quickly.

CASSANDRA: Quick! Be on your guard! The bull—
Keep him clear of the cow.
Caught with a trick, the black horn's point,
She strikes. He falls; lies in the water.
Murder; a trick in a bath. I tell what I see.

CHORUS: I would not claim to be expert in oracles
But these, as I deduce, portend disaster.
Do men ever get a good answer from oracles?
No. It is only through disaster
That their garrulous craft brings home
The meaning of the prophet's panic.

CASSANDRA: And for me also, for me, chance ill-destined!
My own now I lament, pour into the cup my own.
Where is this you have brought me in my misery?
Unless to die as well. What else is meant?

CHORUS: You are mad, mad, carried away by the god,

Raising the dirge, the tuneless
Tune, for yourself. Like the tawny
Unsatisfied singer from her luckless heart
Lamenting 'Itys, Itys,' the nightingale
Lamenting a life luxuriant with grief.

CASSANDRA: Oh the lot of the songful
nightingale!
The gods enclosed her in a winged body,
Gave her a sweet and tearless passing.
But for me remains the two-edged cutting
blade.

CHORUS: From whence these rushing
and God-inflicted
Profitless pains?
Why shape with your sinister crying
The piercing hymn—fear-piercing?
How can you know the evil-worded land-
marks
On the prophetic path?

CASSANDRA: Oh the wedding, the wed-
ding of Paris—death to his people!
O river Scamander, water drunk by my
fathers!
When I was young, alas, upon your
beaches
I was brought up and cared for.
But now it is the River of Wailing and the
banks of Hell
That shall hear my prophecy soon.

CHORUS: What is this clear speech, too
clear?
A child could understand it.
I am bitten with fangs that draw blood
By the misery of your cries,
Cries harrowing the heart.

CASSANDRA: Oh trouble on trouble of
a city lost, lost utterly!
My father's sacrifices before the towers,
Much killing of cattle and sheep,
No cure—availed not at all
To prevent the coming of what came to
Troy,
And I, my brain on fire, shall soon enter
the trap.

CHORUS: This speech accords with the
former.

What god, malicious, over-heavy, per-
sistently pressing,
Drives you to chant of these lamentable
Griefs with death their burden?
But I cannot see the end.

(CASSANDRA now steps down from the car.)

CASSANDRA: The oracle now no longer
from behind veils
Will be peeping forth like a newly-
wedded bride;
But I can feel it like a fresh wind swoop
And rush in the face of the dawn and,
wave-like, wash
Against the sun a vastly greater grief
Than this one. I shall speak no more
conundrums.
And bear me witness, pacing me, that I
Am trailing on the scent of ancient
wrongs.
For this house here a choir never deserts,
Chanting together ill. For they mean ill,
And to puff up their arrogance they have
drunk
Men's blood, this band of revellers that
haunts the house,
Hard to be rid of, fiends that attend the
family.
Established in its rooms they hymn their
hymn
Of that original sin, abhor in turn
The adultery that proved a brother's ruin.
A miss? Or do my arrows hit the
mark?
Or am I a quack prophet who knocks
at doors, a babbler?
Give me your oath, confess I have the
facts,
The ancient history of this house's crimes.

LEADER: And how could an oath's
assurance, however finely assured,
Turn out a remedy? I wonder, though,
that you
Being brought up overseas, of another
tongue,
Should hit on the whole tale as if you had
been standing by.

CASSANDRA: Apollo the prophet set me to prophesy.

LEADER: Was he, although a god, struck by desire?

CASSANDRA: Till now I was ashamed to tell that story.

LEADER: Yes. Good fortune keeps us all fastidious.

CASSANDRA: He wrestled hard upon me, panting love.

LEADER: And did you come, as they do, to child-getting?

CASSANDRA: No. I agreed to him. And I cheated him.

LEADER: Were you already possessed by the mystic art?

CASSANDRA: Already I was telling the townsmen all their future suffering.

LEADER: Then how did you escape the doom of Apollo's anger?

CASSANDRA: I did not escape. No one ever believed me.

LEADER: Yet to us your words seem worthy of belief.

CASSANDRA: Oh misery, misery!
Again comes on me the terrible labor of true
Prophecy, dizzying prelude; distracts. . . .
Do you see these who sit before the house,
Children, like the shapes of dreams?
Children who seem to have been killed by their kinsfolk,
Filling their hands with meat, flesh of themselves,
Guts and entrails, handfuls of lament—
Clear what they hold—the same their father tasted.
For this I declare someone is plotting vengeance—
A lion? Lion but coward, that lurks in bed,
Good watchdog truly against the lord's return—
My lord, for I must bear the yoke of serfdom.

Leader of the ships, overturner of Troy,
He does not know what plots the accursed hound
With the licking tongue and the pricked-up ear will plan
In the manner of a lurking doom, in an evil hour.
A daring criminal! Female murders male.
What monster could provide her with a title?
An amphisbaena or hag of the sea who dwells
In rocks to ruin sailors—
A raving mother of death who breathes against her folk
War to the finish. Listen to her shout of triumph,
Who shirks no horrors, like men in a rout of battle.
And yet she poses as glad at their return.
If you distrust my words, what does it matter?
That which will come will come. You too will soon stand here
And admit with pity that I spoke too truly.

LEADER: Thyestes' dinner of his children's meat
I understood and shuddered, and fear grips me
To hear the truth, not framed in parables.
But hearing the rest I am thrown out of my course.

CASSANDRA: It is Agamemnon's death I tell you you shall witness.

LEADER: Stop! Provoke no evil. Quiet your mouth!

CASSANDRA: The god who gives me words is here no healer.

LEADER: Not if this shall be so. But may some chance avert it.

CASSANDRA: *You* are praying. But others are busy with murder.

LEADER: What man is he promotes this terrible thing?

CASSANDRA: Indeed you have missed my drift by a wide margin!

LEADER: But I do not understand the assassin's method.

CASSANDRA: And yet too well I know the speech of Greece!

LEADER: So does Delphi but the replies are hard.

CASSANDRA: Ah what a fire it is! It comes upon me.
Apollo, Wolf-Destroyer, pity, pity. . . .
It is the two-foot lioness who beds
Beside a wolf, the noble lion away,
It is she will kill me. Brewing a poisoned cup
She will mix my punishment too in the angry draught
And boasts, sharpening the dagger for her husband,
To pay back murder for my bringing here.
Why then do I wear these mockeries of myself,
The wand and the prophet's garland round my neck?
My hour is coming—but you shall perish first.
Destruction! Scattered thus you give me my revenge;
Go and enrich some other woman with ruin.
See: Apollo himself is stripping me
Of my prophetic gear, who has looked on
When in this dress I have been a laughing-stock
To friends and foes alike, and to no purpose;
They call me crazy, like a fortune-teller,
A poor starved beggar-woman—and I bore it.
And now the prophet undoing his prophetess
Has brought me to this final darkness.
Instead of my father's altar the executioner's block
Waits me the victim, red with my hot blood.
But the gods will not ignore me as I die.
One will come after to avenge my death,

A matricide, a murdered father's champion.
Exile and tramp and outlaw he will come back
To gable the family house of fatal crime;
His father's outstretched corpse shall lead him home.
Why need I then lament so pitifully?
For now that I have seen the town of Troy
Treated as she was treated, while her captors
Come to their reckoning thus by the gods' verdict,
I will go in and have the courage to die.
Look, these gates are the gates of Death. I greet them.
And I pray that I may meet a deft and mortal stroke
So that without a struggle I may close
My eyes and my blood ebb in easy death.

LEADER: Oh woman very unhappy and very wise,
Your speech was long. But if in sober truth
You know your fate, why like an ox that the gods
Drive, do you walk so bravely to the altar?

CASSANDRA: There is no escape, strangers. No; not by postponement.

LEADER: But the last moment has the privilege of hope.

CASSANDRA: The day is here. Little should I gain by flight.

LEADER: This patience of yours comes from a brave soul.

CASSANDRA: A happy man is never paid that compliment.

LEADER: But to die with credit graces a mortal man.

CASSANDRA: Oh my father! You and your noble sons!

(*She approaches the door, then suddenly recoils.*)

LEADER: What is it? What is the fear that drives you back?

CASSANDRA: Faugh.

LEADER: Why faugh? Or is this some hallucination?

CASSANDRA: These walls breathe out a death that drips with blood.

LEADER: Not so. It is only the smell of the sacrifice.

CASSANDRA: It is like a breath out of a charnel-house.

LEADER: You think our palace burns odd incense then!

CASSANDRA: But I will go to lament among the dead
My lot and Agamemnon's. Enough of life!
Strangers,
I am not afraid like a bird afraid of a bush
But witness you my words after my death
When a woman dies in return for me a woman
And a man falls for a man with a wicked wife.
I ask this service, being about to die.

LEADER: Alas, I pity you for the death you have foretold.

CASSANDRA: One more speech I have; I do not wish to raise
The dirge for my own self. But to the sun I pray
In face of his last light that my avengers
May make my murderers pay for this my death,
Death of a woman slave, an easy victim.

(*She enters the palace.*)

LEADER: Ah the fortunes of men! When they go well
A shadow sketch would match them, and in ill-fortune
The dab of a wet sponge destroys the drawing.
It is not myself but the life of man I pity.

CHORUS: Prosperity in all men cries
For more prosperity. Even the owner
Of the finger-pointed-at palace never shuts
His door against her, saying "Come no more."
So to our king the blessed gods had granted
To take the town of Priam, and heaven-favored
He reaches home. But now if for former bloodshed
He must pay blood
And dying for the dead shall cause
Other deaths in atonement
What man could boast he was born
Secure, who heard this story?

AGAMEMNON: (*within*) Oh! I am struck a mortal blow—within!

LEADER: Silence! Listen. Who calls out, wounded with a mortal stroke?

AGAMEMNON: Again—the second blow —I am struck again.

LEADER: You heard the king cry out. I think the deed is done.
Let us see if we can concert some sound proposal.

2ND OLD MAN: Well, I will tell you my opinion—
Raise an alarm, summon the folk to the palace.

3RD OLD MAN: I say burst in with all speed possible,
Convict them of the deed while still the sword is wet.

4TH OLD MAN: And I am partner to some such suggestion.
I am for taking some course. No time to dawdle.

5TH OLD MAN: The case is plain. This is but the beginning.
They are going to set up dictatorship in the state.

6TH OLD MAN: We are wasting time. The assassins tread to earth
The decencies of delay and give their hands no sleep.

7TH OLD MAN: I do not know what plan I could hit on to propose.

The man who acts is in the position to plan.

8TH OLD MAN: So I think, too, for I am at a loss
To raise the dead man up again with words.

9TH OLD MAN: Then to stretch out our life shall we yield thus
To the rule of these profaners of the house?

10TH OLD MAN: It is not to be endured. To die is better.
Death is more comfortable than tyranny.

11TH OLD MAN: And are we on the evidence of groans
Going to give oracle that the prince is dead?

12TH OLD MAN: We must know the facts for sure and *then* be angry.
Guesswork is not the same as certain knowledge.

LEADER: Then all of you back me and approve this plan—
To ascertain how it is with Agamemnon.

(*The doors of the palace open, revealing the bodies of* AGAMEMNON *and* CASSANDRA. CLYTEMNESTRA *stands above them.*)

CLYTEMNESTRA: Much having been said before to fit the moment,
To say the opposite now will not outface me.
How else could one serving hate upon the hated,
Thought to be friends, hang high the nets of doom
To preclude all leaping out?
For me I have long been training for this match,
I tried a fall and won—a victory overdue.
I stand here where I struck, above my victims;
So I contrived it—this I will not deny—
That he could neither fly nor ward off death;
Inextricable like a net for fishes

I cast about him a vicious wealth of raiment
And struck him twice and with two groans he loosed
His limbs beneath him, and upon him fallen
I deal him the third blow to the God beneath the earth,
To the safe keeper of the dead a votive gift,
And with that he spits his life out where he lies
And smartly spouting blood he sprays me with
The somber drizzle of bloody dew and I
Rejoice no less than in God's gift of rain
The crops are glad when the ear of corn gives birth.
These things being so, you, elders of Argos,
Rejoice if rejoice you will. Mine is the glory.
And if I could pay this corpse his due libation
I should be right to pour it and more than right;
With so many horrors this man mixed and filled
The bowl—and, coming home, has drained the draught himself.

LEADER: Your speech astonishes us. This brazen boast
Above the man who was your king and husband!

CLYTEMNESTRA: You challenge me as a woman without foresight
But I with unflinching heart to you who know
Speak. And you, whether you will praise or blame,
It makes no matter. Here lies Agamemnon,
My husband, dead, the work of this right hand,
An honest workman. There you have the facts.

CHORUS: Woman, what poisoned
Herb of the earth have you tasted
Or potion of the flowing sea
To undertake this killing and the people's curses?
You threw down, you cut off—The people will cast you out,
Black abomination to the town.

CLYTEMNESTRA: Now your verdict—in my case—is exile
And to have the people's hatred, the public curses,
Though then in no way you opposed this man
Who carelessly, as if it were a head of sheep
Out of the abundance of his fleecy flocks,
Sacrificed his own daughter, to me the dearest
Fruit of travail, charm for the Thracian winds.
He was the one to have banished from this land,
Pay off the pollution. But when you hear what I
Have done, you judge severely. But I warn you—
Threaten me on the understanding that I am ready
For two alternatives—Win by force the right
To rule me, but, if God brings about the contrary,
Late in time you will have to learn self-discipline.

CHORUS: You are high in the thoughts,
You speak extravagant things,
After the soiling murder your crazy heart
Fancies your forehead with a smear of blood.
Unhonored, unfriended, you must
Pay for a blow with a blow.

CLYTEMNESTRA: Listen then to this—the sanction of my oaths:
By the Justice totting up my child's atonement,

By the Avenging Doom and Fiend to whom I killed this man,
For me hope walks not in the rooms of fear
So long as my fire is lit upon my hearth
By Aegisthus, loyal to me as he was before.
The man who outraged me lies here,
The darling of each courtesan at Troy,
And here with him is the prisoner clairvoyante,
The fortune-teller that he took to bed,
Who shares his bed as once his bench on shipboard,
A loyal mistress. Both have their deserts.
He lies so, and she who like a swan
Sang her last dying lament
Lies his lover, and the sight contributes
An appetiser to my own bed's pleasure.

CHORUS: Ah would some quick death come not overpainful,
Not overlong on the sickbed,
Establishing in us the ever-
Lasting unending sleep now that our guardian
Has fallen, the kindest of men,
Who suffering much for a woman
By a woman has lost his life.
O Helen, insane, being one,
One to have destroyed so many
And many souls under Troy,
Now is your work complete, blossomed not for oblivion,
Unfading stain of blood. Here now, if in any home,
Is Discord, here is a man's deep-rooted ruin.

CLYTEMNESTRA: Do not pray for the portion of death
Weighed down by these things, do not turn
Your anger on Helen as destroyer of men,
One woman destroyer of many
Lives of Greek men,
A hurt that cannot be healed.

CHORUS: O Evil Spirit, falling on the family,

On the two sons of Atreus and using
Two sisters in heart as your tools,
A power that bites to the heart—
See on the body
Perched like a raven he gloats
Harshly croaking his hymn.

CLYTEMNESTRA: Ah, now you have
amended your lips' opinion,
Calling upon this family's three times
gorged
Genius—demon who breeds
Blood-hankering lust in the belly:
Before the old sore heals, new pus collects.

CHORUS: It is a great spirit—great—
You tell of, harsh in anger,
A ghastly tale, alas,
Of unsatisfied disaster
Brought by Zeus, by Zeus,
Cause and worker of all.
For without Zeus what comes to pass
among us?
Which of these things is outside Provi-
dence?
    O my king, my king,
    How shall I pay you in tears,
    Speak my affection in words?
    You lie in that spider's web,
    In a desecrating death breathe out your
    life,
    Lie ignominiously
    Defeated by a crooked death
    And the two-edged cleaver's stroke.

CLYTEMNESTRA: You say this is my
work—mine?
Do not cozen yourself that I am Agamem-
non's wife.
Masquerading as the wife
Of the corpse there the old sharp-witted
Genius
Of Atreus who gave the cruel banquet
Has paid with a grown man's life
The due for children dead.

CHORUS: That you are not guilty of
This murder who will attest?
No, but you may have been abetted
By some ancestral Spirit of Revenge.

Wading a millrace of the family's blood
The black Manslayer forces a forward path
To make the requital at last
For the eaten children, the blood-clot cold
with time.
    O my king, my king,
    How shall I pay you in tears,
    Speak my affection in words?
    You lie in that spider's web,
    In a desecrating death breathe out your
    life,
    Lie ignominiously
    Defeated by a crooked death
    And the two-edged cleaver's stroke.

CLYTEMNESTRA: Did he not, too, con-
trive a crooked
Horror for the house? My child by him,
Shoot that I raised, much-wept-for Iphi-
geneia,
He treated her like this;
So suffering like this he need not make
Any great brag in Hell having paid with
death
Dealt by the sword for work of his own
beginning.

CHORUS: I am at a loss for thought, I
lack
All nimble counsel as to where
To turn when the house is falling.
I fear the house-collapsing crashing
Blizzard of blood—of which these drops
are earnest.
Now is Destiny sharpening her justice
On other whetstones for a new infliction.
    O earth, earth, if only you had received
    me
    Before I saw this man lie here as if in
    bed
    In a bath lined with silver.
    Who will bury him? Who will keen
    him?
    Will you, having killed your own hus-
    band,
    Dare now to lament him
    And after great wickedness make
    Unamending amends to his ghost?

And who above this godlike hero's
grave
Pouring praises and tears
Will grieve with a genuine heart?

CLYTEMNESTRA: It is not your business
to attend to that.
By my hand he fell low, lies low and dead,
And I shall bury him low down in the
earth,
And his household need not weep him
For Iphigeneia his daughter
Tenderly, as is right,
Will meet her father at the rapid ferry of
sorrows,
Put her arms round him and kiss him!

CHORUS: Reproach answers reproach,
It is hard to decide,
The catcher is caught, the killer pays for
his kill.
But the law abides while Zeus abides en-
throned
That the wrongdoer suffers. That is es-
tablished.
Who could expel from the house the seed
of the
Curse?
The race is soldered in sockets of Doom
and
Vengeance.

CLYTEMNESTRA: In this you say what is
right and the will of God.
But for my part I am ready to make a con-
tract
With the Evil Genius of the House of
Atreus
To accept what has been till now, hard
though it is,
But that for the future he shall leave this
house
And wear away some other stock with
deaths
Imposed among themselves. Of my posses-
sions
A small part will suffice if only I
Can rid these walls of the mad exchange
of murder.

(Enter AEGISTHUS, *followed by soldiers.)*
AEGISTHUS: O welcome light of a justice-
dealing day!
From now on I will say that the gods,
avenging men,
Look down from above on the crimes of
earth,
Seeing as I do in woven robes of the Furies
This man lying here—a sight to warm my
heart—
Paying for the crooked violence of his
father.
For his father Atreus, when he ruled the
country,
Because his power was challenged,
hounded out
From state and home his own brother
Thyestes.
My father—let me be plain—was this
Thyestes,
Who later came back home a suppliant,
There, miserable, found so much asylum
As not to die on the spot, stain the an-
cestral floor.
But to show his hospitality godless Atreus
Gave him an eager if not a loving wel-
come,
Pretending a day of feasting and rich
meats
Served my father with his children's flesh.
The hands and feet, fingers and toes, he
hid
At the bottom of the dish. My father sit-
ting apart
Took unknowing the unrecognizable por-
tion
And ate of a dish that has proved, as you
see, expensive.
But when he knew he had eaten worse
than poison
He fell back groaning, vomiting their
flesh,
And invoking a hopeless doom on the
sons of Pelops
Kicked over the table to confirm his
curse—
So may the whole race perish!

Result of this—you see this man lie here.
I stitched this murder together; it was my
title.
Me the third son he left, an unweaned in-
fant,
To share the bitterness of my father's exile.
But I grew up and Justice brought me
back,
I grappled this man while still beyond his
door,
Having pieced together the programme of
his ruin.
So now would even death be beautiful to
me
Having seen Agamemnon in the nets of
Justice.

LEADER: Aegisthus. I cannot respect
brutality in distress.
You claim that you deliberately killed this
prince
And that you alone planned this pitiful
murder.
Be sure that in your turn your head shall
not escape
The people's volleyed curses mixed with
stones.

AEGISTHUS: Do you speak so who sit at
the lower oar
While those on the upper bench control
the ship?
Old as you are, you will find it is a heavy
load
To go to school when old to learn the les-
son of tact.
For old age, too, gaol and hunger are fine
Instructors in wisdom, second-sighted doc-
tors.
You have eyes. Cannot you see?
Do not kick against the pricks. The blow
will hurt you.

LEADER: You woman waiting in the
house for those who return from
battle
While you seduce their wives! Was it you
devised
The death of a master of armies?

AEGISTHUS: And these words, too, prepare the way for tears.
Contrast your voice with the voice of Orpheus: he
Led all things after him bewitched with
joy, but you
Having stung me with your silly yelps
shall be
Led off yourself, to prove more mild when
mastered.

LEADER: Indeed! So you are now to be
king of Argos,
You who, when you had plotted the king's
death,
Did not even dare to do that thing yourself!

AEGISTHUS: No. For the trick of it was
clearly woman's work.
I was suspect, an enemy of old.
But now I shall try with Agamemnon's
wealth
To rule the people. Any who is disobedient
I will harness in a heavy yoke, no trace-
horse work for him
Like barley-fed colt, but hateful hunger
lodging
Beside him in the dark will see his temper
soften.

LEADER: Why with your cowardly soul
did you yourself
Not strike this man but left that work to
a woman
Whose presence pollutes our country and
its gods?
But Orestes—does he somewhere see the
light
That he may come back here by favor of
fortune
And kill this pair and prove the final victor?

AEGISTHUS (*summoning his guards*):
Well, if such is your design in deeds and
words, you will quickly learn—
Here my friends, here my guards, there is
work for you at hand.

LEADER: Come then, hands on hilts, be each and all of us prepared.

(*The old men and the guards threaten each other.*)

AEGISTHUS: Very well! I too am ready to meet death with sword in hand.

LEADER: We are glad you speak of dying. We accept your words for luck.

CLYTEMNESTRA: No, my dearest, do not so. Add no more to the train of wrong.
To reap these many present wrongs is harvest enough of misery.
Enough of misery. Start no more. Our hands are red.
But do you, and you old men, go home and yield to fate in time,
In time before you suffer. We have acted as we had to act.
If only our afflictions now could prove enough, we should agree—
We who have been so hardly mauled in the heavy claws of the evil god.
So stands my word, a woman's if any man think fit to hear.

AEGISTHUS: But to think that these should thus pluck the blooms of an idle tongue
And should throw out words like these, giving the evil god his chance,
And should miss the path of prudence and insult their master so!

LEADER: It is not the Argive way to fawn upon a cowardly man.

AEGISTHUS: Perhaps. But I in later days will take further steps with you.

LEADER: Not if the god who rules the family guides Orestes to his home.

AEGISTHUS: Yes. I know that men in exile feed themselves on barren hopes.

LEADER: Go on, grow fat defiling justice . . . while you have your hour.

AEGISTHUS: Do not think you will not pay me a price for your stupidity.

LEADER: Boast on in your self-assurance, like a cock beside his hen.

CLYTEMNESTRA: Pay no heed, Aegisthus, to these futile barkings. You and I,
Masters of this house, from now shall order all things well.

(*They enter the palace.*)

Medea

EURIPIDES

COMMENTARY

 Euripides (484-406 B. C.), like Aeschylus, was a prolific writer of tragedies although he did not win as many first prizes, perhaps because his
plays were more realistic and less traditionally orthodox. His career
spanned the period of Athenian glory; he moved in the circle of the
great philosophers, including Socrates. Late in life, he went into exile
in Macedonia, out of harmony with his countrymen's political and religious beliefs. He was more inventive in his dramatic technique than
either Aeschylus or Sophocles, especially in his psychological intensity
and esthetic detachment. He introduced the *deus ex machina*, a divinity,
or divine force, appearing on stage at the end of the play to resolve the
human action. More of his plays survive than of Aeschylus or Sophocles.
These include *Alcestis, Medea, Hippolytus, The Trojan Women, Orestes,
Iphigeneia at Aulis, The Bacchae, Heracles, The Suppliants, Iphigeneia
at Tauris, Electra.*

   Medea does not neatly fit the classical Aristotelian descriptions of
tragedy. Details of the play are so "horrible," to use H. D. F. Kitto's
formulation, that we may well want to think of it as "melodrama,"
perhaps in defense, to protect ourselves against its enormous force. Certainly the quality of the Euripidean world is different from that of the
Aeschylean and Sophoclean. Euripides would seem to put the burden
of guilt—and of absolution, of forgiveness—on frail yet potentially heroic
human nature itself. Human horror and human heroism do not need
divine impetus. The Euripidean irony, or cynicism, is peculiarly modern
in thrusting the effort of interpretation and judgment on the audience.

   Arrowsmith ("The Criticism of Greek Tragedy" in *Tragedy: Vision
and Form,* ed. Robert W. Corrigan, originally in *Tulane Drama Review,*
III, 3 [March 1959], 31-57) speaks of responding to the characters
and events in Euripides as a member of a "jury." Just how do we judge
Medea and Jason? How do their separate and different guilts compare
with those of Jocasta and Oedipus or of Clytemnestra and Agamemnon?

How do we judge Medea in the company of Mrs. Alving in *Ghosts*, Laura in *The Father*, or of Yerma in *Yerma*? What aspect of the "feminine mystique" does Medea embody?

Euripides in general and *Medea* specifically have been the subjects of many essays. In addition to Kitto's commentary in his *Greek Tragedy*, 3rd ed. (New York, 1961) and Arrowsmith's essay mentioned above, another valuable essay is Arrowsmith's introduction to the Chandler edition of *Medea,* edited by Robert W. Corrigan (San Francisco, 1966). The essays on melodrama by Eric Bentley, James L. Rosenberg, and Robert B. Heilman, in *Tragedy: Vision and Form,* ed. Robert W. Corrigan, provide valuable general concepts. Robinson Jeffers' version, available in various editions, is itself a critical comment. You might want to read it in terms of how that text might be staged as compared with the one here. How might some of the critical issues raised by the play—the intensity of Medea's fury, the "melodramatic" tones—affect a production? In what ways does a close reading suggest that the text itself might justify varying kinds of productions?

Euripides

MEDEA

Translated by Frederic Prokosch

The princess MEDEA of Colchis fell in love with JASON, who had come to her country in quest of the Golden Fleece, and aided him in his enterprise even to the extent of betraying her father, murdering her brother, and leaving her home for ever in order to live with JASON in Greece. After many vicissitudes they arrived at the court of PELIAS, who had sent JASON on his expedition. Here MEDEA contrived that PELIAS should be barbarously killed by his own daughters. The pair fled the country and took refuge in Corinth, where JASON abandoned MEDEA in order to marry GLAUKE, the daughter of KING KREON.

DRAMATIS PERSONÆ

MEDEA	ATTENDANT
JASON	NURSE
KREON	AEGEUS

MEDEA'S CHILDREN
A MESSENGER
CHORUS OF CORINTHIAN WOMEN

SCENE: *Corinth, before the house of Medea.*

(*The* NURSE *enters from the house.*)

NURSE: Oh how I wish that famous ship, the Argo, had never made its way through the blue Symplegades to the land of Colchis! How I wish the pine tree had never been felled in the glades of Pelion, and never been hewn into oars for the heroes who went to fetch the Golden Fleece for Pelias! For then my mistress, Medea, would never have sailed to the towers of the land of Iolcos, her heart on fire with love for Jason! Nor would she ever have beguiled the daughters of Pelias into slaying their father, nor have come to live in Corinth with her husband and children. For a long time she found favor with the people here in the land of exile; and she did all things in complete accord with Jason; and indeed it is this—when a woman stands loyally by a man—which brings to men the only sure salvation. But now their love has fallen into decay; and there's hatred everywhere. For Jason has betrayed his children and my mistress; he has taken a royal bride to his bed, the daughter of Kreon, who is the ruler of this land. And poor Medea, scorned and deserted, can do nothing but appeal to the vows they made to one another, and remind him of the eternal pledge they made with their right hands clasped. And she calls upon the gods to witness how Jason is repaying her for her love. She lies half famished; her body is bowed utterly with grief, wasting away the whole day long. So it has been since she learned that he has betrayed her. Never stirring an eye, never lifting her gaze from the ground; and when her friends speak to her in warning she no more listens than a rock listens, or the surging sea wave. Only now and then she turns her snowy neck and quietly laments, and utters her father's name, and the name of her land and home, which she deserted when she followed the man who now brings her such dishonor. Pitiful woman! She has learned at last through all her sufferings how lucky are those who have never lost their native land. She has come to feel a hatred for her children, and no longer wants to see them. Indeed, I fear she may be moving toward some dreadful plan; for her heart is violent. She will never submit to this cruel treatment. I know her well: her anger is great; and I know that any man who makes an enemy of her will have it hard. . . . Look; here come the children; they have been playing. Little they know of their mother's misery; little the hearts of the young can guess of sorrow!

(*The* ATTENDANT *brings in* MEDEA's *children.*)

ATTEND: Why are you standing here, in front of the gates? You've been maid for so many years to my mistress; why have you left her alone, then, only to stand outside the gates and lament?

NURSE: Listen, old man, who watch over Jason's sons! It's a sad, sad thing for faithful servants like us to see our master's fortunes meet with disaster; it stirs us to the heart. I am so lost in grief, now, that a longing came over me to step outside the gates, and tell the whole wide world and the heavens of my mistress's sorrows!

ATTEND: Poor lady! Hasn't she ceased her weeping yet?

NURSE: Ceased? Far from it! This is only the beginning; there is far more to come.

ATTEND: Poor, foolish lady; though I shouldn't call her that; but how little she knows of this latest trouble!

NURSE: What do you mean, old man? Come! Don't be afraid to tell me!

ATTEND: Nothing at all; I should never have mentioned it.

NURSE: No, no, by your wise old beard I beg you, don't hide anything from your fellow servant! Tell me; and, if you wish, I'll keep it secret.

ATTEND: Well, as I was passing the usual place where the old men sit playing draughts, down by the holy fountain of Pirene, I happened to overhear one of them saying that Kreon, King of the land, intends to send these children, and their mother from Corinth, far away into exile. But whether it was the truth he was speaking, I do not know; I hope and pray it wasn't the truth.

NURSE: And will Jason allow this thing to happen to his sons, even though he is on bad terms with their mother?

ATTEND: Old ties give way to new ones; and his love for this family of ours is dying away.

NURSE: Oh, it looks dark indeed for us; new sorrows are being added to old ones, even before the old ones have faded!

ATTEND: Be still, be still; don't whisper a word of it. This isn't the proper time to tell our mistress.

NURSE: O little children, do you hear how your father feels toward you? May evil befall him! But no; he is still my master. Yet how cruelly he has betrayed his dear ones!

ATTEND: And which of us has not done the same? Haven't you learned long ago, my dear, how each man loves himself far more than his neighbor? Some, perhaps, from honest motives; some for private gain. So you see how Jason deserts his children for the pleasure of his new bride.

NURSE: Go back into the house, children; all will be well. Try to keep them out of the way, old man; keep them far from their mother as long as she feels this desperate anger. I have already seen the fire in her eyes as she watched them, almost as though she were wishing them harm. I am sure her anger won't end till she has found a victim. Let's hope the victim will be an enemy, and not a friend!

(*Within the house.*)

MEDEA: Lost, oh lost! I am lost
In my sufferings. I wish, oh I wish
That I could die. . . .

NURSE: My dear children, what did I
tell you?
Your mother's mind is filled with the
wildest
Fancies; her heart is wild with anger!
Run quickly back into the house.
Keep out of her sight. Do not
Go near her. Beware of the wildness
And bitterness of her heart!

Go, quickly, quickly!
I can feel that her fury will rise
And redouble! I can hear
In that cry the rising thunderstorm,
I can feel the approach of thunder and
lightning!
Oh what will she do, in the pride
And torment of her soul? What
Evil thing will she do?

(*The* ATTENDANT *takes the children into the house.*)

(*Within.*)

MEDEA: Oh, I have suffered
And suffered enough for all these tears!
I call destruction upon you, all, all of you,
Sons of a doomed mother, and the father
too!
May ruin fall on the entire house!

NURSE: I am full of pity,
Full of deep pity for you! Yet why
Do the children share their father's crime?
Why should you hate them? O my poor
children,
I fear some outrage will befall you!
Yes, strange and terrible is the temper of
princes.
There is none they need to obey;
There is none that can check them:
There is nothing to control
The madness of their mood.
How much better off are the rest of us
Who've been taught to live equally
With our neighbors! All I wish
Is to grow old quietly, not in pride,
But only in humble security.
It's the moderate thing that always sounds
Best to our ears; and indeed it is
The moderate thing that is best in practice.
For power grows beyond control;
Power brings comfort to no man.
And I say, the greater the power, the
greater
The ruin when it finally falls.

(*Enter the* CHORUS *of Corinthian women. The following lines are chanted.*)

CHORUS: I heard the voice,
I heard the loud lament
Of the pitiful lady from Colchis:
Oh tell me, mother, is she still
Unquiet? As I stood
By the house with the double gates
I heard the sound of weeping from within.
I grieve for the sorrow of this family
Which I have come to love.

NURSE: There is no family left; it has gone,
It has gone forever. The master now
Has a royal bride in the bed beside him,
And our mistress is withering away
In her chamber, and finds no solace
Or warmth in words
That friends can utter.

(*Within.*)

MEDEA: Oh how I wish that a stroke of lightning
Would fall from heaven and shatter my head!
Why should I live any longer?
Death would bring release; in death
I could leave behind me the horror of living.

CHORUS: Did you hear, almighty Zeus?
O earth, O heaven, did you hear
The cry of woe this woman has uttered?
Oh why, poor lady, should you long
For that unutterable haven of rest?
Death only can bring it; and death comes only too soon!
No, no, there is no need to pray for death.
And if your man is drawn
To a new love, remember,
Such things occur often; do not feel hurt.
For God will be your ultimate friend and judge
In this as in all matters.
So do not mourn too much,
Do not waste away in sorrow
For the loss of the one you loved!

(*Within.*)

MEDEA: Great Themis, O lady Artemis, look down

On all I am suffering; and suffering in spite
Of all the vows my husband made me.
I pray that I may some day see
Him and his bride brought down to ruin
And their palace ruined for all the wrong
They dared to do me without cause.
O my own father, my own country,
Shameful it was of me to leave you,
And to have killed my brother before I left you!

NURSE: Do you hear what she says? Do you hear
How loudly she cries to Themis, the goddess of promises,
And to Zeus, whom men think of as the Emperor of Vows?
One thing I know. It is no small thing
That draws such anger from our mistress!

CHORUS: Let her come forth and see us,
Let her listen to our words of warning,
Let her lay aside the rage and violence of her heart;
Never shall I refuse to help my friends,
Never shall they turn to me in vain.
Go, go, and bring her from the house
That we may see her; speak kindly to her!
Hurry, before she does some violent thing.
I feel her passion rising to a new pitch.

NURSE: Yes; I shall go; but I deeply doubt
Whether I can persuade my mistress.
Still, I shall gladly go and try;
Though she glares upon her servants, those
That approach and dare to speak to her,
With the fiery look of a lioness with cubs!
You would be right, I think,
If you called both ignorant
And trivial those poets of old who wrote
Their songs for festivities and banquets,
Graceful and pleasant sounds for men
Who lived in gaiety and leisure.
For none of them learned a way
For the song or the musicians
To still man's suffering. And suffering it is

From which all killing springs, and all
    calamity
Which falls on the homes of men.
Yet it would be a blessing, surely,
If songs could heal the wounds which
    sorrow
Inflicts on men! What good is music
And singing at an idle banquet? It seems
    to me
That men who are sitting at the banquet
    table
Have pleasure enough already . . .

(*The* NURSE *goes into the house.*)

CHORUS: I heard a cry that was heavy
    and sick with sorrow.
Loud in her bitterness she cries
On the man who betrayed her marriage
    bed!
Full of her wrongs she cries
To the gods, to Themis, to the bride of
    Zeus,
To the Keeper of Vows, who brought her
    away
To the shores of Greece which face the
    shores of Asia,
Through the straits at night to the gate-
    way opening
On the unlimited salty sea.

(*Toward the end of this song,* MEDEA
enters from the house.)

MEDEA: Ladies of Corinth, I have come
forth from my house, lest you should feel
bitterness toward me; for I know that men
often acquire a bad name for their pride—
not only the pride they show in public,
but also the pride of retirement; those who
live in solitude, as I do, are frequently
thought to be proud. For there is no justice in the view one man takes of another,
often hating him before he has suffered
wrong, hating him even before he has seen
his true character. Therefore a foreigner
above all should fit into the ways of a city.
Not even a native citizen, I think, should
risk offending his neighbors by rudeness
or pride.

But this new thing has fallen upon me
so unexpectedly, my strength is broken.
O my friends, my life is shattered; my
heart no longer longs for the blessings of
life, but only for death! There was one
man through whom I came to see the
world's whole beauty: and that was my
husband; and he has turned out utterly
evil. O women, of all creatures that live
and reflect, certainly it is we who are the
most luckless. First of all, we pay a great
price to purchase a husband; and thus
submit our bodies to a perpetual tyrant.
And everything depends on whether our
choice is good or bad—for divorce is not
an honorable thing, and we may not refuse to be married. And then a wife is
plunged into a way of life and behavior
entirely new to her, and must learn what
she never learned at home—she must
learn by a kind of subtle intuition how to
manage the man who lies beside her. And
if we have the luck to handle all these
things with tact and success, and if the
husband is willing to live at our side without resentment, then life can become happy
indeed. But if not, I'd rather be dead. A
man who is disgusted with what he finds
at home, goes forth to put an end to his
boredom, and turns to a friend or companion of his own age; while we at home
continue to think of him, and of him only.

And yet people say that we live in security at home, while the men go forth to
war. How wrong they are! Listen: I'd
rather be sent three times over to the battle-
front than give birth to a single child.

Still, my friends, I realize that all this
applies not to you but to me; you after
all have a city of your own, and a family
home, and a certain pleasure in life, and
the company of your friends. But I am
utterly lonely, an exile, cast off by my own
husband—nothing but a captive brought
here from a foreign land—without a
mother or brother, without a single kins-
man who can give me refuge in this sea

of disaster. Therefore, my ladies, I ask only one thing of you: promise me silence. If I can find some way, some cunning scheme of revenge against my husband for all that he has done to me, and against the man who gave away his daughter, and against the daughter who is now my husband's wife: then please be silent. For though a woman is timid in everything else, and weak, and terrified at the sight of a sword: still, when things go wrong in this thing of love, no heart is so fearless as a woman's; no heart is so filled with the thought of blood.

CHORAG: Yes; I promise this. You will be right, Medea, in avenging yourself on your husband. It does not surprise me to see you lost in despair . . . But look! I see Kreon, our king, approaching: he will have some news to tell us.

(*Enter* KREON, *with his following.*)

KREON: Listen to me, Medea! You, with your angry looks and all that bitterness against your husband: I order you to leave my kingdom! I order you to go with both your children into exile, and immediately. This is my decree. And I will not return to my house until I have hurled you beyond the borders of my kingdom.

MEDEA: Oh, now I am lost indeed! This is the end of all things for me! Now my enemies are bearing down on me in all their force; and I have no refuge left in this hour of ruin. And yet, let me ask you this one thing, Kreon: why is it, Kreon, you are sending me away?

KREON: I am afraid of you. I need no longer pretend otherwise. I am afraid you will do my daughter some mortal harm. And I have many reasons for being afraid of this. You are a cunning woman, Medea, expert in all kinds of magic, so I hear. And you are enraged by the loss of your husband's love. I have also heard them say that you are planning some kind of mischief against Jason and the bride, and the bride's father, myself, as well. It is

against these things I take precautions. I tell you, Medea, I'd rather incur your hatred now than be soft-hearted and later learn to regret it.

MEDEA: This is not the first time, Kreon! Many times before has this strange reputation done me harm. A sensible man should never nowadays bring up his children to be too clever or exceptional. For one thing, these talents never bring them profit; for another, they end by bringing envy and hatred from others. If you present new ideas to a group of fools, they'll think you ignorant as well as idle. And if your fame should come to exceed the established reputations, they'll hate you for it. This has been my own experience. Some think me clever, and resent it; some think me not so very clever after all, and disapprove. And you, Kreon, are somehow afraid that I may do something to harm you. But you need not worry. It isn't for someone like me to quarrel with kings. After all, why should I? You haven't harmed me. You've allowed your daughter to marry as you saw fit. I hate my husband, certainly; but as for you, I feel you have acted reasonably enough. I don't grudge you for your good fortune. I wish you luck with your daughter's marriage, Kreon, but beg you only, let me live on in this land. I have been wronged, but I shall remain quiet, and submit to those above me.

KREON: Your words are gentle enough, Medea. Yet in my heart I can't help dreading that you are planning some evil; and I trust you now even less than before. It is easier to deal with a quick-tempered man or woman than with one who is subtle and soft-spoken. No. You must go at once. Make no more speeches. It is settled. You are my enemy, and there is nothing you can do to prolong your stay in my country.

MEDEA: I implore you! By your knees, by your newly wed daughter!

KREON: You are wasting your words. You will never persuade me.

MEDEA: Then you'll drive me out without listening to my prayers?

KREON: I shall; for I love my own family more than you.

MEDEA: O my country! How my heart goes back to you now!

KREON: I, too, love my country above all things, except my children.

MEDEA: How cruelly passionate love can deal with men!

KREON: And yet, it all depends on the luck men have.

MEDEA: O Zeus, never forget the man who caused this!

KREON: Go now; go. Spare me this useless trouble.

MEDEA: No trouble, no pain, nothing has been spared me!

KREON: Soon one of my men shall lead you away by force.

MEDEA: Not that, Kreon, not that! I beg you, Kreon.

KREON: It seems you insist on creating a disturbance.

MEDEA: I will go. I will go. That is not what I intended.

KREON: Why all this commotion, then? What is it you want?

MEDEA: Let me stay here just a single day longer, Kreon. Let me stay and think over where I shall go in exile, and how I shall find a living for my children, for whom their father has completely failed to provide. Take pity on them, Kreon! You too have children of your own; you too must have a soft place in your heart for them. What happens to me now no longer matters; I only grieve for the suffering that will come to my children.

KREON: I am not a cruel man, Medea. I have often made blunders, out of sheer compassion. Even now I feel I am making a mistake. All the same, have it your way.

But let me warn you! If tomorrow at sunrise still finds you and your children within the frontiers of my land, you shall die for it. That is my verdict; it is final. So stay this one day longer, if you must. One day is not enough to bring disaster.

(*Exit* KREON *with his following.*)

CHORAG: Pitiful woman! Oh we pity
The sorrows you suffer!
Where will you turn now? Who can help
    you?
What home remains, what land
Is left to save you from destruction?
O Medea, you have been hurled by heaven
Into an ocean of despair.

MEDEA: Everything has gone wrong. None can deny it. But not quite everything is lost; don't give up hope, my friends! There still are troubles in store for the young bride, and for the bridegroom too. Do you think I would have fawned on that old man without some plan and purpose? Certainly not. I would never have touched him with my hands. But now, although he could have crushed all my plans by instant exile, he has made a fatal error; he has given me one day's reprieve. One day in which I can bring death to the three creatures that I loathe: the father, the bride, my husband. There are many manners of death which I might use; I don't quite know yet which to try. Shall I set fire to the bridal mansion? Or shall I sharpen a sword and steal into the chamber to the wedding bed and plunge it into their hearts? One thing stands in my way. If I am caught making my way into the bridal room on such an errand, I shall surely be put to death, and my foes will end by triumphing over me. Better to take the shortest way, the way I am best trained in: better to bring them down with poison. That I will do, then. And after that? Suppose them dead. What city will take me in then? What friend will offer me shelter in his land, and safety, and a home? None. Then best to wait a little longer; perhaps some sure defense will appear, and I can set about this murder in stealth and still-ness. And if no help should come from fate, and even if death is certain, still I can take at last the sword in my own hand and go forth boldly to the crime, and kill. Yes, by that dark Queen whom I revere above all others, and whom I now invoke to help me, by Hecate who dwells in my most secret chamber: I swear no man shall injure me and not regret it. I will turn their marriage into sorrow and anguish! Go now, go forward to this dangerous deed! The time has come for courage. Remember the suffering they caused you! Never shall you be mocked because of this wedding of Jason's, you who are sprung from a noble father and whose grandfather was the Sun-God himself! You have the skill; what is more, you are a woman: and it's always a woman who is incapable of a noble deed, yet expert in every kind of mischief!

(STROPHE 1)

CHORUS: The sacred rivers are flowing back to their sources!
The order of the world is being reversed!
Now it is men who have grown deceitful,
Men who have broken their sacred vows.
The name of woman shall rise to favor
Again; and women once again
Shall rise and regain their honor: never
Again shall ill be said of women!

(ANTISTROPHE 1)

Those poets of old shall cease at last
To sing of our faithlessness. Never
On us did Phoebus, the god of music,
Lavish the talents of the lyre,
Else I should long ago have sung
A song of rebuttal to the race
Of men: for the years have many things
To tell of them as well as of us!

(STROPHE 2)

You sailed away from your father's dwelling

With your heart on fire, Medea! And you passed
Between the rocky gates of the seas;
And now you sleep on a foreign shore,
In a lonely bed: now you are driven
Forth, and far away from the land
Once more you go in exile and dishonor!

(ANTISTROPHE 2)

Gone is the dignity of vows,
Gone from great Hellas the sense of honor.
It has flown and vanished in the skies.
And now no father's dwelling house
Stands as a refuge from this storm!
Now another princess lies
In the bed which once was yours, and
rules your home!

(*As the* CHORUS *approaches the end of the song,* JASON *enters.*)

JASON: This is not the first time I have noticed how difficult it is to deal with a violent temper. Ah, Medea, if you had patiently accepted the will of our ruler, you might have stayed on quietly in this land and this house. But now your point-less complaints are driving you into exile. Not that I minded them myself; I didn't mind it at all when you called Jason an evil man. But, considering your references to the King himself, you may count your-self lucky that your punishment is exile. Personally, I have always done my best to calm the King's anger, and would have liked to see you stay on here. But you refused to give up this sort of folly, and kept on slandering him; with the result that you are facing banishment. Never-theless, in spite of your behavior, I feel inclined to do you a favor; I have come to make some sort of provision for you and the children, my dear, so that you won't be penniless when you are in exile; for I know that exile will not be easy. And even though you hate me, Medea, my thoughts of you will continue to be friendly as always.

MEDEA: You filthy coward! That is the only name I can find for you, you and your utter lack of manliness! And now you, who are the worst of my enemies, now you too have chosen to come to me! No; it isn't courage which brings you, nor recklessness in facing the friends you have injured; it is worse than that, it is the worst of all human vices: shamelessness. Still, you did well to come to me, for now I can ease my heart by reviling you: and perhaps you too will suffer as you listen.

Let me begin, then, at the very beginning. I saved your life; every Greek who sailed with you on the Argo knows I saved you, when you were sent to tame the fire-breathing bulls and to yoke them, and to sow the deadly fields. Yes, and I killed the many-folded serpent who lay guarding the Golden Fleece, forever wakeful, coil upon coil. And I raised a beacon of light to bring you to safety. Freely I deserted my own father and my own home; and followed you to Iolcos, to the hills of Pelion; and all this time my love was stronger than my reason. And I brought death to Pelias by his own daughters' hands; I utterly destroyed the household. All of these things I did for you, traitor! And you forsook me, and took another wife, even though I had borne your children. Had you been childless, one might have pardoned your wish for a second wedding. But now all my faith in your vows has vanished. I do not know whether you imagine that the gods by whom you swore have disappeared, or that new rules are now in vogue in such matters; for you must be aware that you have broken your vows to me. Oh this poor right hand, which you so often pressed! These knees, which you so often used to embrace! And all in vain, for it was an evil man that touched me! How wildly all my hopes have fallen through! . . .

Come, Jason, I shall speak to you quite frankly, as though we still were friends. Can I possibly expect any kindness from someone like you? Still, let us assume that I can: it will only make you appear still more ignoble. Very well. Where shall I go? Home to my father? Home to him and the land I betrayed when I followed you? Or back to the pitiful daughters of Pelias? What a fine welcome they would give me, who arranged the death of their own father! So this is how it now stands with me. I am loathed by my friends at home; and for your sake I made enemies of others whom I need never have harmed. And now, to reward me for all this, look, look how doubly happy you've made me among the women of Hellas! Look what a fine, trustworthy husband I have had in you! And now I am to be cast forth into exile, in utter misery, alone with my children and without a single friend! Oh, this will be a shameful shadow upon you, as you lie in your wedding bed! That your own children, and their mother, who saved your life, should go wandering around the world like beggars! . . . O Zeus, why have you given us a way to tell true gold from the counterfeit, but no way, no emblem branded on a man's body whereby we can tell the true man from the false?

CHORAG: Dreadful is the anger, and past all healing, when lovers in fury turn against each other!

JASON: The time has come, it seems, when I must speak, and speak well, and like a good helmsman reef up my sail and weather the tempest of your tongue . . . And since you dwell so heavily on all the favors you did me, Medea, I am certain that I owe the safety of my voyage to Aphrodite alone among gods and men. Not that I doubt your skill; but all the same, I prefer not to dwell on this notion that love, with all its irresistible power, compelled you to save my life. I don't think we need go into details. I admit that you meant well, and did your best. But when it comes to this matter of my safety, let me point out that you got rather more than you gave. First of all, instead of living in a barbaric land, you've come to Greece and enjoyed contact with a country where justice and law prevail, and not brute force; and what is more, the Greeks thought rather highly of you. You even acquired a certain fame here. Whereas, if you had stayed on in that outer fringe of the world, your name would now be quite unknown. Frankly, I'd rather have real fame and distinction than mighty stores of gold in my halls or the talent to sing more sweetly than Orpheus. That is my answer to your version of all my labors; remember, it was you who brought up this matter.

As for your bitter attack on my marriage with the princess, I think I can prove first of all that it was a shrewd move; secondly, a thoroughly sober one; and finally, that I did it in your interest and that of your children . . . Wait! Please remain calm . . . Since I had come from Iolcos involved in every kind of trouble, and an exile, what could be luckier for me than marriage with the King's own daughter? It was not—since it is this that seems to rankle in you—it was not that I grew weary of going to bed with you, and began to look around for a new wife. Nor was it that I was anxious to have more children. The two we have are quite enough; I don't complain. No, it was this, first of all: that we might live in comfort, and not in poverty. Believe me, I have learned how a man's friends desert him the moment he is penniless . . . And then I wanted to bring up my sons in a manner worthy of my position; I even hoped that by having more sons, who would live as brothers to yours, we might draw the entire family into harmony, and all be happy. You yourself need no more children; but I would do well to help the sons I have through

the sons I hope to have. Do you disagree with all this? You would agree if it weren't for this matter of love which rankles in you. But you women have developed such curious notions: you think that all is well as long as your life at night runs smoothly. But if something happens which upsets your way of love, then all that you once found lovely and desirable you now find hateful. Believe me, it would have been better far if men could have thought up some other way of producing children, and done away with women; then no evil would ever have come to men.

CHORAG: O Jason, you have given this speech of yours a convincing enough air; and yet I somehow feel, though perhaps I shouldn't say so, that you have acted wickedly in betraying your wife.

MEDEA: I suppose I am different in many ways from most people, for I feel that the worst punishment should fall on the man who speaks brilliantly for an evil cause, the man who knows he can make an evil thing sound plausible and who dares to do so. And still, such a man isn't really so very wise after all. Listen, Jason. You need not bring forth these clever phrases and specious arguments; for a single word from me will destroy you. Consider: had you not been a coward, Jason, you would have spoken frankly to me first, and not concealed your wedding plans from the one who loved you.

JASON: And you, no doubt, would have done all you could to help me, if I had spoken of this matter: you, who even now cannot control the rage in your heart.

MEDEA: It wasn't this that restrained you. No. It was that you thought it might not be altogether proper, as you grew older, to have a foreign wife.

JASON: You may be quite sure of one thing, Medea. It was not because of any woman that I made this royal marriage. It was as I said before: because I wanted security for you, and also to be the father of royal children bound by blood to our two children: a thing which would have brought welfare to all of us.

MEDEA: I don't want the kind of welfare that is brought by suffering. I don't want the kind of safety which ends in sorrow.

JASON: Reflect on that opinion, Medea; it will make you wiser. Don't search for sorrow in prosperity. Don't keep looking for pain in a piece of good luck.

MEDEA: Go on; mock me. You at least have a home to turn to. But I am going into exile, and alone.

JASON: It was you who made this choice; there is no one else to blame.

MEDEA: How so? By marrying and deserting you?

JASON: You called down an evil curse on the royal house.

MEDEA: I have brought a curse to your own house too, I think.

JASON: Well, I don't propose to go into this any further. But if you'd like to take along some of my money into exile, for your own need and that of the children, please say so. I am prepared to be generous on this point, and even to give you letters to friends of mine abroad who will treat you well. It would be madness for you to refuse this offer. It will be to your own gain, Medea, if you give up your anger.

MEDEA: I will never accept favors from friends of yours; and I'll accept nothing from you, so please don't offer it. Gifts from a coward bring luck to no one.

JASON: Very well then. I call upon the gods to witness that I have tried in every way to help you and the children. It is you who refuse my offers. It is you who are stubbornly rejecting your friends. And for this, Medea, you will surely suffer.

MEDEA: Please go! I can see you are longing to be with your new sweetheart. Aren't you lingering too long outside her bedroom? Go, and taste the joys of your wedding. Go, and God help you; you may end by regretting this kind of wedding!

(JASON *goes out.*)

(STROPHE I)

CHORUS: When love has passed its limits
It brings no longer good:
It brings no peace or comfort to any soul.
Yet while she still moves mildly there is
    no fire
So sweet as that which is lit by the goddess
    of love.
Oh never, upon me, Cypris,
Send forth from your golden bow
The unerring arrow poisoned with desire!

(ANTISTROPHE I)

Let my heart be temperate: for that
Is the wisest gift of the gods.
Let not that terrible goddess drive
Me to jealousy or rage! Oh let me never
Be one of those who incessantly are driven
To some new, forbidden longing!
Let her guide us gently toward the man
    we choose;
Let her bless our beds with repose.

(STROPHE 2)

O my country, my own home
Let me never leave my city,
Let me never lose my way
In that dark and pitiless life
Where each new day brings sorrow!
O, let me first succumb
To death, yes, let me die
Before I suffer the hopeless
Grief of the loss of a home!

(ANTISTROPHE 2)

I have seen it with my own eyes,
I have heard my own heart tell me:
There is no city, no,
No friend who will give you pity
In the hour of your deepest woe.
O, let him perish in darkness

Who is faithless to his friends
And lets his heart stay frozen!
Let no such man be my friend!

(MEDEA *has been sitting in despair on the
stairway during this song.* AEGEUS *enters.*)

AEGEUS: Joy to you, Medea! This is the
best kind of greeting between old friends!

MEDEA: And joy to you, Aegeus, son of
Pandion, King of Athens! How does it
happen that you have set foot in this country?

AEGEUS: I have come from the ancient
oracles of Phoebus.

MEDEA: And why did you visit that
great centre of prophecy?

AEGEUS: I went to ask how I might
bring fertility to my seed.

MEDEA: Tell me, has your life been
childless hitherto?

AEGEUS: Some divine visitation, I think,
has made me childless.

MEDEA: Have you a wife, or not?

AEGEUS: I have, Medea.

MEDEA: And what did Phoebus tell you
about begetting children?

AEGEUS: Words far too subtle for any
man to understand.

MEDEA: Is it proper for you to tell me
what he said?

AEGEUS: Certainly; what I need is
cleverness like yours.

MEDEA: Then what were the God's
words? Tell me, if I may hear them.

AEGEUS: That I shouldn't loosen the
hanging neck of the wine skin . . .

MEDEA: Till when? What must you do
first? Where must you go?

AEGEUS: Till I have returned again to
my native home.

MEDEA: Then why have you come sailing to this land?

AEGEUS: There is a man called Pittheus,
who is King of Troezen.

MEDEA: A son of Pelops, so they say,
and a man of piety.

AEGEUS: I want to discuss this oracle of
the God with him.

MEDEA: He is a man full of skill and
experience in these matters.

AEGEUS: As well as the dearest of my
old spear-bearing friends.

MEDEA: Good luck to you then! And
success to your wishes!

AEGEUS: But why do you look so pale
and woebegone?

MEDEA: O Aegeus, my husband has
turned out to be the vilest of men!

AEGEUS: What do you mean? Tell me
what has made you so unhappy.

MEDEA: Jason is wronging me, and
utterly without provocation.

AEGEUS: What has he done? Tell me
more clearly, Medea.

MEDEA: He has taken another wife to
take my place.

AEGEUS: Does he really dare to do such
a cruel thing!

MEDEA: He does indeed! He loved me
once, but no longer.

AEGEUS: Has he fallen in love? Has he
wearied of your bed?

MEDEA: Ah, he's a great lover! But
never true to his love. . . .

AEGEUS: Let him go, then, if he is really
as bad as you say.

MEDEA: He's in love with the idea of
marrying royalty.

AEGEUS: And who is the father of this
princess? Please go on.

MEDEA: Her father is Kreon, King of
Corinth.

AEGEUS: Indeed, Medea, I understand
your grief.

MEDEA: I am lost. And there is more:
I am being banished!

AEGEUS: Banished? By whom? This is something new you tell me.

MEDEA: Kreon is driving me from Corinth into banishment.

AEGEUS: Does Jason consent? This is a contemptible thing.

MEDEA: Not in so many words, but he has not really opposed it. O Aegeus, I beg you, I implore you, by your beard and by your knees, I beseech you, have pity on me! Have pity on a friend who is in trouble! Don't let me wander about in exile! Let me come to your land of Athens, let me find refuge in your halls! And there, with heaven's consent, you may find your love grow fertile and be blessed with children, and your life at last end happily. You don't know, Aegeus, how good your luck has been, for I shall end your sterility; I shall bring power to your seed; for I know of drugs that can do this.

AEGEUS: There are many reasons, my dear lady, why I should like to do this for you: first, for the sake of the children you promise me (for in that matter, frankly, I'm at my wits' end). But let me state my position. If you arrive in Athens, I shall stand by you as I am bound to do. But I must warn you first, my friend: I won't agree to take you with me. If you arrive at my halls of your own accord, you shall live there in safety; I shan't surrender you to anyone. But you yourself must manage your escape from this land, for I have no wish to incur ill will among my friends here.

MEDEA: Very well. So be it. Make me a formal pledge on this, and I shall be satisfied.

AEGEUS: Do you distrust me? What is it that troubles you?

MEDEA: I trust you, yes. But the house of Pelias, and Kreon as well, both detest me. If you are bound to me by an oath, then, when they come to drag me away

from your country, I know you will remain true to your vow and stand by me. Whereas, if it's only a promise, you might not be in a position to resist their demands; for I am weak, and they have both money and a royal house to help them.

AEGEUS: You show considerable foresight in these matters, I must say. Still, if you insist, I shan't refuse you. From my own point of view, too, it might be just as well to have an excuse like this oath to present to your enemies . . . Now name your gods.

MEDEA: Swear by the plain of Earth, and by my father's father Helios, the Sun God, and in one sweeping phrase by the whole host of the gods. . . .

AEGEUS: Swear to do what, or not to do what? Tell me.

MEDEA: Swear that you will never cast me from your land, nor ever, as long as you live, allow an enemy of mine to carry me away.

AEGEUS: I swear by the Earth, and by the holy light of Helios, the Sun God, and by the entire host of the gods, that I will abide by the terms you have just made.

MEDEA: Very well. And if you should fail, what curse are you willing to incur?

AEGEUS: Whatever happens to such as disregard the gods.

MEDEA: Go in peace, Aegeus. All is well, now; I shall arrive in your city as soon as I possibly can—after I have done what I must do, and accomplished what I desire.

(AEGEUS *goes out.*)

CHORAG: May Hermes, the God of Travelers,
Go with you on your way, Aegeus,
And bring you safely home!
And may you find the thing you have been seeking
For so long; you seem to be a generous man.

MEDEA: O Zeus, and Justice who are the child of Zeus, and light of the Sun God! Now, my friends, has come the hour of my triumph! Now I have started on the road; now I know that I shall bring revenge on the ones I hate. For at the very moment that my doom looked darkest of all, this man Aegeus appeared, like a harbor for all my hopes; and to him I can fasten the cable of my ship when I come to the town and fortress of Pallas Athene. And now let me tell you all of my plans. Listen; they will not be idle words, or pleasant. I shall send a servant to Jason and ask for an interview. And when he comes, I shall be soft and conciliatory; I shall tell him that I've thought better of it; that I agree; that even the treacherous marriage with the princess, which he is celebrating, strikes me as sensible, and all for the best. However, I shall beg him to let the children stay on here: not that I'd dream of leaving my babies to be insulted in a land that loathes me; but purely as a stratagem; and I shall kill the king's own daughter. For I shall send them with gifts in their little hands, to be offered to the bride to preserve them from banishment: a finely woven dress and a golden diadem. And if she takes these things and wears them on her body, she, and whoever touches her, will die in anguish; for I shall rub these things with deadly poison. That will be that; but it is the next thing I must do which sets me weeping. For I will kill my own children! My own dear children, whom none shall take from me. And when I have brought ruin on the house of Jason, I shall flee from the land and flee from the murder of my children; for it will be a terrible deed to do! It isn't easy, my friends, to bear the insults of one's enemies. And so it shall be. For what have I left in life? I have no land, no home, no harbor to protect me. What a fool I was to leave my father's house, to put my faith in the words of a Greek!

And for this he will pay the penalty, so help me God. Never again will he see his sons alive; never will he have a son by this new bride. For she is doomed to die, and die hideously from the power of my poison. Let no man think I am a feeble, frail-hearted woman who sits with folded hands: no, let them know me for the opposite of that—one who knows how to hurt her enemies and help her friends. It is lives like this that are longest remembered!

CHORAG: Since you have told us all your plans, let me say this to you: do not do this thing!

MEDEA: There is nothing else I can do. It is forgivable that you should say this: but remember, you have not suffered as I have!

CHORAG: Woman, can you really bring yourself to destroy your own flesh and blood?

MEDEA: I can; for in that way I can hurt my husband most cruelly.

CHORAG: And yourself as well! You will be the most miserable of women.

MEDEA: Then I will; no matter. No word of warning now can stop me!

(*The* NURSE *enters;* MEDEA *turns to her.*)

MEDEA: Go and tell Jason to come to me. And remember, I send you on a mission of great secrecy. Say nothing of the plans I have prepared; don't say a word, if you are loyal to your mistress and loyal to the race of woman!

(STROPHE 1)
CHORUS: Oh listen! We know of a land
Where dwell the sons of Erechtheus,
Fed on the food of wisdom, and blessed
    with the blood of gods,
Raised on a soil still holy and still unconquered; and there
Moving amid that glittering air where the legends

Say that lovely Harmonia, the golden-
haired,
Brought forth the Sacred Nine, the Pierian
Muses!

(ANTISTROPHE 1)
And where they say that Cypris,
The divine one, sailed to draw the
Water out of the wandering stream of
Cephisus, and the gentle
Winds passed over the land: and over her
glittering
Head the long, sweet-scented rose wreaths
Were wound by the Loves, who sit by
Wisdom's side
And in all virtuous deeds are the friends
of mortals.

(STROPHE 2)
Then how can this city, O how
Can these sacred streams which welcome
Only the ones they love,
O tell, how can they welcome
You who are evil? You
Who are killing your sons? O think
Of the sons you plan to slay,
Of the blood you plan to shed!
We beg, we implore you, Medea:
Do not murder your sons!

(ANTISTROPHE 2)
Oh where can your hand or your heart
Medea, find the hardness
To do this frightful thing
Against your sons? O how
Can you look on them and yet
Not weep, Medea? How
Can you still resolve to slay them?
Ah, when they fall at your feet
For mercy, you will not be able
To dip your hand in their blood!

(JASON *enters*.)

JASON: I have come at your bidding,
Medea. For although you are full of hatred
for me, this small favor I will grant you;
I will listen to you, my lady, and hear
what new favor you are asking.

MEDEA: Jason, I beg your forgiveness
for what I have said! Surely you can afford
to forgive my bad temper: after all, there
has been much love between us! I have
reasoned with myself and reproached myself. 'Poor fool,' I said, 'Why am I so distraught? Why am I so bitter against all
good advice, why am I so angry at the
rulers of this country, and my husband as
well, who does the best he can for me in
marrying a royal princess, and in having
royal children, who will be brothers to
my own? Why not stop complaining?
What is wrong with me, when the gods
are being so generous? Don't I have my
children to consider? Don't I realize that
we are exiles after all, and in need of
friends?' . . . And when I had thought all
this over, Jason, I saw how foolish I'd
been, and how silly my anger. So now I
agree with you. I think you are well advised in taking this new wife; and I was
mad. I should have helped you in your
plans, I should have helped arrange the
wedding. I should have stood by the wedding bed and been happy to wait on your
bride. But we women are—well, I shan't
say entirely worthless; but we are what
we are. And you men shouldn't stoop to
our level: you shouldn't reply to our folly
with folly. I give in. I admit I was wrong.
I have thought better of it all. . . .

(*She turns toward the house.*)

Come, come, my children, come out from
the house, come and greet your father,
and then say good-bye to him. Give up
your anger, as your mother does; be
friends with him again, be reconciled!

(*The* ATTENDANT *enters with the children.*)

We have made peace now; our bitterness
is gone. Take his right hand . . . O God:
I can't help thinking of the things that lie
dark and hidden in the future! . . . My
children, hold out your arms—the way one
holds them in farewell after a long, long
life . . . I am close to tears, my children!

I am full of fear! I have ended my quarrel with your father at last, and look! My eyes are full of tears.

CHORAG: And our eyes too are filling with tears. O, do not let disasters worse than the present descend on you!

JASON: I approve of your conduct, Medea; not that I blame you for anything in the past. It is natural for a woman to be furious with her husband when he begins to have other affairs. But now your heart has grown more sensible, and your mind is changed for the better; you are behaving like a woman of sense. And of you, my sons, your father will take good care, and make full provision, with the help of God. And I trust that in due time you with your brothers will be among the leading men in Corinth. All you need to do is grow up, my sons; and as for your future, you may leave it safely in the hands of your father, and of those among the gods who love him. I want to see you when you've grown to be men, tall and strong, towering over my enemies! . . . Medea, why are your eyes wet with tears? Why are your cheeks so pale? Why are you turning away? Don't these happy words of mine make you happy?

MEDEA: It is nothing. I was only thinking about these children.

JASON: Take heart, then. I shall look after them well.

MEDEA: I will, Jason. It is not that I don't trust you. Women are weak; and tears come easily to them.

JASON: But why should you feel disturbed about the children?

MEDEA: I gave birth to them, Jason. And when you prayed that they might live long, my heart filled with sorrow to think that all these things must happen . . . Well now: I have told you some of the things I called you here to tell you; now let me tell you the rest. Since the ruler of this land

has resolved to banish me, and since I am considered an enemy, I know it will be best for me not to stand in your way, or in the way of the King, by living here. I am going forth from this land into exile. But these children—O let them feel that you are protecting them, and beg of Kreon not to banish them!

JASON: I doubt whether I can persuade him; still, I will try.

MEDEA: Or at least ask your wife to beg her father to do this, and give the children reprieve from exile.

JASON: I will try; and with her I think I shall succeed.

MEDEA: She's a woman, after all; and like all other women. And I will help you in this matter; I will send the children to her with gifts far more exquisite, I am sure, than any now to be found among men—a finely woven dress and a diadem of chased gold. There; let one of the servants go and bring me these lovely ornaments.

(*One of the* ATTENDANTS *goes into the house.*)

And she'll be happy not in one way, but a thousand! With so splendid a man as you to share her bed, and with this marvelous gown as well, which once the Sun God Helios himself, my father's father, gave his descendants.

(*The* ATTENDANT *returns with the poisoned dress and diadem.*)

There, my children, take these wedding presents in your hands and take them as an offering to the royal princess, the lucky bride; give them to her; they are not gifts to be scorned.

JASON: But why do you give them away so rashly, Medea? Do you think the royal palace is lacking in dresses, or in gold? Keep them. Don't give them away. If my wife really loves me, I am sure she values me more highly than gold.

MEDEA: No; don't say that, Jason. For I have heard it said that gifts can persuade even the gods; and men are governed more by gold than by words! Luck has fallen on your bride, and the gods have blessed her fortune. She is young: she's a princess. Yet I'd give not only gold but my life to save my children from exile. Enter that rich palace together, children, and pray to your father's new bride; pray to my mistress, and beg her to save you from banishment. Present this garment to her; and above all let her take the gift from you with her own hands. Go; don't linger. And may you succeed, and bring back to your mother the good news for which she longs!

(*Exit* JASON, *the* ATTENDANT, *and the children bearing the poisoned gifts.*)

(STROPHE 1)

CHORUS: No hope now remains for the children's lives!
No, none. Even now they are moving toward death;
The luckless bride will accept the gown that will kill her,
And take the golden crown, and hold it
In her hand, and over her golden head will
Lift the garment of Hell!

(ANTISTROPHE 1)

The grace and glitter of gold will enchant her:
She will put on the golden robe and wear
The golden crown: and deck herself as the bride
Of Death. And thus, pitiful girl,
Will fall in the trap; will fall and perish.
She will never escape!

(STROPHE 2)

You likewise, O miserable groom,
Who planned a royal wedding ceremony,
Do not see the doom you are bringing
Upon your sons; and the terrible death
Now lying in wait for your bride. Pity
Upon you! O, how you are fallen!

(ANTISTROPHE 2)

And I weep for you too, Medea,
O mother who are killing your sons,
Killing in revenge for the loss
Of your love: you whom your lover Jason
Now has deserted and betrayed
To love and marry another mistress!

(*Enter* ATTENDANT *with the children.*)

ATTEND: My lady, your children are reprieved from exile. The royal bride was delighted to receive your gifts with her own hands. And there is peace between her and your children . . . Medea! Why are you so distraught at this lucky moment? Why are you turning your head away? Are you not happy to hear this news, my lady?

MEDEA: Oh, I am lost!

ATTEND: That cry does not suit the news I have brought you, surely!

MEDEA: I am lost! I am lost!

ATTEND: Have I told you of some disaster, without knowing it? Was I wrong in thinking that my news was good?

MEDEA: You have said what you have said: I do not wish to blame you.

ATTEND: Then why are you so disturbed? Why are you weeping?

MEDEA: Oh, my old friend, I can't help weeping. It was I, it was I and the gods, who planned these things so badly.

ATTEND: Take heart, Medea. Your sons will bring you back to your home some day.

MEDEA: And I'll bring others back to their homes, long before that happens!

ATTEND: And often before this, mothers have been parted from their sons. Bear your troubles, Medea, as all mortals must bear them.

MEDEA: I will, I will. Go back into the house; and plan your daily work for the children.

(*The* ATTENDANT *goes into the house, and* MEDEA *turns to her children.*)

MEDEA: O my children, my children, you will still have a city, you will still have a home where you can dwell forever, far away from me, far forever from your mother! But I am doomed to go in exile to another land, before I can see you grow up and be happy, before I can take pride in you, before I can wait on your brides and make your marriage beds, or hold the torch at your wedding ceremony! What a victim I am of my own self-will! It was all in vain, my children, that I reared you! It was all in vain that I grew weary and worn, and suffered the anguish and pangs of childbirth! Oh pity me! Once I had great hopes for you; I had hopes that you'd look after me in my old age, and that you'd lovingly deck my body with your own hands when I died, as all men hope and desire. But now my lovely dreams are over. I shall love you both. I shall spend my life in grief and solitude. And never again will you see your mother with your own dear eyes; now you will pass into another kind of life. Ah, my dear children, why do you look at me like this? Why are you smiling your sweet little smiles at me? O children, what can I do? My heart gives way when I see the joy shining in my children's eyes. O women, I cannot do it! . . . Farewell to all my plans! I will take my babies away with me from this land. Why should I hurt their father by hurting them? Why should I hurt myself doubly? No: I cannot do it. I shall say good-bye to my plans . . . And yet—O, what is wrong with me? Am I willing to see my enemies go unpunished? Am I willing to be insulted and laughed at? I shall follow this thing to the end. How weak I am! How weak to let my heart be touched by these soft sentiments! Go back into the house, my children . . . And if anyone prefers not to witness my sacrifice, let him do as he wishes! My poor heart—do not do this thing! My poor

heart, have pity on them, let them go, the little children! They'll bring cheer to you, if you let them live with you in exile! . . . No, by all the avenging Furies, this shall not be! Never shall I surrender my children to the insolence and mockery of my enemies! It is settled. I have made my decision. And since they must die, it is their mother who must kill them. Now there is no escape for the young bride! Already the crown is on her head; already the dress is hanging from her body; the royal bride, the princess is dying! This I know. And now—since I am about to follow a dreadful path, and am sending them on a path still more terrible—I will simply say this: I want to speak to my children.

(*She calls and the children come back; she takes them in her arms.*)

Come, come, give me your hands, my babies, let your mother kiss you both. O dear little hands, dear little lips: how I have loved them! How fresh and young your eyes look! How straight you stand! I wish you joy with all my heart; but not here; not in this land. All that you had here your father has stolen from you. . . . How good it is to hold you, to feel your soft young cheeks, the warm young sweetness of your breath. . . . Go now; leave me. I cannot look at you any longer . . . I am overcome. . . .

(*The children go into the house again.*)

Now at last I understand the full evil of what I have planned. At last I see how my passion is stronger than my reason: passion, which brings the worst of woes to mortal man.

(*She goes out at right, toward the palace.*)

CHORAG: Many a time before
I have gone through subtler reasoning,
Many times I have faced graver question-
ing
Than any woman should ever have to face:
But we women have a goddess to help us,
too,

And lead us into wisdom.
Not all of us; perhaps not many;
But some women there are who are capable of wisdom.
And I say this: that those who have never
Known the fullness of life and never had children,
Are happier far than those who are parents.
For the childless, who never discover whether
Their children grow up to be a cause for joy or for pain,
Are spared many troubles:
While those who know in their houses
The sweet presence of children—
We have seen how their lives are wasted by worry.
First they fret about how they shall raise them
Properly; and then how to leave them enough
Money to live on; and then they continue
To worry about whether all this labor
Has gone into children that will turn out well
Or turn out ill: and the question remains unanswered.
And let me tell of one more trouble,
The last of all, and common to all mortals:
For suppose you have found enough
For them to live on, and suppose
You have seen them grow up and turn out well;
Still, if fate so decrees it, Death
Will come and tear away your children!
What use is it, then, that the gods
For the sake of children
Should pile on us mortals,
After all other griefs,
This grief for lost children? This grief
Greater by far than any?

(MEDEA *comes out of the house.*)

MEDEA: I have been waiting in suspense, ladies; I have waited long to learn how things will happen . . . Look! I see one of Jason's servants coming toward us;

he is panting; and the bearer of news, I think; of bad news . . .

(*A* MESSENGER *rushes in.*)

MESS: Fly, Medea, fly! You have done a terrible thing, a thing breaking all human laws: fly, and take with you a ship for the seas, or a chariot for the plains!

MEDEA: Why? What reason have you for asking me to fly?

MESS: She lies dead! The royal princess, and her father Kreon too! They have died: they have been slain by your poisons!

MEDEA: You bring me blessèd news! Now and from now on I count you among my friends, my benefactors!

MESS: What! Are you insane? Are you mad, Medea? You have done an outrage to the royal house: does it make you happy to hear it? Can you hear of this dreadful thing without horror?

MEDEA: I too have words to say in reply to yours. Do not be impatient, my friend. Tell me: how did they die? You will make me doubly happy if you say they died in anguish!

MESS: When those two children, your own babies, Medea, came with their father and entered the palace of the bride, it gave joy to all of us, the servants who have suffered with you; for instantly all through the house we whispered that you had made up your quarrel with your husband. One of us kissed your children's hands, and another their golden hair, and I myself was so overjoyed that I followed them in person to the women's chambers. And there stood our mistress, whom we now serve instead of you; and she kept her eyes fixed longingly on Jason. When she caught sight of your children, she covered up her eyes, and her face grew pale, and she turned away filled with petulance at their coming. But your husband tried to soothe the bride's ill humor, and said: 'Do not look so unkindly at your friends! Do not feel angry: turn your head to me once more, and think of your husband's friends as your own friends! Accept these gifts, and do this for my sake: beg of your father not to let these children be exiled!' And then, when she saw the dress, she grew mild and yielded, and gave in to her husband. And before the father and the children had gone far from her rooms, she took the gorgeous robe and put it on; and she put the golden crown on her curly head, and arranged her hair in the shining mirror, smiling as she saw herself reflected. And then she rose from her chair and walked across the room, stepping softly and delicately on her small white feet, filled with delight at the gift, and glancing again and again at the delicate turn of her ankles. And after that it was a thing of horror we saw. For suddenly her face changed its color, and she staggered back, and began to tremble as she ran, and reached a chair just as she was about to fall to the ground. An old woman servant, thinking no doubt that this was some kind of seizure, a fit sent by Pan, or some other god cried out a prayer: and then, as she prayed, she saw the flakes of foam flow from her mouth, and her eyeballs rolling, and the blood fade from her face. And then it was a different prayer she uttered, a terrible scream, and one of the women ran to the house of the King, and another to the newly wedded groom to tell him what had happened to the bride; and the whole house echoed as they ran to and fro.

Let me tell you, time enough for a man to walk two hundred yards passed before the poor lady awoke from her trance, with a dreadful scream, and opened her eyes again. A twofold torment was creeping over her. The golden diadem on her head was sending forth a violent stream of flame, and the finely woven dress which your children gave her was beginning to eat into the poor girl's snowy soft flesh. And she leapt from her chair, all on fire,

and started to run, shaking her head to and fro, trying to shake off the diadem; but the gold still clung firmly, and as she shook her hair the fire blazed forth with double fury. And then she sank to the ground, helpless, overcome; and past all recognition except to the eye of a father— for her eyes had lost their normal expression, and the familiar look had fled from her face, and from the top of her head a mingled stream of blood and fire was pouring. And it was like the drops falling from the bark of a pine tree when the flesh dropped away from her bones, torn loose by the secret fangs of the poison. And terror kept all of us from touching the corpse; for we were warned by what had happened.

But then her poor father, who knew nothing of her death, came suddenly into the house and stumbled over her body, and cried out as he folded his arms about her, and kissed her, and said: 'O my child, my poor child, which of the gods has so cruelly killed you? Who has robbed me of you, who am old and close to the grave? O my child, let me die with you!' And he grew silent and tried to rise to his feet again, but found himself fastened to the finely spun dress, like vine clinging to a laurel bough, and there was a fearful struggle. And still he tried to lift his knees, and she writhed and clung to him; and as he tugged, he tore the withered flesh from his bones. And at last he could no longer master the pain, and surrendered, and gave up the ghost. So there they are lying together: and it is a sight to send us weeping. . . .

As for you, Medea, I will say nothing of your own problems: you yourself must discover an escape from punishment. I think, and I have always thought, the life of men is a shadow; and I say without fear that those who are wisest among all men, and probe most deeply into the cause of things—they are the ones who suffer most deeply! For, believe me, no man among mortals is happy; if wealth comes to a man, he may be luckier than the rest; but happy—never.

(*Exit* MESSENGER.)

CHORAG: It seems that heaven has sent, today, a heavy load of evils upon Jason; and he deserves them. Alas, poor girl, poor daughter of Kreon! I pity you and your anguish; and now you are gone, all because of your wedding with Jason: gone away to the halls of Hades!

MEDEA: Women, the deed shall be done! Swiftly I will go and kill my children, and then leave the land: and not delay nor let them be killed by a crueler hand. For die they must in any case: and if they must be slain, it is I, their mother who gave them life, who must slay them! O my heart, my heart, arm yourself in steel! Do not shrink back from this hideous thing which has to be done! Come, my hand, and seize the sword, take it and step forward to the place where my life's true sorrow begins! Do not be a coward . . . do not think of the children, and how dear they are to you who are their mother! For one brief day, Medea, forget your children; and then forever after you may mourn; for though you will kill them, they were dear to you, very dear . . . I am a miserable woman!

(*With a cry* MEDEA *rushes into the house.*)

(STROPHE)

CHORUS: O Earth, and the all-brightening
Beam of the Sun, look, look
Upon this lost one, shine upon
This pitiful woman before she raises
Her hand in murder against her sons!
For lo! these are the offspring
Of thine own golden seed, and I fear
That divine blood may now be shed by men!
O Light flung forth by Zeus,
O heavenly Light,

Hold back her hand,
Restrain her, and drive out
This dark demoniac fury from the house!

(ANTISTROPHE)

Was it all in vain, Medea,
What you suffered in bearing your sons?
Was it utterly in vain
You bore the babes you loved, after you left
Behind you that dark passage through the straits
And past the perilous rocks, the blue Symplegades?
Wretched woman, how has it happened
That your soul is torn by anger
And darkened by the shadow of death?
Heavy will be the price
To pay for kindred blood staining the earth!
Heavy the woe sent down by heaven
On the house of the killer for such a crime!

(*A cry is heard from the children within.*)

CHORAG: Listen! Do you hear? Do you hear the children crying?
Hate-hardened heart! O woman born for evil!

(*Crying within.*)

1ST SON: What can I do? How can I run from mother's hands?

(*Crying within.*)

2ND SON: I don't know! We are lost, we are lost, brother!

CHORAG: Shall I enter the house? Oh surely
I must help! I must save these children from murder!

(*Within.*)

1ST SON: Help, in the name of heaven! We need your help!

(*Within.*)

2ND SON: Now, it's coming closer! The sword is falling!

CHORAG: Oh, you must be made of stone
or steel,
To kill the fruit of your womb
With your own hands, unhappy woman!
I have heard of only one,
Of all the women who ever lived, who laid
Her hand upon her children: it was Ino,
Who was driven insane by the Gods
When the wife of Zeus sent her wandering
from her home.
And wild with grief at killing her chil-
dren,
She flung herself from the seat-battered
cliff
And plunged into the sea, and in the sea
Rejoined her two dead children.
Can anything so dreadful ever happen
again?
Woe flows forth from the bed of a woman
Whom fate has touched with trouble!
Great is the grief that they have brought
on men!

(*Enter* JASON *with his attendants.*)

JASON: Ladies, you have been sitting
near this house! Tell me! Is Medea, is the
woman who did this frightful thing, still
in the house? Or has she fled already? O
believe me, she'll have to hide deep under
the earth, or fly on wings through the sky,
if she hopes to escape the vengeance of
the royal house! Does she dream, after
killing the rulers of the land, that she herself can escape from these halls unpunished? But I am thinking of her far less
than of her children; for she herself will
duly suffer at the hands of those she
wronged. Ladies, I have come to save the
lives of my boys, lest the royal house
should harm them in revenge for this vile
thing done by their mother.

CHORAG: O Jason, you do not yet know
the full depth of your misery, or you
would not have spoken those words!

JASON: What do you mean? Is she planning to kill me also?

CHORAG: Your boys are dead; dead at
their mother's hand.

JASON: What have you said, woman?
You are destroying me!

CHORAG: You may be sure of this: your
children are dead.

JASON: Oh where did she kill them?
Was it here, or in the house?

CHORAG: Open the doors, and you will
see their murdered bodies!

JASON: Open the doors! Unlock the
bolts! Undo the fastenings! And let me
see this twofold horror! Let me see my
murdered boys! Let me look on her whom
I shall kill in vengeance!

(*His attendants rush to the door.* MEDEA
*appears above the house in a chariot drawn
by dragons. The dead children are at her
side.*)

MEDEA: Why do you batter at the doors?
Why do you shake these bolts, in quest of
the dead and their murderess? You may
cease your trouble, Jason; and if there is
anything you want to say, then say it!
Never again shall you lay your hand on
me; so swift is the chariot which my
father's father gave me, the Sun God
Helios, to save me from my foes!

JASON: Horrible woman! Now you are
utterly loathed by the gods, and by me,
and by all mankind. You had the heart to
stab your children; you, their own mother,
and to leave me childless; you have done
these fearful things, and still you dare to
gaze as ever at the sun and the earth! O
I wish you were dead! Now at last I see
clearly what I did not see on the day I
brought you, loaded with doom, from your
barbarous home to live in Hellas—a traitress to your father and your native land.
On me too the gods have hurled the curse
which has haunted you. For you killed
your own brother at his fireside, and then
came aboard our beautiful ship the Argo.

And that was how it started. And then you married me, and slept with me, and out of your passion bore me children; and now, out of your passion, you have killed them. There is no woman in all of Greece who would dare to do this. And yet I passed them over, and chose you instead; and chose to marry my own doom! I married not a woman, but a monster, wilder of heart than Scylla in the Tyrrhenian Sea! But even if I hurled a thousand insults at you, Medea, I know I could not wound you: your heart is so hard, so utterly hard. Go, you wicked sorceress; I see the stains of your children's blood upon you! Go; all that is left to me now is to mourn. I shall never lie beside my newly wedded love; I shall never have my sons, whom I bred and brought up, alive beside me to say a last farewell! I have lost them forever, and my life is ended.

MEDEA: O Jason, to these words of yours I could make a long reply; but Zeus, the father, himself well knows all that I did for you, and what you did to me. Destiny has refused to let you scorn my love, and lead a life of pleasure, and mock at me; nor were the royal princess and the matchmaker Kreon destined to drive me into exile, and then go untormented! Call me a monster if you wish; call me the Scylla in the Tyrrhenian Sea. For now I have torn your heart: and this indeed was destined, Jason!

JASON: You too must feel the pain; you will share my grief, Medea.

MEDEA: Yes; but the pain is milder, since you cannot mock me!

JASON: O my sons, it was an unspeakable mother who bore you!

MEDEA: O my sons, it was really your father who destroyed you!

JASON: But I tell you: it was not my hand that slew them!

MEDEA: No; but your insolence, and your new wedding slew them!

JASON: And you thought this wedding cause enough to kill them?

MEDEA: And you think the anguish of love is trifling for a woman?

JASON: Yes, if her heart is sound: but yours makes all things evil.

MEDEA: Your sons are dead, Jason! Does it hurt you when I say this?

JASON: They will live on, Medea, by bringing suffering on you.

MEDEA: The gods are well aware who caused all this suffering.

JASON: Yes, the gods are well aware. They know your brutal heart.

MEDEA: You too are brutal. And I am sick of your bitter words!

JASON: And I am sick of yours. Oh Medea, it will be easy to leave you.

MEDEA: Easy! Yes! And for me too! What, then, do you want?

JASON: Give me those bodies to bury, and to mourn.

MEDEA: Never! I will bury them myself. I will bring them myself to Hera's temple, which hangs over the Cape, where none of their enemies can insult them, and where none can defile their graves! And in this land of Corinth I shall ordain a holy feast and sacrifice, forever after, to atone for this guilt of killing. And I shall go myself to Athens, to live in the house of Aegeus, the son of Pandion. And I predict that you, as you deserve, will die without honor; and your head crushed by a beam of the shattered Argo; and then you will know the bitter end of all my love for you!

JASON: May the avenging fury of our sons destroy you! May Justice destroy you, and repay blood with blood!

MEDEA: What god, what heavenly

power would listen to you? To a breaker of oaths? To a betrayer of love?

JASON: Oh, you are vile! You sorceress! Murderess!

MEDEA: Go to your house. Go, and bury your bride.

JASON: Yes, I shall go; and mourn for my murdered sons.

MEDEA: Wait; do not weep yet, Jason! Wait till age has sharpened your grief!

JASON: Oh my sons, whom I loved! My sons!

MEDEA: It was I, not you, who truly loved them.

JASON: You say you loved them; yet you killed them.

MEDEA: Yes. I killed them to make you suffer.

JASON: Medea, I only long to kiss them one last time.

MEDEA: Now, now, you long to kiss them! Now you long to say farewell: but before, you cast them from you!

JASON: Medea, I beg you, let me touch the little bodies of my boys!

MEDEA: No. Never. You speak in vain.

JASON: O Zeus, high in your heaven, have you heard these words? Have you heard this unutterable cruelty? Have you heard this woman, this monster, this murderess? And now I shall do the only thing I still can do! Yes! I shall cry, I shall cry aloud to heaven, and call on the gods to witness how you killed my sons, and refused to let me kiss them farewell, or touch them, or give them burial! Oh, I'd rather never have seen them live, than have seen them slaughtered so!

(*The chariot carries* MEDEA *away.*)

CHORAG: Many, many are the things
That Zeus determines, high on the Olympian throne;
Many the things beyond men's understanding
That the gods achieve, and bring to pass.
Many the things we think will happen,
Yet never happen.
And many the things we thought could never be,
Yet the gods contrive.
Such things have happened on this day,
And in this place!

Oedipus Rex

SOPHOCLES

COMMENTARY

 Sophocles (495-406 B. C.), born at Colonus, was the son of a rich maker of armor. He seems to have been physically attractive as well as talented, one of the "superior" persons of the world. His first entry for the tragedy prize won over a play by the then leading dramatist, Aeschylus. In this lifetime he won more than twenty first prizes in the tragedy contests, more than either Aeschylus or Euripides. His fellow Athenians repeatedly elected him to public office, and at his death he was virtually revered as having nearly divine insight. Of over a hundred plays, only seven survive: *Antigone, Philoctetes, Oedipus Rex, Oedipus at Colonus, Ajax, Trachiniae,* and *Electra,* all written probably between 445 and 406 B. C.

Oedipus (also called *Oedipus Rex, King Oedipus,* and *Oedipus Tyrannus*) by Sophocles embodies in some form most of the fundamental esthetic, philosophical, psychological, and critical issues in the study of tragedy. The tragedy served the ancient Greeks as basically as it does modern Western man. It provided Aristotle with a nearly ideal model in studying the nature of tragedy; it offered Freud a ready allegory to explore some of the mysterious territory of Western man's unconscious mind. It was first performed in Athens in the early half of the fifth century B. C., during the annual Dionysian celebration.

Oedipus has for many centuries baffled, enchanted, and stimulated readers and students. "I cannot myself pretend to understand that mysterious play," writes William Arrowsmith, a modern translator and critic of Greek drama, "but I wonder if we are perhaps not better off for proceeding from the play rather than from Aristotle" ("The Criticism of Greek Tragedy," in *Tragedy: Vision and Form,* ed. Robert W. Corrigan, p. 336, originally in *Tulane Drama Review,* III, 3 [March 1959], 31-57).

One might look at Oedipus, as Bernard Knox suggests, as "a paradigm, an example to all men; and the fact that he is tyrannos, self-made ruler, the proverbial Greek example of worldly success won by individual intelligence and exertion, makes him an appropriate symbol of civilized man, who was beginning to believe, in the fifth century B. c., that he could seize control of his environment and make his own destiny, become, in fact, equated to the gods" ("Sophocles' *Oedipus*," in *Tragic Themes in Western Literature,* ed. Cleanth Brooks, [New Haven 1955], pp. 7-29). This "paradigmatic" nature of Oedipus, those qualities of his character and ambition that make him in some measure representative of all men, his heroic efforts toward self-fulfillment in the face of the gods, that is, against the handicaps of his own nature and of the hazards of living itself, offer clues to understanding the compelling character of the drama.

Like all great art, *Oedipus* is largely self-contained. We may read it profitably without extensive reference to outside sources, to mythology, to Aristotle, or to Greek history and art, although our understanding would surely be enlarged by such reference. *Oedipus* is especially unique among Greek tragedies in that it needs little background synopsis by way of introduction since previous events are adequately reported or alluded to in the course of the play. The text alone offers enough rich ore for discussion and speculation. Is not Oedipus indeed his parents' son, in his hot temper, intelligence, impetuousness, and in his mixed attitude of casualness and awe toward the gods? To what extent is Oedipus "free" to exercise his own will: to what extent does he do so; in what ways is he determined? Has not Oedipus repeatedly been warned about his fate, in Corinth by a drunkard, at Delphos by the oracle? Are not his rejection of Teiresias and his suspicion of Creon excessive? Why is Iocastê so insistent on Oedipus not pushing his inquiry? Any reader will surely multiply these questions many times.

The play has depths of interlocked riddles. The primary riddle of the Sphinx hovers over the play, as background and perhaps as definition. The answer to the Sphinx is Man. The answer to the specific question Oedipus and the people of Thebes pose, "Who is the murderer of Laïos?," is a man, Oedipus. The large question "What is Man?" becomes for Oedipus, and ultimately for all individuals, the small and focussed one, "Who am I?" and "What am I?" Oedipus becomes a kind of cosmic detective in running down the murderer of Laïos, that is, in running down his own history and identity.

Oedipus is also very much a social play. The young Oedipus becomes savior and king of a city by freeing it from the domination of the Sphinx. The plague that descends on Thebes is in part the consequence of the city's languishing in the hunt for, and in the punishment of, the murderer of Laïos. Social disintegration follows from failure to respect and support order, failure to punish the murderer of a king, the murderer of the "father" of the community.

The play is marked by irony. Not only are few things what they seem to be, they are often exactly the reverse. It is not the sightless Teiresias who is blind about the identity of the murderer, it is the piercingly clear-sighted Oedipus who triumphed over the Sphinx, yet who does not see; and the change in roles is horribly dramatized by Oedipus' climactic self-blinding.

Invariably, any study of tragedy begins with or alludes significantly to *Oedipus,* and the general titles in the bibliography will contain some references to the work. Among the fuller and more provocative recent discussions of the play, in addition to those cited above, are H. D. F. Kitto, "The *Oedipus Tyrannus,*" in his *Greek Tragedy,* 3rd ed. (New York, 1961); Bernard Knox, *Oedipus at Thebes* (New Haven, 1966); and Ernest Jones, *Hamlet and Oedipus* (New York, 1949), a classic distillation of the Freudian formulation and application. Jean Cocteau's adaptation of the play, *The Infernal Machine* (Paris, 1934; Norfolk, Conn., 1964), is itself a commentary, depicting Oedipus as a shallow careerist and Iocastê as a frivolous woman reluctant to acknowledge her age.

Oedipus is frequently produced on stage; an interesting film version has also been made. If you have seen it performed, you might want to consider how your reading of the play was affected. If you have not seen the play acted, speculate how an actor or a director might change some important meaning you have found in your reading.

Sophocles

OEDIPUS REX

An English Version by Dudley Fitts and Robert Fitzgerald

OEDIPUS   IOCASTE
A PRIEST   MESSENGER
CREON   SHEPHERD OF LAÏOS
TEIRESIAS   SECOND MESSENGER
CHORUS OF THEBAN ELDERS

THE SCENE. *Before the palace of Oedipus, King of Thebes. A central door and two lateral doors open onto a platform which runs the length of the façade. On the platform, right and left, are altars; and three steps lead down into the "orchestra," or chorus-ground. At the beginning of the action these steps are crowded by suppliants who have brought branches and chaplets of olive leaves and who lie in various attitudes of despair.* OEDIPUS *enters.*

PROLOGUE

OEDIPUS: My children, generations of the living
In the line of Kadmos, nursed at his ancient hearth:
Why have you strewn yourselves before these altars
In supplication, with your boughs and garlands?
The breath of incense rises from the city
With a sound of prayer and lamentation.

Children,
I would not have you speak through messengers,
And therefore I have come myself to hear you—
I, Oedipus, who bear the famous name.

(*To a* PRIEST:)

You, there, since you are eldest in the company,
Speak for them all, tell me what preys upon you,

Whether you come in dread, or crave some
     blessing:
Tell me, and never doubt that I will help
     you
In every way I can; I should be heartless
Were I not moved to find you suppliant
     here.

> PRIEST: Great Oedipus, O powerful
>   King of Thebes!

You see how all the ages of our people
Cling to your altar steps: here are boys
Who can barely stand alone, and here are
     priests
By weight of age, as I am a priest of God,
And young men chosen from those yet
     unmarried;
As for the others, all that multitude,
They wait with olive chaplets in the
     squares,
At the two shrines of Pallas, and where
     Apollo
Speaks in the glowing embers.
                              Your own eyes
Must tell you: Thebes is tossed on a mur-
     dering sea
And can not lift her head from the death
     surge.
A rust consumes the buds and fruits of
     the earth;
The herds are sick; children die unborn,
And labor is vain. The god of plague and
     pyre
Raids like detestable lightning through the
     city,
And all the house of Kadmos is laid waste,
All emptied, and all darkened: Death
     alone
Battens upon the misery of Thebes.

You are not one of the immortal gods, we
     know;
Yet we have come to you to make our
     prayer
As to the man surest in mortal ways
And wisest in the ways of God. You saved
     us

From the Sphinx, that flinty singer, and
     the tribute
We paid to her so long; yet you were never
Better informed than we, nor could we
     teach you:
It was some god breathed in you to set us
     free.

Therefore, O mighty King, we turn to
     you:
Find us our safety, find us a remedy,
Whether by counsel of the gods or men.
A king of wisdom tested in the past
Can act in a time of troubles, and act well.
Noblest of men, restore
Life to your city! Think how all men call
     you
Liberator for your triumph long ago;
Ah, when your years of kingship are re-
     membered,
Let them not say *We rose, but later fell*—
Keep the State from going down in the
     storm!
Once, years ago, with happy augury,
You brought us fortune; be the same
     again!
No man questions your power to rule the
     land:
But rule over men, not over a dead city!
Ships are only hulls, citadels are nothing,
When no life moves in the empty passage-
     ways.

> OEDIPUS: Poor children! You may be
>   sure I know

All that you longed for in your coming
     here.
I know that you are deathy sick; and yet,
Sick as you are, not one is as sick as I.
Each of you suffers in himself alone
His anguish, not another's; but my spirit
Groans for the city, for myself, for you.

I was not sleeping, you are not waking me.
No, I have been in tears for a long while
And in my restless thought walked many
     ways.

In all my search, I found one helpful
course,
And that I have taken: I have sent Creon,
Son of Menoikeus, brother of the Queen,
To Delphi, Apollo's place of revelation,
To learn there, if he can,
What act or pledge of mine may save the
city.
I have counted the days, and now, this
very day,
I am troubled, for he has overstayed his
time.
What is he doing? He has been gone too
long.
Yet whenever he comes back, I should do
ill
To scant whatever duty God reveals.

PRIEST: It is a timely promise. At this
instant
They tell me Creon is here.

OEDIPUS: O Lord Apollo!
May his news be fair as his face is radiant!

PRIEST: It could not be otherwise: he is
crowned with bay,
The chaplet is thick with berries.

OEDIPUS: We shall soon know;
He is near enough to hear us now.

(*Enter* CREON.)

O Prince:
Brother: son of Menoikeus:
What answer do you bring us from the
god?

CREON: A strong one. I can tell you,
great afflictions
Will turn out well, if they are taken well.

OEDIPUS: What was the oracle? These
vague words
Leave me still hanging between hope and
fear.

CREON: Is it your pleasure to hear me
with all these
Gathered around us? I am prepared to
speak,
But should we not go in?

OEDIPUS: Let them all hear it.
It is for them I suffer, more than for myself.

CREON: Then I will tell you what I
heard at Delphi.

In plain words
The god commands us to expel from the
land of Thebes
An old defilement we are sheltering.
It is a deathly thing, beyond cure;
We must not let it feed upon us longer.

OEDIPUS: What defilement? How shall
we rid ourselves of it?

CREON: By exile or death, blood for
blood. It was
Murder that brought the plague-wind on
the city.

OEDIPUS: Murder of whom? Surely the
god has named him?

CREON: My lord: long ago Laïos was our
king,
Before you came to govern us.

OEDIPUS: I know;
I learned of him from others; I never saw
him.

CREON: He was murdered; and Apollo
commands us now
To take revenge upon whoever killed him.

OEDIPUS: Upon whom? Where are
they? Where shall we find a clue
To solve that crime, after so many years?

CREON: Here in this land, he said.
                If we make enquiry,
We may touch things that otherwise
escape us.

OEDIPUS: Tell me: Was Laïos murdered
in his house,
Or in the fields, or in some foreign country?

CREON: He said he planned to make a
pilgrimage.
He did not come home again.

OEDIPUS: And was there no one,
No witness, no companion, to tell what
    happened?

CREON: They were all killed but one,
    and he got away
So frightened that he could remember one
    thing only.

OEDIPUS: What was that one thing?
    One may be the key
To everything, if we resolve to use it.

CREON: He said that a band of high-
    waymen attacked them,
Outnumbered them, and overwhelmed the
    King.

OEDIPUS: Strange, that a highwayman
    should be so daring—
Unless some faction here bribed him to do
    it.

CREON: We thought of that. But after
    Laïos' death
New troubles arose and we had no aven-
    ger.

OEDIPUS: What troubles could prevent
    your hunting down the killers?

CREON: The riddling Sphinx's song
Made us deaf to all mysteries but her own.

OEDIPUS: Then once more I must bring
    what is dark to light.
It is most fitting that Apollo shows,
As you do, this compunction for the dead.
You shall see how I stand by you, as I
    should,
To avenge the city and the city's god,
And not as though it were for some dis-
    tant friend,
But for my own sake, to be rid of evil.
Whoever killed King Laïos might—who
    knows?—
Decide at any moment to kill me as well.
By avenging the murdered king I protect
    myself.

Come, then, my children: leave the altar
    steps,

Lift up your olive boughs!
                    One of you go
And summon the people of Kadmos to
    gather here.
I will do all that I can; you may tell them
    that.

                    (*Exit a* PAGE)

So, with the help of God,
We shall be saved—or else indeed we are
    lost.

PRIEST: Let us rise, children. It was for
    this we came,
And now the King has promised it him-
    self.
Phoibos has sent us an oracle; may he
    descend
Himself to save us and drive out the
    plague.

(*Exeunt* OEDIPUS *and* CREON *into the palace
by the central door. The* PRIEST *and the*
SUPPLIANTS *disperse R and L. After a short
pause the* CHORUS *enters the orchestra.*)

PÁRODOS

                                    (STROPHE I)
CHORUS: What is God singing in his
    profound
Delphi of gold and shadow?
What oracle for Thebes, the sunwhipped
    city?

Fear unjoints me, the roots of my heart
    tremble.

Now I remember, O Healer, your power,
    and wonder:
Will you send doom like a sudden cloud,
    or weave it
Like nightfall of the past?

Speak, speak to us, issue of holy sound:
Dearest to our expectancy: be tender!

(ANTISTROPHE I)

Let me pray to Athenê, the immortal
   daughter of Zeus,
And to Artemis her sister
Who keeps her famous throne in the
   market ring,
And to Apollo, bowman at the far butts
   of heaven—

O gods, descend! Like three streams leap
   against
The fires of our grief, the fires of darkness;
Be swift to bring us rest!

As in the old time from the brilliant house
Of air you stepped to save us, come again!

(STROPHE 2)

Now our afflictions have no end,
Now all our stricken host lies down
And no man fights off death with his
   mind;

The noble plowland bears no grain,
And groaning mothers can not bear—

See, how our lives like birds take wing,
Like sparks that fly when a fire soars,
To the shore of the god of evening.

(ANTISTROPHE 2)

The plague burns on, it is pitiless,
Though pallid children laden with death
Lie unwept in the stony ways,

And old gray women by every path
Flock to the strand about the altars

There to strike their breasts and cry
Worship of Phoibos in wailing prayers:
Be kind, God's golden child!

(STROPHE 3)

There are no swords in this attack by fire,
No shields, but we are ringed with cries.
Send the besieger plunging from our
   homes

Into the vast sea-room of the Atlantic
Or into the waves that foam eastward of
   Thrace—

For the day ravages what the night
   spares—

Destroy our enemy, lord of the thunder!
Let him be riven by lightning from
   heaven!

(ANTISTROPHE 3)

Phoibos Apollo, stretch the sun's bow-
   string,
That golden cord, until it sing for us,
Flashing arrows in heaven!
                              Artemis, Huntress,
Race with flaring lights upon our moun-
   tains!

O scarlet god, O golden-banded brow,
O Theban Bacchos in a storm of Maenads,
                     (*Enter* OEDIPUS, *C.*)

Whirl upon Death, that all the Undying
   hate!
Come with blinding torches, come in joy!

SCENE I

OEDIPUS: Is this your prayer? It may be
   answered. Come,
Listen to me, act as the crisis demands,
And you shall have relief from all these
   evils.

Until now I was a stranger to this tale,
As I had been a stranger to the crime.
Could I track down the murderer without
   a clue?
But now, friends,
As one who became a citizen after the
   murder,
I make this proclamation to all Thebans:
If any man knows by whose hand Laïos,
   son of Labdakos,

Met his death, I direct that man to tell me
    everything,
No matter what he fears for having so
    long withheld it.
Let it stand as promised that no further
    trouble
Will come to him, but he may leave the
    land in safety.

Moreover: If anyone knows the murderer
    to be foreign,
Let him not keep silent: he shall have his
    reward from me.
However, if he does conceal it; if any man
Fearing for his friend or for himself dis-
    obeys this edict
Hear what I propose to do:

I solemnly forbid the people of this coun-
    try,
Where power and throne are mine, ever to
    receive that man
Or speak to him, no matter who he is, or
    let him
Join in sacrifice, lustration, or in prayer.
I decree that he be driven from every
    house,
Being, as he is, corruption itself to us: the
    Delphic
Voice of Zeus has pronounced this revela-
    tion.
Thus I associate myself with the oracle
And take the side of the murdered king.

As for the criminal, I pray to God—
Whether it be a lurking thief, or one of a
    number—
I pray that that man's life be consumed
    in evil and wretchedness.
And as for me, this curse applies no less
If it should turn out that the culprit is my
    guest here,
Sharing my hearth.
            You have heard the penalty.
I lay it on you now to attend to this
For my sake, for Apollo's, for the sick
Sterile city that heaven has abandoned.

Suppose the oracle had given you no com-
    mand:
Should this defilement go uncleansed for
    ever?
You should have found the murderer:
    your king,
A noble king, had been destroyed!
                      Now I,
Having the power that he held before me,
Having his bed, begetting children there
Upon his wife, as he would have, had he
    lived—
Their son would have been my children's
    brother,
If Laïos had had luck in fatherhood!
(But surely ill luck rushed upon his
    reign)—
I say I take the son's part, just as though
I were his son, to press the fight for him
And see it won! I'll find the hand that
    brought
Death to Labdakos' and Polydoros' child,
Heir of Kadmos' and Agenor's line.
And as for those who fail me,
May the gods deny them the fruit of the
    earth,
Fruit of the womb, and may they rot
    utterly!
Let them be wretched as we are
    wretched, and worse!

For you, for loyal Thebans, and for all
Who find my actions right, I pray the
    favor
Of justice, and of all the immortal gods.

    CHORAGOS: Since I am under oath, my
        lord, I swear
I did not do the murder, I can not name
The murderer. Might not the oracle
That has ordained the search tell where to
    find him?

    OEDIPUS: An honest question. But no
        man in the world
Can make the gods do more than the gods
    will.

    CHORAGOS: There is one last expedient—

OEDIPUS: Tell me what it is.
Though it seem slight, you must not hold
it back.

CHORAGOS: A lord clairvoyant to the lord
Apollo,
As we all know, is the skilled Teiresias.
One might learn much about this from
him, Oedipus.

OEDIPUS: I am not wasting time:
Creon spoke of this, and I have sent for
him—
Twice, in fact; it is strange that he is not
here.

CHORAGOS: The other matter—that old
report—seems useless.

OEDIPUS: Tell me. I am interested in all
reports.

CHORAGOS: The King was said to have
been killed by highwaymen.

OEDIPUS: I know. But we have no witnesses to that.

CHORAGOS: If the killer can feel a par-
ticle of dread,
Your curse will bring him out of hiding!

OEDIPUS: No.
The man who dared that act will fear no
curse.

(*Enter the blind seer* TEIRESIAS, *led by a*
PAGE.)

CHORAGOS: But there is one man who
may detect the criminal.
This is Teiresias, this is the holy prophet
In whom, alone of all men, truth was born.

OEDIPUS: Teiresias: seer, student of mysteries,
Of all that's taught and all that no man
tells,
Secrets of Heaven and secrets of the earth:
Blind though you are, you know the city
lies
Sick with plague; and from this plague,
my lord,
We find that you alone can guard or save
us.

Possibly you did not hear the messengers?
Apollo, when we sent to him,
Sent us back word that this great pesti-
lence
Would lift, but only if we established
clearly
The identity of those who murdered Laïos.
They must be killed or exiled.

Can you use
Birdflight or any art of divination
To purify yourself, and Thebes, and me
From this contagion? We are in your
hands.
There is no fairer duty
Than that of helping others in distress.

TEIRESIAS: How dreadful knowledge of
the truth can be
When there's no help in truth! I knew this
well,
But made myself forget. I should not have
come.

OEDIPUS: What is troubling you? Why
are your eyes so cold?

TEIRESIAS: Let me go home. Bear your
own fate, and I'll
Bear mine. It is better so: trust what I say.

OEDIPUS: What you say is ungracious
and unhelpful
To your native country. Do not refuse to
speak.

TEIRESIAS: When it comes to speech,
your own is neither temperate
Nor opportune. I wish to be more prudent.

OEDIPUS: In God's name, we all beg
you—

TEIRESIAS: You are all ignorant.
No; I will never tell you what I know.
Now it is my misery; then, it would be
yours.

OEDIPUS: What! You do know some-
thing, and will not tell us?
You would betray us all and wreck the
State?

TEIRESIAS: I do not intend to torture myself, or you.
Why persist in asking? You will not persuade me.

OEDIPUS: What a wicked old man you are! You'd try a stone's
Patience! Out with it! Have you no feeling at all?

TEIRESIAS: You call me unfeeling. If you could only see
The nature of your own feelings . . .

OEDIPUS: Why,
Who would not feel as I do? Who could endure
Your arrogance toward the city?

TEIRESIAS: What does it matter!
Whether I speak or not, it is bound to come.

OEDIPUS: Then, if "it" is bound to come, you are bound to tell me.

TEIRESIAS: No, I will not go on. Rage as you please.

OEDIPUS: Rage? Why not!
And I'll tell you what I think:
You planned it, you had it done, you all but
Killed him with your own hands: if you had eyes,
I'd say the crime was yours, and yours alone.

TEIRESIAS: So? I charge you, then,
Abide by the proclamation you have made:
From this day forth
Never speak again to these men or to me;
You yourself are the pollution of this country.

OEDIPUS: You dare say that! Can you possibly think you have
Some way of going free, after such insolence?

TEIRESIAS: I have gone free. It is the truth sustains me.

OEDIPUS: Who taught you shamelessness? It was not your craft.

TEIRESIAS: You did. You made me speak. I did not want to.

OEDIPUS: Speak what? Let me hear it again more clearly.

TEIRESIAS: Was it not clear before? Are you tempting me?

OEDIPUS: I did not understand it. Say it again.

TEIRESIAS: I say that you are the murderer whom you seek.

OEDIPUS: Now twice you have spat out infamy. You'll pay for it!

TEIRESIAS: Would you care for more? Do you wish to be really angry?

OEDIPUS: Say what you will. Whatever you say is worthless.

TEIRESIAS: I say you live in hideous shame with those
Most dear to you. You can not see the evil.

OEDIPUS: It seems you can go on mouthing like this for ever.

TEIRESIAS: I can, if there is power in truth.

OEDIPUS: There is:
But not for you, not for you,
You sightless, witless, senseless, mad old man!

TEIRESIAS: You are the madman. There is no one here
Who will not curse you soon, as you curse me.

OEDIPUS: You child of endless night! You can not hurt me
Or any other man who sees the sun.

TEIRESIAS: True: it is not from me your fate will come.
That lies within Apollo's competence,
As it is his concern.

OEDIPUS: Tell me:
Are you speaking for Creon, or for yourself?

TEIRESIAS: Creon is no threat. You weave your own doom.

OEDIPUS: Wealth, power, craft of states-
    manship!
Kingly position, everywhere admired!
What savage envy is stored up against
    these,
If Creon, whom I trusted, Creon my
    friend,
For this great office which the city once
Put in my hands unsought—if for this
    power
Creon desires in secret to destroy me!

He has bought this decrepit fortune-teller,
    this
Collector of dirty pennies, this prophet
    fraud—
Why, he is no more clairvoyant than I
    am!
         Tell us:
Has your mystic mummery ever ap-
    proached the truth?
When that hellcat the Sphinx was per-
    forming here,
What help were you to these people?
Her magic was not for the first man who
    came along:
It demanded a real exorcist. Your birds—
What good were they? or the gods, for
    the matter of that?
But I came by,
Oedipus, the simple man, who knows
    nothing—
I thought it out for myself, no birds helped
    me!
And this is the man you think you can
    destroy,
That you may be close to Creon when he's
    king!
Well, you and your friend Creon, it seems
    to me,
Will suffer most. If you were not an old
    man,
You would have paid already for your
    plot.

  CHORAGOS: We can not see that his
    words or yours

Have been spoken except in anger, Oedi-
    pus,
And of anger we have no need. How can
    God's will
Be accomplished best? That is what most
    concerns us.

    TEIRESIAS: You are a king. But where
    argument's concerned
I am your man, as much a king as you.
I am not your servant, but Apollo's.
I have no need of Creon to speak for me.

Listen to me. You mock my blindness, do
    you?
But I say that you, with both your eyes,
    are blind:
You can not see the wretchedness of your
    life,
Nor in whose house you live, no, nor
    with whom.
Who are your father and mother? Can
    you tell me?
You do not even know the blind wrongs
That you have done them, on earth and
    in the world below.
But the double lash of your parents' curse
    will whip you
Out of this land some day, with only night
Upon your precious eyes.
Your cries then—where will they not be
    heard?
What fastness of Kithairon will not echo
    them?
And that bridal-descant of yours—you'll
    know it then,
The song they sang when you came here
    to Thebes
And found your misguided berthing.
All this, and more, that you can not guess
    at now,
Will bring you to yourself among your
    children.

Be angry, then. Curse Creon. Curse my
    words.
I tell you, no man that walks upon the
    earth

Shall be rooted out more horribly than
  you.

OEDIPUS: Am I to bear this from him?
  —Damnation
Take you! Out of this place! Out of my
  sight!

TEIRESIAS: I would not have come at all
  if you had not asked me.

OEDIPUS: Could I have told that you'd
  talk nonsense, that
You'd come here to make a fool of yourself, and of me?

TEIRESIAS: A fool? Your parents thought
  me sane enough.

OEDIPUS: My parents again!—Wait:
  who were my parents?

TEIRESIAS: This day will give you a
  father, and break your heart.

OEDIPUS: Your infantile riddles! Your
  damned abracadabra!

TEIRESIAS: You were a great man once
  at solving riddles.

OEDIPUS: Mock me with that if you like;
  you will find it true.

TEIRESIAS: It was true enough. It
  brought about your ruin.

OEDIPUS: But if it saved this town?

TEIRESIAS: (*To the* PAGE:)
              Boy, give me your hand.

OEDIPUS: Yes, boy; lead him away.
              —While you are here
We can do nothing. Go; leave us in peace.

TEIRESIAS: I will go when I have said
  what I have to say.
How can you hurt me? And I tell you
  again:
The man you have been looking for all
  this time,
The damned man, the murderer of Laïos,
That man is in Thebes. To your mind he
  is foreign-born,
But it will soon be shown that he is a
  Theban,
A revelation that will fail to please.

A blind man,
Who has his eyes now; a penniless man,
  who is rich now;
And he will go tapping the strange earth
  with his staff
To the children with whom he lives now
  he will be
Brother and father—the very same; to her
Who bore him, son and husband—the
  very same
Who came to his father's bed, wet with his
  father's blood.

Enough. Go think that over.
If later you find error in what I have said,
You may say that I have no skill in
  prophecy.
(*Exit* TEIRESIAS, *led by his* PAGE. OEDIPUS
              goes into the palace.)

ODE I

(STROPHE I)
CHORUS: The Delphic stone of proph-
  ecies
Remembers ancient regicide
And a still bloody hand.
That killer's hour of flight has come.
He must be stronger than riderless
Coursers of untiring wind,
For the son of Zeus armed with his father's
  thunder
Leaps in lightning after him;
And the Furies follow him, the sad Furies.

(ANTISTROPHE I)
Holy Parnassos' peak of snow
Flashes and blinds that secret man,
That all shall hunt him down:
Though he may roam the forest shade
Like a bull gone wild from pasture
To rage through glooms of stone.
Doom comes down on him; flight will not
  avail him;

For the world's heart calls him desolate,
And the immortal Furies follow, for ever
follow.

(STROPHE 2)

But now a wilder thing is heard
From the old man skilled at hearing Fate
in the wingbeat of a bird.
Bewildered as a blown bird, my soul
hovers and can not find
Foothold in this debate, or any reason or
rest of mind.
But no man ever brought—none can bring
Proof of strife between Thebes' royal
house,
Labdakos' line, and the son of Polybos;
And never until now has any man brought
word
Of Laïos' dark death staining Oedipus the
King.

(ANTISTROPHE 2)

Divine Zeus and Apollo hold
Perfect intelligence alone of all tales ever
told;
And well though this diviner works, he
works in his own night;
No man can judge that rough unknown
or trust in second sight,
For wisdom changes hands among the
wise.
Shall I believe my great lord criminal
At a raging word that a blind old man let
fall?
I saw him, when the carrion woman faced
him of old,
Prove his heroic mind! These evil words
are lies.

SCENE II

CREON: Men of Thebes:
I am told that heavy accusations
Have been brought against me by King
Oedipus.

I am not the kind of man to bear this
tamely.

If in these present difficulties
He holds me accountable for any harm
to him
Through anything I have said or done—
why, then,
I do not value life in this dishonor.
It is not as though this rumor touched
upon
Some private indiscretion. The matter is
grave.
The fact is that I am being called dis-
loyal
To the State, to my fellow citizens, to
my friends.

CHORAGOS: He may have spoken in
anger, not from his mind.

CREON: But did you not hear him say
I was the one
Who seduced the old prophet into lying?

CHORAGOS: The thing was said; I do
not know how seriously.

CREON: But you were watching him!
Were his eyes steady?
Did he look like a man in his right mind?

CHORAGOS: I do not know.
I can not judge the behavior of great
men.
But here is the King himself.

(*Enter* OEDIPUS.)

OEDIPUS: So you dared come back
Why? How brazen of you to come to my
house,
You murderer!
              Do you think I do not know
That you plotted to kill me, plotted to
steal my throne?
Tell me, in God's name: am I coward, a
fool,
That you should dream you could accom-
plish this?
A· fool who could not see your slippery
game?

A coward, not to fight back when I saw it?
You are the fool, Creon, are you not?
      hoping
Without support or friends to get a
      throne?
Thrones may be won or bought: you
      could do neither.

CREON: Now listen to me. You have
      talked; let me talk, too.
You can not judge unless you know the
      facts.

OEDIPUS: You speak well: there is one
      fact; but I find it hard
To learn from the deadliest enemy I
      have.

CREON: That above all I must dispute
      with you.

OEDIPUS: That above all I will not hear
      you deny.

CREON: If you think there is anything
      good in being stubborn
Against all reason, then I say you are
      wrong.

OEDIPUS: If you think a man can sin
      against his own kind
And not be punished for it, I say you are
      mad.

CREON: I agree. But tell me: what have
      I done to you?

OEDIPUS: You advised me to send for
      that wizard, did you not?

CREON: I did. I should do it again.

OEDIPUS: Very well. Now tell me:
How long has it been since Laïos—

CREON: What of Laïos?

OEDIPUS: Since he vanished in that on-
      set by the road?

CREON: It was long ago, a long time.

OEDIPUS: And this prophet,
Was he practicing here then?

CREON: He was; and with honor, as
      now.

OEDIPUS: Did he speak of me at that
      time?

CREON: He never did;
At least, not when I was present.

OEDIPUS: But . . . the enquiry?
I suppose you held one?

CREON: We did, but we learned nothing.

OEDIPUS: Why did the prophet not
      speak against me then?

CREON: I do not know; and I am the
      kind of man
Who holds his tongue when he has no
      facts to go on.

OEDIPUS: There's one fact that you know,
      and you could tell it.

CREON: What fact is that? If I know it,
      you shall have it.

OEDIPUS: If he were not involved with
      you, he could not say
That it was I who murdered Laïos.

CREON: If he says that, you are the one
      that knows it!—
But now it is my turn to question you.

OEDIPUS: Put your questions. I am no
      murderer.

CREON: First, then: You married my
      sister?

OEDIPUS: I married your sister.

CREON: And you rule the kingdom
      equally with her?

OEDIPUS: Everything that she wants
      she has from me.

CREON: And I am the third, equal to
      both of you?

OEDIPUS: That is why I call you a bad
      friend.

CREON: No. Reason it out, as I have
      done.
Think of this first: Would any sane man
      prefer
Power, with all a king's anxieties,
To that same power and the grace of
      sleep?
Certainly not I.
I have never longed for the king's power
      —only his rights.

Would any wise man differ from me in this?

As matters stand, I have my way in everything

With your consent, and no responsibilities.

If I were king, I should be a slave to policy.

How could I desire a scepter more

Than what is now mine—untroubled influence?

No, I have not gone mad; I need no honors,

Except those with the perquisites I have now.

I am welcome everywhere; every man salutes me,

And those who want your favor seek my ear,

Since I know how to manage what they ask.

Should I exchange this ease for that anxiety?

Besides, no sober mind is treasonable.

I hate anarchy

And never would deal with any man who likes it.

Test what I have said. Go to the priestess

At Delphi, ask if I quoted her correctly.

And as for this other thing: if I am found

Guilty of treason with Teiresias,

Then sentence me to death! You have my word

It is a sentence I should cast my vote for—

But not without evidence!

You do wrong

When you take good men for bad, bad men for good.

A true friend thrown aside—why, life itself

Is not more precious!

In time you will know this well:

For time, and time alone, will show the just man,

Though scoundrels are discovered in a day.

CHORAGOS: This is well said, and a prudent man would ponder it.

Judgments too quickly formed are dangerous.

OEDIPUS: But is he not quick in his duplicity?

And shall I not be quick to parry him?

Would you have me stand still, hold my peace, and let

This man win everything, through my inaction?

CREON: And you want—what is it, then? To banish me?

OEDIPUS: No, not exile. It is your death I want,

So that all the world may see what treason means.

CREON: You will persist, then? You will not believe me?

OEDIPUS: How can I believe you?

CREON: Then you are a fool.

OEDIPUS: To save myself?

CREON: In justice, think of me.

OEDIPUS: You are evil incarnate.

CREON: But suppose that you are wrong?

OEDIPUS: Still I must rule.

CREON: But not if you rule badly.

OEDIPUS: O city, city!

CREON: It is my city, too!

CHORAGOS: Now, my lords, be still. I see the Queen,

Iocastê, coming from her palace chambers;

And it is time she came, for the sake of you both.

This dreadful quarrel can be resolved through her.

(*Enter* IOCASTE)

IOCASTE: Poor foolish men, what wicked din is this?

With Thebes sick to death, is it not shameful

That you should rake some private quarrel up?

(*To* OEDIPUS:)

Come into the house.

  —And you, Creon, go now:
Let us have no more of this tumult over
  nothing.

   CREON: Nothing? No, sister: what your
     husband plans for me
Is one of two great evils: exile or death.

   OEDIPUS: He is right.
                    Why, woman I
     have caught him squarely
Plotting against my life.

   CREON: No! Let me die
Accurst if ever I have wished you harm!

   IOCASTE: Ah, believe it, Oedipus!
In the name of the gods, respect this oath
  of his
For my sake, for the sake of these people
   here!

(STROPHE 1)

   CHORAGOS: Open your mind to me, my
     lord. Be ruled by her, I beg you!

   OEDIPUS: What would you have me do?

   CHORAGOS: Respect Creon's word. He
     has never spoken like a fool,
And now he has sworn an oath.

   OEDIPUS: You know what you ask?

   CHORAGOS: I do.

   OEDIPUS: Speak on, then.

   CHORAGOS: A friend so sworn should
     not be baited so,
In blind malice, and without final proof.

   OEDIPUS: You are aware, I hope, that
     what you say
Means death for me, or exile at the least.

(STROPHE 2)

   CHORAGOS: No, I swear by Helios, first
     in Heaven!
May I die friendless and accurst,
The worst of deaths, if ever I meant that!
   It is the withering fields
     That hurt my sick heart:

Must we bear all these ills,
   And now your bad blood as well?

   OEDIPUS: Then let him go. And let me
     die, if I must,
Or be driven by him in shame from the
   land of Thebes.
It is your unhappiness, and not his talk,
That touches me.
              As for him—
Wherever he goes, hatred will follow him.

   CREON: Ugly in yielding, as you were
     ugly in rage!
Natures like yours chiefly torment themselves.

   OEDIPUS: Can you not go? Can you
     not leave me?

   CREON: I can.
You do not know me; but the city knows
   me,
And in its eyes I am just, if not in yours.

(*Exit* CREON)

(ANTISTROPHE 1)

   CHORAGOS: Lady Iocastê, did you not
ask the King to go to his chambers?

   IOCASTE: First tell me what has hap-
     pened.

   CHORAGOS: There was suspicion with-
     out evidence; yet it rankled
As even false charges will.

   IOCASTE: On both sides?

   CHORAGOS: On both.

   IOCASTE: But what was said?

   CHORAGOS: Oh let it rest, let it be done
     with!
Have we not suffered enough?

   OEDIPUS: You see to what your decency
     has brought you:
You have made difficulties where my
   heart saw none.

(ANTISTROPHE 2)

   CHORAGOS: Oedipus, it is not once only
     I have told you—

You must know I should count myself
unwise
To the point of madness, should I now
forsake you—
You, under whose hand,
In the storm of another time,
Our dear land sailed out free.
But now stand fast at the helm!

IOCASTE: In God's name, Oedipus, inform your wife as well:
Why are you so set in this hard anger?

OEDIPUS: I will tell you, for none of
these men deserves
My confidence as you do. It is Creon's
work,
His treachery, his plotting against me.

IOCASTE: Go on, if you can make this
clear to me.

OEDIPUS: He charges me with the murder of Laïos.

IOCASTE: Has he some knowledge? Or
does he speak from hearsay?

OEDIPUS: He would not commit himself
to such a charge,
But he has brought in that damnable
soothsayer
To tell his story.

IOCASTE: Set your mind at rest.
If it is a question of soothsayers, I tell you
That you will find no man whose craft
gives knowledge
Of the unknowable.

Here is my proof:

An oracle was reported to Laïos once
(I will not say from Phoibos himself, but
from
His appointed ministers, at any rate)
That his doom would be death at the
hands of his own son—
His son, born of his flesh and of mine!

Now, you remember the story: Laïos was
killed

By marauding strangers where three highways meet;
But his child had not been three days in
this world
Before the King had pierced the baby's
ankles
And left him to die on a lonely mountain-
side.

Thus, Apollo never caused that child
To kill his father, and it was not Laïos'
fate
To die at the hands of his son, as he had
feared.
This is what prophets and prophecies are
worth!
Have no dread of them.
                    It is God himself
Who can show us what he wills, in his
own way.

OEDIPUS: How strange a shadowy memory crossed my mind,
Just now while you were speaking; it
chilled my heart.

IOCASTE: What do you mean? What
memory do you speak of?

OEDIPUS: If I understand you, Laïos was
killed
At a place where three roads meet.

IOCASTE: So it was said;
We have no later story.

OEDIPUS: Where did it happen?

IOCASTE: Phokis, it is called: at a place
where the Theban Way
Divides into the roads toward Delphi and
Daulia.

OEDIPUS: When?

IOCASTE: We had the news not long
before you came
And proved the right to your succession
here.

OEDIPUS: Ah, what net has God been
weaving for me?

IOCASTE: Oedipus! Why does this trouble you?

OEDIPUS: Do not ask me yet.
First, tell me how Laïos looked, and tell me
How old he was.

IOCASTE: He was tall, his hair just touched
With white; his form was not unlike your own.

OEDIPUS: I think that I myself may be accurst
By my own ignorant edict.

IOCASTE: You speak strangely.
It makes me tremble to look at you, my King.

OEDIPUS: I am not sure that the blind man can not see.
But I should know better if you were to tell me—

IOCASTE: Anything—though I dread to hear you ask it.

OEDIPUS: Was the King lightly escorted, or did he ride
With a large company, as a ruler should?

IOCASTE: There were five men with him in all: one was a herald,
And a single chariot, which he was driving.

OEDIPUS: Alas, that makes it plain enough!
                But who—
Who told you how it happened?

IOCASTE: A household servant,
The only one to escape.

OEDIPUS: And is he still
A servant of ours?

IOCASTE: No; for when he came back at last
And found you enthroned in the place of the dead king,
He came to me, touched my hand with his, and begged
That I would send him away to the frontier district
Where only the shepherds go—
As far away from the city as I could send him.

I granted his prayer; for although the man was a slave,
He had earned more than this favor at my hands.

OEDIPUS: Can he be called back quickly?

IOCASTE: Easily.
But why?

OEDIPUS: I have taken too much upon myself
Without enquiry; therefore I wish to consult him.

IOCASTE: Then he shall come.
                But am I not one also
To whom you might confide these fears of yours?

OEDIPUS: That is your right; it will not be denied you,
Now least of all; for I have reached a pitch
Of wild foreboding. Is there anyone
To whom I should sooner speak?

Polybos of Corinth is my father.
My mother is a Dorian: Meropê.
I grew up chief among the men of Corinth
Until a strange thing happened—
Not worth my passion, it may be, but strange.

At a feast, a drunken man maundering in his cups
Cries out that I am not my father's son!

I contained myself that night, though I felt anger
And a sinking heart. The next day I visited
My father and mother, and questioned them. They stormed,
Calling it all the slanderous rant of a fool;
And this relieved me. Yet the suspicion
Remained always aching in my mind;
I knew there was talk; I could not rest;
And finally, saying nothing to my parents,
I went to the shrine at Delphi.
The god dismissed my question without reply;

He spoke of other things.
                              Some were clear,
Full of wretchedness, dreadful, unbear-
      able:
As, that I should lie with my own mother,
      breed
Children from whom all men would turn
      their eyes;
And that I should be my father's mur-
      derer.

I heard all this, and fled. And from that
      day
Corinth to me was only in the stars
Descending in that quarter of the sky,
As I wandered farther and farther on my
      way
To a land where I should never see the
      evil
Sung by the oracle. And I came to this
      country
Where, so you say, King Laïos was killed.

I will tell you all that happened there, my
      lady.

There were three highways
Coming together at a place I passed;
And there a herald came towards me, and
      a chariot
Drawn by horses, with a man such as you
      describe
Seated in it. The groom leading the horses
Forced me off the road at his lord's com-
      mand;
But as this charioteer lurched over to-
      wards me
I struck him in my rage. The old man
      saw me
And brought his double goad down upon
      my head
As I came abreast.
                        He was paid back, and more!
Swinging my club in this right hand I
      knocked him
Out of his car, and he rolled on the
      ground.
                              I killed him.

I killed them all.
Now if that stranger and Laïos were—
      kin,
Where is a man more miserable than I?
More hated by the gods? Citizen and alien
      alike
Must never shelter me or speak to me—
I must be shunned by all.
                              And I myself
Pronounced this malediction upon myself!

Think of it: I have touched you with
      these hands,
These hands that killed your husband.
      What defilement!

Am I all evil, then? It must be so,
Since I must flee from Thebes, yet never
      again
See my own countrymen, my own country,
For fear of joining my mother in mar-
      riage
And killing Polybos, my father.
                                    Ah,
If I was created so, born to this fate,
Who could deny the savagery of God?

O holy majesty of heavenly powers!
May I never see that day! Never!
Rather let me vanish from the race of men
Than know the abomination destined me!

   CHORAGOS: We too, my lord, have felt
      dismay at this.
But there is hope: you have yet to hear
      the shepherd.

   OEDIPUS: Indeed, I fear no other hope is
      left me.

   IOCASTE: What do you hope from him
      when he comes?

   OEDIPUS: This much:
If his account of the murder tallies with
      yours,
Then I am cleared.

   IOCASTE: What was it that I said
Of such importance?

   OEDIPUS: Why, "marauders," you said,

Killed the King, according to this man's
    story.
If he maintains that still, if there were
    several,
Clearly the guilt is not mine: I was alone.
But if he says one man, singlehanded, did
    it,
Then the evidence all points to me.
    IOCASTE: You may be sure that he said
    there were several;
And can he call back that story now? He
    can not.
The whole city heard it as plainly as I.
But suppose he alters some detail of it:
He can not ever show that Laïos' death
Fulfilled the oracle: for Apollo said
My child was doomed to kill him; and my
    child—
Poor baby!—it was my child that died
    first.

No. From now on, where oracles are con-
    cerned,
I would not waste a second thought on
    any.
    OEDIPUS: You may be right.
              But come: let someone go
For the shepherd at once. This matter
    must be settled.
    IOCASTE: I will send for him.
I would not wish to cross you in anything,
And surely not in this.—Let us go in.

        (Exeunt into the palace)

ODE II

              (STROPHE 1)
CHORUS: Let me be reverent in the ways
    of right,
Lowly the paths I journey on;
Let all my words and actions keep
The laws of the pure universe
From highest Heaven handed down.
For Heaven is their bright nurse,

Those generations of the realms of light;
Ah, never of mortal kind were they begot,
Nor are they slaves of memory, lost in
    sleep:
Their Father is greater than Time, and
    ages not.

             (ANTISTROPHE 1)
The tyrant is a child of Pride
Who drinks from his great sickening cup
Recklessness and vanity,
Until from his high crest headlong
He plummets to the dust of hope.
That strong man is not strong.
But let no fair ambition be denied;
May God protect the wrestler for the State
In government, in comely policy,
Who will fear God, and on His ordinance
    wait.

             (STROPHE 2)
Haughtiness and the high hand of dis-
    dain
Tempt and outrage God's holy law;
And any mortal who dares hold
No immortal Power in awe
Will be caught up in a net of pain:
The price for which his levity is sold.
Let each man take due earnings, then,
And keep his hands from holy things,
And from blasphemy stand apart—
Else the crackling blast of heaven
Blows on his head, and on his desperate
    heart;
Though fools will honor impious men,
In their cities no tragic poet sings.

             (ANTISTROPHE 2)
Shall we lose faith in Delphi's obscurities,
We who have heard the world's core
Discredited, and the sacred wood
Of Zeus at Elis praised no more?
The deeds and the strange prophecies
Must make a pattern yet to be understood.
Zeus, if indeed you are lord of all,
Throned in light over night and day,
Mirror this in your endless mind:

Our masters call the oracle
Words on the wind, and the Delphic
    vision blind!
Their hearts no longer know Apollo,
And reverence for the gods has died away.

SCENE III

(*Enter* IOCASTE)

IOCASTE: Princes of Thebes, it has oc-
    curred to me
To visit the altars of the gods, bearing
These branches as a suppliant, and this
    incense.
Our King is not himself: his noble soul
Is overwrought with fantasies of dread,
Else he would consider
The new prophecies in the light of the old.
He will listen to any voice that speaks dis-
    aster,
And my advice goes for nothing.

(*She approaches the altar, R.*)

                To you, then, Apollo,
Lycean lord, since you are nearest, I turn
    in prayer.
Receive these offerings, and grant us de-
    liverance
From defilement. Our hearts are heavy
    with fear
When we see our leader distracted, as
    helpless sailors
Are terrified by the confusion of their
    helmsman.

(*Enter* MESSENGER)

MESSENGER: Friends, no doubt you can
    direct me:
Where shall I find the house of Oedipus,
Or, better still, where is the King himself?

CHORAGOS: It is this very place, stranger;
    he is inside.
This is his wife and mother of his chil-
    dren.

MESSENGER: I wish her happiness in a
    happy house,

Blest in all the fulfillment of her marriage.

IOCASTE: I wish as much for you: your
    courtesy
Deserves a like good fortune. But now,
    tell me:
Why have you come? What have you to
    say to us?

MESSENGER: Good news, my lady, for
    your house and your husband.

IOCASTE: What news? Who sent you
    here?

MESSENGER: I am from Corinth.
The news I bring ought to mean joy for
    you,
Though it may be you will find some
    grief in it.

IOCASTE: What is it? How can it touch
    us in both ways?

MESSENGER: The word is that the peo-
    ple of the Isthmus
Intend to call Oedipus to be their king.

IOCASTE: But old King Polybos—is he
    not reigning still?

MESSENGER: No. Death holds him in his
    sepulchre.

IOCASTE: What are you saying? Poly-
    bos is dead?

MESSENGER: If I am not telling the
    truth, may I die myself.

IOCASTE: (*To a* MAIDSERVANT:)
Go in, go quickly; tell this to your master.

O riddlers of God's will, where are you
    now!
This was the man whom Oedipus, long
    ago,
Feared so, fled so, in dread of destroying
    him—
But it was another fate by which he died.

(*Enter* OEDIPUS, *C.*)

OEDIPUS: Dearest Iocastê, why have you
    sent for me?

IOCASTE: Listen to what this man says,
    and then tell me

What has become of the solemn prophecies.

OEDIPUS: Who is this man? What is
his news for me?

IOCASTE: He has come from Corinth to
announce your father's death!

OEDIPUS: Is it true, stranger? Tell me
in your own words.

MESSENGER: I can not say it more
clearly: the King is dead.

OEDIPUS: Was it by treason? Or by an
attack of illness?

MESSENGER: A little thing brings old
men to their rest.

OEDIPUS: It was sickness, then?

MESSENGER: Yes, and his many years.

OEDIPUS: Ah!

Why should a man respect the Pythian
hearth, or

Give heed to the birds that jangle above
his head?

They prophesied that I should kill Polybos,

Kill my own father; but he is dead and
buried,

And I am here—I never touched him,
never,

Unless he died of grief for my departure,

And thus, in a sense, through me. No.
Polybos

Has packed the oracles off with him
underground.

They are empty words.

IOCASTE: Had I not told you so?

OEDIPUS: You had; it was my faint
heart that betrayed me.

IOCASTE: From now on never think of
those things again.

OEDIPUS: And yet—must I not fear my
mother's bed?

IOCASTE: Why should anyone in this
world be afraid,

Since Fate rules us and nothing can be
foreseen?

A man should live only for the present
day.

Have no more fear of sleeping with your
mother:

How many men, in dreams, have lain
with their mothers!

No reasonable man is troubled by such
things.

OEDIPUS: That is true; only—

If only my mother were not still alive!

But she is alive. I can not help my dread.

IOCASTE: Yet this news of your father's
death is wonderful.

OEDIPUS: Wonderful. But I fear the
living woman.

MESSENGER: Tell me, who is this woman
that you fear?

OEDIPUS: It is Meropê, man; the wife
of King Polybos.

MESSENGER: Meropê? Why should you
be afraid of her?

OEDIPUS: An oracle of the gods, a dreadful saying.

MESSENGER: Can you tell me about it
or are you sworn to silence?

OEDIPUS: I can tell you, and I will.

Apollo said through his prophet that I
was the man

Who should marry his own mother, shed
his father's blood

With his own hands. And so, for all these
years

I have kept clear of Corinth, and no harm
has come—

Though it would have been sweet to see
my parents again.

MESSENGER: And is this the fear that
drove you out of Corinth?

OEDIPUS: Would you have me kill my
father?

MESSENGER:　　　　　　　　As for that

You must be reassured by the news I
gave you.

OEDIPUS: If you could reassure me, I would reward you.

MESSENGER: I had that in mind, I will confess: I thought
I could count on you when you returned to Corinth.

OEDIPUS: No: I will never go near my parents again.

MESSENGER: Ah, son, you still do not know what you are doing—

OEDIPUS: What do you mean? In the name of God tell me!

MESSENGER: —If these are your reasons for not going home.

OEDIPUS: I tell you, I fear the oracle may come true.

MESSENGER: And guilt may come upon you through your parents?

OEDIPUS: That is the dread that is always in my heart.

MESSENGER: Can you not see that all your fears are groundless?

OEDIPUS: How can you say that? They are my parents, surely?

MESSENGER: Polybos was not your father.

OEDIPUS: Not my father?

MESSENGER: No more your father than the man speaking to you.

OEDIPUS: But you are nothing to me!

MESSENGER: Neither was he.

OEDIPUS: Then why did he call me son?

MESSENGER: I will tell you:
Long ago he had you from my hands, as a gift.

OEDIPUS: Then how could he love me so, if I was not his?

MESSENGER: He had no children, and his heart turned to you.

OEDIPUS: What of you? Did you buy me? Did you find me by chance?

MESSENGER: I came upon you in the crooked pass of Kithairon.

OEDIPUS: And what were you doing there?

MESSENGER: Tending my flocks.

OEDIPUS: A wandering shepherd?

MESSENGER: But your savior, son, that day.

OEDIPUS: From what did you save me?

MESSENGER: Your ankles should tell you that.

OEDIPUS: Ah, stranger, why do you speak of that childhood pain?

MESSENGER: I cut the bonds that tied your ankles together.

OEDIPUS: I have had the mark as long as I can remember.

MESSENGER: That was why you were given the name you bear.

OEDIPUS: God! Was it my father or my mother who did it? Tell me!

MESSENGER: I do not know. The man who gave you to me
Can tell you better than I.

OEDIPUS: It was not you that found me, but another?

MESSENGER: It was another shepherd gave you to me.

OEDIPUS: Who was he? Can you tell me who he was?

MESSENGER: I think he was said to be one of Laïos' people.

OEDIPUS: You mean the Laïos who was king here years ago?

MESSENGER: Yes; King Laïos; and the man was one of his herdsmen.

OEDIPUS: Is he still alive? Can I see him?

MESSENGER: These men here
Know best about such things.

OEDIPUS: Does anyone here
Know this shepherd that he is talking about?
Have you seen him in the fields, or in the town?

If you have, tell me. It is time things were
    made plain.
  CHORAGOS: I think the man he means
    is that same shepherd
You have already asked to see. Iocastê
    perhaps
Could tell you something.
  OEDIPUS: Do you know anything
About him, Lady? Is he the man we
    have summoned?
Is that the man this shepherd means?
  IOCASTE: Why think of him?
Forget this herdsman. Forget it all.
This talk is a waste of time.
  OEDIPUS: How can you say that,
When the clues to my true birth are in
    my hands?
  IOCASTE: For God's love, let us have no
    more questioning!
Is your life nothing to you?
My own is pain enough for me to bear.
  OEDIPUS: You need not worry. Suppose
    my mother a slave,
And born of slaves: no baseness can touch
    you.
  IOCASTE: Listen to me, I beg you: do
    not do this thing!
  OEDIPUS: I will not listen; the truth
    must be made known.
  IOCASTE: Everything that I say is for
    your own good!
  OEDIPUS: My own good
Snaps my patience, then; I want none of it.
  IOCASTE: You are fatally wrong! May
    you never learn who you are!
  OEDIPUS: Go, one of you, and bring the
    shepherd here.
Let us leave this woman to brag of her
    royal name.
  IOCASTE: Ah, miserable!
That is the only word I have for you now.
That is the only word I can ever have.
             (*Exit into the palace*)
  CHORAGOS: Why has she left us, Oedi-
    pus? Why has she gone

In such a passion of sorrow? I fear this
    silence:
Something dreadful may come of it.
  OEDIPUS: Let it come!
However base my birth, I must know
    about it.
The Queen, like a woman, is perhaps
    ashamed
To think of my low origin. But I
Am a child of Luck; I can not be dis-
    honored.
Luck is my mother; the passing months,
    my brothers,
Have seen me rich and poor.
                If this is so,
How could I wish that I were someone
    else?
How could I not be glad to know my
    birth?

ODE III

                    (STROPHE)
  CHORUS: If ever the coming time were
    known
To my heart's pondering,
Kithairon, now by Heaven I see the
    torches
At the festival of the next full moon,
And see the dance, and hear the choir
    sing
A grace to your gentle shade:
Mountain where Oedipus was found,
O mountain guard of a noble race!
May the god who heals us lend his aid,
And let that glory come to pass
For our king's cradling-ground.

                (ANTISTROPHE)
Of the nymphs that flower beyond the
    years,
Who bore you, royal child,
To Pan of the hills or the timberline
    Apollo,
Cold in delight where the upland clears,

Or Hermês for whom Kyllenê's heights
    are piled?
Or flushed as evening cloud,
Great Dionysos, roamer of mountains,
He—was it he who found you there,
And caught you up in his own proud
Arms from the sweet god-ravisher
Who laughed by the Muses' fountains?

SCENE IV

OEDIPUS: Sirs: though I do not know
    the man,
I think I see him coming, this shepherd
    we want:
He is old, like our friend here, and the
    men
Bringing him seem to be servants of my
    house.
But you can tell, if you have ever seen
    him.

(*Enter* SHEPHERD *escorted by servants*)

CHORAGOS: I know him, he was Laïos'
    man. You can trust him.

OEDIPUS: Tell me first, you from Cor-
    inth: is this the shepherd
We were discussing?

MESSENGER: This is the very man.

OEDIPUS: (*To* SHEPHERD:)
Come here. No, look at me. You must
    answer
Everything I ask.—You belonged to Laïos?

SHEPHERD: Yes: born his slave, brought
    up in his house.

OEDIPUS: Tell me: what kind of work
    did you do for him?

SHEPHERD: I was a shepherd of his,
    most of my life.

OEDIPUS: Where mainly did you go for
    pasturage?

SHEPHERD: Sometimes Kithairon, some-
    times the hills near-by.

OEDIPUS: Do you remember ever seeing
    this man out there?

SHEPHERD: What would he be doing
    there? This man?

OEDIPUS: This man standing here. Have
    you ever seen him before?

SHEPHERD: No. At least, not to my
    recollection.

MESSENGER: And that is not strange,
    my lord. But I'll refresh
His memory: he must remember when
    we two
Spent three whole seasons together, March
    to September,
On Kithairon or thereabouts. He had two
    flocks;
I had one. Each autumn I'd drive mine
    home
And he would go back with his to Laïos'
    sheepfold.—
Is this not true, just as I have described
    it?

SHEPHERD: True, yes; but it was all so
    long ago.

MESSENGER: Well, then: do you remem-
    ber, back in those days,
That you gave me a baby boy to bring up
    as my own?

SHEPHERD: What if I did? What are
    you trying to say?

MESSENGER: King Oedipus was once
    that little child.

SHEPHERD: Damn you, hold your
    tongue!

OEDIPUS: No more of that!
It is your tongue needs watching, not
    this man's.

SHEPHERD: My King, my Master, what
    is it I have done wrong?

OEDIPUS: You have not answered his
    question about the boy.

SHEPHERD: He does not know . . . He
    is only making trouble . . .

OEDIPUS: Come, speak plainly, or it
    will go hard with you.

SHEPHERD: In God's name, do not tor-
    ture an old man!

OEDIPUS: Come here, one of you; bind his arms behind him.

SHEPHERD: Unhappy king! What more do you wish to learn?

OEDIPUS: Did you give this man the child he speaks of?

SHEPHERD:　　　　　　I did. And I would to God I had died that very day.

OEDIPUS: You will die now unless you speak the truth.

SHEPHERD: Yet if I speak the truth, I am worse than dead.

OEDIPUS: Very well; since you insist upon delaying—

SHEPHERD: No! I have told you already that I gave him the boy.

OEDIPUS: Where did you get him? From your house? From somewhere else?

SHEPHERD: Not from mine, no. A man gave him to me.

OEDIPUS: Is that man here? Do you know whose slave he was?

SHEPHERD: For God's love, my King, do not ask me any more!

OEDIPUS: You are a dead man if I have to ask you again.

SHEPHERD: Then . . . Then the child was from the palace of Laïos.

OEDIPUS: A slave child? or a child of his own line?

SHEPHERD: Ah, I am on the brink of dreadful speech!

OEDIPUS: And I of dreadful hearing. Yet I must hear.

SHEPHERD: If you must be told, then . . . They said it was Laïos' child; But it is your wife who can tell you about that.

OEDIPUS: My wife!—Did she give it to you?

SHEPHERD:　　　　　　My lord, she did.

OEDIPUS: Do you know why?

SHEPHERD:　　I was told to get rid of it.

OEDIPUS: An unspeakable mother!

SHEPHERD: There had been prophecies . . .

OEDIPUS: Tell me.

SHEPHERD: It was said that the boy would kill his own father.

OEDIPUS: Then why did you give him over to this old man?

SHEPHERD: I pitied the baby, my King, And I thought that this man would take him far away To his own country.
　　　　He saved him—but for what a fate! For if you are what this man says you are, No man living is more wretched than Oedipus.

OEDIPUS: Ah God! It was true!
　　　　All the prophecies!
　　　　　　　　　　—Now,
O Light, may I look on you for the last time!
I, Oedipus,
Oedipus, damned in his birth, in his marriage damned,
Damned in the blood he shed with his own hand!

　　　　(*He rushes into the palace*)

ODE IV

CHORUS: Alas for the seed of men.

What measures shall I give these generations
That breathe on the void and are void
And exist and do not exist?

Who bears more weight of joy
Than mass of sunlight shifting in images,

Or who shall make his thought stay on
That down time drifts away?

Your splendor is all fallen.

O naked brow of wrath and tears,
O change of Oedipus!
I who saw your days call no man blest—
Your great days like ghósts góne.

(ANTISTROPHE 1)

That mind was a strong bow.

Deep, how deep you drew it then, hard
    archer,
At a dim fearful range,
And brought dear glory down!

You overcame the stranger—
The virgin with her hooking lion claws—
And though death sang, stood like a
    tower
To make pale Thebes take heart.

Fortress against our sorrow!

True king, giver of laws,
Majestic Oedipus!
No prince in Thebes had ever such re-
    nown,
No prince won such grace of power.

(STROPHE 2)

And now of all men ever known
Most pitiful is this man's story:
His fortunes are most changed, his state
Fallen to a low slave's
Ground under bitter fate.

O Oedipus, most royal one!
The great door that expelled you to the
    light
Gave at night—ah, gave night to your
    glory:
As to the father, to the fathering son.

All understood too late.

How could that queen whom Laïos won,
The garden that he harrowed at his height,
Be silent when that act was done?

(ANTISTROPHE 2)

But all eyes fail before time's eye,
All actions come to justice there.
Though never willed, though far down
    the deep past,
Your bed, your dread sirings,
Are brought to book at last.
Child by Laïos doomed to die,
Then doomed to lose that fortunate little
    death,
Would God you never took breath in this
    air
That with my wailing lips I take to cry:

For I weep the world's outcast.

I was blind, and now I can tell why:
Asleep, for you had given ease of breath
To Thebes, while the false years went by.

ÉXODOS

(Enter, from the palace, SECOND
MESSENGER*)*

SECOND MESSENGER: Elders of Thebes,
    most honored in this land,
What horrors are yours to see and hear,
    what weight
Of sorrow to be endured, if, true to your
    birth,
You venerate the line of Labdakos!
I think neither Istros nor Phasis, those
    great rivers,
Could purify this place of the corruption
It shelters now, or soon must bring to
    light—
Evil not done unconsciously, but willed.

The greatest griefs are those we cause our-
    selves.

CHORAGOS: Surely, friend, we have grief enough already;
What new sorrow do you mean?

SECOND MESSENGER: The Queen is dead.

CHORAGOS: Iocastê? Dead? But at whose hand?

SECOND MESSENGER: Her own.
The full horror of what happened you can not know,
For you did not see it; but I, who did, will tell you
As clearly as I can how she met her death.

When she had left us,
In passionate silence, passing through the court,
She ran to her apartment in the house,
Her hair clutched by the fingers of both hands.
She closed the doors behind her; then, by that bed
Where long ago the fatal son was conceived—
That son who should bring about his father's death—
We heard her call upon Laïos, dead so many years,
And heard her wail for the double fruit of her marriage,
A husband by her husband, children by her child.

Exactly how she died I do not know:
For Oedipus burst in moaning and would not let us
Keep vigil to the end: it was by him
As he stormed about the room that our eyes were caught.
From one to another of us he went, begging a sword,
Cursing the wife who was not his wife, the mother
Whose womb had carried his own children and himself.
I do not know: it was none of us aided him,

But surely one of the gods was in control!
For with a dreadful cry
He hurled his weight, as though wrenched out of himself,
At the twin doors: the bolts gave, and he rushed in.
And there we saw her hanging, her body swaying
From the cruel cord she had noosed about her neck.
A great sob broke from him, heartbreaking to hear,
As he loosed the rope and lowered her to to the ground.

I would blot out from my mind what happened next!
For the King ripped from her gown the golden brooches
That were her ornament, and raised them, and plunged them down
Straight into his own eyeballs, crying, "No more,
No more shall you look on the misery about me,
The horrors of my own doing! Too long you have known
The faces of those whom I should never have seen,
Too long been blind to those for whom I was searching!
From this hour, go in darkness!" And as he spoke,
He struck at his eyes—not once, but many times;
And the blood spattered his beard,
Bursting from his ruined sockets like red hail.

So from the unhappiness of two this evil has sprung,
A curse on the man and woman alike. The old
Happiness of the house of Labdakos
Was happiness enough: where is it today?
It is all wailing and ruin, disgrace, death— all

The misery of mankind that has a name—
And it is wholly and for ever theirs.

> CHORAGOS: Is he in agony still? Is there
> no rest for him?

> SECOND MESSENGER: He is calling for
> someone to lead him to the gates
So that all the children of Kadmos may
    look upon
His father's murderer, his mother's—no,
I can not say it!
                    And then he will leave Thebes,
Self-exiled, in order that the curse
Which he himself pronounced may depart
    from the house.
He is weak, and there is none to lead him,
So terrible is his suffering.
                    But you will see:
Look, the doors are opening; in a moment
You will see a thing that would crush a
    heart of stone.

> (*The central door is opened;* OEDIPUS,
> *blinded, is led in.*)

> CHORAGOS: Dreadful indeed for men to
> see.
Never have my own eyes
Looked on a sight so full of fear.

Oedipus!
What madness came upon you, what dae-
    mon
Leaped on your life with heavier
Punishment than a mortal man can bear?
No: I can not even
Look at you, poor ruined one.
And I would speak, question, ponder,
If I were able. No.
You make me shudder.

> OEDIPUS: God.   God.
Is there a sorrow greater?
Where shall I find harbor in this world?
My voice is hurled far on a dark wind.
What has God done to me?

> CHORAGOS: Too terrible to think of, or to
> see.

(STROPHE 1)

> OEDIPUS: O cloud of night,
Never to be turned away: night coming
    on,
I can not tell how: night like a shroud!

My fair winds brought me here.
                            O God. Again
The pain of the spikes where I had sight,
The flooding pain
Of memory, never to be gouged out.

> CHORAGOS: This is not strange.
You suffer it all twice over, remorse in
    pain,
Pain in remorse.

(ANTISTROPHE 1)

> OEDIPUS: Ah dear friend
Are you faithful even yet, you alone?
Are you still standing near me, will you
    stay here,
Patient, to care for the blind?
                            The blind man!
Yet even blind I know who it is attends
    me,
By the voice's tone—
Though my new darkness hide the com-
    forter.

> CHORAGOS: Oh fearful act!
What god was it drove you to rake black
Night across your eyes?

(STROPHE 2)

> OEDIPUS: Apollo. Apollo. Dear
Children, the god was Apollo.
He brought my sick, sick fate upon me.
But the blinding hand was my own!
How could I bear to see
When all my sight was horror everywhere?

> CHORAGOS: Everywhere; that is true.

> OEDIPUS: And now what is left?
Images? Love? A greeting even,
Sweet to the senses? Is there anything?
Ah, no, friends: lead me away.
Lead me away from Thebes.

Lead the great wreck
And hell of Oedipus, whom the gods hate.

CHORAGOS: Your fate is clear, you are not
blind to that.
Would God you had never found it out!

　　　　　　　　　　　(ANTISTROPHE 2)

OEDIPUS: Death take the man who un-
bound
My feet on that hillside
And delivered me from death to life! What
life?
If only I had died,
This weight of monstrous doom
Could not have dragged me and my
darlings down.

CHORAGOS: I would have wished the
same.

OEDIPUS: Oh never to have come here
With my father's blood upon me! Never
To have been the man they call his
mother's husband!
Oh accurst! Oh child of evil,
To have entered that wretched bed—
　　　　　　　　　　　　the selfsame one!
More primal than sin itself, this fell to me.

CHORAGOS: I do not know how I can answer you.
You were better dead than alive and blind.

OEDIPUS: Do not counsel me any more.
This punishment
That I have laid upon myself is just.
If I had eyes,
I do not know how I could bear the sight
Of my father, when I came to the house of
Death,
Or my mother: for I have sinned against
them both
So vilely that I could not make my peace
By strangling my own life.
　　　　　　　　Or do you think my children,
Born as they were born, would be sweet to
my eyes?
Ah never, never! Nor this town with its
high walls,
Nor the holy images of the gods.

　　　　　　　　　　　　For I,
Thrice miserable!—Oedipus, noblest of all
the line
Of Kadmos, have condemned myself to en-
joy
These things no more, by my own maledic-
tion
Expelling that man whom the gods de-
clared
To be a defilement in the house of Laïos.
After exposing the rankness of my own
guilt,
How could I look men frankly in the eyes?
No, I swear it,
If I could have stifled my hearing at its
source,
I would have done it and made all this
body
A tight cell of misery, blank to light and
sound:
So I should have been safe in a dark agony
Beyond all recollection.
　　　　　　　　　　　Ah Kithairon!
Why did you shelter me? When I was cast
upon you,
Why did I not die? Then I should never
Have shown the world my execrable birth.

Ah Polybos! Corinth, city that I believed
The ancient seat of my ancestors: how
fair
I seemed, your child! And all the while this
evil
Was cancerous within me!
　　　　　　　　　　　　For I am sick
In my daily life, sick in my origin.

O three roads, dark ravine, woodland and
way
Where three roads met: you, drinking my
father's blood,
My own blood, spilled by my own hand:
can you remember
The unspeakable things I did there, and the
things
I went on from there to do?
　　　　　　　　　　O marriage, marriage!

The act that engendered me, and again the
    act
Performed by the son in the same bed—
                        Ah, the net
Of incest, mingling fathers, brothers, sons,
With brides, wives, mothers: the last evil
That can be known by men: no tongue can
    say
How evil!
        No. For the love of God, conceal me
Somewhere far from Thebes; or kill me;
    or hurl me
Into the sea, away from men's eyes for
    ever.

Come, lead me. You need not fear to touch
    me.
Of all men, I alone can bear this guilt.

                (*Enter* CREON)

    CHORAGOS: We are not the ones to de-
    cide; but Creon here
May fitly judge of what you ask. He only
Is left to protect the city in your place.

    OEDIPUS: Alas, how can I speak to him?
    What right have I
To beg his courtesy whom I have deeply
    wronged?

    CREON: I have not come to mock you,
    Oedipus,
Or to reproach you, either.

                (*To* ATTENDANTS:)

        —You, standing there:
If you have lost all respect for man's
    dignity,
At least respect the flame of Lord Helios:
Do not allow this pollution to show itself
Openly here, an affront to the earth
And Heaven's rain and the light of day.
    No, take him
Into the house as quickly as you can.
For it is proper
That only the close kindred see his grief.

    OEDIPUS: I pray you in God's name,
    since your courtesy
Ignores my dark expectation, visiting

With mercy this man of all men most ex-
    ecrable:
Give me what I ask—for your good, not
    for mine.

    CREON: And what is it that you would
    have me do?

    OEDIPUS: Drive me out of this country
    as quickly as may be
To a place where no human voice can ever
    greet me.

    CREON: I should have done that before
    now—only,
God's will had not been wholly revealed to
    me.

    OEDIPUS: But his command is plain: the
    parricide
Must be destroyed. I am that evil man.

    CREON: That is the sense of it, yes; but
    as things are,
We had best discover clearly what is to be
    done.

    OEDIPUS: You would learn more about a
    man like me?

    CREON: You are ready now to listen to
    the god.

    OEDIPUS: I will listen. But it is to you
That I must turn for help. I beg you, hear
    me.

The woman in there—
Give her whatever funeral you think
    proper:
She is your sister.
                        —But let me go, Creon!
Let me purge my father's Thebes of the
    pollution
Of my living here, and go out to the wild
    hills,
To Kithairon, that has won such fame with
    me,
The tomb my mother and father appointed
    for me,
And let me die there, as they willed I
    should.
And yet I know

Death will not ever come to me through sickness
Or in any natural way: I have been preserved
For some unthinkable fate. But let that be.

As for my sons, you need not care for them.
They are men, they will find some way to live.
But my poor daughters, who have shared my table,
Who never before have been parted from their father—
Take care of them, Creon; do this for me.
And will you let me touch them with my hands
A last time, and let us weep together?
Be kind, my lord,
Great prince, be kind!
                    Could I but touch them,
They would be mine again, as when I had my eyes.

(*Enter* ANTIGONE *and* ISMENE, *attended*)

Ah, God!
Is it my dearest children I hear weeping?
Has Creon pitied me and sent my daughters?

   CREON: Yes, Oedipus: I knew that they were dear to you
In the old days, and know you must love them still.

   OEDIPUS: May God bless you for this—and be a friendlier
Guardian to you than he has been to me!

Children, where are you?
Come quickly to my hands: they are your brother's—
Hands that have brought your father's once clear eyes
To this way of seeing—
                    Ah dearest ones,
I had neither sight nor knowledge then, your father

By the woman who was the source of his own life!
And I weep for you—having no strength to see you—,
I weep for you when I think of the bitterness
That men will visit upon you all your lives.
What homes, what festivals can you attend
Without being forced to depart again in tears?
And when you come to marriageable age,
Where is the man, my daughters, who would dare
Risk the bane that lies on all my children?
Is there any evil wanting? Your father killed
His father; sowed the womb of her who bore him;
Engendered you at the fount of his own existence!
That is what they will say of you.

                            Then, whom
Can you ever marry? There are no bridegrooms for you,
And your lives must wither away in sterile dreaming.

O Creon, son of Menoikeus!
You are the only father my daughters have,
Since we, their parents, are both of us gone for ever.
They are your own blood: you will not let them
Fall into beggary and loneliness;
You will keep them from the miseries that are mine!
Take pity on them; see, they are only children,
Friendless except for you. Promise me this,
Great Prince, and give me your hand in token of it.

   (CREON *clasps his right hand*)

Children:
I could say much, if you could understand
    me,
But as it is, I have only this prayer for you:
Live where you can, be as happy as you
    can—
Happier, please God, than God has made
    your father!

CREON: Enough. You have wept enough.
    Now go within.

OEDIPUS: I must; but it is hard.

CREON: Time eases all things.

OEDIPUS: But you must promise—

CREON: Say what you desire.

OEDIPUS: Send me from Thebes!

CREON: God grant that I may!

OEDIPUS: But since God hates me . . .

CREON: No, he will grant your wish.

OEDIPUS: You promise?

CREON: I can not speak beyond my
    knowledge.

OEDIPUS: Then lead me in.

CREON: Come now, and leave your chil-
    dren.

OEDIPUS: No! Do not take them from
    me!

CREON: Think no longer
That you are in command here, but rather
    think
How, when you were, you served your own
    destruction.

(*Exeunt into the house all but the* CHORUS;
    the CHORAGOS *chants directly to the
    audience:*)

CHORAGOS: Men of Thebes: look upon
    Oedipus.

This is the king who solved the famous
    riddle
And towered up, most powerful of men.
No mortal eyes but looked on him with
    envy,
Yet in the end ruin swept over him.

Let every man in mankind's frailty
Consider his last day; and let none
Presume on his good fortune until he
    find
Life, at his death, a memory without pain.

Everyman

ANONYMOUS

COMMENTARY

 Everyman is the most famous English morality play. It was probably written by a clergyman around 1500 A. D. and was widely produced in England during the early decades of the sixteenth century. Like other medieval works, its intention was to prepare the audience for salvation, to put into proper perspective the relation between material and spiritual demands. It was, of course, an affirmatively Christian work, simply and straightforwardly teaching the Church's doctrines.

The play insists on man's mortality. Man's life after death may be glorious and immortal, which is to be desired and strived for, or inglorious and immortal, which is to be avoided; but here, this side of death, in this world, life is just that: merely life, transient, brief, and all too readily given to self-deceits and vanities, not least to the very loss of awareness of the fragility of life. Everyman is not in any large way sinful; he is, as the title insists, as his personified attributes keep reminding us every time they address him, *every man*. He is, even more than Oedipus, paradigmatic, representing us all in his essential decency, simplicity, and self-delusion. Everyman learns what life is, and what he is: life is a prelude to death, and he is but mortal man who must, in the presence of Death, acknowledge this, put his past and his possessions into perspective, arrange the bookkeeping of his life, accept graciously his ineluctable fate.

In reading the play, you might look for those details that might be lost or blurred in a production, especially since the characters are allegorical types. Would casting, for example, conceivably change the quality of *Everyman*? Think of some leading actors who might differently yet still plausibly interpret Everyman's character. How might different emphases in acting, directing, or staging affect your reading of the text?

It is generally agreed by scholars that *Everyman* was preceded by a Dutch play, *Elckerlijc*, probably its original. (The principal articles arguing this point are listed in A. C. Baugh, ed., *A Literary History of*

England [New York, 1948], p. 286, fn. 38). A full and enlightening discussion of both medieval and modern productions of the work appears in Randolph Goodman's *Drama on Stage* (New York, 1961), pp. 61-115. The definitive history is that by E. K. Chambers, *The Medieval Stage* (Oxford, 1903), in two volumes. Chapter Two of Sir Ifor Evans' *A Short History of English Drama* (Boston, 1965) briefly discusses *Everyman* in relation to other medieval plays. A probing discussion of the character of the play, especially as a tragedy, appears in Cleanth Brooks and Robert B. Heilman, *Understanding Drama* (New York, 1948), pp. 100-110. Two other important large studies are by Lawrence V. Ryan, "Doctrine and Dramatic Structure in *Everyman*," *Speculum,* xxxii (1957), 722-735; and Thomas F. Van Laan, *"Everyman*: A Structural Analysis," *PMLA,* lxxviii (No. 5, 1963), 465-475.

Anonymous

EVERYMAN

A Modernized Version by John Gassner

CHARACTERS

EVERYMAN	STRENGTH
GOD: ADONAI*	DISCRETION
DEATH	FIVE-WITS
MESSENGER	BEAUTY
FELLOWSHIP	KNOWLEDGE
COUSIN	CONFESSION
KINDRED	ANGEL
GOODS	DOCTOR
GOOD-DEEDS	

* The Lord.

Here Beginneth a Treatise How the High Father of Heaven Sendeth Death to Summon All Creatures to Come and Give Account of Their Lives in This World and Is in the Manner of a Moral Play.

PROLOGUE

MESSENGER: I pray you all give your audience,
And hear this matter with reverence,
By figure a moral play—
The *Summoning of Everyman* called it is,
That of our lives and ending shows
How transitory we be all our day.

This matter is wondrous precious,
But the intent of it is more gracious,
And sweet to bear away.
The story saith,—Man, in the beginning,
Look well, and take good heed to the ending,
Be you never so gay!
Ye think sin in the beginning full sweet,
Which in the end causeth the soul to weep,

Everyman, version by John Gassner. By his permission.

When the body lieth in clay.
Here shall you see how Fellowship and
Jollity,
And Strength, Pleasure, and Beauty,
Will fade from thee as flower in May.
For ye shall hear how our heaven's king
Calleth Everyman to a general reckoning.
Give audience, and hear what he doth say.

(GOD *appears and speaks.*)

GOD: I perceive here in my majesty,
How that all creatures be to me unkind,
Living without dread in worldly pros-
perity.
Of spiritual sight the people be so blind,
Drowned in sin, they know me not for
their God;
In worldly riches is all their mind,
They fear not my righteousness, the sharp
rod;
My law that I showed, when I for them
died,
They clean forget, and shedding of my
blood red;
I hung between two, it cannot be denied;
To get men life I suffered to be dead;
I healed their feet, with thorns hurt was
my head—
I could do no more than I did truly,
And now I see the people do clean forsake
me.
They love the seven deadly sins damnable;
And pride, covetize, wrath, and lechery,
Now in the world be made commendable;
And thus they leave of angels the heavenly
company;
Every man liveth so after his own pleasure,
And yet of their life they be nothing sure.
I see the more that I forbear
The worse they be from year to year;
All that liveth impaireth fast,
Therefore I will with all my haste
Have a reckoning of Everyman's person
For if I leave the people thus alone
In their life and wicked tempests,
Verily they will become much worse than
beasts;

For now one would by envy another eat;
Charity they all do clean forget.
I hoped well that every man
In my glory should make his mansion,
And thereto I had them all elect;
But now I see, like traitors abject,
They thank me not for pleasure that I
them meant,
Nor yet for their being that I to them have
lent;
I proffer the people great multitude of
mercy,
But few there be that ask it heartily;
They be so cumbered with worldly riches,
That needs on them I must do justice,
On Everyman living without fear.
Where art thou, Death, thou mighty mes-
senger?

(*Enter* DEATH.)

DEATH: Almighty God, I am here at
Thy will,
Thy commandment to fulfil.

GOD: Go thou to Everyman,
And show him in my name
A pilgrimage he must on him take,
Which he in no wise may escape;
And that he bring with him a sure reckon-
ing
Without delay or any tarrying.

(GOD *withdraws.*)

DEATH: Lord, I will in the world run
over all,
And cruelly search out both great and
small;
Every man I will beset that liveth beastly
Out of God's law, and dreadeth not folly.
He that loveth riches will I strike with my
dart,
His sight to blind, and from heaven him
to part,
Except that Alms be his good friend,
In hell for to dwell, world without end.
Lo, yonder I see Everyman walking;
Full little he thinketh on my coming.
His mind is on fleshly lusts and treasure,

And great pain it shall cause him to endure
Before the Lord, heaven's King.
Everyman, stand still! whither art thou
  going
Thus gaily? Hast thou thy maker forgot?

(*Enter* EVERYMAN.)

EVERYMAN: Why askst thou?
Why would you know?

DEATH: Yea, sir, I will show you.
In great haste I am sent to thee
From God out of his majesty.

EVERYMAN: What, sent to me?

DEATH: Yea, certainly.
Though thou have forgot him here,
He thinketh on thee in the heavenly
  sphere,
As, ere we depart, thou shalt know.

EVERYMAN: What desireth God of me?

DEATH: That shall I show thee;
A reckoning he will needs have
Without any longer respite.

EVERYMAN: To give a reckoning longer
  leisure I crave;
This blind matter troubleth my wit.

DEATH: On thee thou must take a long
  journey.
Therefore thy book of accounts with thee
  thou bring;
For turn again thou canst not by any way,
And look thou be sure of thy reckoning:
For before God thou shalt answer, and
  show
Thy many bad deeds and good but a few;
How thou hast spent thy life, and in what
  wise,
Before the Great Lord of Paradise.
Make preparation that we be on the way,
For know thou well, thou shalt make none
  attorney.

EVERYMAN: Full unready I am such
  reckoning to give,
I know thee not. What messenger art
  thou?

DEATH: I am Death, that no man
  dreadeth.

That every man arrests and no man
  spareth;
For it is God's commandment
That all to me should be obedient.

EVERYMAN: O Death, thou comest when
  I had thee least in mind;
In thy power it lieth me to save,
Yet of my goods will I give thee, if ye will
  be kind,
Yea, a thousand pound shalt thou have,
But defer this matter till another day!

DEATH: Everyman, it may not be by no
  way;
I set not by gold, silver, nor riches,
Nor by pope, emperor, king, duke, nor
  princes,
For if I would receive gifts great,
All the world I might get;
But my custom is clean contrary.
I give thee no respite. Come, do not tarry!

EVERYMAN: Alas, shall I have no longer
  respite?
I may say Death giveth no warning.
To think on thee it maketh my heart sick,
For all unready is my book of reckoning.
But twelve year if I might have abiding,
My counting book I would make so clear
That thy reckoning I should not need to
  fear.
Wherefore, Death, I pray thee, for God's
  mercy,
Spare me till I be provided of remedy.

DEATH: Thee availeth not to cry, weep,
  and pray,
But haste thee lightly that thou go the
  journey,
And prove thy friends if thou can.
For, know thou well, the tide abideth no
  man,
And in the world each living creature
For Adam's sin must die by nature.

EVERYMAN: Death, if I should this pil-
  grimage take,
And my reckoning surely make,
Show me, for Saint Charity,
Should I not come again shortly?

DEATH: No, Everyman. If thou be once there
Thou mayst nevermore come here,
Trust me verily.

EVERYMAN: O Gracious God, in the high seat celestial,
Have mercy on me in this my need;
Shall I have no company from this vale terrestrial
Of mine acquaintance the way to lead?

DEATH: Yea, if any be so hardy
That would go with thee and bear thee company.
Hasten to be gone to God's magnificence,
Thy reckoning to give before his presence.
What, thinkest thou thy life is given thee,
And thy worldly goods also?

EVERYMAN: I had thought so, verily.

DEATH: Nay, nay, it was but lent thee!
For as soon as thou dost go,
Another awhile shall have it and then go therefro
Even as thou hast done.
Everyman, thou art mad. Thou hast thy wits five,
And here on earth will not amend thy life,
For suddenly do I come.

EVERYMAN: O wretched caitiff, whither shall I flee,
That I might escape this endless sorrow!
Now, gentle Death, spare me till to-morrow,
That I may amend me
With good advisement.

DEATH: Nay, thereto I will not consent,
Nor no man will I respite,
But to the heart suddenly I shall smite
Without any advisement.
And now out of thy sight I will me hie.
See thou make thee ready shortly,
For thou mayst say this is the day
That no man living may escape away.

(DEATH *withdraws.*)

EVERYMAN: Alas, I may well weep with signs deep.

Now have I no manner of company
To help me in my journey, and me to keep.
And also my writing is full unready!
What shall I do now for to excuse me?
I would to God I had never been begot!
To my soul a full great profit it would be,
For now I fear pains huge and hot.
The time passeth. Lord, help me that all wrought!
For though I mourn it availeth nought.
The day passeth, and is almost gone.
I know not well what is to be done.
To whom were I best my complaint to make?
What if I to Fellowship thereof spake,
And showed him of this sudden chance?
For in him is all mine affiance,
We have in the world so many a day
Been good friends in sport and play.
I see him yonder, certainly—
I trust that he will bear me company.
Therefore him I will ask to ease my sorrow.

(FELLOWSHIP *enters.*)

Well met, good Fellowship, and good morrow!

FELLOWSHIP: Everyman, good morrow by this day.
Sir, why lookest thou so piteously?
If any thing be amiss, I pray thee, say,
That I may help to remedy.

EVERYMAN: Yea, good Fellowship, yea,
I am in great jeopardy.

FELLOWSHIP: My true friend, show to me your mind;
I will not forsake thee, unto my life's end,
In the way of good company.

EVERYMAN: That was well spoken, and lovingly.

FELLOWSHIP: Sir, I must needs know your heaviness—
I have pity to see you in any distress.
If any have wronged you ye shall revenged be,
Though I on the ground be slain for thee,

Though that I knew before that I should
    die.
    EVERYMAN: Verily, Fellowship, gra-
    mercy.
    FELLOWSHIP: Tush! by thy thanks I set
    not a straw.
Show me your grief and say no more.
    EVERYMAN: If I my heart should to you
    break,
And then you turned your mind from me
And would not comfort me when you hear
    me speak,
Then should I ten times sorrier be.
    FELLOWSHIP: Sir, I say as I will do in-
    deed.
    EVERYMAN: Then be you good friend in
    need—
I have found you true here before.
    FELLOWSHIP: And so ye shall evermore.
For, in faith, if thou go to Hell,
I will not forsake thee by the way!
    EVERYMAN: Ye speak like a friend, I
    believe you well.
I shall try deserve thy love, if I may.
    FELLOWSHIP: I speak of no deserving,
    by this day.
For he that will say and nothing do
Is not worthy with good company to go.
Therefore show me the grief of your mind,
As to your friend most loving and kind.
    EVERYMAN: I shall show you how it is:
Commanded I am to go a journey,
A long way, hard and dangerous,
And give a straight count without delay
Before the high judge Adonai.
Wherefore I pray you, bear me company,
As ye have promised, in this journey.
    FELLOWSHIP: This is matter indeed!
    Promise is duty,
But, if I should take such a voyage on me,
I know it well, it should be to my pain.
Also it maketh me afeard, for certain.
But let us take counsel here as well as we
    can,
For thy words would balk a strong man.

    EVERYMAN: Why, ye said, if I had need,
Ye would me never forsake, quick nor
    dead,
Though it were to Hell truly.
    FELLOWSHIP: So I said, certainly,
But from such pleasures set me aside, thee
    sooth to say!
And also, if we took such a journey,
When should we come again?
    EVERYMAN: Nay, never again till the day
    of doom.
    FELLOWSHIP: In faith, then I will not
    come there!
Who hath thee these tidings brought?
    EVERYMAN: Indeed, Death was with me
    here.
    FELLOWSHIP: Now, by God that all hath
    bought,
If Death were the messenger,
For no man living here to-day
Would I go that loathsome journey—
Nay, nor for the father that begat me!
    EVERYMAN: Ye promised otherwise,
    pardie.
    FELLOWSHIP: I know well I did say so
    truly.
And yet if thou wilt eat, and drink, and
    make good cheer,
Or haunt together women's lusty com-
    pany,
I would not forsake you, while the day is
    clear,
Trust me verily!
    EVERYMAN: Yea, thereto ye would be
    ready—
To go to mirth, solace, and play,
Your mind will sooner apply
Than to bear me company in my far
    journey.
    FELLOWSHIP: Now, in good faith, I will
    not that way.
But if thou wilt murder, or any man kill,
In that I will help thee with a good will!
    EVERYMAN: O that is a simple advice
    indeed!

Gentle fellow, help me in my necessity—
We have loved long, and now I need,
And now, gentle Fellowship, remember me.

FELLOWSHIP: Whether ye have loved me or no,
By Saint John, I will not with thee go.

EVERYMAN: Yet I pray thee, take the labor, and do so much for me
To bring me forward, for Saint Charity,
And comfort me till I come outside the town.

FELLOWSHIP: Nay, if thou wouldst give me a new gown,
I will not a foot with thee go.
But hadst thou tarried I would not leave thee so.
And so now, God speed thee in thy journey,
For from thee I will depart as fast as I may.

EVERYMAN: Whither away, Fellowship? will you forsake me?

FELLOWSHIP: Yea, by my fay, to God I bequeath thee.

EVERYMAN: Farewell, good Fellowship, for thee my heart is sore.
Adieu for ever, I shall see thee no more.

FELLOWSHIP: In faith, Everyman, farewell now at the end;
From you I will remember that parting is mourning.

(*Exit* FELLOWSHIP.)

EVERYMAN: Alack! shall we thus depart indeed?
Our Lady, help, without more comfort,
Lo, Fellowship forsaketh me in my most need:
For help in this world whither shall I resort?
Fellowship before with me would merry make,
And now little sorrow for me doth he take.
It is said, in prosperity men friends may find

Which in adversity be full unkind.
Now whither for succor shall I flee,
Since that Fellowship hath forsaken me?
To my kinsmen go I will truly,
Praying them to help me in my necessity.
I believe that they will do so,
For "kind will creep where it may not go."
I will go try, for yonder I see them go.
Where be ye now, my friends and kinsmen?

(KINDRED *and* COUSIN *appear.*)

KINDRED: Here be we now at your commandment.
Cousin, I pray you show us your intent
In any wise, and do not spare.

COUSIN: Yea, Everyman, and to us declare
If ye be disposed to go any whither,
For know you well we will live and die together.

KINDRED: In wealth and woe we will with you hold,
For with his kin a man may be bold.

EVERYMAN: Gramercy, my friends and kinsmen kind.
Now shall I show you the grief of my mind.
I was commanded by a messenger,
That is an High King's chief officer.
He bade me go a pilgrimage to my pain,
And I know well I shall never come again.
Also I must give a reckoning straight,
For I have a great enemy, that hath me in wait,
And intendeth me to hinder.

KINDRED: What account is that which ye must render?
That would I know.

EVERYMAN: Of all my works I must show
How I have lived and my days spent.
Also of ill deeds, that I have used
In my time, since life was me lent.
And of all virtues that I have refused.

Therefore I pray you go thither with me,
To help to make my account, for Saint
  Charity.

  COUSIN: What, to go thither? Is that the
    matter?
Nay, Everyman, I had liefer fast bread and
  water
All this five year and more.

  EVERYMAN: Alas, that ever I was born!
For now shall I never be merry
If you forsake me.

  KINDRED: Ah, sir, what, ye be a merry
    man!
Take good heart to you, and make no
  moan.
But one thing I warn you, by Saint Anne,
As for me, ye shall go alone.

  EVERYMAN: My Cousin, will you not
    with me go?

  COUSIN: No, by our Lady, I have the
    cramp in my toe.
Wait not for me, for, so God me speed,
I will forsake you in your most need.

  KINDRED: It availeth not us to entice.
You shall have my maid with all my heart;
She loveth to go to feasts, there to be nice,
And to dance, and abroad to start.
I will give her leave to help you in that
  journey,
If that you and she will agree.

  EVERYMAN: Now show me the very ef-
    fect of your mind—
Will you go with me, or abide behind?

  KINDRED: Abide behind? yea, that I will
    if I may!
Therefore farewell until another day.

  EVERYMAN: How should I be merry or
    or glad?
For fair promises men to me make,
But when I have most need they me for-
  sake.
I am deceived, alas—that maketh me sad.

  COUSIN: Cousin Everyman, farewell
    now,
For verily I will not go with you.

Also of mine own an unready reckoning
I have to account; therefore I make tarry-
  ing.
Now, God keep thee, for now I go.

         (*Exit* KINDRED *and* COUSIN.)

  EVERYMAN: Ah, Jesus, is all come
    hereto?
Lo, fair words make fools fain.
They promise and nothing will do certain.
My kinsmen promised me faithfully
For to abide with me steadfastly,
And now fast away do they flee.
Even so Fellowship promised me.
What friend were best for me to provide?
I lose my time here longer to abide.
Yet in my mind a thing there is—
All my life I have loved Riches;
If that my Goods now help me might,
It would make my heart full light.
I will speak to him in this distress.—
Where art thou, my Goods and Riches?

  GOODS: Who calleth me? Everyman,
    what haste thou hast!
I lie here in corners, trussed and piled so
  high,
And in chests I am locked so fast,
Also sacked in bags, thou mayest see with
  thine eye,
I cannot stir; in packs so low I lie.
What would ye have, what do you say?

  EVERYMAN: Come hither, Goods, in all
    the haste thou may,
For of counsel I must desire thee.

  GOODS: Sir, if ye in the world have
    trouble or adversity,
That can I help you to remedy shortly.

  EVERYMAN: It is another disease that
    grieveth me.
In this world it is not, I tell thee so.
I am sent for another way to go,
To give a straight account general
Before the highest Jupiter of all.
And all my life I have had joy and plea-
  sure in thee.
Therefore I pray thee go with me,

For, peradventure, thou mayst before God
    Almighty
My reckoning help to clean and purify.
For it is said ever us among,
That money maketh all right that is
    wrong.
    GOODS: Nay, Everyman, I sing another
        song,
I follow no man in such voyages.
For if I went with thee
Thou shouldst fare much the worse for
    me.
For because on me thou did bend thy
    mind,
Thy reckoning I have made blotted and
    blind,
That thine account thou canst not make
    truly—
And that hast thou for the love of me.
    EVERYMAN: That would grieve me full
        sore,
When I should come to that fearful an-
    swer.
Up, let us go thither together.
    GOODS: Nay, not so, I am too brittle, I
        may not endure.
I will follow no man one foot, be ye sure.
    EVERYMAN: Alas, I have loved thee, and
        had great pleasure
All my life-days on goods and treasure.
    GOODS: That is to thy damnation with-
        out ending.
For love of me is contrary to the love
    everlasting
But if thou hadst loved me moderately,
And to the poor hadst given part of me,
Then shouldst thou not in this dolor be,
Nor in this great sorrow and care.
    EVERYMAN: No, now was I deceived ere
        I was aware,
And all I blame on my misusing of time.
    GOODS: What, thinkest thou that I am
        thine?
    EVERYMAN: I had thought so.
    GOODS: Nay, Everyman, I say no.

But for a while was I lent thee,
A season thou hast had me in prosperity.
My condition it is man's soul to kill—
If I save one, a thousand I do spill.
Thinkest thou that I will follow thee?
Nay, from this world, not verily.
    EVERYMAN: I had thought otherwise.
    GOODS: Therefore to thy soul Goods is
        a thief;
For when thou art dead, this is my game
Another to deceive in ways the same,
As I have done thee, and all to his soul's
    grief.
    EVERYMAN: O false Goods, cursed thou
        be!
Thou traitor to God, that hast deceived
    me,
And snatched me in thy snare.
    GOODS: Marry, thou brought thyself in
        care,
Whereof I am glad—
I must needs laugh; I cannot be sad.
    EVERYMAN: Ah, Goods, thou hast had
        long my heartly love;
I gave thee that which should be the
    Lord's above.
But wilt thou not go with me indeed?
I pray thee truth to say.
    GOODS: No, so God me speed,
Therefore farewell, and have good day.
                    (*Exit* GOODS.)
    EVERYMAN: O, to whom shall I make
        my moan
For to go with me in that heavy journey?
First Fellowship said he would with me
    be gone;
His words were very pleasant and gay,
But afterward he left me alone.
Then spake I to my kinsmen all in des-
    pair,
And they also gave me words fair.
They lacked no fair speaking,
But they forsook me in the ending.
Then went I to my Goods that I loved
    best,

In hope to have comfort, but there had I
   least.
For my Goods sharply did me tell
That he bringeth many into Hell.
Then of myself I was ashamed,
And so I am worthy to be blamed,
Thus may I well myself hate.
Of whom shall I now counsel take?
I think that I shall never speed
Till that I go to my Good-Deed,
But, alas, she is so weak,
That she can neither go nor speak.
Yet will I venture on her now.—
My Good-Deeds, where be you?

(*Enter* GOOD-DEEDS.)

GOOD-DEEDS: Here I lie cold in the
   ground.
Thy sins have me sore-bound
That I cannot stir.

EVERYMAN: O, Good-Deeds, I stand in
   fear;
I must pray you for counsel,
For help now would come right well.

GOOD-DEEDS: Everyman, I have under-
   standing
That you be summoned account to make
Before Messias, of Jerusalem the King.
If you walk by me that journey I would
   take.

EVERYMAN: Therefore I come to you,
   my moan to make—
I pray you, that ye will go with me.

GOOD-DEEDS: I would full fain, but I
   cannot stand, verily.

EVERYMAN: Why, is there anything did
   you befall?

GOOD-DEEDS: Yea, sir, and I may thank
   you of all;
If ye had perfectly cheered me,
Your book of account now full ready
   would be.
Look on the books of your works and
   deeds—
Oh, see how they under your feet lie,
Unto your soul's heaviness.

EVERYMAN: Our Lord Jesus, help me!
For one letter here I cannot see.

GOOD-DEEDS: There is a blind reckoning
   in time of distress!

EVERYMAN: Good-Deeds, I pray you,
   help me in this need.
Or else I am for ever damned indeed.
Therefore help me to a reckoning
Before the Redeemer of all thing,
That king is, and was, and ever shall.

GOOD-DEEDS: Everyman, I am sorry for
   your fall,
And fain would I help you, if I were able.

EVERYMAN: Good-Deeds, your counsel
   I pray you give me.

GOOD-DEEDS: That shall I do verily.
Though that on my feet I may not go,
I have as sister that shall with you also,
Called Knowledge, which shall with you
   abide,
To help you to make that dreadful reckon-
   ing.

(*Enter* KNOWLEDGE.)

KNOWLEDGE: Everyman, I will go with
   thee, and be thy guide,
In utmost need to go by thy side.

EVERYMAN: In good condition I am
   now in every thing,
And am wholly content with this good
   thing.
Thanked be God, my Creator!

GOOD-DEEDS: And when he hath brought
   thee there
Where thou shalt heal me of my smart,
Then go you with your reckoning and
   your Good-Deeds together
For to make you joyful at heart
Before the blessed Trinity.

EVERYMAN: My Good-Deeds, gramercy;
I am well content, certainly,
With your words sweet.

KNOWLEDGE: Now go we together lovingly,
To Confession's cleansing river.

EVERYMAN: For joy I weep. I would
    we were there!
But, I pray you, give me cognition
Where dwelleth that holy man, Confes-
    sion.
    KNOWLEDGE: In the house of salvation.
We shall find him in that place
That shall comfort us by God's grace.

    (CONFESSION *appears.*)

Lo, this is Confession; kneel down and
    ask mercy,
For he is in good conceit with God Al-
    mighty.
    EVERYMAN: O glorious fountain that all
    uncleanness doth clarify,
Wash from me the spots of vices unclean,
That on me no sin may be seen.
I come with Knowledge for my redemp-
    tion,
Repent with hearty and full contrition.
For I am commanded a pilgrimage to
    take,
And straight accounts before God to make.
Now, I pray you, Shrift, mother of Sal-
    vation,
Help my good deeds to make a piteous
    exclamation.
    CONFESSION: I know your sorrow well,
    Everyman.
Because with Knowledge ye come to me,
I will comfort you as well as I can,
And a precious jewel I will give thee,
Called penance, wise voider of adversity.
Therewith shall thy body chastised be,
With abstinence and perseverance in God's
    service.
Here shalt thou receive that scourge of me
Which is penance strong that you must
    endure,
To remember thy Savior was scourged for
    thee
With sharp scourges, and suffered it pa-
    tiently.
So must thou, ere thou escape that pain-
    ful pilgrimage;
Knowledge, keep him in this voyage,

And by that time Good-Deeds will be
    with thee.
And in any wise, be sure of mercy,
For your time draweth fast, if you will
    saved be.
Ask God mercy, and He will grant truly;
When with the scourge of penance man
    bind,
The oil of forgiveness then shall he find.
    EVERYMAN: Thanked be God for his
    gracious work!
For now I will my penance begin.
This hath rejoiced and lighted my heart,
Though the knots be painful and hard
    within.
    KNOWLEDGE: Everyman, look that ye
    your penance fulfil,
Whatever pain it to you be,
And Knowledge shall give you counsel at
    will.
How your accounts ye shall make clearly.
    EVERYMAN: O eternal God, O heavenly
    figure,
O way of righteousness, O goodly vision,
Which descended down in a virgin pure
Because He would Everyman redeem,
Which Adam forfeited by his disobedi-
    ence.
O blessed Godhead, elect and divine,
Forgive my grievous offence,
Here I cry Thee mercy in this presence.
O soul's treasure, O ransomer and re-
    deemer
Of all the world, hope and leader,
Mirror of joy, and founder of mercy,
Which illumineth heaven and earth
    thereby,
Hear my clamorous complaint, though it
    late be,
Receive my prayers. Unworthy in this
    heavy life
Though I be, a sinner most abominable,
Yet let my name be written in Moses'
    table;
O Mary, pray to the Maker of everything,
To help me at my ending,

And save me from the power of my
    enemy,
For Death assaileth me strongly.
And, Lady, that I may by means of thy
    prayer
Of your Son's glory be the partaker,
By the pity of his Passion I it crave,
I beseech you, help my soul to save.—
Knowledge, give me the scourge of pen-
    ance,
My flesh therewith shall give a quittance.
I will now begin, if God give me grace.

    KNOWLEDGE: Everyman, God give you
    time and space.
Thus I bequeath you into the hands of
    our Savior,
Thus may you make your reckoning sure.

    EVERYMAN: In the name of the blessed
    Trinity,
My body sore punished shall be.
Take this body for the sin of the flesh!
Thou that delightest to go gay and fresh,
And in the way of damnation didst me
    bring,
Now suffer therefore strokes and punish-
    ing.
Now of penance I will wade the water
    clear,
To save me from Purgatory, that sharp
    fire.

(GOOD-DEEDS *joins them as he smites*
himself.)

    GOOD-DEEDS: I thank God, now I can
    walk and go,
And am delivered of my sickness and
    woe.
Therefore with Everyman I will go, and
    not spare—
His good works I will help him to declare.

    KNOWLEDGE: Now, Everyman, be merry
    and glad.
Your Good-Deeds cometh now, ye may
    not be sad.
Now is your Good-Deeds whole and
    sound,
Going upright upon the ground.

    EVERYMAN: My heart is light, and shall
    be evermore,
Now I will smite faster than I did before.

    GOOD-DEEDS: Everyman, pilgrim, my
    special friend,
Blessed be thou without end.
For thee is prepared the eternal glory.
Ye have made me whole and sound,
Therefore I will bide by thee in every
    round.

    EVERYMAN: Welcome, my Good-Deeds!
    Now I hear thy voice,
I weep for very sweetness of love.

    KNOWLEDGE: Be no more sad, but ever
    rejoice,
God seeth thy being from his throne aloft.
Put on this garment which is so soft—
Wet with your tears it is.
Or else before God you may it miss,
When you to your journey's end shall
    come.

    EVERYMAN: Gentle Knowledge, what is
    its name?

    KNOWLEDGE: It is a garment of sorrow:
From pain it will divide you;
Contrition it is,
That getteth forgiveness;
It pleaseth God passing well.

    GOOD-DEEDS: Everyman, will you wear
    it for your heal?

    (EVERYMAN *puts on the robe.*)

    EVERYMAN: Now blessed be Jesu, Mary's
    Son!
For now have I on true contrition.
And let us go now without tarrying.
Good-Deeds, have we clear our reckoning?

    GOOD-DEEDS: Yea, indeed I have it here.

    EVERYMAN: Then I trust we need not
    fear;
Now, friends, let us not part in twain.

    KNOWLEDGE: Nay, Everyman, that will
    we not, certain.

    GOOD-DEEDS: Yet must thou lead with
    thee

Three persons of great might.

EVERYMAN: Who should they be?

GOOD-DEEDS: Discretion and Strength they hight,

And thy Beauty may not abide behind.

KNOWLEDGE: Also you must call to mind

Your Five-Wits as for your counselors.

GOOD-DEEDS: You must have them ready at all hours.

EVERYMAN: How shall I get them hither?

KNOWLEDGE: You must call them all together,

And they will hear you incontinent.

EVERYMAN: My friends, come hither and be present,

Discretion, Strength, my Five-Wits, and Beauty.

(DISCRETION, STRENGTH, FIVE-WITS *and* BEAUTY *enter.*)

BEAUTY: Here at your will we be all ready.

What will ye that we should do?

GOOD-DEEDS: That ye would with Everyman go,

And help him in his pilgrimage.

Advise me, will ye with him or not in that voyage?

STRENGTH: We will bring him all thither,

To his help and comfort, ye may believe me.

DISCRETION: So will we go with him all together.

EVERYMAN: Almighty God, loved mayest thou be,

I give thee laud that I have hither brought Strength, Discretion, Beauty, and Five-Wits; I lack nought!

And my Good-Deeds, with Knowledge clear,

All stay in my company at my will here;

I desire no more to my business.

STRENGTH: And I, Strength, will stand by you in distress,

Though thou wouldest in battle fight on the ground.

FIVE-WITS: And though it were through the world round,

We will not depart for sweet nor sour.

BEAUTY: No more will I unto death's hour,

Whatsoever thereof befall.

DISCRETION: Everyman, advise you first of all,

Go with a good advisement and deliberation.

We all give you virtuous monition

That all shall be well.

EVERYMAN: My friends, hearken what I will tell.

I pray God reward you in his heavenly sphere.

Now hearken, all that be here,

For I will make my testament

Here before every one present.

In alms half my good I will give with my hands twain

In the way of charity, with good intent,

And the other half shall remain

In quiet to be returned where it ought to be.

This I do in despite of the fiend of hell,

To go quit of his peril

Ever after and this day.

KNOWLEDGE: Everyman, hearken what I say.

Go to priesthood, I advise,

And receive of him in any wise

The holy sacrament and ointment together,

Then shortly see ye turn again hither.

We will all await you here.

FIVE-WITS: Yea, Everyman, haste you that ye ready be.

There is no emperor, king, duke, nor baron,

That of God hath commission,

As hath the least priest in the world's
  design.
For of the blessed sacraments pure and
  benign,
He beareth the keys and thereof hath the
  cure
For man's redemption, that is ever sure;
Which God for our soul's medicine
Gave us out of his heart with great pine.
Here in this transitory life, for thee and
  me,
The blessed sacraments seven there be,
Baptism, confirmation, with priesthood
  good,
And the sacrament of God's precious flesh
  and blood,
Marriage, the holy extreme unction, and
  penance;
These seven be good to have in remem-
  brance,
Gracious sacraments of high divinity.

EVERYMAN: Fain would I receive that
  holy body
And meekly to my spiritual father I will
  go.

FIVE-WITS: Everyman, that is the best
  that ye can do.
God will you to salvation bring,
For priesthood exceedeth all other thing.
To us Holy Scripture they do teach,
And convert man from his sin heaven to
  reach;
God hath to them more power given
Than to any angel that is in heaven.
With five words he may consecrate
God's body in flesh and blood to make,
And holdeth his maker between his hands,
The priest bindeth and unbindeth all
  bands,
Both in earth and in heaven,
He ministers all the sacraments seven.—
Though we kissed thy feet thou wert
  worthy,
Thou art surgeon that cureth sin deadly.
No remedy we find that is good
But only under priesthood.

Everyman, God gave priests that dignity,
And setteth them in his stead among us to
  be—
Thus be they above angels in degree.

(EVERYMAN *departs.*)

KNOWLEDGE: If priests be good it is so
  surely!
But when Jesus hanged on the cross with
  great smart
There he *gave,* out of his blessed heart,
The same sacrament in great torment:
He *sold* them not to us, that Lord Om-
  nipotent!
Therefore Saint Peter, the apostle, doth
  say
That Jesu's curse have all they
Who God their Savior do buy or sell,
Or for any money do take or tell.
Sinful priests have to sinners bad example
  been.
Their children sit by other men's fires, I
  have seen;
And some priests haunt women's company,
With unclean life, in lusts of lechery:
These be with sin made blind.

FIVE-WITS: I trust to God no such may
  we find.
Therefore let us priesthood honor,
And follow their doctrine for our souls'
  succor.
We be their sheep, and they shepherds be
By whom we all are kept in surety.
Peace, for yonder I see Everyman come,
Who hath made true satisfaction.

GOOD-DEEDS: Methinketh it is he indeed.

(EVERYMAN *returns.*)

EVERYMAN: Now Jesu all our labor
  speed,
I have received the sacrament for my redemption,
And then mine extreme unction.
Blessed be all they that counseled me to
  take it!
And now, friends, let us go without longer
  respite,

I thank God that ye have tarried so long.
Now set each of you on this rod your
hand,
And shortly follow me.
I go before, there I would be, God be our
guide!

KNOWLEDGE STRENGTH: Everyman, we will not from
you go,
Till ye have gone this voyage long.

DISCRETION: I, Discretion, will bide by
you also.

KNOWLEDGE: And though this pilgrimage be never so strong,
I will never part from you, too.

EVERYMAN: I will be as sure by thee
As ever I stood by Judas Maccabee.

(*They approach the grave.*)

EVERYMAN: Alas, I am so faint I may
not stand,
My limbs under me do fold.
Friends, let us not turn again to this land,
Not for all the world's gold,
For into this cave must I creep
And turn to the earth and there sleep.

BEAUTY: What, into this grave? Alas!

EVERYMAN: Yea, there shall you consume more and less.

BEAUTY: And what, should I smother
here?

EVERYMAN: Yea, by my faith, and never
more appear.
In this world live no more we shall,
But in heaven before the highest lord of
all.

BEAUTY: I cross out all this, adieu by
Saint John!
I take my cap in my lap and am gone.

EVERYMAN: What, Beauty, whither will
ye?

BEAUTY: Peace, I am deaf! I look not
behind me,
Not if thou would give me all the gold in
thy chest.

(BEAUTY *departs.*)

EVERYMAN: Alas, in whom may I trust?
Beauty fast away doth hie—
She promised with me to live and die.

STRENGTH: Everyman, I will thee also
forsake and deny.
Thy game liketh me not at all.

EVERYMAN: Why, then ye will forsake
me all.
Sweet Strength, tarry a little space.

STRENGTH: Nay, sir, by the rood of
grace
I will hie me from thee first,
Though thou weep till thy heart burst.

EVERYMAN: Ye would ever bide by me,
ye said.

STRENGTH: Yea, I have you far enough
conveyed.
Ye be old enough, I understand,
Your pilgrimage to take on hand;
I repent me that I hither came.

EVERYMAN: Strength, you to displease I
am to blame;
Will you break promise that is debt?

STRENGTH: In faith, I care not.
Thou art but a fool to complain,
You spend your speech and waste your
brain—
Go thrust thee into the ground!

EVERYMAN: I had thought surer I
should have you found.

(*Exit* STRENGTH.)

He that trusteth in his Strength
She deceiveth him at the length.
Both Strength and Beauty forsaking me,
Yet they promised me fair and lovingly.

DISCRETION: Everyman, I will after
Strength be gone,
As for me I will leave you alone.

EVERYMAN: Why, Discretion, will ye
forsake me?

DISCRETION: Yea, in faith, I will go from
thee,
For when Strength goeth before
I follow after evermore.

EVERYMAN: Yet, I pray thee, for the love of Trinity,
Look in my grave once piteously.

DISCRETION: Nay, so nigh will I not come.
Farewell, every one!

(*Exit* DISCRETION.)

EVERYMAN: O all thing faileth, save God alone;
Beauty, Strength, and Discretion;
For when Death bloweth his blast
They all run from me full fast.

FIVE-WITS: Everyman, my leave now of thee I take;
I will follow the other, for here I thee forsake.

EVERYMAN: Alas! then may I wail and weep,
For I took you for my best friend,

FIVE-WITS: I will not longer thee keep.
Now farewell, and there an end.

(*Exit* FIVE-WITS.)

EVERYMAN: O Jesu, help, all have forsaken me!

GOOD-DEEDS: Nay, Everyman, I will bide with thee,
I will not forsake thee indeed,
Thou shalt find me a good friend at need.

EVERYMAN: Gramercy, Good-Deeds, now, may I true friends see.
They have forsaken me every one.
I loved them better than my Good-Deeds alone.
Knowledge, will ye forsake me also?

KNOWLEDGE: Yea, Everyman, when ye to death do go,
But not yet for no manner of danger.

EVERYMAN: Gramercy, Knowledge, with all my heart.

KNOWLEDGE: Nay, yet I will not from hence depart,
Till I be sure where ye shall come.

EVERYMAN: Methinketh, alas, that I must be on,

To make my reckoning and debts to pay.
For I see my time is nigh spent away.
Take example, all ye that this do hear or see,
How they that I loved best do forsake me,
Except my Good-Deeds that bideth truly.

GOOD-DEEDS: All earthly things are but vanity:
Beauty, Strength, and Discretion, do man forsake,
Foolish friends and kinsmen, that fair spake,
All flee save Good-Deeds, and he am I.

EVERYMAN: Have mercy on me, God most mighty;
And stand by me, thou Mother and Maid, holy Mary.

GOOD-DEEDS: Fear not, I will speak for thee.

EVERYMAN: Here I cry God mercy.

GOOD-DEEDS: Shorten our end, and diminish our pain.
Let us go and never come again.

EVERYMAN: Into Thy hands, Lord, my soul I commend.
Receive it, Lord, that it be not lost!
As thou boughtest me, me so defend,
And rescue from the fiend's boast,
That I may appear with that blessed host
That shall be saved at the day of doom.
In manus tuas—of might's utmost
Forever—*commendo spiritum meum.*

(EVERYMAN *and* GOOD-DEEDS *enter the grave.*)

KNOWLEDGE: Now hath he suffered what we all shall endure,
But Good-Deeds shall make all sure.
Now hath he made ending—
Methinketh I hear angels sing
And make great joy and melody,
Where Everyman's soul received shall be.

(*An* ANGEL *appears.*)

ANGEL: Come, excellent elect spouse to Jesu!
Hereabove thou shalt go

Because of thy singular virtue.
Now the soul is taken from the body so,
Thy reckoning is crystal-clear.
Now shalt thou into the heavenly sphere,
Unto which all ye shall come
That live well before the day of doom.

EPILOGUE

DOCTOR: This moral men may have in
    mind:
Ye hearers, take it of worth, old and
    young,
And forsake pride, for he deceiveth you
    in the end,
And   remember   Beauty,   Five-Wits,
    Strength, and Discretion,
They all at the last do Everyman forsake,
Alone his Good-Deeds there doth he take.

But beware, if they be small
Before God, man hath no help at all.
No excuse may there be for Everyman—
Alas, what shall he do then?
For after death amends may no man
    make,
For then mercy and pity him forsake.
If his reckoning be not clear when he
    come,
God will say—*ite maledicti in ignem
    æternum.*[1]
And he that hath his account whole and
    sound,
High in heaven he shall be crowned,
Unto which place God bring us all thither
That we may live body and soul together.
Thereto help blessed Trinity.
Amen, say ye, for Saint Charity.
Thus endeth this moral play of Everyman.

[1] Go into the eternal fire, ye cursed ones.

The Tragical History
of Doctor Faustus

CHRISTOPHER MARLOWE

COMMENTARY

Christopher Marlowe (1564-1593) was born at Canterbury, England. A shoemaker's son, he studied at King's School in Canterbury and received a B.A. in 1584 and an M.A. in 1587 from Corpus Christi College, Cambridge. After Cambridge, he settled in London, where he became an actor. Not much is specifically known of his life there. Between 1587 and 1593 he wrote *Tamburlaine the Great, The Jew of Malta, Edward II,* and *Doctor Faustus.*

Doctor Faustus, generally dated about 1590, was preceded by a German version a few years earlier. Marlowe may have read an English translation in manuscript. *Doctor Faustus* was one of the most popular of Elizabethan-Jacobean tragedies, performed frequently, and published in successive editions in the early decades of the seventeenth century. Although Marlowe's text evokes the form and pace of *Everyman,* it has as hero a sophisticated, ambitious, restless, defiant man, who is "extraordinary" rather than ordinary. *Faustus* and *Everyman* bear sustained close comparison as Christian tragedies.

The original German Faustbook was dominantly theological in tone. Marlowe's text, however, concentrates on the human aspects of Faustus' career. While we may look for the basis of the tragedy in *Everyman* in the medieval reconciliation of life with death, or in the medieval sense of life as a preparation for death, we should seek the tragedy in *Doctor Faustus* in Renaissance man's restless dissatisfaction with the simple limitations of being human. Tragedy in *Everyman* is to be found in the nature of mortal life itself. *Doctor Faustus* longs to transgress the boundaries of physical and intellectual possibilities. Like Oedipus, Doctor Faustus is aware of the promises of the future, and like Oedipus, he does not hesitate to act. Unlike Oedipus, Faustus is all the time aware of the bargain he must carry out. He does not delude himself into thinking he can escape it. He continues to act, knowing that every act makes his contract that much more certain of fulfillment.

The text of Marlowe's play was probably enlarged, in various passages and scenes, by other hands. It is likely that some of the more slapstick comic scenes were not written by Marlowe. Nevertheless, the play may be read as an esthetic unity: the descents to vulgarity may reflect the ill-use to which Faustus puts his diabolically granted powers: ill-gotten means, however great, can only be used for trivial and foolish ends.

The Complete Plays of Christopher Marlowe, edited by Irving Ribner (New York, 1966), provides a full critical and scholarly survey of Marlowe's works as well as modern authoritative texts. *Christopher Marlowe's Doctor Faustus: Text and Major Criticism* (New York, 1966), also edited by Professor Ribner, offers ten critical essays and a selected bibliography of criticism. Other significant critical comments that may be singled out are "Doctor Faustus" in Richard B. Sewall, *The Vision of Tragedy* (New Haven and London, 1959) and the remarks here and there in George Steiner, *The Death of Tragedy* (New York, 1961). Three important full-length studies are Leslie Hotson, *The Death of Christopher Marlowe* (London, 1925); Frederick S. Boas, *Christopher Marlowe: A Biographical and Critical Study* (Oxford, 1940), and John Bakeless, *The Tragicall History of Christopher Marlowe,* 2 vols. (Cambridge, Mass., 1942).

The present text is based on the several standard modern editions, especially the text of 1616 as edited by F. S. Boas (1932 and 1949). Others include those by Hermann Breymann (1889), A. W. Ward (1901), I. Gollancz (1897), Leo Kirschbaum (1962), and Havelock Ellis (with introduction by J. A. Symonds and additional comment by S. F. Johnson; 1956). A succinct editorial and bibliographical survey appears in *Elizabethan and Jacobean Tragedy,* edited by Robert Ornstein and Hazelton Spencer (Boston, 1964). Kirschbaum's account of the textual problems is important, especially those posed by the works of W. W. Greg (1950). John D. Jump's edition (1962), derived from Greg, provides a good reading and acting version.

Christopher Marlowe

THE TRAGICAL HISTORY OF DOCTOR FAUSTUS

DRAMATIS PERSONÆ

THE CHORUS.
DOCTOR FAUSTUS.
WAGNER, *his servant.*
VALDES   }*friends to*
CORNELIUS }*Faustus.*
THREE SCHOLARS.
AN OLD MAN.

THE POPE.
RAYMOND, *King of Hungary.*
BRUNO.
TWO CARDINALS.
ARCHBISHOP OF RHEIMS.
CARDINAL OF LORRAINE.
CHARLES, *Emperor of Germany.*
MARTINO   }
FREDERICK }*Gentlemen*
BENVOLIO }*of his Court.*
A KNIGHT.
DUKE OF SAXONY.
DUKE OF ANHOLT.
DUCHESS OF ANHOLT.
BISHOPS, MONKS, FRIARS, SOL-
   DIERS *and* ATTENDANTS.

CLOWN.
ROBIN, *an ostler.*
DICK.
RALPH.
A VINTNER.
A HORSE-COURSER.
A CARTER.
HOSTESS.

GOOD ANGEL.
BAD ANGEL.
EVIL ANGEL.
MEPHISTOPHILIS.
LUCIFER.
BELZEBUB.
DEVILS.
THE SEVEN DEADLY SINS.
ALEXANDER THE GREAT }
PARAMOUR
   OF ALEXANDER.
DARIUS   }*Spirits.*
HELEN
TWO CUPIDS }

ACT I

(*Enter* chorus.)

chorus: Not marching now in fields
of Thrasimen,
Where Mars did mate the warlike Carth-
agens;
Nor sporting in the dalliance of love,
In courts of kings, where state is over-
turn'd;
Nor in the pomp of proud audacious
deeds,
Intends our Muse to vaunt his heavenly
verse.
Only this, gentles—we must now perform
The form of Faustus' fortunes, good or
bad:
And now to patient judgments we appeal,
And speak for Faustus in his infancy.
Now is he born, of parents base of stock,
In Germany, within a town call'd Rhode;
At riper years, to Wittenberg he went,
Whereas his kinsmen chiefly brought him
up.
So much he profits in divinity,
The fruitful plot of scholarism grac'd,
That shortly he was grac'd with doctor's
name,
Excelling all and sweetly can dispute
In th' heavenly matters of theology—
Till swol'n with cunning, of a self-conceit,
His waxen wings did mount above his
reach,
And melting, heavens conspir'd his over-
throw!
For falling to a devilish exercise,
And glutted now with learning's golden
gifts
He surfeits upon cursed necromancy:
Nothing so sweet as magic is to him,
Which he prefers before his chiefest
bliss . . .
And this the man that in his study sits.
(*Exit.*)

FAUSTUS *in his Study.*

faust: Settle thy studies Faustus, and
begin
To sound the depth of that thou wilt pro-
fess.
Having commenc'd, be a Divine in show,
Yet level at the end of every art,
And live and die in Aristotle's works.
Sweet Analytics, 'tis thou hast ravish'd
me . . .
Bene disserere est finis logicis.
Is to dispute well logic's chiefest end?
Affords this art no greater miracle?
Then read no more, thou hast attain'd that
end.
A greater subject fitteth Faustus' wit:
Bid ὄν καὶ μὴ ὄν farewell, and Galen come;
Be a physician, Faustus; heap up gold,
And be eterniz'd for some wondrous cure!
Summum bonum medicinæ sanitas,
The end of physic is our body's health.
Why Faustus, hast thou not attain'd that
end?
Are not thy bills hung up as monuments,
Whereby whole cities have escap'd the
plague,
And thousand desp'rate maladies been
cur'd?
Yet art thou still but Faustus and a man.
Couldst thou make men to live eternally
Or, being dead, raise them to life again,
Then this profession were to be esteem'd.
Physic, farewell! Where is Justinian?
(*Reads.*)
*Si una eademque res legatur duobus
Alter rem, alter valorem rei, etc.*
A petty case of paltry legacies . . .
(*Reads.*)
*Exhæreditare filium non potest pater,
nisi—*

Such is the subject of the Institute,
And universal body of the law!
This study fits a mercenary drudge
Who aims at nothing but external trash,
Too servile and illiberal for me.
When all is done, Divinity is best:
Jerome's Bible, Faustus, view it well.
                                    (*Reads.*)
Stipendium peccati mors est. Ha! *Sti-*
    pendium, etc.
The reward of sin is death. That's hard.
                                    (*Reads.*)
Si peccasse negamus, fallimur
Et nulla est in nobis veritas.
If we say that we have no sin,
We deceive ourselves, and there is no truth
    in us.
Why, then, belike we must sin,
And so consequently die.
Ay, we must die an everlasting death.
What doctrine call you this, *Che serà, serà:*
What will be, shall be? Divinity, adieu!
These metaphysics of magicians,
And necromantic books are heavenly;
Lines, circles, letters, characters;
Ay, these are those that Faustus most de-
    sires!
O, what a world of profit and delight,
Of power, of honor, and omnipotence,
Is promised to the studious artisan!
All things that move between the quiet
    poles
Shall be at my command: emperors and
    kings
Are but obey'd in their several provinces
But his dominion that exceeds in this,
Stretcheth as far as doth the mind of
    man—
A sound magician is a demi-god!
Here, tire my brains to get a deity!

(*Enter* WAGNER.)

Wagner, commend me to my dearest
    friends,
The German Valdes and Cornelius.
Request them earnestly to visit me.

WAG: I will, sir.   (*Exit.*)

FAUST: Their conference will be a
    greater help to me
Than all my labours, plod I ne'er so fast.
(*Enter the* GOOD ANGEL *and* BAD ANGEL.)

GOOD ANG: O, Faustus, lay that damned
    book aside,
And gaze not on it, lest it tempt thy soul,
And heap God's heavy wrath upon thy
    head!
Read, read the Scriptures:—that is blas-
    phemy!

BAD ANG: Go forward, Faustus, in that
    famous art
Wherein all nature's treasure is contain'd:
Be thou on earth as Jove is in the sky,
Lord and commander of these elements!
                                    (*Exeunt* ANGELS.)

FAUST: How am I glutted with conceit
    of this!
Shall I make spirits fetch me what I please,
Resolve me of all ambiguities,
Perform what desperate enterprise I will?
I'll have them fly to India for gold,
Ransack the ocean for orient pearl,
And search all corners of the new-found
    world
For pleasant fruits and princely delicates;
I'll have them read me strange philosophy,
And tell the secrets of all foreign kings;
I'll have them wall all Germany with brass,
And make swift Rhine circle fair Witten-
    berg.
I'll have them fill the public schools with
    silk,
Wherewith the students shall be bravely
    clad;
I'll levy soldiers with the coin they bring,
And chase the Prince of Parma from our
    land,
And reign sole king of all the Provinces;
Yea, stranger engines for the brunt of
    war,
Than was the fiery keel at Antwerp's
    bridge,
I'll make my servile spirits to invent.
                                    (*He calls within.*)

(*Enter* VALDES *and* CORNELIUS.)

Come German Valdes and Cornelius,
And make me blest with your sage con-
ference!
Valdes, sweet Valdes, and Cornelius,
Know that your words have won me at
the last
To practice magic and concealed arts:
Philosophy is odious and obscure;
Both law and physic are for petty wits;
Divinity is basest of the three,
Unpleasant, harsh, contemptible, and vile:
'Tis magic, magic, that hath ravish'd me.
Then, gentle friends, aid me in this at-
tempt
And I, that have with subtle syllogisms
Gravell'd the pastors of the German
church,
And made the flowering pride of Witten-
berg
Swarm to my problems, as the infernal
spirits
On sweet Musæus when he came to hell,
Will be as cunning as Agrippa was,
Whose shadows made all Europe honour
him.

VALD: Faustus, these books, thy wit, and
our experience
Shall make all nations to canonize us.
As Indian Moors obey their Spanish lords,
So shall the spirits of every element
Be always serviceable to us three;
Like lions shall they guard us when we
please,
Like Almaine rutters with their horse-
men's staves
Or Lapland giants trotting by our sides;
Sometimes like women, or unwedded
maids
Shadowing more beauty in their airy
brows
Than has the white breasts of the queen
of love:
From Venice shall they drag huge argo-
sies,
And from America the golden fleece

That yearly stuffs old Philip's treasury;
If learned Faustus will be resolute.

FAUST: Valdes, as resolute am I in this
As thou to live: therefore object it not.

CORN: The miracles that magic will
perform
Will make thee vow to study nothing else.
He that is grounded in astrology,
Enrich'd with tongues, well seen in min-
erals,
Hath all the principles magic doth require.
Then doubt not, Faustus, but to be re-
nown'd, /
And more frequented for this mystery
Than heretofore the Delphian oracle.
The spirits tell me they can dry the sea,
And fetch the treasure of all foreign
wrecks,
Yea, all the wealth that our forefathers hid
Within the massy entrails of the earth:
Then tell me, Faustus, what shall we three
want?

FAUST: Nothing, Cornelius. O, this
cheers my soul!
Come, show me some demonstrations
magical,
That I may conjure in some bushy grove
And have these joys in full possession.

VALD: Then haste thee to some solitary
grove,
And bear wise Bacon's and Albertus'
works,
The Hebrew Psalter, and New Testament;
And whatsoever else is requisite
We will inform thee ere our conference
cease.

CORN: Valdes, first let him know the
words of art;
And then, all other ceremonies learn'd,
Faustus may try his cunning by himself.

VALD: First I'll instruct thee in the
rudiments,
And then wilt thou be perfecter than I.

FAUST: Then come and dine with me,
and, after meat

We'll canvass every quiddity thereof—
For ere I sleep I'll try what I can do.
This night I'll conjure though I die therefore!

(*Exeunt omnes.*)

SCENE II

Before FAUSTUS's *house.*

(*Enter* TWO SCHOLARS.)

FIRST SCHOL: I wonder what's become of Faustus, that was wont to make our schools ring with *sic probo.*

(*Enter* WAGNER.)

SEC. SCHOL: That shall we presently know. Here comes his boy.

FIRST SCHOL: How now, sirrah! where's thy master?

WAG: God in Heaven knows.

SEC. SCHOL: Why, dost not thou know then?

WAG: Yes, I know; but that follows not.

FIRST SCHOL: Go to, sirrah! leave your jesting, and tell us where he is.

WAG: That follows not by force of argument, which you, being licentiates, should stand upon; therefore acknowledge your error, and be attentive.

SEC. SCHOL: Then you will not tell us?

WAG: You are deceiv'd, for I will tell you: yet, if you were not dunces, you would never ask me such a question; for is he not *corpus naturale?* and is not that *mobile?* Then wherefore should you ask me such a question? But that I am by nature phlegmatic, slow to wrath, and prone to lechery (to love, I would say), it were not for you to come within forty foot of the place of execution, although I do not doubt but to see you both hang'd the next sessions. Thus having triumph'd over you, I will set my countenance like a precisian, and begin to speak thus:—Truly, my dear brethren, my master is within at dinner, with Valdes and Cornelius, as this wine, if it could speak, would inform your worships: and so, the Lord bless you, preserve you, and keep you, my dear brethren.   (*Exit.*)

FIRST SCHOL: O Faustus. Then I fear that which I have long suspected, That thou are fallen into that damned art For which they two are infamous through the world.

SEC. SCHOL: Were he a stranger, not allied to me, The danger of his soul would make me mourn. But, come, let us go and inform the Rector, It may be his grave counsel may reclaim him.

FIRST SCHOL: I fear me nothing will reclaim him now.

SEC. SCHOL: Yet let us see what we can do.   (*Exeunt.*)

SCENE III

A grove.

(*Enter* FAUSTUS *to conjure.*)

FAUST: Now that the gloomy shadow of the night,
Longing to view Orion's drizzling look,
Leaps from th' antarctic world unto the sky,
And dims the welkin with her pitchy breath,
Faustus, begin thine incantations,
And try if devils will obey thy hest,
Seeing thou hast pray'd and sacrific'd to them.
Within this circle is Jehovah's name
Forward and backward anagrammatiz'd;
Th' abbreviated names of holy saints,
Figures of every adjunct to the heavens,

And characters of signs and erring stars,
By which the spirits are enforc'd to rise:
Then fear not, Faustus, to be resolute
And try the uttermost magic can perform.
                    (*Thunder.*)
'Sint mihi Dii Acherontis propitii! Valeat
numen triplex Jehovæ! Ignis, aeris, aqua-
tici, spiritus salvete! Orientis princeps,
Belzebub, inferni ardentis monarcha, et
Demogorgon, propitiamus vos, ut appar-
eat et surgat Mephistophilis. (*Enter*
Dragon above.) *Quid tu moraris? per*
Jehovam, Gehennam, et consecratam aquam
quam nunc spargo, signumque crucis
quod nunc facio, et per vota nostra, ipse
nunc surgat nobis dicatus Mephistophilis!

        (*Enter* MEPHISTOPHILIS.)

I charge thee to return, and change thy
        shape,
Thou art too ugly to attend on me.
Go, and return an old Franciscan friar:
That holy shape becomes a devil best.

            (*Exit* MEPHISTOPHILIS.)

I see there's virtue in my heavenly words:
Who would not be proficient in this art?
How pliant is this Mephistophilis,
Full of obedience and humility,
Such is the force of magic and my spells!
Now, Faustus, thou are conjurer laureat,
That canst command great Mephistophilis.
Quin redis, Mephistophilis, fratris im-
agine!

    (*Re-enter* MEPHISTOPHILIS *like a*
            Franciscan friar.)

MEPH: Now, Faustus, what would'st
    thou have me do?
FAUST: I charge thee wait upon me
    whilst I live,
To do whatever Faustus shall command,
Be it to make the moon drop from her
    sphere,
Or the ocean to overwhelm the world.
MEPH: I am a servant to great Lucifer,
And may not follow thee without his
    leave;

No more than he commands must we
    perform.
FAUST: Did not he charge thee to ap-
    pear to me?
MEPH: No, I came now hither of mine
    own accord.
FAUST: Did not my conjuring raise
    thee? Speak.
MEPH: That was the cause, but yet *per*
    accidens.
For, when we hear one rack the name of
    God,
Abjure the Scriptures and his saviour
    Christ,
We fly in hope to get his glorious soul.
Nor will we come, unless he use such
    means
Whereby he is in danger to be damn'd.
Therefore the shortest cut for conjuring
Is stoutly to abjure all godliness
And pray devoutly to the prince of hell.
FAUST: So Faustus hath
Already done; and holds this principle,
There is no chief but only Belzebub;
To whom Faustus doth dedicate himself.
This word 'damnation' terrifies not me,
For I confound Hell in Elysium:
My ghost be with the old philosophers!
But, leaving these vain trifles of men's
    souls,
Tell me what is that Lucifer thy lord?
MEPH: Arch-regent and Commander of
    All Spirits.
FAUST: Was not that Lucifer an angel
    once?
MEPH: Yes, Faustus, and most dearly
    lov'd of God.
FAUST: How comes it then that he is
    Prince of Devils?
MEPH: O, by aspiring pride and in-
    solence;
For which God threw him from the face
    of Heaven.
FAUST: And what are you that live
    with Lucifer?

MEPH: Unhappy spirits that fell with Lucifer,
Conspir'd against our God with Lucifer,
And are for ever damn'd with Lucifer.

FAUST: Where are you damn'd?

MEPH: In Hell.

FAUST: How comes it then that thou art out of Hell?

MEPH: Why this is Hell, nor am I out of it . . .
Think'st thou that I who saw the face of God,
And tasted the eternal joys of Heaven,
Am not tormented with ten thousand Hells,
In being depriv'd of everlasting bliss?
O Faustus, leave these frivolous demands
Which strikes a terror to my fainting soul!

FAUST: What, is great Mephistophilis so passionate
For being deprived of the joys of heaven?
Learn thou of Faustus manly fortitude,
And scorn those joys thou never shalt possess.
Go bear these tidings to great Lucifer:
Seeing Faustus hath incurr'd eternal death
By desperate thoughts against Jove's deity,
Say he surrenders up to him his soul,
So he will spare him four-and-twenty years,
Letting him live in all voluptuousness;
Having thee ever to attend on me,
To give me whatsoever I shall ask,
To tell me whatsoever I demand,
To slay mine enemies, and to aid my friends,
And always be obedient to my will.
Go, and return to mighty Lucifer,
And meet me in my study at midnight,
And then resolve me of thy master's mind.

MEPH: I will, Faustus.   (*Exit.*)

FAUST: Had I as many souls as there be stars,
I'd give them all for Mephistophilis.
By him I'll be great emperor of the world.
And make a bridge through the moving air,
To pass the ocean with a band of men;
I'll join the hills that bind the Afric shore,
And make that country continent to Spain,
And both contributary to my crown:
The Emperor shall not live but by my leave,
Nor any potentate of Germany.
Now that I have obtain'd what I desir'd,
I'll live in speculation of this art,
Till Mephistophilis return again. (*Exit.*)

Scene IV

(*Enter* WAGNER *and the* CLOWN.)

WAG: Come hither, sirrah boy.

CLOWN: Boy! O disgrace to my person! Zounds, boy in your face! You have seen many boys with such beards, I am sure.

WAG: Sirrah, hast thou no comings in?

CLOWN: Yes, and goings out too, you may see, sir.

WAG: Alas, poor slave! see how poverty jests in his nakedness! I know the villain's out of service, and so hungry, that I know he would give his soul to the devil for a shoulder of mutton, though it were blood-raw.

CLOWN: Not so, neither. I had need to have it well roasted, and good sauce to it, if I pay so dear, I can tell you.

WAG: Sirrah, wilt thou be my man and wait on me, and I will make thee go like *Qui mihi discipulus?*

CLOWN: What, in verse?

WAG: No slave; in beaten silk and staves-acre.

CLOWN: Staves-acre! that's good to kill vermin. Then, belike, if I serve you, I shall be lousy.

WAG: Why, so thou shalt be, whether thou do'st it or no. For, sirrah, if thou do'st not presently bind thyself to me for seven years, I'll turn all the lice about thee into familiars, and make them tear thee in pieces.

CLOWN: Nay, sir, you may save yourself a labour, for they are as familiar with me as if they had paid for their meat and drink, I can tell you.

WAG: Well, sirrah, leave your jesting and take these guilders.

CLOWN: Yes, marry, sir, and I thank you too.

WAG: So, now thou art to be at an hour's warning, whensoever and wheresoever the devil shall fetch thee.

CLOWN: Here, take your guilders again, I'll none of 'em.

WAG: Not I, thou art press'd, for I will presently raise up two devils to carry thee away—Banio, Belcher!

CLOWN: Belcher! and Belcher come here, I'll belch him. I am not afraid of a devil!

(*Enter two* DEVILS.)

WAG: How now, sir, will you serve me now?

CLOWN: Ay, good Wagner, take away the Devil then.

WAG: Spirits, away! Now, sirrah, follow me.   (*Exeunt* DEVILS.)

CLOWN: I will sir! But hark you, master, will you teach me this conjuring occupation?

WAG: Ay, sirrah, I'll teach thee to turn thyself to a dog, or a cat, or a mouse, or a rat, or anything.

CLOWN: A dog, or a cat, or a mouse, or a rat, O brave Wagner!

WAG: Villain, call me Master Wagner, and see that you walk attentively and let your right eye be always diametrally fixed upon my left heel, that thou may'st *quasi vestigiis nostris insistere.*

CLOWN: Well, sir, I warrant you.
                        (*Exeunt.*)

ACT II

SCENE I

(*Enter* FAUSTUS *in his Study.*)

FAUST: Now, Faustus, must
Thou needs be damn'd, and canst thou
        not be sav'd!
What boots it, then, to think on God or
        Heaven?
Away with such vain fancies, and despair;
Despair in God, and trust in Belzebub:
Now go not backward; Faustus, be reso-
        lute!
Why waver'st thou? O something sound-
        eth in mine ear,
'Abjure this magic, turn to God again!'
Ay, and Faustus will turn to God again.
To God? He loves thee not;
The God thou serv'st is thine own appe-
        tite,
Wherein is fix'd the love of Belzebub:
To him I'll build an altar and a church,
And offer lukewarm blood of new-born
        babes!

(*Enter the two* ANGELS.)

BAD ANG: Go forward, Faustus, in that
        famous art.

GOOD ANG: Sweet Faustus, leave that
        execrable art.

FAUST: Contrition, prayer, repentance—
        what of these?

GOOD ANG: O, they are means to bring
        thee unto heaven!

BAD ANG: Rather illusions, fruits of
        lunacy,
That make them foolish that do use them
        most.

GOOD ANG: Sweet Faustus, think of
heaven and heavenly things.

BAD ANG: No, Faustus; think of honour
        and of wealth.

(*Exeunt* ANGELS.)

FAUST: Wealth! Why, the signiory of
Emden shall be mine.

When Mephistophilis shall stand by me,
What power can hurt me? Faustus, thou art safe:
Cast no more doubts—come, Mephistophilis!
And bring glad tidings from great Lucifer;—
Is't not midnight?—come, Mephistophilis,
Veni, veni, Mephistophilis!

(*Enter* MEPHISTOPHILIS.)

Now tell me what saith Lucifer, thy lord?

MEPH: That I shall wait on Faustus whilst he lives,
So he will buy my service with his soul.

FAUST: Already Faustus hath hazarded that for thee.

MEPH: But now thou must bequeath it solemnly,
And write a deed of gift with thine own blood;
For that security craves Lucifer.
If thou deny it, I must back to Hell.

FAUST: Stay, Mephistophilis, and tell me what good
Will my soul do thy lord?

MEPH: Enlarge his kingdom.

FAUST: Is that the reason why he tempts us thus?

MEPH: *Solamen miseris socios habuisse doloris.*

FAUST: Why, have you any pain that torture others?

MEPH: As great as have the human souls of men.
But tell me, Faustus, shall I have thy soul?
And I will be thy slave, and wait on thee,
And give thee more than thou hast wit to ask.

FAUST: Ay, Mephistophilis, I'll give it him.

MEPH: Then, Faustus, stab thy arm courageously,
And bind thy soul, that at some certain day
Great Lucifer may claim it as his own;

And then be thou as great as Lucifer.

FAUST (*stabbing his arm*): Lo, Mephistophilis, for love of thee,
Faustus hath cut his arm and with his proper blood
Assure his soul to be great Lucifer's,
Chief lord and regent of perpetual night!
View here this blood that trickles from mine arm,
And let it be propitious for my wish.

MEPH: But, Faustus,
Write it in manner of a deed of gift.

FAUST: Ay, so I do. (*Writes.*) But, Mephistophilis,
My blood congeals, and I can write no more.

MEPH: I'll fetch thee fire to dissolve it straight.   (*Exit.*)

FAUST: What might the staying of my blood portend?
Is it unwilling I should write this bill?
Why streams it not, that I may write afresh?
Faustus gives to thee his soul: oh, there it stay'd!
Why shouldst thou not? is not thy soul thine own?
Then write again, *Faustus gives to thee his soul.*

(*Re-enter* MEPHISTOPHILIS *with the chafer of fire.*)

MEPH: See, Faustus, here is fire, set it on.

FAUST: So, now the blood begins to clear again;
Now will I make an end immediately.
(*Writes.*)

MEPH: What will not I do to obtain his soul?   (*Aside.*)

FAUST: *Consummatum est!* This bill is ended,
And Faustus hath bequeath'd his soul to Lucifer.
But what is this inscription on mine arm?
Homo, fuge! Whither should I fly?
If unto God, he'll throw me down to Hell.

My senses are deceiv'd; here's nothing
    writ:—
O yes, I see it plain; even here is writ,
Homo, fuge! Yet shall not Faustus fly.

MEPH: I'll fetch him somewhat to de-
    light his mind.
                    (*Aside, and then exit.*)

(*Enter* DEVILS, *giving crowns and rich ap-
parel to* FAUSTUS. *They dance, and then
depart.*)

(*Enter* MEPHISTOPHILIS.)

FAUST: What means this show? Speak,
    Mephistophilis.

MEPH: Nothing Faustus, but to delight
    thy mind,
And let thee see what magic can perform.

FAUST: But may I raise such spirits
    when I please?

MEPH: Ay, Faustus, and do greater
    things than these.

FAUST: Here, Mephistophilis, receive
    this scroll,
A deed of gift of body and of soul:
But yet conditionally that thou perform
All covenants and articles between us both.

MEPH: Faustus, I swear by Hell and
    Lucifer
To effect all promises between us both.

FAUST: Then hear me read it, Meph-
    istophilis:

On these conditions following.
*First, that Faustus may be a spirit in form
and substance.*
*Secondly, that Mephistophilis shall be his
servant, and be by him commanded.*
*Thirdly, that Mephistophilis shall do for
him, and bring him whatsoever.*
*Fourthly, that he shall be in his chamber
or house invisible.*
*Lastly, that he shall appear to the said
John Faustus at all times, in what form
or shape soever he please.*
I, John Faustus, of Wittenberg, Doctor, by

*these presents, do give both body and
soul to Lucifer Prince of the East, and
his minister Mephistophilis; and fur-
thermore grant unto them that, four
and twenty years being expired, and
these articles above written being inviolate, full power to fetch or carry
the said John Faustus, body and soul,
flesh, blood, or goods, into their habi-
tation wheresoever.*
                    By me, John Faustus.

MEPH: Speak, Faustus, do you deliver
    this as your deed?

FAUST: Ay, take it, and the Devil give
    thee good of it!

MEPH: So, now, Faustus, ask me what
    thou wilt.

FAUST: First I will question with thee
    about Hell.
Tell me, where is the place that men call
    Hell?

MEPH: Under the heavens.

FAUST: Ay, so are all things else, but
    whereabouts?

MEPH: Within the bowels of these ele-
    ments,
Where we are tortur'd and remain for
    ever:
Hell hath no limits, nor is circumscrib'd
In one self place; but where we are is hell,
And where hell is, there must we ever be:
And, to be short, when all the world dis-
    solves,
And every creature shall be purified,
All places shall be Hell that is not Heaven.

FAUST: I think hell's a fable.

MEPH: Ay, think so, till experience
    change thy mind.

FAUST: Why, dost thou think that
    Faustus shall be damn'd?

MEPH: Ay, of necessity, for here's the
    scroll
In which thou hast given thy soul to Luci-
    fer.

FAUST: Ay, and body too: but what of that?

Think'st thou that Faustus is so fond to imagine

That after this life there is any pain?

No, these are trifles and mere old wives' tales.

MEPH: But I am an instance to prove the contrary;

For I tell thee I am damn'd, and now in Hell.

FAUST: Nay, and this be Hell, I'll willingly be damn'd:

What! sleeping, eating, walking, and disputing?

But, leaving off this, let me have a wife,

The fairest maid in Germany, for I

Am wanton and lascivious

And cannot live without a wife.

MEPH: Well, Faustus, thou shalt have a wife.

(*He fetches in a woman-devil.*)

FAUST: What sight is this?

MEPH: Now, Faustus, wilt thou have a wife?

FAUST: Here's a hot whore indeed! No, I'll no wife.

MEPH: Marriage is but a ceremonial toy:

And if thou lovest me, think no more of it.

I'll cull thee out the fairest courtesans

And bring them every morning to thy bed.

She whom thine eye shall like, thy heart shall have,

Were she as chaste as was Penelope,

As wise as Saba, or as beautiful

As was bright Lucifer before his fall.

Here, take this book, and peruse it well.

The iterating of these lines brings gold;

The framing of this circle on the ground

Brings thunder, whirlwinds, storm and lightning;

Pronounce this thrice devoutly to thyself,

And men in harness shall appear to thee,

Ready to execute what thou command'st.

FAUST: Thanks, Mephistophilis, for this sweet book.

This will I keep as chary as my life.

(*Exeunt.*)

SCENE II

(*Enter* FAUSTUS *in his Study and* MEPHISTOPHILIS.)

FAUST: When I behold the heavens, then I repent,

And curse thee, wicked Mephistophilis,

Because thou hast depriv'd me of those joys.

MEPH: 'Twas thine own seeking, Faustus, thank thyself.

But think'st thou Heaven is such a glorious thing?

I tell thee, Faustus, it is not half so fair

As thou, or any man that breathes on earth.

FAUST: How prov'st thou that?

MEPH: 'Twas made for man: then he's more excellent.

FAUST: If heaven was made for man, 'twas made for me:

I will renounce this magic and repent.

(*Enter the two* ANGELS.)

GOOD ANG: Faustus, repent: yet God will pity thee.

BAD ANG: Thou are a spirit: God cannot pity thee.

FAUST: Who buzzeth in mine ears I am a spirit?

Be I a devil, yet God may pity me;

Yea, God will pity me if I repent.

BAD ANG: Ay, but Faustus never shall repent.   (*Exeunt* ANGELS.)

FAUST: My heart is harden'd, I cannot repent.

Scarce can I name salvation, faith, or Heaven,

Poison, swords, halters, and envenom'd steel

Are laid before me to dispatch myself;
And long ere this I should have done the
    deed,
Had not sweet pleasure conquer'd deep
    despair.
Have not I made blind Homer sing to me
Of Alexander's love and Oenon's death?
And hath not he, that built the walls of
    Thebes,
With ravishing sound of his melodious
    harp,
Made music with my Mephistophilis?
Why should I die, then, or basely despair?
I am resolv'd; Faustus shall not repent.—
Come, Mephistophilis, let us dispute again,
And reason of divine astrology.
Speak, are there many spheres above the
    moon?
Are all celestial bodies but one globe,
As is the substance of this centric earth?

MEPH: As are the elements, such are
    the heavens,
Even from the moon unto the empyreal
    orb,
Mutually folded in each others' spheres,
And jointly move upon one axle-tree,
Whose termine is termed the world's wide
    pole;
Nor are the names of Saturn, Mars, or
    Jupiter
Feign'd, but are erring stars.

FAUST: But have they all
One motion, both *situ et tempore?*

MEPH: All move from east to west in
four and twenty hours upon the poles of
the world but differ in their motions upon
the poles of the zodiac.

FAUST: These slender questions Wagner
    can decide:
Hath Mephistophilis no greater skill?
Who knows not the double motion of the
    planets?
That the first is finish'd in a natural day;
The second thus: Saturn in 30 years;
Jupiter in 12; Mars in 4; the Sun, Venus,
and Mercury in a year; the Moon in 28

days. These are freshmen's suppositions.
But, tell me, hath every sphere a dominion
or *intelligentia?*

MEPH: Ay.

FAUST: How many heavens or spheres
are there?

MEPH: Nine; the seven planets, the
firmament, and the empyreal heaven.

FAUST: But is there not *coelum igneum,
et crystallinum?*

MEPH: No, Faustus, they be but fables.

FAUST: Resolve me then in this one
question: why are not conjunctions, op-
positions, aspects, eclipses, all at one time,
but in some years we have more, in some
less?

MEPH: *Per inaequalem motum respectu
totius.*

FAUST: Well, I am answer'd. Now tell
me who made the world.

MEPH: I will not.

FAUST: Sweet Mephistophilis, tell me.

MEPH: Move me not, Faustus.

FAUST: Villain, have not I bound thee
to tell me anything?

MEPH: Ay, that is not against our kingdom.
This is: thou art damn'd; think thou of
    Hell!

FAUST: Think, Faustus, upon God that
    made the world.

MEPH: Remember this!   (*Exit.*)

FAUST: Ay, go, accursed spirit, to ugly
    Hell!
'Tis thou hast damn'd distressed Faustus'
    soul.
Is't not too late?

(*Enter the two* ANGELS.)

BAD ANG: Too late.

GOOD ANG: Never too late, if Faustus
    will repent.

BAD ANG: If thou repent, devils will tear
    thee in pieces.

GOOD ANG: Repent, and they shall never raze thy skin.   (*Exeunt* ANGELS.)

FAUST: O, Christ, my Savior, my Savior! Help to save distressed Faustus' soul!

(*Enter* LUCIFER, BELZEBUB, *and* MEPHISTOPHILIS.)

LUC: Christ cannot save thy soul, for he is just:
There's none but I have interest in the same.

FAUST: O, what art thou that look'st so terribly?

LUC: I am Lucifer,
And this is my companion prince in Hell.

FAUST: O, Faustus, they are come to fetch thy soul!

BELZ: We are come to tell thee thou dost injure us.

LUC: Thou call'st on Christ contrary to thy promise.

BELZ: Thou shouldst not think on God.

LUC: Think on the Devil.

BELZ: And his dam too.

FAUST: Nor will Faustus henceforth: pardon him for this,
And Faustus vows never to look to Heaven.

LUC: So shalt thou show thyself an obedient servant,
And we will highly gratify thee for it.

BELZ: Faustus, we are come from Hell in person to show thee some pastime: sit down, and thou shalt behold the Seven Deadly Sins appear to thee in their own proper shapes and likeness.

FAUST: That sight will be as pleasant to me, as Paradise was to Adam, the first day of his creation.

LUC: Talk not of Paradise or creation; but mark the show. Go, Mephistophilis, fetch them in.

(*Enter the* 7 DEADLY SINS.)

BELZ: Now, Faustus, question them of their names and dispositions.

FAUST: That shall I soon. What are thou, the first?

PRIDE: I am Pride. I disdain to have any parents. I am like to Ovid's flea, I can creep into every corner of a wench; sometimes, like a periwig, I sit upon her brow; next, like a necklace I hang about her neck; then, like a fan of feathers, I kiss her, and then turning myself to a wrought smock do what I list. But, fie, what a smell is here! I'll not speak another word, unless the ground be perfum'd, and cover'd with cloth of arras.

FAUST: Thou art a proud knave, indeed! What are thou, the second?

COVET: I am Covetousness, begotten of an old churl in a leather bag: and might I now obtain my wish, this house, you and all, should turn to gold, that I might lock you safe into my chest. O my sweet gold!

FAUST: And what art thou, the third?

ENVY: I am Envy, begotten of a chimney-sweeper and an oyster-wife. I cannot read, and therefore wish all books burn'd. I am lean with seeing others eat. O, that there would come a famine over all the world, that all might die, and I live alone! then thou should'st see how fat I'd be. But must thou sit and I stand? come down, with a vengeance!

FAUST: Out, envious wretch!—But what art thou, the fourth?

WRATH: I am Wrath. I had neither father nor mother: I leapt out of a lion's mouth when I was scarce an hour old; and ever since have run up and down the world with these case of rapiers, wounding myself when I could get none to fight withal. I was born in hell; and look to it, for some of you shall be my father.

FAUST: And what are thou, the fifth?

GLUT: I am Gluttony. My parents are all dead, and the devil a penny they have left me, but a small pension, and that buys me thirty meals a day and ten bevers—a small trifle to suffice nature. I come of a royal pedigree! my father was a Gammon of Bacon, and my mother was a Hogshead of Claret wine; my godfathers were these, Peter Pickled-herring and Martin Martlemas-beef. But my godmother, O she was an ancient gentlewoman; her name was Margery March-beer. Now, Faustus, thou hast heard all my progeny; wilt thou bid me to supper?

FAUST: Not I.

GLUT: Then the Devil choke thee.

FAUST: Choke thyself, glutton!—What art thou, the sixth?

SLOTH: Heigh ho! I am Sloth. I was begotten on a sunny bank, where I have lain ever since. Heigh ho! I'll not speak a word more for a king's ransom.

FAUST: And what are you, Mistress Minx, the seventh and last?

LECHERY: Who, I, sir? I am one that loves an inch of raw mutton better than an ell of fried stockfish, and the first letter of my name begins with Lechery.

LUC: Away, to hell, away, on Piper!

(*Exeunt the 7 SINS.*)

FAUST: O, how this sight doth delight my soul!

LUC: But, Faustus, in Hell is all manner of delight.

FAUST: O, might I see Hell, and return again safe, how happy were I then!

LUC: Faustus, thou shalt. At midnight I will send for thee. Meanwhile peruse this book and view it thoroughly, and thou shalt turn thyself into what shape thou wilt.

FAUST: Thanks, mighty Lucifer! This will I keep as chary as my life.

LUC: Now, Faustus, farewell.

FAUST: Farewell, great Lucifer. Come, Mephistophilis.

(*Exeunt omnes several ways.*)

SCENE III

An Inn-yard.

(*Enter* ROBIN *with a book.*)

ROBIN: What, Dick, look to the horses there, till I come again. I have gotten one of Doctor Faustus' conjuring books, and now we'll have such knavery, as't passes.

(*Enter* DICK.)

DICK: What, Robin, you must come away and walk the horses.

ROBIN: I walk the horses? I scorn't, 'faith, I have other matters in hand, let the horses walk themselves and they will. (*Reads.*) *A per se; a, t, h, e, the; o per se; o deny orgon, gorgon.* Keep further from me, O thou illiterate and unlearned hostler.

DICK: 'Snails, what hast thou got there? a book? why, thou canst not tell ne'er a word on't.

ROBIN: That thou shalt see presently. Keep out of the circle, I say, lest I send you into the hostry with a vengeance.

DICK: That's life, 'faith: you had best leave your foolery, for an my master come, he'll conjure you, 'faith.

ROBIN: My master conjure me? I'll tell thee what, an my master come here, I'll clap as fair a pair of horns on's head as e'er thou sawest in thy life.

DICK: Thou need'st not do that, for my mistress hath done it.

ROBIN: Ay, there be of us here that have waded as deep into matters as other men, if they were disposed to talk.

DICK: A plague take you, I thought you did not sneak up and down after her for nothing. But I prithee, tell me, in good sadness, Robin, is that a conjuring book?

ROBIN: Do but speak what thou'lt have me to do, and I'll do't: If thou'lt dance naked, put off thy clothes, and I'll conjure thee about presently: or if thou'lt go but to the tavern with me, I'll give thee white

wine, red wine, claret wine, sack, musca-
dine, malmesey, and whippin-crust, hold
belly, hold, and we'll not pay one penny
for it.

DICK: O brave, prithee let's to it presently, for I am as dry as a dog.

ROBIN: Come then, let's away.

(*Exeunt.*)

ACT III

(*Enter the* CHORUS.)

CHOR: Learned Faustus,
To find the secrets of astronomy
Graven in the book of Jove's high firma-
ment,
Did mount him up to scale Olympus' top,
Where sitting in a chariot burning bright,
Drawn by the strength of yoked dragons'
necks,
He views the clouds, the planets, and the
stars,
The tropic zones, and quarters of the sky,
From the bright circle of the hornèd moon,
E'en to the height of *Primum Mobile:*
And whirling round with this circum-
ference,
Within the concave compass of the pole;
From east to west his dragons swiftly
glide,
And in eight days did bring him home
again.
Not long he stayed within his quiet house,
To rest his bones after his weary toil,
But new exploits do hale him out again,
And mounted then upon a dragon's back,
That with his wings did part the subtle
air,
He now is gone to prove cosmography,
That measures coasts, and kingdoms of
the earth:
And, as I guess, will first arrive at Rome,
To see the Pope and manner of his court,
And take some part of holy Peter's feast,
The which this day is highly solemniz'd.

(*Exit.*)

SCENE I

The POPE's *Privy-chamber.*

(*Enter* FAUSTUS *and* MEPHISTOPHILIS.)

FAUST: Having now, my good Mephis-
tophilis,
Pass'd with delight the stately town of
Trier,
Environ'd round with airy mountain-tops,
With walls of flint, and deep entrenched
lakes,
Not to be won by any conquering prince;
From Paris next, coasting the realm of
France,
We saw the river Maine fall into Rhine,
Whose banks are set with groves of fruit-
ful vines;
Then up to Naples, rich Campania,
Whose buildings fair and gorgeous to the
eye,
The streets straight forth, and paved with
finest brick,
Quarters the town in four equivalents;
There saw we learned Maro's golden
tomb,
The way he cut, an English mile in length,
Through a rock of stone, in one night's
space;
From thence to Venice, Padua, and the
East,
In one of which a sumptuous temple
stands,
That threats the stars with her aspiring
top,
Whose frame is paved with sundry col-
oured stones,
And roof'd aloft with curious work in
gold.
Thus hitherto hath Faustus spent his time:
But tell me now, what resting-place is
this?
Hast thou, as erst I did command,
Conducted me within the walls of Rome?

MEPH: I have, my Faustus, and for
proof thereof
This is the goodly Palace of the Pope;

And cause we are no common guests
I choose his privy-chamber for our use.

    FAUST: I hope His Holiness will bid us
    welcome.

    MEPH: All's one, for we'll be bold with
    his venison.

But now, my Faustus, that thou may'st
    perceive
What Rome contains for to delight thine
    eyes,
Know that this city stands upon seven hills
That underprop the groundwork of the
    same:
Just through the midst runs flowing
    Tiber's stream,
With winding banks that cut it in two
    parts;
Over the which four stately bridges lean,
That make safe passage to each part of
    Rome:
Upon the bridge called Ponte Angelo
Erected is a castle passing strong,
Where thou shalt see such store of ordi-
    nance,
As that the double cannons, forg'd of
    brass,
Do match the number of the days con-
    tain'd
Within the compass of one complete year:
Beside the gates, and high pyramides,
That Julius Cæsar brought from Africa.

    FAUST: Now, by the kingdoms of in-
    fernal rule,
Of Styx, of Acheron, and the fiery lake
Of ever-burning Phlegethon, I swear
That I do long to see the monuments
And situation of bright splendent Rome:
Come, therefore, let's away.

    MEPH: Nay, stay, my Faustus; I know
    you'd see the Pope
And take some part of holy Peter's feast,
The which, in state and high solemnity,
This day is held through Rome and Italy,
In honour of the Pope's triumphant vic-
    tory.

    FAUST: Sweet Mephistophilis, thou
    pleasest me,

Whilst I am here on earth, let me be
    cloy'd
With all things that delight the heart of
    man.
My four-and-twenty years of liberty
I'll spend in pleasure and in dalliance,
That Faustus' name, whilst this bright
    frame doth stand,
May be admired through the furthest
    land.

    MEPH: 'Tis well said, Faustus, come
    then, stand by me
And thou shalt see them come immedi-
    ately.

    FAUST: Nay, stay, my gentle Mephis-
    tophilis,
And grant me my request, and then I go.
Thou know'st within the compass of eight
    days
We view'd the face of Heaven, of Earth
    and Hell.
So high our dragons soar'd into the air,
That looking down, the earth appear'd to
    me
No bigger than my hand in quantity.
There did we view the kingdoms of the
    world,
And what might please mine eye, I there
    beheld.
Then in this show let me an actor be,
That this proud Pope may Faustus' cun-
    ning see.

    MEPH: Let it be so, my Faustus, but,
    first stay,
And view their triumphs, as they pass this
    way.
And then devise what best contents thy
    mind
By cunning in thine art to cross the Pope,
Or dash the pride of this solemnity;
To make his monks and abbots stand like
    apes,
And point like antics at his triple crown:
To beat the beads about the friars' pates,
Or clap huge horns upon the Cardinals'
    heads;
Or any villainy thou canst devise,

And I'll perform it, Faustus: Hark! they
    come!
This day shall make thee be admir'd in
    Rome!

(*Enter the* CARDINALS *and* BISHOPS, *some
bearing crosiers, some the pillars,* MONKS
and FRIARS *singing their procession. Then
the* POPE, *and* RAYMOND, KING OF HUNGARY,
with BRUNO *led in chains.*)

POPE: Cast down our footstool.

RAY: Saxon Bruno, stoop,
Whilst on thy back his Holiness ascends
Saint Peter's chair and state pontifical.

BRUNO: Proud Lucifer, that state be-
    longs to me:
But thus I fall to Peter, not to thee!

POPE: To me and Peter shalt thou
    grovelling lie,
And crouch before the papal dignity;
Sound trumpets, then, for thus Saint
    Peter's heir,
From Bruno's back, ascends Saint Peter's
    chair.

(*A flourish while he ascends.*)

Thus, as the gods creep on with feet of
    wool,
Long ere with iron hands they punish
    men,
So shall our sleeping vengeance now arise,
And smite with death thy hated enterprise.
Lord Cardinals of France and Padua,
Go forthwith to our holy Consistory,
And read amongst the Statutes Decretal,
What, by the holy Council held at Trent,
The sacred synod hath decreed for him
That doth assume the Papal government
Without election, and a true consent:
Away, and bring us word with speed!

FIRST CARD: We go, my lord.
                (*Exeunt* CARDINALS.)

POPE: Lord Raymond.

FAUST: Go, haste thee, gentle Mephis-
    tophilis
Follow the cardinals to the consistory;
And as they turn their superstitious books,

Strike them with sloth, and drowsy idle-
    ness
And make them sleep so sound, that in
    their shapes
Thyself and I may parley with this Pope,
This proud confronter of the Emperor!
And in despite of all his holiness
Restore this Bruno to his liberty,
And bear him to the States of Germany.

MEPH: Faustus, I go.

FAUST: Dispatch it soon,
The Pope shall curse that Faustus came
    to Rome.

(*Exeunt* FAUSTUS *and* MEPHISTOPHILIS.)

BRUNO: Pope Adrian, let me have right
    of law,
I was elected by the Emperor.

POPE: We will depose the Emperor for
    that deed,
And curse the people that submit to him;
Both he and thou shalt stand excommuni-
    cate,
And interdict from Church's privilege
And all society of holy men:
He grows too proud in his authority,
Lifting his lofty head above the clouds,
And like a steeple over-peers the Church:
But we'll pull down his haughty insolence.
And as Pope Alexander, our progenitor,
Trod on the neck of German Frederick,
Adding this golden sentence to our praise:
'That Peter's heirs should tread on Em-
    perors,
And walk upon the dreadful adder's back,
Treading the lion and the dragon down,
And fearless spurn the killing basilisk'—
So will we quell that haughty schismatic;
And by authority apostolical
Depose him from his regal government.

BRUNO: Pope Julius swore to princely
    Sigismond,
For him and the succeeding Popes of
    Rome,
To hold the Emperors their lawful lords.

POPE: Pope Julius did abuse the
    Church's rites,

And therefore none of his decrees can
stand.

Is not all power on earth bestowed on us?

And therefore, though we would, we cannot err.

Behold this silver belt, whereto is fix'd

Seven golden keys fast sealed with seven
seals

In token of our sevenfold power from
Heaven,

To bind or loose, lock fast, condemn, or
judge,

Resign, or seal, or whatso pleaseth us.

Then he and thou, and all the world shall
stoop,

Or be assured of our dreadful curse,

To light as heavy as the pains of Hell.

(*Enter* FAUSTUS *and* MEPHISTOPHILIS
like the Cardinals.)

MEPH: Now tell me, Faustus, are we
not fitted well?

FAUST: Yes, Mephistophilis, and two
such Cardinals

Ne'er serv'd a holy Pope as we shall do.

But whilst they sleep within the consistory,

Let us salute his reverend Fatherhood.

RAY: Behold, my Lord, the Cardinals
are return'd.

POPE: Welcome, grave Fathers, answer
presently,

What have our holy Council there decreed,

Concerning Bruno and the Emperor,

In quittance off of their late conspiracy

Against our state and Papal dignity?

FAUST: Most sacred patron of the
Church of Rome

By full consent of all the synod

Of priests and prelates, it is thus decreed:

That Bruno and the German Emperor

Be held as Lollards and bold schismatics

And proud disturbers of the Church's
peace.

And if that Bruno, by his own assent,

Without enforcement of the German peers,

Did seek to wear the triple diadem,

And by your death to climb Saint Peter's
chair,

The Statutes Decretal have thus decreed,

He shall be straight condemn'd of heresy,

And on a pile of fagots burnt to death.

POPE: It is enough: Here, take him to
your charge,

And bear him straight to Ponte Angelo,

And in the strongest tower enclose him
fast;

To-morrow, sitting in our Consistory

With all our college of grave Cardinals,

We will determine of his life or death.

Here, take his triple crown along with
you,

And leave it in the Church's treasury.

Make haste again, my good Lord Cardinals,

And take our blessing apostolical.

MEPH: So, so; was never devil thus
blessed before.

FAUST: Away, sweet Mephistophilis, be
gone,

The Cardinals will be plagu'd for this
anon.

(*Exeunt* FAUSTUS *and* MEPHISTOPHILIS,
with BRUNO.)

POPE: Go presently and bring a banquet
forth,

That we may solemnize Saint Peter's
feast,

And with Lord Raymond, King of Hungary,

Drink to our late and happy victory.

(*Exeunt.*)

SCENE II

(*A Sennet while the banquet is brought
in; and then enter* FAUSTUS *and*
MEPHISTOPHILIS *in their own shapes.*)

MEPH: Now, Faustus, come, prepare
thyself for mirth:

The sleepy Cardinals are hard at hand

To censure Bruno, that is posted hence,
And on a proud-pac'd steed, as swift as
    thought,
Flies o'er the Alps to fruitful Germany,
There to salute the woeful Emperor.

FAUST: The Pope will curse them for
    their sloth to-day,
That slept both Bruno and his crown
    away:
But now, that Faustus may delight his
    mind,
And by their folly make some merriment,
Sweet Mephistophilis, so charm me here,
That I may walk invisible to all,
And do whate'er I please, unseen of any.

MEPH: Faustus, thou shalt, then kneel
    down presently:
Whilst on thy head I lay my hand,
And charm thee with this magic wand.
First wear this girdle, then appear
Invisible to all are here:
The Planets seven, the gloomy air,
Hell and the Furies' forked hair,
Pluto's blue fire, and Hecate's tree,
With magic spells so compass thee,
That no eye may thy body see.
So, Faustus, now for all their holiness,
Do what thou wilt, thou shalt not be
    discern'd.

FAUST: Thanks, Mephistophilis; now,
    friars, take heed,
Lest Faustus make your shaven crowns to
    bleed.

MEPH: Faustus, no more: see where the
    Cardinals come.

(*Enter* POPE *and all the* LORDS. *Enter
the* CARDINALS *with a book.*)

POPE: Welcome, lord cardinals: come,
    sit down.
Lord Raymond, take your seat. Friars,
    attend,
And see that all things be in readiness,
As best beseems this solemn festival.

FIRST CARD: First, may it please your
    sacred Holiness

To view the sentence of the reverend
    synod,
Concerning Bruno and the Emperor?

POPE: What needs this question? Did
    I not tell you,
To-morrow we would sit i' th' consistory,
And there determine of his punishment?
You brought us word even now, it was
    decreed
That Bruno and the cursed Emperor
Were by the holy Council both condemn'd
For loathed Lollards and base schismatics:
Then wherefore would you have me view
    that book?

FIRST CARD: Your Grace mistakes, you
    gave us no such charge.

RAY: Deny it not, we all are witnesses
That Bruno here was late deliver'd you,
With his rich triple crown to be reserv'd
And put into the Church's treasury.

BOTH CARD: By holy Paul, we saw them
    not.

POPE: By Peter, you shall die,
Unless you bring them forth immediately:
Hale them to prison, lade their limbs with
    gyves:
False prelates, for this hateful treachery,
Curs'd be your souls to hellish misery.

(*Exeunt* ATTENDANTS *with the
two* CARDINALS.)

FAUST: So, they are safe: now, Faustus,
    to the feast,
The Pope had never such a frolic guest.

POPE: Lord Archbishop of Rheims, sit
    down with us.

ARCHBISHOP: I thank your Holiness.

FAUST: Fall to, the devil choke you an
    you spare.

POPE: Who's that spoke?—Friars, look
    about.
Lord Raymond, pray fall to. I am behold-
    ing
To the Bishop of Milan for this so rare a
    present.

FAUST: I thank you, sir.
(Snatches the dish.)

POPE: How now? who's that which snatch'd the meat from me?
Villains, why speak you not?—
My good Lord Archbishop, here's a most dainty dish,
Was sent me from a cardinal in France.

FAUST: I'll have that too.
(Snatches the dish.)

POPE: What Lollards do attend our Holiness,
That we receive such great indignity?
Fetch me some wine.

FAUST: Ay, pray do, for Faustus is a-dry.

POPE: Lord Raymond, I drink unto your grace.

FAUST: I pledge your grace.
(Snatches the cup.)

POPE: My wine gone too?—ye lubbers, look about
And find the man that doth this villainy,
Or by our sanctitude, you all shall die.
I pray, my lords, have patience at this
Troublesome banquet.

ARCHBISHOP: Please it your Holiness, I think it be
Some ghost crept out of Purgatory, and now
Is come unto your Holiness for his pardon.

POPE: It may be so:
Go then command our priests to sing a dirge,
To lay the fury of this same troublesome ghost.
(Exit an ATTENDANT.)
Once again, my Lord, fall to. *(The POPE crosseth himself.)*

FAUST: How now?
Must every bit be spiced with a cross?
Nay then, take that.   *(Strikes the POPE.)*

POPE: O I am slain, help me, my lords;
O come and help to bear my body hence:—

Damn'd be his soul for ever for this deed!
(Exeunt the POPE and his train.)

MEPH: Now, Faustus, what will you do now, for I can tell you you'll be curs'd with bell, book, and candle.

FAUST: Bell, book and candle,—candle, book, and bell,—
Forward and backward, to curse Faustus to Hell!

(Enter the FRIARS with bell, book and candle for the Dirge.)

FIRST FRIAR: Come, brethren, let's about our business with good devotion.
Sing this.
Cursed be he that stole his Holiness' meat from the table!
Maledicat Dominus!
Cursed be he that struck his Holiness a blow on the face!
Maledicat Dominus!
Cursed be he that took Friar Sandelo a blow on the pate!
Maledicat Dominus!
Cursed be he that disturbeth our holy dirge!
Maledicat Dominus!
Cursed be he that took away his Holiness' wine!
Maledicat Dominus!
Et omnes Sancti! Amen!

(MEPHISTOPHILIS and FAUSTUS beat the FRIARS, fling fireworks among them; and exeunt.)

SCENE III

A Street, near an Inn.

(Enter ROBIN and DICK, with a Cup.)

DICK: Sirrah Robin, we were best look that your devil can answer the stealing of this same cup, for the vintner's boy follows us at the hard heels.

ROBIN: 'Tis no matter! let him come; an he follow us I'll so conjure him as he was never conjured in his life. I warrant him. Let me see the cup.

(*Enter* VINTNER.)

DICK: Here 'tis. Yonder he comes. Now, Robin, now or never show thy cunning.

VINT: O are you here? I am glad I have found you, you are a couple of fine companions; pray, where's the cup you stole from the tavern?

ROBIN: How, how? we steal a cup? Take heed what you say; we look not like cup-stealers, I can tell you.

VINT: Never deny 't, for I know you have it, and I'll search you.

ROBIN: Search me? Ay, and spare not. Hold the cup, Dick (*aside to* DICK). Come, come, search me, search me!

(VINTNER *searches him.*)

VINT (*to* DICK): Come on, sirrah, let me search you now!

DICK: Ay, ay, do! Hold the cup, Robin (*aside to* ROBIN). I fear not your searching; we scorn to steal your cups, I can tell you.

(VINTNER *searches him.*)

VINT: Never outface me for the matter, for, sure, the cup is between you two.

ROBIN: Nay, there you lie, 'tis beyond us both.

VINT: A plague take you! I thought 't was your knavery to take it away; come, give it me again.

ROBIN: Ay much; when? can you tell? Dick, make me a circle, and stand close at my back, and stir not for thy life. Vintner, you shall have your cup anon. Say nothing, Dick. (*Reads.*) O per se, o Demogorgon, Belcher and Mesphistophilis!

(*Enter* MEPHISTOPHILIS.)

MEPH: You princely legions of infernal rule,
How am I vexed by these villain's charms!

From Constantinople have they brought me now
Only for pleasure of these damned slaves.

(*Exit* VINTNER.)

ROBIN: By Lady, sir, you have had a shrewd journey of it. Will it please you to take a shoulder of mutton to supper, and a tester in your purse, and go back again?

DICK: Aye. I pray you heartily, sir, for we call'd you but in jest, I promise you.

MEPH: To purge the rashness of this cursed deed,
First be thou turned to this ugly shape,
For apish deeds transformed to an ape.

ROBIN: O brave; an Ape! I pray, sir, let me have the carrying of him about to show some tricks.

MEPH: And so thou shalt: be thou transformed to a dog,
And carry him upon thy back. Away, be gone!

ROBIN: A dog! that's excellent; let the maids look well to their porridge-pots, for I'll into the kitchen presently. Come, Dick, come.   (*Exeunt the* TWO CLOWNS.)

MEPH: Now with the flames of everburning fire,
I'll wing myself, and forthwith fly amain
Unto my Faustus, to the Great Turk's Court.   (*Exit.*)

ACT IV

(*Enter* CHORUS.)

CHOR: When Faustus had with pleasure ta'en the view
Of rarest things, and royal courts of kings,
He stay'd his course, and so returned home;
Where such as bear his absence but with grief,
I mean his friends and near'st companions,

Did gratulate his safety with kind words,
And in their conference of what befell,
Touching his journey through the world
    and air,
They put forth questions of astrology,
Which Faustus answer'd with such learned
    skill
As they admir'd and wonder'd at his wit.
Now is his fame spread forth in every
    land:
Amongst the rest the Emperor is one,
Carolus the Fifth at whose palace now
Faustus is feasted 'mongst his noblemen.
What there he did, in trial of his art,
I leave untold; your eyes shall see per-
    form'd.   (*Exit.*)

SCENE I

*A room in the Emperor's Court
at Innsbruck.*

(*Enter* MARTINO, *and* FREDERICK
at several doors.)

MART: What ho, officers, gentlemen,
Hie to the presence to attend the Emperor,
Good Frederick, see the rooms be voided
    straight,
His Majesty is coming to the hall;
Go back, and see the state in readiness.

FRED: But where is Bruno, our elected
    Pope,
That on a fury's back came post from
    Rome?
Will not his Grace consort the Emperor?

MART: O yes, and with him comes the
    German conjurer,
The learned Faustus, fame of Wittenberg,
The wonder of the world for magic art;
And he intends to show great Carolus
The race of all his stout progenitors;
And bring in presence of his Majesty
The royal shapes and warlike semblances
Of Alexander and his beauteous paramour.

FRED: Where is Benvolio?

MART: Fast asleep, I warrant you,
He took his rouse with stoups of Rhenish
    wine
So kindly yesternight to Bruno's health,
That all this day the sluggard keeps his
    bed.

FRED: See, see, his window's ope, we'll
    call to him.

MART: What ho, Benvolio!

(*Enter* BENVOLIO *above, at a window,
in his night-cap; buttoning.*)

BENV: What a devil ail you two?

MART: Speak softly, sir, lest the devil
    hear you:
For Faustus at the court is late arriv'd,
And at his heels a thousand furies wait,
To accomplish whatsoever the doctor
    please,

BENV: What of this?

MART: Come, leave thy chamber first,
    and thou shalt see
This conjuror perform such rare exploits,
Before the Pope and royal Emperor,
As never yet was seen in Germany.

BENV: Has not the Pope enough of con-
    juring yet?
He was upon the Devil's back late enough;
And if he be so far in love with him,
I would he would post with him to Rome
    again.

FRED: Speak, wilt thou come and see
    this sport?

BENV: Not I.

MART: Wilt thou stand in thy window,
    and see it then?

BENV: Ay, an I fall not asleep i' th'
    meantime.

MART: The Emperor is at hand, who
    comes to see
What wonders by black spells may com-
    pass'd be.

BENV: Well, go you attend the Emperor: I am content for this once to thrust
my head out at a window; for they say, if

a man be drunk overnight the Devil cannot hurt him in the morning; if that be true, I have a charm in my head shall control him as well as the conjuror, I warrant you.

(*Exeunt* FREDERICK *and* MARTINO.)

SCENE II

The Presence-Chamber in the Court.

(*A Sennet. Enter* CHARLES, *the* GERMAN EMPEROR, BRUNO, DUKE OF SAXONY, FAUSTUS, MEPHISTOPHILIS, FREDERICK, MARTINO, *and* ATTENDANTS.)

EMP: Wonder of men, renown'd magician,
Thrice-learned Faustus, welcome to our Court.
This deed of thine, in setting Bruno free
From his and our professed enemy,
Shall add more excellence unto thine art,
Than if by powerful necromantic spells,
Thou couldst command the world's obedience:
For ever be belov'd of Carolus,
And if this Bruno thou hast late redeem'd,
In peace possess the triple diadem,
And sit in Peter's chair, despite of chance,
Thou shalt be famous through all Italy,
And honour'd of the German Emperor.

FAUST: These gracious words, most royal Carolus,
Shall make poor Faustus, to his utmost power,
Both love and serve the German Emperor,
And lay his life at holy Bruno's feet.
For proof whereof, if so your Grace be pleas'd,
The doctor stands prepar'd by power of art
To cast his magic charms, that shall pierce through
The ebon gates of ever-burning Hell,
And hale the stubborn Furies from their caves,
To compass whatsoe'er your Grace commands.

BENV (*above*): 'Blood, he speaks terribly: but for all that I do not greatly believe him: he looks as like a conjuror as the Pope to a costermonger.

EMP: Then, Faustus, as thou late did'st promise us,
We would behold that famous conqueror,
Great Alexander and his paramour
In their true shapes and state majestical,
That we may wonder at their excellence.

FAUST: Your Majesty shall see them presently.
Mephistophilis, away.
And with a solemn noise of trumpets' sound
Present before this royal Emperor,
Great Alexander and his beauteous paramour.

MEPH: Faustus, I will.

BENV: Well, master doctor, and your devils come not away quickly, you shall have me asleep presently: zounds, I could eat myself for anger, to think I have been such an ass all this while to stand gaping after the devil's governor, and can see nothing.

FAUST: I'll make you feel something anon, if my art fail me not.—
My lord, I must forewarn your Majesty,
That when my spirits present the royal shapes
Of Alexander and his paramour,
Your Grace demand no questions of the king,
But in dumb silence let them come and go.

EMP: Be it as Faustus please, we are content.

BENV: Ay, ay, and I am content too; and thou bring Alexander and his paramour before the Emperor, I'll be Acteon and turn myself to a stag.

FAUST: And I'll play Diana, and send you the horns presently.

(*Sennet. Enter at one door the* EMPEROR ALEXANDER, *at the other* DARIUS; *they meet,* DARIUS *is thrown down,* ALEXANDER *kills him; takes off his crown and offering to go out, his paramour meets him, he embraceth her, and sets* DARIUS' *crown upon her head; and coming back, both salute the* EMPEROR, *who leaving his state, offers to embrace them, which,* FAUSTUS *seeing, suddenly stays him. Then trumpets cease, and music sounds.*)

My gracious lord, you do forget yourself,
These are but shadows, not substantial.

EMP: O pardon me, my thoughts are
        so ravished
With sight of this renowned Emperor,
That in mine arms I would have com-
        pass'd him.
But, Faustus, since I may not speak to
        them,
To satisfy my longing thoughts at full,
Let me this tell thee: I have heard it said,
That this fair lady whilst she liv'd on
        earth,
Had on her neck, a little wart, or mole;
How may I prove that saying to be true?

FAUST: Your Majesty may boldly go and
        see.

EMP: Faustus, I see it plain,
And in this sight thou better pleasest me,
Than if I gain'd another monarchy.

FAUST: Away, be gone!   (*Exit show.*)
See, see, my gracious lord, what strange
        beast is yon, that thrusts his head
        out at window?

EMP: O wondrous sight: see, Duke of
        Saxony,
Two spreading horns most strangely
        fastened
Upon the head of young Benvolio.

SAX: What, is he asleep, or dead?

FAUST: He sleeps, my lord, but dreams
        not of his horns.

EMP: This sport is excellent; we'll call
        and wake him.
What ho, Benvolio.

BENV: A plague upon you, let me sleep
a while.

EMP: I blame thee not to sleep much,
having such a head of thine own.

SAX: Look up, Benvolio, 'tis the Emperor calls.

BENV: The Emperor? where?—O
zounds, my head!

EMP: Nay, and thy horns hold, 'tis no
matter for thy head, for that's arm'd sufficiently.

FAUST: Why, how now, Sir Knight,
what, hang'd by the horns? this is most
horrible: fie, fie, pull in your head for
shame, let not all the world wonder at
you.

BENV: Zounds, Doctor, is this your villainy?

FAUST: O say not so, sir: the Doctor has
        no skill,
No art, no cunning, to present these lords,
Or bring before this royal Emperor
The mighty monarch, warlike Alexander.
If Faustus do it, you are straight resolv'd
In bold Acteon's shape to turn a stag.
And therefore, my lord, so please your
        Majesty,
I'll raise a kennel of hounds, shall hunt
        him so,
As all his footmanship shall scarce prevail
To keep his carcase from their bloody
        fangs.
Ho, Belimote, Argiron, Asterote.

BENV: Hold, hold! Zounds, he'll raise
up a kennel of devils, I think, anon: good,
my lord, entreat for me: 'sblood, I am
never able to endure these torments.

EMP: Then, good master doctor,
Let me entreat you to remove his horns,
He has done penance now sufficiently.

FAUST: My gracious lord, not so much
for injury done to me, as to delight your
Majesty with some mirth, hath Faustus
justly requited this injurious knight, which
being all I desire, I am content to remove
his horns. Mephistophilis, transform him

(MEPHISTOPHILIS *removes the horns*), and hereafter, sir, look you speak well of scholars.

BENV: Speak well of ye? 'sblood, and scholars be such cuckold-makers to clap horns of honest men's heads o' this order, I'll ne'er trust smooth faces and small ruffs, more. But an I be not reveng'd for this, would I might be turn'd to a gaping oyster, and drink nothing but salt water.

(*Aside, and then exit above.*)

EMP: Come, Faustus, while the Emperor lives,
In recompense of this thy high desert,
Thou shalt command the state of Germany,
And live belov'd of mighty Carolus.

(*Exeunt omnes.*)

Scene III

Near a grove, outside Innsbruck.

(*Enter* BENVOLIO, MARTINO, FREDERICK, *and* SOLDIERS.)

MART: Nay, sweet Benvolio, let us sway thy thoughts
From this attempt against the conjuror.

BENV: Away, you love me not, to urge me thus.
Shall I let slip so great an injury,
When every servile groom jests at my wrongs,
And in their rustic gambols proudly say,
'Benvolio's head was graced with horns to-day'?
O may these eyelids never close again,
Till with my sword I have that conjurer slain.
If you will aid me in this enterprise,
Then draw your weapons, and be resolute:
If not, depart: here will Benvolio die,
But Faustus' death shall quit my infamy.

FRED: Nay, we will stay with thee, betide what may,
And kill that doctor if he come this way.

BENV: Then, gentle Frederick, hie thee to the grove,
And place our servants and our followers
Close in an ambush there behind the trees.
By this (I know) the conjurer is near;
I saw him kneel and kiss the Emperor's hand,
And take his leave laden with rich rewards.
Then, soldiers, boldly fight; if Faustus die,
Take you the wealth, leave us the victory.

FRED: Come, soldiers, follow me unto the grove;
Who kills him shall have gold and endless love.

(*Exit* FREDERICK *with the* SOLDIERS.)

BENV: My head is lighter than it was by th' horns,
But yet my heart's more ponderous than my head,
And pants until I see that conjurer dead.

MART: Where shall we place ourselves, Benvolio?

BENV: Here will we stay to bide the first assault.
O were that damned hell-hound but in place,
Thou soon shouldst see me quit my foul disgrace.

(*Enter* FREDERICK.)

FRED: Close, close, the conjurer is at hand,
And all alone comes walking in his gown;
Be ready then, and strike the peasant down.

BENV: Mine be that honour then: now, sword, strike home,
For horns he gave I'll have his head anon.

(*Enter* FAUSTUS *with the false head.*)

MART: See, see, he comes.

BENV: No words: this blow ends all,
Hell take his soul, his body thus must fall.

(*Stabs* FAUSTUS.)

FAUST (*falling*): Oh!

FRED: Groan you, master doctor?

BENV: Break may his heart with groans:
dear Frederick, see,
Thus will I end his griefs immediately.

MART: Strike with a willing hand.
(BENVOLIO *strikes off* FAUSTUS' *false head.*)
His head is off.

BENV: The devil's dead, the furies now
may laugh.

FRED: Was this that stern aspect, that
awful frown,
Made the grim monarch of internal spirits
Tremble and quake at his commanding
charms?

MART: Was this that damned head,
whose art conspir'd
Benvolio's shame before the Emperor?

BENV: Ay, that's the head, and here
the body lies,
Justly rewarded for his villainies.

FRED: Come, let's devise how we may
add more shame
To the black scandal of his hated name.

BENV: First, on his head, in quittance
of my wrongs,
I'll nail huge forked horns, and let them
hang
Within the window where he yok'd me
first,
That all the world may see my just revenge.

MART: What use shall we put his beard
to?

BENV: We'll sell it to a chimney-
sweeper; it will wear out ten birchen
brooms, I warrant you.

FRED: What shall his eyes do?

BENV: We'll put out his eyes, and they
shall serve for buttons to his lips, to keep
his tongue from catching cold.

MART: An excellent policy: and now,
sirs, having divided him, what shall the
body do?   (FAUSTUS *rises.*)

BENV: Zounds, the devil's alive again.

FRED: Give him his head, for God's
sake.

FAUST: Nay, keep it: Faustus will have
heads and hands,
Ay, all your hearts to recompense this
deed.
Knew you not, traitors, I was limited
For four-and-twenty years to breathe on
earth?
And had you cut my body with your
swords,
Or hew'd this flesh and bones as small as
sand,
Yet in a minute had my spirit return'd,
And I had breath'd a man made free
from harm.
But wherefore do I dally my revenge?
Asteroth, Belimoth, Mephistophilis,

(*Enter* MEPHISTOPHILIS *and other* DEVILS.)

Go, horse these traitors on your fiery
backs,
And mount aloft with them as high as
heaven,
Thence pitch them headlong to the lowest
hell:
Yet, stay, the world shall see their misery,
And Hell shall after plague their treachery.
Go, Belimoth, and take this caitiff hence,
And hurl him in some lake of mud and
dirt:
Take thou this other, drag him through
the woods,
Amongst the pricking thorns, and sharp-
est briers,
Whilst with my gently Mephistophilis,
This traitor flies unto some steepy rock.
That, rolling down, may break the vil-
lain's bones,
As he intended to dismember me.
Fly hence, despatch my charge immedi-
ately.

FRED: Pity us, gentle Faustus, save our
lives!

FAUST: Away!

FRED: He must needs go that the Devil
drives.

(*Exeunt* SPIRITS *with the* KNIGHTS.)

(*Enter the ambushed* SOLDIERS.)

FIRST SOLD: Come, sirs, prepare your-
selves in readiness,
Make haste to help these noble gentlemen,
I heard them parley with the conjurer.

SEC. SOLD: See where he comes, dispatch,
and kill the slave.

FAUST: What's here? an ambush to
betray my life:
Then, Faustus, try thy skill: base peasants,
stand:
For lo! these trees remove at my com-
mand,
And stand as bulwarks 'twixt yourselves
and me,
To shield me from your hated treachery:
Yet to encounter this your weak attempt,
Behold an army comes incontinent.

(FAUSTUS *strikes the door, and enter a
devil playing on a drum, after him another bearing an ensign; and divers with
weapons,* MEPHISTOPHILIS *with fireworks;
they set upon the* SOLDIERS, *and drive them
out. Exit* FAUSTUS.)

SCENE IV

(*Enter at several doors* BENVOLIO, FRED-
ERICK, *and* MARTINO, *their heads and
faces bloody, and besmear'd with mud
and dirt, all having horns on their heads.*)

MART: What ho, Benvolio!

BENV: Here, what, Frederick, ho!

FRED: O help me, gentle friend; where
is Martino?

MART: Dear Frederick, here,
Half smother'd in a lake of mud and dirt,
Through which the furies dragg'd me by
the heels.

FRED: Martino, see Benvolio's horns
again.

MART: O misery, how now, Benvolio?

BENV: Defend me, heaven, shall I be
haunted still?

MART: Nay, fear not, man; we have no
power to kill.

BENV: My friends transformed thus! O
hellish spite,
Your heads are all set with horns.

FRED: You hit it right:
It is your own you mean, feel on your
head.

BENV: 'Zounds, horns again!

MART: Nay, chafe not, man, we all
are sped.

BENV: What devil attends this damn'd
magician,
That, spite of spite, our wrongs are doubled?

FRED: What may we do, that we may
hide our shames?

BENV: If we should follow him to work
revenge,
He'd join long asses' ears to these huge
horns,
And make us laughing-stocks to all the
world.

MART: What shall we then do, dear
Benvolio?

BENV: I have a castle joining near these
woods,
And thither we'll repair and live obscure,
Till time shall alter these our brutish
shapes:
Sith black disgrace hath thus eclips'd our
fame,
We'll rather die with grief than live with
shame.   (*Exeunt omnes.*)

SCENE V

At the entrance to the house of Faustus.

(*Enter* FAUSTUS *and the* HORSE-COURSER.)

HORSE-C: I beseech your worship, accept
of these forty dollars.

FAUST: Friend, thou canst not buy so
good a horse, for so small a price. I have
no great need to sell him, but if thou
likest him for ten dollars more take him,
because I see thou hast a good mind to
him.

HORSE-C: I beseech you, sir, accept of this; I am a very poor man and have lost very much of late by horse-flesh, and this bargain will set me up again.

FAUST: Well, I will not stand with thee, give me the money. (HORSE-COURSER *gives* FAUSTUS *the money*.) Now, sirrah, I must tell you that you may ride him o'er hedge and ditch, and spare him not; but, do you hear? in any case ride him not into the water.

HORSE-C: How, sir, not into the water? Why, will he not drink of all waters?

FAUST: Yes, he will drink of all waters, but ride him not into the water; o'er hedge and ditch, or where thou wilt, but not into the water. Go, bid the hostler deliver him unto you, and remember what I say.

HORSE-C: I warrant you, sir. O joyful day, now am I a made man for ever.
(*Exit.*)

FAUST: What art thou, Faustus, but a
    man condemn'd to die?
Thy fatal time draws to a final end,
Despair doth drive distrust into my
    thoughts.
Confound these passions with a quiet
    sleep.
Tush! Christ did call the thief upon the
    Cross;
Then rest thee, Faustus, quiet in conceit.
(*He sits to sleep.*)

(*Re-enter the* HORSE-COURSER *wet.*)

HORSE-C: O what a cozening doctor was this? I was riding my horse into the water, thinking some hidden mystery had been in the horse, I had nothing under me but a little straw, and had much ado to escape drowning. Well, I'll go rouse him, and make him give me my forty dollars again. Ho, sirrah Doctor, you cozening scab! Master doctor, awake and rise, and give me my money again, for your horse is turned to a bottle of hay,

master doctor (*He pulls off his leg.*) Alas! I am undone, what shall I do? I have pull'd off his leg.

FAUST: O, help, help, the villain hath murder'd me.

HORSE-C: Murder, or not murder, now he has but one leg, I'll outrun him, and cast this leg into some ditch or other. (*Aside, and then runs out.*)

FAUST: Stop him, stop him, stop him!— ha, ha, ha, Faustus hath his leg again, and the horse-courser a bundle of hay for his forty dollars.

(*Enter* WAGNER.)

How now, Wagner, what news with thee?

WAGNER: If it please you, the Duke of Anholt doth earnestly entreat your company, and hath sent some of his men to attend you with provision fit for your journey.

FAUST: The Duke of Anholt's an honourable gentleman, and one to whom I must be no niggard of my cunning. Come away! (*Exeunt.*)

SCENE VI

An Inn.

(*Enter* ROBIN, DICK, *the* HORSE-COURSER, *and a* CARTER.)

CART: Come, my masters, I'll bring you to the best beer in Europe. What ho, hostess!—where be these whores?

(*Enter* HOSTESS.)

HOST: How now, what lack you? What, my old guests, welcome.

ROBIN: Sirra Dick, dost thou know why I stand so mute?

DICK: No, Robin, why is't?

ROBIN: I am eighteen pence on the score, but say nothing, see if she have forgotten me.

HOST: Who's this, that stands so solemnly by himself? what, my old guest?

ROBIN: O hostess, how do you? I hope my score stands still.

HOST: Ay, there's no doubt of that, for methinks you make no haste to wipe it out.

DICK: Why, hostess, I say, fetch us some beer.

HOST: You shall presently: look up in th' hall there, ho!   (*Exit.*)

DICK: Come, sirs, what shall we do now till mine hostess comes?

CART: Marry, sir, I'll tell you the bravest tale how a conjuror served me; you know Doctor Fauster?

HORSE-C: Ay, a plague take him, here's some on's have cause to know him; did he conjure thee too?

CART: I'll tell you how he serv'd me: As I was going to Wittenberg t'other day, with a load of hay, he met me, and asked me what he should give me for as much hay as he could eat; now, sir, I thinking that a little would serve his turn, bade him take as much as he would for three farthings; so he presently gave me my money, and fell to eating; and, as I am a cursen man, he never left eating, till he had eat up all my load of hay.

ALL: O monstrous, eat a whole load of hay!

ROBIN: Yes, yes, that may be; for I have heard of one that has eat a load of logs.

HORSE-C: Now, sirs, you shall hear how villainously he serv'd me: I went to him yesterday to buy a horse of him, and he would by no means sell him under forty dollars; so, sir, because I knew him to be such a horse as would run over hedge and ditch and never tire, I gave him his money. So when I had my horse, Doctor Fauster bade me ride him night and day, and spare him no time; but, quoth he, in any case, ride him not into the water. Now, sir, I thinking the horse had had some rare quality that he would not have me know of, what did I but rid him into a great river, and when I came just in the midst, my horse vanish'd away, and I sat straddling upon a bottle of hay.

ALL: O brave doctor!

HORSE-C: But you shall hear how bravely I serv'd him for it; I went me home to his house, and there I found him asleep; I kept a hallooing and whooping in his ears, but all could not wake him: I seeing that, took him by the leg, and never rested pulling, till I had pull'd me his leg quite off, and now 'tis at home in mine hostry.

DICK: And has the Doctor but one leg then? that's excellent, for one of his devils turn'd me into the likeness of an ape's face.

CART: Some more drink, hostess.

ROBIN: Hark you, we'll into another room and drink a while, and then we'll go seek out the Doctor. (*Exeunt omnes.*)

SCENE VII

The Court of the DUKE OF ANHOLT.

(*Enter the* DUKE OF ANHOLT, *his* DUCHESS, FAUSTUS, *and* MEPHISTOPHILIS.)

DUKE: Thanks, master doctor, for these pleasant sights. Nor know I how sufficiently to recompense your great deserts in erecting that enchanted castle in the air, the sight whereof so delighted me, As nothing in the world could please me more.

FAUST: I do think myself, my good Lord, highly recompensed in that it pleaseth your Grace to think but well of that which Faustus hath performed. But gracious lady, it may be that you have taken no pleasure in those sights; therefore, I pray you tell me, what is the thing you most desire to have; be it in the world, it shall be yours. I have heard that great-bellied women do long for things are rare and dainty.

DUCH: True, master Doctor, and since I find you so kind, I will make known unto you what my heart desires to have; and were it now summer, as it is January, a dead time of the winter, I would request no better meat than a dish of ripe grapes.

FAUST: This is but a small matter. Go, Mephistophilis, away!

(Exit MEPHISTOPHILIS.)

Madam, I will do more than this for your content.

(Enter MEPHISTOPHILIS *again with the grapes.)*

Here now taste ye these, they should be good,
For they come from a far country, I can tell you.

DUKE: This makes me wonder more than all the rest
That at this time of the year, when every tree
Is barren of his fruit, from whence you had
These ripe grapes.

FAUST: Please it your Grace the year is divided into two circles over the whole world, so that when it is winter with us, in the contrary circle it is likewise summer with them, as in India, Saba and such countries that lie far east, where they have fruit twice a year. From whence, by means of a swift spirit that I have, I had these grapes brought, as you see.

DUCH: And trust me, they are the sweetest grapes that e'er I tasted.

(The CLOWNS *bounce at the gate within.)*

DUKE: What rude disturbers have we at the gate?
Go, pacify their fury, set it ope,
And then demand of them what they would have.

(They knock again, and call out to talk with FAUSTUS.)*

A SERVANT: Why, how now, masters, what a coil is there?
What is the reason you disturb the Duke?

DICK: We have no reason for it, therefore a fig for him.

SERV: Why, saucy varlets, dare you be so bold?

HORSE-C: I hope, sir, we have wit enough to be more bold than welcome.

SERV: It appears so, pray be bold elsewhere, and trouble not the Duke.

DUKE: What would they have?

SERV: They all cry out to speak with Doctor Faustus.

CART: Ay, and we will speak with him.

DUKE: Will you, sir? Commit the rascals.

DICK: Commit with us! he were as good commit with his father as commit with us.

FAUST: I do beseech your Grace let them come in,
They are good subjects for a merriment.

DUKE: Do as thou wilt, Faustus, I give thee leave.

FAUST: I thank your Grace.

(Enter ROBIN, DICK, CARTER, *and* HORSE-COURSER.)*

Why, how now, my good friends?
'Faith you are too outrageous, but come near,
I have procur'd your pardons: welcome all.

ROBIN: Nay, sir, we will be welcome for our money, and we will pay for what we take. What ho, give's half a dozen of beer here, and be hang'd.

FAUST: Nay, hark you, can you tell me where you are?

CART: Ay, marry can I; we are under Heaven.

SERV: Ay, but, Sir Sauce-Box, know you in what place?

HORSE-C: Ay, ay, the house is good enough to drink in: Zounds, fill us some beer, or we'll break all the barrels in the house, and dash out all your brains with your bottles.

FAUST: Be not so furious: come, you shall have beer.
My lord, beseech you give me leave a while,
I'll gage my credit, 'twill content your Grace.

DUKE: With all my heart, kind doctor, please thyself;
Our servants and our court's at thy command.

FAUST: I humbly thank your Grace: then fetch some beer.

HORSE-C: Ay, marry, there spake a doctor indeed, and, 'faith, I'll drink a health to thy wooden leg for that word.

FAUST: My wooden leg! what dost thou mean by that?

CART: Ha, ha, ha, dost hear him, Dick? He has forgot his leg.

HORSE-C: Ay, ay, he does not stand much upon that.

FAUST: No, 'faith not much upon a wooden leg.

CART: Good Lord, that flesh and blood should be so frail with your worship! Do not you remember a horse-courser you sold a horse to?

FAUST: Yes, I remember I sold one a horse.

CART: And do you remember you bid he should not ride him into the water?

FAUST: Yes, I do very well remember that.

CART: And do you remember nothing of your leg?

FAUST: No, in good sooth.

CART: Then, I pray, remember your curtsy.

FAUST: I thank you, sir.

CART: 'Tis not so much worth; I pray you tell me one thing.

FAUST: What's that?

CART: Be both your legs bedfellows every night together?

FAUST: Wouldst thou make a colossus of me, that thou askest me such questions?

CART: No, truly, sir: I would make nothing of you, but I would fain know that.

(*Enter* HOSTESS *with drink.*)

FAUST: Then I assure thee certainly they are.

CART: I thank you, I am fully satisfied.

FAUST: But wherefore dost thou ask?

CART: For nothing, sir: but methinks you should have a wooden bedfellow of one of 'em.

HORSE-C: Why, do you hear, sir, did not I pull off one of your legs when you were asleep?

FAUST: But I have it again, now I am awake: look you here, sir.

ALL: O horrible, had the doctor three legs?

CART: Do you remember, sir, how you cozened me and ate up my load of——
        (FAUSTUS *charms him dumb.*)

DICK: Do you remember how you made me wear an ape's——

HORSE-C: You whoreson conjuring scab, do you remember how you cozened me of a ho——

ROBIN: Ha' you forgotten me? you think to carry it away with your *hey-pass* and *re-pass*; do you remember the dog's fa——   (*Exeunt* CLOWNS.)

HOST: Who pays for the ale? Hear you, master doctor, now you have sent away my guests, I pray who shall pay me for my a——   (*Exit* HOSTESS.)

LADY: My lord,
We are much beholding to this learned
man.

DUKE: So are we, Madam, which we
will recompense
With all the love and kindness that we
may.
His artful sport drives all sad thoughts
away.   (*Exeunt.*)

ACT V
SCENE I

(*Thunder and lightning. Enter* DEVILS
with cover'd dishes. MEPHISTOPHILIS *leads
them into* FAUSTUS' *study. Then enter*
WAGNER.)

WAG: I think my master means to die
shortly,
He has made his will, and given me his
wealth,
His house, his goods, and store of golden
plate,
Besides two thousand ducats ready coin'd.
I wonder what he means; if death were
nigh
He would not frolic thus. He's now at
supper
With the scholars, where there's such
belly-cheer
As Wagner in his life ne'er saw the like.
And see where they come, belike the feast
is done.   (*Exit.*)

(*Enter* FAUSTUS, MEPHISTOPHILIS, *and two
or three* SCHOLARS.)

1 SCHOL: Master Doctor Faustus, since
our conference about fair ladies, which
was the beautifulest in all the world, we
have determined with ourselves that Helen
of Greece was the admirablest lady that
ever liv'd: therefore, master doctor, if you
will do us so much favor, as to let us see
that peerless dame of Greece, we should
think ourselves much beholding unto you.

FAUST: Gentlemen,
For that I know your friendship is un-
feign'd,
It is not Faustus' custom to deny
The just request of those that wish him
well,
You shall behold that peerless dame of
Greece,
No otherwise for pomp or majesty
Than when Sir Paris cross'd the seas with
her,
And brought the spoil to rich Dardania.
Be silent, then, for danger is in words.

(*Music sound,* MEPHISTOPHILIS *brings in*
HELEN, *she passeth over the stage.*)

2 SCHOL: Was this fair Helen, whose
admir'd worth
Made Greece with ten years' wars afflict
poor Troy?

3 SCHOL: Too simple is my wit to tell
her praise,
Whom all the world admires for majesty.

1 SCHOL: Now we have seen the pride
. of nature's work,
We'll take our leaves; and for this glorious deed
Happy and blest be Faustus evermore!

FAUST: Gentlemen, farewell: the same
I wish to you.
                        (*Exeunt* SCHOLARS.)

(*Enter an* OLD MAN.)

OLD MAN: O gentle Faustus, leave this
damned art,
This magic, that will charm thy soul to
hell,
And quite bereave thee of salvation.
Though thou hast now offended like a
man,
Do not persever in it like a devil;
Yet, yet, thou hast an amiable soul,
If sin by custom grow not into nature:
Then, Faustus, will repentance come too
late,
Then thou art banish'd from the sight of
Heaven;

No mortal can express the pains of Hell.
It may be this my exhortation
Seems harsh and all unpleasant; let it not,
For, gentle son, I speak it not in wrath,
Or envy of thee, but in tender love,
And pity of thy future misery.
And so have hope, that this my kind
    rebuke,
Checking thy body, may amend thy soul.

    FAUST: Where art thou, Faustus?
    wretch, what hast thou done?
Hell claims his right, and with a roaring
    voice
Says, 'Faustus, come; thine hour is almost
    come';
And Faustus now will come to do thee
    right.

    OLD MAN: Oh, stay, good Faustus, stay
    thy desperate steps!
I see an angel hover o'er thy head,
And, with a vial full of precious grace,
Offers to pour the same into thy soul:
Then call for mercy, and avoid despair.

    FAUST: O friend, I feel
Thy words to comfort my distressed soul!
Leave me a while to ponder on my sins.

    OLD MAN: Faustus, I leave thee; but
    with grief of heart,
Fearing the enemy of thy hapless soul.
                 (*Exit.*)

    FAUST: Accursed Faustus, wretch, what
    hast thou done!
I do repent; and yet I do despair:
Hell strives with grace for conquest in my
    breast:
What shall I do to shun the snares of
    death?

    MEPH: Thou traitor, Faustus, I arrest
    thy soul
For disobedience to my sovereign lord:
Revolt, or I'll in piecemeal tear thy flesh.

    FAUST: I do repent I e'er offended him.
Sweet Mephistophilis, entreat thy lord
To pardon my unjust presumption,
And with my blood again I will confirm
The former vow I made to Lucifer.

    MEPH: Do it, then, Faustus, with un-
    feigned heart,
Lest greater dangers do attend thy drift.

(FAUSTUS *stabs his arm, and writes on a*
    paper with his blood.)

    FAUST: Torment, sweet friend, that base
    and aged man.
That durst dissuade me from thy Lucifer,
With greatest torments that our Hell
    affords.

    MEPH: His faith is great; I cannot
    touch his soul;
But what I may afflict his body with
I will attempt, which is but little worth.

    FAUST: One thing, good servant, let me
    crave of thee,
To glut the longing of my heart's desire,—
That I may have unto my paramour
That heavenly Helen which I saw of late,
Whose sweet embraces may extinguish
    clean
Those thoughts that do dissuade me from
    my vow,
And keep the oath I made to Lucifer.

    MEPH: This, or what else, my Faustus
    shall desire,
Shall be perform'd in twinkling of an eye.

(*Enter* HELEN *again, passing over the stage*
    between two CUPIDS.)

    FAUST: Was this the face that launch'd
    a thousand ships,
And burnt the topless towers of Ilium?—
Sweet Helen, make me immortal with a
    kiss.—   (*She kisses him.*)
Her lips suck forth my soul: see where it
    flies!—
Come, Helen, come, give me my soul
    again.
Here will I dwell, for Heaven is in these
    lips,
And all is dross that is not Helena.
            (*Enter* OLD MAN.)
I will be Paris, and for love of thee,
Instead of Troy, shall Wittenberg be
    sack'd;

And I will combat with weak Menelaus,
And wear thy colours on my plumed
   crest:
Yea, I will wound Achilles in the heel,
And then return to Helen for a kiss.
O, thou art fairer than the evening's air
Clad in the beauty of a thousand stars;
Brighter art thou than flaming Jupiter
When he appear'd to hapless Semele;
More lovely than the monarch of the sky
In wanton Arethusa's azured arms;
And none but thou shalt be my paramour!

(*Exeunt* FAUSTUS, HELEN *and* CUPIDS.)

SCENE II

FAUSTUS's *Study.*

(*Thunder. Enter above* LUCIFER, BELZE-
BUB, *and* MEPHISTOPHILIS.)

LUC: Thus from infernal Dis do we
   ascend
To view the subjects of our monarchy,
Those souls which sin seals the black sons
   of Hell,
'Mong which as chief, Faustus, we come
   to thee,
Bringing with us lasting damnation
To wait upon thy soul; the time is come
Which makes it forfeit.

MEPH: And this gloomy night,
Here in this room will wretched Faustus
   be.

BELZ: And here we'll stay,
To mark him how he doth demean himself.

MEPH: How should he, but in desperate
   lunacy?
Fond worldling, now his heart-blood dries
   with grief,
His conscience kills it and his laboring
   brain
Begets a world of idle fantasies,
To over-reach the Devil; but all in vain,
His store of pleasures must be sauc'd with
   pain.

He and his servant, Wagner, are at hand.
Both come from drawing Faustus' latest
   will.
See where they come!

(*Enter* FAUSTUS *and* WAGNER.)

FAUST: Say, Wagner, thou hast perus'd
   my will,
How dost thou like it?

WAG: Sir, so wondrous well,
As in all humble duty, I do yield
My life and lasting service for your love.

(*Enter the* SCHOLARS.)

FAUST: Gramercies, Wagner. Welcome,
gentlemen.   (*Exit* WAGNER.)

FIRST SCHOL: Now, worthy Faustus,
methinks your looks are changed.

FAUST: O, gentlemen!

SEC. SCHOL: What ails Faustus?

FAUST: Ah, my sweet chamber-fellow,
had I liv'd with thee, then had I lived
still! but now must die eternally. Look,
sirs, comes he not? comes he not?

FIRST SCHOL: O my dear Faustus, what
imports this fear?

SEC. SCHOL: Is all our pleasure turn'd to
melancholy?

THIRD SCHOL: He is not well with being
over-solitary.

SEC. SCHOL: If it be so, we'll have physi-
cians and Faustus shall be cur'd.

THIRD SCHOL: 'Tis but a surfeit, sir; fear
nothing.

FAUST: A surfeit of deadly sin, that
hath damn'd both body and soul.

SEC. SCHOL: Yet, Faustus, look up to
Heaven; remember God's mercy is infinite.

FAUST: But Faustus' offence can ne'er
be pardoned: the serpent that tempted
Eve may be saved, but not Faustus. O,
gentlemen, hear me with patience, and
tremble not at my speeches! Though my

heart pant and quiver to remember that I have been a student here these thirty years, O, would I had never seen Wittenberg, never read book! and what wonders I have done, all Germany can witness, yea, all the world; for which Faustus hath lost both Germany and the world; yea, heaven itself, heaven, the seat of God, the throne of the blessed, the kingdom of joy; and must remain in Hell for ever—Hell, oh, Hell for ever! Sweet friends, what shall become of Faustus, being in Hell for ever?

SEC. SCHOL: Yet, Faustus, call on God.

FAUST: On God, whom Faustus hath abjur'd! on God, whom Faustus hath blasphem'd! Oh, my God, I would weep! but the Devil draws in my tears. Gush forth blood, instead of tears! yea, life and soul—Oh, he stays my tongue! I would lift up my hands; but see, they hold 'em, they hold 'em!

ALL: Who, Faustus?

FAUST: Why, Lucifer and Mephistophilis. O, gentlemen, I gave them my soul for my cunning!

ALL: Oh, God forbid!

FAUST: God forbade it, indeed; but Faustus hath done it: for the vain pleasure of four and twenty years hath Faustus lost eternal joy and felicity. I writ them a bill with mine own blood: the date is expired; this is the time, and he will fetch me.

FIRST SCHOL: Why did not Faustus tell us of this before, that Divines might have pray'd for thee?

FAUST: Oft have I thought to have done so; but the Devil threatened to tear me in pieces, if I nam'd God; to fetch me, body and soul, if I once gave ear to divinity: and now 'tis too late. Gentlemen, away, lest you perish with me.

SEC. SCHOL: O, what may we do to save Faustus?

FAUST: Talk not of me, but save yourselves, and depart.

THIRD SCHOL: God will strengthen me; I will stay with Faustus.

FIRST SCHOL: Tempt not God, sweet friend; but let us into the next room, and pray for him.

FAUST: Ay, pray for me, pray for me; and what noise soever you hear, come not unto me, for nothing can rescue me.

SEC. SCHOL: Pray thou, and we will pray that God may have mercy upon thee.

FAUST: Gentlemen, farewell: if I live till morning, I'll visit you; if not, Faustus is gone to hell.

ALL: Faustus, farewell.

(*Exeunt* SCHOLARS.)

MEPH. (*above*): Ay, Faustus, now thou
    hast no hope of heaven;
Therefore despair, think only upon hell,
For that must be thy mansion, there to
    dwell.

FAUST: O thou bewitching fiend, 'twas
    thy temptation
Hath robb'd me of eternal happiness.

MEPH: I do confess it, Faustus, and
    rejoice;
'Twas I, that when thou wert i' the way
    to heaven,
Damm'd up thy passage; when thou
    took'st the book,
To view the Scriptures, then I turn'd the
    leaves,
And led thine eye.—
What, weep'st thou? 'tis too late, despair,
    farewell!
Fools that will laugh on earth, must weep
    in hell.

(*Exeunt* LUCIFER, BELZEBUB,
MEPHISTOPHILIS.)

(*Enter the* GOOD ANGEL *and the* BAD ANGEL
at several doors.)

GOOD ANG: Oh, Faustus, if thou hadst
    given ear to me,
Innumerable joys had followed thee.
But thou didst love the world.

BAD ANG: Gave ear to me,
And now must taste Hell's pains perpetu-
    ally.

GOOD ANG: O what will all thy riches,
    pleasures, pomps,
Avail thee now?

BAD ANG: Nothing but vex thee more,
To want in Hell, that had on earth such
    store.

(*Music while the throne descends.*)

GOOD ANG: O thou hast lost celestial hap-
    piness,
Pleasures unspeakable, bliss without end.
Hadst thou affected sweet divinity,
Hell, or the Devil, had had no power on
    thee.
Hadst thou kept on that way, Faustus,
    behold,
In what resplendent glory thou hadst sit
In yonder throne, like those bright shining
    saints,
And triumph'd over hell: that hast thou
    lost:
And now, poor soul, must thy good angel
    leave thee,

(*The throne ascends.*)

The jaws of Hell are open to receive thee.
                                    (*Exit.*)

(*Hell is discovered.*)

BAD ANG: Now, Faustus, let thine eyes
    with horror stare
Into that vast perpetual torture-house.
There are the furies tossing damned souls
On burning forks; their bodies boil in
    lead:
There are live quarters broiling on the
    coals,
That ne'er can die: this ever-burning chair
Is for o'er-tortured souls to rest them in;
These that are fed with sops of flaming
    fire,
Were gluttons and lov'd only delicates,
And laugh'd to see the poor starve at their
    gates:
But yet all these are nothing; thou shalt see

Ten thousand tortures that more horrid
    be.

FAUST: O, I have seen enough to tor-
    ture me.

BAD ANG: Nay, thou must feel them,
    taste the smart of all:
He that loves pleasure, must for pleasure
    fall:
And so I leave thee, Faustus, till anon;
Then wilt thou tumble in confusion.
                                    (*Exit.*)

(*Hell disappears.*)
(*The clock strikes eleven.*)

FAUST: Oh, Faustus,
Now hast thou but one bare hour to live,
And then thou must be damn'd perpetu-
    ally!
Stand still, you ever moving spheres of
    Heaven,
That time may cease, and midnight never
    come;
Fair nature's eye, rise, rise again, and make
Perpetual day; or let this hour be but
A year, a month, a week, a natural day,
That Faustus may repent and save his
    soul!
O lente, lente currite, noctis equi!
The stars move still, time runs, the clock
    will strike,
The devil will come, and Faustus must be
    damn'd.
O, I'll leap up to Heaven!—Who pulls me
    down?—
See, see, where Christ's blood streams in
    the firmament!
One drop would save my soul, half a drop:
    Oh, my Christ!—
Ah, rend not my heart for naming of my
    Christ!
Yet will I call on him: O, spare me, Luci-
    fer!—
Where is it now? 'tis gone: and see a
    threatening arm, an angry brow!
Mountains and hills, come, come, and fall
    on me,

And hide me from the heavy wrath of Heaven.

No?

Then will I headlong run into the earth:
Earth, gape! O, no, it will not harbor me!
You stars that reign'd at my nativity,
Whose influence hath allotted death and Hell,
Now draw up Faustus, like a foggy mist,
Into the entrails of yon lab'ring cloud
That, when you vomit forth into the air,
My limbs may issue from your smoky mouths,
So that my soul may but ascend to heaven!

(*The clock strikes.*)

Ah, half the hour is past! 'twill all be passed anon.

O God,
If thou wilt not have mercy on my soul,
Yet for Christ's sake, whose blood hath ransom'd me,
Impose some end to my incessant pain;
Let Faustus live in hell a thousand years,
A hundred thousand, and at last be sav'd!
O, no end is limited to damned souls!
Why wert thou not a creature wanting soul?
Or why is this immortal that thou hast?
Ah, Pythagoras' *metempsychosis,* were that true,
This soul should fly from me, and I be changed
Unto some brutish beast! all beasts are happy,
For, when they die,
Their souls are soon dissolved in elements;
But mine must live still to be plagu'd in Hell.
Curs'd be the parents that engender'd me!
No, Faustus, curse thyself, curse Lucifer
That hath depriv'd thee of the joys of heaven.

(*The clock striketh twelve.*)

O, it strikes, it strikes! Now, body, turn to air,
Or Lucifer will bear thee quick to Hell!

O soul, be changed into little water-drops,
And fall into the ocean, ne'er be found!

(*Thunder and enter the* DEVILS.)

O mercy, Heaven, look not so fierce on me!
Adders and serpents, let me breathe a while!
Ugly Hell, gape not! come not, Lucifer!
I'll burn my books!—Oh, Mephistophilis!

(*Exeunt with him.*)

SCENE III

A room next to FAUSTUS' *study.*

(*Enter the* SCHOLARS.)

FIRST SCHOL: Come, gentlemen, let us go visit Faustus,
For such a dreadful night was never seen,
Since first the world's creation did begin.
Such fearful shrieks and cries were never heard:
Pray heaven the doctor have escap'd the danger.

SEC. SCHOL: O help us Heaven! see, here are Faustus' limbs,
All torn asunder by the hand of death.

THIRD SCHOL: The devils whom Faustus serv'd have torn him thus:
For 'twixt the hours of twelve and one, methought
I heard him shriek and call aloud for help:
At which self time the house seem'd all on fire,
With dreadful horror of these damned fiends.

SEC. SCHOL: Well, gentlemen, though Faustus' end be such
As every Christian heart laments to think on,
Yet for he was a scholar, once admired
For wondrous knowledge in our German schools,
We'll give his mangled limbs due burial;

And all the students, clothed in mourning
 black,
Shall wait upon his heavy funeral.
(*Exeunt.*)

(*Enter* CHORUS.)

CHOR: Cut is the branch that might
 have grown full straight,
And burned is Apollo's laurel-bough,
That sometime grew within this learned
 man.

Faustus is gone: regard his hellish fall,
Whose fiendful fortune may exhort the
 wise,
Only to wonder at unlawful things,
Whose deepness doth entice such forward
 wits
To practise more than heavenly power
 permits.
(*Exit.*)

*Terminat hora diem; terminat Author
opus.*

Othello, The Moor of Venice

WILLIAM SHAKESPEARE

COMMENTARY

 William Shakespeare (1564-1616), the most famous of English writers, was born in Stratford-on-Avon. His plays are commonly grouped under three categories: histories, tragedies, and comedies. *Othello* is generally considered one of the four great tragedies; the other three are *King Lear, Hamlet,* and *Macbeth.*

Othello may be read in almost classical terms. Like Oedipus, Othello is a great and good man who, after a somewhat unusual marriage, moves steadily toward his fall, impelled by exterior and interior forces. He achieves great things and wins great rewards. Yet in spite of his stature in the eyes of the world, he is vulnerable by virtue of his simple gullibility. He is an outsider in a society in which he achieves a stature so substantial that he can readily transcend taboos. But perhaps precisely because he is an outsider, his defences are subject to breach by the canny insider, Iago. Othello's recognition of his transgression comes suddenly, unlike Oedipus' recognition, which is gradual, but it provokes a similar self-destructive punishment for acknowledged guilt.

It is valuable to contrast *Othello* as a tragedy with *Oedipus.* Is a production, with costumes and changing scenes, necessary to emphasize the differences, or can the texts alone suggest some of the more critical contrasts? Which is a "simpler" play? Does the obvious "social" complexity of Shakespeare's world contribute to Othello's tragedy? Or does the more "simple" social context carry the roots of Oedipus' fall? How are Oedipus and Othello similar as men? different? What do outside forces have to do with the tragic consequences in each?

In a very modern sense, Othello may never develop the knowledge and the insight gained by Oedipus. He does not seem to recognize the fundamental incongruity of his marriage to Desdemona, nor is he sensitive to his manipulation by Iago. Sir Laurence Olivier's film interpretation of Othello emphasized two aspects of the tragedy not commonly discussed, that of racial intermarriage and that of homosexuality, modern themes that are not to be discounted simply because they may have had different meanings in Shakespeare's world. Do you think Shakespeare's text justifies Sir Laurence's interpretation, or do you think it denies it?

The tragedy in *Othello,* as in *Oedipus,* has its roots as much in social sources as in personal and psychological ones. Othello's "social" innocence leads him to complacency about his socially unusual marriage. Desdemona's sheltered and tender naiveté is overwhelmed by Othello's exotic, rough history. Her excessive innocence matches Othello's excessive susceptibility, and both thus contribute to their fate.

The criticism of *Othello* is voluminous. An excellent essay is that by Mark Van Doren in his book *Shakespeare* (New York, 1939). One of the classical studies is that by A. C. Bradley in his *Shakespearean Tragedy* (London, New York, 1905). The introduction by M. R. Ridley to the Arden Edition (London and Cambridge, Mass., 1958) is a basic modern survey of the background. Of special scholarly interest is Franklin M. Dickey's *Not Wisely But Too Well* (San Marino, California, 1957).

William Shakespeare

OTHELLO, THE MOOR OF VENICE

Edited by Thomas Marc Parrott and Edward Hubler

THE NAMES OF THE ACTORS

DUKE OF VENICE.

BRABANTIO, *father to* DESDEMONA.

GRATIANO,⎫
LUDOVICO,⎭ *two noble Venetians.*

OTHELLO, THE MOOR.

CASSIO, *an honourable lieutenant.*

IAGO, *a villain.*

RODERIGO, *a gulled gentleman.*

MONTANO, *governor of Cyprus.*

CLOWN.

DESDEMONA, *wife to* OTHELLO.

EMILIA, *wife to* IAGO.

BIANCA, *a courtezan.*

SENATORS, GENTLEMEN *of* CYPRUS, SAILORS, OFFICERS, MESSENGER, HERALD, MUSICIANS, *and* ATTENDANTS.

[This list appears at the end of the play in the Folio.]

SCENE: *Venice; Cyprus.*

ACT I

SCENE I.
Venice. A street.

(*Enter* RODERIGO *and* IAGO.)

ROD: Tush, never tell me! I take it much unkindly
That thou, Iago, who hast had my purse
As if the strings were thine, shouldst know of this.

IAGO: 'Sblood, but you will not hear me.
If ever I did dream of such a matter,   5
Abhor me.

ROD: Thou told'st me thou didst hold him in thy hate.

EDITOR'S NOTE: Line numbers in *Othello* are provided for the convenience of the reader, and do not necessarily correspond to original line numbers in the text cited.

IAGO: Despise me, if I do not. Three great ones of the city,
In personal suit to make me his lieutenant,
Off-capp'd to him; and, by the faith of man,   10
I know my price; I am worth no worse a place.
But he, as loving his own pride and purposes,
Evades them with a bombast circumstance
Horribly stuff'd with epithets of war;
And, in conclusion,   15
Nonsuits my mediators; for, "Certes," says he,
"I have already chose my officer."
And what was he?
Forsooth, a great arithmetician,
One Michael Cassio, a Florentine,   20
(A fellow almost damn'd in a fair wife)
That never set a squadron in the field,
Nor the division of a battle knows
More than a spinster, unless the bookish theoric,
Wherein the toged consuls can propose 25
As masterly as he. Mere prattle without practice
Is all his soldiership. But he, sir, had the election;
And I, of whom his eyes had seen the proof
At Rhodes, at Cyprus, and on other grounds
Christian and heathen, must be be-lee'd and calm'd   30
By debitor and creditor; this counter-caster,
He, in good time, must his lieutenant be,
And I—God bless the mark!—his Moor-ship's ancient.

ROD: By heaven, I rather would have been his hangman.

IAGO: Why, there's no remedy. 'T is the curse of service,   35
Preferment goes by letter and affection,
And not by old gradation, where each second

Stood heir to the first. Now, sir, be judge yourself
Whether I in any just term am affin'd
To love the Moor.

ROD: I would not follow him then:

IAGO: O, sir, content you;   41
I follow him to serve my turn upon him.
We cannot all be masters, nor all masters
Cannot be truly follow'd. You shall mark
Many a duteous and knee-crooking knave,
That, doting on his own obsequious bond-age,   46
Wears out his time, much like his master's ass,
For nought but provender, and when he's old, cashier'd.
Whip me such honest knaves. Others there are
Who, trimm'd in forms and visages of duty,   50
Keep yet their hearts attending on them-selves,
And, throwing but shows of service on their lords,
Do well thrive by 'em, and when they have lin'd their coats
Do themselves homage. These fellows have some soul;
And such a one do I profess myself. For, sir,   55
It is as sure as you are Roderigo,
Were I the Moor, I would not be Iago:
In following him, I follow but myself;
Heaven is my judge, not I for love and duty,
But seeming so, for my peculiar end;   60
For when my outward action does demon-strate
The native act and figure of my heart
In compliment extern, 't is not long after
But I will wear my heart upon my sleeve
For daws to peck at: I am not what I am.   65

ROD: What a full fortune does the thick-lips owe,
If he can carry 't thus!

IAGO: Call up her father,
Rouse him; make after him, poison his de-
    light,
Proclaim him in the streets. Incense her
    kinsmen,
And, though he in a fertile climate dwell,
Plague him with flies; though that his joy
    be joy,   71
Yet throw such changes of vexation on 't,
As it may lose some colour.

ROD: Here is her father's house; I'll call
    aloud.

IAGO: Do, with like timorous accent and
    dire yell   75
As when, by night and negligence, the fire
Is spied in populous cities.

ROD: What, ho, Brabantio! Signior Bra-
    bantio, ho!

IAGO: Awake! what, ho, Brabantio,
    thieves! thieves!
Look to your house, your daughter, and
    your bags!   80
Thieves! thieves!

(*Enter* BRABANTIO *above, at a window.*)

BRA: What is the reason of this terrible
    summons?
What is the matter there?

ROD: Signior, is all your family within?

IAGO: Are your doors lock'd?

BRA: Why, wherefore ask you this?

IAGO: 'Zounds, sir, you 're robb'd! For
    shame, put on your gown;   86
Your heart is burst, you have lost half your
    soul;
Even now, now, very now, an old black
    ram
Is tupping your white ewe. Arise, arise!
Awake the snorting citizens with the
    bell,   90
Or else the devil will make a grandsire
    of you.
Arise, I say!

BRA: What, have you lost your wits?

ROD: Most reverend signior, do you
    know my voice?

BRA: Not I. What are you?

ROD: My name is Roderigo.

BRA: The worser welcome;
I have charg'd thee not to haunt about my
    doors: 96
In honest plainness thou hast heard me say
My daughter is not for thee; and now, in
    madness,
Being full of supper and distempering
    draughts,
Upon malicious bravery dost thou come
To start my quiet.   101

ROD: Sir, sir, sir,—

BRA: But thou must needs be sure
My spirits and my place have in them
    power
To make this bitter to thee.

ROD: Patience, good sir.

BRA: What tell'st thou me of robbing?
    This is Venice;   105
My house is not a grange.

ROD: Most grave Brabantio,
In simple and pure soul I come to you.

IAGO: 'Zounds, sir, you are one of those
that will not serve God, if the devil bid
you. Because we come to do you [110
service and you think we are ruffians,
you'll have your daughter covered with a
Barbary horse; you'll have your nephews
neigh to you; you'll have coursers for
cousins, and gennets for germans. [115

BRA: What profane wretch art thou?

IAGO: I am one, sir, that comes to tell
you your daughter and the Moor are now
making the beast with two backs.

BRA: Thou art a villain.

IAGO: You are—a senator.

BRA: This thou shalt answer. I know
    thee, Roderigo.   121

ROD: Sir, I will answer anything. But, I
    beseech you,
If 't be your pleasure and most wise con-
    sent,

(As partly I find it is) that your fair
   daughter,
At this odd-even and dull watch o' th'
   night,   125
Transported, with no worse nor better
   guard
But with a knave of common hire, a gon-
   dolier,
To the gross clasps of a lascivious Moor,—
If this be known to you and your allow-
   ance,
We then have done you bold and saucy
   wrongs;   130
But if you know not this, my manners
   tell me
We have your wrong rebuke. Do not be-
   lieve
That, from the sense of all civility,
I thus would play and trifle with your
   reverence.
Your daughter, if you have not given her
   leave,   135
I say again, hath made a gross revolt;
Tying her duty, beauty, wit, and fortunes
In an extravagant and wheeling stranger
Of here and everywhere. Straight satisfy
   yourself.
If she be in her chamber or your house,
Let loose on me the justice of the state 141
For thus deluding you.

BRA: Strike on the tinder, ho!
Give me a taper! Call up all my people!
This accident is not unlike my dream;
Belief of it oppresses me already.   145
Light, I say! light!   (*Exit.*)

IAGO: Farewell; for I must leave you.
It seems not meet, nor wholesome to my
   place,
To be produc'd—as, if I stay, I shall—
Against the Moor; for, I do know, the
   state,
However this may gall him with some
   check,   150
Cannot with safety cast him, for he 's
   embark'd
With such loud reason to the Cyprus wars,

Which even now stands in act, that, for
   their souls,
Another of his fathom they have none,
To lead their business; in which regard,
Though I do hate him as I do hell-
   pains,   156
Yet, for necessity of present life,
I must show out a flag and sign of love,
Which is indeed but sign. That you shall
   surely find him,
Lead to the Sagittary the raised search; 160
And there will I be with him. So, farewell.
        (*Exit.*)

(*Enter* BRABANTIO *in his night-gown, and
Servants with torches.*)

BRA: It is too true an evil; gone she is;
And what's to come of my despised time
Is nought but bitterness. Now, Roderigo,
Where didst thou see her? O unhappy
   girl!   165
With the Moor, say'st thou? Who would
   be a father!
How didst thou know 't was she? O, she
   deceives me
Past thought! What said she to you? Get
   more tapers;
Raise all my kindred. Are they married,
   think you?

ROD: Truly, I think they are.   170

BRA: O heaven! How got she out? O
   treason of the blood!
Fathers, from hence trust not your daugh-
   ters' minds
By what you see them act. Is there not
   charms
By which the property of youth and maid-
   hood
May be abus'd? Have you not read,
   Roderigo,   175
Of some such thing?

ROD: Yes, sir, I have indeed.

BRA: Call up my brother. O, would you
   had had her!
Some one way, some another. Do you
   know

Where we may apprehend her and the
    Moor?

ROD: I think I can discover him, if you
    please   180
To get good guard and go along with me.

BRA: Pray you, lead on. At every house
    I'll call;
I may command at most. Get weapons, ho!
And raise some special officers of night.
On, good Roderigo; I'll deserve your
    pains.   (*Exeunt.*)

SCENE II.

Another street.

(*Enter* OTHELLO, IAGO, *and* ATTENDANTS
with torches.)

IAGO: Though in the trade of war I
    have slain men,
Yet do I hold it very stuff o' th' conscience
To do no contriv'd murder: I lack iniquity
Sometimes to do me service. Nine or ten
    times
I had thought to have yerk'd him here
    under the ribs.   5

OTH: 'T is better as it is.

IAGO: Nay, but he prated,
And spoke such scurvy and provoking
    terms
Against your honour
That, with the little godliness I have,
I did full hard forbear him. But, I pray
    you, sir,   10
Are you fast married? Be assur'd of this,
That the magnifico is much belov'd,
And hath in his effect a voice potential
As double as the Duke's: he will divorce
    you;
Or put upon you what restraint or griev-
    ance   15
The law, with all his might to enforce it
    on,
Will give him cable.

OTH: Let him do his spite;
My services which I have done the signiory

Shall out-tongue his complaints. 'T is yet
    to know,—
Which, when I know that boasting is an
    honour,   20
I shall promulgate—I fetch my life and
    being
From men of royal siege, and my demerits
May speak unbonneted to as proud a for-
    tune
As this that I have reach'd; for know,
    Iago,
But that I love the gentle Desdemona, 25
I would not my unhoused free condition
Put into circumscription and confine
For the sea's worth. But, look! what lights
    come yond?

(*Enter* CASSIO, *with lights,* OFFICERS, *and
torches.*)

IAGO: Those are the raised father and
    his friends.
You were best go in.

OTH: Not I; I must be found.
My parts, my title, and my perfect soul 31
Shall manifest me rightly. Is it they?

IAGO: By Janus, I think no.

OTH: The servants of the Duke, and
    my lieutenant!
The goodness of the night upon you,
    friends!   35
What is the news?

CAS: The Duke does greet you, general,
And he requires your haste-post-haste ap-
    pearance,
Even on the instant.

OTH: What is the matter, think you?

CAS: Something from Cyprus, as I may
    divine;
It is a business of some heat. The galleys
Have sent a dozen sequent messengers 41
This very night at one another's heels,
And many of the consuls, rais'd and met,
Are at the Duke's already. You have been
    hotly call'd for;
When, being not at your lodging to be
    found,   45

The Senate hath sent about three several
    quests
To search you out.

OTH: 'T is well I am found by you.
I will but spend a word here in the house,
And go with you.   (*Exit.*)

CAS: Ancient, what makes he here?

IAGO: Faith, he to-night hath boarded a
    land carack: 50
If it proves lawful prize, he 's made for
    ever.

CAS: I do not understand.

IAGO: He 's married.

CAS: To who?

(*Re-enter* OTHELLO)

IAGO: Marry, to—Come, captain, will
    you go?

OTH: Have with you.

CAS: Here comes another troop to seek
    for you.

(*Enter* BRABANTIO, RODERIGO, *and* OFFICERS
with torches and weapons.)

IAGO: It is Brabantio. General, be
    advis'd;   55
He comes to bad intent.

OTH: Holla! stand there!

ROD: Signior, it is the Moor.

BRA: Down with him, thief!

(*They draw on both sides.*)

IAGO: You, Roderigo! come, sir, I am
    for you.

OTH: Keep up your bright swords, for
    the dew will rust them.
Good signior, you shall more command
    with years   60
Than with your weapons.

BRA: O thou foul thief, where hast thou
    stow'd my daughter?
Damn'd as thou art, thou hast enchanted
    her;
For I 'll refer me to all things of sense,
If she in chains of magic were not bound,
Whether a maid so tender, and happy, 66

So opposite to marriage that she shunn'd
The wealthy curled darlings of our nation,
Would ever have, t' incur a general
    mock,
Run from her guardage to the sooty
    bosom   70
Of such a thing as thou—to fear, not to
    delight.
Judge me the world, if 't is not gross in
    sense
That thou hast practis'd on her with foul
    charms,
Abus'd her delicate youth with drugs or
    minerals
That weakens motion. I 'll have 't disputed
    on;   75
'T is probable, and palpable to thinking.
I therefore apprehend and do attach thee
For an abuser of the world, a practiser
Of arts inhibited and out of warrant.
Lay hold upon him; if he do resist,   80
Subdue him at his peril.

OTH: Hold your hands,
Both you of my inclining, and the rest.
Were it my cue to fight, I should have
    known it
Without a prompter. Where will you that
    I go
To answer this your charge?

BRA: To prison, till fit time
Of law and course of direct session   86
Call thee to answer.

OTH: What if I do obey?
How may the Duke be therewith satisfied,
Whose messengers are here about my side
Upon some present business of the state 90
To bring me to him?

OFF: 'T is true, most worthy signior.
The Duke's in council; and your noble
    self,
I am sure, is sent for.

BRA: How? the Duke in council?
In this time of the night? Bring him away;
Mine 's not an idle cause. The Duke him-
    self,   95
Or any of my brothers of the state,

Cannot but feel this wrong as 't were their own;
For if such actions may have passage free,
Bond-slaves and pagans shall our states-
     men be.   (*Exeunt.*)

Scene III.

A council-chamber.

(*The* DUKE *and* SENATORS *set at a table, with lights,* OFFICERS *and* ATTENDANTS.)

DUKE: There is no composition in these news
That gives them credit.

1. SEN: Indeed, they are dispropor-
     tioned;
My letters say a hundred and seven galleys.
DUKE: And mine, a hundred forty.

2. SEN: And mine, two hundred!
But though they jump not on a just ac-
     count,—   5
As in these cases, where the aim reports,
'T is oft with difference—yet do they all
     confirm
A Turkish fleet, and bearing up to Cyprus.
DUKE: Nay, it is possible enough to
     judgement.
I do not so secure me in the error   10
But the main article I do approve
In fearful sense.

SAILOR. (*Within*): What, ho! what ho!
     what, ho!

(*Enter a* SAILOR.)

OFF: A messenger from the galleys.
DUKE: Now, what 's the business?
SAIL: The Turkish preparation makes
     for Rhodes;
So was I bid report here to the state   15
By Signior Angelo.
DUKE: How say you by this change?

1. SEN: This cannot be,
By no assay of reason. 'T is a pageant,

To keep up in false gaze. When we con-
     sider
Th' importancy of Cyprus to the Turk, 20
And let ourselves again but understand
That, as it more concerns the Turk than
     Rhodes,
So may he with more facile question bear
     it,
For that it stands not in such warlike
     brace,
But altogether lacks th' abilities   25
That Rhodes is dress'd in; if we make
     thought of this,
We must not think the Turk is so un-
     skilful
To leave that latest which concerns him
     first,
Neglecting an attempt of ease and gain
To wake and wage a danger profitless. 30
DUKE: Nay, in all confidence, he 's not
     for Rhodes.
OFF: Here is more news.

(*Enter a* MESSENGER.)

MESS: The Ottomites, reverend and
     gracious,
Steering with due course toward the isle
     of Rhodes,
Have there injointed them with an after
     fleet.   35

1. SEN: Ay, so I thought. How many,
     as you guess?

MESS: Of thirty sail; and now they do
     restem
Their backward course, bearing with frank
     appearance
Their purposes toward Cyprus. Signior
     Montano,
Your trusty and most valiant servitor,   40
With his free duty recommends you thus,
And prays you to believe him.
DUKE: 'T is certain, then, for Cyprus.
Marcus Luccicos, is not he in town?

1. SEN: He 's now in Florence.   45
DUKE: Write from us to him; post-post-
     haste dispatch.

1. SEN: Here comes Brabantio and the valiant Moor.

(*Enter* BRABANTIO, OTHELLO, CASSIO, IAGO, RODERIGO, *and* OFFICERS.)

DUKE: Valiant Othello, we must straight employ you
Against the general enemy Ottoman.
(*To* BRABANTIO.) I did not see you; welcome, gentle signior; 50
We lack'd your counsel and your help to-night.

BRA: So did I yours. Good your Grace, pardon me;
Neither my place nor aught I heard of business
Hath rais'd me from my bed, nor doth the general care
Take hold on me; for my particular grief 55
Is of so flood-gate and o'erbearing nature
That it engluts and swallows other sorrows
And it is still itself.

DUKE: Why, what's the matter?

BRA: My daughter! O, my daughter!

SEN: Dead?

BRA: Ay, to me;
She is abus'd, stol'n from me, and corrupted
By spells and medicines bought of mountebanks; 61
For nature so preposterously to err,
Being not deficient, blind, or lame of sense,
Sans witchcraft could not.

DUKE: Whoe'er he be that in this foul proceeding 65
Hath thus beguil'd your daughter of herself
And you of her, the bloody book of law
You shall yourself read in the bitter letter
After your own sense, yea, though our proper son
Stood in your action.

BRA: Humbly I thank your Grace.
Here is the man,—this Moor, whom now, it seems, 71
Your special mandate for the state affairs
Hath hither brought.

ALL: We are very sorry for 't.

DUKE: (*To* OTHELLO.) What, in your own part, can you say to this?

BRA: Nothing, but this is so. 75

OTH: Most potent, grave, and reverend signiors,
My very noble and approv'd good masters,
That I have ta'en away this old man's daughter,
It is most true; true, I have married her:
The very head and front of my offending
Hath this extent, no more. Rude am I in my speech, 81
And little bless'd with the soft phrase of peace;
For since these arms of mine had seven years' pith
Till now, some nine moons wasted, they have us'd
Their dearest action in the tented field,
And little of this great world can I speak
More than pertains to feats of broils and battle, 87
And therefore little shall I grace my cause
In speaking for myself. Yet, by your gracious patience,
I will a round unvarnish'd tale deliver 90
Of my whole course of love; what drugs, what charms,
What conjuration and what mighty magic,
(For such proceeding I am charg'd withal,)
I won his daughter.

BRA: A maiden never bold;
Of spirit so still and quiet, that her motion 95
Blush'd at herself; and she, in spite of nature,
Of years, of country, credit, everything,

To fall in love with what she fear'd to
    look on!
It is a judgement maim'd and most im-
    perfect   99
That will confess perfection so could
    err
Against all rules of nature, and must be
    driven
To find out practices of cunning hell,
Why this should be. I therefore vouch
    again
That with some mixtures powerful o'er
    the blood,
Or with some dram conjur'd to this ef-
    fect,   105
He wrought upon her.

DUKE: To vouch this is no proof,
Without more wider and more overt test
Than these thin habits and poor likeli-
    hoods
Of modern seeming do prefer against him.

1. SEN: But, Othello, speak.   110
Did you by indirect and forced courses
Subdue and poison this young maid's
    affections?
Or came it by request and such fair ques-
    tion
As soul to soul affordeth?

OTH: I do beseech you,
Send for the lady to the Sagittary,   115
And let her speak of me before her father;
If you do find me foul in her report,
The trust, the office I do hold of you,
Not only take away, but let your sentence
Even fall upon my life.

DUKE: Fetch Desdemona hither.

(*Exeunt two or three.*)

OTH: Ancient, conduct them; you best
    know the place. (*Exit* IAGO.) 121
And, till she come, as truly as to heaven
I do confess the vices of my blood,
So justly to your grave ears I'll present
How I did thrive in this fair lady's love,
And she in mine.   126

DUKE: Say it, Othello.

OTH: Her father lov'd me; oft invited
    me;
Still question'd me the story of my life
From year to year, the battles, sieges, for-
    tunes,   130
That I have pass'd.
I ran it through, even from my boyish
    days,
To th' very moment that he bade me tell
    it.
Wherein I spoke of most disastrous
    chances,
Of moving accidents by flood and field,
Of hair-breadth scapes i' th' imminent
    deadly breach,   136
Of being taken by the insolent foe
And sold to slavery, of my redemption
    thence
And portance in my travellers' history;
Wherein of antres vast and deserts idle,
Rough quarries, rocks, and hills whose
    heads touch heaven,   141
It was my hint to speak,—such was my
    process,—
And of the Cannibals that each other
    eat,
The Anthropophagi, and men whose
    heads
Do grow beneath their shoulders. This to
    hear   145
Would Desdemona seriously incline;
But still the house-affairs would draw her
    thence,
Which ever as she could with haste dis-
    patch,
She'd come again, and with a greedy ear
Devour up my discourse: which I observ-
    ing,   150
Took once a pliant hour, and found good
    means
To draw from her a prayer of earnest
    heart
That I would all my pilgrimage dilate,
Whereof by parcels she had something
    heard,
But not intentively. I did consent,   155
And often did beguile her of her tears

When I did speak of some distressful
    stroke
That my youth suffer'd. My story being
    done,
She gave me for my pains a world of
    sighs.
She swore, in faith, 't was strange, 't was
    passing strange,   160
'T was pitiful, 't was wondrous pitiful.
She wish'd she had not heard it; yet she
    wish'd
That Heaven had made her such a man.
    She thank'd me,
And bade me, if I had a friend that lov'd
    her,
I should but teach him how to tell my
    story,   165
And that would woo her. Upon this hint
    I spake:
She lov'd me for the dangers I had pass'd,
And I lov'd her that she did pity them.
This only is the witchcraft I have us'd.
Here comes the lady; let her witness it.

(*Enter* DESDEMONA, IAGO, *and* ATTENDANTS.)

DUKE: I think this tale would win my
    daughter too.   171
Good Brabantio,
Take up this mangled matter at the best;
Men do their broken weapons rather use
Than their bare hands.

BRA: I pray you, hear her speak.
If she confess that she was half the wooer,
Destruction on my head, if my bad blame
Light on the man! Come hither, gentle
    mistress.   178
Do you perceive in all this noble company
Where most you owe obedience?

DES: My noble father,
I do perceive here a divided duty.   181
To you I am bound for life and education;
My life and education both do learn me
How to respect you; you are lord of all
    my duty;
I am hitherto your daughter. But here 's
    my husband;   185
And so much duty as my mother show'd

To you, preferring you before her father,
So much I challenge that I may profess
Due to the Moor, my lord.

BRA: God be with you! I have done.
Please it your Grace, on to the state-affairs.
I had rather to adopt a child than get it.
Come hither, Moor.   192
I here do give thee that with all my heart
Which, but thou hast already, with all my
    heart
I would keep from thee. For your sake,
    jewel,   195
I am glad at soul I have no other child;
For thy escape would teach me tyranny,
To hang clogs on them. I have done, my
    lord.

DUKE: Let me speak like yourself, and
    lay a sentence,
Which, as a grise or step, may help these
    lovers   200
Into your favour.
When remedies are past, the griefs are
    ended
By seeing the worst, which late on hopes
    depended.
To mourn a mischief that is past and gone
Is the next way to draw new mischief on.
What cannot be preserv'd when fortune
    takes,   206
Patience her injury a mockery makes.
The robb'd that smiles steals something
    from the thief;
He robs himself that spends a bootless
    grief.

BRA: So let the Turk of Cyprus us
    beguile;   210
We lose it not, so long as we can smile.
He bears the sentence well that nothing
    bears
But the free comfort which from thence
    he hears,
But he bears both the sentence and the
    sorrow
That, to pay grief, must of poor patience
    borrow.   215
These sentences, to sugar, or to gall,

Being strong on both sides, are equivocal:
But words are words; I never yet did hear
That the bruis'd heart was pierced through
    the ear.
I humbly beseech you, proceed to th' af-
    fairs of state.   220

DUKE: The Turk with a most mighty
preparation makes for Cyprus. Othello, the
fortitude of the place is best known to
you; and though we have there a substi-
tute of most allowed sufficiency, yet opinion, a sovereign mistress of effects, throws
a more safer voice on you: you must therefore be content to slubber the gloss of
your new fortunes with this more stubborn and boisterous expedition.   230

OTH: The tyrant custom, most grave
    senators,
Hath made the flinty and steel couch of
    war
My thrice-driven bed of down. I do agnize
A natural and prompt alacrity
I find in hardness, and do undertake   235
These present wars against the Ottomites.
Most humbly therefore bending to your
    state,
I crave fit disposition for my wife,
Due reference of place and exhibition,
With such accommodation and besort
As levels with her breeding.

DUKE: If you please,   241
Be 't at her father's.

BRA: I'll not have it so.

OTH: Nor I.

DES: Nor I; I would not there reside,
To put my father in impatient thoughts
By being in his eye. Most gracious duke,
To my unfolding lend your prosperous
    ear;   246
And let me find a charter in your voice,
T' assist my simpleness.

DUKE: What would you, Desdemona?

DES: That I did love the Moor to live
    with him,   250

My downright violence and storm of
    fortunes
May trumpet to the world. My heart 's
    subdued
Even to the very quality of my lord:
I saw Othello's visage in his mind,   254
And to his honours and his valiant parts
Did I my soul and fortunes consecrate.
So that, dear lords, if I be left behind,
A moth of peace, and he go to the war,
The rites for which I love him are bereft
    me,
And I a heavy interim shall support
By his dear absence. Let me go with him.

OTH: Let her have your voice.   262
Vouch with me, Heaven, I therefore beg
    it not
To please the palate of my appetite,
Nor to comply with heat, the young af-
    fects   265
In my defunct and proper satisfaction,
But to be free and bounteous to her mind;
And Heaven defend your good souls, that
    you think
I will your serious and great business scant
When she is with me. No, when light-
    wing'd toys   270
Of feather'd Cupid seel with wanton dull-
    ness
My speculative and offic'd instruments
That my disports corrupt and taint my
    business,
Let housewives make a skillet of my helm,
And all indign and base adversities   275
Make head against my estimation!

DUKE: Be it as you shall privately de-
    termine,
Either for her stay or going: th' affair
    cries haste,
And speed must answer it.

1. SEN: You must away to-night.

DES: To-night, my lord?

DUKE: This night.

OTH: With all my heart.

DUKE: At nine i' th' morning here we'll
    meet again.   281

Othello, leave some officer behind,
And he shall our commission bring to
　you,
And such things else of quality and respect
As doth import you.

OTH: So please your Grace, my ancient;
A man he is of honesty and trust:　286
To his conveyance I assign my wife,
With what else needful your good Grace
　shall think
To be sent after me.

DUKE:　　　　　Let it be so.
Good-night to every one. (*To* BRABANTIO.)
And, noble signior,　290
If virtue no delighted beauty lack,
Your son-in-law is far more fair than
　black.

1. SEN: Adieu, brave Moor; use Desdemona well.

BRA: Look to her, Moor, if thou hast
eyes to see;　294
She has deceiv'd her father, and may thee.

(*Exeunt* DUKE, BRABANTIO, SENATORS,
OFFICERS, *etc.*)

OTH: My life upon her faith! Honest
Iago,
My Desdemona must I leave to thee.
I prithee, let thy wife attend on her;
And bring them after in the best advan-
tage.　299
Come, Desdemona; I have but an hour
Of love, of worldly matters and direction,
To spend with thee. We must obey the
time.

(*Exeunt* OTHELLO *and* DESDEMONA.)

ROD: Iago,—

IAGO: What say'st thou, noble heart?

ROD: What will I do, think'st thou?

IAGO: Why, go to bed, and sleep.　306

ROD: I will incontinently drown myself.

IAGO: If thou dost, I shall never love
thee after. Why, thou silly gentleman!

ROD: It is silliness to live when to live is
torment; and then have we a prescription
to die when Death is our physician.　312

IAGO: O villanous! I have looked upon
the world for four times seven years; and
since I could distinguish betwixt a　[315
benefit and an injury, I never found man
that knew how to love himself. Ere I
would say I would drown myself for the
love of a guinea-hen, I would change my
humanity with a baboon.　320

ROD: What should I do? I confess it is
my shame to be so fond, but it is not in my
virtue to amend it.　323

IAGO: Virtue! a fig! 't is in ourselves that
we are thus or thus. Our bodies are our
gardens, to the which our wills are garden-
ers; so that if we will plant nettles, or sow
lettuce, set hyssop and weed up thyme,
supply it with one gender of herbs, or distract it with many, either to have it　[330
sterile with idleness, or manured with industry, why, the power and corrigible
authority of this lies in our wills. If the
balance of our lives had not one scale of
reason to poise another of sensuality,　[335
the blood and baseness of our natures
would conduct us to most preposterous
conclusions. But we have reason to cool
our raging motions, our carnal stings, our
unbitted lusts, whereof I take this that
you call love to be a sect or scion.　341

ROD: It cannot be.

IAGO: It is merely a lust of the blood and
a permission of the will. Come, be a man.
Drown myself? drown cats and blind　[345
puppies. I have professed me thy friend,
and I confess me knit to thy deserving
with cables of perdurable toughness; I
could never better stead thee than now.
Put money in thy purse; follow thou　[350
the wars; defeat thy favour with an
usurped beard. I say, put money in thy
purse. It cannot be long that Desdemona
should continue her love to the Moor,—
put money in thy purse,—nor he his　[355
to her. It was a violent commencement
in her, and thou shalt see an answerable
sequestration: put but money in thy purse.
These Moors are changeable in their wills;

—fill thy purse with money;—the [360
food that to him now is as luscious as
locusts, shall be to him shortly as bitter
as coloquintida. She must change for
youth; when she is sated with his body, she
will find the error of her choice—she [365
must have change, she must—therefore
put money in thy purse. If thou wilt needs
damn thyself, do it a more delicate way
than drowning. Make all the money thou
canst. If sanctimony and a frail vow [370
betwixt an erring barbarian and a super-
subtle Venetian be not too hard for my
wits and all the tribe of hell, thou shalt
enjoy her; therefore make money. A pox
of drowning thyself! it is clean out [375
of the way. Seek thou rather to be hanged
in compassing thy joy than to be drowned
and go without her.

ROD: Wilt thou be fast to my hopes, if
I depend on the issue?   380

IAGO: Thou art sure of me—go, make
money—I have told thee often, and I re-
tell thee again and again, I hate the Moor.
My cause is hearted; thine hath no less
reason. Let us be conjunctive in our [385
revenge against him. If thou canst cuckold
him, thou dost thyself a pleasure, me a
sport. There are many events in the womb
of time which will be delivered. [389
Traverse! go, provide thy money. We will
have more of this to-morrow. Adieu.

ROD: Where shall we meet i' th' morning?

IAGO: At my lodging.

ROD: I'll be with thee betimes.   395

IAGO: Go to; farewell. Do you hear,
Roderigo?

ROD: What say you?

IAGO: No more of drowning, do you
hear?   400

ROD: I am chang'd; I'll go sell all my
land.   (*Exit.*)

IAGO: Thus do I ever make my fool my
    purse;

For I mine own gain'd knowledge should
    profane   404
If I would time expend with such a snipe
But for my sport and profit. I hate the
    Moor;
And it is thought abroad that 'twixt my
    sheets
He has done my office. I know not if 't
    be true;   408
But I, for mere suspicion in that kind,
Will do as if for surety. He holds me well;
The better shall my purpose work on him.
Cassio 's a proper man: let me see now:
To get his place and to plume up my will
In double knavery—How, how?—Let 's
    see:—   414
After some time, to abuse Othello's ear
That he is too familiar with his wife.
He hath a person and a smooth dispose
To be suspected, fram'd to make women
    false.
The Moor is of a free and open nature,
That thinks men honest that but seem to
    be so,   420
And will as tenderly be led by th' nose
As asses are.
I have 't. It is engender'd. Hell and night
Must bring this monstrous birth to the
    world's light.   (*Exit.*) 424

ACT II

Scene I.

A sea-port in Cyprus. An open place.

(*Enter* MONTANO *and two* GENTLEMEN.)

MON: What from the cape can you
    discern at sea?

1. GENT: Nothing at all; it is a high-
    wrought flood.
I cannot, 'twixt the heaven and the main,
Descry a sail.

MON: Methinks the wind hath spoke
    aloud at land;   5
A fuller blast ne'er shook our battlements:
If it hath ruffian'd so upon the sea,

What ribs of oak, when mountains melt
    on them,
Can hold the mortise? What shall we
    hear of this?
  2. GENT: A segregation of the Turkish
    fleet: 10
For do but stand upon the foaming
    shore,
The chidden billow seems to pelt the
    clouds;
The wind-shak'd surge, with high and
    monstrous mane,
Seems to cast water on the burning bear
And quench the guards of th' ever-fixed
    pole: 15
I never did like molestation view
On the enchafed flood.
  MON: If that the Turkish fleet
Be not enshelter'd and embay'd, they are
    drown'd;
It is impossible to bear it out.

    (*Enter a third* GENTLEMAN.)

  3. GENT: News, lads! our wars are
    done.   20
The desperate tempest hath so bang'd the
    Turks,
That their designment halts. A noble ship
    of Venice
Hath seen a grievous wreck and sufferance
On most part of their fleet.
  MON: How? is this true?
  3. GENT: The ship is here put in,
A Veronesa; Michael Cassio,   26
Lieutenant to the warlike Moor Othello,
Is come on shore; the Moor himself at
    sea,
And is in full commission here for Cyprus.
  MON: I am glad on 't; 't is a worthy
    governor.   30
  3. GENT: But this same Cassio, though
    he speak of comfort
Touching the Turkish loss, yet he looks
    sadly,
And prays the Moor be safe; for they
    were parted
With foul and violent tempest.

  MON: Pray heavens he be;
For I have serv'd him, and the man com-
    mands   35
Like a full soldier. Let's to the seaside,
    ho!
As well to see the vessel that 's come in
As to throw out our eyes for brave Othello,
Even till we make the main and th' aerial
    blue
An indistinct regard.
  3. GENT: Come, let 's do so;   40
For every minute is expectancy
Of more arrivance.

    (*Enter* CASSIO.)

  CAS: Thanks, you the valiant of this
    warlike isle,
That so approve the Moor! O, let the
    heavens   44
Give him defence against the elements,
For I have lost him on a dangerous sea.
  MON: Is he well shipp'd?
  CAS: His bark is stoutly timber'd, and
    his pilot
Of very expert and approv'd allowance;
Therefore my hopes, not surfeited to
    death,   50
Stand in bold cure.
    (*Within*) "A sail, a sail, a sail!"

    (*Enter a* MESSENGER.)

  CAS: What noise?
  MESS: The town is empty; on the brow
    o' th' sea
Stand ranks of people, and they cry, "A
    sail!"
  CAS: My hopes do shape him for the
    governor.   (*A shot.*)
  2. GENT: They do discharge their shot
    of courtesy   56
Our friends at least.
  CAS: I pray you, sir, go forth,
And give us truth who 't is that is ar-
    riv'd.
  2. GENT: I shall.   (*Exit.*)

MON: But, good lieutenant, is your general wiv'd?   60

CAS: Most fortunately: he had achiev'd a maid
That paragons description and wild fame;
One that excels the quirks of blazoning pens,
And in th' essential vesture of creation
Does tire the ingener.

(*Re-enter second* GENTLEMAN.)

          How now? who has put in?

2. GENT: 'T is one Iago, ancient to the general.   66

CAS: Has had most favourable and happy speed:
Tempests themselves, high seas, and howling winds,
The gutter'd rocks and congregated sands,
Traitors ensteep'd to clog the guiltless keel,   70
As having sense of beauty do omit
Their mortal natures, letting go safely by
The divine Desdemona.

MON: What is she?

CAS: She that I spake of, our great captain's captain,
Left in the conduct of the bold Iago,   75
Whose footing here anticipates our thoughts
A se'nnight's speed. Great Jove, Othello guard,
And swell his sail with thine own powerful breath,
That he may bless this bay with his tall ship,
Make love's quick pants in Desdemona's arms,   80
Give renew'd fire to our extincted spirits,
And bring all Cyprus comfort!

(*Enter* DESDEMONA, EMILIA, IAGO, RODERIGO, *and* ATTENDANTS)

          O, behold,
The riches of the ship is come on shore!
You men of Cyprus, let her have your knees,
Hail to thee, lady! and the grave of heaven,   85
Before, behind thee, and on every hand,
Enwheel thee round!

DES: I thank you, valiant Cassio.
What tidings can you tell me of my lord?

CAS: He is not yet arriv'd; nor know I aught   89
But that he's well and will be shortly here.

DES: O, but I fear—How lost you company?

CAS: The great contention of the sea and skies
Parted our fellowship.—But, hark! a sail.
(*Within*) "A sail, a sail!" (*Guns heard.*)

2. GENT: They give their greeting to the citadel: 95
This likewise is a friend.

CAS: See for the news.
          (*Exit* GENTLEMEN.)
Good ancient, you are welcome. (*To*
EMILIA.) Welcome, mistress.
Let it not gall your patience, good Iago,
That I extend my manners; 't is my breeding   99
That gives me this bold show of courtesy,
          (*Kissing her.*)

IAGO: Sir, would she give you so much of her lips
As of her tongue she oft bestows on me,
You 'd have enough.

DES: Alas, she has no speech.

IAGO: In faith, too much;
I find it still, when I have list to sleep.   105
Marry, before your ladyship, I grant,
She puts her tongue a little in her heart,
And chides with thinking.

EMIL: You have little cause to say so.

IAGO: Come on, come on; you are pictures out of doors,   110
Bells in your parlours, wild-cats in your kitchens,
Saints in your injuries, devils being offended,

Players in your housewifery, and housewives in your beds.

DES: O, fie upon thee, slanderer!

IAGO: Nay, it is true, or else I am a
Turk.   115
You rise to play and go to bed to work.

EMIL: You shall not write my praise.

IAGO: No, let me not.

DES: What wouldst thou write of me,
if thou shouldst praise me?

IAGO: O gentle lady, do not put me to 't;
For I am nothing, if not critical.   120

DES: Come on, assay.—There's one gone
to the harbour?

IAGO: Ay, madam.

DES: I am not merry; but I do beguile
The thing I am, by seeming otherwise.—
Come, how wouldst thou praise me?   125

IAGO: I am about it; but indeed my in-
vention
Comes from my pate as birdlime does
from frieze;
It plucks out brains and all. But my Muse
labours,
And thus she is deliver'd:
If she be fair and wise, fairness and wit,
The one 's for use, the other useth it.   131

DES: Well prais'd! How if she be black
and witty?

IAGO:
If she be black, and thereto have a wit,
She 'll find a white that shall her black-
ness fit.

DES: Worse and worse.   135

EMIL: How if fair and foolish?

IAGO:
She never yet was foolish that was fair;
For even her folly help'd her to an heir.

DES: These are old fond paradoxes to
make fools laugh i' th' alehouse.   [140
What miserable praise hast thou for her
that 's foul and foolish?

IAGO:
There's none so foul and foolish thereunto,

But does foul pranks which fair and wise
ones do.   144

DES: O heavy ignorance! thou praisest
the worst best. But what praise couldst
thou bestow on a deserving woman indeed, one that, in the authority of her
merit, did justly put on the vouch of [149
very malice itself?

IAGO:
She that was ever fair and never proud,
Had tongue at will and yet was never loud,
Never lack'd gold and yet went never gay,
Fled from her wish and yet said, "Now I
may";   154
She that being anger'd, her revenge being
nigh,
Bade her wrong stay and her displeasure
fly;
She that in wisdom never was so frail
To change the cod's head for the salmon's
tail;
She that could think and ne'er disclose
her mind   159
See suitors following and not look behind,
She was a wight, if ever such wights
were,—

DES: To do what?

IAGO:
To suckle fools and chronicle small beer.

DES: O most lame and impotent   [164
conclusion! Do not learn of him, Emilia,
though he be thy husband. How say you,
Cassio? Is he not a most profane and
liberal counsellor?

CAS: He speaks home, madam: you
may relish him more in the soldier than
in the scholar.   171

IAGO: (*Aside.*) He takes her by the
palm; ay, well said, whisper. With as little
a web as this will I ensnare as great [174
a fly as Cassio. Ay, smile upon her, do; I
will gyve thee in thine own courtship.
—You say true; 't is so, indeed.—If such
tricks as these strip you out of your lieu-
tenantry, it had been better you had [179
not kissed your three fingers so oft,

which now again you are most apt to play
the sir in. Very good; well kissed! an excellent curtsy! 'T is so, indeed. Yet again
your fingers to your lips? Would   [184
they were clyster-pipes for your sake!
(*Trumpet within.*)—The Moor! I know
his trumpet.

CAS: 'T is truly so.

DES: Let 's meet him and receive him.

CAS: Lo, where he comes!   190

(*Enter* OTHELLO *and* ATTENDANTS.)

OTH: O my fair warrior!

DES: My dear Othello!

OTH: It gives me wonder great as my
content
To see you here before me. O my soul's
joy!
If after every tempest come such calms,
May the winds blow till they have
waken'd death!   195
And let the labouring bark climb hills
of seas
Olympus-high, and duck again as low
As hell 's from heaven! If it were now to
die,
'T were now to be most happy; for I fear,
My soul hath her content so absolute 200
That not another comfort like to this
Succeeds in unknown fate.

DES: The heavens forbid
But that our loves and comforts should
increase,   203
Even as our days do grow!

OTH: Amen to that, sweet powers!
I cannot speak enough of this content;
It stops me here; it is too much of joy.
And this, and this, the greatest discords be

(*They kiss.*)

That e'er our hearts shall make!   208

IAGO: (*Aside.*) O, you are well tun'd
now!
But I 'll set down the pegs that make this
music,
As honest as I am.

OTH: Come, let us to the castle.
News, friends: our wars are done, the
Turks are drown'd.
How does my old acquaintance of this
isle?   213
Honey, you shall be well desir'd in
Cyprus;
I have found great love amongst them. O
my sweet,
I prattle out of fashion, and I dote
In mine own comforts. I prithee, good
Iago,   217
Go to the bay and disembark my coffers:
Bring thou the master to the citadel;
He is a good one, and his worthiness
Does challenge much respect. Come,
Desdemona,
Once more, well met at Cyprus.   222

(*Exeunt* OTHELLO, DESDEMONA
and ATTENDANTS.)

IAGO: Do thou meet me presently at
the harbour. Come hither. If thou be'st
valiant,—as, they say, base men being in
love have then a nobility in their natures
more than is native to them,—list me. The
lieutenant tonight watches on the   [228
court of guard;—first, I must tell thee this:
Desdemona is directly in love with him.

ROD: With him? why, 't is not possible.

IAGO: Lay thy finger thus, and let thy
soul be instructed. Mark me with   [233
what violence she first loved the Moor, but
for bragging and telling her fantastical lies.
To love him still for prating,—let not thy
discreet heart think it. Her eye must be
fed; and what delight shall she have   [238
to look on the devil? When the blood is
made dull with the act of sport, there
should be, again to inflame it, and to give
satiety a fresh appetite, loveliness in favour,
sympathy in years, manners, and   [243
beauties; all which the Moor is defective
in. Now, for want of these required con-
veniences, her delicate tenderness will find
itself abused, begin to heave the gorge, dis-
relish and abhor the Moor; very na-   [248

ture will instruct her in it and compel her to some second choice. Now, sir this granted, —as it is a most pregnant and unforced position—who stands so eminent in the degree of this fortune as Cassio does? [253 a knave very voluble; no further conscionable than in putting on the mere form of civil and humane seeming, for the better compassing of his salt and most hidden loose affection? Why, none; why, [258 none; a slipper and subtle knave, a finder of occasion, that has an eye can stamp and counterfeit advantages, though true advantage never present itself; a devilish knave. Besides, the knave is hand- [263 some, young, and hath all those requisites in him that folly and green minds look after; a pestilent complete knave, and the woman hath found him already.

ROD: I cannot believe that in her; she 's full of most blessed condition.   269

IAGO: Blessed fig's-end! The wine she drinks is made of grapes. If she had been blessed, she would never have loved the Moor. Blessed pudding! Didst thou [273 not see her paddle with the palm of his hand? Didst not mark that?

ROD: Yes, that I did; but that was but courtesy.   277

IAGO: Lechery, by this hand; an index and obscure prologue to the history of lust and foul thoughts. They met so near with their lips that their breaths embraced together. Villanous thoughts, Roderigo! When these mutualities so [283 marshal the way, hard at hand comes the master and main exercise, th' incorporate conclusion. Pish! But, sir, be you ruled by me; I have brought you from Venice. Watch you to-night; for the com- [288 mand, I 'll lay 't upon you Cassio knows you not: I 'll not be far from you. Do you find some occasion to anger Cassio, either by speaking too loud, or tainting his discipline; or from what other [293 course you please, which the time shall more favourably minister.

ROD: Well?

IAGO: Sir, he 's rash and very sudden in choler, and haply may strike   [298 at you: provoke him, that he may; for even out of that will I cause these of Cyprus to mutiny, whose qualification shall come into no true taste again but by the displanting of Cassio. So shall   [303 you have a shorter journey to your desires by the means I shall then have to prefer them; and the impediment most profitably removed, without the which there were no expectation of our prosperity.   309

ROD: I will do this, if you can bring it to any opportunity.

IAGO: I warrant thee. Meet me by and by at the citadel; I must fetch his necessaries ashore. Farewell.   314

ROD: Adieu.   (*Exit*)

IAGO: That Cassio loves her, I do well
    believe 't;
That she loves him, 't is apt and of great
    credit;
The Moor, howbeit that I endure him not,
Is of a constant, loving, noble nature,
And I dare think he 'll prove to Desde-
    mona   320
A most dear husband. Now, I do love her
    too;
Not out of absolute lust, though perad-
    venture
I stand accountant for as great a sin,   323
But partly led to diet my revenge,
For that I do suspect the lusty Moor
Hath leap'd into my seat; the thought
    whereof
Doth, like a poisonous mineral, gnaw my
    inwards;   327
And nothing can or shall content my soul
Till I am even'd with him, wife for wife;
Or failing so, yet that I put the Moor
At least into a jealousy so strong
That judgement cannot cure. Which thing
    to do,   332
If this poor trash of Venice, whom I
    trash

For his quick hunting, stand the putting on,
I 'll have our Michael Cassio on the hip,
Abuse him to the Moor in the rank garb—
For I fear Cassio with my night-cap too—
Make the Moor thank me, love me, and
    reward me,   338
For making him egregiously an ass
And practising upon his peace and quiet
Even to madness. 'T is here, but yet con-
    fus'd;
Knavery's plain face is never seen till
    us'd.   342
                        (Exit)

SCENE II.

A street.

(Enter Othello's HERALD, *with a proclamation.* PEOPLE *following.)*

HER: It is Othello's pleasure, our noble and valiant general, that, upon certain tidings now arrived importing the mere perdition of the Turkish fleet, every man put himself into triumph; some to [5 dance, some to make bonfires, each man to what sport and revels his addiction leads him; for, beside these beneficial news, it is the celebration of his nuptial. So much was his pleasure should be [10 proclaimed. All offices are open, and there is full liberty of feasting from this present hour of five till the bell have told eleven. Heaven bless the isle of Cyprus and our noble general Othello!   15
                      (Exeunt.)

SCENE III.

A hall in the castle

(Enter OTHELLO, DESDEMONA, CASSIO, *and* ATTENDANTS.)

OTH: Good Michael, look you to the guard to-night:

Let's teach ourselves that honourable stop,
Not to outsport discretion.

CAS: Iago hath direction what to do;
But, notwithstanding, with my personal
    eye   5
Will I look to 't.

OTH: Iago is most honest.
Michael, good-night; to-morrow with your
    earliest
Let me have speech with you. (*To* DESDE-
    MONA.) Come, my dear love,
The purchase made, the fruits are to ensue;
That profit's yet to come 'tween me and
    you.   10
Good night.

         (Exeunt OTHELLO, DESDEMONA,
              and ATTENDANTS.)
         (Enter IAGO)

CAS: Welcome, Iago; we must to the watch.

IAGO: Not this hour, lieutenant; 't is not yet ten o' th' clock. Our general [15 cast us thus early for the love of his Desdemona; who let us not therefore blame: he hath not yet made wanton the night with her; and she is sport for Jove.

CAS: She 's a most exquisite lady.   20

IAGO: And, I 'll warrant her, full of game.

CAS: Indeed, she's a most fresh and delicate creature.

IAGO: What an eye she has! Methinks its sounds a parley to provocation.   26

CAS: An inviting eye; and yet methinks right modest.

IAGO: And when she speaks, is it not an alarum to love?   30

CAS: She is indeed perfection.

IAGO: Well, happiness to their sheets! Come, lieutenant, I have a stoup of wine; and here without are a brace of Cyprus gallants that would fain have a measure to the health of black Othello.   36

CAS: Not to-night, good Iago: I have very poor and unhappy brains for drinking; I could well wish courtesy would invent some other custom of entertainment.   41

IAGO: O, they are our friends: but one cup; I 'll drink for you.

CAS: I have drunk but one cup to-night, and that was craftily qualified too,   [45 and, behold, what innovation it makes here. I am unfortunate in the infirmity, and dare not task my weakness with any more.

IAGO: What, man! 't is a night of   [50 revels: the gallants desire it.

CAS: Where are they?

IAGO: Here at the door; I pray you, call them in.

CAS: I 'll do 't; but it dislikes me.   55
                              (Exit.)

IAGO: If I can fasten but one cup upon him,
With that which he hath drunk to-night already,
He 'll be as full of quarrel and offence
As my young mistress' dog. Now, my sick fool Roderigo,
Whom love hath turn'd almost the wrong side out,   60
To Desdemona hath to-night carous'd
Potations pottle-deep; and he 's to watch:
Three lads of Cyprus, noble swelling spirits
That hold their honours in a wary distance,
The very elements of this warlike isle,   65
Have I to-night fluster'd with flowing cups,
And they watch too. Now, 'mongst this flock of drunkards
Am I to put our Cassio in some action
That may offend the isle. But here they come.

(Re-enter CASSIO, with him MONTANO and GENTLEMEN. SERVANTS follow with wine.)

If consequence do but approve my dream.
My boat sails freely, both with wind and stream.   71

CAS: 'Fore God, they have given me a rouse already.

MON: Good faith, a little one; not past a pint, as I am a soldier.   75

IAGO: Some wine, ho!

(Sings.)

And let me the canakin clink, clink;
And let me the canakin clink.
  A soldier 's a man;
  O, man's life 's but a span;   80
Why, then, let a soldier drink.

Some wine, boys!

CAS: 'Fore God, an excellent song.

IAGO: I learned it in England, where, indeed, they are most potent in pot-   [85 ting; your Dane, your German, and your swag-bellied Hollander—Drink, ho!—are nothing to your English.

CAS: Is your Englishman so exquisite in his drinking?   90

IAGO: Why, he drinks you, with facility, your Dane dead drunk; he sweats not to overthrow your Almain; he gives your Hollander a vomit ere the next pottle can be filled.   95

CAS: To the health of our general!

MON: I am for it, lieutenant; and I 'll do you justice.

IAGO: O sweet England!   99

King Stephen was and-a worthy peer,
  His breeches cost him but a crown;
He held them sixpence all too dear,
  With that he call'd the tailor lown.
He was a wight of high renown,
  And thou art but of low degree;   105
'T is pride that pulls the country down;
  And take thy auld cloak about thee.

Some wine, ho!

CAS: Why, this is a more exquisite song than the other.   110

IAGO: Will you hear 't again?

CAS: No; for I hold him to be unworthy of his place that does those things. Well, God's above all; and there be souls must

be saved, and there be souls must not
be saved.   116

IAGO: It 's true, good lieutenant.

CAS: For mine own part,—no offence
to the general, nor any man of quality—I
hope to be saved.   120

IAGO: And so do I too, lieutenant.

CAS: Ay, but, by your leave, not before
me; the lieutenant is to be saved before
the ancient. Let 's have no more of this;
let 's to our affairs.—God forgive us [125
our sins!—Gentlemen, let's look to our
business. Do not think, gentlemen, I am
drunk. This is my ancient; this is my
right hand, and this is my left. I am not
drunk now; I can stand well enough, [130
and I speak well enough.

GENT: Excellent well.

CAS: Why, very well then; you must
not think then that I am drunk. (*Exit.*)

MON: To th' platform, masters; come,
let's set the watch.   136

IAGO: You see this fellow that is gone
    before:
He is a soldier fit to stand by Cæsar
And give direction; and do but see his vice.
'T is to his virtue a just equinox,   140
The one as long as the other; 't is pity
    of him.
I fear the trust Othello puts him in,
On some odd time of his infirmity,
Will shake this island.

MON: But is he often thus?

IAGO: 'T is evermore his prologue to
    his sleep.   145
He'll watch the horologe a double set,
If drink rock not his cradle.

MON: It were well
The general were put in mind of it.
Perhaps he sees it not; or his good nature
Prizes the virtue that appears in Cassio,
And looks not on his evils. Is not this
    true?   151

(*Enter* RODERIGO.)

IAGO: (*Aside to him.*) How now,
    Roderigo!
I pray you, after the lieutenant; go.
                    (*Exit* RODERIGO.)

MON: And 't is great pity that the noble
    Moor
Should hazard such a place as his own
    second   155
With one of an ingraft infirmity:
It were an honest action to say
So to the Moor.

IAGO: Not I, for this fair island.
I do love Cassio well; and would do much
To cure him of this evil.—But, hark!
    what noise?   160
            (*Cry within*) "Help! help!"

(*Re-enter* CASSIO, *pursuing* RODERIGO.)

CAS: 'Zounds, you rogue! you rascal!

MON: What's the matter, lieutenant?

CAS: A knave teach me my duty!
I'll beat the knave into a twiggen bottle.

ROD: Beat me?

CAS: Dost thou prate, rogue?
                    (*Striking Roderigo.*)

MON: Nay, good lieutenant;
                    (*Staying him.*)
I pray you, sir, hold your hand.

CAS: Let me go, sir,
Or I 'll knock you o'er the mazzard.   166

MON: Come, come, you 're drunk.

CAS: Drunk!   (*They fight.*)

IAGO: (*Aside to* RODERIGO.) Away, I
    say; go out, and cry a mutiny.
                    (*Exit* RODERIGO.)
Nay, good lieutenant,—God's will, gentle-
    men;—   170
Help, ho!—Lieutenant,—sir,—Montano,—
    sir;—
Help, masters!—Here 's a goodly watch
    indeed!   (*A bell rings.*)
Who's that which rings the bell?—Diablo,
    ho!
The town will rise. God's will, lieutenant,
    hold!
You will be sham'd for ever.   175

(*Re-enter* OTHELLO *and* ATTENDANTS.)

OTH: What is the matter here?

MON: 'Zounds, I bleed still; I am hurt
   to th' death. He dies!

OTH: Hold, for your lives!

IAGO: Hold, ho! Lieutenant,—sir,—
   Montano,—gentlemen,—
Have you forgot all sense of place and
   duty?   180
Hold! the general speaks to you; hold,
   for shame!

OTH: Why, how now, ho! from whence
   ariseth this?
Are we turn'd Turks, and to ourselves do
   that
Which Heaven hath forbid the Ottomites?
For Christian shame, put by this barbarous brawl.   185
He that stirs next to carve for his own
   rage
Holds his soul light; he dies upon his
   motion.
Silence that dreadful bell; it frights the
   isle
From her propriety. What is the matter,
   masters?
Honest Iago, that looks dead with grieving,   190
Speak, who began this? On thy love, I
   charge thee.

IAGO: I do not know: friends but all
   now, even now,
In quarter, and in terms like bride and
   groom
Devesting them for bed; and then, but
   now—
As if some planet had unwitted men—
Swords out, and tilting one at other's
   breast,   196
In opposition bloody. I cannot speak
Any beginning to this peevish odds;
And would in action glorious I had lost
Those legs that brought me to a part of it!

OTH: How comes it, Michael, you are
   thus forgot?   201

CAS: I pray you, pardon me; I cannot
   speak.

OTH: Worthy Montano, you were wont
   to be civil;
The gravity and stillness of your youth
The world hath noted, and your name is
   great   205
In mouths of wisest censure. What's the
   matter,
That you unlace your reputation thus,
And spend your rich opinion for the name
Of a night-brawler? Give me answer
   to it.

MON: Worthy Othello, I am hurt to
   danger.   210
Your officer, Iago, can inform you—
While I spare speech, which something
   now offends me—
Of all that I do know; nor know I aught
By me that's said or done amiss this night,
Unless self-charity be sometimes a vice,
And to defend ourselves it be a sin   216
When violence assails us.

OTH: Now, by heaven,
My blood begins my safer guides to rule;
And passion, having by best judgement
   collied,
Assays to lead the way. If I once stir
Or do but lift this arm, the best of
   you   221
Shall sink in my rebuke. Give me to know
How this foul rout began, who set it on;
And he that is approv'd in this offence,
Though he had twinn'd with me, both
   at a birth,   225
Shall lose me. What! in a town of war,
Yet wild, the people's hearts brimful of
   fear,
To manage private and domestic quarrel,
In night, and on the court and guard of
   safety!
'T is monstrous. Iago, who began 't?

MON: If partially affin'd, or leagued in
   office,   231
Thou dost deliver more or less than truth,
Thou are no soldier.

IAGO: Touch me not so near.
I had rather have this tongue cut from
     my mouth   234
Than it should do offence to Michael
     Cassio;
Yet, I persuade myself, to speak the truth
Shall nothing wrong him. Thus it is,
     general:
Montano and myself being in speech,
There comes a fellow crying out for help;
And Cassio following him with determin'd
     sword   240
To execute upon him. Sir, this gentleman
Steps in to Cassio and entreats his pause;
Myself the crying fellow did pursue,
Lest by his clamour—as it so fell out—
The town might fall in fright. He, swift
     of foot,   245
Outran my purpose; and I return'd the
     rather
For that I heard the clink and fall of
     swords,
And Cassio high in oath; which till to-
     night
I ne'er might say before. When I came
     back—
For this was brief—I found them close
     together,   250
At blow and thrust; even as again they
     were
When you yourself did part them.
More of this matter cannot I report.
But men are men; the best sometimes
     forget.
Though Cassio did some little wrong to
     him,   255
As men in rage strike those that wish
     them best,
Yet surely Cassio, I believe, receiv'd
From him that fled some strange indignity
Which patience could not pass.
     OTH: I know, Iago,
Thy honesty and love doth mince this
     matter   260
Making it light to Cassio, Cassio, I love
     thee;
But never more be officer of mine.

(Re-enter DESDEMONA, *attended.)*

Look, if my gentle love be not rais'd up!
I'll make thee an example.

     DES: What's the matter, dear?

OTH: All's well now, sweeting; come
     away to bed.   265
Sir, for your hurts, myself will be your
     surgeon.—
Lead him off.
     (To MONTANO, *who is led off.)*
Iago, look with care about the town,
And silence those whom this vile brawl
     distracted.
Come, Desdemona; 't is the soldiers' life
To have their balmy slumbers wak'd with
     strife.   271
     (Exeunt all but IAGO *and* CASSIO.*)*

IAGO: What, are you hurt, lieutenant?

CAS: Ay, past all surgery.

IAGO: Marry, God forbid!

CAS: Reputation, reputation, repu- [275
tation! O, I have lost my reputation! I
have lost the immortal part of myself, and
what remains is bestial. My reputation,
Iago, my reputation!

IAGO: As I am an honest man, I [280
thought you had received bodily wound;
there is more sense in that than in reputation. Reputation is an idle and most
false imposition; oft got without merit,
and lost without deserving. You have [285
lost no reputation at all, unless you repute yourself such a loser. What, man!
there are more ways to recover the general
again. You are but now cast in his mood,
a punishment more in policy than in [290
malice; even so as one would beat his
offenceless dog to affright an imperious
lion. Sue to him again, and he 's yours.

CAS: I will rather sue to be despised
than to deceive so good a commander [295
with so slight, so drunken, and so indis-
creet an officer. Drunk? and speak parrot?
and squabble? swagger? swear? and discourse fustian with one's own shadow?

O thou invisible spirit of wine, if [300
thou hast no name to be known by, let
us call thee devil!

IAGO: What was he that you followed
with your sword? What had he done to
you?   305

CAS: I know not.

IAGO: Is 't possible?

CAS: I remember a mass of things, but
nothing distinctly; a quarrel, but nothing
wherefore. O God, that men should [310
put an enemy in their mouths to steal
away their brains! That we should, with
joy, pleasance, revel, and applause, transform ourselves into beasts!

IAGO: Why, but you are now well [315
enough. How came you thus recovered?

CAS: It hath pleased the devil drunkenness to give place to the devil wrath: one
unperfectness shows me another, to make
me frankly despise myself.   320

IAGO: Come, you are too severe a
moraler. As the time, the place, and the
condition of this country stands, I could
heartily wish this had not befallen; but
since it is as it is, mend it for your own
good.   326

CAS: I will ask him for my place again;
he shall tell me I am a drunkard! Had I
as many mouths as Hydra, such an
answer would stop them all. To be [330
now a sensible man, by and by a fool,
and presently a beast! O strange! Every
inordinate cup is unblessed and the in-
gredient is a devil.

IAGO: Come, come, good wine is a [335
good familiar creature, if it be well used;
exclaim no more against it. And, good
lieutenant, I think you think I love you.

CAS: I have well approved it, sir. I
drunk!   340

IAGO: You or any man living may be
drunk at a time, man. I 'll tell you what
you shall do. Our general's wife is now
the general;—I may say so in this respect,
for that he hath devoted and given [345
up himself to the contemplation, mark,
and denotement of her parts and graces;
—confess yourself freely to her; importune
her help to put you in your place again.
She is of so free, so kind, so apt, [350
so blessed a disposition, she holds it a
vice in her goodness not to do more than
she is requested. This broken joint between you and her husband entreat her
to splinter; and, my fortunes against [355
any lay worth naming, this crack of your
love shall grow stronger than it was
before.

CAS: You advise me well.

IAGO: I protest, in the sincerity of love
and honest kindness.   361

CAS: I think it freely; and betimes in
the morning I will beseech the virtuous
Desdemona to undertake for me. I am
desperate of my fortunes if they check
me here.   366

IAGO: You are in the right. Good-night,
lieutenant; I must to the watch.

CAS: Good-night, honest Iago. (*Exit.*)

IAGO: And what's he then that says I
play the villain?   370
When this advice is free I give and honest,
Probal to thinking and indeed the course
To win the Moor again? For 't is most
    easy
The inclining Desdemona to subdue
In any honest suit; she's fram'd as fruit-
    ful   375
As the free elements. And then for her
To win the Moor, were 't to renounce his
    baptism,
All seals and symbols of redeemed sin,
His soul is so enfetter'd to her love,
That she may make, unmake, do what
    she list,   380
Even as her appetite shall play the god
With his weak function. How am I then
    a villain
To counsel Cassio to this parallel course,

Directly to his good? Divinity of hell!
When devils will the blackest sins put
    on,
They do suggest at first with heavenly
    shows,   386
As I do now; for whiles this honest fool
Plies Desdemona to repair his fortunes
And she for him pleads strongly to the
    Moor,
I 'll pour this pestilence into his ear,
That she repeals him for her body's lust;
And by how much she strives to do him
    good,   392
She shall undo her credit with the Moor.
So will I turn her virtue into pitch,
And out of her own goodness make the
    net   395
That shall enmesh them all.

          (*Re-enter* RODERIGO.)

                    How now, Roderigo!

ROD: I do follow here in the chase, not
like a hound that hunts, but one that fills
up the cry. My money is almost spent; I
have been to-night exceedingly well cudg-
elled, and I think the issue will be,   [401
I shall have so much experience for my
pains; and so, with no money at all and
a little more wit, return again to Venice.

    IAGO: How poor are they that have not
        patience!   405
What wound did ever heal but by degrees?
Thou know'st we work by wit, and not
    by witchcraft;
And wit depends on dilatory time.
Does 't not go well? Cassio hath beaten
    thee,
And thou, by that small hurt, hast
    cashier'd Cassio.
Though other things grow fair against the
    sun,   411
Yet fruits that blossom first will first be
    ripe.
Content thyself a while. By the mass, 't
    is morning;
Pleasure and action make the hours seem
    short.

Retire thee; go where thou art billeted:
Away, I say; thou shalt know more here-
    after.   416
Nay, get thee gone. (*Exit* RODERIGO.) Two
    things are to be done:
My wife must move for Cassio to her
    mistress;
I 'll set her on;
My self a while to draw the Moor apart,
And bring him jump when he may Cas-
    sio find   421
Soliciting his wife. Ay, that 's the way;
Dull not device by coldness and delay.
                                    (*Exit.*)

ACT III

SCENE I.

Before the castle

(*Enter* CASSIO, *with* MUSICIANS.)

CAS: Masters, play here; I will content
    your pains;
Something that 's brief; and bid "Good
morrow, General."   (*They play.*)

          (*Enter* CLOWN.)

CLO: Why, masters, have your instruments been in Naples, that they speak
i' th' nose thus?   5

    I. MUS: How, sir, how?

CLO: Are these, I pray you, wind-in-
    struments?

    I. MUS: Ay, marry, are they, sir.

CLO: O, thereby hangs a tail.

    I. MUS: Whereby hangs a tale, sir?   10

CLO: Marry, sir, by many a wind-instru-
ment that I know. But, masters, here 's
money for you; and the General so likes
your music, that he desires you, of all
loves, to make no more noise with it.   15

    I. MUS: Well, sir, we will not.

CLO: If you have any music that may
not be heard, to 't again; but, as they say,

to hear music the General does not greatly care.   20

1. MUS: We have none such, sir.

CLO: Then put up your pipes in your bag, for I 'll away. Go, vanish into air, away!

(*Exeunt* MUSICIANS.)

CAS: Does thou hear, mine honest friend?   26

CLO: No, I hear not your honest friend; I hear you.

CAS: Prithee, keep up thy quillets. There 's a poor piece of gold for thee: [30 if the gentlewoman that attends the general's wife be stirring, tell her there 's one Cassio entreats her a little favour of speech. Wilt thou do this?

CLO: She is stirring, sir; if she will [35 stir hither, I shall seem to notify unto her.

CAS: Do, good my friend. (*Exit* CLOWN.)

(*Enter* IAGO.)

In happy time, Iago.

IAGO: You have not been a-bed, then?

CAS: Why, no; the day had broke Before we parted. I have made bold, Iago, To send in to your wife. My suit to her   41
Is, that she will to virtuous Desdemona Procure me some access.

IAGO: I 'll send her to you presently; And I 'll devise a mean to draw the Moor Out of the way, that your converse and business   46
May be more free.

CAS: I humbly thank you for 't. (*Exit* IAGO.) I never knew A Florentine more kind and honest.

(*Enter* EMILIA.)

EMIL: Good morrow, good lieutenant: I am sorry   50
For your displeasure; but all will sure be well:
The General and his wife are talking of it, And she speaks for you stoutly. The Moor replies,

That he you hurt is of great fame in Cyprus
And great affinity, and that in wholesome wisdom   55
He might not but refuse you; but he protests he loves you,
And needs no other suitor but his likings
To take the safest occasion by the front To bring you in again.

CAS: Yet, I beseech you, If you think fit, or that it may be done, Give me advantage of some brief discourse With Desdemon alone.

EMIL: Pray you, come in. I will bestow you where you shall have time   63
To speak your bosom freely.

CAS: I am much bound to you.
(*Exeunt.*)

SCENE II.

A room in the castle.

(*Enter* OTHELLO, IAGO, *and* GENTLEMEN.)

OTH: These letters give, Iago, to the pilot;
And by him do my duties to the Senate. That done, I will be walking on the works;
Repair there to me.

IAGO: Well, my good lord, I 'll do 't.

OTH: This fortification, gentlemen, shall we see 't?   5

GENT: We 'll wait upon your lordship.
(*Exeunt.*)

SCENE III.

The garden of the castle.

(*Enter* DESDEMONA, CASSIO, *and* EMILIA.)

DES: Be thou assur'd, good Cassio, I will do
All my abilities in thy behalf.

EMIL: Good madam, do: I warrant it
  grieves my husband
As if the cause were his.

DES: O, that 's an honest fellow. Do not
  doubt, Cassio,   5
But I will have my lord and you again
As friendly as you were.

CAS: Bounteous madam,
Whatever shall become of Michael Cassio,
He 's never anything but your true
  servant.

DES: I know 't; I thank you. You do
  love my lord;   10
You have known him long; and be you
  well assur'd
He shall in strangeness stand no farther off
Than in a politic distance.

CAS: Ay, but, lady,
That policy may either last so long,
Or feed upon such nice and waterish
  diet,   15
Or breed itself so out of circumstances,
That, I being absent and my place suppli'd,
My general will forget my love and service.

DES: Do not doubt that; before Emilia
  here
I give thee warrant of thy place. Assure
  thee,   20
If I do vow a friendship, I 'll perform
  it
To the last article. My lord shall never
  rest;
I 'll watch him tame, and talk him out of
  patience;
His bed shall seem a school, his board a
  shrift;
I 'll intermingle everything he does   25
With Cassio's suit: therefore be merry,
  Cassio;
For thy solicitor shall rather die
Than give thy cause away.

(*Enter* OTHELLO *and* IAGO.)

EMIL: Madam, here comes my lord.

CAS: Madam, I 'll take my leave.   30

DES: Why, stay, and hear me speak.

CAS: Madam, not now; I am very ill at
  ease,
Unfit for mine own purposes.

DES: Well, do your discretion.
                     (*Exit* CASSIO.)

IAGO: Ha! I like not that.

OTH: What dost thou say?

IAGO: Nothing, my lord; or if—I know
  not what.   36

OTH: Was not that Cassio parted from
  my wife?

IAGO: Cassio, my lord! No, sure, I
  cannot think it,
That he would steal away so guilty-like,
Seeing your coming.

OTH: I do believe 't was he.   40

DES: How now, my lord!
I have been talking with a suitor here,
A man that languishes in your displeasure.

OTH: Who is 't you mean?

DES: Why, your lieutenant, Cassio.
  Good my lord,   45
If I have any grace or power to move you,
His present reconciliation take;
For if he be not one that truly loves you,
That errs in ignorance and not in cun-
  ning,   49
I have no judgement in an honest face
I prithee, call him back.

OTH: Went he hence now?

DES: Yes, faith; so humbled
That he hath left part of his grief with
  me,
To suffer with him. Good love, call him
  back.

OTH: Not now, sweet Desdemon; some
  other time.   55

DES: But shall 't be shortly?

OTH: The sooner, sweet, for you.

DES: Shall 't be to-night at supper?

OTH: No, not to-night.

DES: To-morrow dinner, then?

OTH: I shall not dine at home;
I meet the captains at the citadel.

DES: Why, then, to-morrow night; on
Tuesday morn;   60
On Tuesday morn, or night; on Wednes-
day morn.
I prithee, name the time, but let it not
Exceed three days. In faith, he 's penitent;
And yet his trespass, in our common rea-
son—
Save that, they say, the wars must make
example   65
Out of their best—is not almost a fault
T' incur a private check. When shall he
come?
Tell me, Othello. I wonder in my soul,
What you would ask me, that I should
deny,
Or stand so mamm'ring on. What! Mi-
chael Cassio,   70
That came a-wooing with you, and so
many a time,
When I have spoke of you dispraisingly,
Hath ta'en your part,—to have so much
to do
To bring him in! Trust me, I could do
much,—
OTH: Prithee, no more; let him come
when he will   75
I will deny thee nothing.
DES: Why, this is not a boon.
'T is as I should entreat you wear your
gloves,
Or feed on nourishing dishes, or keep you
warm,
Or sue to you to do a peculiar profit
To your own person. Nay, when I have
a suit   80
Wherein I mean to touch your love in-
deed,
It shall be full of poise and difficult weight
And fearful to be granted.
OTH: I will deny thee nothing;
Whereon, I do beseech thee, grant me this,
To leave me but a little to myself.   85
DES: Shall I deny you? No. Farewell,
my lord.
OTH: Farewell, my Desdemona; I 'll
come to thee straight.

DES: Emilia, come.—Be as your fancies
teach you;
Whate'er you be, I am obedient.

(*Exeunt* DESDEMONA *and* EMILIA.)

OTH: Excellent wretch! Perdition catch
my soul,   90
But I do love thee! and when I love thee
not,
Chaos is come again.
IAGO: My noble lord,—
OTH: What dost thou say, Iago?
IAGO: Did Michael Cassio, when you
woo'd my lady,
Know of your love?   95
OTH: He did, from first to last. Why
dost thou ask?
IAGO: But for a satisfaction of my
thoughts;
No further harm.
OTH: Why of thy thought, Iago?
IAGO: I did not think he had been ac-
quainted with her.
OTH: O, yes; and went between us very
oft.   100
IAGO: Indeed!
OTH: Indeed! ay, indeed. Discern'st thou
aught in that?
Is he not honest?
IAGO: Honest, my Lord?
OTH: Honest! ay, honest.
IAGO: My lord, for aught I know.
OTH: What dost thou think?
IAGO: Think, my lord?
OTH: Think, my lord!
By heaven, he echoes me,   106
As if there were some monster in his
thought
Too hideous to be shown.—Thou dost
mean something:
I heard thee say even now, thou lik'st not
that,
When Cassio left my wife. What didst
not like?   110
And when I told thee he was of my counsel,

Of my whole course of wooing, thou
   criedst, "Indeed!"
And didst contract and purse thy brow
   together,
As if thou then hadst shut up in thy brain
Some horrible conceit. If thou dost love
   me,   115
Show me thy thought.

    IAGO: My lord, you know I love you.

    OTH: I think thou dost;
And, for I know thou 'rt full of love and
   honesty,
And weigh'st thy words before thou giv'st
   them breath,
Therefore these stops of thine fright me
   the more;   120
For such things in a false disloyal knave
Are tricks of custom; but in a man that 's
   just
They 're close delations, working from the
   heart
That passion cannot rule.

    IAGO: For Michael Cassio,
I dare be sworn I think that he is hon-
   est.   125

    OTH: I think so too.

    IAGO: Men should be what they seem;
Or those that be not, would they might
   seem none!

    OTH: Certain, men should be what they
   seem.

    IAGO: Why, then, I think Cassio 's an
   honest man.

    OTH: Nay, yet there 's more in this. 130
I prithee, speak to me as to thy thinkings,
As thou dost ruminate, and give thy worst
   of thoughts
The worst of words.

    IAGO: Good my lord, pardon me.
Though I am bound to every act of duty,
I am not bound to that all slaves are free
   to.
Utter my thoughts? Why, say they are
   vile and false;   136
As where 's that palace whereinto foul
   things

Sometimes intrude not? Who has a breast
   so pure
But some uncleanly apprehensions
Keep leets and law-days and in sessions
   sit   140
With meditations lawful?

    OTH: Thou dost conspire against thy
   friend, Iago,
If thou but think'st him wrong'd and
   mak'st his ear
A stranger to thy thoughts.

    IAGO: I do beseech you—
Though I perchance am vicious in my
   guess,   145
As, I confess, it is my nature's plague
To spy into abuses, and oft my jealousy
Shapes faults that are not—that your
   wisdom yet,
From one that so imperfectly conceits,
Would take no notice, nor build yourself
   a trouble   150
Out of his scattering and unsure obser-
   vance.
It were not for your quiet nor your good,
Nor for my manhood, honesty, and wis-
   dom,
To let you know my thoughts.

    OTH: What dost thou mean?

    IAGO: Good name in man and woman,
   dear my lord,   155
Is the immediate jewel of their souls.
Who steals my purse steals trash; 't is
   something, nothing;
'T was mine, 't is his, and has been slave
   to thousands;
But he that filches from me my good
   name
Robs me of that which not enriches
   him,   160
And makes me poor indeed.

    OTH: By heaven, I 'll know thy
   thoughts.

    IAGO: You cannot, if my heart were in
   your hand;
Nor shall not, whilst 't is in my cus-
   tody.   164

OTH: Ha!

IAGO: O, beware, my lord, of jealousy;
It is the green-ey'd monster which doth mock
The meat it feeds on. That cuckold lives in bliss
Who, certain of his fate, loves not his wronger;
But, O, what damned minutes tells he o'er
Who dotes, yet doubts, suspects, yet strongly loves!   170

OTH: O misery!

IAGO: Poor and content is rich and rich enough,
But riches fineless is as poor as winter
To him that ever fears he shall be poor.
Good heaven, the souls of all my tribe defend   175
From jealousy!

OTH: Why, why is this?
Think'st thou I'd make a life of jealousy,
To follow still the changes of the moon
With fresh suspicions? No! to be once in doubt
Is once to be resolv'd: exchange me for a goat,   180
When I shall turn the business of my soul
To such exsufflicate and blown surmises,
Matching thy inference. 'T is not to make me jealous
To say my wife is fair, feeds well, loves company,
Is free of speech, sings, plays, and dances well;   185
Where virtue is, there are more virtuous;
Nor from mine own weak merits will I draw
The smallest fear or doubt of her revolt;
For she had eyes, and chose me. No, Iago;
I 'll see before I doubt; when I doubt, prove;   190
And on the proof, there is no more but this,—
Away at once with love or jealousy!

IAGO: I am glad of this, for now I shall have reason
To show the love and duty that I bear you
With franker spirit; therefore, as I am bound,   195
Receive it from me. I speak not yet of proof.
Look to your wife; observe her well with Cassio;
Wear your eyes thus, not jealous nor secure:
I would not have your free and noble nature,
Out of self-bounty, be abus'd; look to 't.
I know our country disposition well;   201
In Venice they do let God see the pranks
They dare not show their husbands. Their best conscience
Is not to leave 't undone, but keep 't unknown.

OTH: Dost thou say so?   205

IAGO: She did deceive her father, marrying you;
And when she seem'd to shake and fear your looks,
She lov'd them most.

OTH: And so she did.

IAGO: Why, go to then.
She that, so young, could give out such a seeming,
To seel her father's eyes up close as oak—   210
He thought 't was witchcraft—but I am much to blame.
I humbly do beseech you of your pardon
For too much loving you.

OTH: I am bound to thee for ever.

IAGO: I see this hath a little dash'd your spirits.   214

OTH: Not a jot, not a jot.

IAGO: I' faith, I fear it has.
I hope you will consider what is spoke
Comes from my love. But I do see you 're mov'd.

I am to pray you not to strain my speech
To grosser issues nor to larger reach
Than to suspicion.   220

  OTH: I will not.

  IAGO: Should you do so, my lord,
My speech should fall into such vile success
Which my thoughts aim'd not at. Cassio
   's my worthy friend,—
My lord, I see you 're mov'd.

  OTH: No, not much mov'd.
I do not think but Desdemona 's honest.   225

  IAGO: Long live she so; and long live
   you to think so!

  OTH: And yet, how nature erring from
   itself,—

  IAGO: Ay, there 's the point; as—to be
   bold with you—
Not to affect many proposed matches
Of her own clime, complexion, and
   degree,   230
Whereto we see in all things nature
   tends—
Foh! one may smell in such, a will most
   rank,
Foul disproportions, thoughts unnatural.
But pardon me; I do not in position
Distinctly speak of her; though I may
   fear   235
Her will, recoiling to her better judgement,
May fall to match you with her country
   forms,
And happily repent.

  OTH: Farewell, farewell!
If more thou dost perceive, let me know
   more;
Set on thy wife to observe. Leave me, Iago.

  IAGO: (Going.) My lord, I take my
   leave.

  OTH: Why did I marry? This honest
   creature doubtless   242
Sees and knows more, much more, than
   he unfolds.

  IAGO: (Returning.) My lord, I would
   I might entreat your honour
To scan this thing no farther; leave it to
   time.   245
Although 't is fit that Cassio have his
   place,
For, sure, he fills it up with great ability,
Yet, if you please to hold him off a while,
You shall by that perceive him and his
   means:
Note if your lady strain his entertainment   250
With any strong or vehement importunity;
Much will be seen in that. In the mean
   time,
Let me be thought too busy in my fears—
As worthy cause I have to fear I am—
And hold her free, I do beseech your
   honour.   255

  OTH: Fear not my government.

  IAGO: I once more take my leave.

                    (Exit.)

  OTH: This fellow 's of exceeding honesty,
And knows all qualities, with a learned
   spirit,
Of human dealings. If I do prove her
   haggard,   260
Though that her jesses were my dear
   heartstrings,
I 'd whistle her off and let her down the
   wind
To prey at fortune. Haply, for I am black
And have not those soft parts of conversation
That chamberers have, or for I am declin'd
Into the vale of years,—yet that 's not
   much—   266
She 's gone. I am abus'd; and my relief
Must be to loathe her. O curse of marriage,
That we can call these delicate creatures
   ours,
And not their appetites! I had rather be
   a toad   270
And live upon the vapour of a dungeon,

Than keep a corner in the thing I love
For others' uses. Yet, 't is the plague of
 great ones;
Prerogativ'd are they less than the base:
'T is destiny unshunnable, like death. 275
Even then this forked plague is fated to us
When we do quicken. Look where she
 comes.

(*Re-enter* DESDEMONA *and* EMILIA.)

If she be false, O, then heaven mocks
 itself!
I 'll not believe 't.

 DES: How now, my dear Othello!
Your dinner, and the generous island-
 ers   280
By you invited, do attend your presence.

 OTH: I am to blame.

 DES: Why do you speak so faintly?
Are you not well?

 OTH: I have a pain upon my forehead
 here.

 DES: Faith, that 's with watching; 't
 will away again. 285
Let me but bind it hard, within this hour
It will be well.

 OTH: Your napkin is too little;

(*He puts the handkerchief from him;
    and it drops.*)

Let it alone. Come, I 'll go in with you.

 DES: I am very sorry that you are not
 well.

(*Exeunt* OTHELLO *and* DESDEMONA.)

 EMIL: I am glad I have found this
 napkin; 290
This was her first remembrance from the
 Moor:
My wayward husband hath a hundred
 times
Woo'd me to steal it; but she so loves the
 token,
For he conjur'd her she should ever keep
 it,
That she reserves it evermore about
 her 295

To kiss and talk to. I 'll have the work
 ta'en out,
And give 't Iago. What he will do with it
Heaven knows, not I;
I nothing but to please his fantasy.

(*Re-enter* IAGO.)

 IAGO: How now! what do you here
 alone? 300

 EMIL: Do not you chide; I have a thing
 for you.

 IAGO: A thing for me? It is a common
 thing—

 EMIL: Ha!

 IAGO: To have a foolish wife.

 EMIL: O, is that all? What will you
 give me now 305
For the same handkerchief?

 IAGO: What handkerchief?

 EMIL: What handkerchief!
Why, that the Moor first gave to Desde-
 mona;
That which so often you did bid me steal.

 IAGO: Hast stol'n it from her? 310

 EMIL: No, faith; she let it drop by
 negligence,
And, to th' advantage, I, bring here, took
 't up.
Look, here it is.

 IAGO: A good wench; give it me.

 EMIL: What will you do with 't, that
 you have been so earnest
To have me filch it? 315

 IAGO: (*Snatching it.*) Why, what is that
 to you?

 EMIL: If it be not for some purpose of
 import,
Give 't me again. Poor lady, she 'll run
 mad
When she shall lack it.

 IAGO: Be not acknown on 't; I have
 use for it. 320
Go, leave me. (*Exit* EMILIA.)
I will in Cassio's lodging lose this napkin,
And let him find it. Trifles light as air

Are to the jealous confirmations strong
As proofs of holy writ; this may do some-
    thing.   325
The Moor already changes with my poi-
    son:
Dangerous conceits are, in their nature,
    poisons,
Which at the first are scarce to distaste,
But with a little act upon the blood,
Burn like the mines of sulphur. I did say
    so.   330

(*Re-enter* OTHELLO.)

Look, where he comes! Not poppy, nor
    mandragora,
Nor all the drowsy syrups of the world
Shall ever medicine thee to that sweet
    sleep
Which thou ow'dst yesterday.

OTH: Ha! ha! false to me?

IAGO: Why, how now, General! no more
    of that.   335

OTH: Avaunt! be gone! thou hast set
    me on the rack.
I swear 't is better to be much abus'd
Than but to know 't a little.

IAGO: How now, my lord!

OTH: What sense had I of her stol'n
    hours of lust?
I saw 't not, thought it not, it harm'd not
    me: 340
I slept the next night well, fed well, was
    free and merry;
I found not Cassio's kisses on her lips:
He that is robb'd, not wanting what is
    stol'n,
Let him not know 't, and he 's not robb'd
    at all.

IAGO: I am sorry to hear this.   345

OTH: I had been happy, if the general
    camp,
Pioneers and all, had tasted her sweet
    body,
So I had nothing known. O, now, for ever
Farewell the tranquil mind! farewell con-
    tent!

Farewell the plumed troop, and the big
    wars,   350
That makes ambition virtue! O, farewell!
Farewell the neighing steed, and the shrill
    trump,
The spirit-stirring drum, th' ear-piercing
    fife,
The royal banner, and all quality,
Pride, pomp, and circumstance of glorious
    war!   355
And, O you mortal engines, whose rude
    throats
Th' immortal Jove's dread clamours count-
    erfeit,
Farewell! Othello's occupation 's gone!

IAGO: Is 't possible, my lord?

OTH: Villain, be sure thou prove my
    love a whore,   360
Be sure of it; give me the ocular proof;
Or, by the worth of mine eternal soul,
Thou hadst been better have been born
    a dog
Than answer my wak'd wrath!

IAGO: Is 't come to this?

OTH: Make me to see 't; or, at the least,
    so prove it,   365
That the probation bear no hinge nor
    loop
To hang a doubt on; or woe upon thy life!

IAGO: My noble lord,—

OTH: If thou dost slander her and tor-
    ture me,
Never pray more; abandon all remorse;
On horror's head horrors accumulate;   371
Do deeds to make heaven weep, all earth
    amaz'd;
For nothing canst thou to damnation add
Greater than that.

IAGO: O grace! O Heaven forgive me!
Are you a man? Have you a soul or sense?
God buy you; take mine office. O wretched
    fool,   376
That lov'st to make thine honesty a vice!
O monstrous world! Take note, take note,
    O world,

To be direct and honest is not safe.
I thank you for this profit; and from hence
I 'll love no friend, sith love breeds such
    offence.   381

OTH: Nay, stay. Thou shouldst be hon-
    est.

IAGO: I should be wise, for honesty 's a
    fool
And loses that it works for.

OTH: By the world,
I think my wife be honest and think she
    is not;   385
I think that thou art just and think thou
    art not.
I 'll have some proof. Her name, that was
    as fresh
As Dian's visage, is now begrim'd and
    black
As mine own face. If there be cords, or
    knives,
Poison, or fire, or suffocating streams,
I 'll not endure it. Would I were satis-
    fied!   391

IAGO: I see, sir, you are eaten up with
    passion;
I do repent me that I put it to you.
You would be satisfied?

OTH: Would! nay, I will.

IAGO: And may; but, how? How satis-
    fied, my lord?   395
Would you, the supervisor, grossly gape
    on—
Behold her tupp'd?

OTH: Death and damnation! O!

IAGO: It were a tedious difficulty, I
    think,
To bring them to that prospect; damn
    them then,
If ever mortal eyes do see them bolster
More than their own! What then? How
    then?   401
What shall I say? Where 's satisfac-
    tion?
It is impossible you should see this,
Were they as prime as goats, as hot as
    monkeys,

As salt as wolves in pride, and fools as
    gross   405
As ignorance made drunk. But yet, I
    say,
If imputation and strong circumstances,
Which lead directly to the door of truth,
Will give you satisfaction, you might
    have 't.

OTH: Give me a living reason she's dis-
    loyal.   410

IAGO: I do not like the office;
But, sith I am enter'd in this cause so far,
Prick'd to 't by foolish honesty and love,
I will go on. I lay with Cassio lately;
And, being troubled with a raging tooth,
I could not sleep.   416
There are a kind of men so loose of soul,
That in their sleeps will mutter their
    affairs;
One of this kind is Cassio.
In sleep I heard him say, "Sweet Desde-
    mona,   420
Let us be wary, let us hide our loves";
And then, sir, would he gripe and wring
    my hand,
Cry, "Oh sweet creature!" and then kiss
    me hard,
As if he pluck'd up kisses by the roots
That grew upon my lips; then laid his leg
Over my thigh, and sigh'd and kiss'd; and
    then   426
Cried, "Cursed fate that gave thee to the
    Moor!"

OTH: O monstrous! monstrous!

IAGO: Nay, this was but his dream.

OTH: But this denoted a foregone con-
    clusion.
'T is a shrewd doubt, though it be but a
    dream.   430

IAGO: And this may help to thicken
    other proofs.
That do demonstrate thinly.

OTH: I'll tear her all to pieces.

IAGO: Nay, but be wise; yet we see
    nothing done.
She may be honest yet. Tell me but this,

Have you not sometimes seen a hand-
    kerchief   435
Spotted with strawberries in your wife's
    hand?

  OTH: I gave her such a one; 't was my
    first gift.

  IAGO: I know not that; but such a
    handkerchief—
I am sure it was your wife's—did I to-day
See Cassio wipe his beard with.

  OTH: If it be that,—

  IAGO: If it be that, or any that was
    hers,   441
It speaks against her with the other proofs.

  OTH: O, that the slave had forty thou-
    sand lives!
One is too poor, too weak for my revenge.
Now do I see 't is true. Look here, Iago;
All my fond love thus do I blow to heaven.
'T is gone.   447
Arise, black vengeance, from the hollow
    hell!
Yield up, O love, thy crown and hearted
    throne
To tyrannous hate! Swell, bosom, with thy
    fraught   450
For 't is of aspics' tongues!

  IAGO: Yet be content.

  OTH: O, blood, blood, blood!

  IAGO: Patience, I say; your mind per-
    haps may change.

  OTH: Never, Iago. Like to the Pontic
    Sea,
Whose icy current and compulsive course
Ne'er feels retiring ebb, but keeps due
    on   456
To the Propontic and the Hellespont,
Even so my bloody thoughts, with violent
    pace,
Shall ne'er look back, ne'er ebb to humble
    love,
Till that a capable and wide revenge   460
Swallow them up. Now, by yond marble
    heaven,
In the due reverence of a sacred vow
I here engage my words.   (*Kneels.*)

  IAGO: Do not rise yet.
Witness, you ever-burning lights above.
You elements that clip us round about,
                  (*Kneels.*)
Witness that here Iago doth give up   466
The execution of his wit, hands, heart,
To wrong'd Othello's service! Let him
    command,
And to obey shall be in me remorse,
What bloody business ever.   (*They rise.*)

  OTH: I greet thy love,
Not with vain thanks, but with accept-
    ance bounteous,   471
And will upon the instant put thee to 't:
Within these three days let me hear thee
    say
That Cassio 's not alive.

  IAGO: My friend is dead; 't is done at
    your request.   475
But let her live.

  OTH: Damn her, lewd minx! O, damn
    her!
Come, go with me apart; I will withdraw
To furnish me with some swift means of
    death
For the fair devil. Now art thou my lieu-
    tenant.   480

  IAGO: I am your own for ever. (*Exeunt.*)

Scene IV.

Before the castle.

(*Enter* DESDEMONA, EMILIA, *and* CLOWN.)

  DES: Do you know, sirrah, where Lieutenant Cassio lies?

  CLO: I dare not say he lies anywhere.

  DES: Why, man?

  CLO: He 's a soldier, and for me to say
a soldier lies, 't is stabbing.   6

  DES: Go to! Where lodges he?

  CLO: To tell you where he lodges, is to
tell you where I lie.

  DES: Can anything be made of this? 10

  CLO: I know not where he lodges, and
for me to devise a lodging and say he lies

here or he lies there, were to lie in mine own throat.

DES: Can you inquire him out, and be edified by report? 16

CLO: I will catechize the world for him; that is, make questions, and by them answer.

DES: Seek him, bid him come hither. [20 Tell him I have moved my lord on his behalf, and hope all will be well.

CLO: To do this is within the compass of man's wit; and therefore I will attempt the doing it. (*Exit*.)

DES: Where should I lose the handkerchief, Emilia? 27

EMIL: I know not, madam.

DES: Believe me, I had rather have lost my purse 30
Full of crusadoes; and, but my noble Moor Is true of mind and made of no such baseness
As jealous creatures are, it were enough To put him to ill thinking.

EMIL: Is he not jealous?

DES: Who, he? I think the sun where he was born 35
Drew all such humours from him.

EMIL: Look, where he comes.
(*Enter* OTHELLO.)

DES: I will not leave him now till Cassio Be call'd to him.—How is 't with you, my lord?

OTH: Well, my good lady. (*Aside*.) O, hardness to dissemble!—
How do you, Desdemona?

DES: Well, my good lord.

OTH: Give me your hand. This hand is moist, my lady. 41

DES: It yet hath felt no age nor known no sorrow.

OTH: This argues fruitfulness and liberal heart;
Hot, hot, and moist. This hand of yours requires

A sequester from liberty, fasting and prayer, 45
Much castigation, exercise devout;
For here 's a young and sweating devil here,
That commonly rebels. 'T is a good hand, A frank one.

DES: You may, indeed, say so;
For 't was that hand that gave away my heart. 50

OTH: A liberal hand. The hearts of old gave hands;
But our new heraldry is hands, not hearts.

DES: I cannot speak of this. Come now, your promise.

OTH: What promise, chuck?

DES: I have sent to bid Cassio come speak with you. 55

OTH: I have a salt and sorry rheum offends me;
Lend me thy handkerchief.

DES: Here, my lord.

OTH: That which I gave you,

DES: I have it not about me.

OTH: Not?

DES: No, faith, my lord.

OTH: That 's a fault. That handkerchief 60
Did an Egyptian to my mother give,
She was a charmer, and could almost read
The thoughts of people. She told her, while she kept it
'T would make her amiable and subdue my father
Entirely to her love, but if she lost it, 65
Or made a gift of it, my father's eye
Should hold her loathed and his spirits should hunt
After new fancies. She, dying, gave it me;
And bid me, when my fate would have me wiv'd,
To give it her. I did so; and take heed on 't; 70
Make it a darling like your precious eye.

To lose 't or give 't away were such perdition
As nothing else could match.

DES: Is 't possible?

OTH: 'T is true; there 's magic in the
web of it.
A sibyl, that had number'd in the world
The sun to course two hundred compasses,
In her prophetic fury sew'd the work; 77
The worms were hallowed that did breed
the silk;
And it was dy'd in mummy which the
skilful
Conserv'd of maidens' hearts.

DES: Indeed! is 't true?

OTH: Most veritable; therefore look to
't well.   81

DES: Then would to God that I had
never seen 't!

OTH: Ha! wherefore?

DES: Why do you speak so startingly
and rash?

OTH: Is 't lost? Is 't gone? Speak, is 't
out o' the way?   85

DES: Heaven bless us!

OTH: Say you?

DES: It is not lost; but what an if it
were?

OTH: How?

DES: I say, it is not lost.

OTH: Fetch 't, let me see 't.

DES: Why, so I can, sir, but I will not
now.   91
This is a trick to put me from my suit:
Pray you, let Cassio be receiv'd again.

OTH: Fetch me the handkerchief; my
mind misgives.

DES: Come, come;   95
You 'll never meet a more sufficient man.

OTH: The handkerchief!

DES: I pray, talk me of Cassio.

OTH: The handkerchief!

DES: A man that all his time

Hath founded his good fortunes on your
love,
Shar'd dangers with you,—   100

OTH: The handkerchief!

DES: I' faith, you are to blame.

OTH: 'Zounds!   (*Exit* OTHELLO.)

EMIL: Is not this man jealous?

DES: I ne'er saw this before.   105
Sure, there 's some wonder in this hand-
kerchief;
I am most unhappy in the loss of it.

EMIL: 'T is not a year or two shows us
a man:
They are all but stomachs, and we all but
food;
They eat us hungerly, and when they are
full   110
They belch us.

(*Enter* CASSIO *and* IAGO.)

Look you, Cassio and my husband!

IAGO: There is no other way, 't is she
must do 't;
And, lo, the happiness! Go, and importune
her.

DES: How now, good Cassio! what 's the
news with you?

CAS: Madam, my former suit. I do be-
seech you   115
That by your virtuous means I may again
Exist, and be a member of his love
Whom I with all the office of my heart
Entirely honour: I would not be delay'd.
If my offence be of such mortal kind 120
That nor my service past, nor present sor-
rows,
Nor purpos'd merit in futurity
Can ransom me into his love again,
But to know so must be my benefit; 124
So shall I clothe me in a forc'd con-
tent,
And shut myself up in some other course,
To fortune's alms.

DES: Alas, thrice-gentle Cassio!
My advocation is not now in tune;

My lord is not my lord, nor should I know
him
Were he in favour as in humour alter'd.
So help me every spirit sanctified   131
As I have spoken for you all my best
And stood within the blank of his dis-
pleasure
For my free speech! You must a while be
patient.
What I can do I will; and more I will 135
Than for myself I dare. Let that suffice
you.

IAGO: Is my lord angry?

EMIL: He went hence but now,
And certainly in strange unquietness.

IAGO: Can he be angry? I have seen the
cannon
When it hath blown his ranks into the
air,   140
And, like the devil, from his very arm
Puff'd his own brother—and can he be
angry?
Something of moment then. I will go meet
him.
There 's matter in 't indeed, if he be angry.
          (*Exit* IAGO.)

DES: I prithee, do so. Something, sure,
of state,   145
Either from Venice, or some unhatch'd
practice
Made demonstrable here in Cyprus to him,
Hath puddled his clear spirit; and in such
cases
Men's natures wrangle with inferior
things,
Though great ones are their object. 'T is
even so;   150
For let our finger ache, and it indues
Our other helpful members even to a
sense
Of pain. Nay, we must think men are not
gods,
Nor of them look for such observancy
As fits the bridal. Beshrew me much,
Emilia,   155
I was, unhandsome warrior as I am,
Arraigning his unkindess with my soul;

But now I find I had suborn'd the witness,
And he 's indicted falsely.

EMIL: Pray Heaven it be state-matters,
as you think,   160
And no conception nor no jealous toy
Concerning you.

DES: Alas the day! I never gave him
cause.

EMIL: But jealous souls will not be an-
swered so;
They are not ever jealous for the cause, 165
But jealous for they 're jealous. It is a
monster.
Begot upon itself, born on itself.

DES: Heaven keep that monster from
Othello's mind!

EMIL: Lady, amen.

DES: I will go seek him. Cassio, walk
hereabout;   170
If I do find him fit, I 'll move your suit
And seek to effect it to my uttermost.

CAS: I humbly thank your ladyship.

          (*Exeunt* DESDEMONA *and* EMILIA.)

          (*Enter* BIANCA.)

BIAN: Save you, friend Cassio!

CAS: What make you from home?
How is it with you, my most fair Bianca?
I' faith, sweet love, I was coming to your
house.   176

BIAN: And I was going to your lodging,
Cassio.
What, keep a week away? Seven days and
nights?
Eightscore eight hours? and lovers' absent
hours,
More tedious than the dial eightscore
times?   180
O weary reck'ning!

CAS: Pardon me, Bianca.
I have this while with leaden thoughts
been press'd;
But I shall, in a more continuate time,
Strike off this score of absence. Sweet
Bianca,

          (*Giving her* DESDEMONA's *handkerchief.*)

Take me this work out.

BIAN: O Cassio, whence came this?
This is some token from a newer friend;
To the felt absence now I feel a cause. 187
Is 't come to this? Well, well.

CAS: Go to, woman!
Throw your vile guesses in the devil's
    teeth,
From whence you have them. You are
    jealous now   190
That this is from some mistress, some re-
    membrance.
No, by my faith, Bianca.

BIAN: Why, whose is it?

CAS: I know not, sweet; I found it in
    my chamber.
I like the work well; ere it be demanded—
As like enough it will—I 'd have it
    copied.   195
Take it, and do 't; and leave me for this
    time.

BIAN: Leave you! Wherefore?

CAS: I do attend here on the General;
And think it no addition, nor my wish, 199
To have him see me woman'd.

BIAN: Why, I pray you?

CAS: Not that I love you not.

BIAN: But that you do not love me.
I pray you, bring me on the way a little,
And say if I shall see you soon at night.

CAS: 'T is but a little way that I can
    bring you,
For I attend here; but I 'll see you soon. 205

BIAN: 'T is very good; I must be cir-
    cumstanc'd.   (*Exeunt.*)

ACT IV

SCENE I.

Cyprus. Before the castle.

(*Enter* OTHELLO *and* IAGO.)

IAGO: Will you think so?

OTH: Think so, Iago!

IAGO: What,
To kiss in private?

OTH: An unauthoriz'd kiss.

IAGO: Or to be naked with her friend
    in bed
An hour or more, not meaning any harm?

OTH: Naked in bed, Iago, and not mean
    harm!   5
It is hypocrisy against the devil:
They that mean virtuously, and yet do so,
The devil their virtue tempts, and they
    tempt heaven.

IAGO: If they do nothing, 't is a venial
    slip;
But if I give my wife a handkerchief,— 10

OTH: What then?

IAGO: Why, then, 't is hers, my lord;
    and, being hers,
She may, I think, bestow 't on any man.

OTH: She is protectress of her honour
    too;
May she give that?   15

IAGO: Her honour is an essence that 's
    not seen;
They have it very oft that have it not:
But, for the handkerchief,—

OTH: By heaven, I would most gladly
    have forgot it.
Thou said'st—O, it comes o'er my mem-
    ory,   20
As doth the raven o'er the infected house,
Boding to all—he had my handkerchief.

IAGO: Ay, what of that?

OTH: That 's not so good now.

IAGO: What
If I had said I had seen him do you
    wrong?
Or heard him say,—as knaves be such
    abroad,   25
Who having, by their own importunate
    suit,
Or voluntary dotage of some mistress,
Convinced or supplied them, cannot choose
But they must blab—

OTH: Hath he said anything?

IAGO: He hath, my lord; but be you well
  assur'd,   30
No more than he 'll unswear.

OTH: What hath he said?

IAGO: Faith, that he did—I know not
  what he did.

OTH: What? what?

IAGO: Lie—

OTH: With her?

IAGO: With her, on her; what you
  will.   34

OTH: Lie with her! lie on her! We say
lie on her, when they belie her. Lie with
her! 'Zounds, that 's fulsome!—Handkerchief—confessions—handkerchief!—   [38
To confess, and be hanged for his labour;
—first, to be hanged, and then to confess.
—I tremble at it. Nature would not invest
herself in such shadowing passion without
some instruction. It is not words that
shakes me thus. Pish! Noses, ears, and
lips—Is 't possible?—Confess—hand- [45
kerchief!—O devil!   (*Falls in a trance.*)

IAGO: Work on,
My medicine, work! Thus credulous fools
  are caught;
And many worthy and chaste dames even
  thus,
All guiltless, meet reproach.—What, ho!
  my lord!   50
My lord, I say! Othello!

(*Enter* CASSIO.)

                    How now, Cassio!

CAS: What 's the matter?

IAGO: My lord is fall'n into an epilepsy.
This is his second fit; he had one yesterday.   54

CAS: Rub him about the temples.

IAGO: No, forbear;
The lethargy must have his quiet course;
If not, he foams at mouth and by and by
Breaks out to savage madness. Look, he
  stirs.
Do you withdraw yourself a little while,

He will recover straight: when he is
  gone,   60
I would on great occasion speak with you.
                    (*Exit* CASSIO.)
How is it, general? Have you not hurt
  your head?

OTH: Dost thou mock me?

IAGO: I mock you not, by heaven.
Would you would bear your fortune like
  a man!

OTH: A horned man 's a monster and a
  beast.   65

IAGO: There 's many a beast then in a
  populous city,
And many a civil monster.

OTH: Did he confess it?

IAGO: Good sir, be a man;
Think every bearded fellow that 's but
  yok'd
May draw with you. There's millions now
  alive   70
That nightly lie in those unproper beds
Which they dare swear peculiar; your case
  is better.
O, 't is the spite of hell, the fiend's arch-
  mock,
To lip a wanton in a secure couch,
And to suppose her chaste! No, let me
  know;   75
And knowing what I am, I know what she
  shall be.

OTH: O, thou art wise; 't is certain.

IAGO: Stand you a while apart;
Confine yourself but in a patient list.
Whilst you were here o'erwhelmed with
  your grief—
A passion most unsuiting such a man— 80
Cassio came hither. I shifted him away,
And laid good 'scuse upon your ecstasy;
Bade him anon return and here speak
  with me,
The which he promis'd. Do but encave
  yourself,
And mark the fleers, the gibes, and notable
  scorns,   85

That dwell in every region of his face;
For I will make him tell the tale anew,
Where, how, how oft, how long ago, and
    when
He hath, and is again to cope your wife.
I say, but mark his gesture. Marry, pa-
    tience;   90
Or I shall say you 're all in all in spleen,
And nothing of a man.

    OTH: Dost thou hear, Iago?
I will be found most cunning in my pa-
    tience;
But—dost thou hear?—most bloody.

    IAGO: That's not amiss;
But yet keep time in all. Will you with-
    draw?   (OTHELLO *retires*.)
Now will I question Cassio of Bianca, 96
A housewife that by selling her desires
Buys herself bread and clothes. It is a
    creature
That dotes on Cassio;—as 't is the strum-
    pet's plague
To beguile many and be beguil'd by
    one;—   100
He, when he hears of her, cannot refrain
From the excess of laughter. Here he
    comes.

    (*Re-enter* CASSIO.)

As he shall smile, Othello shall go mad;
And his unbookish jealousy must construe
Poor Cassio's smiles, gestures, and light
    behaviours   105
Quite in the wrong. How do you lieu-
    tenant?

    CAS: The worser that you give me the
    addition
Whose want even kills me.

    IAGO: Ply Desdemona well, and you are
    sure on 't.   109
Now, if this suit lay in Bianca's power,
How quickly should you speed!

    CAS: Alas, poor caitiff!

    OTH: Look, how he laughs already!

    IAGO: I never knew a woman love man
    so.

    CAS: Alas, poor rogue! I think, i' faith,
    she loves me.

    OTH: Now he denies it faintly, and
    laughs it out.   115

    IAGO: Do you hear, Cassio?

    OTH: Now he importunes him
To tell it o'er. Go to; well said, well said.

    IAGO: She gives it out that you shall
    marry her.
Do you intend it?   120

    CAS: Ha, ha, ha!

    OTH: Do ye triumph, Roman? Do you
    triumph?

    CAS: I marry her! What? a customer!
Prithee, bear some charity to my wit;
do not think it so unwholesome. Ha, ha,
ha!   126

    OTH: So, so, so, so; they laugh that
wins.

    IAGO: Faith, the cry goes that you shall
marry her.   130

    CAS: Prithee, say true.

    IAGO: I am a very villain else.

    OTH: Have you scor'd me? Well.

    CAS: This is the monkey's own giving
out. She is persuaded I will marry her,
out of her own love and flattery, not out
of my promise.   137

    OTH: Iago beckons me; now he begins
the story.

    CAS: She was here even now; she [140
haunts me in every place. I was the other
day talking on the sea-bank with certain
Venetians; and thither comes the bauble,
and, by this hand, she falls me thus about
my neck—   145

    OTH: Crying, "O dear Cassio!" as it
were; his gesture imports it.

    CAS: So hangs, and lolls, and weeps
upon me; so shakes and pulls me. Ha, ha,
ha,!   150

    OTH: Now he tells how she plucked
him to my chamber. O, I see that nose of
yours, but not that dog I shall throw it to.

CAS: Well, I must leave her company.

IAGO: Before me! look, where she comes.   156

(*Enter* BIANCA.)

CAS: 'T is such another fitchew! Marry, a perfumed one.—What do you mean by this haunting of me?   159

BIAN: Let the devil and his dam haunt you! What did you mean by that same handkerchief you gave me even now? I was a fine fool to take it. I must take out the work?—A likely piece of work, that you should find it in your chamber, [165 and know not who left it there! This is some minx's token, and I must take out the work? There; give it your hobby-horse: wheresoever you had it, I 'll take no work on 't.   170

CAS: How now, my sweet Bianca! how now! how now!

OTH: By heaven, that should be my handkerchief!   174

BIAN: If you 'll come to supper to-night, you may; if you will not, come when you are next prepared for.   (*Exit.*)

IAGO: After her, after her.

CAS: Faith, I must; she 'll rail in the streets else.   180

IAGO: Will you sup there?

CAS: Faith, I intend so.

IAGO: Well, I may chance to see you; for I would very fain speak with you.

CAS: Prithee, come; will you?   185

IAGO: Go to; say no more. (*Exit* CASSIO.)

OTH: (*Advancing.*) How shall I murder him, Iago?

IAGO: Did you perceive how he laughed at his vice?   190

OTH: O Iago!

IAGO: And did you see the handkerchief?

OTH: Was that mine?   194

IAGO: Yours, by this hand: and to see how he prizes the foolish woman your wife! She gave it him, and he hath given it his whore.

OTH: I would have him nine years a-killing. A fine woman! a fair woman! a sweet woman!   201

IAGO: Nay, you must forget that.

OTH: Ay, let her rot, and perish, and be damned to-night; for she shall not live. No, my heart is turned to stone; I strike it, and it hurts my hand. O, the world [206 hath not a sweeter creature! She might lie by an emperor's side and command him tasks.

IAGO: Nay, that 's not your way.   210

OTH: Hang her! I do but say what she is. So delicate with her needle! an admirable musician! O! she will sing the savageness out of a bear: of so high and plenteous wit and invention!   215

IAGO: She 's the worse for all this.

OTH: O, a thousand thousand times! And then, of so gentle a condition!

IAGO: Ay, too gentle.   219

OTH: Nay, that 's certain. But yet the pity of it, Iago! O Iago, the pity of it, Iago!

IAGO: If you are so fond over her iniquity, give her patent to offend; for, if it touch not you, it comes near nobody.   225

OTH: I will chop her into messes. Cuckold me!

IAGO: O, 't is foul in her.

OTH: With mine officer!

IAGO: That's fouler.   230

OTH: Get me some poison, Iago, this night. I 'll not expostulate with her, lest her body and beauty unprovide my mind again. This night, Iago.   234

IAGO: Do it not with poison; strangle her in her bed, even the bed she hath contaminated.

OTH: Good, good; the justice of it pleases; very good.   239

IAGO: And for Cassio, let me be his undertaker: you shall hear more by midnight.

OTH: Excellent good!   (*A trumpet.*)
    What trumpet is that same?

IAGO: Something from Venice sure.

(*Enter* LODOVICO, DESDEMONA, *and*
    ATTENDANTS)

                    'T is Lodovico.
Come from the Duke; and, see, your wife
    is with him.   245

LOD: God save you, worthy General!

OTH: With all my heart, sir.

LOD: The Duke and senators of Venice
    greet you.   (*Gives him a letter.*)

OTH: I kiss the instrument of their
    pleasures.
            (*Opens the letter, and reads.*)

DES: And what 's the news, good cousin
    Lodovico?

IAGO: I am very glad to see you, signior;
    Welcome to Cyprus.   250

LOD: I thank you. How does Lieutenant
    Cassio?

IAGO: Lives, sir.

DES: Cousin, there 's falln' between him
    and my lord
An unkind breach; but you shall make all
    well.

OTH: Are you sure of that?   255

DES: My lord!

OTH: (*Reads.*) "This fail you not to do,
    as you will"—

LOD: He did not call; he 's busy in the
    paper.
Is there division 'twixt my lord and
    Cassio?

DES: A most unhappy one. I would do
    much   260
T' atone them, for the love I bear to
    Cassio.

OTH: Fire and brimstone!

DES: My lord?

OTH: Are you wise?

DES: What, is he angry?

LOD: May be the letter mov'd him;

For, as I think, they do command him
    home,
Deputing Cassio in his government.   265

DES: Trust me, I am glad on 't.

OTH: Indeed!

DES: My lord?

OTH: I am glad to see you mad.

DES: Why, sweet Othello,—

OTH: (*Striking her.*) Devil!

DES: I have not deserv'd this.

LOD: My lord, this would not be be-
    liev'd in Venice   270
Though I should swear I saw 't. 'T is very
    much.
Make her amends: she weeps.

OTH: O devil, devil!
If that the earth could teem with woman's
    tears,
Each drop she falls would prove a croco-
    dile.   274
Out of my sight!

DES: I will not stay to offend you.
                         (*Going.*)

LOD: Truly, an obedient lady:
I do beseech your lordship, call her back.

OTH: Mistress!

DES: My lord?

OTH: What would you with her, sir?

LOD: Who, I, my lord?

OTH: Ay; you did wish that I would
    make her turn.   280
Sir, she can turn, and turn, and yet go on,
And turn again; and she can weep, sir,
    weep;
And she's obedient, as you say, obedient,
Very obedient. Proceed you in your tears.
Concerning this, sir,—O well-painted pas-
    sion!—   285
I am commanded home.—Get you away;
I 'll send for you anon.—Sir, I obey the
    mandate,
And will return to Venice.—Hence,
    avaunt!—   (*Exit* DESDEMONA.)
Cassio shall have my place. And, sir, to-
    night,   289

I do entreat that we may sup together.
You are welcome, sir, to Cyprus—Goats
   and monkeys!   (*Exit.*)

LOD: Is this the noble Moor whom our
   full Senate
Call all in all sufficient? Is this the nature
Whom passion could not shake? whose
   solid virtue   294
The shot of accident nor dart of chance.
Could neither graze nor pierce?

IAGO: He is much chang'd.

LOD: Are his wits safe? Is he not light
   of brain?

IAGO: He 's that he is; I may not breathe
   my censure
What he might be. If what he might he is
   not,   299
I would to heaven he were!

LOD: What, strike his wife!

IAGO: Faith, that was not so well; yet
   would I knew
That stroke would prove the worst!

LOD: Is it his use?
Or did the letters work upon his blood,
And new-create this fault?

IAGO: Alas, alas!
It is not honesty in me to speak   305
What I have seen and known. You shall
   observe him,
And his own courses will denote him so
That I may save my speech: do but go
   after,
And mark how he continues.   309

LOD: I am sorry that I am deceiv'd in
   him.   (*Exeunt.*)

Scene II.

A room in the castle.

(*Enter* OTHELLO *and* EMILIA.)

OTH: You have seen nothing then?

EMIL: Nor ever heard, nor ever did
   suspect.

OTH: Yes, you have seen Cassio and she
   together.

EMIL: But then I saw no harm, and
   then I heard
Each syllable that breath made up between them.   5

OTH: What, did they never whisper?

EMIL: Never, my lord.

OTH: Nor send you out o' th' way?

EMIL: Never.

OTH: To fetch her fan, her gloves, her
   mask, nor nothing?

EMIL: Never, my lord.   10

OTH: That 's strange.

EMIL: I durst, my lord, to wager she is
   honest,
Lay down my soul at stake: if you think
   other,
Remove your thought; it doth abuse your
   bosom.
If any wretch have put this in your head,
Let Heaven requite it with the serpent's
   curse!   16
For, if she be not honest, chaste, and true,
There 's no man happy; the purest of their
   wives
Is foul as slander.

OTH: Bid her come hither; go.

(*Exit* EMILIA.)

She says enough; yet she 's a simple bawd
That cannot say as much. This is a subtle
   whore,   21
A closet lock and key of villanous secrets;
And yet she 'll kneel and pray; I have seen
   her do 't.

(*Enter* DESDEMONA *with* EMILIA.)

DES: My lord, what is your will?

OTH: Pray, chuck, come hither.

DES: What is your pleasure?

OTH: Let me see your eyes;   25
Look in my face.

DES: What horrible fancy 's this?

OTH: (*To* EMILIA.) Some of your function, mistress;
Leave procreants alone and shut the door;

Cough, or cry "hem," if anybody come.
Your mystery, your mystery; nay, dispatch.

(*Exit* EMILIA.)

DES: Upon my knees, what doth your
    speech import?   31
I understand a fury in your words,
But not the words.

OTH: Why, what art thou?

DES: Your wife, my lord; your true and
    loyal wife.   35

OTH: Come, swear it, damn thyself,
Lest, being like one of heaven, the devils
    themselves
Should fear to seize thee; therefore be
    double damn'd,
Swear thou art honest.

DES: Heaven doth truly know it.

OTH: Heaven truly knows that thou art
    false as hell.   40

DES: To whom, my lord? With whom?
    How am I false?

OTH: Ah, Desdemon! Away! away!
    away!

DES: Alas the heavy day! Why do you
    weep?
Am I the motive of these tears, my lord?
If haply you my father do suspect   45
An instrument of this your calling back,
Lay not your blame on me: if you have
    lost him,
Why, I have lost him too.

OTH: Had it pleas'd Heaven
To try me with affliction; had they rain'd
All kinds of sores and shames on my bare
    head,   50
Steep' me in poverty to the very lips,
Given to captivity me and my utmost
    hopes,
I should have found in some place of my
    soul
A drop of patience; but, alas, to make
    me
A fixed figure for the time of scorn   55
To point his slow unmoving finger at!
Yet could I bear that too, well, very well;

But there, where I have garner'd up my
    heart,
Where either I must live, or bear no life;
The fountain from the which my current
    runs,   60
Or else dries up; to be discarded thence!
Or keep it as a cistern for foul toads
To knot and gender in! Turn thy com-
    plexion there,
Patience, thou young and rose-lipp'd
    cherubin,
Ay, there look grim as hell!   65

DES: I hope my noble lord esteems me
    honest.

OTH: O, ay; as summer flies are in the
    shambles,
That quicken even with blowing. O thou
    weed,
Who are so lovely fair and smell'st so
    sweet
That the sense aches at thee, would thou
    hadst ne'er been born!   70

DES: Alas, what ignorant sin have I
    committed?

OTH: Was this fair paper, this mostly
    goodly book,
Made to write "whore" upon? What com-
    mitted?   73
Committed! O thou public commoner!
I should make very forges of my cheeks,
That would to cinders burn up modesty,
Did I but speak thy deeds. What com-
    mitted?
Heaven stops the nose at it, and the moon
    winks,
The bawdy wind, that kisses all it meets,
Is hush'd within the hollow mine of
    earth,   80
And will not hear it. What committed!
Impudent strumpet!

DES: By heaven, you do me wrong.

OTH: Are not you a strumpet?

DES: No, as I am a Christian.
If to preserve this vessel for my lord
From any other foul unlawful touch
Be not to be a strumpet, I am none.

OTH: What, not a whore?

DES: No, as I shall be sav'd.

OTH: Is 't possible?

DES: O, Heaven forgive us!

OTH: I cry you mercy, then.
I took you for that cunning whore of
    Venice.   90
That married with Othello.—You, mis-
    tress,

(Re-enter EMILIA.*)*

That have the office opposite to Saint
    Peter,
And keeps the gate of hell! You, you, ay,
    you!
We have done our course; there's money
    for your pains.   94
I pray you, turn the key and keep our
    counsel.   *(Exit.)*

EMIL: Alas, what does this gentleman
    conceive?
How do you, madam? How do you, my
    good lady?

DES: Faith, half asleep.

EMIL: Good madam, what 's the matter
    with my lord?

DES: With who?   100

EMIL: Why, with my lord, madam.

DES: Who is thy lord?

EMIL: He that is yours, sweet lady.

DES: I have none: do not talk to me,
    Emilia;
I cannot weep, nor answers have I none
But what should go by water. Prithee, to-
    night   105
Lay on my bed my wedding sheets, re-
    member;
And call thy husband hither.

EMIL: Here 's a change indeed!
                     (Exit.)

DES: 'T is meet I should be us'd so, very
    meet.
How have I been behav'd, that he might
    stick   109
The small'st opinion on my least misuse?

(Re-enter EMILIA *with* IAGO.*)*

IAGO: What is your pleasure, madam?
    How is 't with you?

DES: I cannot tell. Those that do teach
    young babes
Do it with gentle means and easy tasks.
He might have chid me so; for, in good
    faith,
I am a child to chiding.

IAGO: What 's the matter, lady?

EMIL: Alas, Iago, my lord hath so be-
    whor'd her,   116
Thrown such despite and heavy terms
    upon her,
That true hearts cannot bear.

DES: Am I that name, Iago?

IAGO: What name, fair lady?

DES: Such as she said my lord did say
    I was.   120

EMIL: He call'd her whore: a beggar in
    his drink
Could not have laid such terms upon his
    callet.

IAGO: Why did he so?

DES: I do not know; I am sure I am
    none such.

IAGO: Do not weep, do not weep. Alas
    the day!   125

EMIL: Hath she forsook so many noble
    matches,
Her father and her country and her
    friends,
To be call'd whore? Would it not make
    one weep?

DES: It is my wretched fortune.

IAGO: Beshrew him for 't!
How comes this trick upon him?

DES: Nay, Heaven doth know.

EMIL: I will be hang'd, if some eternal
    villain,   131
Some busy and insinuating rogue,
Some cogging, cozening slave, to get some
    office,

Have not devis'd this slander: I 'll be
    hang'd else.
  IAGO: Fie, there is no such man; it is
    impossible.   135
  DES: If any such there be, Heaven par-
    don him!
  EMIL: A halter pardon him and hell
    gnaw his bones!
Why should he call her whore? Who
    keeps her company?
What place? what time? what form? what
    likelihood?
The Moor 's abus'd by some most villan-
    ous knave,   140
Some base notorious knave, some scurvy
    fellow.
O heaven, that such companions thou 'dst
    unfold,
And put in every honest hand a whip
To lash the rascals naked through the
    world
Even from the east to th' west!
  IAGO: Speak within door.
  EMIL: O, fie upon them! Some such
    squire he was   146
That turn'd your wit the seamy side with-
    out,
And made you to suspect me with the
    Moor.
  IAGO: You are a fool; go to.
  DES: Alas, Iago,
What shall I do to win my lord again? 150
Good friend, go to him; for, by this light
    of heaven,
I know not how I lost him. Here I kneel:
If e'er my will did trespass 'gainst his love,
Either in discourse of thought or actual
    deed,
Or that mine eyes, mine ears, or any sense
Delighted them in any other form;   156
Or that I do not yet, and ever did,
And ever will—though he do shake me off
To beggarly divorcement—love him
    dearly,
Comfort forswear me! Unkindness may do
    much;   160

And his unkindness may defeat my life,
But never taint my love. I cannot say
    "whore."
It does abhor me now I speak the word;
To do the act that might the addition earn
Not the world's mass of vanity could make
    me.   165
  IAGO: I pray you, be content; 't is but
    his humour.
The business of the state does him offence,
And he does chide with you.
  DES: If 't were no other,—
  IAGO: It is but so, I warrant.
               (*Trumpets within.*)
Hark, how these instruments summon to
    supper!   170
The messengers of Venice stays the meat.
Go in, and weep not; all things shall be
    well.
    (*Exeunt* DESDEMONA *and* EMILIA.)
        (*Enter* RODERIGO.)
How now, Roderigo!
  ROD: I do not find that thou deal'st
justly with me.   175
  IAGO: What in the contrary?
  ROD: Every day thou daff'st me with
some device, Iago; and rather, as it seems
to me now, keep'st from me all conven-
iency that suppliest me with the least [180
advantage of hope. I will indeed no longer
endure it, nor am I yet persuaded to put
up in peace what already I have foolishly
suffered.
  IAGO: Will you hear me, Roderigo? [185
  ROD: Faith, I have heard too much, for
your words and performances are no kin
together.
  IAGO: You charge me most unjustly.
  ROD: With nought but truth. I have [190
wasted myself out of my means. The
jewels you have had from me to deliver
Desdemona would half have corrupted a
votarist. You have told me she hath received them and returned me expectations

and comforts of sudden respect and acquaintance, but I find none.   197

IAGO: Well; go to; very well.

ROD: Very well! go to! I cannot go to,
man; nor 't is not very well. By this hand,
I say 't is scurvy, and begin to find myself
fopped in it.   202

IAGO: Very well.

ROD: I tell you 't is not very well. I will
make myself known to Desdemona: [205
if she will return me my jewels, I will give
over my suit and repent my unlawful
solicitation; if not, assure yourself I will
seek satisfaction of you.

IAGO: You have said now.   210

ROD: Ay, and said nothing but what I
protest intendment of doing.

IAGO: Why, now I see there 's mettle in
thee, and even from this instant do build
on thee a better opinion than ever   [215
before. Give me thy hand, Roderigo: thou
hast taken against me a most just excep-
tion; but yet, I protest, I have dealt most
directly in thy affair.

ROD: It hath not appeared.   220

IAGO: I grant indeed it hath not appeared, and your suspicion is not without
wit and judgement. But, Roderigo, if thou
hast that in thee indeed, which I have
greater reason to believe now than [225
ever—I mean purpose, courage, and valour
—this night show it. If thou the next night
following enjoy not Desdemona, take me
from this world with treachery and devise
engines for my life.   230

ROD: Well, what is it? Is it within
reason and compass?

IAGO: Sir, there is especial commission
come from Venice to depute Cassio in
Othello's place.   235

ROD: Is that true? Why, then Othello
and Desdemona return again to Venice.

IAGO: O, no; he goes into Mauritania
and takes away with him the fair Des-

demona, unless his abode be lingered [240
here by some accident; wherein none can
be so determinate as the removing of
Cassio.   243

ROD: How do you mean, removing him?

IAGO: Why, by making him uncapable
of Othello's place; knocking out his
brains.

ROD: And that you would have me to
do?

IAGO: Ay, if you dare do yourself a
profit and a right. He sups to-night with
a harlotry, and thither will I go to [252
him; he knows not yet of this honourable fortune. If you will watch his
going thence, which I will fashion to fall
out between twelve and one, you may
take him at your pleasure. I will be [257
near to second your attempt, and he shall
fall between us. Come, stand not amazed
at it, but go along with me; I will show
you such a necessity in his death that you
shall think yourself bound to put it on
him. It is now high suppertime, and the
night grows to waste. About it.   264

ROD: I will hear further reason for this.

IAGO: And you shall be satisfied.

                         (*Exeunt.*)

SCENE III.

Another room in the castle.

(*Enter* OTHELLO, LODOVICO, DESDEMONA,
EMILIA, *and* ATTENDANTS.)

LOD: I do beseech you, sir, trouble yourself no further.

OTH: O, pardon me; 't will do me good
to walk.

LOD: Madam, good-night; I humbly
thank your ladyship.

DES: Your honour is most welcome.

OTH: Will you walk, sir?
O, Desdemona,—

DES: My lord?

OTH: Get you to bed on th' instant; I will be returned forthwith. Dismiss your attendant there. Look 't be done.

DES: I will, my lord.   10

(*Exeunt* OTHELLO, LODOVICO, *and*
ATTENDANTS.)

EMIL: How goes it now? He looks gentler than he did.

DES: He says he will return incontinent; And hath commanded me to go to bed, And bade me to dismiss you.

EMIL: Dismiss me?

DES: It was his bidding; therefore, good Emilia,   15
Give me my nightly wearing, and adieu. We must not now displease him.

EMIL: I would you had never seen him!

DES: So would not I: my love doth so approve him, That even his stubbornness, his checks, his frowns,—   20
Prithee, unpin me,—have grace and favour in them.

EMIL: I have laid those sheets you bade me on the bed.

DES: All 's one. Good faith, how foolish are our minds!
If I do die before thee, prithee, shroud me In one of those same sheets.

EMIL: Come, come, you talk.

DES: My mother had a maid call'd Barbara;   26
She was in love, and he she lov'd prov'd mad
And did forsake her. She had a song of "willow";
An old thing 't was, but it express'd her fortune,
And she died singing it. That song tonight   30
Will not go from my mind; I have much to do
But to go hang my head all at one side

And sing it like poor Barbara. Prithee, dispatch.

EMIL: Shall I go fetch your night-gown?

DES: No, unpin me here.
This Lodovico is a proper man.   35

EMIL: A very handsome man.

DES: He speaks well.

EMIL: I know a lady in Venice would have walked barefoot to Palestine for a touch of his nether lip.   40

DES: (*Singing.*)
The poor soul sat sighing by a sycamore tree,
    Sing all a green willow;
Her hand on her bosom, her head on her knee,
    Sing willow, willow, willow.
The fresh streams ran by her, and murmur'd her moans;
    Sing willow, willow, willow;
Her salt tears fell from her, and soften'd the stones;
    Sing willow, willow, willow;
Lay by these;—
(*Singing.*) "*Willow, willow;*"—
Prithee, hie thee; he 'll come anon;—   50
Sing all a green willow must be my garland.
Let nobody blame him, his scorn I approve,—
Nay, that 's not next.—Hark! who is 't that knocks?

EMIL: It 's the wind.

DES: (*Singing.*)
I call'd my love false love; but what said he then?   55
    Sing willow, willow, willow.
If I court moe women, you'll couch with me men.—
So, get thee gone; good-night. Mine eyes do itch;
Doth that bode weeping?

EMIL: 'T is neither here nor there.

DES: I have heard it said so. O, these men, these men!

Dost thou in conscience think,—tell me,
Emilia,—
That there be women do abuse their husbands
In such gross kind?

EMIL: There be some such, no question.

DES: Would thou do such a deed for all
the world? 64

EMIL: Why, would not you?

DES: No, by this heavenly light!

EMIL: Nor I neither by this heavenly
light;
I might do 't as well i' th' dark.

DES: Wouldst thou do such a deed for
all the world?

EMIL: The world 's a huge thing; it is a
great price 69
For a small vice.

DES: In troth, I think thou wouldst not.

EMIL: In troth, I think I should; and
undo 't when I had done. Marry, I would
not do such a thing for a joint-ing, nor for
measures of lawn, nor for gowns, petticoats, nor caps, nor any petty exhibition;
but, for all the whole world,—'ud's [76
pity, who would not make her husband a
cuckold to make him a monarch? I should
venture purgatory for 't.

DES: Beshrew me, if I would do such a
wrong 80
For the whole world.

EMIL: Why, the wrong is but a wrong
i' th' world; and having the world for
your labour, 't is a wrong in your own
world, and you might quickly make it
right. 86

DES: I do not think there is any such
woman.

EMIL: Yes, a dozen; and as many to th'
vantage as would store the world they
play'd for. 90
But I do think it is their husbands' faults
If wives do fall. Say that they slack their
duties

And pour our treasures into foreign laps,
Or else break out in peevish jealousies,
Throwing restraint upon us; or say they
strike us, 95
Or scant our former having in despite;
Why, we have galls, and though we have
some grace,
Yet have we some revenge. Let husbands
know
Their wives have sense like them; they see
and smell
And have their palates both for sweet and
sour 100
As husbands have. What is it that they do
When they change us for others? Is it
sport?
I think it is. And doth affection breed it?
I think it doth. Is 't frailty that thus errs?
It is so too. And have not we affections,
Desires for sport, and frailty, as men
have? 106
Then let them use us well; else let them
know,
The ills we do, their ills instruct us so.

DES: Good-night, good-night. Heaven
me such uses send, 109
Not to pick bad from bad, but by bad
mend. (*Exeunt.*)

ACT V

SCENE I

Cyprus. A street.

(*Enter* IAGO *and* RODERIGO.)

IAGO: Here, stand behind this bulk;
straight will he come:
Wear thy good rapier bare, and put it
home.
Quick, quick; fear nothing; I 'll be at thy
elbow.
It makes us, or it mars us; think on that,
And fix most firm thy resolution. 5

ROD: Be near at hand; I may miscarry
in 't.

IAGO: Here, at thy hand; be bold, and take thy stand.   (*Retires.*)

ROD: I have no great devotion to the deed,
And yet he hath given me satisfying reasons:
'T is but a man gone. Forth, my sword: he dies.   10

IAGO: I have rubb'd this young quat almost to the sense,
And he grows angry. Now, whether he kill Cassio,
Or Cassio him, or each do kill the other,
Every way makes my gain. Live Roderigo,
He calls me to a restitution large   15
Of gold and jewels that I bobb'd from him,
As gifts to Desdemona;
It must not be. If Cassio do remain,
He hath a daily beauty in his life
That makes me ugly; and, besides, the Moor   20
May unfold me to him; there stand I in much peril.
No, he must die. Be 't so. I hear him coming.

          (*Enter* CASSIO.)

ROD: I know his gait, 't is he.—Villain, thou diest! (*Makes a pass at* CASSIO.)

CAS: That thrust had been mine enemy indeed,
But that my coat is better than thou know'st.   25
I will make proof of thine.

          (*Draws, and wounds* RODERIGO.)

ROD: O, I am slain.

          (IAGO *from behind wounds* CASSIO
          in the leg, and exit.)

CAS: I am maim'd for ever. Help, ho! murder! murder!   (*Falls.*)

          (*Enter* OTHELLO.)

OTH: The voice of Cassio! Iago keeps his word.

ROD: O, villain that I am!

OTH: It is even so.

CAS: O, help, ho! light! a surgeon!   30

OTH: 'T is he!—O brave Iago, honest and just,
That hast such noble sense of thy friends' wrong!
Thou teachest me. Minion, your dear lies dead,
And your unblest fate hies; strumpet, I come.
Forth of my heart those charms, thine eyes, are blotted;   35
Thy bed, lust-stain'd, shall with lust's blood be spotted.   (*Exit.*)

          (*Enter* LODOVICO *and* GRATIANO.)

CAS: What, ho! no watch? no passage? Murder! murder!

GRA: 'T is some mischance; the voice is very direful.

CAS: O, help!

LOD: Hark!   40

ROD: O wretched villain!

LOD: Two or three groan. It is a heavy night,
These may be counterfeits; let 's think 't unsafe
To come in to the cry without more help.

ROD: Nobody come? Then shall I bleed to death.   45

          (*Re-enter* IAGO, *with a light.*)

LOD: Hark!

GRA: Here 's one comes in his shirt, with light and weapons.

IAGO: Who 's there? Whose noise is this that cries on murder?

LOD: We do not know.

IAGO: Do not you hear a cry?

CAS: Here, here! for Heaven's sake, help me!

IAGO: What 's the matter?

GRA: This is Othello's ancient, as I take it.   51

LOD: The same indeed; a very valiant fellow.

IAGO: What are you here that cry so grievously?

CAS: Iago? O, I am spoil'd, undone by villains!

Give me some help.   55

IAGO: O me, lieutenant! what villains have done this?

CAS: I think that one of them is hereabout,

And cannot make away.

IAGO: O treacherous villains!

What are you there?—Come in, and give some help.

    (*To* LODOVICO *and* GRATIANO.)

ROD: O, help me there!   60

CAS: That 's one of them.

IAGO: O murderous slave! O villain!

    (*Stabs* RODERIGO.)

ROD: O damn'd Iago! O inhuman dog!

IAGO: Kill men i' th' dark!—Where be these bloody thieves?—

How silent in this town!—Ho! murder! murder!—

What may you be? Are you of good or evil?   65

LOD: As you shall prove us, praise us.

IAGO: Signior Lodovico?

LOD: He, sir.

IAGO: I cry you mercy. Here 's Cassio hurt by villains.

GRA: Cassio!   70

IAGO: How is 't, brother!

CAS: My leg is cut in two.

IAGO: Marry, heaven forbid!

Light, gentlemen! I 'll bind it with my shirt.

    (*Enter* BIANCA.)

BIAN: What is the matter, ho? Who is 't that cried?

IAGO: Who is 't that cried!   75

BIAN: O my dear Cassio! my sweet Cassio!

O Cassio, Cassio, Cassio!

IAGO: O notable strumpet! Cassio, may you suspect

Who they should be that have thus mangled you?

CAS: No.   80

GRA: I am sorry to find you thus; I have been to seek you.

IAGO: Lend me a garter. So. O, for a chair,

To bear him easily hence!

BIAN: Alas, he faints! O Cassio, Cassio, Cassio!

IAGO: Gentlemen all, I do suspect this trash   85

To be a party in this injury.

Patience a while, good Cassio. Come, come;

Lend me a light. Know we this face or no?

Alas, my friend and my dear countryman

Roderigo! No:—yes, sure:—O heaven! Roderigo.   90

GRA: What, of Venice?

IAGO: Even he, sir; did you know him?

GRA: Know him, ay.

IAGO: Signior Gratiano? I cry your pardon;

These bloody accidents must excuse my manners,

That so neglected you.

GRA: I am glad to see you.

IAGO: How do you, Cassio? O, a chair, a chair!   96

GRA: Roderigo!

IAGO: He, he, 't is he. (*A chair brought in.*) O, that 's well said; the chair.

Some good man bear him carefully from hence;

I 'll fetch the General's surgeon. (*To Bianca.*) For you, mistress,   100

Save you your labour. He that lies slain here, Cassio,

Was my dear friend. What malice was between you?

CAS: None in the world; nor do I know the man.

IAGO: (*To* BIAN.) What, look you pale?
O, bear him out o' th' air.

(CASSIO *and* RODERIGO *are borne off.*)

Stay you, good gentlemen. Look you pale,
mistress?   105
Do you perceive the gastness of her eye?
Nay, if you stare, we shall hear more anon.
Behold her well; I pray you, look upon her.
Do you see, gentlemen? Nay, guiltiness
will speak,
Though tongues were out of use.   110

(*Enter* EMILIA.)

EMIL: Alas, what 's the matter? What
's the matter, husband?

IAGO: Cassio hath here been set on in
the dark
By Roderigo and fellows that are scap'd.
He 's almost slain, and Roderigo dead.

EMIL: Alas, good gentlemen; alas, good
Cassio!   115

IAGO: This is the fruits of whoring.
Prithee, Emilia,
Go know of Cassio where he supp'd to-
night.
(*To* BIANCA.) What, do you shake at that?

BIAN: He supp'd at my house; but I
therefore shake not.

IAGO: O, did he so? I charge you, go
with me.   120

EMIL: Oh, fie upon thee, strumpet!

BIAN: I am no strumpet, but of life as
honest
As you that thus abuse me.

EMIL: As I? Fie upon thee!

IAGO: Kind gentlemen, let 's go see poor
Cassio dress'd.
Come, mistress, you must tell 's another
tale.   125
Emilia, run you to the citadel,
And tell my lord and lady what hath
happ'd.
Will you go on afore? (*Aside.*) This is
the night
That either makes me or fordoes me quite.
(*Exeunt.*)

Scene II.

*A bedchamber in the castle:
Desdemona in bed asleep.*

(*Enter* OTHELLO *with a light.*)

OTH: It is the cause, it is the cause, my
soul,—
Let me not name it to you, you chaste
stars!—
It is the cause. Yet I 'll not shed her blood,
Nor scar that whiter skin of hers than
snow,
And smooth as monumental alabaster. 5
Yet she must die, else she 'll betray more
men.
Put out the light, and then put out the
light:
If I quench thee, thou flaming minister,
I can again thy former light restore,
Should I repent me; but once put out thy
light,   10
Thou cunning'st pattern of excelling na-
ture,
I know not where is that Promethean heat
That can thy light relume. When I have
pluck'd the rose
I cannot give it vital growth again,
It needs must wither; I 'll smell it on the
tree.   (*Kisses her.*) 15
Oh, balmy breath, that dost almost per-
suade
Justice to break her sword! One more,
one more.
Be thus when thou are dead, and I will
kill thee
And love thee after. One more, and that's
the last;
So sweet was ne'er so fatal. I must weep,
But they are cruel tears: this sorrow 's
heavenly;   21
It strikes where it doth love. She wakes.

DES: Who 's there? Othello?

OTH: Ay, Desdemona.

DES: Will you come to bed, my lord?

OTH: Have you pray'd to-night, Desdemon?

DES: Ay, my lord.   25

OTH: If you bethink yourself of any
crime
Unreconcil'd as yet to heaven and grace,
Solicit for it straight.

DES: Alack, my lord, what may you
mean by that?

OTH: Well, do it, and be brief; I will
walk by.   30
I would not kill thy unprepared spirit;
No; heaven forfend! I would not kill thy
soul.

DES: Talk you of killing?

OTH: Ay, I do.

DES: Then heaven
Have mercy on me!

OTH: Amen, with all my heart!

DES: If you say so, I hope you will not
kill me.   35

OTH: Hum!

DES: And yet I fear you; for you 're
fatal then
When your eyes roll so. Why I should fear
I know not,
Since guiltiness I know not; but yet I
feel I fear.

OTH: Think on thy sins.

DES: They are loves I bear to you.

OTH: Ay, and for that thou diest.   41

DES: That death 's unnatural that kills
for loving.
Alas, why gnaw you so your nether lip?
Some bloody passion shakes your very
frame.
These are portents; but yet I hope, I
hope,   45
They do not point on me.

OTH: Peace, and be still!

DES: I will so. What 's the matter?

OTH: That handkerchief which I so
lov'd and gave thee
Thou gav'st to Cassio.

DES: No, by my life and soul!
Send for the man, and ask him.

OTH: Sweet soul, take heed,
Take heed of perjury; thou art on thy
death-bed.   51

DES: Ay, but not yet to die.

OTH: Yes, presently:
Therefore confess thee freely of thy sin;
For to deny each article with oath
Cannot remove nor choke the strong con-
ception   55
That I do groan withal. Thou art to die.

DES: Then Lord have mercy on me!

OTH: I say, amen.

DES: And have you mercy too; I never
did
Offend you in my life; never lov'd Cassio
But with such general warranty of heaven
As I might love; I never gave him
token.   61

OTH: By heaven, I saw my handker-
chief in 's hand.
O perjur'd woman! thou dost stone my
heart,
And makes me call what I intend to do
A murder, which I thought a sacrifice. 65
I saw the handkerchief.

DES: He found it then;
I never gave it him: send for him hither;
Let him confess a truth.

OTH: He hath confess'd.

DES: What, my lord?   69

OTH: That he hath us'd thee.

DES: How? unlawfully?

OTH: Ay.

DES: He will not say so.

OTH: No, his mouth is stopp'd;
Honest Iago hath ta'en order for 't.

DES: O! my fear interprets. What, is he
dead?

OTH: Had all his hairs been lives, my
great revenge
Had stomach for them all.   75

DES: Alas! he is betray'd and I undone.

OTH: Out, strumpet! weep'st thou for
him to my face?

DES: O, banish me, my lord, but kill me not!

OTH: Down, strumpet!

DES: Kill me to-morrow; let me live to-night!   80

OTH: Nay, if you strive,—

DES: But half an hour!

OTH: Being done, there is no pause.

DES: But while I say one prayer!

OTH: It is too late.

(*He smothers her.*)

EMIL: (*At the door.*) My lord, my lord! What, ho! my lord, my lord!

OTH: What noise is this? Not dead? not yet quite dead?   85
I that am cruel am yet merciful;
I would not have thee linger in thy pain.
So, so.

EMIL: (*Within.*) What, ho! my lord, my lord!

OTH: Who's there?

EMIL: (*Within.*) O, good my lord, I would speak a word with you!   90

OTH: Yes:—'t is Emilia.—By and by.— She 's dead.
'T is like she comes to speak of Cassio's death.
The noise was high. Ha! no more moving?
Still as the grave. Shall she come in? Were 't good?—
I think she stirs again:—no. What 's best to do?   95
If she come in, she 'll sure speak to my wife.
My wife! my wife! what wife? I have no wife.
O, insupportable! O heavy hour!
Methinks it should be now a huge eclipse
Of sun and moon, and that th' affrighted globe   100
Did yawn at alteration.

EMIL: (*Within.*) I do beseech you

That I may speak with you, O, good my lord!

OTH: I had forgot thee. O, come in, Emilia.
Soft; by and by.—Let me the curtains draw.—
Where art thou?   (*Opens the door.*)

(*Enter* EMILIA.)

What's the matter with thee now?

EMIL: O, my good lord, yonder's foul murders done!   106

OTH: What, now?

EMIL: But now, my lord.

OTH: It is the very error of the moon;
She comes more nearer earth than she was wont,   110
And makes men mad.

EMIL: Cassio, my lord, hath kill'd a young Venetian
Call'd Roderigo.

OTH: Roderigo kill'd!
And Cassio kill'd!

EMIL: No, Cassio is not kill'd.

OTH: Not Cassio kill'd! Then murder 's out of tune,   115
And sweet revenge grows harsh.

DES: O, falsely, falsely murder'd!

EMIL: O Lord, what cry is that?

OTH: That! what?

EMIL: Out, and alas! that was my lady's voice.   119
Help! help, ho! help! O lady, speak again!
Sweet Desdemona! O sweet mistress, speak!

DES: A guiltless death I die.

EMIL: O, who hath done this deed?

DES: Nobody; I myself. Farewell!   124
Commend me to my kind lord. O, farewell!   (*Dies.*)

OTH: Why, how should she be murder'd?

EMIL: Alas! who knows?

OTH: You heard her say herself, it was
   not I.

EMIL: She said so; I must needs report
   the truth.

OTH: She 's, like a liar, gone to burning
   hell.
'T was I that kill'd her.

EMIL: O, the more angel she,
And you the blacker devil!   131

OTH: She turn'd to folly, and she was
   a whore.

EMIL: Thou dost belie her, and thou
   art a devil.

OTH: She was false as water.

EMIL: Thou art rash as fire, to say
That she was false: O, she was heavenly
   True!   135

OTH: Cassio did tup her; ask thy husband else.
O, I were damn'd beneath all depth in
   hell
But that I did proceed upon just grounds
To this extremity. Thy husband knew it
   all.

EMIL: My husband?   140

OTH: Thy husband.

EMIL: That she was false to wedlock?

OTH: Ay, with Cassio. Nay, had she
   been true,
If Heaven would make me such another
   world
Of one entire and perfect chrysolite, 145
I 'd not have sold her for it.

EMIL: My husband?

OTH: Ay, 't was he that told me on her
   first.
An honest man he is and hates the slime
That sticks on filthy deeds.

EMIL: My husband?

OTH: What needs this iterance, woman?
   I say thy husband.   150

EMIL: O mistress, villainy hath made
   mocks with love!
My husband say that she was false?

OTH: He, woman;
I say thy husband; dost understand the
   word?
My friend, thy husband, honest, honest
   Iago.

EMIL: If he say so, may his pernicious
   soul   155
Rot half a grain a day! He lies to th'
   heart:
She was too fond of her most filthy bargain.

OTH: Ha!

EMIL: Do thy worst!
This deed of thine is no more worthy
   heaven   160
Than thou wast worthy her.

OTH: Peace, you were best.

EMIL: Thou hast not half that power
   to do me harm
As I have to be hurt. O gull! O dolt!
As ignorant as dirt! Thou hast done a
   deed—
I care not for thy sword; I 'll make thee
   known,   165
Though I lost twenty lives.—Help! help,
   ho! help!
The Moor hath kill'd my mistress! Murder! murder!

(*Enter* MONTANO, GRATIANO, IAGO, *and
   others.*)

MON: What is the matter? How now,
   General!

EMIL: O, are you come, Iago? You
   have done well,
That men must lay their murders on your
   neck.   170

GRA: What is the matter?

EMIL: Disprove this villain, if thou
   be'st a man.
He says thou told'st him that his wife
   was false:
I know thou didst not, thou 'rt not such
   a villain.
Speak, for my heart is full.   175

IAGO: I told him what I thought, and told no more
Than what he found himself was apt and true.

EMIL: But did you ever tell him she was false?

IAGO: I did.

EMIL: You told a lie, an odious, damned lie;   180
Upon my soul, a lie, a wicked lie.
She false with Cassio!—did you say with Cassio?

IAGO: With Cassio, mistress. Go to, charm your tongue.

EMIL: I will not charm my tongue; I am bound to speak.
My mistress here lies murdered in her bed,—   185

ALL: O heavens forfend!

EMIL: And your reports have set the murderer on.

OTH: Nay, stare not, masters; it is true, indeed.

GRA: 'T is a strange truth.

MON: O monstrous act!

EMIL: Villainy, villainy, villainy!
I think upon 't, I think: I smell 't,—O villainy!   191
I thought so then,—I'll kill myself for grief—
O villainy, villainy!

IAGO: What, are you mad? I charge you, get you home.

EMIL: Good gentlemen, let me have leave to speak;   195
'T is proper I obey him, but not now.
Perchance, Iago, I will ne'er go home.

OTH: O! O! O!   (He falls on the bed.)

EMIL: Nay, lay thee down and roar;
For thou hast kill'd the sweetest innocent
That e'er did lift up eye.

OTH: (Rising.) O, she was foul!   200
I scarce did know you, uncle; there lies your niece,

Whose breath, indeed, these hands have newly stopp'd.
I know this act shows horrible and grim.

GRA: Poor Desdemon! I am glad thy father's dead:
Thy match was mortal to him, and pure grief   205
Shore his old thread in twain. Did he live now,
This sight would make him do a desperate turn,
Yea, curse his better angel from his side,
And fall to reprobance.   209

OTH: 'T is pitiful; but yet Iago knows
That she with Cassio hath the act of shame
A thousand times committed. Cassio confess'd it;
And she did gratify his amorous works
With that recognizance and pledge of love
Which I first gave her: I saw it in his hand;   215
It was a handkerchief, an antique token
My father gave my mother.

EMIL: O God! O heavenly God!

IAGO: 'Zounds, hold your peace.

EMIL: 'T will out, 't will out! I peace!
No, I will speak as liberal as the north:
Let Heaven and men and devils, let them all,   221
All, all, cry shame against me, yet I 'll speak.

IAGO: Be wise, and get you home.

EMIL: I will not.

(Iago offers to stab Emilia.)

GRA: Fie!
Your sword upon a woman?

EMIL: O thou dull Moor! that handkerchief thou speak'st of   225
I found by fortune and did give my husband;
For often, with a solemn earnestness,
More than indeed belong'd to such a trifle,
He begg'd of me to steal it.

IAGO: Villanous whore!

EMIL: She give it Cassio! No, alas! I found it, 230
And I did give 't my husband.

IAGO: Filth, thou liest!

EMIL: By heaven, I do not, I do not, gentlemen.
O murderous coxcomb! what should such a fool
Do with so good a wife?

OTH: Are there no stones in heaven
But what serves for the thunder?—Precious villain! 235

(*He runs at* IAGO: IAGO *kills his wife.*)

GRA: The woman falls; sure, he hath kill'd his wife.

EMIL: Ay, ay! O, lay me by my mistress' side. (*Exit* IAGO.)

GRA: He 's gone, but his wife 's kill'd.

MON: 'T is a notorious villain. Take you this weapon
Which I have here recover'd from the Moor: 240
Come, guard the door without; let him not pass,
But kill him rather. I 'll after that same villain,
For 't is a damned slave.

(*Exeunt* MONTANO *and* GRATIANO.)

OTH: I am not valiant neither,
But every punny whipster gets my sword.
But why should honour outlive honesty?
Let it go all.

EMIL: What did thy song bode, lady?
Hark, canst thou hear me? I will play the swan, 247
And die in music. (*Singing.*) "Willow, willow, willow!"—
Moor, she was chaste; she lov'd thee, cruel Moor; 249
So come my soul to bliss, as I speak true;
So speaking as I think, alas, I die. (*Dies.*)

OTH: I have another weapon in this chamber;
It was a sword of Spain, the ice-brook's temper,—
O, here it is. Uncle, I must come forth.

GRA: (*Within.*) If thou attempt it, it will cost thee dear: 255
Thou hast no weapon, and perforce must suffer.

OTH: Look in upon me then and speak with me,
Or, naked as I am, I will assault thee.

(*Re-enter* GRATIANO.)

GRA: What is the matter?

OTH: Behold, I have a weapon;
A better never did itself sustain 260
Upon a soldier's thigh. I have seen the day
That, with this little arm and this good sword,
I have made my way through more impediments
Than twenty times your stop. But, O vain boast!
Who can control his fate? 't is not so now. 265
Be not afraid though you do see me weapon'd;
Here is my journey's end, here is my butt
And very sea-mark of my utmost sail.
Do you go back dismay'd? 'T is a lost fear;
Man but a rush against Othello's breast
And he retires. Where should Othello go? 271
Now, how dost thou look now? O ill-starr'd wench!
Pale as thy smock! when we shall meet at compt,
This look of thine will hurl my soul from heaven,
And fiends will snatch at it. Cold, cold, my girl! 275
Even like thy chastity. O cursed, cursed slave!
Whip me, ye devils,
From the possession of this heavenly sight!

Blow me about in winds; roast me in
    sulphur!
Wash me in steep-down gulfs of liquid
    fire!
O Desdemona, Desdemona! dead!   281
Oh! Oh! Oh!

(*Enter* LODOVICO, MONTANO, CASSIO *carried in a chair, and* OFFICERS, *with* IAGO *prisoner.*)

LOD: Where is this rash and most un-
    fortunate man?

OTH: That 's he that was Othello; here
    I am.

LOD: Where is that viper? Bring the
    villain forth.   285

OTH: I look down towards his feet; but
    that's a fable.
If that thou be 'st a devil, I cannot kill
    thee.

          (*Wounds Iago.*)

LOD: Wrench his sword from him.

IAGO: I bleed, sir; but not kill'd.

OTH: I am not sorry neither. I'd have
    thee live;   289
For, in my sense, 't is happiness to die.

LOD: O thou Othello, that wert once
    so good,
Fallen in the practice of a cursed slave,
What shall be said to thee?

OTH: Why, anything.
An honourable murderer, if you will; [294
For nought did I in hate, but all in honour.

LOD: This wretch hath part confess'd
    his villainy.
Did you and he consent in Cassio's death?

OTH: Ay.

CAS: Dear General, I never gave you
    cause.

OTH: I do believe it, and I ask your
    pardon.   300
Will you, I pray, demand that demi-devil
Why he hath thus ensnar'd my soul and
    body?

IAGO: Demand me nothing; what you
    know, you know.
From this time forth I never will speak
    word.

LOD: What, not to pray?

GRA: Torments will ope your lips.

OTH: Well, thou dost best.   306

LOD: Sir, you small understand what
    hath befall'n,
Which, as I think, you know not. Here
    is a letter
Found in the pocket of the slain Roderigo,
And here another. The one of them im-
    ports   310
The death of Cassio to be undertook
By Roderigo.

OTH: O villain!

CAS: Most heathenish and most gross!

LOD: Now here 's another discontented
    paper,
Found in his pocket too; and this, it seems,
Roderigo meant t' have sent this damned
    villain;   316
But that belike Iago in the interim
Came in and satisfi'd him.

OTH: O thou pernicious caitiff!—
How came you, Cassio, by that handker-
    chief
That was my wife's?

CAS: I found it in my chamber;
And he himself confess'd but even
    now   321
That there he dropp'd it for a special pur-
    pose
Which wrought to his desire.

OTH: O fool! fool! fool!

CAS: There is besides in Roderigo's let-
    ter,
How he upbraids Iago, that he made him
Brave me upon the watch, whereon it
    came   326
That I was cast; and even but now he
    spake,
After long seeming dead, Iago hurt him,
Iago set him on.

LOD: You must forsake this room, and go with us.   330
Your power and your command is taken off,
And Cassio rules in Cyprus. For this slave,
If there be any cunning cruelty
That can torment him much and hold him long,
It shall be his. You shall close prisoner rest,   335
Till that the nature of your fault be known
To the Venetian state. Come, bring away.

OTH: Soft you; a word or two before you go.
I have done the state some service, and they know 't.
No more of that. I pray you, in your letters,   340
When you shall these unlucky deeds relate,
Speak of me as I am, nothing extenuate,
Nor set down aught in malice. Then must you speak
Of one that lov'd not wisely but too well;
Of one not easily jealous, but being wrought   345
Perplex'd in the extreme; of one whose hand,
Like the base Indian, threw a pearl away
Richer than all his tribe; of one whose subdued eyes,
Albeit unused to the melting mood,   349
Drops tears as fast as the Arabian trees
Their medicinal gum. Set you down this;
And say besides, that in Aleppo once,
Where a malignant and a turban'd Turk
Beat a Venetian and traduc'd the state,
I took by th' throat the circumcised dog,   355
And smote him, thus.   (Stabs himself.)

LOD: O bloody period!

GRA: All that 's spoke is marr'd.

OTH: I kiss'd thee ere I kill'd thee: no way but this,
Killing myself, to die upon a kiss.

(Falls on the bed, and dies.)

CAS: This did I fear, but thought he had no weapon;   360
For he was great of heart.

LOD: (To IAGO.) O Spartan dog,
More fell than anguish, hunger, or the sea!
Look on the tragic loading of this bed;
This is thy work. The object poisons sight;
Let it be hid. Gratiano, keep the house,
And seize upon the fortunes of the Moor,
For they succeed on you. To you, lord governor,   367
Remains the censure of this hellish villain;
The time, the place, the torture. O, enforce it!
Myself will straight aboard; and to the state
This heavy act with heavy heart relate.   371

(Exeunt.)

Phaedra

JEAN RACINE

COMMENTARY

 Jean Racine (1639-1699) was born some eighty miles from Paris. When he was sixteen, he fell under the influence of Greek tragedy. In 1660 he went to live in Paris. His first significantly successful play was *Andromache* (1667); this was followed by *Brittanicus* (1669), *Bérénice* (1670), *Bajazet* (1672), *Mithridates* (1673), *Iphigenia* (1674), and *Phèdre* (in English, *Phaedra*) (1677). He did not write another play for a dozen years; his last two plays, using Biblical material, were *Esther* (1689) and *Athalia* (1691).

Racine's *Phaedra* offers an immediate paradox. Within the tight neoclassical rules governing the form, style, and content of tragedy, Racine provides a study of the disordering and destructive effects of passion. Racine anticipates Lorca in depicting a conflict between a private compulsion, Phaedra's love for Hippolytus, and social expectation, that form of honor which is more important to Hippolytus than "mere" love. Lorca's *Yerma* might indeed be read in company with *Phaedra,* for each illuminates the other.

Phaedra oscillates between the poles of Phaedra's emotion and Hippolytus' reason. The emotion and the reason are so extreme that they contribute to the breakdown of communication. The offering of love and the rejection of it are unmodulated. Tragedy becomes inevitable since neither love nor honor, passion nor reason, can be qualified without being diminished. If you are familiar with classical opera, you might consider how music might heighten the effect of the play.

Phaedra illustrates well Suzanne Langer's notion, in her essay "The Tragic Rhythm" (from *Feeling and Form* [New York, 1953], pp. 351-366; also in *Tragedy: Vision and Form,* ed. Robert W. Corrigan), that tragedy records an abstraction of growth, maturity, and decline. Also provocative is Lionel Abel's comment that Phaedra's "death, when it comes, is . . . less pathetic and less terrible than would be the death of someone who had all along desired life" (in *Metatheatre, A New View of Dramatic Form* [New York, 1963], p. 26).

Racine's portrait of a woman torn by a great emotional force beyond her control is also to be compared with Euripides' study of Medea. It may be fruitful to consider whether Racine's dignity and decorum contribute to or detract from the total tragic effect. Another valuable critical exercise would be the examination of how O'Neill enlarges, diminishes, and otherwise modifies the Phaedra-Hippolytus story in *Desire Under the Elms*.

An illuminating essay is Henri Peyre's "The Tragedy of Passion: Racine's *Phèdre*," in *Tragic Themes in Western Literature*, ed. Cleanth Brooks (New Haven and London, 1955). Also valuable is Eugène Vinaver's *Racine and Poetic Tragedy* (New York, 1959). *Phaedra and Hippolytus: Myth and Dramatic Form* (Boston, 1966) is a collection of five plays (*Hippolytus* by Euripides, *Phaedra* by Seneca, *Phaedra* by Racine, *The Cretan Women* by Robinson Jeffers, and *Desire Under the Elms* by O'Neill) and essays on the plays by Robert Graves, Sir James George Frazer, Richmond Lattimore, and others.

Jean Racine

PHAEDRA

✿ Translated by Robert Lowell

CHARACTERS

THESEUS, *son of Aegeus and King of Athens*
PHAEDRA, *wife of Theseus and daughter of Minos and Pasiphaë*
HIPPOLYTUS, *son of Theseus and Antiope, Queen of the Amazons*
ARICIA, *princess of the royal blood of Athens*
OENONE, *nurse of Phaedra*
THERAMENES, *tutor of Hippolytus*
ISMENE, *friend of Aricia*
PANOPE, *waiting-woman of Phaedra*
Guards

Pronunciation:

Phaedra=Pheédra	Aricia=Arísha
Oenone=Eenónee	Theramenes=Therámeneés
Ismene=Ismeénee	Panope=Pánopeé
	Pasiphaë=Pásiphá-ee

ACT 1

SCENE I

Hippolytus, Theramenes

HIPPOLYTUS: No, no, my friend, we're off! Six months have passed since Father heard the ocean howl and cast his galley on the Aegean's skull-white froth.
Listen! the blank sea calls us—off, off, off!
I'll follow Father to the fountainhead and marsh of hell. We're off. Alive or dead,
I'll find him.

Racine, *Phaedra*, trans. Robert Lowell. Reprinted from *Phaedra and Figaro* translated by Robert Lowell, by permission of Farrar, Straus & Giroux, Inc. Copyright © 1960, 1961 by Robert Lowell.

THERAMENES: Where, my lord? I've sent a host
of veteran seamen up and down the coast;
each village, creek and cove from here to Crete
has been ransacked and questioned by my fleet;
my flagship skirted Hades' rapids, furled
sail there a day, and scoured the underworld.
Have you fresh news? New hopes? One even doubts
if noble Theseus wants his whereabouts
discovered. Does he need helpers to share
the plunder of his latest love affair;
a shipload of spectators and his son
to watch him ruin his last Amazon—
some creature, taller than a man, whose tanned
and single bosom slithers from his hand,
when he leaps to crush her like a waterfall
of honeysuckle?

HIPPOLYTUS: You are cynical,
my friend. Your insinuations wrong a king,
sick as myself of his philandering.
His heart is Phaedra's and no rivals dare
to challenge Phaedra's sole possession there.
I sail to find my father. The command
of duty calls me from this stifling land.

THERAMENES: This stifling land? Is that how you deride
this gentle province where you used to ride
the bridle-paths, pursuing happiness?
You cured your orphaned childhood's loneliness
and found a peace here you preferred to all
the blaze of Athens' brawling protocol.
A rage for exploits blinds you. Your disease
is boredom.

HIPPOLYTUS: Friend, this kingdom lost its peace,
when Father left my mother for defiled

bull-serviced Pasiphaë's child. The child
of homicidal Minos is our queen!

THERAMENES: Yes, Phaedra reigns and rules here. I have seen
you crouch before her outbursts like a cur.
When she first met you, she refused to stir
until your father drove you out of court.
The news is better now; our friends report
the queen is dying. Will you cross the seas,
desert your party and abandon Greece?
Why flee from Phaedra? Phaedra fears the night
less than she fears the day that strives to light
the universal ennui of her eye—
this dying woman, who desires to die!

HIPPOLYTUS: No, I despise her Cretan vanity,
hysteria and idle cruelty.
I fear Aricia; she alone survives
the blood-feud that destroyed her brothers' lives.

THERAMENES: Prince, Prince, forgive my laughter. Must you fly
beyond the limits of the world and die,
floating in flotsam, friendless, far from help,
and clubbed to death by Tartars in the kelp?
Why arm the shrinking violet with a knife?
Do you hate Aricia, and fear for your life, Prince?

HIPPOLYTUS: If I hated her, I'd trust myself
and stay.

THERAMENES: Shall I explain you to yourself?
Prince, you have ceased to be that hard-mouthed, proud
and pure Hippolytus, who scorned the crowd
of common lovers once and rose above
your wayward father by despising love.
Now you justify your father, and you feel

love's poison running through you, now
        you kneel
and breathe the heavy incense, and a god
possesses you and revels in your blood!
Are you in love?

    HIPPOLYTUS: Theramenes, when I call
and cry for help, you push me to the wall.
Why do you plague me, and try to make
        me fear
the qualities you taught me to revere?
I sucked in prudence with my mother's
        milk.
Antiope, no harlot draped in silk,
first hardened me. I was my mother's son
and not my father's. When the Amazon,
my mother, was dethroned, my mind ap-
        proved
her lessons more than ever. I still loved
her bristling chastity. Later, you told
stories about my father's deeds that made
        me hold
back judgment—how he stood for Her-
        cules,
a second Hercules who cleared the Cretan
        seas
of pirates, throttled Scirron, Cercyon,
Procrustes, Sinnis, and the giant man
of Epidaurus writing in his gore.
He pierced the maze and killed the Mino-
        taur.
Other things turned my stomach: that
        long list
of women, all refusing to resist.
Helen, caught up with all her honeyed
        flesh
from Sparta; Periboea, young and fresh,
already tired of Salinis. A hundred more,
their names forgotten by my father—
        whore
and virgin, child and mother, all deceived,
if their protestations can be believed!
Ariadne declaiming to the rocks,
her sister, Phaedra, kidnapped. Phaedra
        locks
the gate at last! You know how often I
would weary, fall to nodding and deny
the possibility of hearing the whole

ignoble, dull, insipid boast unroll.
And now I too must fall. The gods have
        made me creep.
How can I be in love? I have no specious
        heap
of honors, friend. No mastered monsters
        drape
my shoulders—Theseus' excuse to rape
at will. Suppose I chose a woman. Why
choose an orphan? Aricia is eternally
cut off from marriage, lest she breed
successors to her fierce brothers, and seed
the land with treason. Father only grants
her life on one condition. This—he wants
no bridal torch to burn for her. Unwooed
and childless, she must answer for the
        blood
her brothers shed. How can I marry her,
gaily subvert our kingdom's character,
and sail on the high seas of love?

    THERAMENES: You'll prove
nothing by reason, for you are in love.
Theseus' injustice to Aricia throws
her in the light; your eyes he wished to
        close
are open. She dazzles you. Her pitiful
seclusion makes her doubly terrible.
Does this innocent passion freeze your
        blood?
There's sweetness in it. Is your only good
the dismal famine of your chastity?
You shun your father's path? Where
        would you be,
Prince, if Antiope had never burned
chastely for Theseus? Love, my lord, has
        turned
the head of Hercules, and thousands—
        fired
the forge of Vulcan! All your uninspired,
cold moralizing is nothing, Prince. You
        have changed!
Now no one sees you riding, half-deranged
along the sand-bars, where you drove your
        horse
and foaming chariot with all your force,
tilting and staggering upright through the
        surf—

far from their usual course across the turf.
The woods are quiet . . . How your eyes
    hang down!
You often murmur and forget to frown.
All's out, Prince. You're in love; you burn.
    Flames, flames,
Prince! A dissimulated sickness maims
the youthful quickness of your daring.
    Does
lovely Aricia haunt you?

    HIPPOLYTUS: Friend, spare us.
I sail to find my father.

    THERAMENES: Will you see
Phaedra before you go?

    HIPPOLYTUS: I mean to be
here when she comes. Go, tell her. I will
    do
my duty. Wait, I see her nurse. What new
troubles torment her?

SCENE II

Hippolytus, Theramenes, Oenone

    OENONE: Who has griefs like mine,
my lord? I cannot help the queen in her
    decline.
Although I sit beside her day and night,
she shuts her eyes and withers in my sight.
An eternal tumult roisters through her
    head,
panics her sleep, and drags her from her
    bed.
Just now she fled me at the prime
of day to see the sun for the last time.
She's coming.

    HIPPOLYTUS: So! I'll steal away. My
    flight
removes a hateful object from her sight.

SCENE III

Phaedra, Oenone

PHAEDRA: Dearest, we'll go no further.
    I must rest.

I'll sit here. My emotions shake my breast,
the sunlight throws black bars across my
    eyes.
My knees give. If I fall, why should I rise,
Nurse?

    OENONE: Heaven help us! Let me com-
    fort you.

    PHAEDRA: Tear off these gross, official
    rings, undo
these royal veils. They drag me to the
    ground.
Why have you frilled me, laced me,
    crowned me, and wound
my hair in turrets? All your skill torments
and chokes me. I am crushed by orna-
    ments.
Everything hurts me, and drags me to my
    knees!

    OENONE: Now this, now that, Madam.
    You never cease
commanding us, then cancelling your com-
    mands.
You feel your strength return, summon all
    hands
to dress you like a bride, then say you
    choke!
We open all the windows, fetch a cloak,
rush you outdoors. It's no use, you decide
that sunlight kills you, and only want to
    hide.

    PHAEDRA: I feel the heavens' royal radi-
    ance cool
and fail, as if it feared my terrible
shame has destroyed its right to shine on
    men.
I'll never look upon the sun again.

    OENONE: Renunciation or renunciation!
Now you slander the source of your cre-
    ation.
Why do you run to death and tear your
    hair?

    PHAEDRA: Oh God, take me to some
    sunless forest lair . . .
There hoof-beats raise a dust-cloud, and
    my eye
follows a horseman outlined on the sky!

OENONE: What's this, my lady?

PHAEDRA: I have lost my mind.
Where am I? Oh forget my words! I find
I've lost the habit now of talking sense.
My face is red and guilty—evidence
of treason! I've betrayed my darkest fears,
Nurse, and my eyes, despite me, fill with
    tears.

OENONE: Lady, if you must weep, weep
    for your silence
that filled your days and mine with vio-
    lence.
Ah deaf to argument and numb to care,
you have no mercy. Spare me, spare
yourself. Your blood is like polluted water,
fouling a mind desiring its own slaughter.
The sun has died and shadows filled the
    skies
thrice now, since you have closed your
    eyes;
the day has broken through the night's
    content
thrice now, since you have tasted nourish-
    ment.
Is your salvation from your terrified
conscience this passive, servile suicide?
Lady, your madness harms the gods who
    gave
you life, betrays your husband. Who will
    save
your children? Your downfall will orphan
    them,
deprive them of their kingdom, and con-
    demn
their lives and future to the discipline
of one who abhors you and all your kin,
a tyrant suckled by an amazon,
Hippolytus . . .

PHAEDRA: Oh God!

OENONE: You still hate someone;
thank heaven for that, Madam!

PHAEDRA: You spoke his name!

OENONE: Hippolytus, Hippolytus!
    There's hope
in hatred, Lady. Give your anger rope.
I love your anger. If the winds of love

and fury stir you, you will live. Above
your children towers this foreigner, this
    child
of Scythian cannibals, now wild
to ruin the kingdom, master Greece, and
    choke
the children of the gods beneath his yoke.
Why dawdle? Why deliberate at length?
Oh, gather up your dissipated strength.

PHAEDRA: I've lived too long.

OENONE: Always, always agonized!
Is your conscience still stunned and para-
    lyzed?
Do you think you have washed your hands
    in blood?

PHAEDRA: Thank God, my hands are
    clean still. Would to God
my heart were innocent!

OENONE: Your heart, your heart!
What have you done that tears your soul
    apart?

PHAEDRA: I've said too much. Oenone,
    let me die;
by dying I shall escape blasphemy.

OENONE: Search for another hand to
    close your eyes.
Oh cruel Queen, I see that you despise
my sorrow and devotion. I'll die first,
and end the anguish of this service cursed
by your perversity. A thousand roads
always lie open to the killing gods.
I'll choose the nearest. Lady, tell me how
Oenone's love has failed you. Will you
    allow
your nurse to die, your nurse, who gave
    up all—
nation, parents, children, to serve in thrall.
I saved you from your mother, King
    Minos' wife!
Will your death pay me for giving up my
    life?

PHAEDRA: What I could tell you, I have
    told you. Nurse,
only my silence saves me from the curse
of heaven.

OENONE: How could you tell me anything
worse than watching you dying?

PHAEDRA: I would bring
my life and rank dishonor. What can I say
to save myself, or put off death a day.

OENONE: Ah Lady, I implore you by
my tears,
and by your suffering body. Heaven hears,
and knows the truth already. Let me see.

PHAEDRA: Stand up.

OENONE: Your hesitation's killing me!

PHAEDRA: What can I tell you? How the
gods reprove
me!

OENONE: Speak!

PHAEDRA: Oh Venus, murdering Venus!
love
gored Pasiphaë with the bull.

OENONE: Forget
your mother! When she died, she paid
her debt.

PHAEDRA: Oh Ariadne, oh my Sister,
lost
for love of Theseus on that rocky coast.

OENONE: Lady, what nervous languor
makes you rave
against your family; they are in the grave.

PHAEDRA: Remorseless Aphrodite drives
me. I,
my race's last and worst love-victim, die.

OENONE: Are you in love?

PHAEDRA: I am insane with love!

OENONE: Who
is he?

PHAEDRA: I'll tell you. Nothing love can
do
could equal . . . Nurse, I am in love. The
shame
kills me. I love the . . . Do not ask his
name.

OENONE: Who?

PHAEDRA: Nurse, you know my old
loathing for the son
of Theseus and the barbarous amazon?

OENONE: Hippolytus! My God, oh my
God!

PHAEDRA: You,
not I, have named him.

OENONE: What can you do,
but die? Your words have turned my blood
to ice.
Oh righteous heavens, must the blas-
phemies
of Pasiphaë fall upon her daughter?
Her Furies strike us down across the
water.
Why did we come here?

PHAEDRA: My evil comes from farther
off. In May,
in brilliant Athens, on my marriage day,
I turned aside for shelter from the smile
of Theseus. Death was frowning in an
aisle—
Hippolytus! I saw his face, turned white!
My lost and dazzled eyes saw only night,
capricious burnings flickered through my
bleak
abandoned flesh. I could not breathe or
speak.
I faced my flaming executioner,
Aphrodite, my mother's murderer!
I tried to calm her wrath by flowers and
praise,
I built her a temple, fretted months and
days
on decoration. I even hoped to find
symbols and stays for my distracted mind,
searching the guts of sacrificial steers.
Yet when my erring passions, mutineers
to virtue, offered incense at the shrine
of love, I failed to silence the malign
Goddess. Alas, my hungry open mouth,
thirsting with adoration, tasted drouth—
Venus resigned her altar to my new lord—
and even while I was praying, I adored
Hippolytus above the sacred flame,
now offered to his name I could not name.
I fled him, yet he stormed me in disguise,
and seemed to watch me from his father's
eyes.
I even turned against myself, screwed up

my slack courage to fury, and would not
    stop
shrieking and raging, till half-dead with
    love
and the hatred of a stepmother, I drove
Hippolytus in exile from the rest
and strenuous wardship of his father's
    breast.
Then I could breathe, Oenone; he was
    gone;
my lazy, nerveless days meandered on
through dreams and daydreams, like a
    stately carriage
touring the level landscape of my mar-
    riage.
Yet nothing worked. My husband sent me
    here
to Troezen, far from Athens; once again
    the dear
face shattered me; I saw Hippolytus
each day, and felt my ancient, venomous
passion tear my body limb from limb;
naked Venus was clawing down her
    victim.
What could I do? Each moment, terrified
by loose diseased emotions, now I cried
for death to save my glory and expel
my gloomy frenzy from this world, my
    hell.
And yet your tears and words bewildered
    me,
and so endangered my tranquillity,
at last I spoke. Nurse, I shall not repent,
if you will leave me the passive content
of dry silence and solitude.

Scene IV

Phaedra, Oenone, Panope

PANOPE: My heart breaks. Would to
    God, I could refuse
to tell your majesty my evil news.
The King is dead! Listen, the heavens
    ring
with shouts and lamentations for the King.

PHAEDRA: The King is dead? What's
    this?

PANOPE: In vain
you beg the gods to send him back again.
Hippolytus has heard the true report,
he is already heading for the port.

PHAEDRA: Oh God!

PANOPE: They've heard in Athens.
    Everyone
is joining factions—some salute your son,
others are calling for Hippolytus;
they want him to reform and harden us—
even Aricia claims the loyalty
of a fanatical minority.
The Prince's captains have recalled their
    men.
His flag is up and now he sails again
for Athens. Queen, if he appear there now,
he'll drag the people with him!

OENONE: Stop, allow
the Queen a little respite for her grief.
She hears you, and will act for our relief.

Scene V

Phaedra, Oenone

OENONE: I'd given up persuading you
    to live;
death was your refuge, only death could
    give
you peace and save your troubled glory. I
myself desired to follow you, and die.
But this catastrophe prescribes new laws:
the king is dead, and for the king who
    was,
fate offers you his kingdom. You have a
    son;
he should be king! If you abandon
him, he'll be a slave. The gods, his ances-
    tors,
will curse and drive you on your fatal
    course.
Live! Who'll condemn you if you love and
    woo
the Prince? Your stepson is no kin to you,
now that your royal husband's death has
    cut
and freed you from the throttling mar-
    riage-knot.

Do not torment the Prince with persecution,
and give a leader to the revolution;
no, win his friendship, bind him to your
side.
Give him this city and its countryside.
He will renounce the walls of Athens, piled
stone on stone by Minerva for your child.
Stand with Hippolytus, annihilate
Aricia's faction, and possess the state!

PHAEDRA: So be it! Your superior force
has won.
I will live if compassion for my son,
devotion to the Prince, and love of power
can give me courage in this fearful hour.

ACT 2

SCENE I

Aricia, Ismene

ARICIA: What's this? The Prince has
sent a messenger?
The Prince begs me to wait and meet him
here?
The Prince begs! Goose, you've lost your
feeble wits!

ISMENE: Lady, be calm. These are the
benefits
of Theseus' death: first Prince Hippolytus
comes courting favors; soon the populous
cities of Greece will follow—they will eat
out of your hand, Princess, and kiss your
feet.

ARICIA: This felon's hand, this slave's!
My dear, your news
is only frivolous gossip, I refuse
to hope.

ISMENE: Ah Princess, the just powers
of hell
have struck. Theseus has joined your
brothers!

ARICIA: Tell
me how he died.

ISMENE: Princess, fearful tales
are circulating. Sailors saw his sails,
his infamous black sails, spin round and
round
in Charybdis' whirlpool; all hands were
drowned.
Yet others say on better evidence
that Theseus and Pirithoüs passed the
dense
darkness of hell to rape Persephone.
Pirithoüs was murdered by the hound;
Theseus, still living, was buried in the
ground.

ARICIA: This is an old wives' tale. Only
the dead
enter the underworld, and see the bed
of Queen Persephone. What brought him
there?

ISMENE: Princess, the King is dead—
dead! Everywhere
men know and mourn. Already our wor-
shipping
townsmen acclaim Hippolytus for their
king;
in her great palace, Phaedra, the self-
styled
regent, rages and trembles for her child.

ARICIA: What makes you think the puri-
tanical
son of Theseus is human. Will he recall
my sentence and relent?

ISMENE: I know he will.

ARICIA: You know nothing about him.
He would kill
a woman, rather than be kind to one.
That wolf-cub of a fighting amazon
hates me above all women. He would walk
from here to hell, rather than hear me talk.

ISMENE: Do you know Hippolytus?
Listen to me.
His famous, blasphemous frigidity,
what is it, when you've seen him close at
hand?
I've watched him like a hawk, and seen
him stand
shaking beside you—all his reputation

for hating womenkind bears no relation
to what I saw. He couldn't take his eyes
off you! His eyes speak what his tongue
    denies.
    ARICIA: I can't believe you. Your story's
    absurd!
How greedily I listen to each word!
Ismene, you know me, you know how my
    heart
was reared on death, and always set apart
from what it cherished—can this play-
    thing of
the gods and furies feel the peace of love?
What sights I've seen, Ismene! "Heads
    will roll,"
my brothers told me, "we will rule." I,
    the sole
survivor of those fabulous kings, who
    tilled
the soil of Greece, have seen my brothers
    killed,
six brothers murdered! In a single hour,
the tyrant, Theseus, lopped them in their
    flower.
The monster spared my life, and yet de-
    creed
the torments of this childless life I lead
in exile, where no Greek can look on me;
my forced, perpetual virginity
preserves his crown; no son shall bear my
    name
or blow my brothers' ashes into flame.
Ismene, you know how well his tyranny
favors my temperament and strengthens
    me
to guard the honor of my reputation;
his rigor fortified my inclination.
How could I test his son's civilities?
I'd never even seen him with my eyes!
I'd never seen him. I'd restrained my eye,
that giddy nerve, from dwelling thought-
    lessly
upon his outward grace and beauty—on
    mere
embellishments of nature, a veneer
the Prince himself despises and ignores.
My heart loves nobler virtues, and adores

in him his father's hard intelligence.
He has his father's daring and a sense
of honor his father lacks. Let me confess,
I love him for his lofty haughtiness
never submitted to a woman's yoke.
How could Phaedra's splendid marriage
    provoke
my jealousy? Have I so little pride,
I'd snatch at a rake's heart, a heart denied
to none—all riddled, opened up to let
thousands pass in like water through a net?
To carry sorrows to a heart, alone
untouched by passion, inflexible as stone,
to fasten my dominion on a force
as nervous as a never-harnessed horse—
this stirs me, this enflames me. Devilish
    Zeus
is easier mastered than Hippolytus;
heaven's love-infatuated emperor
confers less glory on his conqueror!
Ismene, I'm afraid. Why should I boast?
His very virtues I admire most
threaten to rise and throw me from the
    brink
of hope. What girlish folly made me think
Hippolytus could love Aricia?
    ISMENE: Here
he is. He loves you, Princess. Have no fear.

SCENE II

Aricia, Ismene, Hippolytus

HIPPOLYTUS: Princess, before
I leave here, I must tell you what's in store
for you in Greece. Alas, my father's dead.
The fierce forebodings that disquieted
my peace are true. Death, only death,
    could hide
his valor from this world he pacified.
The homicidal Fates will not release
the comrade, friend and peer of Hercules.
Princess, I trust your hate will not resent
honors whose justice is self-evident.
A single hope alleviates my grief,
Princess, I hope to offer you relief.
I now revoke a law whose cruelty

has pained my conscience. Princess, you
  are free
to marry. Oh enjoy this province, whose
honest, unhesitating subjects choose
Hippolytus for king. Live free as air,
here, free as I am, much more free!

ARICIA: I dare
not hope. You are too gracious. Can you
  free
Aricia from your father's stern decree?

HIPPOLYTUS: Princess, the Athenian
  people, torn in two
between myself and Phaedra's son, want
  you.

ARICIA: Want me, my Lord!

HIPPOLYTUS: I've no illusions. Lame
Athenian precedents condemn my claim,
because my mother was a foreigner.
But what is that? If my only rival were
my younger brother, his minority
would clear my legal disability.
However, a better claim than his or mine
now favors you, ennobled by the line
of great Erectheus. Your direct descent
sets you before my father; he was only lent
this kingdom by adoption. Once the
  common
Athenian, dazed by Theseus' superhuman
energies, had no longing to exhume
the rights that rushed your brothers to
  their doom.
Now Athens calls you home; the ancient
  feud
too long has stained the sacred olive wood;
blood festers in the furrows of our soil
to blight its fruits and scorch the farmer's
  toil.
This province suits me; let the vines of
  Crete
offer my brother a secure retreat.
The rest is yours. All Attica is yours;
I go to win you what your right assures.

ARICIA: Am I awake, my lord? Your
  sayings seem
like weird phantasmagoria in a dream.
How can your sparkling promises be true?

Some god, my lord, some god, has entered
  you!
How justly you are worshiped in this
  town;
oh how the truth surpasses your renown!
You wish to endow me with your heritage!
I only hoped you would not hate me. This
  rage
your father felt, how can you put it by
and treat me kindly?

HIPPOLYTUS: Princess, is my eye
blind to beauty? Am I a bear, a bull, a
  boar,
some abortion fathered by the Minotaur?
Some one-eyed Cyclops, able to resist
Aricia's loveliness and still exist?
How can a man stand up against your
  grace?

ARICIA: My lord, my lord!

HIPPOLYTUS: I cannot hide my face,
Princess! I'm driven. Why does my violence
so silence reason and intelligence?
Must I be still, and let my adoration
simmer away in silent resignation?
Princess, I've lost all power to restrain
myself. You see a madman, whose insane
pride hated love, and hoped to sit ashore,
watching the galleys founder in the war;
I was Diana's liegeman, dressed in steel.
I hoped to trample love beneath my heel—
alas, the flaming Venus burns me down,
I am the last dependent on her crown.
What left me charred and writhing in her
  clutch?
A single moment and a single touch.
Six months now, bounding like a wounded
  stag,
I've tried to shake this poisoned dart, and
  drag
myself to safety from your eyes that blind
when present, and when absent leave
  behind
volleys of burning arrows in my mind.
Ah Princess, shall I dive into the sea,
or steal the wings of Icarus to flee

love's Midas' touch that turns my world to
gold?
Your image drives me stumbling through
the cold,
floods my deserted forest caves with light,
darkens the day and dazzles through my
night.
I'm grafted to your side by all I see;
all things unite us and imprison me.
I have no courage for the Spartan exercise
that trained my hand and steeled my
energies.
Where are my horses? I forget their
names.
My triumphs with my chariot at the games
no longer give me strength to mount a
horse.
The ocean drives me shuddering from its
shores.
Does such a savage conquest make you
blush?
My boorish gestures, headlong cries that
rush
at you like formless monsters from the
sea?
Ah, Princess, hear me! Your serenity
must pardon the distortions of a weak
and new-born lover, forced by you, to
speak
love's foreign language, words that snarl
and yelp . . .
I never could have spoken without your
help.

Scene III

Aricia, Ismene, Hippolytus, Theramenes

THERAMENES: I announce the Queen.
She comes hurriedly,
looking for you.

HIPPOLYTUS: For me!

THERAMENES: Don't ask me why;
she insisted. I promised I'd prevail
on you to speak with her before you sail.

HIPPOLYTUS: What can she want to
hear? What can I say?

ARICIA: Wait for her, here! You cannot turn away.
Forget her malice. Hating her will serve
no purpose. Wait for her! Her tears deserve
your pity.

HIPPOLYTUS: You're going, Princess?
And I must go
to Athens, far from you. How shall I
know
if you accept my love.

ARICIA: My lord, pursue
your gracious promise. Do what you must
do,
make Athens tributary to my rule.
Nothing you offer is unacceptable;
yet this empire, so great, so glorious,
is the least precious of your gifts to us.

Scene IV

Hippolytus, Theramenes

HIPPOLYTUS: We're ready. Wait, the
Queen's here. I need you.
You must interrupt this tedious interview.
Hurry down to the ship, then rush back,
pale
and breathless. Say the wind's up and we
must sail.

Scene V

Hippolytus, Oenone, Phaedra

PHAEDRA: He's here! Why does he
scowl and look away
from me? What shall I do? What shall
I say?

OENONE: Speak for your son, he has
no other patron.

PHAEDRA: Why are you so impatient
to be gone
from us, my lord? Stay! we will weep
together.
Pity my son; he too has lost his father.

My own death's near. Rebellion, sick with
    wrongs,
now like a sea-beast, lifts its slimy prongs,
its muck, its jelly. You alone now stand
to save the state. Who else can understand
a mother? I forget. You will not hear
me! An enemy deserves no pity. I fear
your anger. Must my son, your brother,
    Prince,
be punished for his cruel mother's sins?

    HIPPOLYTUS: I've no such thoughts.

    PHAEDRA: I persecuted you
blindly, and now you have good reason to
return my impudence. How could you
    find
the motivation of this heart and mind
that scourged and tortured you, till you
    began
to lose the calm composure of a man,
and dwindle to a harsh and sullen boy,
a thing of ice, unable to enjoy
the charms of any civilized resource
except the heavy friendship of your horse,
that whirled you far from women, court
    and throne,
to course the savage woods for wolves
    alone?
You have good reason, yet if pain's a
    measure,
no one has less deserved your stern dis-
    pleasure.
My lord, no one has more deserved com-
    passion.

    HIPPOLYTUS: Lady, I understand a
        mother's passion,
a mother jealous for her children's rights.
How can she spare a first wife's son?
    Long nights
of plotting, devious ways of quarrelling—
a madhouse! What else can remarriage
    bring?
Another would have shown equal hostility,
pushed her advantage more outrageously.

    PHAEDRA: My lord, if you had known
        how far my love
and yearning have exalted me above

this usual weakness . . . Our afflicting kin-
    ship
is ending . . .

    HIPPOLYTUS: Madam, the precious min-
        utes slip
by, I fatigue you. Fight against your fears.
Perhaps Poseidon has listened to our tears,
perhaps your husband's still alive. He
    hears
us, he is surging home—only a short
day's cruise conceals him, as he scuds for
    port.

    PHAEDRA: That's folly, my lord. Who
        has twice visited
black Hades and the river of the dead
and returned? No, the poisonous Acheron
never lets go. Theseus drifts on and on,
a gutted galley on that clotted waste—
he woos, he wins Persephone, the chaste . . .
What am I saying? Theseus is not dead.
He lives in you. He speaks, he's taller by
    a head,
I see him, touch him, and my heart—a
    reef . . .
Ah Prince, I wander. Love betrays my
    grief . . .

    HIPPOLYTUS: No, no, my father lives.
        Lady, the blind
furies release him; in your loyal mind,
love's fullness holds him, and he cannot
    die.

    PHAEDRA: I hunger for Theseus. Always
        in my eye
he wanders, not as he appeared in hell,
lascivious eulogist of any belle
he found there, from the lowest to the
    Queen;
no, faithful, airy, just a little mean
through virtue, charming all, yet young
    and new,
as we would paint a god—as I now see
    you!
Your valiant shyness would have graced
    his speech,
he would have had your stature, eyes, and
    reach,

Prince, when he flashed across our Cretan
  waters,
the loved enslaver of King Minos' daughters.
Where were you? How could he con-
  script the flower
of Athens' youth against my father's
  power,
and ignore you? You were too young,
  they say;
you should have voyaged as a stowaway.
No dawdling bypath would have saved
  our bull,
when your just vengeance thundered
  through its skull.
There, light of foot, and certain of your
  goal,
you would have struck my brother's monstrous soul,
and pierced our maze's slow meanders,
  led
by Ariadne and her subtle thread.
By Ariadne? Prince, I would have fought
for precedence; my every flaming thought,
love-quickened, would have shot you
  through the dark,
straight as an arrow to your quaking
  mark.
Could I have waited, panting, perishing,
entrusting your survival to a string,
like Ariadne, when she skulked behind,
there at the portal, to bemuse her mind
among the solemn cloisters of the porch?
No, Phaedra would have snatched your
  burning torch,
and lunged before you, reeling like a
  priest
of Dionysus to distract the beast.
I would have reached the final corridor
a lap before you, and killed the Minotaur!
Lost in the labyrinth, and at your side,
would it have mattered, if I lived or died?

HIPPOLYTUS: What are you saying,
  Madam? You forget
my father is your husband!

PHAEDRA: I have let

you see my grief for Theseus! How could I
forget my honor and my majesty,
Prince?

  HIPPOLYTUS: Madam, forgive me! My
    foolish youth
conjectured hideous untruths from your
  truth.
I cannot face my insolence. Farewell . . .

  PHAEDRA: You monster! You under-
    stood me too well!
Why do you hang there, speechless, petrified,
polite! My mind whirls. What have I to
  hide?
Phaedra in all her madness stands before
  you.
I love you! Fool, I love you, I adore you!
Do not imagine that my mind approved
my first defection, Prince, or that I loved
your youth light-heartedly, and fed my
  treason
with cowardly compliance, till I lost my
  reason.
I wished to hate you, but the gods corrupt
us; though I never suffered their abrupt
seductions, shattering advances, I
too bear their sensual lightnings in my
  thigh.
I too am dying. I have felt the heat
that drove my mother through the fields
  of Crete,
the bride of Minos, dying for the full
magnetic April thunders of the bull.
I struggled with my sickness, but I found
no grace or magic to preserve my sound
intelligence and honor from this lust,
plowing my body with its horny thrust.
At first I fled you, and when this fell short
of safety, Prince, I exiled you from court.
Alas, my violence to resist you made
my face inhuman, hateful. I was afraid
to kiss my husband lest I love his son.
I made you fear me (this was easily done);
you loathed me more, I ached for you no
  less.
Misfortune magnified your loveliness.

I grew so wrung and wasted, men mistook
me for the Sibyl. If you could bear to look
your eyes would tell you. Do you believe
    my passion
is voluntary? That my obscene confession
is some dark trick, some oily artifice?
I came to beg you not to sacrifice
my son, already uncertain of his life.
Ridiculous, mad embassy, for a wife
who loves her stepson! Prince, I only spoke
about myself! Avenge yourself, invoke
your father; a worse monster threatens you
than any Theseus ever fought and slew.
The wife of Theseus loves Hippolytus!
See, Prince! Look, this monster, ravenous
for her execution, will not flinch.
I want your sword's spasmodic final inch.

OENONE: Madam, put down this weap-
    on. Your distress
attracts the people. Fly these witnesses.
Hurry! Stop kneeling! What a time to
    pray!

SCENE VI

Theramenes, Hippolytus

THERAMENES: Is this Phaedra, fleeing,
    or rather dragged away
sobbing? Where is your sword? Who tore
this empty scabbard from your belt?

HIPPOLYTUS: No more!
Oh let me get away! I face disaster.
Horrors unnerve me. Help! I cannot
    master
my terror. Phaedra . . . No, I won't expose
her. No! Something I do not dare dis-
    close . . .

THERAMENES: Our ship is ready, but
    before you leave,
listen! Prince, what we never would believe
has happened: Athens has voted for your
    brother.
The citizens have made him king. His
    mother
is regent.

HIPPOLYTUS: Phaedra is in power!

THERAMENES: An envoy sent from
    Athens came this hour
to place the scepter in her hands. Her son
is king.

HIPPOLYTUS: Almighty gods, you know
    this woman!
Is it her spotless virtue you reward?

THERAMENES: I've heard a rumor. Some-
    one swam aboard
a ship off Epirus. He claims the King
is still alive. I've searched. I know the
    thing
is nonsense.

HIPPOLYTUS: Search! Nothing must be
    neglected.
If the king's dead, I'll rouse the disaffected
people, crown Aricia, and place our lands,
our people, and our lives in worthy hands.

ACT 3

SCENE I

Phaedra, Oenone

PHAEDRA: Why do my people rush to
    crown me queen?
Who can even want to see me? They have
    seen
my downfall. Will their praise deliver me?
Oh bury me at the bottom of the sea!
Nurse, I have said too much! Led on by
    you,
I've said what no one should have listened
    to.
He listened. How could he pretend my
    drift
was hidden? Something held him, and
    made him shift
his ground . . . He only wanted to depart
and hide, while I was pouring out my
    heart.
Oh how his blushing multiplied my
    shame!
Why did you hold me back! You are to
    blame,

Oenone. But for you, I would have killed
myself. Would he have stood there, iron-
willed
and merciless, while I fell upon his sword?
He would have snatched it, held me, and
restored
my life. No! No!

OENONE: Control yourself! No peace
comes from surrendering to your disease,
Madam. Oh daughter of the kings of Crete,
why are you weeping and fawning at the
feet
of this barbarian, less afraid of fate
than of a woman? You must rule the state.

PHAEDRA: Can I, who have no courage
to restrain
the insurrection of my passions, reign?
Will the Athenians trust their sovereignty
to me? Love's despotism is crushing me,
I am ruined.

OENONE: Fly!

PHAEDRA: How can I leave him?

OENONE: Lady, you have already banished him.
Can't you take flight?

PHAEDRA: The time for flight has passed.
He knows me now. I rushed beyond the
last
limits of modesty, when I confessed.
Hope was no longer blasting through my
breast;
I was resigned to hopelessness and death,
and gasping out my last innocent breath,
Oenone, when you forced me back to life.
You thought I was no longer Theseus'
wife,
and let me feel that I was free to love.

OENONE: I would have done anything to
remove
your danger. Whether I'm guilty or innocent
is all the same to me. Your punishment
should fall on one who tried to kill you,
not
on poor Oenone. Lady, you must plot
and sacrifice this monster, whose unjust

abhorrence left you dying in the dust.
Oh humble him, undo him, oh despise
him! Lady, you must see him with my
eyes.

PHAEDRA: Oenone, he was nourished in
the woods;
he is all shyness and ungracious moods
because the forests left him half-inhuman.
He's never heard love spoken by a woman!
We've gone too far. Oenone, we're unwise;
perhaps the young man's silence was surprise.

OENONE: His mother, the amazon, was
never moved by men.

PHAEDRA: The boy exists. She must have
loved!

OENONE: He has a sullen hatred for our
sex.

PHAEDRA: Oh, all the better; rivals will
not vex
my chances. Your advice is out of season;
now you must serve my frenzy, not my
reason!
You tell me love has never touched his
heart;
we'll look, we'll find an undefended part.
He's turned his bronze prows seaward;
look, the wind
already blows like a trumpeter behind
his bulging canvas! The Acropolis
of Athens and its empire shall be his!
Hurry, Oenone, hunt the young man
down,
blind him with dazzling visions of the
crown.
Go tell him I relinquish my command,
I only want the guidance of his hand.
Let him assume these powers that weary
me,
he will instruct my son in sovereignty.
Perhaps he will adopt my son, and be
the son and mother's one divinity!
Oenone, rush to him, use every means
to bend and win him; if he fears the
Queen's
too proud, he'll listen to her slave. Plead,
groan,

insist, say I am giving him my throne . . .
No, say I'm dying!

Scene II

Phaedra

PHAEDRA: Implacable Aphrodite, now
    you see
the depths to which your tireless cruelty
has driven Phaedra—here is my bosom;
every thrust and arrow has struck home!
Oh Goddess, if you hunger for renown,
rise now, and shoot a worthier victim
    down!
Conquer the barbarous Hippolytus,
who mocks the graces and the power of
    Venus,
and gazes on your godhead with disgust.
Avenge me, Venus! See, my cause is just,
my cause is yours. Oh bend him to my
    will! . . .
You're back, Oenone? Does he hate me
    still?

Scene III

Phaedra, Oenone

OENONE: Your love is folly, dash it from
    your soul,
gather your scattered pride and self-con-
    trol,
Madam! I've seen the royal ship arrive.
Theseus is back, Theseus is still alive!
Thousands of voices thunder from the
    docks.
People are waving flags and climbing
    rocks.
While I was looking for Hippolytus . . .
    PHAEDRA: My husband's living! Must
        you trouble us
by talking? What am I living for?
He lives, Oenone, let me hear no more
about it.
    OENONE: Why?
    PHAEDRA: I told you, but my fears

were stilled, alas, and smothered by your
    tears.
Had I died this morning, I might have
    faced
the gods. I heeded you and die disgraced!
    OENONE: You are disgraced!
    PHAEDRA: Oh Gods of wrath,
how far I've travelled on my dangerous
    path!
I go to meet my husband; at his side
will stand Hippolytus. How shall I hide
my thick adulterous passion for this youth,
who has rejected me, and knows the truth?
Will the stern Prince stand smiling and
    approve
the labored histrionics of my love
for Theseus, see my lips, still languishing
for his, betray his father and his King?
Will he not draw his sword and strike me
    dead?
Suppose he spares me? What if nothing's
    said?
Am I a gorgon, or Circe, or the infidel
Medea, stifled by the flames of hell,
yet rising like Aphrodite from the sea,
refreshed and radiant with indecency?
Can I kiss Theseus with dissembled poise?
I think each stone and pillar has a voice.
The very dust rises to disabuse
my husband—to defame me and accuse!
Oenone, I want to die. Death will give
me freedom; oh it's nothing not to live;
death to the unhappy's no catastrophe!
I fear the name that must live after me,
and crush my son until the end of time.
Is his inheritance his mother's crime,
his right to curse me, when my pollution
    stains
the blood of heaven bubbling in his veins?
The day will come, alas, the day will come,
when nothing will be left to save him from
the voices of despair. If he should live
he'll flee his subjects like a fugitive.
    OENONE: He has my pity. Who has ever
        built
firmer foundations to expose her guilt?

But why expose your son? Is your contri-
bution
for his defense to serve the prosecution?
Suppose you kill yourself? The world will
say
you fled your outraged husband in dismay.
Could there be stronger evidence and
proof
than Phaedra crushed beneath the horse's
hoof
of blasphemous self-destruction to convince
the crowds who'll dance attendance on the
Prince?
The crowds will mob your children when
they hear
their defamation by a foreigner!
Wouldn't you rather see earth bury us?
Tell me, do you still love Hippolytus?

PHAEDRA: I see him as a beast, who'd
murder us.

OENONE: Madam, let the positions be
reversed!
You fear the Prince; you must accuse him
first.
Who'll dare assert your story is untrue,
if all the evidence shall speak for you:
your present grief, your past despair of
mind,
the Prince's sword so luckily left behind?
Do you think Theseus will oppose his
son's
second exile? He has consented once!

PHAEDRA: How dare I take this murderous, plunging course?

OENONE: I tremble, Lady, I too feel
remorse.
If death could rescue you from infamy,
Madam, I too would follow you and die.
Help me by being silent. I will speak
in such a way the King will only seek
a bloodless exile to assert his rights.
A father is still a father when he smites,
You shudder at this evil sacrifice,
but nothing's evil or too high a price
to save your menaced honor from defeat.
Ah Minos, Minos, you defended Crete

by killing young men? Help us! If the cost
for saving Phaedra is a holocaust
of virtue, Minos, you must sanctify
our undertaking, or watch your daughter
die.
I see the King.

PHAEDRA: I see Hippolytus!

Scene IV

Phaedra, Theseus, Hippolytus, Oenone

THESEUS: Fate's heard me, Phaedra, and
removed the bar
that kept me from your arms.

PHAEDRA: Theseus, stop where you are!
Your raptures and endearments are profane.
Your arm must never comfort me again.
You have been wronged, the gods who
spared your life
have used your absence to disgrace your
wife,
unworthy now to please you or come near.
My only refuge is to disappear.

Scene V

Theseus, Hippolytus

THESEUS: What a strange welcome!
This bewilders me.
My son, what's happened?

HIPPOLYTUS: Phaedra holds the key.
Ask Phaedra. If you love me, let me leave
this kingdom. I'm determined to achieve
some action that will show my strength.
I fear
Phaedra. I am afraid of living here.

THESEUS: My son, you want to leave
me?

HIPPOLYTUS: I never sought
her grace or favor. Your decision brought
her here from Athens. Your desires prevailed

against my judgment, Father, when you
  sailed
leaving Phaedra and Aricia in my care.
I've done my duty, now I must prepare
for sterner actions, I must test my skill
on monsters far more dangerous to kill
than any wolf or eagle in this wood.
Release me, I too must prove my manhood.
Oh Father, you were hardly half my age,
when herds of giants writhed before your
  rage—
you were already famous as the scourge
of insolence. Our people saw you purge
the pirates from the shores of Greece and
  Thrace,
the harmless merchantman was free to
  race
the winds, and weary Hercules could pause
from slaughter, knowing you upheld his
  cause.
The world revered you. I am still unknown;
even my mother's deeds surpass my own.
Some tyrants have escaped you; let me
  meet
with them and throw their bodies at your
  feet.
I'll drag them from their wolf-holes; if
  I die,
my death will show I struggled worthily.
Oh, Father, raise me from oblivion;
my deeds shall tell the universe I am your
  son.
  THESEUS: What do I see? Oh gods,
    what horror drives
my queen and children fleeing for their
  lives
before me? If so little warmth remains,
oh why did you release me from my
  chains?
Why am I hated, and so little loved?
I had a friend, just one. His folly moved
me till I aided his conspiracy
to ravish Queen Persephone.
The gods, tormented by our blasphemous
designs, befogged our minds and blinded
  us—

we invaded Epirus instead of hell.
There a diseased and subtle tyrant fell
upon us as we slept, and while I stood
by, helpless, monsters crazed for human
  blood
consumed Pirithoüs. I myself was chained
fast in a death-deep dungeon. I remained
six months there, then the gods had pity,
and put me in possession of the city.
I killed the tyrant; now his body feasts
the famished, pampered bellies of his
  beasts.
At last, I voyaged home, cast anchor,
  furled
my sails. When I was rushing to my
  world—
what am I saying? When my heart and
  soul
were mine again, unable to control
themselves for longing—who receives me?
  All run
and shun me, as if I were a skeleton.
Now I myself begin to feel the fear
I inspire. I wish I were a prisoner
again or dead. Speak! Phaedra says my
  home
was outraged. Who betrayed me? Someone come
and tell me. I have fought for Greece.
  Will Greece,
sustained by Theseus, give my enemies
asylum in my household? Tell me why
I've no avenger? Is my son a spy?
You will not answer. I must know my
  fate.
Suspicion chokes me, while I hesitate
and stand here pleading. Wait, let no one
  stir.
Phaedra shall tell me what has troubled
  her.

Scene VI

Hippolytus

HIPPOLYTUS: What now? His anger
  turns my blood to ice.
Will Phaedra, always uncertain, sacrifice

herself? What will she tell the King?
How hot
the air's becoming here! I feel the rot
of love seeping like poison through this
house.
I feel the pollution. I cannot rouse
my former loyalties. When I try to gather
the necessary strength to face my father,
my mind spins with some dark presenti-
ment . . .
How can such terror touch the innocent?
I LOVE ARICIA! Father, I confess
my treason to you is my happiness!
I LOVE ARICIA! Will this bring you joy,
our love you have on power to destroy?

ACT 4

SCENE I

Theseus, Oenone

THESEUS: What's this, you tell me he
dishonors me,
and has assaulted Phaedra's chastity?
Oh heavy fortune, I no longer know
who loves me, who I am, or where I go.
Who has ever seen such disloyalty
after such love? Such sly audacity!
His youth made no impression on her
soul,
so he fell back on force to reach his goal!
I recognize this perjured sword; I gave
him this myself to teach him to be brave!
Oh Zeus, are blood-ties no impediment?
Phaedra tried to save him from punishment!
Why did her silence spare this parricide?

OENONE: She hoped to spare a trusting
father's pride.
She felt so sickened by your son's attempt,
his hot eyes leering at her with contempt,
she had no wish to live. She read out her
will
to me, then lifted up her arm to kill
herself. I struck the sword out of her hand.
Fainting, she babbled the secret she had
planned

to bury with her in the grave. My ears
unwillingly interpreted her tears.

THESEUS: Oh traitor! I know why he
seemed to blanch
and toss with terror like an aspen branch
when Phaedra saw him. Now I know why
he stood
back, then embraced me so coldly he froze
my blood.
Was Athens the first stage for his obscene
attentions? Did he dare attack the Queen
before our marriage?

OENONE: Remember her disgust
and hate then? She already feared his lust.

THESEUS: And when I sailed, this
started up again?

OENONE: I've hidden nothing. Do you
want your pain
redoubled? Phaedra calls me. Let me go,
and save her. I have told you what I know.

SCENE II

Theseus, Hippolytus

THESEUS: My son returns! Oh God,
reserved and cool,
dressed in a casual freedom that could fool
the sharpest. Is it right his brows should
blaze
and dazzle me with virtue's sacred rays?
Are there not signs? Should not ADULTERER
in looping scarlet script be branded there?

HIPPOLYTUS: What cares becloud your
kingly countenance,
Father! What is this irritated glance?
Tell me! Are you afraid to trust your son?

THESEUS: How dare you stand here?
May the great Zeus stone
me, if I let my fondness and your birth
protect you! Is my strength which rid the
earth
of brigands paralysed? Am I so sick
and senile, any coward with a stick
can strike me? Am I a schoolboy's target?
Oh God,

am I food for vultures? Some carrion you
  must prod
and poke to see if it's alive or dead?
Your hands are moist and itching for my
  bed,
Coward! Wasn't begetting you enough
dishonor to destroy me? Must I snuff
your perjured life, my own son's life, and
  stain
a thousand glories? Let the gods restrain
my fury! Fly! live hated and alone—
there are places where my name may be
  unknown.
Go, find them, follow your disastrous star
through filth; if I discover where you
  are,
I'll add another body to the hill
of vermin I've extinguished by my skill.
Fly from me, let the grieving storm-
  winds bear
your contagion from me. You corrupt the
  air.
I call upon Poseidon. Help me, Lord
of Ocean, help your servant! Once my
  sword
heaped crucified assassins on your shore
and let them burn like beacons. God, you
  swore
my first request would be fulfilled. My
  first!
I never made it. Even through the worst
torments of Epirus I held my peace;
no threat or torture brought me to my
  knees
beseeching favors; even then I knew
some greater project was reserved for you!
Poseidon, now I kneel. Avenge me, dash
my incestuous son against your rocks, and
  wash
his dishonor from my household; wave on
  wave
of roaring nothingness shall be his grave.

 HIPPOLYTUS: Phaedra accuses me of
  lawless love!
Phaedra! My heart stops, I can hardly
  move
my lips and answer. I have no defense,
if you condemn me without evidence.

THESEUS: Oh coward, you were counting on the Queen
to hide your brutal insolence and screen
your outrage with her weakness! You
  forgot
something. You dropped your sword and
  spoiled your plot.
You should have kept it. Surely you had
  time
to kill the only witness to your crime!

 HIPPOLYTUS: Why do I stand this, and
  forbear to clear
away these lies, and let the truth appear?
I could so easily. Where would you be,
if I spoke out? Respect my loyalty,
Father, respect your own intelligence.
Examine me. What am I? My defense
is my whole life. When have I wavered,
  when
have I pursued the vices of young men?
Father, you have no scaffolding to rig
your charges on. Small crimes precede the
  big.
Phaedra accused me of attempting rape!
Am I some Proteus, who can change his
  shape?
Nature despises such disparities.
Vice, like virtue, advances by degrees.
Bred by Antiope to manly arms,
I hate the fever of this lust that warms
the loins and rots the spirit. I was taught
uprightness by Theramenes. I fought
with wolves, tamed horses, gave my soul
  to sport,
and shunned the joys of women and the
  court.
I dislike praise, but those who know me
  best
grant me one virtue—it's that I detest
the very crimes of which I am accused.
How often you yourself have been amused
and puzzled by my love of purity,
pushed to the point of crudeness. By the
  sea
and in the forests, I have filled my heart
with freedom, far from women.

 THESEUS: When this part

was dropped, could only Phaedra violate
the cold abyss of your immaculate
reptilian soul. How could this funeral urn
contain a heart, a living heart, or burn
for any woman but my wife?

HIPPOLYTUS: Ah no!
Father, I too have seen my passions blow
into a tempest. Why should I conceal
my true offense? I feel, Father, I feel
what other young men feel. I love, I love
Aricia. Father, I love the sister of
your worst enemies. I worship her!
I only feel and breathe and live for her!

THESEUS: You love Aricia? God! No,
  this is meant
to blind my eyes and throw me off the
  scent.

HIPPOLYTUS: Father, for six months I
  have done my worst
to kill this passion. You shall be the first
to know . . . You frown still. Nothing can
  remove
your dark obsession. Father, what will
  prove
my innocence? I swear by earth and sky,
and nature's solemn, shining majesty. . . .

THESEUS: Oaths and religion are the
  common cant
of all betrayers. If you wish to taunt
me, find a better prop than blasphemy.

HIPPOLYTUS: All's blasphemy to eyes
  that cannot see.
Could even Phaedra bear me such ill will?

THESEUS: Phaedra, Phaedra! Name her
  again, I'll kill
you! My hand's already on my sword.

HIPPOLYTUS: Explain
my terms of exile. What do you ordain?

THESEUS: Sail out across the ocean.
  Everywhere
on earth and under heaven is too near.

HIPPOLYTUS: Who'll take me in? Oh
  who will pity me,
and give me bread, if you abandon me?

THESEUS: You'll find fitting companions. Look for friends

who honor everything that most offends.
Pimps and jackals who praise adultery
and incest will protect your purity!

HIPPOLYTUS: Adultery! Is it your privilege
to fling this word in my teeth? I've
  reached the edge
of madness . . . No, I'll say no more. Compare
my breeding with Phaedra's. Think and
  beware . . .
She had a mother . . . No, I must not
  speak.

THESEUS: You devil, you'll attack the
  queen still weak
from your assault. How can you stand
  and face
your father? Must I drive you from this
  place
with my own hand. Run off, or I will flog
you with the flat of my sword like a dog!

Scene III

Theseus

THESEUS: You go to your inevitable fate,
Child—by the river immortals venerate.
Poseidon gave his word. You cannot fly:
death and the gods march on invisibly.
I loved you once; despite your perfidy,
my bowels writhe inside me. Must you
  die?
Yes; I am in too deep now to draw back.
What son has placed his father on such a
  rack?
What father groans for such a monstrous
  birth?
Oh gods, your thunder throws me to the
  earth.

Scene IV

Theseus, Phaedra

PHAEDRA: Theseus, I heard the deluge
  of your voice,

and stand here trembling. If there's time
  for choice,
hold back your hand, still bloodless; spare
  your race!
I supplicate you, I kneel here for grace.
Oh, Theseus, Theseus, will you drench the
  earth
with your own blood? His virtue, youth
  and birth
cry out for him. Is he already slain
by you for me—spare me this incestuous
  pain!

THESEUS: Phaedra, my son's blood has
  not touched my hand;
and yet I'll be avenged. On sea and land,
spirits, the swift of foot, shall track him
  down.
Poseidon owes me this. Why do you frown?

PHAEDRA: Poseidon owes you this?
  What have you done
in anger?

THESEUS: What! You wish to help my
  son?
No, stir my anger, back me to the hilt,
call for blacker colors to paint his guilt.
Lash, strike and drive me on! You cannot guess
the nerve and fury of his wickedness.
Phaedra, he slandered your sincerity,
he told me your accusation was a lie.
He swore he loved Aricia, he wants to wed
Aricia. . . .

PHAEDRA: What, my lord!

THESEUS: That's what he said.
Of course, I scorn his shallow artifice.
Help me, Poseidon, hear me, sacrifice
my son. I seek the altar. Come! Let us both
kneel down and beg the gods to keep their
  oath.

Scene V

Phaedra

PHAEDRA: My husband's gone, still
  rumbling his own name

and fame. He has no inkling of the flame
his words have started. If he hadn't
  spoken,
I might have . . . I was on my feet, I'd
  broken
loose from Oenone, and had just begun
to say I know not what to save his son.
Who knows how far I would have gone?
  Remorse,
longing and anguish shook me with such
  force,
I might have told the truth and suffered
  death,
before this revelation stopped my breath:
Hippolytus is not insensible,
only insensible to me! His dull
heart chases shadows. He is glad to rest
upon Aricia's adolescent breast!
Oh thin abstraction! When I saw his firm
repugnance spurn my passion like a worm,
I thought he had some magic to withstand
the lure of any woman in the land,
and now I see a schoolgirl leads the boy,
as simply as her puppy or a toy.
Was I about to perish for this sham,
this panting hypocrite? Perhaps I am
the only woman that he could refuse!

Scene VI

Phaedra, Oenone

PHAEDRA: Oenone, dearest, have you
  heard the news?

OENONE: No, I know nothing, but I
  am afraid.
How can I follow you? You have betrayed
your life and children. What have you
  revealed,
Madam?

PHAEDRA: I have a rival in the field,
Oenone.

OENONE: What?

PHAEDRA: Oenone, he's in love—
this howling monster, able to disprove
my beauty, mock my passion, scorn each
  prayer,

and face me like a tiger in its lair—
he's tamed, the beast is harnessed to a
    cart;
Aricia's found an entrance to his heart.

OENONE: Aricia?

PHAEDRA: Nurse, my last calamity
has come. This is the bottom of the sea.
All that preceded this had little force—
the flames of lust, the horrors of remorse,
the prim refusal by my grim young
    master,
were only feeble hints of this disaster.
They love each other! Passion blinded me.
I let them blind me, let them meet and see
each other freely! Was such bounty
    wrong?
Oenone, you have known this all along,
you must have seen their meetings,
    watched them sneak
off to their forest, playing hide-and-seek!
Alas, such rendezvous are no offence:
innocent nature smiles of innocence,
for them each natural impulse was al-
    lowed,
each day was summer and without a
    cloud.
Oenone, nature hated me. I fled
its light, as if a price were on my head.
I shut my eyes and hungered for my end.
Death was the only God my vows could
    bend.
And even while my desolation served
me gall and tears, I knew I was observed;
I never had security or leisure
for honest weeping, but must steal this
    pleasure.
Oh hideous pomp; a monarch only wears
the robes of majesty to hide her tears!

    OENONE: How can their folly help
        them? They will never
enjoy its fruit.

    PHAEDRA: Ugh, they will love forever—
even while I am talking, they embrace,
they scorn me, they are laughing in my
    face!
In the teeth of exile, I hear them swear

they will be true forever, everywhere.
Oenone, have pity on my jealous rage;
I'll kill this happiness that jeers at age.
I'll summon Theseus; hate shall answer
    hate!
I'll drive my husband to annihilate
Aricia—let no trivial punishment,
her instant death, or bloodless banish-
    ment . . .
What am I saying? Have I lost my mind?
I am jealous, and call my husband! Bind
me, gag me; I am frothing with desire.
My husband is alive, and I'm on fire!
For whom? Hippolytus. When I have
    said
his name, blood fills my eyes, my heart
    stops dead.
Imposture, incest, murder! I have passed
the limits of damnation; now at last,
my lover's lifeblood is my single good.
Nothing else cools my murderous thirst
    for blood.
Yet I live on! I live, looked down upon
by my progenitor, the sacred sun,
by Zeus, by Europa, by the universe
of gods and stars, my ancestors. They
    curse
their daughter. Let me die. In the great
    night
of Hades, I'll find shelter from their sight.
What am I saying? I've no place to turn:
Minos, my father, holds the judge's urn.
The gods have placed damnation in his
    hands,
the shades in Hades follow his commands.
Will he not shake and curse his fatal star
that brings his daughter trembling to his
    bar?
His child by Pasiphaë forced to tell
a thousand sins unclassified in hell?
Father, when you interpret what I speak,
I fear your fortitude will be too weak
to hold the urn. I see you fumbling for
new punishments for crimes unknown be-
    fore.
You'll be your own child's executioner!
You cannot kill me; look, my murderer

is Venus, who destroyed our family;
Father, she has already murdered me.
I killed myself—and what is worse I
    wasted
my life for pleasures I have never tasted.
My lover flees me still, and my last gasp
is for the fleeting flesh I failed to clasp.

OENONE: Madam, Madam, cast off this
    groundless terror!
Is love now an unprecedented error?
You love! What then? You love! Accept
    your fate.
You're not the first to sail into this strait.
Will chaos overturn the earth and Jove,
because a mortal woman is in love?
Such accidents are easy, all too common.
A woman must submit to being woman.
You curse a failure in the source of things.
Venus has feasted on the hearts of kings;
even the gods, man's judges, feel desire,
Zeus learned to live with his adulterous fire.

PHAEDRA: Must I still listen and drink
    your poisoned breath?
My death's redoubled on the edge of
    death.
I'd fled Hippolytus and I was free
till your entreaties stabbed and blinded
    me,
and dragged me howling to the pit of lust.
Oenone, I was learning to be just.
You fed my malice. Attacking the young
    Prince
was not enough; you clothed him with my
    sins.
You wished to kill him; he is dying now,
because of you, and Theseus' brutal vow.
You watch my torture; I'm the last un-
    gorged
scrap rotting in this trap your plots have
    forged.
What binds you to me? Leave me, go, and
    die,
may your punishment be to terrify
all those who ruin princes by their lies,
hints, acquiescence, filth, and blas-
    phemies—

panders who grease the grooves of in-
    clination,
and lure our willing bodies from salvation.
Go die, go frighten false flatterers, the
    worst
friends the gods can give to kings they've
    cursed!

OENONE: I have given all and left all
    for her service,
almighty gods! I have been paid my price!

ACT 5

Scene I

Hippolytus, Aricia

ARICIA: Take a stand, speak the truth,
    if you respect
your father's glory and your life. Protect
yourself! I'm nothing to you. You consent
without a struggle to your banishment.
If you are weary of Aricia, go;
at least do something to prevent the blow
that dooms your honor and existence—
    both
at a stroke! Your father must recall his
    oath;
there is time still, but if the truth's con-
    cealed,
you offer your accuser a free field.
Speak to your father!

HIPPOLYTUS: I've already said
what's lawful. Shall I point to his soiled
    bed,
tell Athens how his marriage was fore-
    sworn,
make Theseus curse the day that he was
    born?
My aching heart recoils. I only want
God and Aricia for my confidants.
See how I love you; love makes me confide
in you this horror I have tried to hide
from my own heart. My faith must not be
    broken;
forget, if possible, what I have spoken.
Ah Princess, if even a whisper slips

past you, it will perjure your pure lips.
God's justice is committed to the cause
of those who love him, and uphold his
    laws;
sooner or later, heaven itself will rise
in wrath and punish Phaedra's blasphe-
    mies.
I must not. If I rip away her mask,
I'll kill my father. Give me what I ask.
Do this! Then throw away your chains;
    it's right
for you to follow me, and share my flight.
Fly from this prison; here the vices seethe
and simmer, virtue has no air to breathe.
In the confusion of my exile, none
will even notice that Aricia's gone.
Banished and broken, Princess, I am still
a force in Greece. Your guards obey my
    will,
powerful intercessors wish us well:
our neighbors, Argos' citadel
is armed, and in Mycenae our allies
will shelter us, if lying Phaedra tries
to hurry us from our paternal throne,
and steal our sacred titles for her son.
The gods are ours, they urge us to attack.
Why do you tremble, falter and hold back?
Your interests drive me to this sacrifice.
While I'm on fire, your blood has changed
    to ice.
Princess, is exile more than you can face?

ARICIA: Exile with you, my lord? What
    sweeter place
is under heaven? Standing at your side,
I'd let the universe and heaven slide.
You're my one love, my king, but can I
    hope
for peace and honor, Prince, if I elope
unmarried? This . . . I wasn't questioning
the decency of flying from the King.
Is he my father? Only an abject
spirit honors tyrants with respect.
You say you love me. Prince, I am afraid.

HIPPOLYTUS: Aricia, you shall never be
    betrayed;
accept me! Let our love be sanctified,

then flee from your oppressor as my bride.
Bear witness, oh you gods, our love re-
    leased
by danger, needs no temple or a priest.
It's faith, not ceremonial, that saves.
Here at the city gates, among these graves
the resting places of my ancient line,
there stands a sacred temple and a shrine.
Here, where no mortal ever swore in vain,
here in these shadows, where eternal pain
is ready to engulf the perjurer;
here heaven's scepter quivers to confer
its final sanction; here, my Love, we'll
    kneel,
and pray the gods to consecrate and seal
our love. Zeus, the father of the world will
    stand
here as your father and bestow your hand.
Only the pure shall be our witnesses:
Hera, the guarantor of marriages,
Demeter and the virgin Artemis.

ARICIA: The King is coming. Fly. I'll
    stay and meet
his anger here and cover your retreat.
Hurry. Be off, send me some friend to
    guide
my timid footsteps, husband, to your side.

SCENE II

Theseus, Ismene, Aricia

THESEUS: Oh God, illuminate my trou-
    bled mind.
Show me the answer I have failed to find.
ARICIA: Go, Ismene, be ready to escape.

SCENE III

Theseus, Aricia

THESEUS: Princess, you are disturbed.
    You twist your cape
and blush. The Prince was talking to you.
    Why
is he running?

ARICIA: We've said our last goodbye,
my lord.

THESEUS: I see the beauty of your eyes
moves even my son, and you have gained
      a prize
no woman hoped for.

ARICIA: He hasn't taken on
your hatred for me, though he is your son.

THESEUS: I follow. I can hear the oaths
      he swore.
He knelt, he wept. He has done this before
and worse. You are deceived.

ARICIA: Deceived, my lord?

THESEUS: Princess, are you so rich? Can
      you afford
to hunger for this lover that my queen
rejected? Your betrayer loves my wife.

ARICIA: How can you bear to blacken
      his pure life?
Is kingship only for the blind and strong,
unable to distinguish right from wrong?
What insolent prerogative obscures
a light that shines in every eye but yours?
You have betrayed him to his enemies.
What more, my lord? Repent your blas-
      phemies.
Are you not fearful lest the gods so loathe
and hate you they will gratify your oath?
Fear God, my lord, fear God. How many
      times
he grants men's wishes to expose their
      crimes.

THESEUS: Love blinds you, Princess, and
      beclouds your reason.
Your outburst cannot cover up his treason.
My trust's in witnesses that cannot lie.
I have seen Phaedra's tears. She tried to
      die.

ARICIA: Take care, your Highness.
      What your killing hand
drove all the thieves and reptiles from the
      land,
you missed one monster, one was left alive,
one . . . No, I must not name her, Sire,
      or strive

to save your helpless son; he wants to spare
your reputation. Let me go. I dare
not stay here. If I stayed I'd be too weak
to keep my promise. I'd be forced to speak.

SCENE IV

Theseus

THESEUS: What was she saying? I must
      try to reach
the meaning of her interrupted speech.
Is it a pitfall? A conspiracy?
Are they plotting together to torture me?
Why did I let the rash, wild girl depart?
What is this whisper crying in my heart?
A secret pity fills my soul with pain.
I must question Oenone once again.
My guards, summon Oenone to the
      throne.
Quick, bring her. I must talk with her
      alone.

SCENE V

Theseus, Panope

PANOPE: The Queen's deranged, your
      Highness. Some accursed
madness is driving her; some fury stalks
behind her back, possesses her, and talks
its evil through her, and blasphemes the
      world.
She cursed Oenone. Now Oenone's hurled
herself into the ocean, Sire, and drowned.
Why did she do it. No reason can be
      found.

THESEUS: Oenone's drowned?

PANOPE: Her death has brought no
      peace.
The cries of Phaedra's troubled soul in-
      crease.
Now driven by some sinister unrest,
she snatches up her children to her breast,
pets them and weeps, till something makes
      her scoff
at her affection, and she drives them off.

Her glance is drunken and irregular,
she looks through us and wonders who we
    are;
thrice she has started letters to you, Sire,
thrice tossed the shredded fragments in
    the fire.
Oh call her to you. Help her!

    THESEUS: The nurse is drowned? Phae-
    dra wishes to die?
Oh gods! Summon my son. Let him de-
    fend
himself, tell him I'm ready to attend.
I want him!

        (*Exit* PANOPE)

    Neptune, hear me, spare my son!
My vengeance was too hastily begun.
Oh why was I so eager to believe
Oenone's accusation? The gods deceive
the victims they are ready to destroy!

SCENE VI

Theseus, Theramenes

    THESEUS: Here is Theramenes. Where
    is my boy,
my first-born? He was yours to guard
    and keep.
Where is he? Answer me. What's this?
    You weep?

    THERAMENES: Oh, tardy, futile grief,
    his blood is shed.
My lord, your son, Hippolytus, is dead.

    THESEUS: Oh gods, have mercy!

    THERAMENES: I saw him die. The most
lovely and innocent of men is lost.

    THESEUS: He's dead? The gods have
    hurried him away
and killed him? . . . just as I began to
    pray . . .
What sudden thunderbolt has struck him
    down?

    THERAMENES: We'd started out, and
    hardly left the town.
He held the reins; a few feet to his rear,

a single, silent guard held up a spear.
He followed the Mycenae highroad, deep
in thought, reins dangling, as if half
    asleep;
his famous horses, only he could hold,
trudged on with lowered heads, and some-
    times rolled
their dull eyes slowly—they seemed to
    have caught
their master's melancholy, and aped his
    thought.
Then all at once winds struck us like a
    fist,
we heard a sudden roaring through the
    mist;
from underground a voice in agony
answered the prolonged groaning of the
    sea.
We shook, the horses' manes rose on their
    heads,
and now against a sky of blacks and reds,
we saw the flat waves hump into a moun-
    tain
of green-white water rising like a foun-
    tain,
as it reached land and crashed with a last
    roar
to shatter like a galley on the shore.
Out of its fragments rose a monster, half
dragon, half bull; a mouth that seemed
    to laugh
drooled venom on its dirty yellow scales
and python belly, forking to three tails.
The shore was shaken like a tuning fork,
ships bounced on the stung sea like bits
    of cork,
the earth moved, and the sun spun round
    and round,
a sulphur-colored venom swept the
    ground.
We fled; each felt his useless courage
    falter,
and sought asylum at a nearby altar.
Only the Prince remained; he wheeled
    about,
and hurled a javelin through the mon-
    ster's snout.

Each kept advancing. Flung from the
  Prince's arm,
dart after dart struck where the blood
  was warm.
The monster in its death-throes felt defeat,
and bounded howling to the horses' feet.
There its stretched gullet and its armor
  broke,
and drenched the chariot with blood and
  smoke,
and then the horses, terror-struck, stam-
  peded.
Their master's whip and shouting went
  unheeded,
they dragged his breathless body to the
  spray.
Their red mouths bit the bloody surf,
  men say
Poseidon stood beside them, that the god
was stabbing at their bellies with a goad.
Their terror drove them crashing on a
  cliff,
the chariot crashed in two, they ran as if
the Furies screamed and crackled in their
  manes,
their fallen hero tangled in the reins,
jounced on the rocks behind them. The
  sweet light
of heaven never will expunge this sight:
the horses that Hippolytus had tamed,
now dragged him headlong, and their
  mad hooves maimed
his face past recognition. When he tried
to call them, calling only terrified;
faster and ever faster moved their feet,
his body was a piece of bloody meat.
The cliffs and ocean trembled to our
  shout,
at last their panic failed, they turned
  about,
and stopped not far from where those
  hallowed graves,
the Prince's fathers, overlook the waves.
I ran on breathless, guards were at my
  back,
my master's blood had left a generous
  track.

The stones were red, each thistle in the
  mud
was stuck with bits of hair and skin and
  blood.
I came upon him, called; he stretched his
  right
hand to me, blinked his eyes, then closed
  them tight.
"I die," he whispered, "it's the gods'
  desire.
Friend, stand between Aricia and my
  sire—
some day enlightened, softened, dis-
  abused,
he will lament his son, falsely accused;
then when at last he wishes to appease
my soul, he'll treat my lover well, release
and honor Aricia. . . ." On this word, he
  died.
Only a broken body testified
he'd lived and loved once. On the sand
  now lies
something his father will not recognize.

THESEUS: My son, my son! Alas, I
  stand alone
before the gods. I never can atone.

THERAMENES: Meanwhile Aricia, rushing down the path,
approached us. She was fleeing from your
  wrath,
my lord, and wished to make Hippolytus
her husband in God's eyes. Then nearing
  us,
she saw the signs of struggle in the waste,
she saw (oh what a sight) her love de-
  faced,
her young love lying lifeless on the sand.
At first she hardly seemed to understand;
while staring at the body in the grass,
she kept on asking where her lover was.
At last the black and fearful truth broke
  through
her desolation! She seemed to curse the
  blue
and murdering ocean, as she caught his
  head

up in her lap; then fainting lay half dead,
until Ismene somehow summoned back
　　her breath,
restored the child to life—or rather death.
I come, great King, to urge my final task,
your dying son's last outcry was to ask
mercy for poor Aricia, for his bride.
Now Phaedra comes. She killed him. She
　　has lied.

Scene VII

Theseus, Phaedra, Panope

THESEUS: Ah Phaedra, you have won.
　　He's dead. A man
was killed. Were you watching? His
　　horses ran
him down, and tore his body limb from
　　limb.
Poseidon struck him, Theseus murdered
　　him.
I served you! Tell me why Oenone died?
Was it to save you? Is her suicide
A proof of your truth? No, since he's
　　dead, I must
accept your evidence, just or unjust.
I must believe my faith has been abused;
you have accused him; he shall stand ac-
　　cused.
He's friendless even in the world below.
There the shades fear him! Am I forced
　　to know
the truth? Truth cannot bring my son to
　　life.
If fathers murder, shall I kill my wife
too? Leave me, Phaedra. Far from you,
　　exiled
from Greece, I will lament my murdered
　　child.
I am a murdered gladiator, whirled
in black circles. I want to leave the world;
my whole life rises to increase my guilt—
all those dazzled, dazzling eyes, my glory
　　built
on killing killers. Less known, less mag-
　　nified,

I might escape, and find a place to hide.
Stand back, Poseidon. I know the gods
　　are hard
to please. I pleased you. This is my re-
　　ward:
I killed my son. I killed him! Only a god
spares enemies, and wants his servants'
　　blood!

　　PHAEDRA: No, Theseus, I must disobey
　　　　your prayer.
Listen to me. I'm dying. I declare
Hippolytus was innocent.

　　THESEUS: Ah Phaedra, on your evi-
　　　　dence, I sent
him to his death. Do you ask me to forgive
my son's assassin? Can I let you live?

　　PHAEDRA: My time's too short, your
　　　　highness. It was I,
who lusted for your son with my hot eye.
The flames of Aphrodite maddened me;
I loathed myself, and yearned outrageously
like a starved wolf to fall upon the sheep.
I wished to hold him to me in my sleep
and dreamt I had him. Then Oenone's
　　tears,
troubled my mind; she played upon my
　　fears,
until her pleading forced me to declare
I loved your son. He scorned me. In
　　despair,
I plotted with my nurse, and our con-
　　spiracy
made you believe your son assaulted me.
Oenone's punished; fleeing from my
　　wrath,
she drowned herself, and found a too easy
　　path
to death and hell. Perhaps you wonder
　　why
I still survive her, and refuse to die?
Theseus, I stand before you to absolve
your noble son. Sire, only this resolve
upheld me, and made me throw down my
　　knife.
I've chosen a slower way to end my life—
Medea's poison; chills already dart

along my boiling veins and squeeze my
    heart.
A cold composure I have never known
gives me a moment's poise. I stand alone
and seem to see my outraged husband fade
and waver into death's dissolving shade.
My eyes at last give up their light, and
    see
the day they've soiled resume its purity.

PANOPE: She's dead, my lord.

THESEUS: Would God, all memory

of her and me had died with her! Now I
must live. This knowledge that has come
    too late
must give me strength and help me ex-
    piate
my sacrilegious vow. Let's go, I'll pay
my son the honors he has earned today.
His father's tears shall mingle with his
    blood.
My love that did my son so little good
asks mercy from his spirit. I declare
Aricia is my daughter and my heir.

Samson Agonistes

JOHN MILTON

COMMENTARY

John Milton (1608-1674) was born eight years before Shakespeare's death and died while John Dryden was poet laureate. His life thus ranged through the great literary periods of the seventeenth century in England. He had a classical Renaissance education, studying Latin, Greek, Hebrew, and Italian. Although he felt himself destined early in life to be a poet, he devoted his middle years to writing prose tracts, in English and Latin, most of them in behalf of the Puritan Commonwealth under Oliver Cromwell. Milton's three great works were published when he was blind, after the Restoration of the monarchy in 1660: *Paradise Lost* in 1667, and *Paradise Regained* and *Samson Agonistes* in 1671.

Samson Agonistes combines Greek, Christian, and Jewish elements and has, perhaps partly because of this synthesis, provided many different sorts of problems for critics. Samuel Johnson, for example, complained in 1779 that it has "been too much admired." George Steiner wrote in *The Death of Tragedy* (New York, 1961) that the work "is difficult to get into focus, exactly because it comes so near to making good its presumptions" (Page 31). In part to counter autobiographical readings, some scholarship has argued that the play was written at some earlier period than the Restoration. The choruses, the occasional rhyme, and the generally "static" middle, have produced other critical and scholarly discussions.

Milton did not conceive of his work as appropriate for the theater. Do you agree that it could not be produced successfully? Would a production in which the Philistines were costumed as Restoration rakes and Samson and the Chorus as Puritans enhance your reading, or obscure it? Would a concert reading do it justice? an oratorio? (You might try to hear a performance of Handel's *Samson*.)

Samson differs significantly from a Greek tragic hero in finally making his own fate. He rises rather than falls. He progresses from Samson the Impotent, doubly blind, in spirit and in sight, to Samson the Actor, "seeing" at last that he can fulfill the mission he had once betrayed. Each of the three confrontations—with his father, with Dálila, with Harapha—is an occasion for Samson's new growth, for his regeneration.

In his essay on *Samson,* in *Tragic Themes in Western Literature* (New Haven, 1955), Chauncey B. Tinker points out the disparity between the loutishness, boorishness, and brutality of the Old Testament Samson and the hero of Milton's play. This disparity seems essential to an understanding of the tragedy; we know how much Milton relied on his fit audience, though few, to have in mind the right context for his work. In Milton's *Samson,* then, we may well have an early example of the non-hero, or even anti-hero, as tragic hero. Samson's metamorphosis, from fallen folk hero to his peoples' avenger, reverses the decline we have become accustomed to in classical, neoclassical, or Shakespearean tragedy. The "catharsis" we feel at the conclusion of *Samson* seems more emotionally related to triumph than to defeat: Samson's fulfillment of his search for identity climaxes in an action that simultaneously fulfills his divinely proclaimed destiny.

Introductions to the play in collections of Milton's poetry are valuable, especially those by Douglas Bush, Merritt Y. Hughes, and James Holly Hanford. Some of the academic criticism of *Samson* has been gathered by Ralph E. Hone (San Francisco, 1966) together with early versions of the Samson myth. Miss Marjorie Nicolson's *John Milton: A Reader's Guide to the Poetry* (New York, 1963) provides background and interpretation. Two basic studies are F. M. Krouse, *Milton's Samson and the Christian Tradition* (Princeton, 1949) and Arnold Stein, *Heroic Knowledge* (Minneapolis, 1957).

John Milton

SAMSON AGONISTES

A DRAMATIC POEM

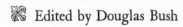 Edited by Douglas Bush

Aristotle, *Poetics*, c. 6. Τραγῳδία μίμησις πράξεως σπονδαίας, &c.

Tragoedia est imitatio actionis seriae, &c., per misericordiam et metum perficiens talium affectuum lustrationem.

Of That Sort of Dramatic Poem Which
Is Called Tragedy

Tragedy, as it was anciently composed, hath been ever held the gravest, moralest, and most profitable of all other poems: therefore said by Aristotle to be of power, by raising pity and fear, or terror, to purge the mind of those and suchlike passions, that is, to temper and reduce them to just measure with a kind of delight, stirred up by reading or seeing those passions well imitated. Nor is nature wanting in her own effects to make good his assertion; for so in physic, things of melancholic hue and quality are used against melancholy, sour against sour, salt to remove salt humors. Hence philosophers and other gravest writers, as Cicero, Plutarch, and others, frequently cite out of tragic poets, both to adorn and illustrate their discourse. The Apostle Paul himself thought it not unworthy to insert a verse of Euripides into the text of Holy Scripture, I Cor. 15:33; and Pareus, commenting on the Revelation, divides the whole book as a tragedy, into acts distinguished each by a chorus of heavenly harpings and song between. Heretofore men in highest dignity have labored not a little to be thought able to compose a tragedy. Of that honor Dionysius the elder was no less ambitious than before of his attaining to the tyranny. Augustus Caesar also had begun his *Ajax*, but, unable to please his own judgment with what he had begun, left it unfinished. Seneca the philosopher is by some thought

John Milton, *Samson Agonistes* in *The Complete Poetical Works of John Milton*, ed. Douglas Bush (Boston: Houghton Mifflin Co., 1965), pp. 517-558. Used by permission.

the author of those tragedies (at least the best of them) that go under that name. Gregory Nazianzen, a Father of the Church, thought it not unbeseeming the sanctity of his person to write a tragedy, which he entitled *Christ Suffering*. This is mentioned to vindicate tragedy from the small esteem, or rather infamy, which in the account of many it undergoes at this day with other common interludes; happening through the poet's error of intermixing comic stuff with tragic sadness and gravity, or introducing trivial and vulgar persons, which by all judicious hath been counted absurd, and brought in without discretion, corruptly to gratify the people. And though ancient tragedy use no prologue, yet using sometimes, in case of self-defense, or explanation, that which Martial calls an epistle; in behalf of this tragedy, coming forth after the ancient manner, much different from what among us passes for best, thus much beforehand may be epistled: that chorus is here introduced after the Greek manner, not ancient only but modern, and still in use among the Italians. In the modeling therefore of this poem, with good reason, the ancients and Italians are rather followed, as of much more authority and fame. The measure of verse used in the chorus is of all sorts, called by the Greeks *monostrophic,* or rather *apolelymenon,* without regard had to strophe, antistrophe, or epode, which were a kind of stanzas framed only for the music, then used with the chorus that sung; not essential to the poem, and therefore not material; or, being divided into stanzas or pauses, they may be called *alloeostropha.* Division into act and scene, referring chiefly to the stage (to which this work never was intended), is here omitted.

It suffices if the whole drama be found not produced beyond the fifth act. Of the style and uniformity, and that commonly called the plot, whether intricate or explicit—which is nothing indeed but such economy, or disposition of the fable, as may stand best with verisimilitude and decorum—they only will best judge who are not unacquainted with Aeschylus, Sophocles, and Euripides, the three tragic poets unequaled yet by any, and the best rule to all who endeavor to write tragedy. The circumscription of time wherein the whole drama begins and ends is, according to ancient rule and best example, within the space of twenty-four hours.

The Argument

Samson, made captive, blind, and now in the prison at Gaza, there to labor as in a common workhouse, on a festival day, in the general cessation from labor, comes forth into the open air, to a place nigh, somewhat retired, there to sit a while and bemoan his condition. Where he happens at length to be visited by certain friends and equals of his tribe, which make the chorus, who seek to comfort him what they can; then by his old father, Manoa, who endeavors the like, and withal tells him his purpose to procure his liberty by ransom; lastly, that this feast was proclaimed by the Philistines as a day of thanksgiving for their deliverance from the hands of Samson, which yet more troubles him. Manoa then departs to prosecute his endeavor with the Philistian lords for Samson's redemption; who in the meanwhile is visited by other persons; and lastly by a public officer to require his coming to the feast before the lords and people, to play or show his strength in their presence. He at first refuses, dismissing the public officer with absolute denial to come; at length persuaded inwardly that this was from God, he yields to go along with him, who came now the second time with great threatenings to fetch him. The chorus yet remaining on the place, Manoa returns full of joyful hope to procure ere long his son's deliverance; in midst of which discourse an Hebrew comes in haste, confusedly at first, and afterward more distinctly, relating the catastrophe, what Samson had done to the Philistines, and by accident to himself; wherewith the tragedy ends.

THE PERSONS

SAMSON.
MANOA, *the father of Samson.*
DÁLILA, *his wife.*
HARAPHA *of Gath.*
PUBLIC OFFICER.
MESSENGER.
CHORUS OF DANITES.

The Scene, before the Prison in Gaza.

SAMSON: A little onward lend thy guiding hand
To these dark steps, a little further on,
For yonder bank hath choice of sun or shade;
There I am wont to sit, when any chance
Relieves me from my task of servile toil,
Daily in the common prison else enjoined me,
Where I, a prisoner chained, scarcely freely draw
The air imprisoned also, close and damp,
Unwholesome draught. But here I feel amends,
The breath of heav'n fresh-blowing, pure and sweet,
With day-spring born; here leave me to respire.
This day a solemn feast the people hold
To Dagon their sea-idol, and forbid
Laborious works; unwillingly this rest
Their superstition yields me; hence with leave
Retiring from the popular noise, I seek
This unfrequented place to find some ease,
Ease to the body some, none to the mind
From restless thoughts, that like a deadly swarm
Of hornets armed, no sooner found alone,
But rush upon me thronging, and present
Times past, what once I was, and what am now.
O wherefore was my birth from Heaven foretold
Twice by an angel, who at last in sight
Of both my parents all in flames ascended
From off the altar, where an off'ring burned,
As in a fiery column charioting

His godlike presence, and from some great act
Or benefit revealed to Abraham's race?
Why was my breeding ordered and prescribed
As of a person separate to God,
Designed for great exploits, if I must die
Betrayed, captíved, and both my eyes put out,
Made of my enemies the scorn and gaze;
To grind in brazen fetters under task
With this Heav'n-gifted strength? O glorious strength,
Put to the labor of a beast, debased
Lower than bondslave! Promise was that I
Should Israel from Philistian yoke deliver;
Ask for this great deliverer now, and find him
Eyeless in Gaza at the mill with slaves,
Himself in bonds under Philistian yoke;
Yet stay, let me not rashly call in doubt
Divine prediction; what if all foretold
Had been fulfilled but through mine own default?
Whom have I to complain of but myself?
Who this high gift of strength committed to me,
In what part lodged, how easily bereft me,
Under the seal of silence could not keep,
But weakly to a woman must reveal it,
O'ercome with importunity and tears.
O impotence of mind, in body strong!
But what is strength without a double share
Of wisdom? Vast, unwieldy, burdensome,
Proudly secure, yet liable to fall
By weakest subtleties; not made to rule,
But to subserve where wisdom bears command.
God, when he gave me strength, to show withal
How slight the gift was, hung it in my hair.
But peace! I must not quarrel with the will

Of highest dispensation, which herein
Haply had ends above my reach to know:
Suffices that to me strength is my bane,
And proves the source of all my miseries,
So many, and so huge, that each apart
Would ask a life to wail; but chief of all,
O loss of sight, of thee I most complain!
Blind among enemies, O worse than chains,
Dungeon, or beggary, or decrepit age!
Light, the prime work of God, to me is extinct,
And all her various objects of delight
Annulled, which might in part my grief have eased,
Inferior to the vilest now become
Of man or worm; the vilest here excel me,
They creep, yet see; I, dark in lights exposed
To daily fraud, contempt, abuse and wrong,
Within doors, or without, still as a fool,
In power of others, never in my own;
Scarce half I seem to live, dead more than half.
O dark, dark, dark, amid the blaze of noon,
Irrecoverably dark, total eclipse
Without all hope of day!
O first-created beam, and thou great Word,
"Let there be light, and light was over all";
Why am I thus bereaved thy prime decree?
The sun to me is dark
And silent as the moon,
When she deserts the night,
Hid in her vacant interlunar cave.
Since light so necessary is to life,
And almost life itself, if it be true
That light is in the soul,
She all in every part, why was the sight
To such a tender ball as th' eye confined?
So obvious and so easy to be quenched,
And not, as feeling, through all parts diffused,

That she might look at will through every
    pore?
Then had I not been thus exiled from
    light,
As in the land of darkness, yet in light,
To live a life half dead, a living death,
And buried; but O yet more miserable!
Myself my sepulchre, a moving grave,
Buried, not yet exempt
By privilege of death and burial
From worst of other evils, pains and
    wrongs,
But made hereby obnoxious more
To all the miseries of life,
Life in captivity
Among inhuman foes.
But who are these? For with joint pace
    I hear
The tread of many feet steering this way;
Perhaps my enemies who come to stare
At my affliction, and perhaps to insult,
Their daily practice to afflict me more.

    CHORUS: This, this is he; softly a while;
Let us not break in upon him.
O change beyond report, thought, or be-
    lief!
See how he lies at random, carelessly
    diffused,
With languished head unpropped,
As one past hope, abandoned,
And by himself given over;
In slavish habit, ill-fitted weeds
O'erworn and soiled;
Or do my eyes misrepresent? Can this
    be he,
That heroic, that renowned,
Irresistible Samson? Whom unarmed
No strength of man, or fiercest wild beast
    could withstand;
Who tore the lion, as the lion tears the
    kid,
Ran on embattled armies clad in iron,
And, weaponless himself,
Made arms ridiculous, useless the forgery
Of brazen shield and spear, the hammered
    cuirass,

Chalýbean-tempered steel, and frock of
    mail
Adamantean proof;
But safest he who stood aloof,
When insupportably his foot advanced,
In scorn of their proud arms and warlike
    tools,
Spurned them to death by troops. The
    bold Ascalonite
Fled from his lion ramp, old warriors
    turned
Their plated backs under his heels;
Or grov'ling soiled their crested helmets
    in the dust.
Then with what trivial weapon came to
    hand,
The jaw of a dead ass, his sword of bone,
A thousand foreskins fell, the flower of
    Palestine,
In Ramath-lechi, famous to this day;
Then by main force pulled up, and on his
    shoulders bore
The gates of Azza, post and massy bar,
Up to the hill by Hebron, seat of giants
    old,
No journey of a Sabbath day, and loaded
    so;
Like whom the Gentiles feign to bear up
    heav'n.
Which shall I first bewail,
Thy bondage or lost sight,
Prison within prison
Inseparably dark?
Thou art become (O worst imprison-
    ment!)
The dungeon of thyself; thy soul
(Which men enjoying sight oft without
    cause complain)
Imprisoned now indeed,
In real darkness of the body dwells,
Shut up from outward light
To incorporate with gloomy night;
For inward light, alas,
Puts forth no visual beam.
O mirror of our fickle state,
Since man on earth unparalleled!
The rarer thy example stands,

By how much from the top of wondrous
    glory,
Strongest of mortal men,
To lowest pitch of abject fortune thou art
    fall'n.
For him I reckon not in high estate
Whom long descent of birth
Or the sphere of fortune raises;
But thee whose strength, while virtue was
    her mate,
Might have subdued the earth,
Universally crowned with highest praises.

    SAM: I hear the sound of words; their
        sense the air
Dissolves unjointed ere it reach my ear.

    CHOR: He speaks; let us draw nigh.
        Matchless in might,
The glory late of Israel, now the grief!
We come thy friends and neighbors not
    unknown
From Eshtaol and Zora's fruitful vale
To visit or bewail thee, or if better,
Counsel or consolation we may bring,
Salve to thy sores; apt words have power
    to swage
The tumors of a troubled mind,
And are as balm to festered wounds.

    SAM: Your coming, friends, revives me,
        for I learn
Now of my own experience, not by talk,
How counterfeit a coin they are who
    "friends"
Bear in their superscription (of the most
I would be understood). In prosperous
    days
They swarm, but in adverse withdraw their
    head,
Not to be found, though sought. Ye see, O
    friends,
How many evils have enclosed me round;
Yet that which was the worst now least
    afflicts me,
Blindness, for had I sight, confused with
    shame,
How could I once look up, or heave the
    head,

Who like a foolish pilot have shipwracked
My vessel trusted to me from above,
Gloriously rigged; and for a word, a tear,
Fool, have divulged the secret gift of God
To a deceitful woman? Tell me, friends,
Am I not sung and proverbed for a fool
In every street, do they not say, "How
    well
Are come upon him his deserts"? Yet
    why?
Immeasurable strength they might behold
In me, of wisdom nothing more than
    mean;
This with the other should, at least, have
    paired;
These two proportioned ill drove me trans-
    verse.

    CHOR: Tax not divine disposal; wisest
        men
Have erred, and by bad women been
    deceived;
And shall again, pretend they ne'er so
    wise.
Deject not then so overmuch thyself,
Who hast of sorrow thy full load besides.
Yet truth to say, I oft have heard men
    wonder
Why thou shouldst wed Philistian women
    rather
Than of thine own tribe fairer, or as fair,
At least of thy own nation, and as noble.

    SAM: The first I saw at Timna, and she
        pleased
Me, not my parents, that I sought to wed,
The daughter of an infidel: they knew not
That what I motioned was of God; I knew
From intimate impulse, and therefore
    urged
The marriage on; that by occasion hence
I might begin Israel's deliverance,
The work to which I was divinely called.
She proving false, the next I took to wife
(O that I never had! fond wish too late!)
Was in the vale of Sorec, Dálila,
That specious monster, my accomplished
    snare.

I thought it lawful from my former act,
And the same end, still watching to op-
press
Israel's oppressors. Of what now I suffer
She was not the prime cause, but I myself,
Who vanquished with a peal of words (O
weakness!)
Gave up my fort of silence to a woman.

CHOR: In seeking just occasion to pro-
voke
The Philistine, thy country's enemy,
Thou never wast remiss, I bear thee wit-
ness:
Yet Israel still serves with all his sons.

SAM: That fault I take not on me, but
transfer
On Israel's governors and heads of tribes,
Who, seeing those great acts which God
had done
Singly by me against their conquerors,
Acknowledged not, or not at all con-
sidered,
Deliverance offered: I on th' other side
Used no ambition to commend my deeds;
The deeds themselves, though mute, spoke
loud the doer;
But they persisted deaf, and would not
seem
To count them things worth notice, till at
length
Their lords the Philistines with gathered
powers
Entered Judea seeking me, who then
Safe to the rock of Etham was retired,
Not flying, but forecasting in what place
To set upon them, what advantaged best;
Meanwhile the men of Judah, to prevent
The harass of their land, beset me round;
I willingly on some conditions came
Into their hands, and they as gladly yield
me
To the uncircumcised a welcome prey,
Bound with two cords; but cords to me
were threads
Touched with the flame: on their whole
host I flew

Unarmed, and with a trivial weapon
felled
Their choicest youth; they only lived who
fled.
Had Judah that day joined, or one whole
tribe,
They had by this possessed the towers of
Gath,
And lorded over them whom now they
serve;
But what more oft in nations grown cor-
rupt,
And by their vices brought to servitude,
Than to love bondage more than liberty,
Bondage with ease than strenuous liberty;
And to despise, or envy, or suspect
Whom God hath of his special favor
raised
As their deliverer; if he aught begin,
How frequent to desert him, and at last
To heap ingratitude on worthiest deeds?

CHOR: Thy words to my remembrance
bring
How Succoth and the fort of Penuel
Their great deliverer contemned,
The matchless Gideon in pursuit
Of Madian and her vanquished kings:
And how ingrateful Ephraim
Had dealt with Jephtha, who by argu-
ment,
Not worse than by his shield and spear,
Defended Israel from the Ammonite,
Had not his prowess quelled their pride
In that sore battle when so many died
Without reprieve adjudged to death,
For want of well pronouncing *Shibboleth.*

SAM: Of such examples add me to the
roll;
Me easily indeed mine may neglect,
But God's proposed deliverance not so.

CHOR: Just are the ways of God,
And justifiable to men;
Unless there be who think not God at all:
If any be, they walk obscure;
For of such doctrine never was there
school,

But the heart of the fool,
And no man therein doctor but himself.
    Yet more there be who doubt his ways
      not just,
As to his own edícts, found contradicting,
Then give the reins to wand'ring thought,
Regardless of his glory's diminution;
Till by their own perplexities involved
They ravel more, still less resolved,
But never find self-satisfying solution.
    As if they would confine th' Intermin-
      able,
And tie him to his own prescript,
Who made our laws to bind us, not him-
    self,
And hath full right to exempt
Whomso it pleases him by choice
From national obstriction, without taint
Of sin, or legal debt;
For with his own laws he can best dis-
    pense.
    He would not else, who never wanted
      means,
Nor in respect of the enemy just cause,
To set his people free,
Have prompted this heroic Nazarite,
Against his vow of strictest purity,
To seek in marriage that fallacious bride,
Unclean, unchaste.
    Down, Reason, then, at least vain rea-
      sonings down,
Though Reason here aver
That moral verdict quits her of unclean:
Unchaste was subsequent; her stain, not
    his.
    But see, here comes thy reverend sire
With careful step, locks white as down,
Old Manoa: advise
Forthwith how thou ought'st to receive
    him.

    SAM: Ay me, another inward grief
      awaked
With mention of that name renews th'
    assault.

    MANOA: Brethren and men of Dan, for
      such ye seem,

Though in this uncouth place; if old re-
    spect,
As I suppose, towards your once gloried
    friend,
My son now captive, hither hath informed
Your younger feet, while mine cast back
    with age
Came lagging after; say if he be here.

    CHOR: As signal now in low dejected
      state,
As erst in highest, behold him where he
    lies.

    MAN: O miserable change! is this the
      man,
That invincible Samson, far renowned,
The dread of Israel's foes, who with a
    strength
Equivalent to angels' walked their streets,
None offering fight; who single com-
    batant
Duelled their armies ranked in proud
    array,
Himself an army, now unequal match
To save himself against a coward armed
At one spear's length? O ever-failing
    trust
In mortal strength! and oh what not in
    man
Deceivable and vain! Nay, what thing
    good
Prayed for, but often proves our woe, our
    bane?
I prayed for children, and thought barren-
    ness
In wedlock a reproach; I gained a son,
And such a son as all men hailed me
    happy:
Who would be now father in my stead?
O wherefore did God grant me my re-
    quest,
And as a blessing with such pomp
    adorned?
Why are his gifts desirable, to tempt
Our earnest prayers, then giv'n with sol-
    emn hand
As graces, draw a scorpion's tail behind?

For this did the angel twice descend? For
     this
Ordained thy nurture holy, as of a plant;
Select and sacred, glorious for a while,
The miracle of men; then in an hour
Ensnared, assaulted, overcome, led bound,
Thy foes' derision, captive, poor, and
     blind,
Into a dungeon thrust, to work with
     slaves?
Alas, methinks whom God hath chosen
     once
To worthiest deeds, if he through frailty
     err,
He should not so o'erwhelm, and as a
     thrall
Subject him to so foul indignities,
Be it but for honor's sake of former deeds.
     SAM: Appoint not heavenly disposition,
     father.
Nothing of all these evils hath befall'n me
But justly; I myself have brought them on,
Sole author I, sole cause: if aught seem
     vile,
As vile hath been my folly, who have pro-
     faned
The mystery of God giv'n me under
     pledge
Of vow, and have betrayed it to a woman,
A Canaanite, my faithless enemy.
This well I knew, nor was at all surprised,
But warned by oft experience: did not she
Of Timna first betray me, and reveal
The secret wrested from me in her highth
Of nuptial love professed, carrying it
     straight
To them who had corrupted her, my spies,
And rivals? In this other was there found
More faith? Who also in her prime of
     love,
Spousal embraces, vitiated with gold,
Though offered only, by the scent con-
     ceived
Her spurious first-born, treason against
     me.
Thrice she assayed with flattering prayer
     and sighs

And amorous reproaches to win from me
My capital secret, in what part my strength
Lay stored, in what part summed, that
     she might know:
Thrice I deluded her, and turned to sport
Her importunity, each time perceiving
How openly, and with what impudence,
She purposed to betray me, and (which
     was worse
Than undissembled hate) with what con-
     tempt
She sought to make me traitor to myself;
Yet the fourth time, when must'ring all
     her wiles,
With blandished parleys, feminine as-
     saults,
Tongue-batteries, she surceased not day
     nor night
To storm me over-watched, and wearied
     out,
At times when men seek most repose and
     rest,
I yielded, and unlocked her all my heart,
Who with a grain of manhood well re-
     solved
Might easily have shook off all her snares;
But foul effeminacy held me yoked
Her bondslave; O indignity, O blot
To honor and religion! servile mind
Rewarded well with servile punishment!
The base degree to which I now am fall'n,
These rags, this grinding, is not yet so
     base
As was my former servitude, ignoble,
Unmanly, ignominious, infamous,
True slavery, and that blindness worse
     than this,
That saw not how degenerately I served.
     MAN: I cannot praise thy marriage
     choices, son,
Rather approved them not; but thou didst
     plead
Divine impulsion prompting how thou
     might'st
Find some occasion to infest our foes.
I state not that; this I am sure, our foes
Found soon occasion thereby to make thee

Their captive, and their triumph; thou the
    sooner
Temptation   found'st,   or   over-potent
    charms,
To violate the sacred trust of silence
Deposited within thee; which to have kept
Tacit was in thy power; true; and thou
    bear'st
Enough, and more, the burden of that
    fault;
Bitterly hast thou paid, and still art pay-
    ing,
That rigid score. A worse thing yet re-
    mains:
This day the Philistines a popular feast
Here celebrate in Gaza, and proclaim
Great pomp, and sacrifice, and praises
    loud
To Dagon, as their god who hath delivered
Thee, Samson, bound and blind into their
    hands,
Them out of thine, who slew'st them many
    a slain.
So Dagon shall be magnified, and God,
Besides whom is no god, compared with
    idols,
Disglorified, blasphemed, and had in
    scorn
By th' idolatrous rout amidst their wine;
Which to have come to pass by means of
    thee,
Samson, of all thy sufferings think the
    heaviest,
Of all reproach the most with shame that
    ever
Could have befall'n thee and thy father's
    house.
    SAM: Father, I do acknowledge and con-
    fess
That I this honor, I this pomp have
    brought
To Dagon, and advanced his praises high
Among the heathen round; to God have
    brought
Dishonor, obloquy, and oped the mouths
Of idolists and atheists; have brought
    scandal
To Israel, diffidence of God, and doubt

In feeble hearts, propense enough before
To waver, or fall off and join with idols:
Which is my chief affliction, shame and
    sorrow,
The anguish of my soul, that suffers not
Mine eye to harbor sleep, or thoughts to
    rest.
This only hope relieves me, that the
    strife
With me hath end; all the contést is now
'Twixt God and Dagon; Dagon hath pre-
    sumed,
Me overthrown, to enter lists with God,
His deity comparing and preferring
Before the God of Abraham. He, be sure,
Will not connive, or linger, thus provoked,
But will arise and his great name assert:
Dagon must stoop, and shall ere long
    receive
Such a discomfit, as shall quite despoil
    him
Of all these boasted trophies won on me,
And with confusion blank his worshipers.

    MAN: With cause this hope relieves
    thee, and these words
I as a prophecy receive; for God,
Nothing more certain, will not long defer
To vindicate the glory of his name
Against all competition, nor will long
Endure it doubtful whether God be Lord,
Or Dagon. But for thee what shall be
    done?
Thou must not in the meanwhile, here
    forgot,
Lie in this miserable loathsome plight
Neglected. I already have made way
To some Philistian lords, with whom to
    treat
About thy ransom: well they may by this
Have satisfied their utmost of revenge
By pains and slaveries, worse than death,
    inflicted
On thee, who now no more canst do them
    harm.

    SAM: Spare that proposal, father, spare
    the trouble
Of that solicitation; let me here,

As I deserve, pay on my punishment;
And expiate, if possible, my crime,
Shameful garrulity. To have revealed
Secrets of men, the secrets of a friend,
How heinous had the fact been, how de-
    serving
Contempt, and scorn of all, to be excluded
All friendship, and avoided as a blab,
The mark of fool set on his front! But I
God's counsel have not kept, his holy
    secret
Presumptuously have published, impi-
    ously,
Weakly at least, and shamefully: a sin
That Gentiles in their parables condemn
To their abyss and horrid pains confined.

   MAN: Be penitent and for thy fault
    contríte,
But act not in thy own affliction, son;
Repent the sin, but if the punishment
Thou canst avoid, self-preservation bids;
Or th' execution leave to high disposal,
And let another hand, not thine, exact
Thy penal forfeit from thyself; perhaps
God will relent, and quit thee all his debt;
Who ever more approves and more ac-
    cepts
(Best pleased with humble and filial sub-
    mission)
Him who imploring mercy sues for life,
Than who self-rigorous chooses death as
    due;
Which argues over-just, and self-displeased
For self-offense, more than for God of-
    fended.
Reject not then what offered means who
    knows
But God hath set before us, to return thee
Home to thy country and his sacred house,
Where thou may'st bring thy off'rings,
    to avert
His further ire, with prayers and vows
    renewed.

   SAM: His pardon I implore; but as for
    life,
To what end should I seek it? When in
    strength

All mortals I excelled, and great in hopes
With youthful courage and magnanimous
    thoughts
Of birth from Heav'n foretold and high
    exploits,
Full of divine instinct, after some proof
Of acts indeed heroic, far beyond
The sons of Anak, famous now and
    blazed,
Fearless of danger, like a petty god
I walked about admired of all and dreaded
On hostile ground, none daring my af-
    front.
Then swoll'n with pride into the snare
    I fell
Of fair fallacious looks, venereal trains,
Softened with pleasure and voluptuous
    life;
At length to lay my head and hallowed
    pledge
Of all my strength in the lascivious lap
Of a deceitful concubine who shore me
Like a tame wether, all my precious
    fleece,
Then turned me out ridiculous, despoiled,
Shav'n, and disarmed among my enemies.

   CHOR: Desire of wine and all delicious
    drinks,
Which many a famous warrior overturns,
Thou couldst repress, nor did the dancing
    ruby
Sparkling outpoured, the flavor, or the
    smell,
Or taste that cheers the heart of gods and
    men,
Allure thee from the cool crystálline
    stream.

   SAM: Wherever fountain or fresh cur-
    rent flowed
Against the eastern ray, translucent, pure
With touch ethereal of heav'n's fiery rod,
I drank, from the clear milky juice allay-
    ing
Thirst, and refreshed; nor envied them the
    grape
Whose heads that turbulent liquor fills
    with fumes.

CHOR: O madness, to think use of
strongest wines
And strongest drinks our chief support of
health,
When God with these forbidd'n made
choice to rear
His mighty champion, strong above compare,
Whose drink was only from the liquid
brook.

SAM: But what availed this temperance,
not complete
Against another object more enticing?
What boots it at one gate to make defense,
And at another to let in the foe,
Effeminately vanquished? By which
means,
Now blind, disheartened, shamed, dis-
honored, quelled,
To what can I be useful, wherein serve
My nation, and the work from Heav'n
imposed,
But to sit idle on the household hearth,
A burdenous drone? To visitants a gaze,
Or pitied object; these redundant locks,
Robustious to no purpose, clust'ring down,
Vain monument of strength; till length of
years
And sedentary numbness craze my limbs
To a contemptible old age obscure.
Here rather let me drudge and earn my
bread,
Till vermin or the draff of servile food
Consume me, and oft-invocated death
Hasten the welcome end of all my pains.

MAN: Wilt thou then serve the Philistines with that gift
Which was expressly giv'n thee to annoy
them?
Better at home lie bed-rid, not only idle,
Inglorious, unemployed, with age out-
worn.
But God, who caused a fountain at thy
prayer
From the dry ground to spring, thy thirst
to allay

After the brunt of battle, can as easy
Cause light again within thy eyes to
spring,
Wherewith to serve him better than thou
hast;
And I persuade me so; why else this
strength
Miraculous yet remaining in those locks?
His might continues in thee not for
naught,
Nor shall his wondrous gifts be frustrate
thus.

SAM: All otherwise to me my thoughts
portend,
That these dark orbs no more shall treat
with light,
Nor th' other light of life continue long,
But yield to double darkness nigh at hand:
So much I feel my genial spirits droop,
My hopes all flat; nature within me seems
In all her functions weary of herself;
My race of glory run, and race of shame,
And I shall shortly be with them that
rest.

MAN: Believe not these suggestions,
which proceed
From anguish of the mind and humors
black,
That mingle with thy fancy. I however
Must not omit a father's timely care
To prosecute the means of thy deliverance
By ransom or how else: meanwhile be
calm,
And healing words from these thy friends
admit.

SAM: O that torment should not be
confined
To the body's wounds and sores,
With maladies innumerable
In heart, head, breast, and reins;
But must secret passage find
To th' inmost mind,
There exercise all his fierce accidents,
And on her purest spirits prey,
As on entrails, joints, and limbs,
With answerable pains, but more intense,

Though void of corporal sense.
  My griefs not only pain me
As a ling'ring disease,
But finding no redress, ferment and rage,
Nor less than wounds immedicable
Rankle, and fester, and gangrene,
To black mortification.
Thoughts, my tormentors, armed with
    deadly stings
Mangle my apprehensive tenderest parts,
Exasperate, exulcerate, and raise
Dire inflammation which no cooling herb
Or med'cinal liquor can assuage,
Nor breath of vernal air from snowy Alp.
Sleep hath forsook and giv'n me o'er
To death's benumbing opium as my only
    cure.
Thence faintings, swoonings of despair,
And sense of Heav'n's desertion.
  I was his nursling once and choice
    delight,
His destined from the womb,
Promised by heavenly message twice de-
    scending.
Under his special eye
Abstemious I grew up and thrived amain;
He led me on to mightiest deeds
Above the nerve of mortal arm
Against the uncircumcised, our enemies.
But now hath cast me off as never known,
And to those cruel enemies,
Whom I by his appointment had pro-
    voked,
Left me all helpless with th' irreparable
    loss
Of sight, reserved alive to be repeated
The subject of their cruelty or scorn.
Nor am I in the list of them that hope;
Hopeless are all my evils, all remédiless;
This one prayer yet remains, might I be
    heard,
No long petition—speedy death,
The close of all my miseries, and the
    balm.
  CHOR: Many are the sayings of the wise
In ancient and in modern books enrolled,
Extolling patience as the truest fortitude;

And to the bearing well of all calamities,
All chances incident to man's frail life,
Consolatories writ
With studied argument, and much per-
    suasion sought,
Lenient of grief and anxious thought;
But with th' afflicted in his pangs their
    sound
Little prevails, or rather seems a tune
Harsh, and of dissonant mood from his
    complaint,
Unless he feel within
Some source of consolation from above,
Secret refreshings that repair his strength,
And fainting spirits uphold.
  God of our fathers, what is man!
That thou towards him with hand so
    various—
Or might I say contrarious?—
Temper'st thy providence through his
    short course,
Not evenly, as thou rul'st
The angelic orders and inferior creatures
    mute,
Irrational and brute.
Nor do I name of men the common rout,
That wand'ring loose about
Grow up and perish, as the summer fly,
Heads without name no more remem-
    bered;
But such as thou hast solemnly elected,
With gifts and graces eminently adorned
To some great work, thy glory,
And people's safety, which in part they
    effect;
Yet toward these thus dignified, thou oft
Amidst their highth of noon
Changest thy countenance and thy hand,
    with no regard
Of highest favors past
From thee on them, or them to thee of
    service.
  Nor only dost degrade them, or remit
To life obscured, which were a fair dis-
    mission,
But throw'st them lower than thou didst
    exalt them high,

Unseemly falls in human eye,
Too grievous for the trespass or omission;
Oft leav'st them to the hostile sword
Of heathen and profane, their carcasses
To dogs and fowls a prey, or else cap-
    tíved,
Or to the unjust tribunals, under change
    of times,
And condemnation of the ingrateful mul-
    titude.
If these they scape, perhaps in poverty
With sickness and disease thou bow'st
    them down,
Painful diseases and deformed,
In crude old age;
Though not disordinate, yet causeless
    suff'ring
The punishment of dissolute days; in fine,
Just or unjust, alike seem miserable,
For oft alike, both come to evil end.
    So deal not with this once thy glorious
        champion,
The image of thy strength, and mighty
    minister.
What do I beg? How hast thou dealt
    already?
Behold him in this state calamitous, and
    turn
His labors, for thou canst, to peaceful end.
    But who is this, what thing of sea or
        land?
Female of sex it seems,
That so bedecked, ornate, and gay,
Comes this way sailing
Like a stately ship
Of Tarsus, bound for th' isles
Of Javan or Gadire,
With all her bravery on, and tackle trim,
Sails filled, and streamers waving,
Courted by all the winds that hold them
    play,
An amber scent of odorous perfume
Her harbinger, a damsel train behind;
Some rich Philistian matron she may
    seem,
And now at nearer view, no other certain
Than Dálila thy wife.

SAM: My wife, my traitress, let her not
    come near me.

CHOR: Yet on she moves, now stands
    and eyes thee fixed,
About t' have spoke; but now, with head
    declined
Like a fair flower surcharged with dew,
    she weeps,
And words addressed seem into tears dis-
    solved,
Wetting the borders of her silken veil;
But now again she makes address to
    speak.

DAL: With doubtful feet and wavering
    resolution
I came, still dreading thy displeasure,
    Samson,
Which to have merited, without excuse,
I cannot but acknowledge; yet if tears
May expiate (though the fact more evil
    drew
In the perverse event than I foresaw),
My penance hath not slackened, though
    my pardon
No way assured. But conjugal affection,
Prevailing over fear and timorous doubt,
Hath led me on, desirous to behold
Once more thy face, and know of thy
    estate;
If aught in my ability may serve
To lighten what thou suffer'st, and ap-
    pease
Thy mind with what amends is in my
    power,
Though late, yet in some part to recom-
    pense
My rash but more unfortunate misdeed.

SAM: Out, out, hyena! These are thy
    wonted arts,
And arts of every woman false like
    thee,
To break all faith, all vows, deceive, be-
    tray;
Then as repentant to submit, beseech,
And reconcilement move with feigned
    remorse,

Confess, and promise wonders in her change,
Not truly penitent, but chief to try
Her husband, how far urged his patience bears,
His virtue or weakness which way to assail;
Then with more cautious and instructed skill
Again transgresses, and again submits;
That wisest and best men, full oft beguiled,
With goodness principled not to reject
The penitent, but ever to forgive,
Are drawn to wear out miserable days,
Entangled with a poisonous bosom snake,
If not by quick destruction soon cut off,
As I by thee, to ages an example.

DAL: Yet hear me, Samson; not that I endeavor
To lessen or extenuate my offense,
But that on th' other side if it be weighed
By itself, with aggravations not surcharged,
Or else with just allowance counterpoised,
I may, if possible, thy pardon find
The easier towards me, or thy hatred less.
First granting, as I do, it was a weakness
In me, but incident to all our sex,
Curiosity, inquisitive, importúne
Of secrets, then with like infirmity
To publish them, both common female faults;
Was it not weakness also to make known
For importunity, that is for naught,
Wherein consisted all thy strength and safety?
To what I did thou show'dst me first the way.
But I to enemies revealed, and should not?
Nor shouldst thou have trusted that to woman's frailty:
Ere I to thee, thou to thyself wast cruel.
Let weakness then with weakness come to parle,
So near related, or the same of kind;

Thine forgive mine, that men may censure thine
The gentler, if severely thou exact not
More strength from me than in thyself was found.
And what if love, which thou interpret'st hate,
The jealousy of love, powerful of sway
In human hearts, nor less in mine towards thee,
Caused what I did? I saw thee mutable
Of fancy, feared lest one day thou wouldst leave me
As her at Timna, sought by all means therefore
How to endear, and hold thee to me firmest:
No better way I saw than by impórtuning
To learn thy secrets, get into my power
Thy key of strength and safety. Thou wilt say,
"Why then revealed?" I was assured by those
Who tempted me that nothing was designed
Against thee but safe custody and hold:
That made for me; I knew that liberty
Would draw thee forth to perilous enterprises,
While I at home sat full of cares and fears,
Wailing thy absence in my widowed bed;
Here I should still enjoy thee day and night,
Mine and love's prisoner, not the Philistines',
Whole to myself, unhazarded abroad,
Fearless at home of partners in my love.
These reasons in love's law have passed for good,
Though fond and reasonless to some perhaps;
And love hath oft, well meaning, wrought much woe,
Yet always pity or pardon hath obtained.
Be not unlike all others, not austere
As thou art strong, inflexible as steel.
If thou in strength all mortals dost exceed,
In uncompassionate anger do not so.

SAM: How cunningly the sorceress dis-
  plays
Her own transgressions, to upbraid me
  mine!
That malice, not repentance, brought thee
  hither,
By this appears: I gave, thou say'st, th'
  example,
I led the way—bitter reproach, but true;
I to myself was false ere thou to me;
Such pardon therefore as I give my folly,
Take to thy wicked deed; which when
  thou seest
Impartial, self-severe, inexorable,
Thou wilt renounce thy seeking, and much
  rather
Confess it feigned. Weakness is thy ex-
  cuse,
And I believe it, weakness to resist
Philistian gold; if weakness may excuse,
What murtherer, what traitor, parricide,
Incestuous, sacrilegious, but may plead it?
All wickedness is weakness: that plea
  therefore
With God or man will gain thee no re-
  mission.
But love constrained thee? Call it furious
  rage
To satisfy thy lust: love seeks to have
  love;
My love how couldst thou hope, who
  took'st the way
To raise in me inexpiable hate,
Knowing, as needs I must, by thee be-
  trayed?
In vain thou striv'st to cover shame with
  shame,
Or by evasions thy crime uncover'st more.
  DAL: Since thou determin'st weakness
    for no plea
In man or woman, though to thy own
  condemning,
Hear what assaults I had, what snares
  besides,
What sieges girt me round, ere I con-
  sented;
Which might have awed the best-resolved
  of men,

The constantest, to have yielded without
  blame.
It was not gold, as to my charge thou
  lay'st,
That wrought with me: thou know'st the
  magistrates
And princes of my country came in per-
  son,
Solicited, commanded, threatened, urged,
Adjured by all the bonds of civil duty
And of religion, pressed how just it
  was.
How honorable, how glorious to entrap
A common enemy, who had destroyed
Such numbers of our nation: and the
  priest
Was not behind, but ever at my ear,
Preaching how meritorious with the gods
It would be to ensnare an irreligious
Dishonorer of Dagon. What had I
To oppose against such powerful argu-
  ments?
Only my love of thee held long debate;
And combated in silence all these reasons
With hard contést. At length that
  grounded maxim,
So rife and celebrated in the mouths
Of wisest men, that to the public good
Private respects must yield, with grave
  authority
Took full possession of me and prevailed;
Virtue, as I thought, truth, duty, so en-
  joining.
  SAM: I thought where all thy circling
    wiles would end,
In feigned religion, smooth hypocrisy.
But had thy love, still odiously pretended,
Been, as it ought, sincere, it would have
  taught thee
Far other reasonings, brought forth other
  deeds.
I before all the daughters of my tribe
And of my nation chose thee from among
My enemies, loved thee, as too well thou
  knew'st,
Too well; unbosomed all my secrets to
  thee,
Not out of levity, but overpow'red

By thy request, who could deny thee
    nothing;
Yet now am judged an enemy. Why then
Didst thou at first receive me for thy
    husband,
Then, as since then, thy country's foe
    professed?
Being once a wife, for me thou wast to
    leave
Parents and country; nor was I their
    subject,
Nor under their protection, but my own;
Thou mine, not theirs. If aught against my
    life
Thy country sought of thee, it sought
    unjustly,
Against the law of nature, law of nations;
No more thy country, but an impious crew
Of men conspiring to uphold their state
By worse than hostile deeds, violating the
    ends
For which our country is a name so dear;
Not therefore to be obeyed. But zeal
    moved thee;
To please thy gods thou didst it; gods
    unable
To acquit themselves and prosecute their
    foes
But by ungodly deeds, the contradiction
Of their own deity, gods cannot be:
Less therefore to be pleased, obeyed, or
    feared.
These false pretexts and varnished colors
    failing,
Bare in thy guilt how foul must thou
    appear!

    DAL: In argument with men a woman
    ever
Goes by the worse, whatever be her cause.

    SAM: For want of words, no doubt, or
    lack of breath;
Witness when I was worried with thy
    peals.

    DAL: I was a fool, too rash, and quite
    mistaken
In what I thought would have succeeded
    best.

Let me obtain forgiveness of thee, Sam-
    son;
Afford me place to show what recompense
Towards thee I intend for what I have
    misdone,
Misguided; only what remains past cure
Bear not too sensibly, nor still insist
To afflict thyself in vain. Though sight
    be lost,
Life yet hath many solaces, enjoyed
Where other senses want not their delights
At home in leisure and domestic ease,
Exempt from many a care and chance to
    which
Eyesight exposes daily men abroad.
I to the lords will intercede, not doubting
Their favorable ear, that I may fetch thee
From forth this loathsome prison-house,
    to abide
With me, where my redoubled love and
    care
With nursing diligence, to me glad office,
May ever tend about thee to old age
With all things grateful cheered, and so
    supplied,
That what by me thou hast lost thou least
    shall miss.

    SAM: No, no, of my condition take no
    care;
It fits not; thou and I long since are twain;
Nor think me so unwary or accurst
To bring my feet again into the snare
Where once I have been caught; I know
    thy trains,
Though dearly to my cost, thy gins, and
    toils;
Thy fair enchanted cup and warbling
    charms
No more on me have power, their force
    is nulled;
So much of adder's wisdom I have learnt
To fence my ear against thy sorceries.
If in my flower of youth and strength,
    when all men
Loved, honored, feared me, thou alone
    could hate me,
Thy husband, slight me, sell me, and
    forgo me,

How wouldst thou use me now, blind,
    and thereby
Deceivable, in most things as a child
Helpless, thence easily contemned, and
    scorned,
And last neglected? How wouldst thou
    insult
When I must live uxorious to thy will
In perfect thraldom, how again betray me,
Bearing my words and doings to the lords
To gloss upon, and censuring, frown or
    smile?
This jail I count the house of liberty
To thine whose doors my feet shall never
    enter.

    DAL: Let me approach at least, and
    touch thy hand.

    SAM: Not for thy life, lest fierce re-
    membrance wake
My sudden rage to tear thee joint by joint.
At distance I forgive thee, go with that;
Bewail thy falsehood, and the pious works
It hath brought forth to make thee mem-
    orable
Among illustrious women, faithful wives;
Cherish thy hastened widowhood with the
    gold
Of matrimonial treason: so farewell.

    DAL: I see thou art implacable, more
    deaf
To prayers than winds and seas; yet winds
    to seas
Are reconciled at length, and sea to shore:
Thy anger, unappeasable, still rages,
Eternal tempest never to be calmed.
Why do I humble thus myself, and suing
For peace, reap nothing but repulse and
    hate?
Bid go with evil omen and the brand
Of infamy upon my name denounced?
To mix with thy concernments I desist
Henceforth, nor too much disapprove my
    own.
Fame, if not double-faced, is double-
    mouthed,
And with contráry blast proclaims most
    deeds;

On both his wings, one black, th' other
    white,
Bears greatest names in his wild airy
    flight.
My name perhaps among the circumcised
In Dan, in Judah, and the bordering
    tribes,
To all posterity may stand defamed,
With malediction mentioned, and the blot
Of falsehood most unconjugal traduced.
But in my country where I most desire,
In Ekron, Gaza, Asdod, and in Gath,
I shall be named among the famousest
Of women, sung at solemn festivals,
Living and dead recorded, who, to save
Her country from a fierce destroyer, chose
Above the faith of wedlock bands; my
    tomb
With odors visited and annual flowers:
Not less renowned than in Mount Eph-
    raim
Jael, who with inhospitable guile
Smote Sisera sleeping, through the temples
    nailed.
Nor shall I count it heinous to enjoy
The public marks of honor and reward
Conferred upon me, for the piety
Which to my country I was judged to have
    shown.
At this whoever envies or repines,
I leave him to his lot, and like my own.

    CHOR: She's gone, a manifest serpent
    by her sting
Discovered in the end, till now concealed.

    SAM: So let her go; God sent her to
    debase me,
And aggravate my folly who committed
To such a viper his most sacred trust
Of secrecy, my safety, and my life.

    CHOR: Yet beauty, though injurious,
    hath strange power,
After offense returning, to regain
Love once possessed, nor can be easily
Repulsed, without much inward passion
    felt
And secret sting of amorous remorse.

SAM: Love-quarrels oft in pleasing con-
cord end,
Not wedlock-treachery endangering life.
CHOR: It is not virtue, wisdom, valor,
wit,
Strength, comeliness of shape, or amplest
merit
That woman's love can win or long in-
herit;
But what it is, hard is to say,
Harder to hit,
(Which way soever men refer it),
Much like thy riddle, Samson, in one day
Or seven, though one should musing sit;
If any of these, or all, the Timnian
bride
Had not so soon preferred
Thy paranymph, worthless to thee com-
pared,
Successor in thy bed,
Nor both so loosely disallied
Their nuptials, nor this last so treacher-
ously
Had shorn the fatal harvest of thy head.
Is it for that such outward ornament
Was lavished on their sex, that inward
gifts
Were left for haste unfinished, judgment
scant,
Capacity not raised to apprehend
Or value what is best
In choice, but oftest to affect the wrong?
Or was too much of self-love mixed,
Of constancy no root infixed,
That either they love nothing, or not long?
Whate'er it be, to wisest men and best
Seeming at first all heavenly under virgin
veil,
Soft, modest, meek, demure,
Once joined, the contrary she proves, a
thorn
Intestine, far within defensive arms
A cleaving mischief, in his way to virtue
Adverse and turbulent; or by her charms
Draws him awry enslaved
With dotage, and his sense depraved
To folly and shameful deeds which ruin
ends.

What pilot so expert but needs must
wreck,
Embarked with such a steers-mate at the
helm?
Favored of Heav'n who finds
One virtuous, rarely found,
That in domestic good combines:
Happy that house; his way to peace is
smooth;
But virtue which breaks through all op-
position,
And all temptation can remove,
Most shines and most is ácceptáble above.
Therefore God's universal law
Gave to the man despotic power
Over his female in due awe,
Nor from that right to part an hour,
Smile she or lour:
So shall he least confusion draw
On his whole life, not swayed
By female usurpation, nor dismayed.
But had we best retire? I see a storm.
SAM: Fair days have oft contracted
wind and rain.
CHOR: But this another kind of tempest
brings.
SAM: Be less abstruse, my riddling days
are past.
CHOR: Look now for no enchanting
voice, nor fear
The bait of honied words; a rougher
tongue
Draws hitherward; I know him by his
stride,
The giant Harapha of Gath, his look
Haughty as is his pile high-built and
proud.
Comes he in peace? What wind hath
blown him hither
I less conjecture than when first I saw
The sumptuous Dálila floating this way;
His habit carries peace, his brow defiance.
SAM: Or peace or not, alike to me he
comes.
CHOR: His fraught we soon shall know,
he now arrives.

HARAPHA: I come not, Samson, to con-
dole thy chance,
As these perhaps, yet wish it had not
been,
Though for no friendy intent. I am of
Gath;
Men call me Harapha, of stock renowned
As Og or Anak and the Emims old
That Kiriathaim held; thou know'st me
now,
If thou at all art known. Much I have
heard
Of thy prodigious might and feats per-
formed
Incredible to me, in this displeased,
That I was never present on the place
Of those encounters where we might have
tried
Each other's force in camp or listed
field:
And now am come to see of whom such
noise
Hath walked about, and each limb to sur-
vey,
If thy appearance answer loud report.

SAM: The way to know were not to see
but taste.

HAR: Dost thou already single me? I
thought
Gyves and the mill had tamed thee. O that
fortune
Had brought me to the field where thou
art famed
To have wrought such wonders with an
ass's jaw;
I should have forced thee soon wish other
arms,
Or left thy carcass where the ass lay
thrown:
So had the glory of prowess been recovered
To Palestine, won by a Philistine
From the unforeskinned race, of whom
thou bear'st
The highest name for valiant acts; that
honor,

Certain to have won by mortal duel from
thee.
I lose, prevented by thy eyes put out.

SAM: Boast not of what thou wouldst
have done, but do
What then thou wouldst; thou seest it in
thy hand.

HAR: To combat with a blind man I
disdain,
And thou hast need much washing to be
touched.

SAM: Such usage as your honorable
lords
Afford me, assassinated and betrayed;
Who durst not with their whole united
powers
In fight withstand me single and un-
armed,
Nor in the house with chamber ambushes
Close-banded durst attack me, no, not
sleeping,
Till they had hired a woman with their
gold,
Breaking her marriage faith, to circum-
vent me.
Therefore without feigned shifts let be
assigned
Some narrow place enclosed, where sight
may give thee,
Or rather flight, no great advantage on
me;
Then put on all thy gorgeous arms, thy
helmet
And brigandine of brass, thy broad haber-
geon,
Vant-brace and greaves, and gauntlet;
add thy spear,
A weaver's beam, and seven-times-folded
shield;
I only with an oaken staff will meet thee,
And raise such outcries on thy clattered
iron,
Which long shall not withhold me from
thy head,
That in a little time while breath remains
thee,

Thou oft shalt wish thyself at Gath to
  boast
Again in safety what thou wouldst have
  done
To Samson, but shalt never see Gath
  more.

    HAR: Thou durst not thus disparage
      glorious arms
Which greatest heroes have in battle worn,
Their ornament and safety, had not spells
And black enchantments, some magician's
  art,
Armed thee or charmed thee strong, which
  thou from Heaven
Feign'dst at thy birth was giv'n thee in thy
  hair,
Where strength can least abide, though all
  thy hairs
Were bristles ranged like those that ridge
  the back
Of chafed wild boars, or ruffled porcupines.

    SAM: I know no spells, use no forbidden
      arts;
My trust is in the living God who gave me
At my nativity this strength, diffused
No less through all my sinews, joints and
  bones,
Than thine, while I preserved these locks
  unshorn,
The pledge of my unviolated vow.
For proof hereof, if Dagon be thy god,
Go to his temple, invocate his aid
With solemnest devotion, spread before
  him
How highly it concerns his glory now
To frustrate and dissolve these magic
  spells,
Which I to be the power of Israel's God
Avow, and challenge Dagon to the test,
Offering to combat thee, his champion
  bold,
With th' utmost of his godhead seconded:
Then thou shalt see, or rather to thy sor-
  row
Soon feel, whose God is strongest, thine
  or mine.

    HAR: Presume not on thy God, whate'er
      he be;
Thee he regards not, owns not, hath cut
  off
Quite from his people, and delivered up
Into thy enemies' hand; permitted them
To put out both thine eyes, and fettered
  send thee
Into the common prison, there to grind
Among the slaves and asses, thy comrádes,
As good for nothing else, no better service
With those thy boist'rous locks; no worthy
  match
For valor to assail, nor by the sword
Of noble warrior, so to stain his honor,
But by the barber's razor best subdued.

    SAM: All these indignities, for such they
      are
From thine, these evils I deserve and more,
Acknowledge them from God inflicted on
  me
Justly, yet despair not of his final pardon
Whose ear is ever open, and his eye
Gracious to readmit the suppliant;
In confidence whereof I once again
Defy thee to the trial of mortal fight,
By combat to decide whose god is God,
Thine or whom I with Israel's sons adore.

    HAR: Fair honor that thou dost thy
      God, in trusting
He will accept thee to defend his cause,
A murtherer, a revolter, and a robber.

    SAM: Tongue-doughty giant, how dost
      thou prove me these?

    HAR: Is not thy nation subject to our
      lords?
Their magistrates confessed it, when they
  took thee
As a league-breaker and delivered bound
Into our hands: for hadst thou not com-
  mitted
Notorious murder on those thirty men
At Ascalon, who never did thee harm,
Then like a robber stripp'dst them of their
  robes?

The Philistines, when thou hadst broke
  the league,
Went up with armèd powers thee only
  seeking,
To others did no violence nor spoil.
  SAM: Among the daughters of the Phi-
  listines
I chose a wife, which argued me no foe,
And in your city held my nuptial feast;
But your ill-meaning politician lords,
Under pretense of bridal friends and
  guests,
Appointed to await me thirty spies,
Who threat'ning cruel death constrained
  the bride
To wring from me and tell to them my
  secret,
That solved the riddle which I had pro-
  posed.
When I perceived all set on enmity,
As on my enemies, wherever chanced,
I used hostility, and took their spoil
To pay my underminers in their coin.
My nation was subjected to your lords?
It was the force of conquest; force with
  force
Is well ejected when the conquered can.
But I a private person, whom my country
As a league-breaker gave up bound, pre-
  sumed
Single rebellion and did hostile acts?
I was no private but a person raised
With strength sufficient and command
  from Heav'n
To free my country; if their servile minds
Me their deliverer sent would not receive,
But to their masters gave me up for
  naught,
Th' unworthier they; whence to this day
  they serve.
I was to do my part from Heav'n assigned,
And had performed it if my known of-
  fense
Had not disabled me, not all your force.
These shifts refuted, answer thy appellant,
Though by his blindness maimed for high
  attempts,

Who now defies thee thrice to single fight,
As a petty enterprise of small enforce.
  HAR: With thee, a man condemned, a
  slave enrolled,
Due by the law to capital punishment?
To fight with thee no man of arms will
  deign.
  SAM: Cam'st thou for this, vain boaster,
  to survey me,
To descant on my strength, and give thy
  verdict?
Come nearer, part not hence so slight in-
  formed;
But take good heed my hand survey not
  thee.
  HAR: O Baal-zebub! can my ears un-
  used
Hear these dishonors, and not render
  death?
  SAM: No man withholds thee, nothing
  from thy hand
Fear I incurable; bring up thy van;
My heels are fettered, but my fist is free.
  HAR: This insolence other kind of an-
  swer fits.
  SAM: Go, baffled coward, lest I run upon
  thee,
Though in these chains, bulk without
  spirit vast,
And with one buffet lay thy structure low,
Or swing thee in the air, then dash thee
  down
To the hazard of thy brains and shattered
  sides.
  HAR: By Astaroth, ere long thou shalt
  lament
These braveries in irons loaden on thee.
  CHOR: His giantship is gone somewhat
  crestfall'n,
Stalking with less unconscionable strides,
And lower looks, but in a sultry chafe.
  SAM: I dread him not, nor all his giant
  brood,

Though fame divulge him father of five
  sons,
All of gigantic size, Goliah chief.

CHOR: He will directly to the lords, I
  fear,
And with malicious counsel stir them up
Some way or other yet further to afflict
  thee.

SAM: He must allege some cause, and
  offered fight
Will not dare mention, lest a question rise
Whether he durst accept the offer or not,
And that he durst not plain enough ap-
  peared.
Much more affliction than already felt
They cannot well impose, nor I sustain,
If they intend advantage of my labors,
The work of many hands, which earns my
  keeping
With no small profit daily to my owners.
But come what will, my deadliest foe will
  prove
My speediest friend, by death to rid me
  hence,
The worst that he can give, to me the
  best.
Yet so it may fall out, because their end
Is hate, not help to me, it may with mine
Draw their own ruin who attempt the
  deed.

CHOR: Oh how comely it is and how re-
  viving
To the spirits of just men long oppressed,
When God into the hands of their de-
  liverer
Puts invincible might
To quell the mighty of the earth, th' op-
  pressor,
The brute and boist'rous force of violent
  men,
Hardy and industrious to support
Tyrannic power, but raging to pursue
The righteous and all such as honor truth!
He all their ammunition
And feats of war defeats
With plain heroic magnitude of mind

And celestial vigor armed;
Their armories and magazines contemns,
Renders them useless, while
With winged expedition
Swift as the lightning glance he executes
His errand on the wicked, who surprised
Lose their defense, distracted and amazed.
  But patience is more oft the exercise
Of saints, the trial of their fortitude,
Making them each his own deliverer,
And victor over all
That tyranny or fortune can inflict;
Either of these is in thy lot,
Samson, with might endued
Above the sons of men; but sight bereaved
May chance to number thee with those
Whom patience finally must crown.
  This Idol's day hath been to thee no
  day of rest,
Laboring thy mind
More than the working day thy hands;
And yet perhaps more trouble is behind.
For I descry this way
Some other tending; in his hand
A scepter or quaint staff he bears,
Comes on amain, speed in his look.
By his habit I discern him now
A public officer, and now at hand.
His message will be short and voluble.

OFF: Hebrews, the pris'ner Samson here
  I seek.

CHOR: His manacles remark him; there
  he sits.

OFF: Samson, to thee our lords thus bid
  me say:
This day to Dagon is a solemn feast,
With sacrifices, triumph, pomp, and
  games;
Thy strength they know surpassing human
  rate,
And now some public proof thereof require
To honor this great feast, and great assembly;
Rise therefore with all speed and come
  along,

Where I will see thee heartened and fresh
    clad
To appear as fits before th' illustrious
    lords.
    SAM: Thou know'st I am an Hebrew,
      therefore tell them
Our Law forbids at their religious rites
My presence; for that cause I cannot come.
    OFF: This answer, be assured, will not
      content them.
    SAM: Have they not sword-players, and
      ev'ry sort
Of gymnic artists, wrestlers, riders, run-
    ners,
Jugglers and dancers, antics, mummers,
    mimics,
But they must pick me out with shackles
    tired,
And over-labored at their public mill,
To make them sport with blind activity?
Do they not seek occasion of new quarrels,
On my refusal, to distress me more,
Or make a game of my calamities?
Return the way thou cam'st; I will not
    come.
    OFF: Regard thyself; this will offend
      them highly.
    SAM: Myself? My conscience and in-
      ternal peace.
Can they think me so broken, so debased
With corporal servitude, that my mind
    ever
Will condescend to such absurd com-
    mands?
Although their drudge, to be their fool or
    jester,
And in my midst of sorrow and heart-
    grief
To show them feats and play before their
    god,
The worst of all indignities, yet on me
Joined with extreme contempt? I will not
    come.
    OFF: My message was imposed on me
      with speed,
Brooks no delay; is this thy resolution?

    SAM: So take it with what speed thy
      message needs.
    OFF: I am sorry what this stoutness
      will produce.
    SAM: Perhaps thou shalt have cause to
      sorrow indeed.
    CHOR: Consider, Samson; matters now
      are strained
Up to the highth, whether to hold or
    break;
He's gone, and who knows how he may
    report
Thy words by adding fuel to the flame?
Expect another message more imperious,
More lordly thund'ring than thou well wilt
    bear.
    SAM: Shall I abuse this consecrated gift
Of strength, again returning with my hair
After my great transgression, so requite
Favor renewed, and add a greater sin
By prostituting holy things to idols;
A Nazarite in place abominable
Vaunting my strength in honor to their
    Dagon?
Besides, how vile, contemptible, ridiculous,
What act more execrably unclean, pro-
    fane?
    CHOR: Yet with this strength thou serv'st
      the Philistines,
Idolatrous, uncircumcised, unclean.
    SAM: Not in their idol-worship, but by
      labor
Honest and lawful to deserve my food
Of those who have me in their civil power.
    CHOR: Where the heart joins not, out-
      ward acts defile not.
    SAM: Where outward force constrains,
      the sentence holds;
But who constrains me to the temple of
    Dagon,
Not dragging? The Philistian lords com-
    mand.
Commands are no constraints. If I obey
    them,
I do it freely, venturing to displease

God for the fear of man, and man prefer,
Set God behind; which in his jealousy
Shall never, unrepented, find forgiveness.
Yet that he may dispense with me or thee,
Present in temples at idolatrous rites
For some important cause, thou need'st not
doubt.

CHOR: How thou wilt here come off
surmounts my reach.

SAM: Be of good courage; I begin to
feel
Some rousing motions in me which dispose
To something extraordinary my thoughts.
I with this messenger will go along,
Nothing to do, be sure, that may dishonor
Our Law, or stain my vow of Nazarite.
If there be aught of presage in the mind,
This day will be remarkable in my life
By some great act, or of my days the last.

CHOR: In time thou hast resolved; the
man returns.

OFF: Samson, this second message from
our lords
To thee I am bid say: art thou our slave,
Our captive, at the public mill our drudge,
And dar'st thou at our sending and com-
mand
Dispute thy coming? Come without delay;
Or we shall find such engines to assail
And hamper thee, as thou shalt come of
force,
Though thou wert firmlier fastened than
a rock.

SAM: I could be well content to try
their art,
Which to no few of them would prove
pernicious.
Yet knowing their advantages too many,
Because they shall not trail me through
their streets
Like a wild beast, I am content to go.
Masters' commands come with a power
resistless
To such as owe them absolute subjection;
And for a life who will not change his
purpose?

(So mutable are all the ways of men.)
Yet this be sure, in nothing to comply
Scandalous or forbidden in our Law.

OFF: I praise thy resolution; doff these
links.
By this compliance thou wilt win the lords
To favor, and perhaps to set thee free.

SAM: Brethren, farewell; your company
along
I will not wish, lest it perhaps offend them
To see me girt with friends; and how the
sight
Of me as of a common enemy,
So dreaded once, may now exasperate
them,
I know not. Lords are lordliest in their
wine;
And the well-feasted priest then soonest
fired
With zeal, if aught religion seem con-
cerned;
No less the people on their holy-days
Impetuous, insolent, unquenchable;
Happen what may, of me expect to hear
Nothing dishonorable, impure, unworthy
Our God, our Law, my nation, or my-
self;
The last of me or no I cannot warrant.

CHOR: Go, and the Holy One
Of Israel be thy guide
To what may serve his glory best, and
spread his name
Great among the heathen round;
Send thee the angel of thy birth, to stand
Fast by thy side, who from thy father's
field
Rode up in flames after his message told
Of thy conception, and be now a shield
Of fire; that spirit that first rushed on thee
In the camp of Dan,
Be efficacious in thee now at need.
For never was from Heaven imparted
Measure of strength so great to mortal
seed,
As in thy wondrous actions hath been
seen.

But wherefore comes old Manoa in such
  haste
With youthful steps? Much livelier than
  erewhile
He seems: supposing here to find his son,
Or of him bringing to us some glad news?

  MAN: Peace with you, brethren; my in-
    ducement hither
Was not at present here to find my son,
By order of the lords new parted hence
To come and play before them at their
  feast.
I heard all as I came, the city rings,
And numbers thither flock; I had no will,
Lest I should see him forced to things un-
  seemly.
But that which moved my coming now
  was chiefly
To give ye part with me what hope I have
With good success to work his liberty.

  CHOR: That hope would much rejoice us
    to partake
With thee; say, reverend sire; we thirst
  to hear.

  MAN: I have attempted one by one the
    lords,
Either at home, or through the high street
  passing,
With supplication prone and father's tears
To accept of ransom for my son their
  pris'ner.
Some much averse I found and wondrous
  harsh,
Contemptuous, proud, set on revenge and
  spite;
That part most reverenced Dagon and his
  priests;
Others more moderate seeming, but their
  aim
Private reward, for which both God and
  State
They easily would set to sale; a third
More generous far and civil, who con-
  fessed
They had enough revenged, having re-
  duced

Their foe to misery beneath their fears;
The rest was magnanimity to remit,
If some convenient ransom were proposed.
What noise or shout was that? It tore the
  sky.

  CHOR: Doubtless the people shouting to
    behold
Their once great dread, captive and blind
  before them,
Or at some proof of strength before them
  shown.

  MAN: His ransom, if my whole in-
    heritance
May compass it, shall willingly be paid
And numbered down; much rather I shall
  choose
To live the poorest in my tribe, than
  richest,
And he in that calamitous prison left.
No, I am fixed not to part hence without
  him.
For his redemption all my patrimony,
If need be, I am ready to forgo
And quit; not wanting him, I shall want
  nothing.

  CHOR: Fathers are wont to lay up for
    their sons,
Thou for thy son art bent to lay out all;
Sons wont to nurse their parents in old
  age,
Thou in old age car'st how to nurse thy
  son,
Made older than thy age through eyesight
  lost.

  MAN: It shall be my delight to tend his
    eyes,
And view him sitting in the house, en-
  nobled
With all those high exploits by him
  achieved,
And on his shoulders waving down those
  locks
That of a nation armed the strength con-
  tained.
And I persuade me God had not permitted

His strength again to grow up with his
hair
Garrisoned round about him like a camp
Of faithful soldiery, were not his purpose
To use him further yet in some great
service,
Not to sit idle with so great a gift
Useless, and thence ridiculous, about him.
And since his strength with eyesight was
not lost,
God will restore him eyesight to his
strength.

CHOR: Thy hopes are not ill-founded nor
seem vain
Of his delivery, and thy joy thereon
Conceived, agreeable to a father's love;
In both which we, as next, participate.

MAN: I know your friendly minds
and—O what noise!
Mercy of Heav'n, what hideous noise was
that!
Horribly loud, unlike the former shout.

CHOR: Noise call you it, or universal
groan,
As if the whole inhabitation perished?
Blood, death, and dreadful deeds are in
that noise,
Ruin, destruction at the utmost point.

MAN: Of ruin indeed methought I
heard the noise.
Oh it continues, they have slain my son.

CHOR: Thy son is rather slaying them;
that outcry
From slaughter of one foe could not
ascend.

MAN: Some dismal accident it needs
must be;
What shall we do, stay here or run and
see?

CHOR: Best keep together here, lest run-
ning thither
We unawares run into danger's mouth.
This evil on the Philistines is fall'n;
From whom could else a general cry be
heard?

The sufferers then will scarce molest us
here;
From other hands we need not much to
fear.
What if his eyesight (for to Israel's God
Nothing is hard) by miracle restored,
He now be dealing dole among his foes,
And over heaps of slaughtered walk his
way?

MAN: That were a joy presumptuous to
be thought.

CHOR: Yet God hath wrought things as
incredible
For his people of old; what hinders now?

MAN: He can, I know, but doubt to
think he will;
Yet hope would fain subscribe, and tempts
belief.
A little stay will bring some notice hither.

CHOR: Of good or bad so great, of bad
the sooner;
For evil news rides post, while good news
baits.
And to our wish I see one hither speeding,
An Hebrew, as I guess, and of our tribe.

MESSENGER: O whither shall I run, or
which way fly
The sight of this so horrid spectacle
Which erst my eyes beheld and yet behold?
For dire imagination still pursues me.
But providence or instinct of nature seems,
Or reason, though disturbed and scarce
consulted,
To have guided me aright, I know not
how,
To thee first, reverend Manoa, and to these
My countrymen, whom here I knew re-
maining,
As at some distance from the place of hor-
ror,
So in the sad event too much concerned.

MAN: The accident was loud, and here
before thee
With rueful cry, yet what it was we hear
not;

No preface needs, thou seest we long to know.

MESS: It would burst forth; but I recover breath

And sense distract, to know well what I utter.

MAN: Tell us the sum, the circumstance defer.

MESS: Gaza yet stands, but all her sons are fall'n,

All in a moment overwhelmed and fall'n.

MAN: Sad, but thou know'st to Israelites not saddest

The desolation of a hostile city.

MESS: Feed on that first, there may in grief be surfeit.

MAN: Relate by whom.

MESS: By Samson.

MAN: That still lessens

The sorrow, and converts it night to joy.

MESS: Ah, Manoa, I refrain, too suddenly

To utter what will come at last too soon;

Lest evil tidings, with too rude irruption

Hitting thy aged ear, should pierce too deep.

MAN: Suspense in news is torture, speak them out.

MESS: Then take the worst in brief: Samson is dead.

MAN: The worst indeed! O all my hope's defeated

To free him hence! But Death who sets all free

Hath paid his ransom now and full discharge.

With windy joy this day had I conceived,

Hopeful of his delivery, which now proves

Abortive as the first-born bloom of spring

Nipped with the lagging rear of winter's frost.

Yet ere I give the reins to grief, say first,

How died he? Death to life is crown or shame.

All by him fell, thou say'st; by whom fell he,

What glorious hand gave Samson his death's wound?

MESS: Unwounded of his enemies he fell.

MAN: Wearied with slaughter then, or how? Explain.

MESS: By his own hands.

MAN: Self-violence? What cause

Brought him so soon at variance with himself

Among his foes?

MESS: Inevitable cause

At once both to destroy and be destroyed;

The edifice where all were met to see him,

Upon their heads and on his own he pulled.

MAN: O lastly over-strong against thyself!

A dreadful way thou took'st to thy revenge.

More than enough we know; but while things yet

Are in confusion, give us, if thou canst,

Eye-witness of what first or last was done,

Relation more particular and distinct.

MESS: Occasions drew me early to this city,

And as the gates I entered with sunrise,

The morning trumpets festival proclaimed

Through each high street. Little I had despatched

When all aboard was rumored that this day

Samson should be brought forth to show the people

Proof of his mighty strength in feats and games;

I sorrowed at his captive state, but minded

Not to be absent at that spectacle.

The building was a spacious theater

Half round on two main pillars vaulted high,

With seats where all the lords, and each degree
Of sort, might sit in order to behold;
The other side was open, where the throng
On banks and scaffolds under sky might stand;
I among these aloof obscurely stood.
The feast and noon grew high, and sacrifice
Had filled their hearts with mirth, high cheer, and wine,
When to their sports they turned. Immediately
Was Samson as a public servant brought,
In their state livery clad; before him pipes
And timbrels; on each side went armèd guards,
Both horse and foot before him and behind
Archers, and slingers, cataphracts and spears.
At sight of him the people with a shout
Rifted the air, clamoring their god with praise,
Who had made their dreadful enemy their thrall.
He, patient but undaunted, where they led him,
Came to the place; and what was set before him,
Which without help of eye might be assayed,
To heave, pull, draw, or break, he still performed,
All with incredible, stupendious force,
None daring to appear antagonist.
At length for intermission sake they led him
Between the pillars; he his guide requested
(For so from such as nearer stood we heard),
As over-tired, to let him lean a while
With both his arms on those two massy pillars
That to the archèd roof gave main support.
He unsuspicious led him; which when Samson

Felt in his arms, with head a while inclined,
And eyes fast fixed he stood, as one who prayed,
Or some great matter in his mind revolved.
At last with head erect thus cried aloud:
"Hitherto, Lords, what your commands imposed
I have performed, as reason was, obeying,
Not without wonder or delight beheld.
Now of my own accord such other trial
I mean to show you of my strength, yet greater,
As with amaze shall strike all who behold."
This uttered, straining all his nerves he bowed;
As with the force of winds and waters pent
When mountains tremble, those two massy pillars
With horrible convulsion to and fro
He tugged, he shook, till down they came and drew
The whole roof after them, with burst of thunder
Upon the heads of all who sat beneath,
Lords, ladies, captains, counselors, or priests,
Their choice nobility and flower, not only
Of this but each Philistian city round,
Met from all parts to solemnize this feast.
Samson, with these inmixed, inevitably
Pulled down the same destruction on himself;
The vulgar only scaped who stood without.

    CHOR: O dearly bought revenge, yet glorious!
Living or dying thou hast fulfilled
The work for which thou wast foretold
To Israel, and now li'st victorious
Among thy slain self-killed,
Not willingly, but tangled in the fold
Of dire necessity, whose law in death conjoined

Thee with thy slaughtered foes, in number
      more
Than all thy life had slain before.

    SEMICHOR: While their hearts were
      jocund and sublime,
Drunk with idolatry, drunk with wine,
And fat regorged of bulls and goats,
Chanting their idol, and preferring
Before our living Dread who dwells
In Silo, his bright sanctuary,
Among them he a spirit of frenzy sent,
Who hurt their minds,
And urged them on with mad desire
To call in haste for their destroyer;
They only set on sport and play
Unweetingly importuned
Their own destruction to come speedy
      upon them.
So fond are mortal men
Fall'n into wrath divine,
As their own ruin on themselves to invite,
Insensate left, or to sense reprobate,
And with blindness internal struck.

    SEMICHOR: But he, though blind of
      sight,
Despised and thought extinguished quite,
With inward eyes illuminated,
His fiery virtue roused
From under ashes into sudden flame,
And as an ev'ning dragon came,
Assailant on the perchèd roosts
And nests in order ranged
Of tame villatic fowl; but as an eagle
His cloudless thunder bolted on their
      heads.
So virtue, giv'n for lost,
Depressed, and overthrown, as seemed,
Like that self-begotten bird
In the Arabian woods embost,
That no second knows nor third,
And lay erewhile a holocaust,
From out her ashy womb now teemed,
Revives, reflourishes, then vigorous most
When most unactive deemed,
And though her body die, her fame sur-
      vives,
A secular bird, ages of lives.

MAN: Come, come, no time for lamen-
      tation now,
Nor much more cause; Samson hath quit
      himself
Like Samson, and heroicly hath finished
A life heroic, on his enemies
Fully revenged; hath left them years of
      mourning,
And lamentation to the sons of Caphtor
Through all Philistian bounds. To Israel
Honor hath left, and freedom—let but
      them
Find courage to lay hold on this occasion;
To himself and father's house eternal
      fame;
And, which is best and happiest yet, all
      this
With God not parted from him, as was
      feared,
But favoring and assisting to the end.
Nothing is here for tears, nothing to wail
Or knock the breast, no weakness, no con-
      tempt,
Dispraise, or blame; nothing but well and
      fair,
And what may quiet us in a death so
      noble.
Let us go find the body where it lies
Soaked in his enemies' blood, and from
      the stream
With lavers pure and cleansing herbs wash
      off
The clotted gore. I with what speed the
      while
(Gaza is not in plight to say us nay)
Will send for all my kindred, all my
      friends,
To fetch him hence and solemnly attend
With silent obsequy and funeral train
Home to his father's house: there will I
      build him
A monument, and plant it round with
      shade
Of laurel ever green, and branching palm,
With all his trophies hung, and acts en-
      rolled
In copious legend, or sweet lyric song.
Thither shall all the valiant youth resort,

And from his memory inflame their
    breasts
To matchless valor and adventures high;
The virgins also shall on feastful days
Visit his tomb with flowers, only bewailing
His lot unfortunate in nuptial choice,
From whence captivity and loss of eyes.

    CHOR: All is best, though we oft doubt,
What th' unsearchable dispose
Of Highest Wisdom brings about,
And ever best found in the close.
Oft he seems to hide his face,

But unexpectedly returns
And to his faithful champion hath in
    place
Bore witness gloriously; whence Gaza
    mourns,
And all that band them to resist
His uncontrollable intent:
His servants he, with new acquist
Of true experience from this great event,
With peace and consolation hath dis-
    missed,
And calm of mind, all passion spent.

                (1660?–1670)

All For Love

JOHN DRYDEN

COMMENTARY

John Dryden (1631-1700) was England's great poet, dramatist, and critic of the later seventeenth century. Although his schooling was not significantly different from that of John Milton, he has generally been taken to be a post-Renaissance literary figure, a man of the Augustan age: rational, controlled, and guided by rules.

All for Love (1677), indeed, seems to be a carefully edited, smoothed down, neat version of the sprawling, turbulent, landscape of Shakespeare's *Antony and Cleopatra*. In addition, it is almost neo-classical in the French manner of Racine, and it invites comparison in terms of form and tone with *Phaedra*. Yet Dryden's work suggests a pairing as well with Milton's *Samson Agonistes,* the other great classically modeled tragedy written in blank verse in the same decade. Do Milton and Dryden observe the "Unities" (see Introduction) in the same way? What might be in *All for Love* the equivalent of the Chorus in *Samson*? How are Samson and Antony similar as heroes? different? Might *All for Love* lend itself more easily to modern production than *Samson*? How and why?

Dryden's Antony is neither the divinely driven classical hero nor the greatly human, individually responsible giant of Shakespeare. He has somehow been diminished, in ambition and in stature; *All for Love,* as has been suggested, is the first "domestic tragedy": Antony's tragedy in Dryden is less "public," more intimate than in Shakespeare. Cleopatra also is somehow reduced in intensity and private whimsicality, although she has gained in dignity.

In his preface to the play, Dryden seemed troubled by his material. "That which is wanting to work up the pity to a greater height," he wrote, "was not afforded me by the story; for the crimes of love which they both committed were not occasioned by any necessity, or fatal ignorance, but were wholly voluntary; since our passions are, or ought to be, within our power." Shakespeare's Antony chooses between passion and honor. Dryden's Antony may be read as making a third choice, doing nothing, waiting, like Samson, for some force to impel him. Unlike Samson, however, Dryden's Antony in the end simply mucks things up.

Like *Samson Agonistes* before it, and *The Father* long after it, *All for Love* is also a study of the emasculating effects of passion. Very specifically, the "unmanning" of Antony is a significantly organic element in the drama. How might a stage production blur or emphasize this aspect?

Dryden's own critical comments, particularly in his *Essay of Dramatic Poesy* (1668), raise important questions about the structure of *All for Love* in relation to the unities, and about its use of blank verse instead of rhymed couplets, the only play of his written in this form. F. R. Leavis' sustained comparison (*Scrutiny*, V, No. 2 [1936], 158-169) of *All for Love* with *Antony and Cleopatra* is provocative in opening up possibilities for further critical exercises of this nature. Significant essays on Dryden have been collected by Bernard N. Schilling (Englewood Cliffs, N. J., 1963); particularly relevant is R. J. Kaufmann's "On the Poetics of Terminal Tragedy: Dryden's *All for Love*," which was originally the introduction to the Chandler edition of the play (San Francisco, 1962). Arthur C. Kirsch's *Dryden's Heroic Drama* (Princeton, 1965) is a full study of Dryden's serious plays and takes an unconventional position on *All for Love*.

John Dryden

ALL FOR LOVE

✦ Edited by John Harold Wilson

DRAMATIS PERSONÆ

MARK ANTONY
VENTIDIUS, *his General*
DOLABELLA, *his Friend*
ALEXAS, *the Queen's Eunuch*
SERAPION, *Priest of Isis*
MYRIS, *another Priest*
Servants to Antony

CLEOPATRA, *Queen of Egypt*
OCTAVIA, *Antony's Wife*
CHARMION ⎫
IRAS ⎬ *Cleopatra's Maids*
Antony's two little Daughters

SCENE: *Alexandria*

PROLOGUE

What flocks of critics hover here today,
As vultures wait on armies for their prey,
All gaping for the carcass of a play!
With croaking notes they bode some dire
    event,
And follow dying poets by the scent.
Ours gives himself for gone; y'have
    watched your time!
He fights this day unarmed—without his
    rhyme—
And brings a tale which often has been
    told,

John Dryden, *All For Love* in *Six Restoration Plays*, ed. John Harold Wilson (Boston: Houghton Mifflin Co., 1959), pp. 169-243. Used by permission.

As sad as Dido's and almost as old.
His hero, whom you wits his bully call,
Bates of his mettle[1] and scarce rants at
    all.
He's somewhat lewd, but a well-meaning
    mind;
Weeps much, fights little, but is wond'rous
    kind;
In short, a pattern and companion fit
For all the keeping tonies[2] of the pit.
I could name more: a wife, and mistress
    too,
Both (to be plain) too good for most of
    you;
The wife well-natured, and the mistress
    true.
    Now, poets, if your fame has been his
    care,
Allow him all the candor you can spare.
A brave man scorns to quarrel once a day,
Like Hectors,[3] in at every petty fray.
Let those find fault whose wit's so very
    small,
They've need to show that they can think
    at all.
Errors, like straws, upon the surface flow;
He who would search for pearls must dive
    below.
Fops may have leave to level all they can,
As pigmies would be glad to lop a man.
Half-wits are fleas, so little and so light,
We scarce could know they live but that
    they bite.
But as the rich, when tired with daily
    feasts,
For change become their next poor ten-
    ant's guests,
Drink hearty draughts of ale from plain
    brown bowls,
And snatch the homely rasher from the
    coals,
So you, retiring from much better cheer,
For once may venture to do penance here.
And since that plenteous autumn now is
    past,

---

1 Blunts his edge; abates his bombast.
2 Dissolute fools (with a play on Antony).
3 Bullies; street-brawlers.

Whose grapes and peaches have indulged
    your taste,
Take in good part, from our poor poet's
    board,
Such rivelled[4] fruits as winter can afford.

ACT I

Scene I

The Temple of Isis

(*Enter* SERAPION, MYRIS, *Priests of Isis.*)

    SERAPION: Portents and prodigies are
    grown so frequent
That they have lost their name. Our fruit-
    ful Nile
Flowed ere the wonted season with a tor-
    rent
So unexpected and so wondrous fierce
That the wild deluge overtook the haste
Even of the hinds that watched it. Men
    and beasts
Were borne above the tops of trees that
    grew
On th' utmost margin of the water-mark
Then, with so swift an ebb the flood drove
    backward,
It slipt from underneath the scaly herd:
Here monstrous phocae[1] panted on the
    shore;
Forsaken dolphins there with their broad
    tails
Lay lashing the departing waves; hard by
    'em,
Sea-horses, floundering in the slimy mud,
Tossed up their heads, and dashed the
    ooze about them.

    (*Enter* ALEXAS *behind them.*)

    MYRIS: Avert these omens, Heaven!
    SERAPION: Last night, between the hours
    of twelve and one,
In a lone aisle of the temple while I
    walked,

---

4 Shriveled.
1 Seals.

A whirlwind rose that with a violent blast
Shook all the dome; the doors around me
    clapped;
The iron wicket that defends the vault
Where the long race of Ptolemies is laid
Burst open and disclosed the mighty dead.
From out each monument, in order placed,
An armèd ghost starts up: the boy-king[2]
    last
Reared his inglorious head. A peal of
    groans
Then followed, and a lamentable voice
Cried, "Egypt is no more!" My blood
    ran back,
My shaking knees against each other
    knocked;
On the cold pavement down I fell en-
    tranced,
And so unfinished left the horrid scene.

ALEXAS: (*Showing himself.*) And
    dreamed you this? or did invent
    the story
To frighten our Egyptian boys withal,
And train them up betimes in fear of
    priesthood?

SERAPION: My lord, I saw you not,
Nor meant my words should reach your
    ears; but what
I uttered was most true.

ALEXAS: A foolish dream,
Bred from the fumes of indigested feasts
And holy luxury.

SERAPION: I know my duty;
This goes no farther.

ALEXAS: 'Tis not fit it should,
Nor would the times now bear it, were
    it true.
All southern, from yon hills, the Roman
    camp
Hangs o'er us black and threatening like
    a storm
Just breaking on our heads.

SERAPION: Our faint Egyptians pray
    for Antony;

2 Cleopatra's dead brother.

But in their servile hearts they own Oc-
    tavius.

MYRIS: Why then does Antony dream
    out his hours,
And tempts not fortune for a noble day
Which might redeem what Actium lost?

ALEXAS: He thinks 'tis past recovery.

SERAPION: Yet the foe
Seems not to press the siege.

ALEXAS: Oh, there's the wonder.
Maecenas and Agrippa, who can most
With Caesar, are his foes. His wife Oc-
    tavia,
Driven from his house, solicits her re-
    venge;
And Dolabella, who was once his friend,
Upon some private grudge now seeks his
    ruin;
Yet still war seems on either side to sleep.

SERAPION: 'Tis strange that Antony,
    for some days past,
Has not beheld the face of Cleopatra,
But here in Isis' temple lives retired,
And makes his heart a prey to black de-
    spair.

ALEXAS: 'Tis true; and we much fear
    he hopes by absence
To cure his mind of love.

SERAPION: If he be vanquished
Or makes his peace, Egypt is doomed to be
A Roman province, and our plenteous
    harvests
Must then redeem the scarceness of their
    soil.
While Antony stood firm, our Alexandria
Rivaled proud Rome (dominion's other
    seat),
And Fortune, striding like a vast Colossus,
Could fix an equal foot of empire here.

ALEXAS: Had I my wish, these tyrants of
    all nature
Who lord it o'er mankind, should perish
    —perish
Each by the other's sword; but, since our
    will

Is lamely followed by our power, we
    must
Depend on one, with him to rise or fall.

    SERAPION: How stands the queen
      affected?

    ALEXAS: Oh, she dotes,
She dotes, Serapion, on this vanquished
    man,
And winds herself about his mighty ruins;
Whom would she yet forsake, yet yield
    him up,
This hunted prey, to his pursuer's hands,
She might preserve us all; but 'tis in vain—
This changes my designs, this blasts my
    counsels,
And makes me use all means to keep him
    here,
Whom I could wish divided from her
    arms
Far as the earth's deep center. Well, you
    know
The state of things; no more of your ill
    omens
And black prognostics; labor to confirm
The people's hearts.

(*Enter* VENTIDIUS, *talking aside with a
    Gentleman of* ANTONY'S.)

    SERAPION: These Romans will o'erhear
    us.
But who's that stranger? By his warlike
    port,
His fierce demeanor, and erected look,
He's of no vulgar note.

    ALEXAS: Oh, 'tis Ventidius,
Our emperor's great lieutenant in the East,
Who first showed Rome that Parthia
    could be conquered.
When Antony returned from Syria last,
He left this man to guard the Roman
    frontiers.

    SERAPION: You seem to know him well.

    ALEXAS: Too well. I saw him in Cilicia
    first,
When Cleopatra there met Antony.
A mortal foe he was to us and Egypt.

But—let me witness to the worth I hate—
A braver Roman never drew a sword;
Firm to his prince, but as a friend, not
    slave.
He ne'er was of his pleasures; but presides
O'er all his cooler hours and morning
    counsels;
In short, the plainness, fierceness, rugged
    virtue
Of an old true-stamped Roman lives in
    him.
His coming bodes I know not what of ill
To our affairs. Withdraw, to mark him
    better;
And I'll acquaint you why I sought you
    here,
And what's our present work.

(*They withdraw to a corner of the stage;
and* VENTIDIUS, *with the other, comes
    forward to the front.*)

    VENTIDIUS: Not see him, say you?
I say I must and will.

    GENTLEMAN: He has commanded,
On pain of death, none should approach
    his presence.

    VENTIDIUS: I bring him news will raise
    his drooping spirits,
Give him new life.

    GENTLEMAN: He sees not Cleopatra.

    VENTIDIUS: Would he had never seen
    her!

    GENTLEMAN: He eats not, drinks not,
    sleeps not, has no use
Of anything but thought; or, if he talks,
'Tis to himself, and then 'tis perfect rav-
    ing.
Then he defies the world, and bids it pass;
Sometimes he gnaws his lip and curses
    loud
The boy Octavius; then he draws his
    mouth
Into a scornful smile and cries, "Take all,
The world's not worth my care."

    VENTIDIUS: Just, just his nature.

Virtue's his path; but sometimes 'tis too
        narrow
For his vast soul; and then he starts out
        wide,
And bounds into a vice that bears him
        far
From his first course and plunges him in
        ills;
But when his danger makes him find his
        fault,
Quick to observe, and full of sharp re-
        morse,
He censures eagerly his own misdeeds,
Judging himself with malice to himself,
And not forgiving what as man he did,
Because his other parts are more than
        man.
He must not thus be lost.

(ALEXAS *and the Priests come forward.*)

ALEXAS: You have your full instruc-
        tions, now advance;
Proclaim your orders loudly.

SERAPION: Romans, Egyptians, hear the
        queen's command!
Thus Cleopatra bids: let labor cease;
To pomp and triumphs give this happy
        day
That gave the world a lord: 'tis Antony's.
Live, Antony; and Cleopatra, live!
Be this the general voice sent up to
        heaven,
And every public place repeat this echo.

VENTIDIUS: (*Aside*) Fine pageantry!

SERAPION: Set out before your doors
The images of all your sleeping fathers,
With laurels crowned; with laurels wreathe
        your posts
And strew with flowers the pavement; let
        the priests
Do present[3] sacrifice; pour out the wine
And call the gods to join with you in
        gladness.

VENTIDIUS: Curse on the tongue that
        bids this general joy!

[3] Immediate.

Can they be friends of Antony, who revel
When Antony's in danger? Hide, for
        shame,
You Romans, your great grandsires'
        images,
For fear their souls should animate their
        marbles,
To blush at their degenerate progeny.

ALEXAS: A love which knows no bounds
        to Antony
Would mark the day with honors when
        all heaven
Labored for him, when each propitious
        star
Stood wakeful in his orb to watch that
        hour
And shed his better influence. Her own
        birthday
Our queen neglected like a vulgar fate
That passed obscurely by.

VENTIDIUS: Would it had slept,
Divided far from his, till some remote
And future age had called it out, to ruin
Some other prince, not him!

ALEXAS: Your emperor,
Though grown unkind, would be more
        gentle than
T' upbraid my queen for loving him too
        well.

VENTIDIUS: Does the mute sacrifice up-
        braid the priest?
He knows him not his executioner.
Oh, she has decked his ruin with her love,
Led him in golden bands to gaudy slaugh-
        ter,
And made perdition pleasing. She has
        left him
The blank of what he was.
I tell thee, eunuch, she has quite un-
        manned him.
Can any Roman see and know him now,
Thus altered from the lord of half man-
        kind,
Unbent, unsinewed, made a woman's toy,
Shrunk from the vast extent of all his
        honors,

And cramped within a corner of the
  world?
O Antony!
Thou bravest soldier and thou best of
  friends!
Bounteous as nature; next to nature's God!
Couldst thou but make new worlds, so
  wouldst thou give 'em,
As bounty were thy being; rough in battle
As the first Romans when they went to
  war;
Yet, after victory, more pitiful
Than all their praying virgins left at
  home!

  ALEXAS: Would you could add to those
  more shining virtues,
His truth to her who loves him.

  VENTIDIUS: Would I could not!
But wherefore waste I precious hours with
  thee?
Thou art her darling mischief, her chief
  engine,
Antony's other fate. Go, tell thy queen
Ventidius is arrived to end her charms.
Let your Egyptian timbrels play alone,
Nor mix effeminate sounds with Roman
  trumpets.
You dare not fight for Antony; go pray,
And keep your coward's holiday in tem-
  ples.   (*Exeunt* ALEXAS, SERAPION.)

(*Enter a second Gentleman of* MARK
  ANTONY.)

  SECOND GENTLEMAN: The emperor approaches and commands
On pain of death that none presume to
  stay.

  FIRST GENTLEMAN: I dare not disobey
  him.
            (*Going out with the other.*)

  VENTIDIUS: Well, I dare.
But I'll observe him first unseen, and
  find
Which way his humor drives. The rest
  I'll venture.   (*Withdraws.*)

(*Enter* ANTONY, *walking with a disturbed
  motion before he speaks.*)

  ANTONY: They tell me 'tis my birthday,
  and I'll keep it
With double pomp of sadness.
'Tis what the day deserves which gave me
  breath.
Why was I raised the meteor of the world,
Hung in the skies and blazing as I
  travelled,
Till all my fires were spent, and then cast
  downward
To be trod out by Caesar?

  VENTIDIUS: (*Aside*)   On my soul,
'Tis mournful, wondrous mournful!

  ANTONY: Count thy gains.
Now, Antony, wouldst thou be born for
  this?
Glutton of fortune, thy devouring youth
Has starved thy wanting age.

  VENTIDIUS: (*Aside*)   How sorrow
  shakes him!
So now the tempest tears him up by the
  roots,
And on the ground extends the noble
  ruin.

  ANTONY: (*Having thrown himself
  down*) Lie there, thou shadow of
  an emperor;
The place thou pressest on thy mother
  earth
Is all thy empire now; now it contains
  thee;
Some few days hence, and then 'twill be
  too large,
When thou'rt contracted in thy narrow
  urn,
Shrunk to a few cold ashes. Then Octavia
(For Cleopatra will not live to see it),
Octavia then will have thee all her own,
And bear thee in her widowed hand to
  Caesar;
Caesar will weep, the crocodile will weep,
To see his rival of the universe
Lie still and peaceful there. I'll think no
  more on't.

Give me some music; look that it be
    sad.
I'll soothe my melancholy till I swell
And burst myself with sighing.—
                (*Soft music.*)
'Tis somewhat to my humor. Stay, I fancy
I'm now turned wild, a commoner of
    nature;
Of all forsaken and forsaking all,
Live in a shady forest's sylvan scene,
Stretched at my length beneath some
    blasted oak,
I lean my head upon the mossy bark
And look just of a piece as I grew from it;
My uncombed locks, matted like mistle-
    toe,
Hang o'er my hoary face; a murm'ring
    brook
Runs at my foot.

  VENTIDIUS: (*Aside.*) Methinks I fancy
Myself there, too.

  ANTONY: The herd come jumping by
    me,
And, fearless, quench their thirst while I
    look on,
And take me for their fellow-citizen.
More of this image, more it lulls my
    thoughts.   (*Soft music again.*)

  VENTIDIUS: I must disturb him; I can
    hold no longer.
             (*Stands before him.*)

  ANTONY: (*Starting up.*) Art thou Ven-
    tidius?

  VENTIDIUS: Are you Antony?
I'm liker what I was than you to him
I left you last.

  ANTONY: I'm angry.

  VENTIDIUS: So am I.

  ANTONY: I would be private. Leave me.

  VENTIDIUS: Sir, I love you,
And therefore will not leave you.

  ANTONY: Will not leave me!
Where have you learned that answer!
    Who am I?

  VENTIDIUS: My emperor; the man I love
    next Heaven;
If I said more, I think 'twere scarce a
    sin—
You're all that's good and good-like.

  ANTONY: All that's wretched.
You will not leave me then?

  VENTIDIUS: 'Twas too presuming
To say I would not; but I dare not leave
    you,
And 'tis unkind in you to chide me hence
So soon, when I so far have come to see
    you.

  ANTONY: Now thou hast seen me, art
    thou satisfied?
For, if a friend, thou hast beheld enough;
And, if a foe, too much.

  VENTIDIUS: (*Weeping.*) Look, emperor,
    this is no common dew.
I have not wept this forty years; but now
My mother comes afresh into my eyes;
I cannot help her softness.

  ANTONY: By heaven, he weeps! poor,
    good old man, he weeps!
The big round drops course one another
    down
The furrows of his cheeks.—Stop 'em,
    Ventidius,
Or I shall blush to death; they set my
    shame,
That caused 'em, full before me.

  VENTIDIUS: I'll do my best.

  ANTONY: Sure, there's contagion in the
    tears of friends—
See, I have caught it, too. Believe me, 'tis
    not
For my own griefs, but thine.—Nay,
    father!

  VENTIDIUS: Emperor!

  ANTONY: Emperor! Why, that's the
    style of victory;
The conqu'ring soldier, red with unfelt
    wounds,
Salutes his general so; but never more
Shall that sound reach my ears.

VENTIDIUS: I warrant you.

ANTONY: Actium, Actium! Oh!—

VENTIDIUS: It sits too near you.

ANTONY: Here, here it lies, a lump of
    lead by day,
And, in my short, distracted, nightly slum-
    bers,
The hag that rides my dreams.

VENTIDIUS: Out with it; give it vent.

ANTONY: Urge not my shame.
I lost a battle.

VENTIDIUS: So has Julius done.

ANTONY: Thou favor'st me, and speak'st
    not half thou think'st;
For Julius fought it out, and lost it fairly,
But Antony—

VENTIDIUS: Nay, stop not.

ANTONY: Antony,
(Well, thou wilt have it), like a coward
    fled,
Fled while his soldiers fought; fled first,
    Ventidius.
Thou long'st to curse me, and I give thee
    leave.
I know thou cam'st prepared to rail.

VENTIDIUS: I did.

ANTONY: I'll help thee.—I have been a
    man, Ventidius.

VENTIDIUS: Yes, and a brave one; but—

ANTONY: I know thy meaning.
But I have lost my reason, have disgraced
The name of soldier with inglorious ease.
In the full vintage of my flowing honors,
Sat still, and saw it pressed by other hands.
Fortune came smiling to my youth, and
    wooed it,
And purple greatness met my ripened
    years.
When first I came to empire, I was borne
On tides of people crowding to my tri-
    umphs—
The wish of nations! and the willing
    world
Received me as its pledge of future peace.

I was so great, so happy, so beloved,
Fate could not ruin me, till I took pains,
And worked against my fortune, chid her
    from me,
And turned her loose; yet still she came
    again.
My careless days and my luxurious nights
At length have wearied her, and now
    she's gone,
Gone, gone, divorced for ever. Help me,
    soldier,
To curse this madman, this industrious
    fool,
Who labored to be wretched. Pr'ythee,
    curse me.

VENTIDIUS: No.

ANTONY: Why?

VENTIDIUS: You are too sensible already
Of what you've done, too conscious of
    your failings;
And, like a scorpion, whipped by others
    first
To fury, sting yourself in mad revenge.
I would bring balm and pour it in your
    wounds,
Cure your distempered mind and heal
    your fortunes.

ANTONY: I know thou would'st.

VENTIDIUS: I will.

ANTONY: Ha, ha, ha, ha!

VENTIDIUS: You laugh.

ANTONY: I do, to see officious love
Give cordials to the dead.

VENTIDIUS: You would be lost, then?

ANTONY: I am.

VENTIDIUS: I say you are not. Try your
    fortune.

ANTONY: I have, to th' utmost. Dost
    thou think me desperate
Without just cause? No, when I found all
    lost
Beyond repair, I hid me from the world,
And learned to scorn it here; which now
    I do

So heartily, I think it is not worth
The cost of keeping.

VENTIDIUS: Caesar thinks not so.
He'll thank you for the gift he could not
take.
You would be killed like Tully, would
you? Do,
Hold out your throat to Caesar, and die
tamely.

ANTONY: No, I can kill myself; and so
resolve.

VENTIDIUS: I can die with you, too,
when time shall serve,
But fortune calls upon us now to live,
To fight, to conquer.

ANTONY: Sure, thou dream'st, Ventidius.

VENTIDIUS: No; 'tis you dream. You
sleep away your hours
In desperate sloth, miscalled philosophy.
Up, up, for honor's sake! Twelve legions
wait you
And long to call you chief. By painful
journeys
I led them, patient both of heat and
hunger,
Down from the Parthian marches to the
Nile.
'Twill do you good to see their sunburnt
faces,
Their scarred cheeks, and chopped⁵ hands.
There's virtue in 'em.
They'll sell those mangled limbs at dearer
rates
Than yon trim bands can buy.

ANTONY: Where left you them?

VENTIDIUS: I said in Lower Syria.

ANTONY: Bring them hither;
There may be life in these.

VENTIDIUS: They will not come.

ANTONY: Why didst thou mock my
hopes with promised aids,
To double my despair? They're mutinous.

⁵ Chapped.

VENTIDIUS: Most firm and loyal.

ANTONY: Yet they will not march
To succor me. O trifler!

VENTIDIUS: They petition
You would make haste to head them.

ANTONY: I'm besieged.

VENTIDIUS: There's but one way shut
up.
How came I hither?

ANTONY: I will not stir.

VENTIDIUS: They would perhaps desire
A better reason.

ANTONY: I have never used
My soldiers to demand a reason of
My actions. Why did they refuse to
march?

VENTIDIUS: They said they would not
fight for Cleopatra.

ANTONY: What was't they said?

VENTIDIUS: They said they would not
fight for Cleopatra.
Why should they fight, indeed, to make
her conquer,
And make you more a slave? to gain you
kingdoms
Which, for a kiss at your next midnight
feast,
You'll sell to her? Then she new-names
her jewels
And calls this diamond such or such a
tax;
Each pendant in her ear shall be a province.

ANTONY: Ventidius, I allow your tongue
free license
On all my other faults; but, on your life,
No word of Cleopatra. She deserves
More worlds than I can lose.

VENTIDIUS: Behold, you powers,
To whom you have intrusted humankind!
See Europe, Afric, Asia, put in balance
And all weighed down by one light,
worthless woman!
I think the gods are Antonies and give,

Like prodigals, this nether world away
To none but wasteful hands.

ANTONY: You grow presumptuous.

VENTIDIUS: I take the privilege of plain
   love to speak.

ANTONY: Plain love! plain arrogance,
   plain insolence!
Thy men are cowards, thou, an envious
   traitor,
Who, under seeming honesty, hast vented
The burden of thy rank, o'erflowing gall.
O that thou wert my equal, great in arms
As the first Caesar was, that I might kill
   thee
Without a stain to honor!

VENTIDIUS: You may kill me;
You have done more already,—called me
   traitor.

ANTONY: Art thou not one?

VENTIDIUS: For showing you yourself,
Which none else durst have done? But
   had I been
That name which I disdain to speak again,
I needed not have sought your abject for-
   tunes,
Come to partake your fate, to die with
   you.
What hindered me t' have led my con-
   quering eagles
To fill Octavius' bands? I could have been
A traitor then, a glorious, happy traitor,
And not have been so called.

ANTONY: Forgive me, soldier;
I've been too passionate.

VENTIDIUS: You thought me false;
Thought my old age betrayed you. Kill
   me, sir,
Pray, kill me. Yet you need not; your un-
   kindness
Has left your sword no work.

ANTONY: I did not think so.
I said it in my rage. Pr'ythee, forgive me.
Why didst thou tempt my anger by dis-
   covery
Of what I would not hear?

VENTIDIUS: No prince but you

Could merit that sincerity I used,
Nor durst another man have ventured it;
But you, ere love misled your wandering
   eyes,
Were sure the chief and best of human
   race,
Framed in the very pride and boast of
   nature;
So perfect that the gods who formed you
   wondered
At their own skill, and cried, "A lucky hit
Has mended our design." Their envy
   hindered,
Else you had been immortal, and a pat-
   tern,
When Heaven would work for ostenta-
   tion's sake
To copy out again.

ANTONY: But Cleopatra—
Go on, for I can bear it now.

VENTIDIUS: No more.

ANTONY: Thou dar'st not trust my passion, but thou may'st;
Thou only lov'st, the rest have flattered
   me.

VENTIDIUS: Heaven's blessing on your
   heart for that kind word!
May I believe you love me? Speak again.

ANTONY: Indeed I do. Speak this, and
   this, and this.   (Hugging him.)
Thy praises were unjust, but I'll deserve
   them,
And yet mend all. Do with me what thou
   wilt;
Lead me to victory! Thou know'st the
   way.

VENTIDIUS: And will you leave this—

ANTONY: Pr'ythee, do not curse her,
And I will leave her; though Heaven
   knows I love
Beyond life, conquest, empire, all but
   honor;
But I will leave her.

VENTIDIUS: That's my royal master;
And shall we fight?

ANTONY: I warrant thee, old soldier.

Thou shalt behold me once again in iron;
And at the head of our old troops that beat
The Parthians, cry aloud, "Come, follow
me!"

VENTIDIUS: Oh, now I hear my em-
peror! In that word
Octavius fell. Gods, let me see that day,
And, if I have ten years behind, take all;
I'll thank you for th' exchange.

ANTONY: O Cleopatra!

VENTIDIUS: Again?

ANTONY: I've done. In that last sigh,
she went.
Caesar shall know what 'tis to force a
lover
From all he holds most dear.

VENTIDIUS: Methinks you breathe
Another soul. Your looks are more divine;
You speak a hero, and you move a god.

ANTONY: Oh, thou hast fired me! My
soul's up in arms,
And mans each part about me. Once
again
That noble eagerness of fight has seized
me,
That eagerness with which I darted up-
ward
To Cassius' camp. In vain the steepy hill
Opposed my way; in vain a war of spears
Sung round my head and planted all my
shield;
I won the trenches while my foremost
men
Lagged on the plain below.

VENTIDIUS: Ye gods, ye gods,
For such another hour!

ANTONY: Come on, my soldier!
Our hearts and arms are still the same. I
long
Once more to meet our foes, that thou
and I,
Like time and death, marching before our
troops,
May taste fate[6] to them, mow them out a
passage,

[6] Act as tasters of their fate.

And, entering where the foremost squad-
rons yield,
Begin the noble harvest of the field.

                    (*Exeunt.*)

ACT II
SCENE I

(*Enter* CLEOPATRA, IRAS, *and* ALEXAS.)

CLEOPATRA: What shall I do or whither
shall I turn?
Ventidius has o'ercome, and he will go.

ALEXAS: He goes to fight for you.

CLEOPATRA: Then he would see me ere
he went to fight.
Flatter me not. If once he goes, he's lost,
And all my hopes destroyed.

ALEXAS: Does this weak passion
Become a mighty queen?

CLEOPATRA: I am no queen.
Is this to be a queen, to be besieged
By yon insulting Roman, and to wait
Each hour the victor's chain? These ills
are small;
For Antony is lost, and I can mourn
For nothing else but him. Now come,
Octavius,
I have no more to lose! Prepare thy bands;
I'm fit to be a captive; Antony
Has taught my mind the fortune of a
slave.

IRAS: Call reason to assist you.

CLEOPATRA: I have none,
And none would have. My love's a noble
madness,
Which shows the cause deserved it. Mod-
erate sorrow
Fits vulgar love, and for a vulgar man,
But I have loved with such transcendent
passion,
I soared, at first, quite out of reason's
view,
And now am lost above it. No, I'm proud

'Tis thus. Would Antony could see me
  now!
Think you he would not sigh? Though he
  must leave me,
Sure, he would sigh, for he is noble-
  natured,
And bears a tender heart. I know him
  well.
Ah, no, I know him not; I knew him
  once,
But now 'tis past.

  IRAS: Let it be past with you.
Forget him, madam.

  CLEOPATRA: Never, never, Iras.
He once was mine; and once, though now
  'tis gone,
Leaves a faint image of possession still.

  ALEXAS: Think him unconstant, cruel,
  and ungrateful.

  CLEOPATRA: I cannot. If I could, those
  thoughts were vain.
Faithless, ungrateful, cruel though he be,
I still must love him.

  (*Enter* CHARMION.)
          Now, what news, my Charmion?
Will he be kind? And will he not forsake
  me?
Am I to live, or die?—nay, do I live?
Or am I dead? For when he gave his
  answer,
Fate took the word, and then I lived or
  died.

  CHARMION: I found him, madam—

  CLEOPATRA: A long speech preparing?
If thou bring'st comfort, haste, and give
  it me,
For never was more need.

  IRAS: I know he loves you.

  CLEOPATRA: Had he been kind, her
  eyes had told me so
Before her tongue could speak it. Now
  she studies
To soften what he said; but give me death
Just as he sent it, Charmion, undisguised,
And in the words he spoke.

  CHARMION: I found him, then,
Encompassed round, I think, with iron
  statues;
So mute, so motionless his soldiers stood,
While awfully he cast his eyes about
And every leader's hopes or fears sur-
  veyed.
Methought he looked resolved, and yet
  not pleased.
When he beheld me struggling in the
  crowd,
He blushed, and bade make way.

  ALEXAS: There's comfort yet.

  CHARMION: Ventidius fixed his eyes
  upon my passage
Severely, as he meant to frown me back,
And sullenly gave place. I told my mes-
  sage,
Just as you gave it, broken and disordered;
I numbered in it all your sighs and tears,
And while I moved your pitiful request,
That you but only begged a last farewell,
He fetched an inward groan; and every
  time
I named you, sighed as if his heart were
  breaking,
But shunned my eyes and guiltily looked
  down.
He seemed not now that awful Antony
Who shook an armed assembly with his
  nod;
But, making show as he would rub his
  eyes,
Disguised and blotted out a falling tear.

  CLEOPATRA: Did he then weep? And
  was I worth a tear?
If what thou hast to say be not as pleasing,
Tell me no more, but let me die contented.

  CHARMION: He bid me say, he knew
  himself so well,
He could deny you nothing if he saw you;
And therefore—

  CLEOPATRA: Thou wouldst say, he
  would not see me?

CHARMION: And therefore begged you not to use a power
Which he could ill resist; yet he should ever
Respect you as he ought.

CLEOPATRA: Is that a word
For Antony to use to Cleopatra?
O that faint word, *respect!* how I disdain it!
Disdain myself for loving, after it!
He should have kept that word for cold Octavia.
Respect is for a wife. Am I that thing,
That dull, insipid lump, without desires,
And without power to give them?

ALEXAS: You misjudge;
You see through love, and that deludes your sight,
As what is straight seems crooked through the water.
But I, who bear my reason undisturbed,
Can see this Antony, this dreaded man,
A fearful slave who fain would run away,
And shuns his master's eyes. If you pursue him,
My life on't, he still drags a chain along
That needs must clog his flight.

CLEOPATRA: Could I believe thee!—

ALEXAS: By every circumstance I know he loves,
True, he's hard pressed by int'rest and by honor;
Yet he but doubts and parleys and casts out
Many a long look for succor.

CLEOPATRA: He sends word
He fears to see my face.

ALEXAS: And would you more?
He shows his weakness who declines the combat,
And you must urge your fortune. Could he speak
More plainly? To my ears the message sounds—
"Come to my rescue, Cleopatra, come;

Come, free me from Ventidius—from my tyrant;
See me and give me a pretense to leave him!"
I hear his trumpets. This way he must pass.
Please you, retire a while; I'll work him first,
That he may bend more easy.

CLEOPATRA: You shall rule me;
But all, I fear, in vain.

(*Exit with* CHARMION *and* IRAS.)

ALEXAS: I fear so, too,
Though I concealed my thoughts, to make her bold,
But 'tis our utmost means, and fate befriend it! (*Withdraws.*)

(*Enter Lictors with fasces, one bearing the eagle; then enter* ANTONY *with* VENTIDIUS, *followed by other commanders.*)

ANTONY: Octavius is the minion of blind chance
But holds from virtue nothing.

VENTIDIUS: Has he courage?

ANTONY: But just enough to season him from coward.
Oh, 'tis the coldest youth upon a charge,
The most deliberate fighter! If he ventures
(As in Illyria once, they say, he did,
To storm a town), 'tis when he cannot choose;
When all the world have fixed their eyes upon him,
And then he lives on that for seven years after;
But at a close revenge he never fails.

VENTIDIUS: I heard you challenged him.

ANTONY: I did, Ventidius.
What think'st thou was his answer? 'Twas so tame!—
He said he had more ways than one to die;
I had not.

VENTIDIUS: Poor!

ANTONY: He has more ways than one,

But he would choose them all before that
one.

   VENTIDIUS: He first would choose an
ague or a fever.

   ANTONY: No; it must be an ague, not
a fever;

He has not warmth enough to die by that.

   VENTIDIUS: Or old age and a bed.

   ANTONY: Ay, there's his choice,

He would live like a lamp to the last
wink,

And crawl upon the utmost verge of life.

O Hercules! Why should a man like this,

Who dares not trust his fate for one great
action,

Be all the care of Heaven? Why should
he lord it

O'er fourscore thousand men, of whom
each one

Is braver than himself?

   VENTIDIUS: You conquered for him.

Philippi knows it; there you shared with
him

That empire which your sword made all
your own.

   ANTONY: Fool that I was, upon my
eagle's wings

I bore this wren till I was tired with soar-
ing,

And now he mounts above me.

Good heavens, is this—is this the man who
braves me?

Who bids my age make way? Drives me
before him

To the world's ridge and sweeps me off
like rubbish?

   VENTIDIUS: Sir, we lose time; the troops
are mounted all.

   ANTONY: Then give the word to march.

I long to leave this prison of a town,

To join thy legions, and in open field

Once more to show my face. Lead, my
deliverer.

            (Enter ALEXAS.)

   ALEXAS: Great emperor,

In mighty arms renowned above mankind,

But in soft pity to th' oppressed, a god,

This message sends the mournful Cleopatra

To her departing lord.

   VENTIDIUS: Smooth sycophant!

   ALEXAS: A thousand wishes and ten
thousand prayers,

Millions of blessings wait you to the wars;

Millions of sighs and tears she sends you,
too,

And would have sent

As many parting kisses to your lips,

But those, she fears, have wearied you
already.

   VENTIDIUS: *(Aside.)* False crocodile!

   ALEXAS: And yet she begs not now you
would not leave her;

That were a wish too mighty for her
hopes,

Too presuming

For her low fortune and your ebbing
love;

That were a wish for her more prosperous
days,

Her blooming beauty and your growing
kindness.

   ANTONY: *(Aside.)* Well, I must man it
out.—What would the queen?

   ALEXAS: First, to these noble warriors
who attend

Your daring courage in the chase of
fame,—

Too daring and too dangerous for her
quiet,—

She humbly recommends all she holds
dear,

All her own cares and fears,—the care of
you.

   VENTIDIUS: Yes, witness Actium.

   ANTONY: Let him speak, Ventidius.

   ALEXAS: You, when his matchless valor
bears him forward

With ardor too heroic, on his foes,

Fall down, as she would do, before his
    feet;
Lie in his way and stop the paths of death.
Tell him this god is not invulnerable,
That absent Cleopatra bleeds in him,
And, that you may remember her petition,
She begs you wear these trifles as a pawn
Which, at your wished return, she will
    redeem

    (*Gives jewels to the commanders.*)

With all the wealth of Egypt.
This to the great Ventidius she presents,
Whom she can never count her enemy,
Because he loves her lord.

VENTIDIUS: Tell her, I'll none on't;
I'm not ashamed of honest poverty;
Not all the diamonds of the east can bribe
Ventidius from his faith. I hope to see
These and the rest of all her sparkling
    store
Where they shall more deservingly be
    placed.

ANTONY: And who must wear 'em
    then?

VENTIDIUS: The wronged Octavia.

ANTONY: You might have spared that
    word.

VENTIDIUS: And he, that bribe.

ANTONY: But have I no remembrance?

ALEXAS: Yes, a dear one;
Your slave the queen—

ANTONY: My mistress.

ALEXAS: Then your mistress;
Your mistress would, she says, have sent
    her soul,
But that you had long since; she humbly
    begs
This ruby bracelet, set with bleeding
    hearts,
The emblems of her own, may bind your
    arm.

    (*Presenting a bracelet.*)

VENTIDIUS: Now, my best lord, in
    honor's name, I ask you,

For manhood's sake and for your own
    dear safety,
Touch not these poisoned gifts,
Infected by the sender; touch 'em not;
Myriads of bluest plagues lie underneath
    them,
And more than aconite has dipped the
    silk.

ANTONY: Nay, now you grow too cyni-
    cal, Ventidius;
A lady's favors may be worn with honor.
What, to refuse her bracelet! On my soul,
When I lie pensive in my tent alone,
'Twill pass the wakeful hours of winter
    nights
To tell these pretty beads upon my arm,
To count for every one a soft embrace,
A melting kiss at such and such a time,
And now and then the fury of her love
When—And what harm's in this?

ALEXAS: None, none, my lord,
But what's to her, that now 'tis past for
    ever.

ANTONY: (*Going to tie it.*) We soldiers
    are so awkward—help me tie it.

ALEXAS: In faith, my lord, we courtiers,
    too, are awkward
In these affairs; so are all men indeed,
Even I, who am not one. But shall I
    speak?

ANTONY: Yes, freely.

ALEXAS: Then, my lord, fair hands alone
Are fit to tie it; she who sent it can.

VENTIDIUS: Hell! death! this eunuch
    pander ruins you.
You will not see her?

(ALEXAS *whispers an attendant, who goes
out.*)

ANTONY: But to take my leave.

VENTIDIUS: Then I have washed an
    Aethiop. You're undone;
You're in the toils; you're taken; you're
    destroyed;
Her eyes do Caesar's work.

ANTONY: You fear too soon.
I'm constant to myself; I know my
    strength;
And yet she shall not think me barbarous
    neither,
Born in the depths of Afric. I'm a Roman,
Bred to the rules of soft humanity.
A guest, and kindly used, should bid
    farewell.

VENTIDIUS: You do not know
How weak you are to her, how much an
    infant;
You are not proof against a smile or
    glance;
A sigh will quite disarm you.

ANTONY: See, she comes!
Now you shall find your error.—Gods, I
    thank you.
I formed the danger greater than it was,
And now 'tis near, 'tis lessened.

VENTIDIUS: Mark the end yet.

(*Enter* CLEOPATRA, CHARMION, *and* IRAS.)

ANTONY: Well, madam, we are met.

CLEOPATRA: Is this a meeting?
Then, we must part?

ANTONY: We must.

CLEOPATRA: Who says we must?

ANTONY: Our own hard fates.

CLEOPATRA: We make those fates our-
    selves.

ANTONY: Yes, we have made them; we
    have loved each other
Into our mutual ruin.

CLEOPATRA: The gods have seen my
    joys with envious eyes;
I have no friends in heaven, and all the
    world,
As 'twere the business of mankind to part
    us,
Is armed against my love. Even you your-
    self
Join with the rest; you, you are armed
    against me.

ANTONY: I will be justified in all I do

To late posterity, and therefore hear me.
If I mix a lie
With any truth, reproach me freely with
    it;
Else, favor me with silence.

CLEOPATRA: You command me,
And I am dumb.

VENTIDIUS: (*Aside*) I like this well; he
    shows authority.

ANTONY: That I derive my ruin
From you alone—

CLEOPATRA: O heavens! I ruin you!

ANTONY: You promised me your si-
    lence, and you break it
Ere I have scarce begun.

CLEOPATRA: Well, I obey you.

ANTONY: When I beheld you first, it
    was in Egypt.
Ere Caesar saw your eyes, you gave me
    love,
And were too young to know it; that I
    settled
Your father in his throne was for your
    sake;
I left th' acknowledgment for time to
    ripen.
Caesar stepped in and with a greedy hand
Plucked the green fruit ere the first blush
    of red,
Yet cleaving to the bough. He was my
    lord,
And was, beside, too great for me to rival.
But I deserved you first, though he en-
    joyed you.
When, after, I beheld you in Cilicia,
An enemy to Rome, I pardoned you.

CLEOPATRA: I cleared myself—

ANTONY: Again you break your promise.
I loved you still and took your weak ex-
    cuses,
Took you into my bosom, stained by
    Caesar,
And not half mine. I went to Egypt with
    you,

And hid me from the business of the world,
Shut out inquiring nations from my sight
To give whole years to you.

VENTIDIUS: (*Aside*) Yes, to your shame be't spoken.

ANTONY: How I loved,
Witness, ye days and nights and all your hours
That danced away with down upon your feet,
As all your business were to count my passion!
One day passed by and nothing saw but love;
Another came and still 'twas only love.
The suns were wearied out with looking on,
And I untired with loving.
I saw you every day, and all the day;
And every day was still but as the first,
So eager was I still to see you more.

VENTIDIUS: 'Tis all too true.

ANTONY: Fulvia, my wife, grew jealous,
As she indeed had reason; raised a war
In Italy to call me back.

VENTIDIUS: But yet
You went not.

ANTONY: While within your arms I lay,
The world fell moldering from my hands each hour,
And left me scarce a grasp—I thank your love for't.

VENTIDIUS: Well pushed: that last was home.

CLEOPATRA: Yet may I speak?

ANTONY: If I have urged a falsehood, yes; else, not.
Your silence says I have not. Fulvia died
(Pardon, you gods, with my unkindness died);
To set the world at peace I took Octavia,
This Caesar's sister; in her pride of youth

And flower of beauty did I wed that lady,
Whom, blushing, I must praise, because I left her.
You called; my love obeyed the fatal summons.
This raised the Roman arms; the cause was yours,
I would have fought by land where I was stronger;
You hindered it; yet, when I fought at sea,
Forsook me fighting; and (O stain to honor!
O lasting shame!) I knew not that I fled,
But fled to follow you.

VENTIDIUS: What haste she made to hoist her purple sails!
And, to appear magnificent in flight,
Drew half our strength away.

ANTONY: All this you caused.
And would you multiply more ruins on me?
This honest man, my best, my only friend,
Has gathered up the shipwreck of my fortunes;
Twelve legions I have left, my last recruits,
And you have watched the news, and bring your eyes
To seize them, too. If you have aught to answer,
Now speak, you have free leave.

ALEXAS (*Aside*): She stands confounded.
Despair is in her eyes.

VENTIDIUS: Now lay a sigh i'th' way to stop his passage;
Prepare a tear and bid it for his legions;
'Tis like they shall be sold.

CLEOPATRA: How shall I plead my cause when you, my judge,
Already have condemned me? Shall I bring
The love you bore me for my advocate?
That now is turned against me, that destroys me;

For love, once past, is, at the best, for-
gotten,
But oft'ner sours to hate. 'Twill please
my lord
To ruin me, and therefore I'll be guilty.
But could I once have thought it would
have pleased you,
That you would pry, with narrow search-
ing eyes,
Into my faults, severe to my destruction,
And watching all advantages with care
That serve to make me wretched? Speak,
my lord,
For I end here. Though I deserve this
usage,
Was it like you to give it?

ANTONY: Oh, you wrong me
To think I sought this parting or desired
To accuse you more than what will clear
myself
And justify this breach.

CLEOPATRA: Thus low I thank you,
And, since my innocence will not offend,
I shall not blush to own it.

VENTIDIUS (*Aside*):   After this,
I think she'll blush at nothing.

CLEOPATRA: You seem grieved
(And therein you are kind) that Caesar
first
Enjoyed my love, though you deserved it
better.
I grieve for that, my lord, much more
than you;
For, had I first been yours, it would have
saved
My second choice: I never had been his,
And ne'er had been but yours. But Caesar
first,
You say, possessed my love. Not so, my
lord.
He first possessed my person; you, my
love.
Caesar loved me, but I loved Antony.
If I endured him after, 'twas because
I judged it due to the first name of men,

And, half constrained, I gave as to a
tyrant
What he would take by force.

VENTIDIUS: O Siren! Siren!
Yet grant that all the love she boasts were
true,
Has she not ruined you? I still urge that,
The fatal consequence.

CLEOPATRA: The consequence, indeed,
For I dare challenge him, my greatest foe,
To say it was designed. 'Tis true I loved
you,
And kept you far from an uneasy wife,—
Such Fulvia was.
Yes, but he'll say you left Octavia for
me;—
And can you blame me to receive that love
Which quitted such desert for worthless
me?
How often have I wished some other
Caesar,
Great as the first, and as the second, young,
Would court my love to be refused for
you!

VENTIDIUS: Words, words; but Actium,
sir; remember Actium.

CLEOPATRA: Even there I dare his mal-
ice. True, I counseled
To fight at sea, but I betrayed you not.
I fled, but not to the enemy. 'Twas fear.
Would I had been a man, not to have
feared!
For none would then have envied me your
friendship,
Who envy me your love.

ANTONY: We're both unhappy.
If nothing else, yet out ill fortune parts us.
Speak; would you have me perish by my
stay?

CLEOPATRA: If, as a friend, you ask my
judgment, go;
If as a lover, stay. If you must perish—
'Tis a hard word—but stay.

VENTIDIUS: See now th' effects of her
so boasted love!

She strives to drag you down to ruin with
    her;
But could she 'scape without you, oh, how
    soon
Would she let go her hold and haste to
    shore
And never look behind!

CLEOPATRA: Then judge my love by
    this.
            (Giving Antony a writing.)
Could I have borne
A life or death, a happiness or woe
From yours divided, this had given me
    means.

ANTONY: By Hercules, the writing of
    Octavius!
I know it well; 'tis that proscribing hand,
Young as it was, that led the way to mine
And left me but the second place in mur-
    der.—
See, see, Ventidius! here he offers Egypt,
And joins all Syria to it as a present,
So, in requital, she forsake my fortunes
And join her arms with his.

CLEOPATRA: And yet you leave me!
You leave me, Antony; and yet I love
    you,
Indeed I do. I have refused a kingdom;
That's a trifle;
For I could part with life, with anything,
But only you. Oh, let me die but with
    you!
Is that a hard request?

ANTONY: Next living with you,
'Tis all that Heaven can give.

ALEXAS *(Aside)*: He melts; we conquer.

CLEOPATRA: No; you shall go. Your in-
    terest calls you hence;
Yes, your dear interest pulls too strong
    for these
Weak arms to hold you here.
            (Takes his hand.)
Go; leave me, soldier
(For you're no more a lover), leave me
    dying;

Push me, all pale and panting, from your
    bosom,
And, when your march begins, let one
    run after,
Breathless almost for joy, and cry, "She's
    dead."
The soldiers shout; you then perhaps
    may sigh
And muster all your Roman gravity.
Ventidius chides; and straight your brow
    clears up,
As I had never been.

ANTONY: Gods, 'tis too much—
Too much for man to bear.

CLEOPATRA: What is't for me, then,
A weak, forsaken woman and a lover?—
Here let me breathe my last. Envy me not
This minute in your arms. I'll die apace,
As fast as e'er I can, and end your trouble.

ANTONY: Die! Rather let me perish;
    loosened nature
Leap from its hinges! Sink the props of
    heaven,
And fall the skies to crush the nether
    world!
My eyes, my soul, my all!
            (Embraces her.)

VENTIDIUS: And what's this toy
In balance with your fortune, honor,
    fame?

ANTONY: What is't, Ventidius? It out-
    weighs 'em all;
Why, we have more than conquered
    Caesar now.
My queen's not only innocent, but loves
    me.
This, this is she who drags me down to
    ruin!
"But could she 'scape without me, with
    what haste
Would she let slip her hold and make to
    shore
And never look behind!"
Down on thy knees, blasphemer as thou
    art,

And ask forgiveness of wronged innocence.

VENTIDIUS: I'll rather die than take it.
Will you go?

ANTONY: Go! Whither? Go from all
that's excellent!

Faith, honor, virtue, all good things forbid

That I should go from her who sets my
love

Above the price of kingdoms. Give, you
gods,

Give to your boy, your Caesar,

This rattle of a globe to play withal,

This gewgaw world, and put him cheaply
off.

I'll not be pleased with less than Cleopatra.

CLEOPATRA: She's wholly yours. My
heart's so full of joy

That I shall do some wild extravagance

Of love in public, and the foolish world,

Which knows not tenderness, will think
me mad.

VENTIDIUS: O women! women! women!
all the gods

Have not such power of doing good to
man

As you of doing harm.

(*Exit.*)

ANTONY: Our men are armed.

Unbar the gate that looks to Caesar's
camp.

I would revenge the treachery he meant
me;

And long security makes conquest easy.

I'm eager to return before I go,

For all the pleasures I have known beat
thick

On my remembrance.—How I long for
night!

That both the sweets of mutual love may
try,

And once triumph o'er Caesar [ere] we
die.   (*Exeunt.*)

ACT III
SCENE I

(*At one door enter* CLEOPATRA, *CHARM-
ION,* IRAS, *and* ALEXAS, *a train of Egyptians;
at the other,* ANTONY *and Romans. The
entrance on both sides is prepared by
music; the trumpets first sounding on*
ANTONY's *part, then answered by timbrels,
etc., on* CLEOPATRA's. CHARMION *and* IRAS
*hold a laurel wreath betwixt them. A
dance of Egyptians. After the ceremony*
CLEOPATRA *crowns* ANTONY.)

ANTONY: I thought how those white
arms would fold me in,

And strain me close and melt me into
love;

So pleased with that sweet image, I
sprung forwards,

And added all my strength to every blow.

CLEOPATRA: Come to me, come, my
soldier, to my arms!

You've been too long away from my embraces,

But, when I have you fast and all my own,

With broken murmurs and with amorous
sighs

I'll say you were unkind, and punish you,

And mark you red with many an eager
kiss.

ANTONY: My brighter Venus!

CLEOPATRA: O my greater Mars!

ANTONY: Thou join'st us well, my love!

Suppose me come from the Phlegraean
plains[1]

Where gasping giants lay, cleft by my
sword,

And mountain-tops pared off each other
blow

To bury those I slew. Receive me, goddess!

Let Caesar spread his subtle nets, like
Vulcan;

[1] In Macedonia, scene of the battle between
the Gods and the Titans.

In thy embraces I would be beheld
By heaven and earth at once;
And make their envy what they meant
  their sport.
Let those who took us blush; I would love
  on
With awful state, regardless of their
  frowns,
As their superior god.
There's no satiety of love in thee:
Enjoyed, thou still art new; perpetual
  spring
Is in thy arms; the ripened fruit but falls,
And blossoms rise to fill its empty place,
And I grow rich by giving.

(*Enter* VENTIDIUS, *and stands apart.*)

ALEXAS: Oh, now the danger's past,
  your general comes!
He joins not in your joys, nor minds your
  triumphs;
But with contracted brows looks frowning on,
As envying your success.

ANTONY: Now, on my soul, he loves
  me; truly loves me;
He never flattered me in any vice,
But awes me with his virtue. Even this
  minute
Methinks, he has a right of chiding me.—
Lead to the temple—I'll avoid his presence;
It checks too strong upon me.

(*Exeunt the rest.*)

(*As* ANTONY *is going,* VENTIDIUS *pulls him
  by the robe.*)

VENTIDIUS: Emperor!

ANTONY: (*Looking back*) 'Tis the old
  argument. I pr'ythee, spare me.

VENTIDIUS: But this one hearing, emperor.

ANTONY: Let go
My robe; or, by my father Hercules—

VENTIDIUS: By Hercules his father,
  that's yet greater,

I bring you somewhat you would wish to
  know.

ANTONY: Thou see'st we are observed;
  attend me here,
And I'll return.   (*Exit.*)

VENTIDIUS: I'm waning in his favor,
  yet I love him;
I love this man who runs to meet his ruin;
And sure the gods, like me, are fond of
  him.
His virtues lie so mingled with his crimes,
As would confound their choice to pun-
  ish one
And not reward the other.

(*Enter* ANTONY.)

ANTONY: We can conquer,
You see, without your aid.
We have dislodged their troops;
They look on us at distance and, like curs
'Scaped from the lion's paw, they bay far
  off,
And lick their wounds and faintly threat-
  en war.
Five thousand Romans with their faces
  upward
Lie breathless on the plain.

VENTIDIUS: 'Tis well; and he
Who lost them could have spared ten
  thousand more.
Yet if, by this advantage, you could gain
An easier peace while Caesar doubts the
  chance
Of arms—

ANTONY: Oh, think not on't, Ventidius!
The boy pursues my ruin, he'll no peace;
His malice is considerate in advantage.
Oh, he's the coolest murderer! so staunch,
He kills, and keeps his temper.

VENTIDIUS: Have you no friend
In all his army who has power to move
  him?
Maecenas, or Agrippa, might do much.

ANTONY: They're both too deep in
  Caesar's interests.

We'll work it out by dint of sword, or
    perish.
    VENTIDIUS: Fain I would find some
    other.
    ANTONY: Thank thy love.
Some four or five such victories as this
Will save thy further pains.
    VENTIDIUS: Expect no more—Caesar is
    on his guard.
I know, sir, you have conquered against
    odds,
But still you draw supplies from one poor
    town,
And of Egyptians. He has all the world,
And at his back nations come pouring in
To fill the gaps you make. Pray, think
    again,
    ANTONY: Why dost thou drive me
    from myself, to search
For foreign aid?—to hunt my memory,
And range all o'er a waste and barren
    place
To find a friend? The wretched have no
    friends.—
Yet I had one, the bravest youth of Rome,
Whom Caesar loves beyond the love of
    women;
He could resolve his mind as fire does
    wax,
From that hard, rugged image melt him
    down,
And mold him in what softer form he
    pleased.
    VENTIDIUS: Him would I see—that man
    of all the world;
Just such a one we want.
    ANTONY: He loved me, too;
I was his soul; he lived not but in me.
We were so closed within each other's
    breasts,
The rivets were not found that joined us
    first.
That does not reach us yet; we were so
    mixed
As meeting streams, both to ourselves were
    lost;

We were one mass; we could not give or
    take
But from the same, for he was I, I he.
    VENTIDIUS (*Aside*): He moves as I
    would wish him.
    ANTONY: After this
I need not tell his name.—'Twas Dola-
    bella.
    VENTIDIUS: He's now in Caesar's camp.
    ANTONY: No matter where,
Since he's no longer mine. He took un-
    kindly
That I forbade him Cleopatra's sight,
Because I feared he loved her. He con-
    fessed
He had a warmth which, for my sake, he
    stifled,
For 'twere impossible that two, so one,
Should not have loved the same. When
    he departed,
He took no leave, and that confirmed my
    thoughts.
    VENTIDIUS: It argues that he loved you
    more than her,
Else he had stayed. But he perceived you
    jealous,
And would not grieve his friend. I know
    he loves you.
    ANTONY: I should have seen him, then,
    ere now.
    VENTIDIUS: Perhaps
He has thus long been laboring for your
    peace.
    ANTONY: Would he were here!
    VENTIDIUS: Would you believe he loved
    you?
I read your answer in your eyes—you
    would.
Not to conceal it longer, he has sent
A messenger from Caesar's camp with let-
    ters.
    ANTONY: Let him appear.
    VENTIDIUS: I'll bring him instantly.
(*Exit* VENTIDIUS, [*and*] *re-enters imme-
    diately with* DOLABELLA.)

ANTONY: 'Tis he himself, by holy friendship!

(*Runs to embrace him.*)

Art thou returned at last, my better half?
Come, give me all myself! Let me not live,
If the young bridegroom, longing for his night,
Was ever half so fond!

DOLABELLA: I must be silent, for my soul is busy
About a nobler work: she's new come home,
Like a long absent man, and wanders o'er
Each room, a stranger to her own, to look
If all be safe.

ANTONY: Thou hast what's left of me;
For I am now so sunk from what I was,
Thou find'st me at my lowest water-mark.
The rivers that ran in and raised my fortunes
Are all dried up, or take another course;
What I have left is from my native spring.
I've still a heart that swells in scorn of fate
And lifts me to my banks.

DOLABELLA: Still you are lord of all the world to me.

ANTONY: Why, then I yet am so; for thou art all.
If I had any joy when thou wert absent,
I grudged it to myself; methought I robbed
Thee of thy part. But, O my Dolabella!
Thou hast beheld me other than I am.
Hast thou not seen my morning chambers filled
With sceptred slaves who waited to salute me?
With eastern monarchs who forgot the sun
To worship my uprising?—menial kings
Ran coursing up and down my palace-yard
Stood silent in my presence, watched my eyes,

And at my least command all started out
Like racers to the goal.

DOLABELLA: Slaves to your fortune.

ANTONY: Fortune is Caesar's now; and what am I?

VENTIDIUS: What you have made yourself; I will not flatter.

ANTONY: Is this friendly done?

DOLABELLA: Yes; when his end is so, I must join with him;
Indeed, I must; and yet you must not chide;
Why am I else your friend?

ANTONY: Take heed, young man,
How thou upbraid'st my love. The queen has eyes,
And thou, too, hast a soul. Canst thou remember
When, swelled with hatred, thou beheld'st her first,
As accessory to thy brother's death?

DOLABELLA: Spare my remembrance; 'twas a guilty day,
And still the blush hangs here.

ANTHONY: To clear herself
For sending him no aid, she came from Egypt.
Her galley down the silver Cydnos rowed,
The tackling silk, the streamers waved with gold;
The gentle winds were lodged in purple sails;
Her nymphs, like Nereids, round her couch were placed,
Where she, another sea-born Venus, lay.

DOLABELLA: No more; I would not hear it.

ANTONY: Oh, you must!
She lay, and leant her cheek upon her hand,
And cast a look so languishingly sweet
As if, secure of all beholders' hearts,
Neglecting, she could take them. Boys like Cupids

Stood fanning with their painted wings
   the winds
That played about her face; but if she
   smiled,
A darting glory seemed to blaze abroad,
That men's desiring eyes were never
   wearied,
But hung upon the object. To soft flutes
The silver oars kept time; and while they
   played,
The hearing gave new pleasure to the
   sight,
And both, to thought. 'Twas heaven or
   somewhat more;
For she so charmed all hearts, that gazing
   crowds
Stood panting on the shore, and wanted
   breath
To give their welcome voice.
Then, Dolabella, where was then thy soul?
Was not thy fury quite disarmed with
   wonder?
Didst thou not shrink behind me from
   those eyes
And whisper in my ear "Oh, tell her not
That I accused her of my brother's
   death?"

   DOLABELLA: And should my weakness
   be a plea for yours?
Mine was an age when love might be
   excused,
When kindly warmth, and when my
   springing youth,
Made it a debt to nature. Yours—

   VENTIDIUS: Speak boldly.
Yours, he would say, in your declining
   age,
When no more heat was left but what
   you forced,
When all the sap was needful for the
   trunk,
When it went down, then you constrained
   the course,
And robbed from nature to supply desire;
In you (I would not use so harsh a word)
'Tis but plain dotage.

ANTONY: Ha!

   DOLABELLA: 'Twas urged too home.—
But yet the loss was private that I made;
Twas but myself I lost. I lost no legions;
I had no world to lose, no people's love.

ANTONY: This from a friend?

   DOLABELLA: Yes, Antony, a true one;
A friend so tender that each word I speak
Stabs my own heart before it reach your
   ear.
Oh, judge me not less kind because I
   chide!
To Caesar I excuse you.

ANTONY: O ye gods!
Have I then lived to be excused to Caesar?

   DOLABELLA: As to your equal.

ANTONY: Well, he's but my equal;
While I wear this, he never shall be more.

   DOLABELLA: I bring conditions from
   him.

ANTONY: Are they noble?
Methinks thou shouldst not bring them
   else; yet he
Is full of deep dissembling; knows no
   honor
Divided from his interest. Fate mistook
   him,
For nature meant him for an usurer;
He's fit indeed to buy, not conquer, king-
   doms.

   VENTIDIUS: Then, granting this,
What power was theirs who wrought so
   hard a temper
To honorable terms?

ANTONY: It was my Dolabella, or some
   god.

   DOLABELLA: Nor I, not yet Maecenas,
   nor Agrippa;
They were your enemies, and I, a friend,
Too weak alone; yet 'twas a Roman's
   deed.

ANTONY: 'Twas like a Roman done;
   show me that man

Who has preserved my life, my love, my
    honor;
Let me but see his face.

VENTIDIUS: That task is mine,
And, Heaven, thou know'st how pleasing.
                (*Exit* VENTIDIUS.)

DOLABELLA: You'll remember
To whom you stand obliged?

ANTONY: When I forget it,
Be thou unkind, and that's my greatest
    curse.
My queen shall thank him, too.

DOLABELLA: I fear she will not.

ANTONY: But she shall do't—the queen,
    my Dolabella!
Hast thou not still some grudgings of thy
    fever?

DOLABELLA: I would not see her lost.

ANTONY: When I forsake her,
Leave me, my better stars! for she has
    truth
Beyond her beauty. Caesar tempted her,
At no less price than kingdoms, to betray
    me,
But she resisted all; and yet thou chid'st
    me
For loving her too well. Could I do so?

(*Re-enter* VENTIDIUS *with* OCTAVIA, *leading*
ANTONY's *two little Daughters.*)

DOLABELLA: Yes; there's my reason.

ANTONY: Where?—Octavia there!
                (*Starting back.*)

VENTIDIUS: What—is she poison to you?
    a disease?
Look on her, view her well, and those she
    brings.
Are they all strangers to your eyes? has
    nature
No secret call, no whisper they are yours?

DOLABELLA: For shame, my lord, if not
    for love, receive them
With kinder eyes. If you confess a man,
Meet them, embrace them, bid them wel-
    come to you.

Your arms should open, even without
    your knowledge,
To clasp them in; your feet should turn to
    wings,
To bear you to them; and your eyes dart
    out
And aim a kiss ere you could reach the
    lips.

ANTONY: I stood amazed to think how
    they came hither.

VENTIDIUS: I sent for 'em; I brought
    'em in, unknown
To Cleopatra's guards.

DOLABELLA: Yet are you cold?

OCTAVIA: Thus long have I attended
    for my welcome,
Which, as a stranger, sure I might expect.
Who am I?

ANTONY: Caesar's sister.

OCTAVIA: That's unkind.
Had I been nothing more than Caesar's
    sister,
Know, I had still remained in Caesar's
    camp.
But your Octavia, your much injured
    wife,
Though banished from your bed, driven
    from your house,
In spite of Caesar's sister, still is yours.
'Tis true, I have a heart disdains your
    coldness,
And prompts me not to seek what you
    should offer;
But a wife's virtue still surmounts that
    pride.
I come to claim you as my own; to show
My duty first; to ask, nay beg, your kind-
    ness.
Your hand, my lord; 'tis mine, and I will
    have it.   (*Taking his hand.*)

VENTIDIUS: Do, take it; thou deserv'st it.

DOLABELLA: On my soul,
And so she does; she's neither too sub-
    missive,
Nor yet too haughty; but so just a mean

Shows, as it ought, a wife and Roman too.

ANTONY: I fear, Octavia, you have begged my life.

OCTAVIA: Begged it, my lord?

ANTONY: Yes, begged it, my ambassadress;
Poorly and basely begged it of your brother.

OCTAVIA: Poorly and basely I could never beg.
Nor could my brother grant.

ANTONY: Shall I, who, to my kneeling slave, could say,
"Rise up and be a king," shall I fall down
And cry, "Forgive me, Caesar?" Shall I set
A man, my equal, in the place of Jove,
As he could give me being? No—that word
"Forgive" would choke me up
And die upon my tongue.

DOLABELLA: You shall not need it.

ANTONY: I will not need it. Come, you've all betrayed me—
My friend too!—to receive some vile conditions.
My wife has bought me with her prayers and tears,
And now I must become her branded slave.
In every peevish mood she will upbraid
The life she gave; if I but look awry,
She cries, "I'll tell my brother."

OCTAVIA: My hard fortune
Subjects me still to your unkind mistakes.
But the conditions I have brought are such
You need not blush to take; I love your honor,
Because 'tis mine. It never shall be said
Octavia's husband was her brother's slave.
Sir, you are free—free, even from her you loathe;
For, though my brother bargains for your love,

Makes me the price and cément of your peace,
I have a soul like yours; I cannot take
Your love as alms, nor beg what I deserve.
I'll tell my brother we are reconciled;
He shall draw back his troops, and you shall march
To rule the East. I may be dropped at Athens—
No matter where. I never will complain,
But only keep the barren name of wife,
And rid you of the trouble.

VENTIDIUS: Was ever such a strife of sullen honor!
Both scorn to be obliged.

DOLABELLA: Oh, she has touched him in the tenderest part;
See how he reddens with despite and shame,
To be outdone in generosity!

VENTIDIUS: See how he winks! how he dries up a tear,
That fain would fall!

ANTONY: Octavia, I have heard you, and must praise
The greatness of your soul;
But cannot yield to what you have proposed,
For I can ne'er be conquered but by love,
And you do all for duty. You would free me,
And would be dropped at Athens; was't not so?

OCTAVIA: It was, my lord.

ANTONY: Then I must be obliged
To one who loves me not; who, to herself,
May call me thankless and ungrateful man.—
I'll not endure it—no.

VENTIDIUS (Aside): I am glad it pinches there.

OCTAVIA: Would you triumph o'er poor Octavia's virtue?
That pride was all I had to bear me up;

That you might think you owed me for
    your life,
And owed it to my duty, not my love.
I have been injured, and my haughty soul
Could brook but ill the man who slights
    my bed.

ANTONY: Therefore you love me not.

OCTAVIA: Therefore, my lord,
I should not love you.

ANTONY: Therefore you would leave
    me?

OCTAVIA: And therefore I should leave
    you—if I could.

DOLABELLA: Her soul's too great, after
    such injuries,
To say she loves; and yet she lets you see it.
Her modesty and silence plead her cause.

ANTONY: O Dolabella, which way shall
    I turn?
I find a secret yielding in my soul;
But Cleopatra, who would die with me,
Must she be left? Pity pleads for Octavia,
But does it not plead more for Cleopatra?

VENTIDIUS: Justice and pity both plead
    for Octavia;
For Cleopatra, neither.
One would be ruined with you, but she
    first
Had ruined you; the other, you have
    ruined,
And yet she would preserve you.
In everything their merits are unequal.

ANTONY: O my distracted soul!

OCTAVIA: Sweet Heaven, compose it!—
Come, come, my lord, if I can pardon you,
Methinks you should accept it. Look on
    these—
Are they not yours? or stand they thus
    neglected
As they are mine? Go to him, children,
    go;
Kneel to him, take him by the hand, speak
    to him,
For you may speak and he may own you,
    too,

Without a blush—and so he cannot all
His children. Go, I say, and pull him to
    me,
And pull him to yourselves from that bad
    woman.
You, Agrippina, hang upon his arms,
And you, Antonia, clasp about his waist.
If he will shake you off, if he will dash
    you
Against the pavement, you must bear it,
    children,
For you are mine, and I was born to
    suffer.

(*Here the Children go to him, etc.*)

VENTIDIUS: Was ever sight so moving?
    —Emperor!

DOLABELLA: Friend!

OCTAVIA: Husband!

BOTH CHILDREN: Father!

ANTONY: I am vanquished. Take me,
Octavia—take me, children—share me all.
        (*Embracing them.*)
I've been a thriftless debtor to your loves,
And run out much, in riot, from your
    stock,
But all shall be amended.

OCTAVIA: O blest hour!

DOLABELLA: O happy change!

VENTIDIUS: My joy stops at my tongue,
But it has found two channels here for
    one,
And bubbles out above.

ANTONY: (*To Octavia.*) This is thy
    triumph. Lead me where thou wilt,
Even to thy brother's camp.

OCTAVIA: All there are yours.

(*Enter* ALEXAS *hastily.*)

ALEXAS: The queen, my mistress, sir,
    and yours—

ANTONY: 'Tis past.—
Octavia, you shall stay this night. To-
    morrow
Caesar and we are one.

(*Exit, leading* OCTAVIA; DOLABELLA *and
the Children follow.*)

VENTIDIUS: There's news for you! Run,
my officious eunuch,
Be sure to be the first—haste forward!
Haste, my dear eunuch, haste!   (*Exit.*)

ALEXAS: This downright fighting fool,
this thick-skulled hero,
This blunt, unthinking instrument of
death,
With plain, dull virtue has outgone my
wit.
Pleasure forsook my earliest infancy;
The luxury of others robbed my cradle,
And ravished thence the promise of a
man.
Cast out from nature, disinherited
Of what her meanest children claim by
kind,
Yet greatness kept me from contempt.
That's gone
Had Cleopatra followed my advice,
Then he had been betrayed who now for-
sakes.
She dies for love, but she has known its
joys.
Gods, is this just that I, who know no joys,
Must die because she loves?

(*Enter* CLEOPATRA, CHARMION, IRAS, [*and*]
train.)

O madam, I have seen what blasts my
eyes!
Octavia's here.

CLEOPATRA: Peace with that raven's
note.
I know it, too, and now am in
The pangs of death.

ALEXAS: You are no more a queen—
Egypt is lost.

CLEOPATRA: What tell'st thou me of
Egypt?
My life, my soul is lost! Octavia has
him!—
O fatal name to Cleopatra's love!
My kisses, my embraces now are hers,

While I—But thou hast seen my rival.
Speak—
Does she deserve this blessing? Is she fair?
Bright as a goddess? and is all perfection
Confined to her?—It is. Poor I was made
Of that coarse matter which, when she
was finished,
The gods threw by for rubbish.

ALEXAS: She's indeed a very miracle.

CLEOPATRA: Death to my hopes, a
miracle!

ALEXAS: (*Bowing.*)   A miracle—
I mean, of goodness; for in beauty,
madam,
You make all wonders cease.

CLEOPATRA: I was too rash.
Take this in part of recompense. But, oh!

(*Giving a ring.*)

I fear thou flatter'st me.

CHARMION: She comes! She's here!

IRAS: Fly, madam, Caesar's sister!

CLEOPATRA: Were she the sister of the
thunderer Jove,
And bore her brother's lightning in her
eye,
Thus would I face my rival.

(*Meets* OCTAVIA *with* VENTIDIUS. OCTAVIA
*bears up to her. Their trains come up on
either side.*)

OCTAVIA: I need not ask if you are Cleopatra,
Your haughty carriage—

CLEOPATRA: Shows I am a queen.
Nor need I ask you who you are.

OCTAVIA: A Roman;
A name that makes and can unmake a
queen.

CLEOPATRA: Your lord, the man who
serves me, is a Roman.

OCTAVIA: He was a Roman, till he lost
that name
To be a slave in Egypt; but I come
To free him thence.

CLEOPATRA: Peace, peace, my lover's Juno.
When he grew weary of that household clog,
He chose my easier bonds.

OCTAVIA: I wonder not
Your bonds are easy. You have long been practised
In that lascivious art. He's not the first
For whom you spread your snares: let Caesar witness.

CLEOPATRA: I loved not Caesar; 'twas but gratitude
I paid his love. The worst your malice can
Is but to say the greatest of mankind
Has been my slave. The next, but far above him
In my esteem, is he whom law calls yours,
But whom his love made mine.

OCTAVIA: (Coming up closer to her)
I would view nearer
That face which has so long usurped my right,
To find the inevitable charms that catch
Mankind so sure, that ruined my dear lord.

CLEOPATRA: Oh, you do well to search, for had you known
But half these charms, you had not lost his heart.

OCTAVIA: Far be their knowledge from a Roman lady—
Far from a modest wife! Shame of our sex,
Dost thou not blush to own those black endearments
That make sin pleasing?

CLEOPATRA: You may blush, who want them.
If bounteous nature, if indulgent heaven
Have given me charms to please the bravest man,
Should I not thank them? Should I be ashamed,
And not be proud? I am, that he has loved me.

And when I love not him, heaven change this face
For one like that.

OCTAVIA: Thou lov'st him not so well.

CLEOPATRA: I love him better, and deserve him more.

OCTAVIA: You do not—cannot. You have been his ruin.
Who made him cheap at Rome but Cleopatra?
Who made him scorned abroad but Cleopatra?
At Actium, who betrayed him? Cleopatra!
Who made his children orphans, and poor me
A wretched widow? Only Cleopatra.

CLEOPATRA: Yet she who loves him best is Cleopatra.
If you have suffered, I have suffered more.
You bear the specious title of a wife
To gild your cause and draw the pitying world
To favor it. The world contemns poor me,
For I have lost my honor, lost my fame,
And stained the glory of my royal house,
And all to bear the branded name of mistress.
There wants but life, and that, too, I would lose
For him I love.

OCTAVIA: Be't so, then; take thy wish.

(Exit with her train.)

CLEOPATRA: And 'tis my wish,
Now he is lost for whom alone I lived.
My sight grows dim, and every object dances
And swims before me in the maze of death.
My spirits, while they were opposed, kept up;
They could not sink beneath a rival's scorn,
But now she's gone, they faint.

ALEXAS: Mine have had leisure
To recollect their strength and furnish counsel
To ruin her, who else must ruin you.

CLEOPATRA: Vain promiser!
Lead me, my Charmion; nay, your hand,
    too, Iras.
My grief has weight enough to sink you
    both.
Conduct me to some solitary chamber,
And draw the curtains round;
Then leave me to myself, to take alone
My fill of grief.
There I till death will his unkindness
    weep,
As harmless infants moan themselves
    asleep.

                                (*Exeunt.*)

ACT IV
SCENE I

([*Enter*] ANTONY [*and*] DOLABELLA.)

DOLABELLA: Why would you shift it
    from yourself on me?
Can you not tell her you must part?
    ANTONY: I cannot.
I could pull out an eye and bid it go,
And t'other should not weep. O Dolabella,
How many deaths are in this word, *Depart!*
I dare not trust my tongue to tell her so—
One look of hers would thaw me into
    tears,
And I should melt till I were lost again.
    DOLABELLA: Then let Ventidius—
He's rough by nature.
    ANTONY: Oh, he'll speak too harshly;
He'll kill her with the news. Thou, only
    thou!
    DOLABELLA: Nature has cast me in so
    soft a mould
That but to hear a story feigned for
    pleasure,
Of some sad lover's death moistens my
    eyes,

And robs me of my manhood. I should
    speak
So faintly, with such fear to grieve her
    heart,
She'd not believe it earnest.
    ANTONY: Therefore—therefore
Thou, only thou are fit. Think thyself me,
And when thou speak'st (but let it first
    be long),
Take off the edge from every sharper
    sound,
And let our parting be as gently made
As other loves begin. Wilt thou do this?
    DOLABELLA: What you have said so
    sinks into my soul
That, if I must speak, I shall speak just so.
    ANTONY: I leave you then to your sad
    task.
Farewell!
I sent her word to meet you.

        (*Goes to the door and comes back.*)
                                    I forgot.
Let her be told I'll make her peace with
    mine.
Her crown and dignity shall be preserved,
If I have power with Caesar.—Oh, be
    sure
To think on that!
    DOLABELLA: Fear not, I will remember.

    (ANTONY *goes again to the door and
            comes back.*)

    ANTONY: And tell her, too, how much
    I was constrained;
I did not this but with extremest force.
Desire her not to hate my memory,
For I still cherish hers;—insist on that.
    DOLABELLA: Trust me, I'll not forget it.
    ANTONY: Then that's all.
        (*Goes out and returns again.*)
Wilt thou forgive my fondness this once
    more?
Tell her, though we shall never meet
    again,
If I should hear she took another love,

The news would break my heart.—Now
    I must go,
For every time I have returned, I feel
My soul more tender, and my next com-
    mand
Would be to bid her stay, and ruin both.

                                (*Exit.*)

DOLABELLA: Men are but children of a
    larger growth;
Our appetites as apt to change as theirs,
And full as craving, too, and full as vain;
And yet the soul, shut up in her dark
    room,
Viewing so clear abroad, at home sees
    nothing;
But like a mole in earth, busy and blind,
Works all her folly up and casts it out-
    ward
To the world's open view. Thus I dis-
    covered,
And blamed, the love of ruined Antony,
Yet wish that I were he, to be so ruined.

        (*Enter* VENTIDIUS *above.*)

VENTIDIUS: Alone, and talking to him-
    self? concerned, too?
Perhaps my guess is right; he loved her
    once,
And may pursue it still.

DOLABELLA: O friendship! friendship!
Ill canst thou answer this; and reason,
    worse.
Unfaithful in the attempt; hopeless to win;
And, if I win, undone; mere madness all.
And yet the occasion's fair. What injury
To him, to wear the robe which he throws
    by?

VENTIDIUS: None, none at all. This hap-
    pens as I wish,
To ruin her yet more with Antony.

(*Enter* CLEOPATRA, *talking with* ALEXAS;
    CHARMION, IRAS *on the other side.*)

DOLLABELLA: She comes! What charms
    have sorrow on that face!
Sorrow seems pleased to dwell with so
    much sweetness;

Yet, now and then, a melancholy smile
Breaks loose like lightning in a winter's
    night,
And shows a moment's day.

    VENTIDIUS: If she should love him, too
        —her eunuch there!
That porc-pisce[1] bodes ill weather. Draw,
    draw nearer,
Sweet devil, that I may hear.

    ALEXAS: Believe me, try

(DOLABELLA *goes over to* CHARMION *and*
    IRAS; *seems to talk with them.*)

To make him jealous; jealousy is like
A polished glass held to the lips when
    life's in doubt;
If there be breath, 'twil catch the damp,
    and show it.

    CLEOPATRA: I grant you, jealousy's a
        proof of love,
But 'tis a weak and unavailing medicine;
It puts out the disease, and makes it show,
But has no power to cure.

    ALEXAS: 'Tis your last remedy, and
        strongest, too.
And then this Dolabella—who so fit
To practise on? He's handsome, valiant,
    young,
And looks as he were laid for nature's
    bait
To catch weak women's eyes.
He stands already more than half sus-
    pected
Of loving you. The least kind word or
    glance
You give this youth will kindle him with
    love;
Then, like a burning vessel set adrift,
You'll send him down amain before the
    wind
To fire the heart of jealous Antony.

    CLEOPATRA: Can I do this? Ah, no. My
        love's so true
That I can neither hide it where it is,

---

[1] Porcus pisces; porpoise.

Nor show it where it is not. Nature meant
    me
A wife—a silly, harmless, household dove,
Fond without art, and kind without de-
    ceit;
But Fortune, that has made a mistress of
    me,
[Has] thrust me out to the wide world,
    unfurnished
Of falsehood to be happy.

    ALEXAS: Force yourself.
The event will be, your lover will return
Doubly desirous to possess the good
Which once he feared to lose.

    CLEOPATRA: I must attempt it,

                      (*Exit* ALEXAS.)
But oh, with what regret!

    (*She comes up to* DOLABELLA.)

    VENTIDIUS: So, now the scene draws
      near; they're in my reach.

    CLEOPATRA: (*To* DOLABELLA) Discours-
      ing with my women! Might not I
Share in your entertainment?

    CHARMION: You have been
The subject of it, madam.

    CLEOPATRA: How! and how?

    IRAS: Such praises of your beauty!

    CLEOPATRA: Mere poetry.
Your Roman wits, your Gallus and Tibul-
    lus;
Have taught you this from Cytheris and
    Delia.

    DOLABELLA: Those Roman wits have
      never been in Egypt;
Cytheris and Delia else had been unsung.
I, who have seen—had I been born a poet,
Should choose a nobler name.

    CLEOPATRA: You flatter me.
But 'tis your nation's vice. All of your
    country
Are flatterers, and all false. Your friend's
    like you.
I'm sure he sent you not to speak these
    words.

    DOLABELLA: No, madam, yet he sent
      me—

    CLEOPATRA: Well, he sent you—

    DOLABELLA: Of a less pleasing errand.

    CLEOPATRA: How less pleasing?
Less to yourself, or me?

    DOLABELLA: Madam, to both.
For you must mourn, and I must grieve
    to cause it.

    CLEOPATRA: You, Charmion, and your
      fellow, stand at distance—
(*Aside*) Hold up, my spirits.—Well, now
    your mournful matter,
For I'm prepared—perhaps can guess it,
    too.

    DOLABELLA: I wish you would, for 'tis a
      thankless office
To tell ill news; and I, of all your sex,
Most fear displeasing you.

    CLEOPATRA: Of all your sex
I soonest could forgive you if you should.

    VENTIDIUS: Most delicate advances!
      Woman! woman!
Dear, damned, inconstant sex!

    CLEOPATRA: In the first place,
I am to be forsaken. Is't not so?

    DOLABELLA: I wish I could not answer
      to that question.

    CLEOPATRA: Then pass it o'er, because
      it troubles you;
I should have been more grieved another
    time.
Next, I'm to lose my kingdom—Farewell,
    Egypt!
Yet, is there any more?

    DOLABELLA: Madam, I fear
Your too deep sense of grief has turned
    your reason.

    CLEOPATRA: No, no, I'm not run mad;
      I can bear fortune,
And love may be expelled by other love,
As poisons are by poisons.

    DOLABELLA: You o'erjoy me, madam,
To find your griefs so moderately borne.

You've heard the worst; all are not false like him.

CLEOPATRA: No. Heaven forbid they should.

DOLABELLA: Some men are constant.

CLEOPATRA: And constancy deserves reward, that's certain.

DOLABELLA: Deserves it not, but give it leave to hope.

VENTIDIUS: I'll swear thou hast my leave. I have enough.—
But how to manage this! Well, I'll consider.   (*Exit.*)

DOLABELLA: I came prepared
To tell you heavy news—news which, I thought,
Would fright the blood from your pale cheeks to hear,
But you have met it with a cheerfulness
That makes my task more easy; and my tongue,
Which on another's message was employed,
Would gladly speak its own.

CLEOPATRA: Hold, Dolabella.
First tell me, were you chosen by my lord?
Or sought you this employment?

DOLABELLA: He picked me out; and, as his bosom friend,
He charged me with his words.

CLEOPATRA: The message then
I know was tender, and each accent smooth,
To mollify that rugged word, Depart.

DOLABELLA: Oh, you mistake. He chose the harshest words;
With fiery eyes and with contracted brows
He coined his face in the severest stamp;
And fury shook his fabric like an earthquake;
He heaved for vent, and burst like bellowing Aetna.
In sounds scarce human—"Hence, away, for ever,

Let her begone, the blot of my renown,
And bane of all my hopes!

(*All the time of this speech* CLEOPATRA *seems more and more concerned till she sinks quite down.*)

Let her be driven as far as men can think
From man's commèrce! she'll poison to the center."

CLEOPATRA: Oh, I can bear no more!

DOLABELLA: Help, help!—O wretch! O cursèd, cursèd wretch!
What have I done!

CHARMION: Help, chafe her temples, Iras.

IRAS: Bend, bend her forward quickly.

CHARMION: Heaven be praised,
She comes again.

CLEOPATRA: Oh, let him not approach me.
Why have you brought me back to this loathed being,
The abode of falsehood, violated vows,
And injured love? For pity, let me go;
For, if there be a place of long repose,
I'm sure I want it. My disdainful lord
Can never break that quiet, nor awake
The sleeping soul with hollowing in my tomb
Such words as fright her hence.—Unkind, unkind!

DOLABELLA: (*Kneeling*) Believe me, 'tis against myself I speak.
That sure deserves belief—I injured him:
My friend ne'er spoke those words. Oh, had you seen
How often he came back, and every time
With something more obliging and more kind
To add to what he said; what dear farewells;
How almost vanquished by his love he parted,
And leaned to what unwillingly he left!
I, traitor as I was, for love of you

(But what can you not do, who made me
    false?)
I forged that lie; for whose forgiveness
    kneels
This self-accused, self-punished criminal.
    CLEOPATRA: With how much ease be-
    lieve we what we wish!
Rise, Dolabella; if you have been guilty,
I have contributed, and too much love
Has made me guilty too.
The advance of kindness which I made
    was feigned
To call back fleeting love by jealousy,
But 'twould not last. Oh, rather let me
    lose
Than so ignobly trifle with his heart!
    DOLABELLA: I find your breast fenced
    round from human reach,
Transparent as a rock of solid crystal,
Seen through, but never pierced. My
    friend, my friend!
What endless treasure hast thou thrown
    away,
And scattered, like an infant, in the ocean,
Vain sums of wealth, which none can
    gather thence!
    CLEOPATRA: Could you not beg
An hour's admittance to his private ear?
Like one who wanders through long bar-
    ren wilds,
And yet foreknows no hospitable inn
Is near to succor hunger, eats his fill
Before his painful march,
So would I feed a while my famished eyes
Before we part, for I have far to go,
If death be far, and never must return.
    ([Enter] VENTIDIUS with OCTAVIA, behind.)
    VENTIDIUS: From hence you may dis-
    cover—Oh, sweet, sweet!
Would you, indeed? The pretty hand in
    earnest?
    DOLABELLA: I will, for this reward.
        (Takes her hand)
                Draw it not back,
'Tis all I e'er will beg.
    VENTIDIUS: They turn upon us.

OCTAVIA: What quick eyes has guilt!
VENTIDIUS: Seem not to have observed
    them, and go on.
                        (They enter.)
DOLABELLA: Saw you the emperor,
    Ventidius?
VENTIDIUS: No.
I sought him, but I heard that he was
    private,
None with him but Hipparchus, his freed-
    man.
DOLABELLA: Know you his business?
VENTIDIUS: Giving him instructions
And letters to his brother Caesar.
DOLABELLA: Well,
He must be found.
    (Exeunt DOLABELLA and CLEOPATRA.)
OCTAVIA: Most glorious impudence!
VENTIDIUS: She looked, methought,
As she would say, "Take your old man,
    Octavia,
Thank you, I'm better here." Well, but
    what use
Make we of this discovery?
OCTAVIA: Let it die.
VENTIDIUS: I pity Dolabella. But she's
    dangerous;
Her eyes have power beyond Thessalian
    charms
To draw the moon from heaven; for elo-
    quence,
The sea-green Syrens taught her voice
    their flatt'ry;
And while she speaks, night steals upon
    the day,
Unmarked of those that hear. Then she's
    so charming
Age buds at sight of her, and swells to
    youth;
The holy priests gaze on her when she
    smiles,
And with heaved hands, forgetting
    gravity,
They bless her wanton eyes. Even I, who
    hate her,

With a malignant joy behold such beauty,
And while I curse, desire it. Antony
Must needs have some remains of passion
　　still,
Which may ferment into a worse relapse
It now not fully cured. I know, this
　　minute,
With Caesar he's endeavoring her peace.

OCTAVIA: You have prevailed:—But for
　　a further purpose

　　　　　　　　　(Walks off.)

I'll prove how he will relish this discovery.
What, make a strumpet's peace! it swells
　　my heart;
It must not, shall not be.

VENTIDIUS: 　　　His guards appear.
Let me begin, and you shall second me.

　　　　　(Enter ANTONY.)

ANTONY: Octavia, I was looking you,
　　my love.
What, are your letters ready? I have given
My last instructions.

OCTAVIA: 　　Mine, my lord, are written.

ANTONY: Ventidius.

　　　　　(Drawing him aside.)

VENTIDIUS: 　　　My lord?

ANTONY: 　　　A word in private.—
When saw you Dolabella?

VENTIDIUS: 　　　　Now, my lord,
He parted hence; and Cleopatra with him.

ANTONY: Speak softly.—'Twas by my
　　command he went
To bear my last farewell.

VENTIDIUS: (Aloud) It looked indeed
　　Like your farewell.

ANTONY: 　　More softly.—My farewell?
What secret meaning have you in those
　　words
Of "my farewell?" He did it by my
　　order.

VENTIDIUS: (Aloud) Then he obeyed
　　your order. I suppose
You bid him do it with all gentleness,
All kindness, and all—love.

ANTONY: 　　　　How she mourned,
The poor forsaken creature!

VENTIDIUS: She took it as she ought;
　　she bore your parting
As she did Caesar's, as she would an-
　　other's,
Were a new love to come.

ANTONY: (Aloud) Thou dost belie her;
Most basely and maliciously belie her.

VENTIDIUS: I thought not to displease
　　you; I have done.

OCTAVIA: (Coming up) You seem dis-
　　turbed, my lord.

ANTONY: 　　　　A very trifle.
Retire, my love.

VENTIDIUS: It was indeed a trifle.
He sent—

ANTONY: (Angrily) No more. Look
　　how thou disobey'st me;
Thy life shall answer it.

OCTAVIA: 　　　Then 'tis no trifle.

VENTIDIUS: (To OCTAVIA) 'Tis less—a
　　very nothing. You too saw it,
As well as I, and therefore 'tis no secret.

ANTONY: She saw it!

VENTIDIUS: Yes. She saw young Dola-
　　bella—

ANTONY: Young Dolabella!

VENTIDIUS: Young, I think him young,
And handsome too, and so do others think
　　him.
But what of that? He went by your
　　command,
Indeed, 'tis probable, with some kind mes-
　　sage,
For she received it graciously; she smiled;
And then he grew familiar with her hand,
Squeezed it, and worried it with ravenous
　　kisses;
She blushed, and sighed, and smiled, and
　　blushed again;
At last she took occasion to talk softly,
And brought her cheek up close, and
　　leaned on his;

At which, he whispered kisses back on
  hers;
And then she cried aloud that constancy
Should be rewarded.

OCTAVIA: This I saw and heard.

ANTONY: What woman was it whom
  you heard and saw
So playful with my friend? Not Cleopatra?

VENTIDIUS: Even she, my lord.

ANTONY: My Cleopatra?

VENTIDIUS: Your Cleopatra;
Dolabella's Cleopatra;
Every man's Cleopatra.

ANTONY: Thou liest.

VENTIDIUS: I do not lie, my lord.
Is this so strange? Should mistresses be
  left,
And not provide against a time of change?
You know she's not much used to lonely
  nights.

ANTONY: I'll think no more on't.
I know 'tis false, and see the plot betwixt
  you.—
You needed not have gone this way,
  Octavia.
What harms it you that Cleopatra's just?
She's mine no more. I see, and I forgive.
Urge it no further, love.

OCTAVIA: Are you concerned
That she's found false?

ANTONY: I should be, were it so,
For though 'tis past, I would not that the
  world
Should tax my former choice, that I loved
  one
Of so light note, but I forgive you both.

VENTIDIUS: What has my age deserved
  that you should think
I would abuse your ears with perjury?
If Heaven be true, she's false.

ANTONY: Though heaven and earth
Should witness it, I'll not believe her
  tainted.

VENTIDIUS: I'll bring you, then, a witness
From hell to prove her so.—Nay, go not
  back,

(*Seeing* ALEXAS *just entering, and starting
  back.*)

For stay you must and shall.

ALEXAS: What means my lord?

VENTIDIUS: To make you do what most
  you hate,—speak truth.
You are of Cleopatra's private counsel,
Of her bed-counsel, her lascivious hours;
Are conscious of each nightly change she
  makes,
And watch her, as Chaldaeans do the
  moon,
Can tell what signs she passes through,
  what day.

ALEXAS: My noble lord!

VENTIDIUS: My most illustrious pander,
No fine set speech, no cadence, no turned
  periods,
But a plain homespun truth is what I ask:
I did myself o'erhear your queen make
  love
To Dolabella. Speak. For I will know
By your confession what more passed be-
  twixt them;
How near the business draws to your
  employment;
And when the happy hour.

ANTONY: Speak truth, Alexas; whether
  it offend
Or please Ventidius, care not. Justify
Thy injured queen from malice. Dare his
  worst.

OCTAVIA: (*Aside*) See how he gives him
  courage! how he fears
To find her false! and shuts his eyes to
  truth,
Willing to be misled!

ALEXAS: As far as love may plead for
  woman's frailty,
Urged by desert and greatness of the
  lover,

So far, divine Octavia, may my queen
Stand even excused to you for loving him
Who is your lord; so far, from brave
Ventidius,
May her past actions hope a fair report.

ANTONY: 'Tis well, and truly spoken.
Mark, Ventidius.

ALEXAS: To you, most noble emperor,
her strong passion
Stands not excused, but wholly justified.
Her beauty's charms alone, without her
crown,
From Ind and Meroë[2] drew the distant
vows
Of sighing kings; and at her feet were laid
The sceptres of the earth exposed on heaps,
To choose where she would reign.
She thought a Roman only could deserve
her,
And of all Romans only Antony;
And, to be less than wife to you, disdained
Their lawful passion.

ANTONY: 'Tis but truth.

ALEXAS: And yet, though love and
your unmatched desert
Have drawn her from the due regard of
honor,
At last Heaven opened her unwilling
eyes
To see the wrongs she offered fair Octavia,
Whose holy bed she lawlessly usurped.
The sad effects of this improsperous war
Confirmed those pious thoughts.

VENTIDIUS: (Aside) Oh, wheel you
there?
Observe him now; the man begins to
mend,
And talk substantial reason.—Fear not,
eunuch,
The emperor has given thee leave to
speak.

ALEXAS: Else had I never dared to
offend his ears
With what the last necessity has urged

2 Upper Egypt.

On my forsaken mistress; yet I must not
Presume to say her heart is wholly altered.

ANTONY: No, dare not for thy life, I
charge thee dare not
Pronounce that fatal word!

OCTAVIA: (Aside) Must I bear this?
Good heaven, afford me patience!

VENTIDIUS: On, sweet eunuch; my dear
half-man, proceed.

ALEXAS: Yet Dolabella
Has loved her long. He, next my god-
like lord,
Deserves her best; and should she meet
his passion,
Rejected as she is by him she loved—

ANTONY: Hence from my sight! for I
can bear no more.
Let furies drag thee quick to hell; let all
The longer damned have rest; each tor-
turing hand
Do thou employ till Cleopatra comes;
Then join thou too, and help to torture
her!

(Exit ALEXAS, thrust out by ANTONY.)

OCTAVIA: 'Tis not well,
Indeed, my lord, 'tis much unkind to me,
To show this passion, this extreme con-
cernment
For an abandoned, faithless prostitute.

ANTONY: Octavia, leave me. I am much
disordered.
Leave me, I say.

OCTAVIA: My lord!

ANTONY: I bid you leave me.

VENTIDIUS: Obey him, madam. Best
withdraw a while,
And see how this will work.

OCTAVIA: Wherein have I offended you,
my lord,
That I am bid to leave you? Am I false
Or infamous? Am I a Cleopatra?
Were I she,
Base as she is, you would not bid me
leave you,

But hang upon my neck, take slight
excuses,
And fawn upon my falsehood.

ANTONY: 'Tis too much,
Too much, Octavia. I am pressed with
sorrows
Too heavy to be borne, and you add more.
I would retire and recollect what's left
Of man within, to aid me.

OCTAVIA: You would mourn
In private for your love, who has betrayed
you.
You did but half return to me; your kind-
ness
Lingered behind with her. I hear, my lord,
You make conditions for her,
And would include her treaty. Wondrous
proofs
Of love to me!

ANTONY: Are you my friend, Ventidius?
Or are you turned a Dolabella too,
And let this Fury loose?

VENTIDIUS: Oh, be advised,
Sweet madam, and retire.

OCTAVIA: Yes, I will go, but never to
return.
You shall no more be haunted with this
Fury.
My lord, my lord, love will not always last
When urged with long unkindness and
disdain.
Take her again whom you prefer to me;
She stays but to be called. Poor cozened
man!
Let a feigned parting give her back your
heart,
Which a feigned love first got; for injured
me,
Though my just sense of wrongs forbid
my stay,
My duty shall be yours.
To the dear pledges of our former love
My tenderness and care shall be trans-
ferred,
And they shall cheer, by turns, my wid-
owed nights.

So, take my last farewell, for I despair
To have you whole, and scorn to take you
half.

VENTIDIUS: I combat Heaven, which
blasts my best designs;
My last attempt must be to win her back;
But oh! I fear in vain.   (Exit.)

ANTONY: Why was I framed with this
plain, honest heart,
Which knows not to disguise its griefs and
weakness,
But bears its workings outward to the
world?
I should have kept the mighty anguish in,
And forced a smile at Cleopatra's false-
hood.
Octavia had believed it, and had stayed.
But I am made a shallow-forded stream,
Seen to the bottom; all my clearness
scorned,
And all my faults exposed.—See where he
comes

(Enter DOLABELLA.)

Who has profaned the sacred name of
friend,
And worn it into vileness!
With how secure a brow, and specious
form,
He gilds the secret villain! Sure that face
Was meant for honesty, But Heaven mis-
matched it,
And furnished treason out with nature's
pomp
To make its work more easy.

DOLABELLA: O my friend!

ANTONY: Well, Dolabella, you performed my message?

DOLABELLA: I did, unwillingly.

ANTONY: Unwillingly?
Was it so hard for you to bear our parting?
You should have wished it.

DOLABELLA: Why?

ANTONY: Because you love me.
And she received my message with as
true,

With as unfeigned a sorrow as you brought
   it?

DOLABELLA: She loves you, even to madness.

ANTONY: Oh, I know it.
You, Dolabella, do not better know
How much she loves me. And should I
Forsake this beauty? This all-perfect crea-
   ture?

DOLABELLA: I could not, were she mine.

ANTONY: And yet you first
Persuaded me. How come you altered
   since?

DOLABELLA: I said at first I was not fit
   to go;
I could not hear her sighs and see her
   tears,
But pity must prevail. And so perhaps
It may again with you, for I have prom-
   ised
That she should take her last farewell.
   And see,
She comes to claim my word.

          (*Enter* CLEOPATRA.)

ANTONY: False Dolabella!
DOLABELLA: What's false, my lord?

ANTONY: Why Dolabella's false,
And Cleopatra's false—both false and
   faithless.
Drew near, you well-joined wickedness,
   you serpents
Whom I have in my kindly bosom
   warmed,
Till I am stung to death.

DOLABELLA: My lord, have I
Deserved to be thus used?

CLEOPATRA: Can Heaven prepare
A newer torment? Can it find a curse
Beyond our separation?

ANTONY: Yes, if fate
Be just, much greater. Heaven should be
   ingenious
In punishing such crimes. The rolling
   stone

And gnawing vulture were slight pains,
   invented
When Jove was young, and no examples
   known
Of mighty ills. But you have ripened sin
To such a monstrous growth 'twill pose
   the gods
To find an equal torture. Two, two such!—
Oh, there's no farther name,—two such!
   to me,
To me, who locked my soul within your
   breasts,
Had no desires, no joys, no life, but you.
When half the globe was mine, I gave it
   you
In dowry with my heart; I had no use,
No fruit of all, but you. A friend and
   mistress
Was what the world could give. O Cleo-
   patra!
O Dolabella! how could you betray
This tender heart which with an infant
   fondness
Lay lulled betwixt your bosoms and there
   slept,
Secure of injured faith?

DOLABELLA: If she has wronged you,
Heaven, hell, and you, revenge it.

ANTONY: If she wronged me!
Thou wouldst evade thy part of guilt.
   But swear
Thou lov'st not her.

DOLABELLA: Not so as I love you.

ANTONY: Not so? Swear, swear, I say,
   thou dost not love her.

DOLABELLA: No more than friendship
   will allow.

ANTONY: No more?
Friendship allows thee nothing. Thou are
   perjured—
And yet thou dist not swear thou lov'd'st
   her not,
But not so much, no more. O trifling
   hypocrite,
Who dar'st not own to her, thou dost not
   love,

Nor own to me, thou dost. Ventidius
　　heard it;
Octavia saw it.

CLEOPATRA: They are enemies.

ANTONY: Alexas is not so. He, he confessed it;
He, who, next hell, best knew it, he
　　avowed it.
Why do I seek a proof beyond yourself?

　　　　　　　　(To DOLABELLA.)

You, whom I sent to bear my last farewell,
Returned to plead her stay.

DOLABELLA:　　What shall I answer?
If to have loved be guilt, then I have
　　sinned;
But if to have repented of that love
Can wash away my crime, I have repented.
Yet, if I have offended past forgiveness,
Let not her suffer. She is innocent.

CLEOPATRA: Ah, what will not a woman
　　do who loves?
What means will she refuse to keep that
　　heart
Where all her joys are placed? 'Twas I
　　encouraged,
'Twas I blew up the fire that scorched his
　　soul,
To make you jealous, and by that regain
　　you.
But all in vain. I could not counterfeit;
In spite of all the dams, my love broke
　　o'er,
And drowned my heart again; fate took
　　the occasion,
And thus one minute's feigning has de-
　　stroyed
My whole life's truth.

ANTONY: Thin cobweb arts of falsehood,
Seen, and broke through at first

DOLABELLA:　　Forgive your mistress.

CLEOPATRA: Forgive your friend.

ANTONY: You have convinced[3] your-
　　selves.

[3] Convicted.

You plead each other's cause. What wit-
　　ness have you
That you but meant to raise my jealousy?

CLEOPATRA: Ourselves, and Heaven.

ANTONY: Guilt witnesses for guilt.
　　Hence, love and friendship!
You have no longer place in human
　　breasts;
These two have driven you out. Avoid
　　my sight!
I would not kill the man whom I have
　　loved,
And cannot hurt the woman. But avoid
　　me,
I do not know how long I can be tame,
For, if I stay one minute more, to think
How I am wronged, my justice and re-
　　venge
Will cry so loud within me that my pity
Will not be heard for either.

DOLABELLA:　　　　Heaven has but
Our sorrow for our sins, and then de-
　　lights
To pardon erring man. Sweet mercy
　　seems
Its darling attribute, which limits justice
As if there were degrees in infinite,
And infinite would rather want perfection
Than punish to extent.

ANTONY:　　　　I can forgive
A foe, but not a mistress and a friend.
Treason is there in its most horrid shape
Where trust is greatest, and the soul, re-
　　signed,
Is stabbed by its own guards. I'll hear no
　　more.—
Hence from my sight forever!

CLEOPATRA:　　　　How? Forever?
I cannot go one moment from your sight,
And must I go forever?
My joys, my only joys, are centered here.
What place have I to go to? My own
　　kingdom?
That I have lost for you. Or to the Ro-
　　mans?

They hate me for your sake. Or must I wander
The wide world o'er, a helpless, banished woman,
Banished for love of you—banished from you?
Aye, there's the banishment! Oh, hear me, hear me
With strictest justice, for I beg no favor,
And if I have offended you, then kill me,
But do not banish me.

ANTONY: I must not hear you.
I have a fool within me takes your part,
But honor stops my ears.

CLEOPATRA: For pity hear me!
Would you cast off a slave who followed you?
Who crouched beneath your spurn?—He has no pity!
See if he gives one tear to my departure,
One look, one kind farewell. O iron heart!
Let all the gods look down and judge betwixt us,
If he did ever love!

ANTONY: No more.—Alexas!

DOLABELLA: A perjured villain!

ANTONY: (*To* CLEOPATRA.) Your Alexas, yours.

CLEOPATRA: Oh, 'twas his plot, his ruinous design,
T' engage you in my love by jealousy.
Hear him. Confront him with me. Let him speak.

ANTONY: I have, I have.

CLEOPATRA: And if he clear me not—

ANTONY: Your creature! one who hangs upon your smiles!
Watches your eye to say or to unsay
Whate'er you please! I am not to be moved.

CLEOPATRA: Then must we part? Farewell, my cruel lord!
Th' appearance is against me, and I go,
Unjustified, forever from your sight.

How I have loved, you know; how yet I love,
My only comfort is, I know myself.
I love you more, even now you are unkind,
Than when you loved me most; so well, so truly
I'll never strive against it but die pleased
To think you once were mine.

ANTONY: Good heaven, they weep at parting!
Must I weep too? That calls them innocent.
I must not weep. And yet I must, to think
That I must not forgive.—
Live, but live wretched; 'tis but just you should,
Who made me so. Live from each other's sight.
Let me not hear, you meet. Set all the earth
And all the seas betwixt your sundered loves;
View nothing common but the sun and skies.
Now, all take several ways;
And each your own sad fate, with mine, deplore;
That you were false, and I could trust no more.

(*Exeunt severally.*)

ACT V
SCENE I

([*Enter*] CLEOPATRA, CHARMION, [*and*] IRAS.)

CHARMION: Be juster, Heaven; such virtue punished thus
Will make us think that chance rules all above,
And shuffles with a random hand the lots
Which man is forced to draw.

CLEOPATRA: I could tear out these eyes
  that gained his heart,
And had not power to keep it. O the curse
Of doting on, even when I find it dotage!
Bear witness, gods, you heard him bid
  me go;
You whom he mocked with imprecating
  vows
Of promised faith!—I'll die! I will not
  bear it.
You may hold me—

  (*She pulls out her dagger, and
      they hold her.*)

But I can keep my breath; I can die inward,
And choke this love.

  (*Enter* ALEXAS.)

IRAS: Help, O Alexas, help!
The queen grows desperate; her soul
  struggles in her
With all the agonies of love and rage,
And strives to force its passage.

CLEOPATRA: Let me go.
Art thou there, traitor!—Oh,
Oh, Oh, for a little breath, to vent my
  rage!
Give, give me way, and let me loose upon
  him.

ALEXAS: Yes, I deserve it for my ill-
  timed truth.
Was it for me to prop
The ruins of a falling majesty?
To place myself beneath the mighty flaw,
Thus to be crushed and pounded into
  atoms
By its o'erwhelming weight? 'Tis too
  presuming
For subjects to preserve that wilful power
Which courts its own destruction.

CLEOPATRA: I would reason
More calmly with you. Did not you
  o'errule
And force my plain, direct, and open love
Into these crooked paths of jealousy?
Now, what's the event? Octavia is re-
  moved,

But Cleopatra's banished. Thou, thou
  villain,
[Hast] pushed my boat to open sea, to
  prove
At my sad cost, if thou canst steer it back.
It can not be; I'm lost too far; I'm
  ruined!—
Hence, thou imposter, traitor, monster,
  devil!—
I can no more. Thou, and my griefs, have
  sunk
Me down so low that I want voice to curse
  thee.

ALEXAS: Suppose some shipwrecked sea-
  man near the shore,
Dropping and faint with climbing up the
  cliff;
If, from above, some charitable hand
Pull him to safety, hazarding himself
To draw the other's weight, would he
  look back
And curse him for his pains?   The case
  is yours;
But one step more, and you have gained
  the height.

CLEOPATRA: Sunk, never more to rise.

ALEXAS: Octavia's gone, and Dolabella
  banished.
Believe me, madam, Antony is yours.
His heart was never lost, but started off
To jealousy, love's last retreat and covert,
Where it lies hid in shades, watchful in
  silence,
And listening for the sound that calls it
  back.
Some other, any man ('tis so advanced)
May perfect this unfinished work, which I
(Unhappy only to myself) have left
So easy to his hand.

CLEOPATRA: Look well thou do't; else—

ALEXAS: Else what your silence threatens.—Antony
Is mounted up the Pharos, from whose
  turret
He stands surveying our Egyptian galleys
Engaged with Caesar's fleet. Now death
  or conquest!

If the first happen, fate acquits my promise;
If we o'ercome, the conqueror is yours.

(*A distant shout within.*)

CHARMION: Have comfort, madam. Did
you mark that shout?

(*Second shout nearer.*)

IRAS: Hark! they redouble it.

ALEXAS: 'Tis from the port.
The loudness shows it near. Good news,
kind heavens!

CLEOPATRA: Osiris make it so!

(*Enter* SERAPION).

SERAPION: Where, where's the queen?

ALEXAS: How frightfully the holy
coward stares
As if not yet recovered of the assault,
When all his gods and, what's more dear
to him,
His offerings were at stake!

SERAPION: O horror, horror!
Egypt has been; our latest hour is come;
The queen of nations from her ancient
seat
Is sunk forever in the dark abyss;
Time has unrolled her glories to the last,
And now closed up the volume.

CLEOPATRA: Be more plain.
Say whence thou comest, though fate is
in thy face,
Which from thy haggard eyes looks wildly
out,
And threatens ere thou speakest.

SERAPION: I came from Pharos—
From viewing (spare me, and imagine it)
Our land's last hope, your navy—

CLEOPATRA: Vanquished?

SERAPION: No.
They fought not.

CLEOPATRA: Then they fled!

SERAPION: Nor that. I saw,
With Antony, your well-appointed fleet
Row out; and thrice he waved his hand
on high,

And thrice with cheerful cries they shouted
back.
'Twas then false Fortune like a fawning
strumpet
About to leave the bankrupt prodigal,
With a dissembled smile would kiss at
parting,
And flatter to the last; the well-timed oars
Now dipt from every bank, now smoothly
run
To meet the foe; and soon indeed they met,
But not as foes. In few, we saw their caps
On either side thrown up. The Egyptian
galleys,
Received like friends, passed through and
fell behind
The Roman rear. And now they all come
forward,
And ride within the port.

CLEOPATRA: Enough, Serapion.
I've heard my doom.—This needed not,
you gods:
When I lost Antony, your work was done.
'Tis but superfluous malice.—Where's my
lord?
How bears he this last blow?

SERAPION: His fury can not be expressed
by words.
Thrice he attempted headlong to have
fallen
Full on his foes, and aimed at Caesar's
galley;
Withheld, he raves on you; cries he's betrayed.
Should he now find you—

ALEXAS: Shun him. Seek your safety
Till you can clear your innocence.

CLEOPATRA: I'll stay.

ALEXAS: You must not. Haste you to
your monument,
While I make speed to Caesar.

CLEOPATRA: Caesar! No,
I have no business with him.

ALEXAS: I can work him
To spare your life, and let this madman
perish.

CLEOPATRA: Base, fawning wretch! wouldst thou betray him too?
Hence from my sight! I will not hear a traitor.
'Twas thy design brought all this ruin on us.—
Serapion, thou art honest. Counsel me—
But haste, each moment's precious.

SERAPION: Retire. You must not yet see Antony.
He who began this mischief,
'Tis just he tempt the danger. Let him clear you;
And, since he offered you his servile tongue,
To gain a poor precarious life from Caesar
Let him expose that fawning eloquence,
And speak to Antony.

ALEXAS: O heaven! I dare not;
I meet my certain death.

CLEOPATRA: Slave, thou deservest it.—
Not that I fear my lord, will I avoid him;
I know him noble. When he banished me,
And thought me false, he scorned to take my life;
But I'll be justified, and then die with him.

ALEXAS: O pity me, and let me follow you!

CLEOPATRA: To death, if thou stir hence. Speak if thou canst
Now for thy life which basely thou wouldst save,
While mine I prize at—this. Come, good Serapion.

(*Exeunt* CLEOPATRA, SERAPION, CHARMION, *and* IRAS.)

ALEXAS: O that I less could fear to lose this being,
Which, like a snowball in my coward hand,
The more 'tis grasped, the faster melts away.
Poor reason! what a wretched aid art thou!
For still, in spite of thee,
These two long lovers, soul and body, dread
Their final separation. Let me think;
What can I say to save myself from death,
No matter what becomes of Cleopatra?

ANTONY: (*Within.*) Which way? where?

VENTIDIUS: (*Within.*) This leads to the monument.

ALEXAS: Ah me! I hear him; yet I'm unprepared,
My gift of lying's gone;
And this court-devil, which I so oft have raised,
Forsakes me at my need. I dare not stay,
Yet can not far go hence.   (*Exit.*)

(*Enter* ANTONY *and* VENTIDIUS.)

ANTONY: O happy Caesar! thou hast men to lead!
Think not 'tis thou hast conquered Antony,
But Rome has conquered Egypt. I'm betrayed.

VENTIDIUS: Curse on this treacherous train!
Their soul and heaven infect them all with baseness,
And their young souls come tainted to the world
With the first breath they draw.

ANTONY: The original villain sure no god created;
He was a bastard of the sun by Nile,
Aped into man; with all his mother's mud[1]
Crusted about his soul.

VENTIDIUS: The nation is
One universal traitor, and their queen
The very spirit and extract of them all.

ANTONY: Is there yet left
A possibility of aid from valor?
Is there one god unsworn to my destruction?

[1] I.e., bred by the sun from the mud of the Nile.

The least unmortgaged hope? for, if there
  be,
Methinks I can not fall beneath the fate
Of such a boy as Caesar.
The world's one half is yet in Antony,
And from each limb of it that's hewed
  away,
The soul comes back to me.

VENTIDIUS: There yet remain
Three legions in the town. The last assault
Lopt off the rest. If death be your design—
As I must wish it now—these are sufficient
To make a heap about us of dead foes,
An honest pile for burial.

ANTONY: They're enough.
We'll not divide our stars, but, side by
  side,
Fight emulous, and with malicious eyes
Survey each other's acts, so every death
Thou giv'st, I'll take on me as a just debt,
And pay thee back a soul.

VENTIDIUS: Now you shall see I love
  you. Not a word
Of chiding more. By my few hours of life,
I am so pleased with this grave Roman
  fate
That I would not be Caesar to outlive you.
When we put off this flesh and mount to-
  gether,
I shall be shown to all the ethereal
  crowd,—
"Lo, this is he who died with Antony!"

ANTONY: Who knows but we may
  pierce through all their troops,
And reach my veterans yet? 'tis worth the
  'tempting
To o'erleap this gulf of fate,
And leave our wondering destinies behind.

(Enter ALEXAS, trembling.)

VENTIDIUS: See, see, that villain!
See Cleopatra stamped upon that face
With all her cunning, all her arts of false-
  hood!
How she looks out through those dissem-
  bling eyes!

How he has set out his count'nance for
  deceit,
And promises a lie before he speaks!
(Drawing) Let me dispatch him first.

ALEXAS: O spare me, spare me!

ANTONY: Hold. He's not worth your
  killing.—On thy life,
Which thou may'st keep because I scorn
  to take it,
No syllable to justify thy queen.
Save thy base tongue its office.

ALEXAS: Sir, she's gone
Where she shall never be molested more
By love, or you.

ANTONY: Fled to her Dolabella!
Die, traitor! I revoke my promise! die!

(Going to kill him.)

ALEXAS: O hold! she is not fled.

ANTONY: She is. My eyes
Are open to her falsehood; my whole life
Has been a golden dream of love and
  friendship;
But, now I wake, I'm like a merchant
  roused
From soft repose to see his vessel sinking,
And all his wealth cast o'er. Ingrateful
  woman!
Who followed me but as the swallow
  summer,
Hatching the young ones in my kindly
  beams,
Singing her flatteries to my morning
  wake;
But now my winter comes, she spreads
  her wings,
And seeks the spring of Caesar.

ALEXAS: Think not so:
Her fortunes have in all things mixed
  with yours.
Had she betrayed her naval force to Rome,
How easily might she have gone to
  Caesar,
Secure by such a bribe.

VENTIDIUS: She sent it first,
To be more welcome after.

ANTONY: 'Tis too plain,
Else would she have appeared to clear
    herself.

ALEXAS: Too fatally she has. She could
    not bear
To be accused by you, but shut herself
Within her monument, looked down and
    sighed,
While from her unchanged face the silent
    tears
Dropped, as they had not leave, but stole
    their parting.
Some undistinguished words she inly mur-
    mured;
At last she raised her eyes, and, with such
    looks
As dying Lucrece cast—

ANTONY: My heart forebodes—

VENTIDIUS: All for the best;—go on.

ALEXAS: She snatched her poniard,
And, ere we could prevent the fatal blow,
Plunged it within her breast, then turned
    to me:
"Go, bear my lord," said she, "my last
    farewell,
And ask him if he yet suspect my faith."
More she was saying, but death rushed
    betwixt.
She half pronounced your name with her
    last breath,
And buried half within her.

VENTIDIUS: Heaven be praised!

ANTONY: Then art thou innocent, my
    poor dear love?
And art thou dead?
O those two words! their sound should be
    divided;
Hadst thou been false, and died; or hadst
    thou lived,
And hadst been true—But innocence and
    death!
This shows not well above. Then what
    am I,
The murderer of this truth, this inno-
    cence!

Thoughts can not form themselves in
    words so horrid
As can express my guilt!

VENTIDIUS: Is't come to this? The gods
    have been too gracious,
And thus you thank 'em for't!

ANTONY: (To ALEXAS) Why stayest
    thou here?
Is it for thee to spy upon my soul
And see its inward mourning? Get thee
    hence.
Thou are not worthy to behold what now
Becomes a Roman emperor to perform.

ALEXAS: (Aside) He loves her still:
His grief betrays it. Good! the joy to find
She's yet alive completes the reconcile-
    ment.
I've saved myself and her. But, oh! the
    Romans!
Fate comes too fast upon my wit,
Hunts me too hard, and meets me at each
        double.   (Exit.)

VENTIDIUS: Would she had died a little
    sooner, though,
Before Octavia went; you might have
    treated;
Now 'twill look tame, and would not be
    received.
Come, rouse yourself, and let's die warm
    together.

ANTONY: I will not fight: there's no
    more work for war.
The business of my angry hours is done.

VENTIDIUS: Caesar is at your gates.

ANTONY: Why, let him enter;
He's welcome now.

VENTIDIUS: What lethargy has crept
    into your soul?

ANTONY: 'Tis but a scorn of life, and
    just desire
To free myself from bondage.

VENTIDIUS: Do it bravely.

ANTONY: I will; but not by fighting. O
    Ventidius!

What should I fight for now?—my queen
is dead.
I was but great for her; my power, my
empire,
Were but my merchandise to buy her love,
And conquered kings, my factors. Now
she's dead,
Let Caesar take the world,—
An empty circle since the jewel's gone
Which made it worth my strife; my
being's nauseous;
For all the bribes of life are gone away.

VENTIDIUS: Would you be taken?

ANTONY: Yes, I would be taken,
But as a Roman ought,—dead, my Ven-
tidius.
For I'll convey my soul from Caesar's
reach,
And lay down life myself. 'Tis time the
world
Should have a lord, and know whom to
obey.
We two have kept its homage in suspense,
And bent the globe, on whose each side
we trod,
Till it was dinted inwards. Let him walk
Alone upon't; I'm weary of my part.
My torch is out; and the world stands
before me
Like a black desert at th' approach of
night.
I'll lay me down and stray no farther on.

VENTIDIUS: I could be grieved,
But that I'll not outlive you. Choose your
death,
For I have seen him in such various shapes,
I care not which I take—I'm only trou-
bled,
The life I bear is worn to such a rag,
'Tis scarce worth giving. I could wish,
indeed,
We threw it from us with a better grace;
That, like two lions taken in the toils,
We might at least thrust out our paws
and wound
The hunters that inclose us.

ANTONY: I have thought on it.
Ventidius, you must live.

VENTIDIUS: I must not, sir.

ANTONY: Wilt thou not live to speak
some good of me?
To stand by my fair fame and guard the
approaches
From the ill tongues of men?

VENTIDIUS: Who shall guard mine
For living after you?

ANTONY: Say I command it.

VENTIDIUS: If we die well, our deaths
will speak themselves,
And need no living witness.

ANTONY: Thou hast loved me,
And fain I would reward thee. I must die.
Kill me, and take the merit of my death
To make the friends with Caesar.

VENTIDIUS: Thank your kindness.
You said I love you; and in recompense
You bid me turn a traitor.—Did I think
You would have used me thus?—that I
should die
With a hard thought of you?

ANTONY: Forgive me, Roman.
Since I have heard of Cleopatra's death,
My reason bears no rule upon my tongue,
But lets my thoughts break all at random
out.
I've thought better; do not deny me twice.

VENTIDIUS: By Heaven, I will not.
Let it not be to outlive you.

ANTONY: Kill me first,
And then die thou; for 'tis but just thou
serve
Thy friend before thyself.

VENTIDIUS: Give me your hand.
We soon shall meet again. Now farewell,
emperor!— (Embrace.)
Methinks that word's too cold to be my
last:
Since death sweeps all distinctions, fare-
well, friend!
That's all—
I will not make a business of a trifle;

And yet I can not look on you and kill you;
Pray turn your face.

ANTONY: I do. Strike home, be sure.

VENTIDIUS: Home as my sword will reach.   (*Kills himself.*)

ANTONY: Oh, thou mistak'st;
That wound was none of thine; give it me back;
Thou robb'st me of my death.

VENTIDIUS: I do, indeed;
But think 'tis the first time I e'er deceived you,
If that may plead my pardon.—And you, gods,
Forgive me if you will; for I die perjured
Rather than kill my friend.   (*Dies.*)

ANTONY: Farewell! Ever my leader, even in death!
My queen and thou have got the start of me,
And I'm the lag of honor.—Gone so soon?
Is death no more? he used him carelessly,
With a familiar kindness; ere he knocked,
Ran to the door and took him in his arms,
As who should say, "You're welcome at all hours,
A friend need give no warning." Books had spoiled him,
For all the learn'd are cowards by profession.
'Tis not worth
My farther thought; for death, for aught I know,
Is but to think no more. Here's to be satisfied.   (*Falls on his sword.*)
I've missed my heart. O unperforming hand!
Thou never couldst have erred in a worse time.
My fortune jades me to the last; and death,
Like a great man, takes state, and makes me wait
For my admittance—
    (*Trampling within.*)

Some, perhaps, from Caesar
If he should find me living, and suspect
That I played booty[2] with my life! I'll mend
My work ere they can reach me.
    (*Rises upon his knees.*)

(*Enter* CLEOPATRA, CHARMION, [*and*] IRAS.)

CLEOPATRA: Where is my lord? where is he?

CHARMION: There he lies,
And dead Ventidius by him.

CLEOPATRA: My fear were prophets; I am come too late.
    (*Runs to him.*)
O that accursed Alexas!

ANTONY: Art thou living?
Or am I dead before I knew, and thou
The first kind ghost that meets me?

CLEOPATRA: Help me seat him.
Send quickly, send for help!
    (*They place him in a chair.*)

ANTONY: I am answered.
We live both. Sit thee down, my Cleopatra;
I'll make the most I can of life, to stay
A moment more with thee.

CLEOPATRA: How is it with you?

ANTONY: 'Tis as with a man
Removing in a hurry; all packed up,
But one dear jewel that his haste forgot;
And he, for that, returns upon the spur;
So I come back for thee.

CLEOPATRA: Too long, you heavens, you have been cruel to me;
Now show your mended faith, and give me back
His fleeting life!

ANTONY: It will not be, my love;
I keep my soul by force.
Say but, thou are not false.

CLEOPATRA: 'Tis now too late

---

2 Shammed suicide to gain pity.

To say I'm true: I'll prove it, and die
with you.
Unknown to me, Alexas feigned my
death,
Which, when I knew, I hasted to prevent
This fatal consequence. My fleet betrayed
Both you and me.

ANTONY: And Dolabella—

CLEOPATRA: Scarce
Esteemed before he loved; but hated now.

ANTONY: Enough. My life's not long
enough for more.
Thou say'st thou wilt come after: I believe
thee,
For I can now believe whate'er thou say-
est,
That we may part more kindly.

CLEOPATRA: I will come.
Doubt not, my life, I'll come, and quickly
too;
Caesar shall triumph o'er no part of thee.

ANTONY: But grieve not, while thou
stay'st,
My last disastrous times.
Think we have had a clear and glorious
day,
And Heaven did kindly to delay the storm
Just till our close of evening. Ten years'
love,
And not a moment lost, but all improved
To the utmost joys,—what ages have we
lived!
And now to die each other's; and, so
dying,
While hand in hand we walk in groves
below,
Whole troops of lovers' ghosts shall flock
about us,
And all the train be ours.

CLEOPATRA: Your words are like the
notes of dying swans,
Too sweet to last. Were there so many
hours
For your unkindness, and not one for
love?

ANTONY: No, not a minute.—This one
kiss—more worth
Than all I leave to Caesar.   (Dies.)

CLEOPATRA: O tell me so again,
And take ten thousand kisses for that
word.
My lord, my lord! Speak, if you yet have
being;
Sign to me, if you can not speak; or cast
One look! Do anything that shows you live.

IRAS: He's gone too far to hear you,
And this you see, a lump of senseless clay,
The leavings of a soul.

CHARMION: Remember, madam,
He charged you not to grieve.

CLEOPATRA: And I'll obey him.
I have not loved a Roman not to know
What should become his wife—his wife,
my Charmion!
For 'tis to that high title I aspire,
And now I'll not die less. Let dull Octavia
Survive to mourn him, dead. My nobler
fate
Shall knit our spousals with a tie too
strong
For Roman laws to break.

IRAS: Will you then die?

CLEOPATRA: Why shouldst thou make
that question?

IRAS: Caesar is merciful.

CLEOPATRA: Let him be so
To those that want his mercy. My poor
lord
Made no such covenant with him to spare
me
When he was dead. Yield me to Caesar's
pride?
What! to be led in triumph through the
streets,
A spectacle to base plebian eyes,
While some dejected friend of Antony's
Close in a corner, shakes his head, and
mutters
A secret curse on her who ruined him?
I'll none of that.

CHARMION: Whatever you resolve,
I'll follow, even to death.

IRAS: I only feared
For you, but more should fear to live
    without you.

CLEOPATRA: Why, now, 'tis as it should
    be. Quick, my friends,
Dispatch. Ere this, the town's in Caesar's
    hands.
My lord looks down concerned, and fears
    my stay,
Lest I should be surprised.
Keep him not waiting for his love too
    long.
You, Charmion, bring my crown and rich-
    est jewels;
With them, the wreath of victory I made
(Vain augury!) for him who now lies
    dead.
You, Iras, bring the cure of all our ills.

IRAS: The aspics, madam?

CLEOPATRA: Must I bid you twice?

                    (*Exeunt* CHARMION *and* IRAS.)

'Tis sweet to die when they would force
    life on me,
To rush into the dark abode of death,
And seize him first. If he be like my love,
He is not frightful, sure.
We're now alone in secrecy and silence;
And is not this like lovers? I may kiss
These pale, cold lips; Octavia does not see
    me.
And oh! 'tis better far to have him thus
Than see him in her arms.—Oh, welcome,
    welcome!

                    (*Enter* CHARMION [*and*] IRAS.)

CHARMION: What must be done?

CLEOPATRA: Short ceremony, friends,
But yet it must be decent. First, this
    laurel
Shall crown my hero's head; he fell not
    basely,
Nor left his shield behind him.—Only
    thou

Couldst triumph o'er thyself; and thou
    alone
Wert worthy so to triumph.

CHARMION: To what end
These ensigns of your pomp and royalty?

CLEOPATRA: Dull that thou art! why,
    'tis to meet my love
As when I saw him first on Cydnos' bank,
All sparkling, like a goddess; so adorned,
I'll find him once again. My second
    spousals
Shall match my first in glory. Haste, haste,
    both,
And dress the bride of Antony.

CHARMION: —'Tis done.

CLEOPATRA: Now seat me by my lord.
    I claim this place,
For I must conquer Caesar, too, like him,
And win my share o' th' world.—Hail,
    you dear relics
Of my immortal love!
O let no impious hand remove you hence,
But rest forever here! Let Egypt give
His death that peace which it denied his
    life.—
Reach me the casket.

IRAS: Underneath the fruit
The aspic lies.

CLEOPATRA: Welcome, thou kind de-
    ceiver!

                    (*Putting aside the leaves.*)

Thou best of thieves, who, with an easy
    key,
Dost open life and, unperceived by us,
Even steal us from ourselves, discharging
    so
Death's dreadful office better than himself,
Touching our limbs so gently into slumber
That Death stands by, deceived by his
    own image,
And thinks himself but sleep.

SERAPION: (*Within*)   The queen,
    where is she?
The town is yielded, Caesar's at the gates.

CLEOPATRA: He comes too late to invade the rights of death.
Haste, bare my arm, and rouse the serpent's fury.

(*Holds out her arm, and draws it back.*)

Coward flesh,
Wouldst thou conspire with Caesar to betray me
As thou wert none of mine? I'll force thee to 't,
And not be sent by him,
But bring, myself, my soul to Antony.

(*Turns aside, and then shows her arm bloody.*)

Take hence. The work is done.

SERAPION: (*Within*) Break ope the door
And guard the traitor well.

CHARMION: The next is ours.
IRAS: Now, Charmion, to be worthy
Of our great queen and mistress.

(*They apply the aspics.*)

CLEOPATRA: Already, death, I feel thee in my veins.
I go with such a will to find my lord
That we shall quickly meet.
A heavy numbness creeps through every limb,
And now 'tis at my head. My eyelids fall,
And my dear love is vanished in a mist.—
Where shall I find him—where? O turn me to him,
And lay me on his breast!—Caesar, thy worst.
Now part us, if thou canst.   (*Dies.*)

(IRAS *sinks down at her feet, and dies;*
CHARMION *stands behind her chair, as dressing her head.*)

(*Enter* SERAPION, *two Priests,* ALEXAS, *bound, Egyptians.*)

PRIEST: Behold, Serapion,
What havoc death has made!

SERAPION: 'Twas what I feared.—
Charmion, is this well done?

CHARMION: Yes, 'tis well done, and like a queen, the last
Of her great race. I follow her.

(*Sinks down [and] dies.*)

ALEXAS: 'Tis true,
She has done well. Much better thus to die
Than live to make a holiday in Rome.

SERAPION: See, see how the lovers sit in state together,
As they were giving laws to half mankind!
Th' impression of a smile, left in her face,
Shows she died pleased with him for whom she lived,
And went to charm him in another world.
Caesar's just entering; grief has now no leisure.
Secure the villain as our pledge of safety
To grace the imperial triumph.—Sleep, blest pair,
Secure from human chance, long ages out,
While all the storms of fate fly o'er your tomb;
And fame to late posterity shall tell,
No lovers lived so great or died so well.

(*Exeunt.*)

EPILOGUE

Poets, like disputants when reasons fail,
Have one sure refuge left—and that's to rail.
Fop, coxcomb, fool, are thundered through the pit;
And this is all their equipage of wit.
We wonder how the devil this difference grows
Betwixt our fools in verse, and yours in prose;
For, 'faith, the quarrel rightly understood,
'Tis civil war with their own flesh and blood.
The threadbare author hates the gaudy coat;

And swears at the gilt coach, but swears
    afoot;
For 'tis observed of every scribbling man,
He grows a fop as fast as e'er he can;
Prunes up, and asks his oracle, the glass,
If pink or purple best become his face.
For our poor wretch, he neither rails
    nor prays;
Nor likes your wit just as you like his
    plays;
He has not yet so much of Mr. Bayes.[1]
He does his best; and if he can not please,
Would quickly sue out his writ of ease.[2]
Yet, if he might his own grand jury
    call,

[1] See Buckingham's *The Rehearsal,* a satire
on Dryden.
[2] Certificate of discharge.

By the fair sex he begs to stand or fall.
Let Caesar's power the men's ambition
    move,
But grace you him who lost the world for
    love!
Yet if some antiquated lady say,
The last age is not copied in his play;
Heaven help the man who for that face
    must drudge,
Which only has the wrinkles of a judge.
Let not the young and beauteous join with
    those;
For should you raise such numerous hosts
    of foes,
Young wits and sparks he to his aid must
    call;
'Tis more than one man's work to please
    you all.

Ghosts

HENRIK IBSEN

COMMENTARY

Henrik Johan Ibsen (1828-1906) grew up in small Norwegian towns. He left Skien at 16 to be a pharmacist's assistant in Grivestad, where, at 20, he wrote his first play, a defense of Catiline, the Roman politician known to us mainly because of Cicero's orations attacking him. In his early 20's, Ibsen left for Oslo, planning to study medicine at the University there, but he soon became an assistant stage manager at Ole Bull's famous theatre in Bergen. After six years, he moved to Oslo as director of the Norwegian Theatre, in which post he spent five years. During this period, he helped stage the "well-made" plays of Europe's leading contemporary dramatists and wrote his own, largely derivative historical plays. In 1864 he left Norway to live in Italy and Germany.

His most famous early plays, *Brand* (1866), *Peer Gynt* (1867), and *Emperor and Galilean* (1873), are mystical, philosophical, and poetic. His next plays were realistic, concerned with current social problems: *Pillars of Society* (1877), *A Doll's House* (1879), *Ghosts* (1881), *An Enemy of the People* (1882), and *The Wild Duck* (1884). Most of the final plays were complex and subtle psychological studies: *Rosmersholm* (1886), *The Master Builder* (1892), *John Gabriel Borkman* (1896), and *When We Dead Awaken* (1899).

Ghosts is a study of a woman who does not leave her husband and home in spite of substantial cause to do so. It is commonly taken as a kind of "response" to the critics of *A Doll's House,* which depicted a woman who did leave the home where she was treated as a "doll." Yet *Ghosts* has a power and meaning independent of its relation to the earlier play.

Mrs. Alving is a woman of great will and determination, able to sustain a convincing presentation of proper domesticity in spite of having to live with a prodigiously profligate husband, and having to run a household in which the maid is his illegitimate child. Francis Fergusson has compared *Ghosts* with *Oedipus* in *The Idea of a Theatre* (Princeton, 1949). It is clear that the main motivators of the action in both plays are absent personages, the late King Laïos and the late Captain Alving; the final action in both works is preceded by a long past.

But the moral disorder of Mrs. Alving's universe is perhaps more Aeschylean, dominated by disease, fire, and hints of incest, mercy killing, and prostitution. Mrs. Alving is rooted in a conformist, bourgeois context while she strains for enlightenment, freedom, and tolerance. As in all tragedy perhaps, one of the crucial questions is, to what extent, in what ways, she may be responsible for her own fate. How far is she to blame for the captain's secret indulgences? She describes him, for instance, to Oswald, their son, as a man full of the joy of living. Does her tragedy come from her being rooted in the world of *A Doll's House* while she tries to enter an "advanced" world where she can read liberal works, flirt with a shallow and pompous clergyman, and countenance incest? In her efforts to control a hostile destiny, Mrs. Alving is to be compared with other dominating women of tragedy, Clytemnestra, Medea, Laura in *The Father,* and Yerma. You might consider how differently the character of Mrs. Alving would be played by different actresses.

In addition to Fergusson's essay, other relevant critical materials are Shaw's remarks in *The Quintessence of Ibsenism* (London, 1891, 1913; New York, 1909, 1925), which include a small anthology of the scurrilous reviews that greeted the play's early performances, and Morris Freedman's "The Morality of Paradox: Ibsen's Social Plays," in *The Moral Impulse* (Boston, 1964). James W. McFarlane's collection *Discussions of Henrik Ibsen* (Boston, 1962) collects various critical essays.

Henrik Ibsen

GHOSTS

A FAMILY-DRAMA IN THREE ACTS

Translated by William Archer

CHARACTERS

MRS. HELEN ALVING, *widow of Captain Alving, late Chamberlain*[1] *to the King.*
OSWALD ALVING, *her son, a painter.*
PASTOR MANDERS.
JACOB ENGSTRAND, *a carpenter.*
REGINA ENGSTRAND, *Mrs. Alving's maid.*

The action takes place at Mrs. Alving's country house, beside one of the large fjords in Western Norway.

ACT FIRST

A spacious garden-room, with one door to the left, and two doors to the right. In the middle of the room a round table, with chairs about it. On the table lie books, periodicals, and newspapers. In the foreground to the left a window, and by it a small sofa, with a work-table in front of it. In the background, the room is continued into a somewhat narrower conservatory, the walls of which are formed by large panes of glass. In the right-hand wall of the conservatory is a door leading down into the garden. Through the glass wall a gloomy fjord-landscape is faintly visible, veiled by steady rain.

ENGSTRAND, *the carpenter, stands by the*

[1] Chamberlain (Kammerherre) is the only title of honour now existing in Norway. It is a distinction conferred by the King on men of wealth and position, and is not hereditary.

Ghosts is reprinted with the permission of Charles Scribner's Sons from Volume VII, *The Collected Works of Henrik Ibsen*, translated by William Archer.

garden door. His left leg is somewhat bent; he has a clump of wood under the sole of his boot. REGINA, *with an empty garden syringe in her hand, hinders him from advancing.*

REGINA: (*In a low voice.*) What do you want? Stop where you are. You're positively dripping.

ENGSTRAND: It's the Lord's own rain, my girl.

REGINA: It's the devil's rain, *I* say.

ENGSTRAND: Lord, how you talk, Regina. (*Limps a step or two forward into the room.*) It's just this as I wanted to say——

REGINA: Don't clatter so with that foot of yours, I tell you! The young master's asleep upstairs.

ENGSTRAND: Asleep? In the middle of the day?

REGINA: It's no business of yours.

ENGSTRAND: I was out on the loose last night——

REGINA: I can quite believe that.

ENGSTRAND: Yes, we're weak vessels, we poor mortals, my girl——

REGINA: So it seems.

ENGSTRAND: ——and temptations are manifold in this world, you see. But all the same, I was hard at work, God knows, at half-past five this morning.

REGINA: Very well; only be off now. I won't stop here and have *rendezvous's*[1] with you.

ENGSTRAND: What do you say you won't have?

REGINA: I won't have any one find you here; so just you go about your business.

ENGSTRAND: (*Advances a step or two.*) Blest if I go before I've had a talk with you. This afternoon I shall have finished my ·work at the school-house, and then I shall take to-night's boat and be off home to the town.

[1] This and other French words used by Regina are in that language in the original.

REGINA: (*Mutters.*) Pleasant journey to you!

ENGSTRAND: Thank you, my child. To-morrow the Orphanage is to be opened, and then there'll be fine doings, no doubt, and plenty of intoxicating drink going, you know. And nobody shall say of Jacob Engstrand that he can't keep out of temptation's way.

REGINA: Oh!

ENGSTRAND: You see, there's to be heaps of grand folks here tomorrow. Pastor Manders is expected from town, too.

REGINA: He's coming to-day.

ENGSTRAND: There, you see! And I should be cursedly sorry if he found out anything against me, don't you understand?

REGINA: Oho! is that your game?

ENGSTRAND: Is what my game?

REGINA: (*Looking hard at him.*) What are you going to fool Pastor Manders into doing, this time?

ENGSTRAND: Sh! sh! Are you crazy? Do *I* want to fool Pastor Manders? Oh, no! Pastor Manders has been far too good a friend to me for that. But I just wanted to say, you know—that I mean to be off home again to-night.

REGINA: The sooner the better, say I.

ENGSTRAND: Yes, but I want you with me, Regina.

REGINA: (*Open-mouthed.*) You want me——? What are you talking about?

ENGSTRAND: I want you to come home with me, I say.

REGINA: (*Scornfully.*) Never in this world shall you get me home with you.

ENGSTRAND: Oh, we'll see about that.

REGINA: Yes, you may be sure we'll see about it! Me, that have been brought up by a lady like Mrs. Alving! Me, that am treated almost as a daughter here! Is it m e you want to go home with you?—to a house like yours? For shame?

ENGSTRAND: What the devil do you mean? Do you set yourself up against your father, you hussy?

REGINA: (*Mutters without looking at him.*) You've said often enough I was no concern of yours.

ENGSTRAND: Pooh! Why should you bother about t h a t ——

REGINA: Haven't you many a time sworn at me and called me a——? *Fi donc*!

ENGSTRAND: Curse me, now, if ever I used such an ugly word.

REGINA: Oh, I remember very well what word you used.

ENGSTRAND: Well, but that was only when I was a bit on, don't you know? Temptations are manifold in this world, Regina.

REGINA: Ugh!

ENGSTRAND: And besides, it was when your mother was that aggravating—I h a d to find something to twit her with, my child. She was always setting up for a fine lady. (*Mimics.*) "Let me go, Engstrand; let me be. Remember I was three years in Chamberlain Alving's family at Rosenvold." (*Laughs.*) Mercy on us! She could never forget that the Captain was made a Chamberlain while she was in service here.

REGINA: Poor mother! you very soon tormented her into her grave.

ENGSTRAND: (*With a twist of his shoulders.*) Oh, of course! I'm to have the blame for everything.

REGINA: (*Turns away; half aloud.*) Ugh——! And that leg too!

ENGSTRAND: What do you say, my child?

REGINA: *Pied de mouton.*

ENGSTRAND: Is that English, eh?

REGINA: Yes.

ENGSTRAND: Ay, ay; you've picked up some learning out here; and that may come in useful now, Regina.

REGINA: (*After a short silence.*) What do you want with me in town?

ENGSTRAND: Can you ask what a father wants with his only child? A'n't I a lonely, forlorn widower?

REGINA: Oh, don't try on any nonsense like that with m e ! Why do you want me?

ENGSTRAND: Well, let me tell you, I've been thinking of setting up in a new line of business.

REGINA: (*Contemptuously.*) You've tried that often enough, and much good you've done with it.

ENGSTRAND: Yes, but this time you shall see, Regina! Devil take me——

REGINA: (*Stamps.*) Stop your swearing!

ENGSTRAND: Hush, hush; you're right enough there, my girl. What I wanted to say was just this—I've laid by a very tidy pile from this Orphanage job.

REGINA: Have you? That's a good thing for you.

ENGSTRAND: What can a man spend his ha'pence on here in this country hole?

REGINA: Well, what then?

ENGSTRAND: Why, you see, I thought of putting the money into some paying speculation. I thought of a sort of a sailor's tavern——

REGINA: Pah!

ENGSTRAND: A regular high-class affair, of course; not any sort of pig-sty for common sailors. No! damn it! it would be for captains and mates, and—and—regular swells, you know.

REGINA: And I was to——?

ENGSTRAND: You were to help, to be sure. Only for the look of the thing, you understand. Devil a bit of hard work shall you have, my girl. You shall do exactly what you like.

REGINA: Oh, indeed!

ENGSTRAND: But there must be a petti-coat in the house; that's as clear as daylight. For I want to have it a bit lively-like in the evenings, with singing and dancing, and so on. You must remember they're weary wanderers on the ocean of life. (*Nearer.*) Now don't be a fool and stand in your own light, Regina. What's to become of you out here? Your mistress has given you a lot of learning; but what good is t h a t to you? You're to look after the children at the new Orphanage, I hear. Is t h a t the sort of thing for you, eh? Are you so dead set on wearing your life out for a pack of dirty brats?

REGINA: No; if things go as I want them to—— Well there's no saying—there's no saying.

ENGSTRAND: What do you mean by "there's no saying"?

REGINA: Never you mind.—How much money have you saved?

ENGSTRAND: What with one thing and another, a matter of seven or eight hundred crowns.[1]

REGINA: That's not so bad.

ENGSTRAND: It's enough to make a start with, my girl.

REGINA: Aren't you thinking of giving me any?

ENGSTRAND: No, I'm blest if I am!

REGINA: Not even of sending me a scrap of stuff for a new dress?

ENGSTRAND: Come to town with me, my lass, and you'll soon get dresses enough.

REGINA: Pooh! I can do that on my own account, if I want to.

ENGSTRAND: No, a father's guiding hand is what you want, Regina. Now, I've got my eye on a capital house in Little Harbour Street. They don't want much ready-money; and it could be a sort of a Sailors' Home, you know.

[1] A "krone" is equal to one shilling and three-halfpence.

REGINA: But I will n o t live with you! I have nothing whatever to do with you. Be off!

ENGSTRAND: You wouldn't stop long with me, my girl. No such luck! If you knew how to play your cards, such a fine figure of a girl as you've grown in the last year or two——

REGINA: Well?

ENGSTRAND: You'd soon get hold of some mate—or maybe even a captain——

REGINA: I won't marry any one of that sort. Sailors have no *savoir vivre*.

ENGSTRAND: What's that they haven't got?

REGINA: I know what sailors are, I tell you. They're not the sort of people to marry.

ENGSTRAND: Then never mind about marrying them. You can make it pay all the same. (*More confidentially.*) He—the Englishman—the man with the yacht—he came down with three hundred dollars, he did; and she wasn't a bit handsomer than you.

REGINA: (*Making for him.*) Out you go!

ENGSTRAND: (*Falling back.*) Come, come! You're not going to hit me, I hope.

REGINA: Yes, if you begin talking about mother I shall hit you. Get away with you, I say! (*Drives him back towards the garden door.*) And don't slam the doors. Young Mr. Alving——

ENGSTRAND: He's asleep; I know. You're mightily taken up about young Mr. Alving —— (*More softly.*) Oho! you don't mean to say it's him as——?

REGINA: Be off this minute! You're crazy, I tell you! No, not that way. There comes Pastor Manders. Down the kitchen stairs with you.

ENGSTRAND: (*Towards the right.*) Yes, yes, I'm going. But just you talk to him as is coming there. H e ' s the man to tell you what a child owes its father. For I a m your father all the same, you know. I can prove it from the church register.

(*He goes out through the second door to the right, which* REGINA *has opened, and closes again after him.* REGINA *glances hastily at herself in the mirror, dusts herself with her pocket handkerchief, and settles her necktie; then she busies herself with the flowers.*)

(PASTOR MANDERS, *wearing an overcoat, carrying an umbrella, and with a small travelling-bag on a strap over his shoulder, comes through the garden door into the conservatory.*)

MANDERS: Good-morning, Miss Engstrand.

REGINA: (*Turning round, surprised and pleased.*) No, really! Good-morning, Pastor Manders. Is the steamer in already?

MANDERS: It is just in. (*Enters the sitting-room.*) Terrible weather we have been having lately.

REGINA: (*Follows him.*) It's such blessëd weather for the country, sir.

MANDERS: No doubt; you are quite right. We townspeople give too little thought to that.

(*He begins to take off his overcoat.*)

REGINA: Oh, mayn't I help you?— There! Why, how wet it is! I'll just hang it up in the hall. And your umbrella, too— I'll open it and let it dry.

(*She goes out with the things through the second door on the right.* PASTOR MANDERS *takes off his travelling-bag and lays it and his hat on a chair. Meanwhile* REGINA *comes in again.*)

MANDERS: Ah, it's a comfort to get safe under cover. I hope everything is going on well here?

REGINA: Yes, thank you, sir.

MANDERS: You have your hands full, I suppose, in preparation for to-morrow?

REGINA: Yes, there's plenty to do, of course.

MANDERS: And Mrs. Alving is at home, I trust?

REGINA: Oh dear, yes. She's just upstairs, looking after the young master's chocolate.

MANDERS: Yes, by-the-bye—I heard down at the pier that Oswald had arrived.

REGINA: Yes, he came the day before yesterday. We didn't expect him before to-day.

MANDERS: Quite strong and well, I hope?

REGINA: Yes, thank you, quite; but dreadfully tired with the journey. He has made one rush right through from Paris —the whole way in one train, I believe. He's sleeping a little now, I think; so perhaps we'd better talk a little quietly.

MANDERS: Sh!—as quietly as you please.

REGINA: (*Arranging an arm-chair beside the table.*) Now, do sit down, Pastor Manders, and make yourself comfortable. (*He sits down; she places a footstool under his feet.*) There! Are you comfortable now, sir?

MANDERS: Thanks, thanks, extremely so. (*Looks at her.*) Do you know, Miss Engstrand, I positively believe you have grown since I last saw you.

REGINA: Do you think so, sir? Mrs. Alving says I've filled out too.

MANDERS: Filled out? Well, perhaps a little; just enough.

(*Short pause.*)

REGINA: Shall I tell Mrs. Alving you are here?

MANDERS: Thanks, thanks, there is no hurry, my dear child.—By-the-bye, Regina, my good girl, tell me: how is your father getting on out here?

REGINA: Oh, thank you, sir, he's getting on well enough.

MANDERS: He called upon me last time he was in town.

REGINA: Did he, indeed? He's always so glad of a chance of talking to you, sir.

MANDERS: And you often look in upon him at his work, I daresay?

REGINA: I? Oh, of course, when I have time, I——

MANDERS: Your father is not a man of strong character, Miss Engstrand. He stands terribly in need of a guiding hand.

REGINA: Oh, yes; I daresay he does.

MANDERS: He requires some one near him whom he cares for, and whose judgment he respects. He frankly admitted as much when he last came to see me.

REGINA: Yes, he mentioned something of the sort to me. But I don't know whether Mrs. Alving can spare me; especially now that we've got the new Orphanage to attend to. And then I should be so sorry to leave Mrs. Alving; she has always been so kind to me.

MANDERS: But a daughter's duty, my good girl—— Of course, we should first have to get your mistress's consent.

REGINA: But I don't know whether it would be quite proper for me, at my age, to keep house for a single man.

MANDERS: What! My dear Miss Engstrand! When the man is your own father!

REGINA: Yes, that may be; but all the same—— Now, if it were in a thoroughly n i c e house, and with a real gentleman——

MANDERS: Why, my dear Regina——

REGINA: ——one I could love and respect, and be a daughter to——

MANDERS: Yes, but my dear, good child——

REGINA: Then I should be glad to go to town. It's very lonely out here; you know

yourself, sir, what it is to be alone in the world. And I can assure you I'm both quick and willing. Don't you know of any such place for me, sir?

MANDERS: I? No, certainly not.

REGINA: But, dear, dear sir, do remember me if——

MANDERS: (*Rising.*) Yes, yes, certainly, Miss Engstrand.

REGINA: For if I——

MANDERS: Will you be so good as to tell your mistress I am here?

REGINA: I will, at once, sir.

(*She goes out to the left.*)

MANDERS: (*Paces the room two or three times, stands a moment in the background with his hands behind his back, and looks out over the garden. Then he returns to the table, takes up a book, and looks at the title-page; starts, and looks at several books.*) Ha—indeed!

(MRS. ALVING *enters by the door on the left; she is followed by* REGINA, *who immediately goes out by the first door on the right.*)

MRS. ALVING: (*Holds out her hand.*) Welcome, my dear Pastor.

MANDERS: How do you do, Mrs. Alving? Here I am as I promised.

MRS. ALVING: Always punctual to the minute.

MANDERS: You may believe it was not so easy for me to get away. With all the Boards and Committees I belong to——

MRS. ALVING: That makes it all the kinder of you to come so early. Now we can get through our business before dinner. But where is your portmanteau?

MANDERS: (*Quickly.*) I left it down at the inn. I shall sleep there to-night.

MRS. ALVING: (*Suppressing a smile.*) Are you really not to be persuaded, even now, to pass the night under my roof?

MANDERS: No, no, Mrs. Alving; many thanks. I shall stay at the inn, as usual. It is so conveniently near the landing-stage.

MRS. ALVING: Well, you must have your own way. But I really should have thought we two old people——

MANDERS: Now you are making fun of me. Ah, you're naturally in great spirits to-day—what with to-morrow's festival and Oswald's return.

MRS. ALVING: Yes; you can think what a delight it is to me! It's more than two years since he was home last. And now he has promised to stay with me all the winter.

MANDERS: Has he really? That is very nice and dutiful of him. For I can well believe that life in Rome and Paris has very different attractions from any we can offer here.

MRS. ALVING: Ah, but here he has his mother, you see. My own darling boy—he hasn't forgotten his old mother!

MANDERS: It would be grievous indeed, if absence and absorption in art and that sort of thing were to blunt his natural feelings.

MRS. ALVING: Yes, you may well say so. But there's nothing of that sort to fear with him. I'm quite curious to see whether you know him again. He'll be down presently; he's upstairs just now, resting a little on the sofa. But do sit down, my dear Pastor.

MANDERS: Thank you. Are you quite at liberty——?

MRS. ALVING: Certainly.

(*She sits by the table.*)

MANDERS: Very well. Then let me show you—— (*He goes to the chair where his travelling-bag lies, takes out a packet of papers, sits down on the opposite side of the table, and tries to find a clear space for the papers.*) Now, to begin with, here

is—— (*Breaking off.*) Tell me, Mrs. Alving, how do these books come to be here?

MRS. ALVING: These books? They are books I am reading.

MANDERS: Do you read this sort of literature?

MRS. ALVING: Certainly I do.

MANDERS: Do you feel better or happier for such reading?

MRS. ALVING: I feel, so to speak, more secure.

MANDERS: That is strange. How do you mean?

MRS. ALVING: Well, I seem to find explanation and confirmation of all sorts of things I myself have been thinking. For that is the wonderful part of it, Pastor Manders—there is really nothing new in these books, nothing but what most people think and believe. Only most people either don't formulate it to themselves, or else keep quiet about it.

MANDERS: Great heavens! Do you really believe that most people——?

MRS. ALVING: I do, indeed.

MANDERS: But surely not in this country? Not here among us?

MRS. ALVING: Yes, certainly; here as elsewhere.

MANDERS: Well, I really must say——!

MRS. ALVING: For the rest, what do you object to in these books?

MANDERS: Object to in them? You surely do not suppose that I have nothing better to do than to study such publications as these?

MRS. ALVING: That is to say, you know nothing of what you are condemning?

MANDERS: I have read enough a b o u t these writings to disapprove of them.

MRS. ALVING: Yes; but your own judgment——

MANDERS: My dear Mrs. Alving, there are many occasions in life when one must rely upon others. Things are so ordered in this world; and it is well that they are. Otherwise, what would become of society?

MRS. ALVING: Well, well, I daresay you're right there.

MANDERS: Besides, I of course do not deny that there may be much that is attractive in such books. Nor can I blame you for wishing to keep up with the intellectual movements that are said to be going on in the great world—where you have let your son pass so much of his life. But——

MRS. ALVING: But?

MANDERS: (*Lowering his voice.*) But one should not talk about it, Mrs. Alving. One is certainly not bound to account to everybody for what one reads and thinks within one's own four walls.

MRS. ALVING: Of course not; I quite agree with you.

MANDERS: Only think, now, how you are bound to consider the interests of this Orphanage, which you decided on founding at a time when—if I understand you rightly—you thought very differently on spiritual matters.

MRS. ALVING: Oh, yes, I quite admit that. But it was about the Orphanage——

MANDERS: It was about the Orphanage we were to speak; yes. All I say is: prudence, my dear lady! And now let us get to business. (*Opens the packet, and takes out a number of papers.*) Do you see these?

MRS. ALVING: The documents?

MANDERS: All—and in perfect order. I can tell you it was hard work to get them in time. I had to put on strong pressure. The authorities are almost morbidly scrupulous when there is any decisive step to be taken. But here they are at last. (*Looks through the bundle.*) See! here is the formal deed of gift of the parcel of ground known as Solvik in the Manor of Rosenvold, with all the newly constructed buildings, schoolrooms, master's house, and chapel. And here is the legal fiat for the endowment and for the Bye-laws of the Institution. Will you look at them? (*Reads.*) "Bye-laws for the Children's Home to be known as 'Captain Alving's Foundation.'"

MRS. ALVING: (*Looks long at the paper.*) So there it is.

MANDERS: I have chosen the designation "Captain" rather than "Chamberlain." "Captain" looks less pretentious.

MRS. ALVING: Oh, yes; just as you think best.

MANDERS: And here you have the Bank Account of the capital lying at interest to cover the current expenses of the Orphanage.

MRS. ALVING: Thank you; but please keep it—it will be more convenient.

MANDERS: With pleasure. I think we will leave the money in the Bank for the present. The interest is certainly not what we could wish—four per cent. and six months' notice of withdrawal. If a good mortgage could be found later on—of course it must be a first mortgage and an unimpeachable security—then we could consider the matter.

MRS. ALVING: Certainly, my dear Pastor Manders. You are the best judge in these things.

MANDERS: I will keep my eyes open at any rate.—But now there is one thing more which I have several times been intending to ask you.

MRS. ALVING: And what is that?

MANDERS: Shall the Orphanage buildings be insured or not?

MRS. ALVING: Of course they must be insured.

MANDERS: Well, wait a moment, Mrs. Alving. Let us look into the matter a little more closely.

MRS. ALVING: I have everything insured; buildings and movables and stock and crops.

MANDERS: Of course you have—on your own estate. And so have I—of course. But here, you see, it is quite another matter. The Orphanage is to be consecrated, as it were, to a higher purpose.

MRS. ALVING: Yes, but that's no reason——

MANDERS: For my own part, I should certainly not see the smallest impropriety in guarding against all contingencies——

MRS. ALVING: No, I should think not.

MANDERS: But what is the general feeling in the neighbourhood? You, of course, know better than I.

MRS. ALVING: Well—the general feeling ——

MANDERS: Is there any considerable number of people—really responsible people—who might be scandalised?

MRS. ALVING: What do you mean by "really responsible people"?

MANDERS: Well, I mean people in such independent and influential positions that one cannot help attaching some weight to their opinions.

MRS. ALVING: There are several people of that sort here, who would very likely be shocked if——

MANDERS: There, you see! In town we have many such people. Think of all my colleague's adherents! People would be only too ready to interpret our action as a sign that neither you nor I had the right faith in a Higher Providence.

MRS. ALVING: But for your own part, my dear Pastor, you can at least tell yourself that——

MANDERS: Yes, I know—I know; my conscience would be quite easy, that is true enough. But nevertheless we should not escape grave misinterpretation; and

that might very likely react unfavourably upon the Orphanage.

MRS. ALVING: Well, in that case——

MANDER: Nor can I entirely lose sight of the difficult—I may even say painful—position in which *I* might perhaps be placed. In the leading circles of the town, people take a lively interest in this Orphanage. It is, of course, founded partly for the benefit of the town, as well; and it is to be hoped it will, to a considerable extent, result in lightening our Poor Rates. Now, as I have been your adviser, and have had the business arrangements in my hands, I cannot but fear that I may have to bear the brunt of fanaticism——

MRS. ALVING: Oh, you mustn't run the risk of that.

MANDERS: To say nothing of the attacks that would assuredly be made upon me in certain papers and periodicals, which——

MRS. ALVING: Enough, my dear Pastor Manders. That consideration is quite decisive.

MANDERS: Then you do not wish the Orphanage to be insured?

MRS ALVING: No. We will let it alone.

MANDERS: (*Leaning back in his chair.*) But if, now, a disaster were to happen? One can never tell—— Should you be able to make good the damage?

MRS. ALVING: No; I tell you plainly I should do nothing of the kind.

MANDERS: Then I must tell you, Mrs. Alving—we are taking no small responsibility upon ourselves.

MRS. ALVING: Do you think we can do otherwise?

MANDERS: No, that is just the point; we really cannot do otherwise. We ought not to expose ourselves to misinterpretation; and we have no right whatever to give offence to the weaker brethren.

MRS. ALVING: You, as a clergyman, certainly should not.

MANDERS: I really think, too, we may trust that such an institution has fortune on its side; in fact, that it stands under a special providence.

MRS. ALVING: Let us hope so, Pastor Manders.

MANDERS: Then we will let it take its chance?

MRS. ALVING: Yes, certainly.

MANDERS: Very well. So be it. (*Makes a note.*) Then—no insurance.

MRS. ALVING: It's odd that you should just happen to mention the matter to-day——

MANDERS: I have often thought of asking you about it——

MRS. ALVING: ——for we very nearly had a fire down there yesterday.

MANDERS: You don't say so!

MRS. ALVING: Oh, it was a trifling matter. A heap of shavings had caught fire in the carpenter's workshop.

MANDERS: Where Engstrand works?

MRS. ALVING: Yes. They say he's often very careless with matches.

MANDERS: He has so much on his mind, that man—so many things to fight against. Thank God, he is now striving to lead a decent life, I hear.

MRS. ALVING: Indeed! Who says so?

MANDERS: He himself assures me of it. And he is certainly a capital workman.

MRS. ALVING: Oh, yes; so long as he's sober——

MANDERS: Ah, that melancholy weakness! But he is often driven to it by his injured leg, he says. Last time he was in town I was really touched by him. He came and thanked me so warmly for having got him work here, so that he might be near Regina.

MRS. ALVING: He doesn't see much of her.

MANDERS: Oh, yes, he has a talk with her every day. He told me so himself.

MRS. ALVING: Well, it may be so.

MANDERS: He feels so acutely that he needs some one to keep a firm hold on him when temptation comes. That is what I cannot help liking about Jacob Engstrand: he comes to you so helplessly, accusing himself and confessing his own weakness. The last time he was talking to me—— Believe me, Mrs. Alving, supposing it were a real necessity for him to have Regina home again——

MRS. ALVING: (*Rising hastily.*) Regina!

MANDERS: ——you must not set yourself against it.

MRS. ALVING: Indeed I s h a l l set myself against it. And besides—Regina is to have a position in the Orphanage.

MANDERS: But, after all, remember he is her father——

MRS. ALVING: Oh, I know very well what sort of a father he has been to her. No! She shall never go to him with my goodwill.

MANDERS: (*Rising.*) My dear lady, don't take the matter so warmly. You sadly misjudge poor Engstrand. You seem to be quite terrified——

MRS. ALVING: (*More quietly.*) It makes no difference. I have taken Regina into my house, and there she shall stay. (*Listens.*) Hush, my dear Mr. Manders; say no more about it. (*Her face lights up with gladness.*) Listen! there is Oswald coming downstairs. Now we'll think of no one but him.

(OSWALD ALVING, *in a light overcoat, hat in hand, and smoking a large meerschaum, enters by the door on the left; he stops in the doorway.*)

OSWALD: Oh, I beg your pardon; I thought you were in the study. (*Comes forward.*) Good-morning, Pastor Manders.

MANDERS: *(Staring.)* Ah——! How strange——!

MRS. ALVING: Well now, what do you think of him, Mr. Manders?

MANDERS: I—I—can it really be——?

OSWALD: Yes, it's really the Prodigal Son, sir.

MANDERS: *(Protesting.)* My dear young friend——

OSWALD: Well, then, the Lost Sheep Found.

MRS. ALVING: Oswald is thinking of the time when you were so much opposed to his becoming a painter.

MANDERS: To our human eyes many a step seems dubious, which afterwards proves—— *(Wrings his hand.)* But first of all, welcome, welcome home! Do not think, my dear Oswald—I suppose I may call you by your Christian name?

OSWALD: What else should you call me?

MANDERS: Very good. What I wanted to say was this, my dear Oswald—you must not think that I utterly condemn the artist's calling. I have no doubt there are many who can keep their inner self unharmed in that profession, as in any other.

OSWALD: Let us hope so.

MRS. ALVING: *(Beaming with delight.)* I know one who has kept both his inner and his outer self unharmed. Just look at him, Mr. Manders.

OSWALD: *(Moves restlessly about the room.)* Yes, yes, my dear mother; let's say no more about it.

MANDERS: Why, certainly—that is undeniable. And you have begun to make a name for yourself already. The newspapers have often spoken of you, most favourably. Just lately, by-the-bye, I fancy I haven't seen your name quite so often.

OSWALD: *(Up in the conservatory.)* I haven't been able to paint so much lately.

MRS. ALVING: Even a painter needs a little rest now and then.

MANDERS: No doubt, no doubt. And meanwhile he can be preparing himself and mustering his forces for some great work.

OSWALD: Yes.—Mother, will dinner soon be ready?

MRS. ALVING: In less than half an hour. He has a capital appetite, thank God.

MANDERS: And a taste for tobacco, too.

OSWALD: I found my father's pipe in my room——

MANDERS: Aha—then that accounts for it!

MRS. ALVING: For what?

MANDERS: When Oswald appeared there, in the doorway, with the pipe in his mouth, I could have sworn I saw his father, large as life.

OSWALD: No, really?

MRS. ALVING: Oh, how can you say so? Oswald takes after me.

MANDERS: Yes, but there is an expression about the corners of the mouth—something about the lips—that reminds one exactly of Alving: at any rate, now that he is smoking.

MRS. ALVING: Not in the least. Oswald has rather a clerical curve about his mouth, I think.

MANDERS: Yes, yes; some of my colleagues have much the same expression.

MRS. ALVING: But put your pipe away, my dear boy; I won't have smoking in here.

OSWALD: *(Does so.)* By all means. I only wanted to try it; for I once smoked it when I was a child.

MRS. ALVING: You?

OSWALD: Yes. I was quite small at the time. I recollect I came up to father's room one evening when he was in great spirits.

MRS. ALVING: Oh, you can't recollect anything of those times.

OSWALD: Yes, I recollect it distinctly. He took me on his knee, and gave me the pipe. "Smoke, boy," he said; "smoke away, boy!" And I smoked as hard as I could, until I felt I was growing quite pale, and the perspiration stood in great drops on my forehead. Then he burst out laughing heartily——

MANDERS: That was most extraordinary.

MRS. ALVING: My dear friend, it's only something Oswald has dreamt.

OSWALD: No, mother, I assure you I didn't dream it. For—don't you remember t h i s ?—you came and carried me out into the nursery. Then I was sick, and I saw that you were crying.—Did father often play such practical jokes?

MANDERS: In his youth he overflowed with the joy of life——

OSWALD: And yet he managed to do so much in the world; so much that was good and useful; although he died so early.

MANDERS: Yes, you have inherited the name of an energetic and admirable man, my dear Oswald Alving. No doubt it will be an incentive to you——

OSWALD: It ought to, indeed.

MANDERS: It was good of you to come home for the ceremony in his honour.

OSWALD: I could do no less for my father.

MRS. ALVING: And I am to keep him so long! That is the best of all.

MANDERS: You are going to pass the winter at home, I hear.

OSWALD: My stay is indefinite, sir.— But, ah! it is good to be at home!

MRS. ALVING: (*Beaming.*) Yes, isn't it, dear?

MANDERS: (*Looking sympathetically at him.*) You went out into the world early, my dear Oswald.

OSWALD: I did. I sometimes wonder whether it wasn't t o o early.

MRS. ALVING: Oh, not at all. A healthy lad is all the better for it; especially when he's an only child. He oughtn't to hang on at home with his mother and father, and get spoilt.

MANDERS: That is a very disputable point, Mrs. Alving. A child's proper place is, and must be, the home of his fathers.

OSWALD: There I quite agree with you, Pastor Manders.

MANDERS: Only look at your own son— there is no reason why we should not say it in his presence—what has the consequence been for him? He is six or seven and twenty, and has never had the opportunity of learning what a well-ordered home really is.

OSWALD: I beg your pardon, Pastor; there you're quite mistaken.

MANDERS: Indeed? I thought you had lived almost exclusively in artistic circles.

OSWALD: So I have.

MANDERS: And chiefly among the younger artists?

OSWALD: Yes, certainly.

MANDERS: But I thought few of those young fellows could afford to set up house and support a family.

OSWALD: There are many who cannot afford to marry, sir.

MANDERS: Yes, that is just what I say.

OSWALD: But they may have a home for all that. And several of them have, as a matter of fact; and very pleasant, well-ordered homes they are, too.

(MRS. ALVING *follows with breathless interest; nods, but says nothing.*)

MANDERS: But I'm not talking of bachelors' quarters. By a "home" I understand the home of a family, where a man lives with his wife and children.

OSWALD: Yes; or with his children and his children's mother.

MANDERS: (*Starts; clasps his hands.*) But, good heavens——

OSWALD: Well?

MANDERS: Lives with—his children's mother!

OSWALD: Yes. Would you have him turn his children's mother out of doors?

MANDERS: Then it is illicit relations you are talking of! Irregular marriages, as people call them!

OSWALD: I have never noticed anything particularly irregular about the life these people lead.

MANDERS: But how is it possible that a—a young man or young woman with any decency of feeling can endure to live in that way?—in the eyes of all the world!

OSWALD: What are they to do? A poor young artist—a poor girl—marriage costs a great deal. What are they to do?

MANDERS: What are they to do? Let me tell you, Mr. Alving, what they ought to do. They ought to exercise self-restraint from the first; that is what they ought to do.

OSWALD: That doctrine will scarcely go down with warm-blooded young people who love each other.

MRS. ALVING: No, scarcely!

MANDERS: (*Continuing.*) How can the authorities tolerate such things! Allow them to go on in the light of day; (*Confronting* MRS. ALVING.) Had I not cause to be deeply concerned about your son? In circles where open immorality prevails, and has even a sort of recognised position——!

OSWALD: Let me tell you, sir, that I have been in the habit of spending nearly all my Sundays in one or two such irregular homes——

MANDERS: Sundays of all days!

OSWALD: Isn't that the day to enjoy one's self? Well, never have I heard an offensive word, and still less have I witnessed anything that could be called immoral. No; do you know when and where I have come across immorality in artistic circles?

MANDERS: No, thank heaven, I don't!

OSWALD: Well, then, allow me to inform you. I have met with it when one or other of our pattern husbands and fathers has come to Paris to have a look round on his own account, and has done the artists the honour of visiting their humble haunts. T h e y knew what was what. These gentlemen could tell us all about places and things we had never dreamt of.

MANDERS: What! Do you mean to say that respectable men from home here would——?

OSWALD: Have you never heard these respectable men, when they got home again, talking about the way in which immorality runs rampant abroad?

MANDERS: Yes, no doubt——

MRS. ALVING: I have too.

OSWALD: Well, you may take their word for it. They know what they are talking about! (*Presses his hands to his head.*) Oh! that that great, free, glorious life out there should be defiled in such a way!

MRS. ALVING: You mustn't get excited, Oswald. It's not good for you.

OSWALD: Yes; you're quite right, mother. It's bad for me, I know. You see, I'm wretchedly worn out. I shall go for a little turn before dinner. Excuse me, Pastor: I know you can't take my point of view; but I couldn't help speaking out.

(*He goes out by the second door to the right.*)

MRS. ALVING: My poor boy!

MANDERS: You may well say so. Then this is what he has come to!

(MRS. ALVING *looks at him silently.*)

MANDERS: (*Walking up and down.*) He called himself the Prodigal Son. Alas! alas!

(MRS. ALVING *continues looking at him.*)

MANDERS: And what do y o u say to all this?

MRS. ALVING: I say that Oswald was right in every word.

MANDERS: (*Stands still.*) Right? Right! In such principles?

MRS. ALVING: Here, in my loneliness, I have come to the same way of thinking, Pastor Manders. But I have never dared to say anything. Well! now my boy shall speak for me.

MANDERS: You are greatly to be pitied, Mrs. Alving. But now I must speak seriously to you. And now it is no longer your business manager and adviser, your own and your husband's early friend, who stands before you. It is the priest—the priest who stood before you in the moment of your life when you had gone farthest astray.

MRS. ALVING: And what has the priest to say to me?

MANDERS: I will first stir up your memory a little. The moment is well chosen. To-morrow will be the tenth anniversary of your husband's death. To-morrow the memorial in his honour will be unveiled. To-morrow I shall have to speak to the whole assembled multitude. But to-day I will speak to you alone.

MRS. ALVING: Very well, Pastor Manders. Speak.

MANDERS: Do you remember that after less than a year of married life you stood on the verge of an abyss? That you forsook your house and home? That you fled from your husband? Yes, Mrs. Alving—fled, fled, and refused to return to him, however much he begged and prayed you?

MRS. ALVING: Have you forgotten how infinitely miserable I was in that first year?

MANDERS: It is the very mark of the spirit of rebellion to crave for happiness in this life. What right have we human beings to happiness? We have simply to do our duty, Mrs. Alving! And your duty was to hold firmly to the man you had once chosen, and to whom you were bound by the holiest ties.

MRS. ALVING: You know very well what sort of life Alving was leading—what excesses he was guilty of.

MANDERS: I know very well what rumours there were about him; and I am the last to approve the life he led in his young days, if report did not wrong him. But a wife is not appointed to be her husband's judge. It was your duty to bear with humility the cross which a Higher Power had, in its wisdom, laid upon you. But instead of that you rebelliously throw away the cross, desert the backslider whom you should have supported, go and risk your good name and reputation, and— nearly succeed in ruining other people's reputation into the bargain.

MRS. ALVING: Other people's? One other person's, you mean.

MANDERS: It was incredibly reckless of you to seek refuge with me.

MRS. ALVING: With our clergyman? With our intimate friend?

MANDERS: Just on that account. Yes, you may thank God that I possessed the necessary firmness; that I succeeded in dissuading you from your wild designs; and that it was vouchsafed me to lead you back to the path of duty, and home to your lawful husband.

MRS. ALVING: Yes, Pastor Manders, t h a t was certainly your work.

MANDERS: I was but a poor instrument in a Higher Hand. And what a blessing has it not proved to you, all the days of your life, that I induced you to resume the yoke of duty and obedience! Did not everything happen as I foretold? Did not Alving turn his back on his errors, as a man should? Did he not live with you from that time, lovingly and blamelessly, all his days? Did he not become a benefactor to the whole district? And did he not help you to rise to his own level, so that you, little by little, became his assistant in all his undertakings? And a capital assistant, too—oh, I know, Mrs. Alving, t h a t praise is due to you.—But now I come to the next great error in your life.

MRS. ALVING: What do you mean?

MANDERS: Just as you once disowned a wife's duty, so you have since disowned a mother's.

MRS. ALVING: Ah——!

MANDERS: You have been all your life under the dominion of a pestilent spirit of self-will. The whole bias of your mind has been towards insubordination and lawlessness. You have never known how to endure any bond. Everything that has weighed upon you in life you have cast away without care or conscience, like a burden you were free to throw off at will. It did not please you to be a wife any longer, and you left your husband. You found it troublesome to be a mother, and you sent your child forth among strangers.

MRS. ALVING: Yes, that is true. I did so.

MANDERS: And thus you have become a stranger to him.

MRS. ALVING: No! no! I am not.

MANDERS: Yes, you are; you m u s t be. And in what state of mind has he returned to you? Bethink yourself well, Mrs. Alving. You sinned greatly against your husband;—that you recognise by raising yonder memorial to him. Recognise now, also, how you have sinned against your son—there may yet be time to lead him back from the paths of error. Turn back yourself, and save what may yet be saved in him. For (*With uplifted forefinger*) verily, Mrs. Alving, you are a guilt-laden mother!—This I have thought it my duty to say to you.   (*Silence.*)

MRS. ALVING: (*Slowly and with self-control.*) You have now spoken out, Pastor Manders; and to-morrow you are to speak publicly in memory of my husband. I shall not speak to-morrow. But now I will speak frankly to you, as you have spoken to me.

MANDERS: To be sure; you will plead excuses for your conduct——

MRS. ALVING: No. I will only tell you a story.

MANDERS: Well——?

MRS. ALVING: All that you have just said about my husband and me, and our life after you had brought me back to the path of duty—as you called it—about all that you know nothing from personal observation. From that moment you, who had been our intimate friend, never set foot in our house again.

MANDERS: You and your husband left the town immediately after.

MRS. ALVING: Yes; and in my husband's lifetime you never came to see us. It was business that forced you to visit me when you undertook the affairs of the Orphanage.

MANDERS: (*Softly and hesitatingly.*) Helen—if that is meant as a reproach, I would beg you to bear in mind——

MRS. ALVING: ——the regard you owed to your position, yes; and that I was a runaway wife. One can never be too cautious with such unprincipled creatures.

MANDERS: My dear—Mrs. Alving, you know that is an absurd exaggeration——

MRS. ALVING: Well well, suppose it is. My point is that your judgment as to my married life is founded upon nothing but common knowledge and report.

MANDERS: I admit that. What then?

MRS. ALVING: Well, then, Pastor Manders—I will tell you the truth. I have sworn to myself that one day you should know it—you alone!

MANDERS: What is the truth, then?

MRS. ALVING: The truth is that my husband died just as dissolute as he had lived all his days.

MANDERS: (*Feeling after a chair.*) What do you say?

MRS. ALVING: After nineteen years of marriage, as dissolute—in his desires at any rate—as he was before you married us.

MANDERS: And those—those wild oats—those irregularities—those excesses, if you like—you call "a dissolute life"?

MRS. ALVING: Our doctor used the expression.

MANDERS: I do not understand you.

MRS. ALVING: You need not.

MANDERS: It almost makes me dizzy. Your whole married life, the seeming union of all these years, was nothing more than a hidden abyss!

MRS. ALVING: Neither more nor less. Now you know it.

MANDERS: This is—this is inconceivable to me. I cannot grasp it! I cannot realise it! But how was it possible to——? How could such a state of things be kept secret?

MRS. ALVING: That has been my ceaseless struggle, day after day. After Oswald's birth, I thought Alving seemed to be a little better. But it did not last long. And then I had to struggle twice as hard, fighting as though for life or death, so that nobody should know what sort of man my child's father was. And you know what power Alving had of winning people's hearts. Nobody seemed able to

believe anything but good of him. He was one of those people whose life does not bite upon their reputation. But at last, Mr. Manders—for you must know the whole story—the most repulsive thing of all happened.

MANDERS: More repulsive than what you have told me!

MRS. ALVING: I had gone on bearing with him, although I knew very well the secrets of his life out of doors. But when he brought the scandal within our own walls——

MANDERS: Impossible! Here!

MRS. ALVING: Yes; here in our own home. It was there (*Pointing towards the first door on the right*), in the dining-room, that I first came to know of it. I was busy with something in there, and the door was standing ajar. I heard our housemaid come up from the garden, with water for those flowers.

MANDERS: Well——?

MRS. ALVING: Soon after, I heard Alving come in too. I heard him say something softly to her. And then I heard—(*With a short laugh*)—oh! it still sounds in my ears, so hateful and yet so ludicrous—I heard my own servant-maid whisper, "Let me go, Mr. Alving! Let me be!"

MANDERS: What unseemly levity on his part! But it cannot have been more than levity, Mrs. Alving; believe me, it cannot.

MRS. ALVING: I soon knew what to believe. Mr. Alving had his way with the girl; and that connection had consequences, Mr. Manders.

MANDERS: (*As though petrified.*) Such things in this house! in this house!

MRS. ALVING: I had borne a great deal in this house. To keep him at home in the evenings, and at night, I had to make myself his boon companion in his secret orgies up in his room. There I had had to sit alone with him, to clink glasses and drink with him, and to listen to his ribald, silly talk. I have had to fight with him to get him dragged to bed——

MANDERS: (*Moved.*) And you were able to bear all this!

MRS. ALVING: I had to bear it for my little boy's sake. But when the last insult was added; when my own servant-maid ——; then I swore to myself: This shall come to an end! And so I took the reins into my own hand—the whole control—over him and everything else. For now I had a weapon against him, you see; he dared not oppose me. It was then I sent Oswald away from home. He was nearly seven years old, and was beginning to observe and ask questions, as children do. That I could not bear. It seemed to me the child must be poisoned by merely breathing the air of this polluted home. That was why I sent him away. And now you can see, too, why he was never allowed to set foot inside his home so long as his father lived. No one knows what that cost me.

MANDERS: You have indeed had a life of trial.

MRS. ALVING: I could never have borne it if I had not had my work. For I may truly say that I have worked! All the additions to the estate—all the improvements—all the labour-saving appliances, that Alving was so much praised for having introduced—do you suppose he had energy for anything of the sort?—h e, who lay all day on the sofa, reading an old Court Guide! No; but I may tell you t h i s too; when he had his better intervals, it was I who urged him on; it was I who had to drag the whole load when he relapsed into his evil ways, or sank into querulous wretchedness.

MANDERS: And it is to this man that you raise a memorial?

MRS. ALVING: There you see the power of an evil conscience.

MANDERS: Evil——? What do you mean?

MRS. ALVING: It always seemed to me impossible but that the truth must come out and be believed. So the Orphanage was to deaden all rumours and set every doubt at rest.

MANDERS: In that you have certainly not missed your aim, Mrs. Alving.

MRS. ALVING: And besides, I had one other reason. I was determined that Oswald, my own boy, should inherit nothing whatever from his father.

MANDERS: Then it is Alving's fortune that——?

MRS. ALVING: Yes. The sums I have spent upon the Orphanage, year by year, make up the amount—I have reckoned it up precisely—the amount which made Lieutenant Alving "a good match" in his day.

MANDERS: I don't understand——

MRS. ALVING: It was my purchase-money. I do not choose that that money should pass into Oswald's hands. My son shall have everything from me—everything.

OSWALD ALVING *enters through the second door to the right; he has taken off his hat and overcoat in the hall.*)

MRS. ALVING: (*Going towards him.*) Are you back again already? My dear, dear boy!

OSWALD: Yes. What can a fellow do out of doors in this eternal rain? But I hear dinner is ready. That's capital!

REGINA: (*With a parcel, from the dining-room.*) A parcel has come for you, Mrs. Alving. (*Hands it to her.*)

MRS. ALVING: (*With a glance at* MR. MANDERS.) No doubt copies of the ode for to-morrow's ceremony.

MANDERS: H'm——

REGINA: And dinner is ready.

MRS. ALVING: Very well. We will come directly. I will just——

(*Begins to open the parcel.*)

REGINA: (*To* OSWALD.) Would Mr. Alving like red or white wine?

OSWALD: Both, if you please.

REGINA: *Bien.* Very well, sir.

(*She goes into the dining-room.*)

OSWALD: I may as well help to uncork it.

(*He also goes into the dining-room, the door of which swings half open behind him.*)

MRS. ALVING: (*Who has opened the parcel.*) Yes, I thought so. Here is the Ceremonial Ode, Pastor Manders.

MANDERS: (*With folded hands.*) With what countenance I am to deliver my discourse to-morrow——!

MRS. ALVING: Oh, you will get through it somehow.

MANDERS: (*Softly, so as not to be heard in the dining-room.*) Yes; it would not do to provoke scandal.

MRS. ALVING: (*Under her breath, but firmly.*) No. But t h e n this long, hateful comedy will be ended. From the day after to-morrow, I shall act in every way as though he who is dead had never lived in this house. There shall be no one here but my boy and his mother.

(*From the dining-room comes the noise of a chair overturned, and at the same moment is heard:*)

REGINA: (*Sharply, but in a whisper.*) Oswald! take care! are you mad? Let me go!

MRS. ALVING: (*Starts in terror.*) Ah——!

(*She stares wildly towards the half-open door.* OSWALD *is heard laughing and humming. A bottle is uncorked.*)

MANDERS: (*Agitated.*) What c a n be the matter? What is it Mrs. Alving?

MRS. ALVING: (*Hoarsely.*) Ghosts! The couple from the conservatory—risen again!

MANDERS: Is it possible! Regina——? Is s h e——?

MRS. ALVING: Yes. Come. Not a word——!

(*She seizes* PASTOR MANDERS *by the arm, and walks unsteadily towards the dining-room.*)

ACT SECOND

The same room. The mist still lies heavy over the landscape.

(MANDERS *and* MRS. ALVING *enter from the dining-room.*)

MRS. ALVING: (*Still in the doorway.*) *Velbekomme,*[1] Mr. Manders. (*Turns back towards the dining-room.*) Aren't you coming too, Oswald?

OSWALD: (*From within.*) No, thank you. I think I shall go out a little.

MRS. ALVING: Yes, do. The weather seems a little brighter now. (*She shuts the dining-room door, goes to the hall door, and calls:*) Regina!

REGINA: (*Outside.*) Yes, Mrs. Alving?

MRS. ALVING: Go down to the laundry, and help with the garlands.

REGINA: Yes, Mrs. Alving.

(MRS. ALVING *assures herself that* REGINA *goes; then shuts the door.*)

MANDERS: I suppose he cannot overhear us in there?

MRS. ALVING: Not when the door is shut. Besides, he's just going out.

[1] A phrase equivalent to the German *Prosit die Mahlzeit*—"May good digestion wait on appetite."

MANDERS: I am still quite upset. I don't know how I could swallow a morsel of dinner.

MRS. ALVING: (*Controlling her nervousness, walks up and down.*) Nor I. But what is to be done now?

MANDERS: Yes; what is to be done? I am really quite at a loss. I am so utterly without experience in matters of this sort.

MRS. ALVING: I feel sure that, so far, no mischief has been done.

MANDERS: No; heaven forbid! But it is an unseemly state of things, nevertheless.

MRS. ALVING: It is only an idle fancy on Oswald's part; you may be sure of that.

MANDERS: Well, as I say, I am not accustomed to affairs of the kind. But I should certainly think——

MRS. ALVING: Out of the house she must go, and that immediately. That is as clear as daylight——

MANDERS: Yes, of course she must.

MRS. ALVING: But where to? It would not be right to——

MANDERS: Where to? Home to her father, of course.

MRS. ALVING: To whom did you say?

MANDERS: To her—— But then, Engstrand is not——? Good God, Mrs. Alving, it's impossible! You must be mistaken after all.

MRS. ALVING: Unfortunately there is no possibility of mistake. Johanna confessed everything to me; and Alving could not deny it. So there was nothing to be done but to get the matter hushed up.

MANDERS: No, you could do nothing else.

MRS. ALVING: The girl left our service at once, and got a good sum of money to hold her tongue for the time. The rest she managed for herself when she got to town. She renewed her old acquaintance with Engstrand, no doubt let him see that she had money in her purse, and told him some tale about a foreigner who put in here with a yacht that summer. So she and Engstrand got married in hot haste. Why, you married them yourself.

MANDERS: But then how to account for——? I recollect distinctly Engstrand coming to give notice of the marriage. He was quite overwhelmed with contrition, and bitterly reproached himself for the misbehaviour he and his sweetheart had been guilty of.

MRS. ALVING: Yes; of course he had to take the blame upon himself.

MANDERS: But such a piece of duplicity on his part! And towards m e too! I never could have believed it of Jacob Engstrand. I shall not fail to take him seriously to task; he may be sure of that.—And then the immorality of such a connection! For money——! How much did the girl receive?

MRS. ALVING: Three hundred dollars.

MANDERS: Just think of it—for a miserable three hundred dollars, to go and marry a fallen woman!

MRS. ALVING: Then what have you to say of me? I went and married a fallen man.

MANDERS: Why—good heavens!—what are you talking about! A fallen man.

MRS. ALVING: Do you think Alving was any purer when I went with him to the altar than Johanna was when Engstrand married her?

MANDERS: Well, but there is a world of difference between the two cases——

MRS. ALVING: Not so much difference after all—except in the price:—a miserable three hundred dollars and a whole fortune.

MANDERS: How can you compare such absolutely dissimilar cases? you had taken counsel with your own heart and with your natural advisers.

MRS. ALVING: (*Without looking at him.*) I thought you understood where what you call my heart had strayed to at the time.

MANDERS: (*Distantly.*) Had I understood anything of the kind, I should not have been a daily guest in your husband's house.

MRS. ALVING: At any rate, the fact remains that with myself I took no counsel whatever.

MANDERS: Well then, with your nearest relatives—as your duty bade you—with your mother and your two aunts.

MRS. ALVING: Yes, that is true. Those three cast up the account for me. Oh, it's marvellous how clearly they made out that it would be downright madness to refuse such an offer. If mother could only see me now, and know what all that grandeur has come to!

MANDERS: Nobody can be held responsible for the result. This, at least, remains clear: your marriage was in full accordance with law and order.

MRS. ALVING: (*At the window.*) Oh, that perpetual law and order! I often think t h a t is what does all the mischief in this world of ours.

MANDERS: Mrs. Alving, that is a sinful way of talking.

MRS. ALVING: Well, I can't help it; I must have done with all this constraint and insincerity. I can endure it no longer. I must work my way out to freedom.

MANDERS: What do you mean by that?

MRS. ALVING: (*Drumming on the window-frame.*) I ought never to have concealed the facts of Alving's life. But at that time I dared not do anything else— I was afraid, partly on my own account. I was such a coward.

MANDERS: A coward?

MRS. ALVING: If people had come to know anything, they would have said— "Poor man! with a runaway wife, no wonder he kicks over the traces."

MANDERS: Such remarks might have been made with a certain show of right.

MRS. ALVING: (*Looking steadily at him.*) If I were what I ought to be, I should go to Oswald and say, "Listen, my boy: your father led a vicious life——"

MANDERS: Merciful heavens——!

MRS. ALVING: ——and then I should tell him all I have told you—every word of it.

MANDERS: You shock me unspeakably, Mrs. Alving.

MRS. ALVING: Yes; I know that. I know that very well. I myself am shocked at the idea. (*Goes away from the window.*) I am such a coward.

MANDERS: You call it "cowardice" to do your plain duty? Have you forgotten that a son ought to love and honour his father and mother?

MRS. ALVING: Do not let us talk in such general terms. Let us ask: Ought Oswald to love and honour Chamberlain Alving?

MANDERS: Is there no voice in your mother's heart that forbids you to destroy your son's ideals?

MRS. ALVING: But what about the truth?

MANDERS: But what about the ideals?

MRS. ALVING: Oh—ideals, ideals! If only I were not such a coward!

MANDERS: Do not despise ideals, Mrs. Alving; they will avenge themselves cruelly. Take Oswald's case: he, unfortunately, seems to have few enough ideals as it is; but I can see that his father stands before him as an ideal.

MRS. ALVING: Yes, that is true.

MANDERS: And this habit of mind you have yourself implanted and fostered by your letters.

MRS. ALVING: Yes; in my superstitious

awe for duty and the proprieties, I lied to my boy, year after year. Oh, what a coward—what a coward I have been!

MANDERS: You have established a happy illusion in your son's heart, Mrs. Alving; and assuredly you ought not to undervalue it.

MRS. ALVING: H'm; who knows whether it is so happy after all——? But, at any rate, I will not have any tampering with Regina. He shall not go and wreck the poor girl's life.

MANDERS: No; good God—that would be terrible!

MRS. ALVING: If I knew he was in earnest, and that it would be for his happiness——

MANDERS: What? What then?

MRS. ALVING: But it couldn't be; for unfortunately Regina is not the right sort of woman.

MANDERS: Well, what then? What do you mean?

MRS. ALVING: If I weren't such a pitiful coward, I should say to him, "Marry her, or make what arrangement you please, only let us have nothing underhand about it."

MANDERS: Merciful heavens, would you let them m a r r y! Anything so dreadful ——! so unheard of——

MRS. ALVING: Do you really mean "unheard of"? Frankly, Pastor Manders, do you suppose that throughout the country there are not plenty of married couples as closely akin as they?

MANDERS: I don't in the least understand you.

MRS. ALVING: Oh yes, indeed you do.

MANDERS: Ah, you are thinking of the possibility that—— Alas! yes, family life is certainly not always so pure as it ought to be. But in such a case as you point to, one can never know—at least with any certainty. Here, on the other hand—that you, a mother, can think of letting your son——!

MRS. ALVING: But I cannot—I wouldn't for anything in the world; that is precisely what I am saying.

MANDERS: No, because you are a "coward," as you put it. But if you were not a "coward," then——? Good God! a connection so shocking!

MRS. ALVING: So far as that goes, they say we are all sprung from connections of that sort. And who is it that arranged the world so, Pastor Manders?

MANDERS: Questions of that kind I must decline to discuss with you, Mrs. Alving; you are far from being in the right frame of mind for them. But that you dare do call your scruples "cowardly"——!

MRS. ALVING: Let me tell you what I mean. I am timid and fainthearted because of the ghosts that hang about me, and that I can never quite shake off.

MANDERS: What do you say hangs about you?

MRS. ALVING: Ghosts! When I heard Regina and Oswald in there, it was as though ghosts rose up before me. But I almost think we are all of us ghosts, Pastor Manders. It is not only what we have inherited from our father and mother that "walks" in us. It is all sorts of dead ideas, and lifeless old beliefs, and so forth. They have no vitality, but they cling to us all the same, and we cannot shake them off. Whenever I take up a newspaper, I seem to see ghosts gliding between the lines. There must be ghosts all the country over, as thick as the sands of the sea. And then we are, one and all, so pitifully afraid of the light.

MANDERS: Aha—here we have the fruits of your reading. And pretty fruits they are, upon my word! Oh, those horrible, revolutionary, freethinking books!

MRS. ALVING: You are mistaken, my dear Pastor. It was you yourself who set me thinking; and I thank you for it with all my heart.

MANDERS: I!

MRS. ALVING: Yes—when you forced me under the yoke of what you called duty and obligation; when you lauded as right and proper what my whole soul rebelled against as something loathsome. It was then that I began to look into the seams of your doctrines. I wanted only to pick at a single knot; but when I had got that undone, the whole thing ravelled out. And then I understood that it was all machine-sewn.

MANDERS: (*Softly, with emotion.*) And was that the upshot of my life's hardest battle?

MRS. ALVING: Call it rather your most pitiful defeat.

MANDERS: It was my greatest victory, Helen—the victory over myself.

MRS. ALVING: It was a crime against us both.

MANDERS: When you went astray, and came to me crying, "Here I am; take me!" I commanded you, saying, "Woman, go home to your lawful husband." Was t h a t a crime?

MRS. ALVING: Yes, I think so.

MANDERS: We two do not understand each other.

MRS. ALVING: Not now, at any rate.

MANDERS: Never—never in my most secret thoughts have I regarded you otherwise than as another's wife.

MRS. ALVING: Oh—indeed?

MANDERS: Helen——!

MRS. ALVING: People so easily forget their past selves.

MANDERS: I do not. I am what I always was.

MRS. ALVING: (*Changing the subject.*) Well, well, well; don't let us talk of old times any longer. You are now over head and ears in Boards and Committees, and I am fighting my battle with ghosts, both within me and without.

MANDERS: Those without I shall help you to lay. After all the terrible things I have heard from you to-day, I cannot in conscience permit an unprotected girl to remain in your house.

MRS. ALVING: Don't you think the best plan would be to get her provided for?— I mean, by a good marriage.

MANDERS: No doubt. I think it would be desirable for her in every respect. Regina is now at the age when—— Of course I don't know much about these things, but——

MRS. ALVING: Regina matured very early.

MANDERS: Yes, I thought so. I have an impression that she was remarkably well developed, physically, when I prepared her for confirmation. But in the meantime, she ought to be at home, under her father's eye—— Ah! but Engstrand is not—— That he—that h e—could so hide the truth from me!

(*A knock at the door into the hall.*)

MRS. ALVING: Who can this be? Come in!

ENGSTRAND: (*In his Sunday clothes, in the doorway.*) I humbly beg your pardon, but——

MANDERS: Aha! H'm——

MRS. ALVING: Is that you, Engstrand?

ENGSTRAND: ——there was none of the servants about, so I took the great liberty of just knocking.

MRS. ALVING: Oh, very well. Come in. Do you want to speak to me?

ENGSTRAND: (*Comes in.*) No, I'm obliged to you, ma'am; it was with his Reverence I wanted to have a word or two.

MANDERS: (*Walking up and down the room.*) Ah—indeed! You want to speak to me, do you?

ENGSTRAND: Yes, I'd like so terrible much to——

MANDERS: (*Stops in front of him.*) Well; may I ask what you want?

ENGSTRAND: Well, it was just this, your Reverence: we've been paid off down yonder—my grateful thanks to you, ma'am,—and now everything's finished, I've been thinking it would be but right and proper if we, that have been working so honestly together all this time—well, I was thinking we ought to end up with a little prayer-meeting to-night.

MANDERS: A prayer-meeting? Down at the Orphanage?

ENGSTRAND: Oh, if your Reverence doesn't think it proper——

MANDERS: Oh yes, I do; but—h'm——

ENGSTRAND: I've been in the habit of offering up a little prayer in the evenings, myself——

MRS. ALVING: Have you?

ENGSTRAND: Yes, every now and then—just a little edification, in a manner of speaking. But I'm a poor, common man, and have little enough gift, God help me! —and so I thought, as the Reverend Mr. Manders happened to be here, I'd—

MANDERS: Well, you see, Engstrand, I have a question to put to you first. Are you in the right frame of mind for such a meeting? Do you feel your conscience clear and at ease?

ENGSTRAND: Oh, God help us, your Reverence! we'd better not talk about conscience.

MANDERS: Yes, that is just what we must talk about. What have you to answer?

ENGSTRAND: Why—a man's conscience —it can be bad enough now and then.

MANDERS: Ah, you admit that. Then perhaps you will make a clean breast of it, and tell me—the real truth about Regina?

MRS. ALVING: (*Quickly.*) Mr. Manders!

MANDERS: (*Reassuringly.*) Please allow me——

ENGSTRAND: About Regina! Lord, what a turn you gave me! (*Looks at* MRS. AL-VING.) There's nothing wrong about Regina, is there?

MANDERS: We will hope not. But I mean, what is the truth about you and Regina? You pass for her father, eh!

ENGSTRAND: (*Uncertain.*) Well—h'm— your Reverence knows all about me and poor Johanna.

MANDERS: Come now, no more prevarication! Your wife told Mrs. Alving the whole story before quitting her service.

ENGSTRAND: Well, then, may——! Now, did she really?

MANDERS: You see we know you now, Engstrand.

ENGSTRAND: And she swore and took her Bible oath——

MANDERS: Did she take her Bible oath?

ENGSTRAND: No; she only swore; but she did it that solemn-like.

MANDERS: And you have hidden the truth from me all these years? Hidden it from me, who have trusted you without reserve, in everything.

ENGSTRAND: Well, I can't deny it.

MANDERS: Have I deserved this of you, Engstrand? Have I not always been ready to help you in word and deed, so far as it lay in my power? Answer me. Have I not?

ENGSTRAND: It would have been a poor look-out for me many a time but for the Reverend Mr. Manders.

MANDERS: And this is how you reward me! You cause me to enter falsehoods in the Church Register, and you withhold from me, year after year, the explanations you owed alike to me and to the truth. Your conduct has been wholly inexcusable, Engstrand; and from this time forward I have done with you!

ENGSTRAND: (*With a sigh.*) Yes! I suppose there's no help for it.

MANDERS: How can you possibly justify yourself?

ENGSTRAND: Who could ever have thought she'd have gone and made bad worse by talking about it? Will your Reverence just fancy yourself in the same trouble as poor Johanna——

MANDERS: I!

ENGSTRAND: Lord bless you, I don't mean just exactly the same. But I mean, if your Reverence had anything to be ashamed of in the eyes of the world, as the saying goes. We menfolk oughtn't to judge a poor woman too hardly, your Reverence.

MANDERS: I am not doing so. It is you I am reproaching.

ENGSTRAND: Might I make so bold as to ask your Reverence a bit of a question?

MANDERS: Yes, if you want to.

ENGSTRAND: Isn't it right and proper for a man to raise up the fallen?

MANDERS: Most certainly it is.

ENGSTRAND: And isn't a man bound to keep his sacred word?

MANDERS: Why, of course he is; but——

ENGSTRAND: When Johanna had got into trouble through that Englishman—or it might have been an American or a Russian, as they call them—well, you see, she came down into the town. Poor thing, she'd sent me about my business once or twice before: for she couldn't bear the sight of anything as wasn't handsome; and I'd got this damaged leg of mine. Your Reverence recollects how I ventured up into a dancing saloon, where seafaring men was carrying on with drink and devilry, as the saying goes. And then, when I was for giving them a bit of an admonition to lead a new life——

MRS. ALVING: (*At the window.*) H'm——

MANDERS: I know all about that, Engstrand; the ruffians threw you downstairs. You have told me of the affair already. Your infirmity is an honour to you.

ENGSTRAND: I'm not puffed up about it, your Reverence. But what I wanted to say was, that when she came and confessed all to me, with weeping and gnashing of teeth, I can tell your Reverence I was sore at heart to hear it.

MANDERS: Were you indeed, Engstrand? Well, go on.

ENGSTRAND: So I says to her, "The American, he's sailing about on the boundless sea. And as for you, Johanna," says I, "you've committed a grievous sin, and you're a fallen creature. But Jacob Engstrand," says I, "he's got two good legs to stand upon, h e has——" You see, your Reverence, I was speaking figurative-like.

MANDERS: I understand quite well. Go on.

ENGSTRAND: Well, that was how I raised her up and made an honest woman of her, so as folks shouldn't get to know how as she'd gone astray with foreigners.

MANDERS: In all that you acted very well. Only I cannot approve of your stooping to take money——

ENGSTRAND: Money? I? Not a farthing!

MANDERS: (*Inquiringly to* MRS. ALVING.) But——

ENGSTRAND: Oh, wait a minute!—now I recollect. Johanna d i d have a trifle of money. But I would have nothing to do with t h a t. "No," says I, "that's mammon; that's the wages of sin. This dirty gold—or notes, or whatever it was—we'll just fling that back in the American's face," says I. But he was off and away, over the stormy sea, your Reverence.

MANDERS: Was he really, my good fellow?

ENGSTRAND: He was indeed, sir. So Johanna and I, we agreed that the money should go to the child's education; and so it did, and I can account for every blessed farthing of it.

MANDERS: Why, this alters the case considerably.

ENGSTRAND: That's just how it stands, your Reverence. And I make so bold as to say as I've been an honest father to Regina, so far as my poor strength went; for I'm but a weak vessel, worse luck!

MANDERS: Well, well, my good fellow——

ENGSTRAND: All the same, I bear myself witness as I've brought up the child, and lived kindly with poor Johanna, and ruled over my own house, as the Scripture has it. But it couldn't never enter my head to go to your Reverence and puff myself up and boast because even the likes of me had done some good in the world. No, sir; when anything of that sort happens to Jacob Engstrand, he holds his tongue about it. It don't happen so terrible often, I daresay. And when I do come to see your Reverence, I find a mortal deal that's wicked and weak to talk about. For I said it before, and I says it again—a man's conscience isn't always as clean as it might be.

MANDERS: Give me your hand, Jacob Engstrand.

ENGSTRAND: Oh, Lord! your Reverence——

MANDER: Come, no nonsense (*wrings his hand*). There we are!

ENGSTRAND: And if I might humbly beg your Reverence's pardon——

MANDERS: You? On the contrary, it is I who ought to beg your pardon——

ENGSTRAND: Lord, no, sir!

MANDERS: Yes, assuredly. And I do it with all my heart. Forgive me for misunderstanding you. I only wish I. could give you some proof of my hearty regret, and of my goodwill towards you——

ENGSTRAND: Would your Reverence do it?

MANDERS: With the greatest pleasure.

ENGSTRAND: Well then, here's the very chance. With the bit of money I've saved here, I was thinking I might set up a Sailors' Home down in the town.

MRS. ALVING: Y o u?

ENGSTRAND: Yes; it might be a sort of Orphanage, too, in a manner of speaking. There's such a many temptations for seafaring folk ashore. But in this Home of mine, a man might feel like as he was under a father's eye, I was thinking.

MANDERS: What do you say to this, Mrs. Alving?

ENGSTRAND: It isn't much as I've got to start with, Lord help me! But if I could only find a helping hand, why——

MANDERS: Yes, yes; we will look into the matter more closely. I entirely approve of your plan. But now, go before me and make everything ready, and get the candles lighted, so as to give the place an air of festivity. And then we will pass an edifying hour together, my good fellow; for now I quite believe you are in the right frame of mind.

ENGSTRAND: Yes, I trust I am. And so I'll say good-bye, ma'am, and thank you kindly; and take good care of Regina for me—(*Wipes a tear from his eye*)—poor Johanna's child. Well, it's a queer thing, now; but it's just like as if she'd growd into the very apple of my eye. It is, indeed.

(*He bows and goes out through the hall.*)

MANDERS: Well, what do you say of that man now, Mrs. Alving? T h a t was a very different account of matters, was it not?

MRS. ALVING: Yes, it certainly was.

MANDERS: It only shows how excessively careful one ought to be in judging one's fellow creatures. But what a heartfelt joy it is to ascertain that one has been mistaken! Don't you think so?

MRS. ALVING: I think you are, and will always be, a great baby, Manders.

MANDERS: I?

MRS. ALVING: (*Laying her two hands upon his shoulders.*) And I say that I have half a mind to put my arms round your neck, and kiss you.

MANDERS: (*Stepping hastily back.*) No, no! God bless me! What an idea!

MRS. ALVING: (*With a smile.*) Oh, you needn't be afraid of me.

MANDERS: (*By the table.*) You have sometimes such an exaggerated way of expressing yourself. Now, let me just collect all the documents, and put them in my bag. (*He does so.*) There, that's all right. And now, good-bye for the present. Keep your eyes open when Oswald comes back. I shall look in again later.

(*He takes his hat and goes out through the hall door.*)

MRS. ALVING: (*Sighs, looks for a moment out of the window, sets the room in order a little, and is about to go into the dining-room, but stops at the door with a half-suppressed cry.*) Oswald, are you still at table?

OSWALD: (*In the dining room.*) I'm only finishing my cigar.

MRS. ALVING: I thought you had gone for a little walk.

OSWALD: In such weather as this?

(*A glass clinks. MRS. ALVING leaves the door open, and sits down with her knitting on the sofa by the window.*)

OSWALD: Wasn't that Pastor Manders that went out just now?

MRS. ALVING: Yes; he went down to the Orphanage.

OSWALD: H'm.

(*The glass and decanter clink again.*)

MRS. ALVING: (*With a troubled glance.*) Dear Oswald, you should take care of that liqueur. It is strong.

OSWALD: It keeps out the damp.

MRS. ALVING: Wouldn't you rather come in here, to me?

OSWALD: I mayn't smoke in there.

MRS. ALVING: You know quite well you may smoke cigars.

OSWALD: Oh, all right then; I'll come in. Just a tiny drop more first.—There! (*He comes into the room with his cigar, and shuts the door after him. A short silence.*) Where has the pastor gone to?

MRS. ALVING: I have just told you; he went down to the Orphanage.

OSWALD: Oh, yes; so you did.

MRS. ALVING: You shouldn't sit so long at table, Oswald.

OSWALD: (*Holding his cigar behind him.*) But I find it so pleasant, mother. (*Strokes and caresses her.*) Just think what it is for me to come home and sit at mother's own table, in mother's room, and eat mother's delicious dishes.

MRS. ALVING: My dear, dear boy!

OSWALD: (*Somewhat impatiently, walks about and smokes.*) And what else can I do with myself here? I can't set to work at anything.

MRS. ALVING: Why can't you?

OSWALD: In such weather as this? Without a single ray of sunshine the whole day? (*Walks up the room.*) Oh, not to be able to work——!

MRS. ALVING: Perhaps it was not quite wise of you to come home?

OSWALD: Oh, yes, mother; I had to.

MRS. ALVING: You know I would ten

times rather forgo the joy of having you here, than let you——

OSWALD: (*Stops beside the table.*) Now just tell me, mother: does it really make you so very happy to have me home again?

MRS. ALVING: D o e s it make me happy!

OSWALD: (*Crumpling up a newspaper.*) I should have thought it must be pretty much the same to you whether I was in existence or not.

MRS. ALVING: Have you the heart to say that to your mother, Oswald?

OSWALD: But you've got on very well without me all this time.

MRS. ALVING: Yes; I have got on without you. That is true.

(*A silence. Twilight slowly begins to fall.* OSWALD *paces to and fro across the room. He has laid his cigar down.*)

OSWALD: (*Stops beside* MRS. ALVING.) Mother, may I sit on the sofa beside you?

MRS. ALVING: (*Makes room for him.*) Yes, do, my dear boy.

OSWALD: (*Sits down.*) There is something I must tell you, mother.

MRS. ALVING: (*Anxiously.*) Well?

OSWALD: (*Looks fixedly before him.*) For I can't go on hiding it any longer.

MRS. ALVING: Hiding what? What is it?

OSWALD: (*As before.*) I could never bring myself to write to you about it; and since I've come home——

MRS. ALVING: (*Seizes him by the arm.*) Oswald, what i s the matter?

OSWALD: Both yesterday and to-day I have tried to put the thoughts away from me—to cast them off; but it's no use.

MRS. ALVING: (*Rising.*) Now you must tell me everything, Oswald!

OSWALD: (*Draws her down to the sofa again.*) Sit still; and then I will try to tell you.—I complained of fatigue after my journey——

MRS. ALVING: Well? What then?

OSWALD: But it isn't that that is the matter with me; not any ordinary fatigue——

MRS. ALVING: (*Tries to jump up.*) You are not ill, Oswald?

OSWALD: (*Draws her down again.*) Sit still, mother. Do take it quietly. I'm not downright ill, either; not what is commonly called "ill." (*Clasps his hands above his head.*) Mother, my mind is broken down—ruined—I shall never be able to work again!

(*With his hands before his face, he buries his head in her lap, and breaks into bitter sobbing.*)

MRS. ALVING: (*White and trembling.*) Oswald! Look at me! No, no; it's not true.

OSWALD: (*Looks up with despair in his eyes.*) Never to be able to work again! Never!—never! A living death! Mother, can you imagine anything so horrible?

MRS. ALVING: My poor boy! How has this horrible thing come upon you?

OSWALD: (*Sitting upright again.*) That's just what I cannot possibly grasp or understand. I have never led a dissipated life—never, in any respect. You mustn't believe that of me, mother! I've never done that.

MRS. ALVING: I am sure you haven't, Oswald.

OSWALD: And yet this has come upon me just the same—this awful misfortune!

MRS. ALVING: Oh, but it will pass over, my dear, blessëd boy. It's nothing but overwork. Trust me, I am right.

OSWALD: (*Sadly.*) I thought so too, at first; but it isn't so.

MRS. ALVING: Tell me everything, from beginning to end.

OSWALD: Yes, I will.

MRS. ALVING: When did you first notice it?

OSWALD: It was directly after I had been home last time, and had got back to Paris again. I began to feel the most violent pains in my head—chiefly in the back of my head, they seemed to come. It was as though a tight iron ring was being screwed round my neck and upwards.

MRS. ALVING: Well, and then?

OSWALD: At first I thought it was nothing but the ordinary headache I had been so plagued with while I was growing up——

MRS. ALVING: Yes, yes——

OSWALD: But it wasn't that. I soon found that out. I couldn't work any more. I wanted to begin upon a big new picture, but my powers seemed to fail me; all my strength was crippled; I could form no definite images; everything swam before me—whirling round and round. Oh, it was an awful state! At last I sent for a doctor—and from him I learned the truth.

MRS. ALVING: How do you mean?

OSWALD: He was one of the first doctors in Paris. I told him my symptoms; and then he set to work asking me a string of questions which I thought had nothing to do with the matter. I couldn't imagine what the man was after——

MRS. ALVING: Well?

OSWALD: At last he said: "There has been something worm-eaten in you from your birth." He used that very word—*vermoulu.*

MRS. ALVING: (*Breathlessly.*) What did he mean by that?

OSWALD: I didn't understand either, and begged him to explain himself more clearly. And then the old cynic said— (*Clenching his fist.*) Oh——!

MRS. ALVING: What did he say?

OSWALD: He said, "The sins of the fathers are visited upon the children."

MRS. ALVING: (*Rising slowly.*) The sins of the fathers——!

OSWALD: I very nearly struck him in the face——

MRS. ALVING: (*Walks away across the room.*) The sins of the fathers——

OSWALD: (*Smiles sadly.*) Yes; what do you think of that? Of course I assured him that such a thing was out of the question. But do you think he gave in? No, he stuck to it; and it was only when I produced your letters and translated the passages relating to father——

MRS. ALVING: But t h e n——?

OSWALD: Then of course he had to admit that he was on the wrong track; and so I learned the truth—the incomprehensible truth! I ought not to have taken part with my comrades in that light-hearted, glorious life of theirs. It had been too much for my strength. So I had brought it upon myself!

MRS. ALVING: Oswald! No, no; do not believe it!

OSWALD: No other explanation was possible, he said. T h a t ' s the awful part of it. Incurably ruined for life—by my own heedlessness! All that I meant to have done in the world—I never dare think of it again—I'm not a b l e to think of it. Oh! if I could only live over again, and undo all I have done!

(*He buries his face in the sofa.*)

MRS. ALVING: (*Wrings her hands and walks, in silent struggle, backwards and forwards.*)

OSWALD: (*After a while, looks up and remains resting upon his elbow.*) If it had only been something inherited—something one wasn't responsible for! But this! To have thrown away so shamefully, thoughtlessly, recklessly, one's own happiness, one's own health, everything in the world —one's future, one's very life——!

MRS. ALVING: No, no, my dear, darling boy; this is impossible! (*Bends over him.*) Things are not so desperate as you think.

OSWALD: Oh, you don't know—— (*Springs up.*) And then, mother, to cause you all this sorrow! Many a time I have almost wished and hoped that at bottom you didn't care so very much about me.

MRS. ALVING: I, Oswald? My only boy! You are all I have in the world! The only thing I care about!

OSWALD: (*Seizes both her hands and kisses them.*) Yes, yes, I see it. When I'm at home, I see it, of course; and that's almost the hardest part for me.—But now you know the whole story; and now we won't talk any more about it to-day. I daren't think of it for long together. (*Goes up the room.*) Get me something to drink, mother.

MRS. ALVING: To drink? What do you want to drink now?

OSWALD: Oh, anything you like. You have some cold punch in the house.

MRS. ALVING: Yes, but my dear Oswald——

OSWALD: Don't refuse me, mother. Do be kind, now! I m u s t have something to wash down all these gnawing thoughts. (*Goes into the conservatory.*) And then ——it's so dark here! (MRS. ALVING *pulls a bell-rope on the right.*) And this ceaseless rain! It may go on week after week, for months together. Never to get a glimpse of the sun! I can't recollect ever having seen the sun shine all the times I've been at home.

MRS. ALVING: Oswald—you are thinking of going away from me.

OSWALD: H'm—*Drawing a heavy breath.*) I'm not thinking of anything. I c a n n o t think of anything! (*In a low voice.*) I let thinking alone.

REGINA: (*From the dining-room.*) Did you ring, ma'am?

MRS. ALVING: Yes; let us have the lamp in.

REGINA: Yes, ma'am. It's ready lighted.
(*Goes out.*)

MRS. ALVING: (*Goes across to* OSWALD.) Oswald, be frank with me.

OSWALD: Well, so I am, mother. (*Goes to the table.*) I think I have told you enough.

(REGINA *brings the lamp and sets it upon the table.*)

MRS. ALVING: Regina, you may bring us a small bottle of champagne.

REGINA: Very well, ma'am.
(*Goes out.*)

OSWALD: (*Puts his arm round* MRS. ALVING's *neck.*) That's just what I wanted. I knew mother wouldn't let her boy go thirsty.

MRS. ALVING: My own, poor, darling Oswald; how could I deny you anything now?

OSWALD: (*Eagerly.*) Is that true, mother? Do you mean it?

MRS. ALVING: How? What?

OSWALD: That you couldn't deny me anything.

MRS. ALVING: My dear Oswald——

OSWALD: Hush!

REGINA: (*Brings a tray with a half-bottle of champagne and two glasses, which she sets on the table.*) Shall I open it?

OSWALD: No, thanks. I will do it my-self.   (REGINA *goes out again.*)

MRS. ALVING: (*Sits down by the table.*) What was it you meant—that I mustn't deny you?

OSWALD: (*Busy opening the bottle.*) First let us have a glass—or two.

(*The cork pops; he pours wine into one glass, and is about to pour it into the other.*)

MRS. ALVING: (*Holding her hand over it.*) Thanks; not for me.

OSWALD: Oh, won't you? Then I will!

(*He empties the glass, fills, and empties it
again; then he sits down by the table.*)

MRS. ALVING: (*In expectancy.*) Well?

OSWALD: (*Without looking at her.*)
Tell me—I thought you and Pastor
Manders seemed so odd—so quiet—at
dinner to-day.

MRS ALVING: Did you notice it?

OSWALD: Yes. H'm—— (*After a short
silence.*) Tell me: what do you think of
Regina?

MRS. ALVING: What do I think?

OSWALD: Yes; isn't she splendid?

MRS. ALVING: My dear Oswald, you
don't know her as I do——

OSWALD: Well?

MRS. ALVING: Regina, unfortunately,
was allowed to stay at home too long. I
ought to have taken her earlier into my
house.

OSWALD: Yes, but isn't she splendid to
look at, mother?   (*He fills his glass.*)

MRS. ALVING: Regina has many serious
faults——

OSWALD: Oh, what does that matter?
                              (*He drinks again.*)

MRS. ALVING: But I am fond of her,
nevertheless, and I am responsible for her.
I wouldn't for all the world have any
harm happen to her.

OSWALD: (*Springs up.*) Mother, Regina is my only salvation!

MRS. ALVING: (*Rising.*) What do you
mean by that?

OSWALD: I cannot go on bearing all this
anguish of soul alone.

MRS. ALVING: Have you not your
mother to share it with you?

OSWALD: Yes; that's what I thought;
and so I came home to you. But that will
not do. I see it won't do. I cannot endure
my life here.

MRS. ALVING: Oswald!

OSWALD: I must live differently, mother.
That is why I must leave you. I will not
have you looking on at it.

MRS. ALVING: My unhappy boy! But,
Oswald, while you are so ill as this——

OSWALD: If it were only the illness, I
should stay with you, mother, you may be
sure; for you are the best friend I have
in the world.

MRS. ALVING: Yes, indeed I am, Oswald;
am I not?

OSWALD: (*Wanders restlessly about.*)
But it's all the torment, the gnawing re-
morse—and then, the great, killing dread.
Oh—that awful dread!

MRS. ALVING: (*Walking after him.*)
Dread? What dread? What do you mean?

OSWALD: Oh, you mustn't ask me any
more. I don't know. I can't describe it.

MRS. ALVING: (*Goes over to the right
and pulls the bell.*)

OSWALD: What is it you want?

MRS. ALVING: I want my boy to be
happy—that is what I want. He sha'n't go
on brooding over things. (*To* REGINA, *who
appears at the door:*) More champagne—
a large bottle.   (REGINA *goes.*)

OSWALD: Mother!

MRS. ALVING: Do you think we don't
know how to live here at home?

OSWALD: Isn't she splendid to look at?
How beautifully she's built! And so thoroughly healthy!

MRS. ALVING: (*Sits by the table.*) Sit
down, Oswald; let us talk quietly together.

OSWALD: (*Sits.*) I daresay you don't
know, mother, that I owe Regina some
reparation.

MRS. ALVING: You!

OSWALD: For a bit of thoughtlessness, or
whatever you like to call it—very innocent, at any rate. When I was home last
time——

MRS. ALVING: Well?

OSWALD: She used often to ask me about Paris, and I used to tell her one thing and another. Then I recollect I happened to say to her one day, "Shouldn't you like to go there yourself?"

MRS. ALVING: Well?

OSWALD: I saw her face flush, and then she said, "Yes, I should like it of all things." "Ah, well," I replied, "it might perhaps be managed"—or something like that.

MRS. ALVING: And then?

OSWALD: Of course I had forgotten all about it; but the day before yesterday I happened to ask her whether she was glad I was to stay at home so long——

MRS. ALVING: Yes?

OSWALD: And then she gave me such a strange look, and asked, "But what's to become of my trip to Paris?"

MRS. ALVING: Her trip!

OSWALD: And so it came out that she had taken the thing seriously; that she had been thinking of me the whole time, and had set to work to learn French——

MRS. ALVING: So t h a t was why——!

OSWALD: Mother—when I saw that fresh, lovely, splendid girl standing there before me—till then I had hardly noticed her—but when she stood there as though with open arms ready to receive me——

MRS. ALVING: Oswald!

OSWALD: ——then it flashed upon me that in her lay my salvation; for I saw that she was full of the joy of life.

MRS. ALVING: (*Starts.*) The joy of life ——? Can there be salvation in t h a t?

REGINA: (*From the dining-room, with a bottle of champagne.*) I'm sorry to have been so long, but I had to go to the cellar. (*Places the bottle on the table.*)

OSWALD: And now bring another glass.

REGINA: (*Looks at him in surprise.*) There is Mrs. Alving's glass, Mr. Alving.

OSWALD: Yes, but bring one for yourself, Regina. (REGINA *starts and gives a lightning-like side glance at* MRS. ALVING.) Why do you wait?

REGINA: (*Softly and hesitatingly.*) Is it Mrs. Alving's wish?

MRS. ALVING: Bring the glass, Regina.

(REGINA *goes out into the dining-room.*)

OSWALD: (*Follows her with his eyes.*) Have you noticed how she walks?—so firmly and lightly!

MRS. ALVING: This can never be, Oswald!

OSWALD: It's a settled thing. Can't you see that? It's no use saying anything against it.

(REGINA *enters with an empty glass, which she keeps in her hand.*)

OSWALD: Sit down, Regina.

(REGINA *looks inquiringly at* MRS. ALVING.)

MRS. ALVING: Sit down. (REGINA *sits on a chair by the dining-room door, still holding the empty glass in her hand.*) Oswald —what were you saying about the joy of life?

OSWALD: Ah, the joy of life, mother— that's a thing you don't know much about in these parts. I have never felt it here.

MRS. ALVING: Not when you are with me?

OSWALD: Not when I'm at home. But you don't understand that.

MRS. ALVING: Yes, yes; I think I almost understand it—now.

OSWALD: And then, too, the joy of work! At bottom, it's the same thing. But that, too, you know nothing about.

MRS. ALVING: Perhaps you are right. Tell me more about it, Oswald.

OSWALD: I only mean that here people are brought up to believe that work is a curse and a punishment for sin, and that life is something miserable, something it would be best to have done with, the sooner the better.

MRS. ALVING: "A vale of tears," yes; and we certainly do our best to make it one.

OSWALD: But in the great world people won't hear of such things. There, nobody really believes such doctrines any longer. There, you feel it a positive bliss and ecstasy merely to draw the breath of life. Mother, have you noticed that everything I have painted has turned upon the joy of life?—always, always upon the joy of life?—light and sunshine and glorious air—and faces radiant with happiness. That is why I'm afraid of remaining at home with you.

MRS. ALVING: Afraid? What are you afraid of here, with me?

OSWALD: I'm afraid lest all my instincts should be warped into ugliness.

MRS. ALVING: (Looks steadily at him.) Do you think t h a t is what would happen?

OSWALD: I know it. You may live the same life here as there, and yet it won't be the same life.

MRS. ALVING: (Who has been listening eagerly, rises, her eyes big with thought, and says:) Now I see the sequence of things.

OSWALD: What is it you see?

MRS. ALVING: I see it now for the first time. And now I can speak.

OSWALD: (Rising.) Mother, I don't understand you.

REGINA: (Who has also risen.) Perhaps I ought to go?

MRS. ALVING: No. Stay here. Now I can speak. Now, my boy, you shall know the whole truth. And then you can choose. Oswald! Regina!

OSWALD: Hush! The Pastor——

MANDERS: (Enters by the hall door.) There! We have had a most edifying time down there.

OSWALD: So have we.

MANDERS: We must stand by Engstrand and his Sailors' Home. Regina must go to him and help him——

REGINA: No thank you, sir.

MANDERS: (Noticing her for the first time.) What——? You here? And with a glass in your hand!

REGINA: (Hastily putting the glass down.) Pardon!

OSWALD: Regina is going with m e, Mr. Manders.

MANDERS: Going! With you!

OSWALD: Yes; as my wife—if she wishes it.

MANDERS: But, merciful God——!

REGINA: I can't help it, sir.

OSWALD: Or she'll stay here, if I stay.

REGINA: (Involuntarily.) Here!

MANDERS: I am thunderstruck at your conduct, Mrs. Alving.

MRS. ALVING: They will do neither one thing nor the other; for now I can speak out plainly.

MANDERS: You surely will not do that! No, no, no!

MRS. ALVING: Yes, I can speak and I will. And no ideals shall suffer after all.

OSWALD: Mother—what is it you are hiding from me?

REGINA: (Listening.) Oh, ma'am, listen! Don't you hear shouts outside.

(She goes into the conservatory and looks out.)

OSWALD: (At the window on the left.) What's going on? Where does that light come from?

REGINA: (Cries out.) The Orphanage is on fire!

MRS. ALVING: (*Rushing to the window.*) On fire!

MANDERS: On fire! Impossible! I've just come from there.

OSWALD: Where's my hat? Oh, never mind it—Father's Orphanage——! (*He rises out through the garden door.*)

MRS. ALVING: My shawl, Regina! The whole place is in a blaze!

MANDERS: Terrible! Mrs. Alving, it is a judgment upon this abode of lawlessness.

MRS. ALVING: Yes, of course. Come Regina.

(*She and* REGINA *hasten out through the hall.*)

MANDERS: (*Clasps his hands together.*) And we left it uninsured!

(*He goes out the same way.*)

ACT THIRD

The room as before. All the doors stand open. The lamp is still burning on the table. It is dark out of doors; there is only a faint glow from the conflagration in the background to the left.

MRS. ALVING, *with a shawl over her head, stands in the conservatory, looking out.* REGINA, *also with a shawl on, stands a little behind her.*

MRS. ALVING: The whole thing burnt!— burnt to the ground!

REGINA: The basement is still burning.

MRS. ALVING: How is it Oswald doesn't come home? There's nothing to be saved.

REGINA: Should you like me to take down his hat to him?

MRS. ALVING: Has he not even got his hat on?

REGINA: (*Pointing to the hall.*) No; there it hangs.

MRS. ALVING: Let it be. He must come up now. I shall go and look for him myself.

(*She goes out through the garden door*).

MANDERS: (*Comes in from the hall.*) Is not Mrs. Alving here?

REGINA: She has just gone down the garden.

MANDERS: This is the most terrible night I ever went through.

REGINA: Yes; isn't it a dreadful misfortune, sir?

MANDERS: Oh, don't talk about it! I can hardly bear to think of it.

REGINA: How c a n it have happened ——?

MANDERS: Don't ask me, Miss Engstrand! How should *I* know? Do y o u, too——? Is it not enough that your father ——?

REGINA: What about him?

MANDERS: Oh, he has driven me distracted——

ENGSTRAND: (*Enters through the hall.*) Your Reverence——

MANDERS: (*Turns round in terror.*) Are you after me here, too?

ENGSTRAND: Yes, strike me dead, but I must——! Oh, Lord! what am I saying? But this is a terrible ugly business, your Reverence.

MANDERS: (*Walks to and fro.*) Alas! alas!

REGINA: What's the matter?

ENGSTRAND: Why, it all came of this here prayer-meeting, you see. (*Softly.*) The bird's limed, my girl. (*Aloud.*) And to think it should be m y doing that such a thing should be his Reverence's doing!

MANDERS: But I assure you, Engstrand ——

ENGSTRAND: There wasn't another soul except your Reverence as ever laid a finger on the candles down there.

MANDERS: (*Stops.*) So you declare. But I certainly cannot recollect that I ever had a candle in my hand.

ENGSTRAND: And I s a w as clear as daylight how your Reverence took the candle and snuffed it with your fingers, and threw away the snuff among the shavings.

MANDERS: And you stood and looked on?

ENGSTRAND: Yes; I saw it as plain as a pike-staff, I did.

MANDERS: It's quite beyond my comprehension. Besides, it has never been my habit to snuff candles with my fingers.

ENGSTRAND: And terrible risky it looked, too, that it did! But is there such a deal of harm done after all, your Reverence?

MANDERS: (*Walks restlessly to and fro.*) Oh, don't ask me!

ENGSTRAND: (*Walks with him.*) And your Reverence hadn't insured it, neither?

MANDERS: (*Continuing to walk up and down.*) No, no, no; I have told you so.

ENGSTRAND: (*Following him.*) Not insured! And then to go straight away down and set light to the whole thing! Lord, Lord, what a misfortune!

MANDERS: (*Wipes the sweat from his forehead.*) Ay, you may well say that, Engstrand.

ENGSTRAND: And to think that such a thing should happen to a benevolent Institution, that was to have been a blessing both to town and country, as the saying goes! The newspapers won't be for handling your Reverence very gently, I expect.

MANDERS: No; that is just what I am thinking of. That is almost the worst of the whole matter. All the malignant attacks and imputations——! Oh, it makes me shudder to think of it!

MRS. ALVING: (*Comes in from the garden.*) He is not to be persuaded to leave the fire.

MANDERS: Ah, there you are, Mrs. Alving.

MRS. ALVING: So you have escaped your Inaugural Address, Pastor Manders.

MANDERS: Oh, I should so gladly——

MRS. ALVING: (*In an undertone.*) It is all for the best. That Orphanage would have done no one any good.

MANDERS: Do you think not?

MRS. ALVING: Do you think it would?

MANDERS: It is a terrible misfortune, all the same.

MRS. ALVING: Let us speak of it plainly, as a matter of business.—Are you waiting for Mr. Manders, Engstrand?

ENGSTRAND: (*At the hall door.*) That's just what I'm a-doing of, ma'am.

MRS. ALVING: Then sit down meanwhile.

ENGSTRAND: Thank you, ma'am; I'd as soon stand.

MRS. ALVING: (*To* MANDERS.) I suppose you are going by the steamer?

MANDERS: Yes; it starts in an hour.

MRS. ALVING: Then be so good as to take all the papers with you. I won't hear another word about this affair. I have other things to think of——

MANDERS: Mrs. Alving——

MRS. ALVING: Later on I shall send you a Power of Attorney to settle everything as you please.

MANDERS: That I will very readily undertake. The original destination of the endowment must now be completely changed, alas!

MRS. ALVING: Of course it must.

MANDERS: I think, first of all, I shall arrange that the Solvik property shall pass to the parish. The land is by no means without value. It can always be turned to account for some purpose or other. And the interest of the money in the Bank I could, perhaps, best apply for the benefit of some undertaking of acknowledged value to the town.

MRS. ALVING: Do just as you please. The whole matter is now completely indifferent to me.

ENGSTRAND: Give a thought to my Sailors' Home, your Reverence.

MANDERS: Upon my word, that is not a bad suggestion. That must be considered.

ENGSTRAND: Oh, devil take considering —Lord forgive me!

MANDERS: (*With a sigh.*) And unfortunately I cannot tell how long I shall be able to retain control of these things— whether public opinion may not compel me to retire. It entirely depends upon the result of the official inquiry into the fire
——

MRS. ALVING: What are you talking about?

MANDERS: And the result can by no means be foretold.

ENGSTRAND: (*Comes close to him.*) Ay, but it can though. For here stands old Jacob Engstrand.

MANDERS: Well well, but——?

ENGSTRAND: (*More softly.*) And Jacob Engstrand isn't the man to desert a noble benefactor in the hour of need, as the saying goes.

MANDERS: Yes, but my good fellow— how——?

ENGSTRAND: Jacob Engstrand may be likened to a sort of a guardian angel, he may, your Reverence.

MANDERS: No, no; I really cannot accept that.

ENGSTRAND: Oh, that'll be the way of it, all the same. I know a man as has taken others' sins upon himself before now, I do.

MANDERS: Jacob! (*Wrings his hand.*) Yours is a rare nature. Well, you shall be helped with your Sailors' Home. That you may rely upon.

(ENGSTRAND *tries to thank him, but cannot for emotion.*)

MANDERS: (*Hangs his travelling-bag over his shoulder.*) And now let us set out. We two will go together.

ENGSTRAND: (*At the dining-room door, softly to* REGINA.) You come along too, my lass. You shall live as snug as the yolk in an egg.

REGINA: (*Tosses her head.*) *Merci!*

(*She goes out into the hall and fetches* MANDER'S *overcoat.*)

MANDERS: Good-bye, Mrs. Alving! and may the spirit of Law and Order descend upon this house, and that quickly.

MRS. ALVING: Good-bye, Pastor Manders.

(*She goes up towards the conservatory, as she sees* OSWALD *coming in through the garden door.*)

ENGSTRAND: (*While he and* REGINA *help* MANDERS *to get his coat on.*) Good-bye, my child. And if any trouble should come to you, you know where Jacob Engstrand is to be found. (*Softly.*) Little Harbour Street, h'm——! (*To* MRS. ALVING *and* OSWALD.) And the refuge for wandering mariners shall be called "Chamberlain Alving's Home," that it shall! And if so be as I'm spared to carry on that house in my own way, I make so bold as to promise that it shall be worthy of the Chamberlain's memory.

MANDERS: (*In the doorway.*) H'm— h'm!—Come along, my dear Engstrand. Good-bye! Good-bye!

(*He and* ENGSTRAND *go out through the hall.*)

OSWALD: (*Goes towards the table.*) What house was he talking about?

MRS ALVING: Oh, a kind of Home that he and Pastor Manders want to set up.

OSWALD: It will burn down like the other.

MRS. ALVING: What makes you think so?

OSWALD: Everything will burn. All that recalls father's memory is doomed. Here am I, too, burning down.

(REGINA *starts and looks at him.*)

MRS. ALVING: Oswald! You oughtn't to have remained so long down there, my poor boy.

OSWALD: (*Sits down by the table.*) I almost think you are right.

MRS. ALVING: Let me dry your face, Oswald; you are quite wet.

(*She dries his face with her pocket-hand-kerchief.*)

OSWALD: (*Stares indifferently in front of him.*) Thanks, mother.

MRS. ALVING: Are you not tired, Oswald? Should you like to sleep?

OSWALD: (*Nervously.*) No, no—not to sleep! I never sleep. I only pretend to. (*Sadly.*) That will come soon enough.

MRS. ALVING: (*Looking sorrowfully at him.*) Yes, you really are ill, my blessèd boy.

REGINA: (*Eagerly.*) Is Mr. Alving ill?

OSWALD: (*Impatiently.*) Oh, do shut all the doors! This killing dread——

MRS. ALVING: Close the doors, Regina.

(REGINA *shuts them and remains standing by the hall door.* MRS. ALVING *takes her shawl off.* REGINA *does the same.* MRS. ALVING *draws a chair across to* OSWALD's, *and sits by him.*)

MRS. ALVING: There now! I am going to sit beside you——

OSWALD: Yes, do. And Regina shall stay here too. Regina shall be with me always. You will come to the rescue, Regina, won't you?

REGINA: I don't understand——

MRS. ALVING: To the rescue?

OSWALD: Yes—when the need comes.

MRS. ALVING: Oswald, have you not your mother to come to the rescue?

OSWALD: You? (*Smiles.*) No, mother; that rescue you will never bring me. (*Laughs sadly.*) You; ha ha! (*Looks earnestly at her.*) Though, after all, who ought to do it if not you? (*Impetuously.*) Why can't you say "thou"[1] to me, Regina? Why don't you call me "Oswald"?

REGINA: (*Softly.*) I don't think Mrs. Alving would like it.

MRS. ALVING: You shall have leave to, presently. And meanwhile sit over here beside us.

(REGINA *seats herself demurely and hesitatingly at the other side of the table.*)

MRS. ALVING: And now, my poor suffering boy, I am going to take the burden off your mind——

OSWALD: You, mother?

MRS. ALVING: ——all the gnawing remorse and self-reproach you speak of.

OSWALD: And you think you can do that?

MRS. ALVING: Yes, now I can, Oswald. A little while ago you spoke of the joy of life; and at that word a new light burst for me over my life and everything connected with it.

OSWALD: (*Shakes his head.*) I don't understand you.

MRS. ALVING: You ought to have known your father when he was a young lieutenant. He was brimming over with the joy of life!

OSWALD: Yes, I know he was.

MRS. ALVING: It was like a breezy day only to look at him. And what exuberant strength and vitality there was in him!

OSWALD: Well——?

[1] "Sige du"=Fr. *tutoyer.*

MRS. ALVING: Well then, child of joy as he was—for he w a s like a child in those days—he had to live at home here in a half-grown town, which had no joys to offer him—only dissipations. He had no object in life—only an official position. He had no work into which he could throw himself heart and soul; he had only business. He had not a single comrade that could realise what the joy of life meant— only loungers and boon-companions——

OSWALD: Mother——!

MRS. ALVING: So the inevitable happened.

OSWALD: The inevitable?

MRS. ALVING: You told me yourself, this evening, what would become of y o u if you stayed at home.

OSWALD: Do you mean to say that father——?

MRS. ALVING: Your poor father found no outlet for the overpowering joy of life that was in him. And I brought no brightness into his home.

OSWALD: Not even you?

MRS. ALVING: They had taught me a great deal about duties and so forth, which I went on obstinately believing in. Everything was marked out into duties—into m y duties, and h i s duties, and—I am afraid I made his home intolerable for your poor father, Oswald.

OSWALD: Why have you never spoken of this in writing to me?

MRS. ALVING: I have never before seen it in such a light that I could speak of it to you, his son.

OSWALD: In what light did you see it, then?

MRS. ALVING: (Slowly.) I saw only this one thing: that your father was a broken-down man before you were born.

OSWALD: (Softly.) Ah——!

(He rises and walks away to the window.)

MRS. ALVING: And then, day after day, I dwelt on the one thought that by rights Regina should be at home in this house —just like my own boy.

OSWALD: (Turning round quickly.) Regina——!

REGINA: (Springs up and asks, with bated breath.) I——?

MRS. ALVING: Yes, now you know it, both of you.

OSWALD: Regina!

REGINA: (To herself.) So mother w a s that kind of woman.

MRS. ALVING: Your mother had many good qualities, Regina.

REGINA: Yes, but she was one of that sort, all the same. Oh, I've often suspected it; but—— And now, if you please, ma'am, may I be allowed to go away at once?

MRS. ALVING: Do you really wish it, Regina?

REGINA: Yes, indeed I do.

MRS. ALVING: Of course you can do as you like; but——

OSWALD: (Goes towards REGINA.) Go away now? Your place is here.

REGINA: Merci, Mr. Alving!—or now, I suppose, I may say Oswald. But I can tell you t h i s wasn't at all what I expected.

MRS. ALVING: Regina, I have not been frank with you——

REGINA: No, that you haven't indeed. If I'd known that Oswald was an invalid, why—— And now, too, that it can never come to anything serious between us—— I really can't stop out here in the country and wear myself out nursing sick people.

OSWALD: Not even one who is so near to you?

REGINA: No, that I can't. A poor girl must make the best of her young days, or she'll be left out in the cold before she knows where she is. And I, too, have the joy of life in me, Mrs. Alving!

MRS. ALVING: Unfortunately, you have. But don't throw yourself away, Regina.

REGINA: Oh, what must be, must be. If Oswald takes after his father, I take after my mother, I daresay.—May I ask, ma'am, if Pastor Manders knows all this about me?

MRS. ALVING: Pastor Manders knows all about it.

REGINA: (*Busied in putting on her shawl.*) Well then, I'd better make haste and get away by this steamer. The Pastor is such a nice man to deal with; and I certainly think I've as much right to a little of that money as h e has—that brute of a carpenter.

MRS. ALVING: You are heartily welcome to it, Regina.

REGINA: (*Looks hard at her.*) I think you might have brought me up as a gentleman's daughter, ma'am; it would have suited me better. (*Tosses her head.*) But pooh—what does it matter! (*With a bitter side glance at the corked bottle.*) I may come to drink champagne with gentlefolks yet.

MRS. ALVING: And if you ever need a home, Regina, come to me.

REGINA: No, thank you, ma'am. Pastor Manders will look after me, I know. And if the worst comes to the worst, I know of one house where I've every right to a place.

MRS. ALVING: Where is that?

REGINA: "Chamberlain Alving's Home."

MRS. ALVING: Regina—now I see it— you are going to your ruin.

REGINA: Oh, stuff! Good-bye.

(*She nods and goes out through the hall.*)

OSWALD: (*Stands at the window and looks out.*) Is she gone?

MRS. ALVING: Yes.

OSWALD: (*Murmuring aside to himself.*) I think it was a mistake, this.

MRS. ALVING: (*Goes up behind him and lays her hands on his shoulders.*) Oswald, my dear boy—has it shaken you very much?

OSWALD: (*Turns his face towards her.*) All that about father, do you mean?

MRS. ALVING: Yes, about your unhappy father. I am so afraid it may have been too much for you.

OSWALD: Why should you fancy that? Of course it came upon me as a great surprise; but it can make no real difference to me.

MRS. ALVING: (*Draws her hands away.*) No difference! That your father was so infinitely unhappy!

OSWALD: Of course I can pity him, as I would anybody else; but——

MRS. ALVING: Nothing more! Your own father!

OSWALD: (*Impatiently.*) Oh, "father," —"father"! I never knew anything of father. I remember nothing about him, except that he once made me sick.

MRS. ALVING: This is terrible to think of! Ought not a son to love his father, whatever happens?

OSWALD: When a son has nothing to thank his father for—has never known him? Do you really cling to that old superstition?—you who are so enlightened in other ways?

MRS. ALVING: Can it be only a superstition——?

OSWALD: Yes; surely you can see t h a t, mother. It's one of those notions that are current in the world, and so——

MRS. ALVING: (*Deeply moved.*) Ghosts!

OSWALD: (*Crossing the room.*) Yes; you may call them ghosts.

MRS. ALVING: (*Wildly.*) Oswald—then you don't love me, either!

OSWALD: You I know, at any rate——

MRS. ALVING: Yes, you know me; but is that all!

OSWALD: And, of course, I know how fond you are of me, and I can't but be grateful to you. And then you can be so useful to me, now that I am ill.

MRS. ALVING: Yes, cannot I, Oswald? Oh, I could almost bless the illness that has driven you home to me. For I see very plainly that you are not mine: I have to win you.

OSWALD: (*Impatiently.*) Yes, yes, yes; all these are just so many phrases. You must remember that I am a sick man, mother. I can't be much taken up with other people; I have enough to do thinking about myself.

MRS. ALVING: (*In a low voice.*) I shall be patient and easily satisfied.

OSWALD: And cheerful too, mother!

MRS. ALVING: Yes, my dear boy, you are quite right. (*Goes towards him.*) Have I relieved you of all remorse and self-reproach now?

OSWALD: Yes, you have. But now who will relieve me of the dread?

MRS. ALVING: The dread?

OSWALD: (*Walks across the room.*) Regina could have been got to do it.

MRS. ALVING: I don't understand you. What is this about dread—and Regina?

OSWALD: Is it very late, mother?

MRS. ALVING: It is early morning. (*She looks out through the conservatory.*) The day is dawning over the mountains. And the weather is clearing, Oswald. In a little while you shall see the sun.

OSWALD: I'm glad of that. Oh, I may still have much to rejoice in and live for——

MRS. ALVING: I should think so, indeed!

OSWALD: Even if I can't work——

MRS. ALVING: Oh, you'll soon be able to work again, my dear boy—now that you haven't got all those gnawing and depressing thoughts to brood over any longer.

OSWALD: Yes, I'm glad you were able to rid me of all those fancies. And when I've got over this one thing more—— (*Sits on the sofa.*) Now we will have a little talk, mother——

MRS. ALVING: Yes, let us.

(*She pushes an arm-chair towards the sofa, and sits down close to him.*)

OSWALD: And meantime the sun will be rising. And then you will know all. And then I shall not feel this dread any longer.

MRS. ALVING: What is it that I am to know?

OSWALD: (*Not listening to her.*) Mother, did you not say a little while ago, that there was nothing in the world you would not do for me, if I asked you?

MRS. ALVING: Yes, indeed I said so!

OSWALD: And you'll stick to it, mother?

MRS. ALVING: You may rely on that, my dear and only boy! I have nothing in the world to live for but you alone.

OSWALD: Very well, then; now you shall hear—— Mother, you have a strong, steadfast mind, I know. Now you're to sit quite still when you hear it.

MRS. ALVING: What dreadful thing can it be——?

OSWALD: You're not to scream out. Do you hear? Do you promise me that? We will sit and talk about it quietly. Do you promise me, mother?

MRS. ALVING: Yes, yes; I promise. Only speak!

OSWALD: Well, you must know that all this fatigue—and my inability to think of work—all that is not the illness itself——

MRS. ALVING: Then what is the illness itself?

OSWALD: The disease I have as my birthright—(*He points to his forehead and adds very softly*)—is seated here.

MRS. ALVING: (*Almost voiceless.*) Oswald! No—no!

OSWALD: Don't scream. I can't bear it. Yes, mother, it is seated here—waiting. And it may break out any day—at any moment.

MRS. ALVING: Oh, what horror——!

OSWALD: Now, quiet, quiet. That is how it stands with me——

MRS. ALVING: (*Springs up.*) It's not true, Oswald! It's impossible! It cannot be so!

OSWALD: I have had o n e attack down there already. It was soon over. But when I came to know the state I had been in, then the dread descended upon me, raging and ravening: and so I set off home to you as fast as I could.

MRS. ALVING: Then this is the dread——!

OSWALD: Yes—it's so indescribably loathsome, you know. Oh, if it had only been an ordinary mortal disease——! For I'm not so afraid of death—though I should like to live as long as I can.

MRS. ALVING: Yes, yes, Oswald, you must!

OSWALD: But this is so unutterably loathsome. To become a little baby again! To have to be fed! To have to—— Oh, it's not to be spoken of!

MRS. ALVING: The child has his mother to nurse him.

OSWALD: (*Springs up.*) No, never that! That is just what I will not have. I can't endure to think that perhaps I should lie in that state for many years—and get old and grey. And in the meantime you might die and leave me. (*Sits in* MRS. ALVING'S *chair.*) For the doctor said it wouldn't necessarily prove fatal at once. He called it a sort of softening of the brain—or

something like that. (*Smiles sadly.*) I think that expression sounds so nice. It always sets me thinking of cherry-coloured velvet—something soft and delicate to stroke.

MRS. ALVING: (*Shrieks.*) Oswald!

OSWALD: (*Springs up and paces the room.*) And now you have taken Regina from me. If I could only have had her! She would have come to the rescue, I know.

MRS. ALVING: (*Goes to him.*) What do you mean by that, my darling boy? Is there any help in the world that I would not give you?

OSWALD: When I got over my attack in Paris, the doctor told me that when it comes again—and it w i l l come—there will be no more hope.

MRS. ALVING: He was heartless enough to——

OSWALD: I demanded it of him. I told him I had preparations to make—— (*He smiles cunningly.*) And so I had. (*He takes a little box from his inner breast pocket and opens it.*) Mother, do you see this?

MRS. ALVING: What is it?

OSWALD: Morphia.

MRS. ALVING: (*Looks at him horror-struck.*) Oswald—my boy!

OSWALD: I've scraped together twelve pilules——

MRS. ALVING: (*Snatches at it.*) Give me the box, Oswald.

OSWALD: Not yet, mother.

(*He hides the box again in his pocket.*)

MRS. ALVING: I shall never survive this!

OSWALD: It must be survived. Now if I'd had Regina here, I should have told her how things stood with me—and begged her to come to the rescue at the last. She would have done it. I know she would.

MRS. ALVING: Never!

OSWALD: When the horror had come upon me, and she saw me lying there helpless, like a little new-born baby, impotent, lost, hopeless—past all saving——

MRS. ALVING: Never in all the world would Regina have done this!

OSWALD: Regina would have done it. Regina was so splendidly light-hearted. And she would soon have wearied of nursing an invalid like me.

MRS. ALVING: Then heaven be praised that Regina is not here!

OSWALD: Well then, it is you that must come to the rescue, mother.

MRS. ALVING: (*Shrieks aloud.*) I!

OSWALD: Who should do it if not you?

MRS. ALVING: I! your mother!

OSWALD: For that very reason.

MRS. ALVING: I, who gave you life!

OSWALD: I never asked you for life. And what sort of a life have you given me? I will not have it! You shall take it back again!

MRS. ALVING: Help! Help!
(*She runs out into the hall.*)

OSWALD: (*Going after her.*) Do not leave me! Where are you going?

MRS. ALVING: (*In the hall.*) To fetch the doctor, Oswald! Let me pass!

OSWALD: (*Also outside.*) You shall not go out. And no one shall come in.
(*The locking of a door is heard.*)

MRS. ALVING: (*Comes in again.*) Oswald! Oswald—my child!

OSWALD: (*Follows her.*) Have you a mother's heart for me—and yet can see me suffer from this unutterable dread?

MRS. ALVING: (*After a moment's silence, commands herself, and says:*) Here is my hand upon it.

OSWALD: Will you——?

MRS. ALVING: If it should ever be necessary. But it will never be necessary. No, no; it is impossible.

OSWALD: Well, let us hope so. And let us live together as long as we can. Thank you, mother.

(*He seats himself in the arm-chair which* MRS. ALVING *has moved to the sofa. Day is breaking. The lamp is still burning on the table.*)

MRS. ALVING: (*Drawing near cautiously.*) Do you feel calm now?

OSWALD: Yes.

MRS. ALVING: (*Bending over him.*) It has been a dreadful fancy of yours, Oswald—nothing but a fancy. All this excitement has been too much for you. But now you shall have a long rest; at home with your mother, my own blessëd boy. Everything you point to you shall have, just as when you were a little child. —There now. The crisis is over. You see how easily it passed! Oh, I was sure it would.—And do you see, Oswald, what a lovely day we are going to have? Brilliant sunshine! Now you can really see your home.

(*She goes to the table and puts out the lamp. Sunrise. The glacier and the snow-peaks in the background glow in the morning light.*)

OSWALD: (*Sits in the arm-chair with his back towards the landscape, without moving. Suddenly he says:*) Mother, give me the sun.

MRS. ALVING: (*By the table, starts and looks at him.*) What do you say?

OSWALD: (*Repeats, in a dull, toneless voice.*) The sun. The sun.

MRS. ALVING: (*Goes to him.*) Oswald, what is the matter with you?

OSWALD: (*Seems to shrink together in the chair; all his muscles relax; his face is expressionless, his eyes have a glassy stare.*)

MRS. ALVING: (*Quivering with terror.*) What is this? (*Shrieks.*) Oswald! what is the matter with you? (*Falls on her knees beside him and shakes him.*) Oswald! Oswald! look at me! Don't you know me?

OSWALD: (*Tonelessly as before.*) The sun.—The sun.

MRS. ALVING: (*Springs up in despair, entwines her hands in her hair and shrieks.*) I cannot bear it! (*Whispers, as though petrified*) I cannot bear it! Never! (*Suddenly.*) Where has he got them? (*Fumbles hastily in his breast.*) Here! (*Shrinks back a few steps and screams:*) No; no; no!—Yes!—No; no!

(*She stands a few steps away from him with her hands twisted in her hair, and stares at him in speechless horror.*)

OSWALD: (*Sits motionless as before and says.*) The sun.—The sun.

THE END.

The Father

AUGUST STRINDBERG

COMMENTARY

 August Strindberg (1849-1912) was born in Stockholm, Sweden. His father was an unsuccessful businessman of a good family; his mother, a barmaid. His parents married just before August was born. When he was thirteen, his mother died and his father married again. His later life was as irregular, as marked by shock, as was his earlier life. He entered the universities at Uppsala and Stockholm for short periods and tried several careers. When he was around twenty, he began writing plays and soon gained the encouragement of the king. He married and divorced three times: much of his marital agony became the raw material of his plays. For a while he was mad. Throughout his life, however, his literary energies rarely flagged, and when he died, he was recognized as one of the great dramatists of all time. His plays may be divided into three groups, the realistic ones, like *Comrades* (1886), *The Father* (1886), and *Miss Julie* (1888); the surrealistic or dream plays, like *The Dream Play* (1902) and *The Ghost Sonata* (1907); and the history plays, about early Swedish rulers, *Gustave Vasa* (1899) and *Erik XIV* (1899). A play like *Easter* (1901) mixes the realistic and the dream forms and, in its calmness particularly, suggests the depths of understanding and sympathy Strindberg could achieve.

The Father is a turbulent work. The hero is an inflexible man, driven by a nearly monomaniacal sense of principle into a whimpering infantilism. Although his wife may remind us of Clytemnestra or of Medea, in her assertion of self-interest and in the fierceness of her maternal instincts, the captain seems finally the victim of his own softness of character and will. His doubts about his paternity may be read as doubts about his own identity, about his own capacity to assume and properly play the role of father.

The play invites comparison with archetypal tragedies. The *Agamemnon* is an obvious if remote model, and the differences between the central characters in both works suggests the significance of the personal and modern elements in Strindberg. Oedipus' need to find truth is related to the captain's similar compulsion, yet is critically different: Oedipus' question does have a conclusive answer; the captain's answer, short of incontrovertible blood tests proving paternity, can only be based on a plausible faith. Othello's flaw of jealousy had at its source a naiveté similiar to the captain's uncertainty of self, and we may ask whether the quality of tragedy in *Othello* and in *The Father* is affected by the depth and the reasonableness of the sources of jealous doubt in each. *Ghosts* had curious parallels with *The Father,* in the persons of the two captains and the two women; Strindberg did propose "woman-hate" as a balance for Ibsen's "woman-love."

Miss Julie and *The Stronger* (1890), the latter a short play in the form of a monologue, illuminate the background of *The Father* in their descriptions of the elemental battle between the sexes in which Strindberg felt himself totally involved. Eric Bentley's essay in *The Playwright as Thinker* (New York, 1946) and Robert Brustein's chapter in *The Theatre of Revolt* (Boston, 1964) are valuable; Morris Freedman's "Strindberg's Positive Nihilism," in *The Moral Impulse* (Carbondale and Edwardsville, 1967), surveys five representative plays, including *The Father.*

August Strindberg

THE FATHER

A TRAGEDY IN THREE ACTS

Translated by Elizabeth Sprigge

CHARACTERS

THE CAPTAIN
LAURA, *his wife*
BERTHA, *their daughter*
DOCTOR ÖSTERMARK
THE PASTOR
THE NURSE
NÖJD
THE ORDERLY

The whole play takes place in the central living-room of the Captain's home. He is a cavalry officer in a remote country district of Sweden.

It is about 1886, shortly before Christmas.

At the back of the room, towards the right, a door leads to the hall. In the left wall there is a door to other rooms, and in the right-hand corner another, smaller door, covered in the same wall-paper as the walls, opens on to a staircase leading to the Captain's room above.

In the centre of the room stands a large round table on which are newspapers, magazines, a big photograph album and a lamp. On the right are a leather-covered sofa, arm chairs and a smaller table. On the left is a writing-bureau with a pendulum clock upon it. Arms, guns and gun-bags hang on the walls, and military coats on pegs by the door to the hall.

August Strindberg, *The Father*, trans. Elizabeth Sprigge (New York, 1955). By permission of Collins-Knowlton-Wing, Inc., Agent for the Proprietor.

ACT ONE

(*Early evening. The lamp on the table is lighted. The* CAPTAIN *and the* PASTOR *are sitting on the sofa talking. The* CAPTAIN *is in undress uniform with riding-boots and spurs; the* PASTOR *wears black, with a white cravat in place of his clerical collar, and is smoking a pipe.*
The CAPTAIN *rises and rings a bell. The* ORDERLY *enters from the hall.*)

ORDERLY: Yes, sir?

CAPTAIN: Is Nöjd there?

ORDERLY: Nöjd's in the kitchen, sir, waiting for orders.

CAPTAIN: In the kitchen again, is he? Send him here at once.

ORDERLY: Yes, sir.

(*Exit.*)

PASTOR: Why, what's the trouble?

CAPTAIN: Oh, the ruffian's been at his tricks again with one of the servant girls! He's a damn nuisance, that fellow!

PASTOR: Was it Nöjd you said? Didn't he give you some trouble back in the spring?

CAPTAIN: Ah, you remember that, do you? Look here, you give him a bit of a talking to, there's a good chap. That might have some effect. I've sworn at him and thrashed him, without making the least impression.

PASTOR: So now you want me to preach to him. How much impression do you think God's word is likely to make on a trooper?

CAPTAIN: Well, my dear brother-in-law, it makes none at all on me, as you know, but . . .

PASTOR: As I know only too well.

CAPTAIN: But on him? Worth trying anyhow.

(*Enter* NÖJD.)

What have you been up to now, Nöjd?

NÖJD? God bless you, sir, I can't talk about that—not with Pastor here.

PASTOR: Don't mind me, my lad.

NÖJD: Well you see, sir, it was like this. We was at a dance at Gabriel's, and then, well then Ludwig said as . . .

CAPTAIN: What's Ludwig got to do with it? Stick to the point.

NÖJD: Well then Emma said as we should go in the barn.

CAPTAIN: I see. I suppose it was Emma who led you astray.

NÖJD: Well, not far from it. What I mean is if the girl's not game, nothing don't happen.

CAPTAIN: Once and for all—are you the child's father or are you not?

NÖJD: How's one to know?

CAPTAIN: What on earth do you mean? Don't you know?

NÖJD: No, you see, sir, that's what you never can know.

CAPTAIN: You mean you weren't the only man?

NÖJD: That time I was. But you can't tell if you've always been the only one.

CAPTAIN: Are you trying to put the blame on Ludwig? Is that the idea?

NÖJD: It's not easy to know who to put the blame on.

CAPTAIN: But, look here, you told Emma you would marry her.

NÖJD: Oh well, you always have to say that, you know.

CAPTAIN: (*to the* PASTOR.) This is atrocious.

PASTOR: It's the old story. Come now, Nöjd, surely you are man enough to know if you are the father.

NÖJD: Well, sir, it's true, I did go with

her, but you know yourself, Pastor, that don't always lead to nothing.

PASTOR: Look here, my lad, it's you we are talking about. And you are not going to leave that girl destitute with a child. You can't be forced to marry her, but you must make provision for the child. That you must do.

NÖJD: So must Ludwig then.

CAPTAIN: If that's how it is, the case will have to go before the Magistrate. I can't settle it, and it's really nothing to do with me. Dismiss!

PASTOR: One moment, Nöjd. Ahem. Don't you think it's rather a dirty trick to leave a girl destitute with a child like that? Don't you think so—eh?

NÖJD: Yes, if I knew I was the father, it would be, but I tell you, Pastor, you never can know that. And it wouldn't be much fun slaving all your life for another chap's brat. You and the Captain must see that for yourselves.

CAPTAIN: That will do, Nöjd.

NÖJD: Yes, sir, thank you, sir.

CAPTAIN: And keep out of the kitchen, you scoundrel!

(*Exit* NÖJD.)

Why didn't you haul him over the coals?

PASTOR: What do you mean? Didn't I?

CAPTAIN: No, you just sat there muttering to yourself.

PASTOR: As a matter of fact, I scarcely knew what to say to him. It's hard on the girl, of course, but it's hard on the boy too. Supposing he's not the father? The girl can nurse the baby for four months at the orphanage, and after that it will be taken care of for good. But the boy can't nurse the child, can he? Later on, the girl will get a good place in some respectable family, but if the boy is cashiered, his future may be ruined.

CAPTAIN: Upon my soul, I'd like to be the magistrate and judge this case! Maybe the boy is responsible—that's what you can't know. But one thing you *can* know —if anybody's guilty, the girl is.

PASTOR: Well, I never sit in judgment. Now what was it we were talking about when this blessed business interrupted us? Yes, Bertha and her confirmation, wasn't it?

CAPTAIN: It's not just a question of confirmation, but of her whole future. The house is full of women, all trying to mould this child of mine. My mother-in-law wants to turn her into a spiritualist; Laura wants her to be an artist; the governess would have her a Methodist, old Margaret a Baptist, and the servant girls a Salvation Army lass. You can't make a character out of patchwork. Meanwhile I . . . I, who have more right than all the rest to guide her, am opposed at every turn. So I must send her away.

PASTOR: You have too many women running your house.

CAPTAIN: You're right there. It's like going into a cage of tigers. They'd soon tear me to pieces, if I didn't hold a red-hot poker under their noses. It's all very well for you to laugh, you blackguard. It wasn't enough that I married your sister; you had to palm off your old stepmother on me too.

PASTOR: Well, good Lord, one can't have stepmothers in one's house!

CAPTAIN: No, you prefer mothers-in-law—in someone else's house, of course.

PASTOR: Well, well, we all have our burdens to bear.

CAPTAIN: I daresay, but I have more than my share. There's my old nurse too, who treats me as if I still wore a bib. She's a good old soul, to be sure, but she shouldn't be here.

PASTOR: You should keep your women-folk in order, Adolf. You give them too much rope.

CAPTAIN: My dear fellow, can you tell me how to keep women in order?

PASTOR: To tell the truth, although she's my sister, Laura was always a bit of a handful.

CAPTAIN: Laura has her faults, of course, but they are not very serious ones.

PASTOR: Oh come now, I know her!

CAPTAIN: She was brought up with romantic ideas and has always found it a little difficult to come to terms with life. But she is my wife and . . .

PASTOR: And because she is your wife she must be the best of women. No, brother-in-law, it's she not you who wears the trousers.

CAPTAIN: In any case, the whole household has gone mad. Laura's determined Bertha shan't leave her, and I won't let her stay in this lunatic asylum.

PASTOR: So Laura's determined, is she? Then there's bound to be trouble, I'm afraid. As a child she used to lie down and sham dead until they gave in to her. Then she would calmly hand back whatever she'd set her mind on, explaining it wasn't the thing she wanted, but simply to get her own way.

CAPTAIN: So she was like that even then, was she? Hm. As a matter of fact, she does sometimes get so overwrought I'm frightened for her and think she must be ill.

PASTOR: What is it you want Bertha to do that's such a bone of contention? Can't you come to some agreement?

CAPTAIN: Don't think I want to turn her into a prodigy—or into some image of myself. But I will not play pander and have my daughter fitted for nothing but the marriage market. For then, if she didn't marry after all, she'd have a

wretched time of it. On the other hand, I don't want to start her off in some man's career with a long training that would be entirely wasted if she did marry.

PASTOR: Well, what do you want then?

CAPTAIN: I want her to be a teacher. Then, if she doesn't marry she'll be able to support herself, and at least be no worse off than those unfortunate schoolmasters who have to support families on their earnings. And if she does marry, she can educate her own children. Isn't that reasonable?

PASTOR: Reasonable, yes—but what about her artistic talent? Wouldn't it be against the grain to repress that?

CAPTAIN: No. I showed her attempts to a well-known painter who told me they were nothing but the usual sort of thing learnt at school. Then, during the summer, some young jackanapes came along who knew better and said she was a genius—whereupon the matter was settled in Laura's favour.

PASTOR: Was he in love with Bertha?

CAPTAIN: I take that for granted.

PASTOR: Well, God help you, old boy, I don't see any solution. But it's a tiresome business, and I suppose Laura has supporters . . . (indicates other rooms) in there.

CAPTAIN: You may be sure of that. The whole household is in an uproar, and between ourselves the method of attack from that quarter is not exactly chivalrous.

PASTOR: (rising.) Do you think I haven't been through it?

CAPTAIN: You too?

PASTOR: Yes, indeed.

CAPTAIN: But to me the worst thing about it is that Bertha's future should be decided in there from motives of sheer hate. They do nothing but talk about men being made to see that women can do this and do that. It's man versus woman the whole day long ... Must you go? Won't you stay to supper? I don't know what there is, but do stay. I'm expecting the new doctor, you know. Have you seen him yet?

PASTOR: I caught a glimpse of him on my way here. He looks a decent, reliable sort of man.

CAPTAIN: That's good. Do you think he may be my ally?

PASTOR: Maybe. It depends how well he knows women.

CAPTAIN: But won't you stay?

PASTOR: Thank you, my dear fellow, but I promised to be home this evening, and my wife gets anxious if I'm late.

CAPTAIN: Anxious! Furious, you mean. Well, as you please. Let me help you on with your coat.

PASTOR: It's certainly very cold tonight. Thank you. You must look after yourself, Adolf. You seem a bit on edge.

CAPTAIN: On edge? Do I?

PASTOR: Yes. You aren't very well, are you?

CAPTAIN: Did Laura put this into your head? For the last twenty years she's been treating me as if I had one foot in the grave.

PASTOR: Laura? No, it's just that I'm ... I'm worried about you. Take my advice and look after yourself. Goodbye, old man. By the way, didn't you want to talk about the confirmation?

CAPTAIN: By no means. But I give you my word this shall take its own course—and be chalked up to the official conscience. I am neither a witness to the truth, nor a martyr. We have got past that sort of thing. Goodbye. Remember me to your wife.

PASTOR: Goodbye, Adolf. Give my love to Laura.

(*Exit* PASTOR. *The* CAPTAIN *opens the bureau and settles down to his accounts.*)

CAPTAIN: Thirty-four—nine, forty-three —seven, eight, fifty-six.

LAURA: (*entering from the next room.*) Will you please ...

CAPTAIN: One moment!—Sixty-six, seventy-one, eighty-four, eighty-nine, ninety-two, a hundred. What is it?

LAURA: Am I disturbing you?

CAPTAIN: Not in the least. Housekeeping money, I suppose?

LAURA: Yes, housekeeping money.

CAPTAIN: If you put the acounts down there, I will go through them.

LAURA: Accounts?

CAPTAIN: Yes.

LAURA: Do you expect me to keep accounts now?

CAPTAIN: Of course you must keep accounts. Our position's most precarious, and if we go bankrupt, we must have accounts to show. Otherwise we could be accused of negligence.

LAURA: It's not my fault if we're in debt.

CAPTAIN: That's what the accounts will show.

LAURA: It's not my fault the tenant farmer doesn't pay.

CAPTAIN: Who was it recommended him so strongly? You. Why did you recommend such a—shall we call him a scatterbrain?

LAURA: Why did you take on such a scatterbrain?

CAPTAIN: Because I wasn't allowed to eat in peace, sleep in peace or work in peace till you got him here. You wanted him because your brother wanted to get rid of him; my mother-in-law wanted him because I didn't; the governess wanted him because he was a Methodist, and old Margaret because she had known his grandmother as a child. That's why, and if I hadn't taken him I should be in a lunatic asylum by now, or else in the family vault. However, here's the house-keeping allowance and your pin money. You can give me the accounts later.

LAURA: (*with an ironic bob.*) Thank you so much.—By the way, do you keep accounts yourself—of what you spend outside the household?

CAPTAIN: That's none of your business.

LAURA: True. As little my business as the future of my own child. Did you gentlemen come to any decision at this evening's conference?

CAPTAIN: I had already made my decision, so I merely had to communicate it to the only friend I have in the family. Bertha is going to live in town. She will leave in a fortnight's time.

LAURA: Where, if I may ask, is she going to stay?

CAPTAIN: At Sävberg's—the solicitor's.

LAURA: That Freethinker!

CAPTAIN: According to the law as it now stands, children are brought up in their father's faith.

LAURA: And the mother has no say in the matter?

CAPTAIN: None whatever. She sells her birthright by legal contract and surrenders all her rights. In return the husband supports her and her children.

LAURA: So she has no rights over her own child?

CAPTAIN: None at all. When you have sold something, you don't expect to get it back and keep the money too.

LAURA: But supposing the father and mother were to decide things together . . . ?

CAPTAIN: How would that work out? I want her to live in town; you want her to live at home. The mathematical mean would be for her to stop at the railway station, midway between home and town. You see? It's a deadlock.

LAURA: Then the lock must be forced. . . . What was Nöjd doing here?

CAPTAIN: That's a professional secret.

LAURA: Which the whole kitchen knows.

CAPTAIN: Then doubtless you know it too.

LAURA: I do.

CAPTAIN: And are ready to sit in judgment?

LAURA: The law does that.

CAPTAIN: The law doesn't say who the child's father is.

LAURA: Well, people know that for themselves.

CAPTAIN: Discerning people say that's what one never can know.

LAURA: How extraordinary! Can't one tell who a child's father is?

CAPTAIN: Apparently not.

LAURA: How perfectly extraordinary! Then how can the father have those rights over the mother's child?

CAPTAIN: He only has them when he takes on the responsibility—or has it forced on him. But of course in marriage there is no doubt about the paternity.

LAURA: No doubt?

CAPTAIN: I should hope not.

LAURA: But supposing the wife has been unfaithful?

CAPTAIN: Well, such a supposition has no bearing on our problem. Is there anything else you want to ask me about?

LAURA: No, nothing.

CAPTAIN: Then I shall go up to my room. Please let me know when the doctor comes. (*Closes the bureau and rises.*)

LAURA: I will.

CAPTAIN: (*going out by the wall-*

papered door.) As soon as he comes, mind. I don't want to be discourteous, you understand.

(*Exit.*)

LAURA: I understand. (*She looks at the bank-notes she is holding.*)

MOTHER-IN-LAW: (*off.*) Laura!

LAURA: Yes, Mother?

MOTHER-IN-LAW: Is my tea ready?

LAURA: (*at the door to the next room.*) It's coming in a moment.

(*The* ORDERLY *opens the hall door.*)

ORDERLY: Dr. Östermark.

(*Enter* DOCTOR. *Exit* ORDERLY, *closing the door.*)

LAURA: (*shaking hands.*) How do you do, Dr. Östermark. Let me welcome you to our home. The Captain is out, but he will be back directly.

DOCTOR: I must apologize for calling so late, but I have already had to pay some professional visits.

LAURA: Won't you sit down?

DOCTOR: Thank you.

LAURA: Yes, there is a lot of illness about just now, but I hope all the same that you will find this place suits you. It is so important for people in a lonely country district like this to have a doctor who takes a real interest in his patients. I have heard you so warmly spoken of, Dr. Östermark, I hope we shall be on the best of terms.

DOCTOR: You are too kind, dear lady. I hope, however, for your sake that my visits here will not often be of a professional nature. I take it that the health of your family is, on the whole, good, and that . . .

LAURA: Yes, we have been fortunate enough not to have any serious illnesses, but all the same things are not quite as they should be.

DOCTOR: Indeed?

LAURA: No, I'm afraid not really at all as one would wish.

DOCTOR: Dear, dear, you quite alarm me!

LAURA: In a family there are sometimes things which honour and duty compel one to keep hidden from the world.

DOCTOR: But not from one's doctor.

LAURA: No. That is why it is my painful duty to tell you the whole truth from the start.

DOCTOR: May we not postpone this conversation until I have had the honour of meeting the Captain?

LAURA: No. You must hear what I have to say before you see him.

DOCTOR: Does it concern him then?

LAURA: Yes, him. My poor, dear husband.

DOCTOR: You are making me most uneasy. Whatever your trouble, Madam, you can confide in me.

LAURA: (*taking out her hankerchief.*) My husband's mind is affected. Now you know, and later on you will be able to judge for yourself.

DOCTOR: You astound me. The Captain's learned treatise on mineralogy, for which I have the greatest admiration, shows a clear and powerful intellect.

LAURA: Does it? I shall be overjoyed if we—his relatives—are mistaken.

DOCTOR: It is possible, of course, that his mind is disturbed in other ways. Tell me . . .

LAURA: That is exactly what we fear. You see, at times he has the most peculiar ideas, which wouldn't matter much for a scientist, if they weren't such a burden on his family. For instance, he has an absolute mania for buying things.

DOCTOR: That is significant. What kind of things?

LAURA: Books. Whole cases of them, which he never reads.

DOCTOR: Well, that a scholar should buy books isn't so alarming.

LAURA: You don't believe what I am telling you?

DOCTOR: I am convinced, Madam, that you believe what you are telling me.

LAURA: Well, then, is it possible for anyone to see in a microscope what's happening on another planet?

DOCTOR: Does he say he can do that?

LAURA: Yes, that's what he says.

DOCTOR: In a microscope?

LAURA: In a microscope. Yes.

DOCTOR: That is significant, if it is so.

LAURA: If it is so! You don't believe me, Doctor. And here have I let you in to the family secret.

DOCTOR: My dear lady, I am honoured by your confidence, but as a physician I must observe and examine before giving an opinion. Has the Captain shown any symptoms of instability, any lack of will power?

LAURA: Has he, indeed! We have been married twenty years, and he has never yet made a decision without going back on it.

DOCTOR: Is he dogmatic?

LAURA: He certainly lays down the law, but as soon as he gets his own way, he loses interest and leaves everything to me.

DOCTOR: That is significant and requires careful consideration. The will, you see, Madam, is the backbone of the mind. If it is injured, the mind falls to pieces.

LAURA: God knows how I have schooled myself to meet his every wish during these long hard years. Oh, if you knew what I have been through with him, if you only knew!

DOCTOR: I am profoundly distressed to learn of your trouble, Madam, and I promise I will do what I can. You have my deepest sympathy and I beg you to rely on me implicitly. But now you have told me this, I am going to ask one thing of you. Don't allow anything to prey on the patient's mind. In a case of instability, ideas can sometimes take hold and grow into an obsession—or even monomania. Do you follow me?

LAURA: . . . You mean don't let him get ideas into his head.

DOCTOR: Precisely. For a sick man can be made to believe anything. He is highly susceptible to suggestion.

LAURA: I see . . . I understand. Yes, indeed. (*A bell rings within.*) Excuse me. That's my mother ringing. I won't be a moment . . . Oh, here's Adolf!

(*As* LAURA *goes out, the* CAPTAIN *enters by the wall-papered door.*)

CAPTAIN: Ah, so you have arrived, Doctor! You are very welcome.

DOCTOR: How do you do, Captain. It's a great honour to meet such a distinguished scientist.

CAPTAIN: Oh please! Unfortunately, my military duties don't give me much time for research . . . All the same, I do believe I am now on the brink of a rather exciting discovery.

DOCTOR: Really?

CAPTAIN: You see, I have been subjecting meteoric stones to spectrum analysis, and I have found carbon—an indication of organic life. What do you say to that?

DOCTOR: Can you see that in a microscope?

CAPTAIN: No, in a spectroscope, for heaven's sake!

DOCTOR: Spectroscope! I beg your pardon. Then you will soon be telling us what is happening on Jupiter.

CAPTAIN: Not what is happening, what *has* happened. If only that blasted Paris bookseller would send my books. I really think the whole book-trade must be in league against me. Think of it, for two months I've not had one single answer to my orders, my letters or my abusive telegrams! It's driving me mad. I can't make out what's happened.

DOCTOR: Well, what could it be but ordinary carelessness? You shouldn't let it upset you.

CAPTAIN: Yes, but the devil of it is I shan't be able to get my article finished in time.—I know they're working on the same lines in Berlin . . . However, that's not what we should be talking about now, but about you. If you would care to live here, we can give you a small suite of rooms in that wing. Or would you prefer your predecessor's house?

DOCTOR: Whichever you please.

CAPTAIN: No, whichever *you* please. You have only to say.

DOCTOR: It's for you to decide, Captain.

CAPTAIN: Nothing of the kind. It's for you to say which you prefer. I don't care one way or the other.

DOCTOR: But I really can't . . .

CAPTAIN: For Christ's sake, man, say what you want! I haven't any opinion, any inclination, any choice, any preference at all. Are you such a milksop that you don't know what you want? Make up your mind, or I shall lose my temper.

DOCTOR: If I am to choose, I should like to live here.

CAPTAIN: Good!—Thank you. (*Rings.*) Oh dear me!—I apologise, Doctor, but nothing irritates me so much as to hear people say they don't care one way or the other.

(*The* NURSE *enters.*)

Ah, it's you, Margaret. Look here, my dear, do you know if the rooms in the wing are ready for the doctor?

NURSE: Yes, Captain, they're ready.

CAPTAIN: Good. Then I won't detain you, Doctor, for you must be tired. Goodnight, and once again—welcome. I look forward to seeing you in the morning.

DOCTOR: Thank you. Goodnight.

CAPTAIN: By the way, I wonder if my wife told you anything about us—if you know at all how the land lies?

DOCTOR: Your good lady did suggest one or two things it might be as well for a newcomer to know. Goodnight, Captain.

(*The* NURSE *shows the* DOCTOR *out and returns.*)

CAPTAIN: What is it, old girl? Anything the matter?

NURSE: Now listen, Mr. Adolf, dear.

CAPTAIN: Yes, go on, Margaret, talk. You're the only one whose talk doesn't get on my nerves.

NURSE: Then listen, Mr. Adolf. Couldn't you go halfway to meet the mistress in all this bother over the child? Think of a mother . . .

CAPTAIN: Think of a father, Margaret.

NURSE: Now, now, now! A father has many things besides his child, but a mother has nothing but her child.

CAPTAIN: Quite so, my friend. She has only one burden, while I have three and bear hers too. Do you think I'd have been stuck in the army all my life if I hadn't had her and her child to support?

NURSE: I know, but that wasn't what I wanted to talk about.

CAPTAIN: Quite. What you want is to make out I'm in the wrong.

NURSE: Don't you believe I want what's best for you, Mr. Adolf?

CAPTAIN: I'm sure you do, my dear, but you don't know what is best for me. You see, it's not enough to have given the child life. I want to give her my very soul.

NURSE: Oh, that's beyond me, but I do think you two ought to come to terms.

CAPTAIN: Margaret, you are not my friend.

NURSE: Not your friend! Ah God, what are you saying, Mr. Adolf? Do you think I ever forget you were my baby when you were little?

CAPTAIN: Well, my dear, am I likely to forget it? You have been like a mother to me, and stood by me against all the others. But now that things have come to a head, you're deserting—going over to the enemy.

NURSE: Enemy?

CAPTAIN: Yes, enemy. You know perfectly well how things are here. You've seen it all from beginning to end.

NURSE: Aye, I've seen plenty. But, dear God, why must two people torment the lives out of each other? Two people who are so good and kind to everyone else. The mistress never treats me wrong or . . .

CAPTAIN: Only me. I know. And I tell you, Margaret, if you desert me now, you'll be doing a wicked thing. For a net is closing round me, and that doctor is no friend of mine.

NURSE: Oh, goodness, Mr. Adolf, you believe the worst of everyone! But that's what comes of not having the true faith. That's your trouble.

CAPTAIN: While you and the Baptists have found the one true faith, eh? You're lucky.

NURSE: Aye, luckier than you, Mr. Adolf. Humble your heart and you will see how happy God will make you in your love for your neighbour.

CAPTAIN: Isn't it strange—as soon as you mention God and love, your voice grows hard and your eyes fill with hate. No, Margaret, I'm sure you haven't found the true faith.

MARGARET: However proud you are and stuffed with booklearning, that won't get you anywhere when the pinch comes.

CAPTAIN: How arrogantly thou speakest, O humble heart! I'm well aware that learning means nothing to creatures like you.

NURSE: Shame on you! Still, old Margaret loves her great big boy best of all. And when the storm breaks, he'll come back to her, sure enough, like the good child he is.

CAPTAIN: Forgive me, Margaret. You see, you really are the only friend I have here. Help me, for something is going to happen. I don't know what, but I know it's evil, this thing that's on its way. (*A scream from within.*) What's that? Who's screaming?

(BERTHA *runs in.*)

BERTHA: Father, Father! Help me! Save me!

CAPTAIN: What is it? My darling, tell me.

BERTHA: Please protect me. I know she'll do something terrible to me.

CAPTAIN: Who? What do you mean? Tell me at once.

BERTHA: Grandmother. But it was my fault. I played a trick on her.

CAPTAIN: Go on.

BERTHA: Yes, but you mustn't tell anyone. Promise you won't.

CAPTAIN: Very well, but what happened?

(*Exit* NURSE.)

BERTHA: You see, sometimes in the evening she turns the lamp down and makes me sit at the table holding a pen over a piece of paper. And then she says the spirits write.

CAPTAIN: Well, I'll be damned! And you never told me.

BERTHA: I'm sorry, I didn't dare.

Grandmother says spirits revenge themselves on people who talk about them. And then the pen writes, but I don't know if it's me doing it or not. Sometimes it goes well, but sometimes it doesn't work at all. And when I get tired nothing happens, but I have to make something happen all the same. This evening I thought I was doing rather well, but then Grandmother said it was all out of Stagnelius* and I had been playing a trick on her. And she was simply furious.

CAPTAIN: Do you believe there are spirits?

BERTHA: I don't know.

CAPTAIN: But I know there are not.

BERTHA: Grandmother says you don't understand, and that you have worse things that can see into other planets.

CAPTAIN: She says that, does she? And what else does she say?

BERTHA: That you can't work miracles.

CAPTAIN: I never said I could. You know what meteorites are, don't you?—stones that fall from other heavenly bodies. Well, I examine these and see if they contain the same elements as the earth. That's all I do.

BERTHA: Grandmother says there are things she can see and you can't.

CAPTAIN: My dear, she is lying.

BERTHA: Grandmother doesn't lie.

CAPTAIN: How do you know?

BERTHA: Then Mother does too.

CAPTAIN: Hm!

BERTHA: If you say Mother is a liar, I'll never believe a word you say again.

CAPTAIN: I didn't say that, so now you must believe me. Listen. Your happiness, your whole future depends on your leaving home. Will you do this? Will you go and live in town and learn something useful?

* Erik Johan Stagnelius, Swedish poet and dramatist. (1793-1823.)

BERTHA: Oh yes, I'd love to live in town—anywhere away from here! It's always so miserable in there, as gloomy as a winter night. But when you come home, Father, it's like a spring morning when they take the double windows down.

CAPTAIN: My darling, my beloved child!

BERTHA: But, Father, listen, you must be kind to Mother. She often cries.

CAPTAIN: Hm! . . . So you would like to live in town?

BERTHA: Oh yes!

CAPTAIN: But supposing your mother doesn't agree?

BERTHA: She must.

CAPTAIN: But supposing she doesn't?

BERTHA: Then I don't know what will happen. But she must, she must!

CAPTAIN: Will you ask her?

BERTHA: No, you must ask her—very nicely. She wouldn't pay any attention to me.

CAPTAIN: Hm! . . . Well now, if you want this and I want it and she doesn't want it, what are we to do then?

BERTHA: Oh, then the fuss will begin all over again! Why can't you both . . .

(*Enter* LAURA.)

LAURA: Ah, so you're here, Bertha! Well now, Adolf, as the question of her future is still to be decided, let's hear what she has to say herself.

CAPTAIN: The child can hardly have anything constructive to say about the development of young girls, but you and I ought to be able to sum up the pros and cons. We've watched a good number grow up.

LAURA: But as we don't agree, Bertha can give the casting vote.

CAPTAIN: No. I won't allow anyone to interfere with my rights—neither woman nor child. Bertha, you had better leave us.

(*Exit* BERTHA.)

LAURA: You were afraid to hear her opinion because you knew she would agree with me.

CAPTAIN: I know she wants to leave home, but I also know you have the power to make her change her mind.

LAURA: Oh, have I much power?

CAPTAIN: Yes, you have a fiendish power of getting your own way, like all people who are unscrupulous about the means they employ. How, for instance, did you get rid of Dr. Norling? And how did you get hold of the new doctor?

LAURA: Yes, how did I?

CAPTAIN: You ran the old doctor down until he had to leave, and then you got your brother to canvass for this one.

LAURA: Well, that was quite simple and perfectly legal. Then is Bertha to leave home?

CAPTAIN: Yes, in a fortnight's time.

LAURA: I warn you I shall do my best to prevent it.

CAPTAIN: You can't.

LAURA: Can't I? Do you expect me to give up my child to be taught by wicked people that all she has learnt from her mother is nonsense? So that I would be despised by my own daughter for the rest of my life.

CAPTAIN: Do you expect me to allow ignorant and bumptious women to teach my daughter that her father is a charlatan?

LAURA: That shouldn't matter so much to you—now.

CAPTAIN: What on earth do you mean?

LAURA: Well, the mother's closer to the child, since the discovery that no one can tell who the father is.

CAPTAIN: What's that got to do with us?

LAURA: You don't know if you are Bertha's father.

CAPTAIN: Don't know?

LAURA: How can you know what nobody knows?

CAPTAIN: Are you joking?

LAURA: No, I'm simply applying your own theory. How do you know I haven't been unfaithful to you?

CAPTAIN: I can believe a good deal of you, but not that. And if it were so, you wouldn't talk about it.

LAURA: Supposing I were prepared for anything, for being turned out and ostracised, anything to keep my child under my own control. Supposing I am telling the truth now when I say: Bertha is my child but not yours. Supposing . . .

CAPTAIN: Stop it!

LAURA: Just supposing . . . then your power would be over.

CAPTAIN: Not till you had proved I wasn't the father.

LAURA: That wouldn't be difficult. Do you want me to?

CAPTAIN: Stop.

LAURA: I should only have to give the name of the real father—with particulars of place and time, of course. For that matter—when was Bertha born? In the third year of our marriage . . .

CAPTAIN: Will you stop it now, or . . .

LAURA: Or what? Very well, let's stop. All the same, I should think twice before you decide anything. And, above all, don't make yourself ridiculous.

CAPTAIN: I find the whole thing tragic.

LAURA: Which makes you still more ridiculous.

CAPTAIN: But not you?

LAURA: No, we're in such a strong position.

CAPTAIN: That's why we can't fight you.

LAURA: Why try to fight a superior enemy?

CAPTAIN: Superior?

LAURA: Yes. It's odd, but I have never been able to look at a man without feeling myself his superior.

CAPTAIN: One day you may meet your master—and you'll never forget it.

LAURA: That will be fascinating.

(*Enter* NURSE.)

NURSE: Supper's ready. Come along now, please.

LAURA: Yes, of course. (*The* CAPTAIN *lingers and sits down in an armchair near the sofa.*) Aren't you coming?

CAPTAIN: No, thank you, I don't want any supper.

LAURA: Why not? Has anything upset you?

CAPTAIN: No, but I'm not hungry.

LAURA: Do come, or they'll start asking questions, and that's not necessary. Do be sensible. You won't? Well, stay where you are then!

(*Exit.*)

NURSE: Mr. Adolf, whatever is it now?

CAPTAIN: I don't know yet. Tell me— why do you women treat a grown man as if he were a child?

NURSE: Well, goodness me, you're all some woman's child, aren't you?—All you men, big or small . . .

CAPTAIN: While no woman is born of man, you mean. True. But I must be Bertha's father. You believe that, Margaret, don't you? Don't you?

NURSE: Lord, what a silly boy you are! Of course you're your own child's father. Come along and eat now. Don't sit here sulking. There now, come along, do.

CAPTAIN: (*rising.*) Get out, woman! To hell with the hags! (*At the hall door.*) Svärd! Svärd!

ORDERLY: (*entering.*) Yes, sir?

CAPTAIN: Have the small sleigh got ready at once.

(*Exit* ORDERLY.)

NURSE: Now listen, Captain . . .

CAPTAIN: Get out, woman! Get out, I say!

NURSE: God preserve us, whatever's going to happen now?

CAPTAIN: (*putting on his cap.*) Don't expect me home before midnight.

(*Exit.*)

NURSE: Lord Jesus! What *is* going to happen?

ACT TWO

(*The same as before, late that night. The* DOCTOR *and* LAURA *are sitting talking.*)

DOCTOR: My conversation with him has led me to the conclusion that your suspicions are by no means proved. To begin with, you were mistaken in saying that he had made these important astronomical discoveries by using a microscope. Now I have learnt that it was a spectroscope. Not only is there no sign in this of mental derangement—on the contrary, he has rendered a great service to science.

LAURA: But I never said that.

DOCTOR: I made a memorandum of our conversation, Madam, and I remember questioning you on this vital point, because I thought I must have misheard. One must be scrupulously accurate when bringing charges which might lead to a man being certified.

LAURA: Certified?

DOCTOR: I presume you are aware that if a person is certified insane, he loses both his civil and his family rights.

LAURA: No, I didn't know that.

DOCTOR: There is one other point I should like to be clear about. He spoke of not getting any replies from his booksellers. May I ask whether—from the best of intentions, of course—you have been intercepting his correspondence?

LAURA: Yes, I have. It is my duty to protect the family. I couldn't let him ruin us all and do nothing about it.

DOCTOR: Excuse me, I do not think you understand the possible consequences of your action. If he realises you have been interfering with his affairs behind his back, his suspicions will be aroused and mght even develop into a persecution mania. Particularly, as by thwarting his will, you have already driven him to the end of his tether. Surely you know how enraging it is to have your will opposed and your dearest wishes frustrated.

LAURA: Do I not!

DOCTOR: Then think what this means to him.

LAURA: (*rising.*) It's midnight and he's not back yet. Now we can expect the worst.

DOCTOR: Tell me what happened this evening after I saw him. I must know everything.

LAURA: He talked in the wildest way and said the most fantastic things. Can you believe it—he even suggested he wasn't the father of his own child!

DOCTOR: How extraordinary! What can have put that into his head?

LAURA: Goodness knows, unless it was an interview he had with one of his men about maintenance for a child. When I took the girl's part, he got very excited and said no one could ever tell who a child's father was. God knows I did everything I could to calm him, but I don't believe anything can help him now. (*Weeps.*)

DOCTOR: This can't go on. Something must be done—without rousing his sus-

picions. Tell me, has he had any such delusions before?

LAURA: As a matter of fact, he was much the same six years ago, and then he actually admitted—in a letter to his doctor —that he feared for his reason.

DOCTOR: I see, I see. A deep-seated trouble. But . . . er . . . the sanctity of family life . . . and so forth . . . I mustn't probe too far . . . must keep to the surface. Unfortunately what is done cannot be undone, yet the remedy should have been applied to what is done . . . Where do you think he is now?

LAURA: I can't imagine. He has such wild notions these days . . .

DOCTOR: Would you like me to stay until he comes in? I could explain my presence by saying—well, that your mother is ill and I came to see her.

LAURA: That's a very good idea. Please stand by us, Doctor. If you only knew how worried I am! . . . But wouldn't it be better to tell him straight out what you think of his condition?

DOCTOR: We never do that with mental patients, unless they bring the subject up themselves, and rarely even then. Everything depends on how the case develops. But we had better not stay here. May I go into some other room, to make it more convincing?

LAURA: Yes, that will be best, and Margaret can come in here. She always waits up for him. (*At the door.*) Margaret! Margaret! She is the only one who can manage him.

NURSE: (*entering.*) Did you call, Madam? Is Master back?

LAURA: No, but you are to wait here for him. And when he comes, tell him that my mother is unwell and the doctor is with her.

NURSE: Aye, aye. Leave all that to me.

LAURA: (*opening the door.*) If you

will be so good as to come in here, Doctor . . .

DOCTOR: Thank you.

(*They go out. The* NURSE *sits at the table, puts on her glasses and picks up her hymn-book.*)

NURSE: Ah me! Ah me! (*Reads softly:*)

A sorrowful and grievous thing
Is life, so swiftly passing by,
Death shadows with his angel's wing
The whole earth, and this his cry:
'Tis Vanity, all Vanity!

Ah me! Ah me!

All that on earth has life and breath,
Falls low before his awful might,
Sorrow alone is spared by Death,
Upon the yawning grave to write:
'Tis Vanity, all Vanity!

Ah me! Ah me!

(*During the last lines,* BERTHA *enters, carrying a tray with a coffee-pot and a piece of embroidery.*)

BERTHA: (*softly.*) Margaret, may I sit in here with you? It's so dismal up there.

NURSE: Saints alive! Bertha, are you still up?

BERTHA: Well, you see, I simply must get on with Father's Christmas present. And here's something nice for you.

NURSE: But, sweetheart, this won't do. You have to be up bright and early, and it's past twelve now.

BERTHA: Oh, that doesn't matter! I daren't stay up there all alone. I'm sure there are ghosts.

NURSE: There now! What did I tell you? Mark my words, there's no good fairy in this house. What was it? Did you hear something, Bertha?

BERTHA: Oh Margaret, someone was singing in the attic!

NURSE: In the attic? At this time of night?

BERTHA: Yes. It was such a sad song; the saddest I ever heard. And it seemed to come from the attic—you know, the one on the left where the cradle is.

NURSE: Oh dear, dear, dear! And such a fearful night too. I'm sure the chimneys will blow down. "Alas, what is this earthly life? Sorrow, trouble, grief and strife. Even when it seems most fair, Nought but tribulation there."—Ah, dear child, God grant us a happy Christmas!

BERTHA: Margaret, is it true Father's ill?

NURSE: Aye, that's true enough.

BERTHA: Then I don't expect we shall have a Christmas party. But why isn't he in bed if he's ill?

NURSE: Well, dearie, staying in bed doesn't help his kind of illness. Hush! I hear someone in the porch. Go to bed now—take the tray with you, or the Master will be cross.

BERTHA: (*going out with the tray.*) Goodnight, Margaret.

NURSE: Goodnight, love. God bless you.

(*Enter the* CAPTAIN.)

CAPTAIN: (*taking off his overcoat.*) Are you still up? Go to bed.

NURSE: Oh, I was only biding till . . .

(*The* CAPTAIN *lights a candle, opens the bureau, sits down at it and takes letters and newspapers from his pocket.*)

Mr. Adolf . . .

CAPTAIN: What is it?

NURSE: The old mistress is ill. Doctor's here.

CAPTAIN: Anything serious?

NURSE: No, I don't think so. Just a chill.

CAPTAIN: (*rising.*) Who was the father of your child, Margaret?

NURSE: I've told you often enough, it was that heedless fellow Johansson.

CAPTAIN: Are you sure it was he?

NURSE: Don't talk so silly. Of course I'm sure, seeing he was the only one.

CAPTAIN: Yes, but was he sure he was the only one? No, he couldn't be sure, only you could be. See? That's the difference.

NURSE: I don't see any difference.

CAPTAIN: No, you don't see it, but it's there all the same.

(*Turns the pages of the photograph album on the table.*)

Do you think Bertha's like me?

NURSE: You're as like as two peas in a pod.

CAPTAIN: Did Johansson admit he was the father?

NURSE: Well, he was forced to.

CAPTAIN: How dreadful!—Here's the doctor.

(*Enter* DOCTOR.)

Good evening, Doctor. How is my mother-in-law?

DOCTOR: Oh, it's nothing much. Just a slight sprain of the left ankle.

CAPTAIN: I thought Margaret said it was a chill. There appear to be different diagnoses of the case. Margaret, go to bed.

(*Exit* NURSE. *Pause.*)

Won't you sit down, Dr. Östermark?

DOCTOR: (*sitting.*) Thank you.

CAPTAIN: Is it true that if you cross a mare with a zebra you get striped foals?

DOCTOR: (*astonished.*) Perfectly true.

CAPTAIN: And that if breeding is then continued with a stallion, the foals may still be striped?

DOCTOR: That is also true.

CAPTAIN: So, in certain circumstances, a stallion can sire striped foals, and vice versa.

DOCTOR: That would appear to be the case.

CAPTAIN: So the offspring's resemblance to the father proves nothing.

DOCTOR: Oh . . .

CAPTAIN: You're a widower, aren't you? Any children?

DOCTOR: Ye-es.

CAPTAIN: Didn't you sometimes feel rather ridiculous as a father? I myself don't know anything more ludicrous than the sight of a man holding his child's hand in the street, or hearing a father say: "My child." "My wife's child," he ought to say. Didn't you ever see what a false position you were in? Weren't you ever haunted by doubts—I won't say suspicions, as a gentleman I assume your wife was above suspicion?

DOCTOR: No, I certainly wasn't. There it is, Captain, a man—as I think Goethe says—must take his children on trust.

CAPTAIN: Trust, where a woman's concerned? A bit of a risk.

DOCTOR: Ah, but there are many kinds of women!

CAPTAIN: The latest research shows there is only one kind . . . when I was a young fellow and not, if I may say so, a bad specimen, I had two little experiences which afterwards gave me to think. The first was on a steamer. I was in the saloon with some friends, and the young stewardess told us—with tears running down her cheeks—how her sweetheart had been drowned at sea. We condoled with her and I ordered champagne. After the second glass I touched her foot, after the fourth her knee, and before morning I had consoled her.

DOCTOR: One swallow doesn't make a summer.

CAPTAIN: My second experience was a summer swallow. I was staying at Lysekil and got to know a young married woman who was there with her children—her husband was in town. She was religious and high-minded, kept preaching at me and was—or so I thought—the soul of virtue. I lent her a book or two which, strange to relate, she returned. Three months later, I found her card in one of those books with a pretty outspoken declaration of love. It was innocent—as innocent, that's to say, as such a declaration from a married woman could be—to a stranger who had never made any advances. Moral: don't believe in anyone too much.

DOCTOR: Don't believe too little either.

CAPTAIN: The happy mean, eh? But you see, Doctor, that woman was so unaware of her motives she actually told her husband of her infatuation for me. That's where the danger lies, in the fact that women are unconscious of their instinctive wickedness. An extenuating circumstance, perhaps, but that can only mitigate the judgment, not revoke it.

DOCTOR: You have a morbid turn of mind, Captain. You should be on your guard against this.

CAPTAIN: There's nothing morbid about it. Look here. All steam-boilers explode when the pressure-gauge reaches the limit, but the limit isn't the same for all boilers. Got that? After all, you're here to observe me. Now if I were not a man I could sniff and snivel and explain the case to you, with all its past history. But as unfortunately I am a man, like the ancient Roman I must cross my arms upon my breast and hold my breath until I die. Goodnight.

DOCTOR: If you are ill, Captain, there's no reflection on your manhood in telling me about it. Indeed, it is essential for me to hear both sides of the case.

CAPTAIN: I thought you were quite satisfied with one side.

DOCTOR: You're wrong. And I should like you to know, Captain, that when I heard that Mrs. Alving* blackening her

* Reference to Mrs. Alving in Ibsen's GHOSTS.

late husband's memory, I thought what a damned shame it was that the fellow should be dead.

CAPTAIN: Do you think if he'd been alive he'd have said anything? Do you think if any husband rose from the dead he'd be believed? Goodnight, Doctor. Look how calm I am. It's quite safe for you to go to bed.

DOCTOR: Then I will bid you goodnight. I wash my hands of the whole business.

CAPTAIN: So we're enemies?

DOCTOR: By no means. It's just a pity we can't be friends. Goodnight.

(*The* CAPTAIN *shows the* DOCTOR *out by the hall door, then crosses to the other and slightly opens it.*)

CAPTAIN: Come in and let's talk. I knew you were eavesdropping.

(*Enter* LAURA, *embarrassed. The* CAPTAIN *sits at the bureau.*)

It's very late, but we'd better have things out now. Sit down. (*She sits. Pause.*) This evening it was I who went to the post office and fetched the mail, and from my letters it is clear to me that you have been intercepting my correspondence—both in and out. The result of this has been a loss of time which has pretty well shattered the expectations I had for my work.

LAURA: I acted from the best of intentions. You were neglecting your military duties for this other work.

CAPTAIN: Scarcely the best of intentions. You knew very well that one day I should win more distinction in this field than in the Army, but what you wanted was to stop me winning laurels of any kind, because this would stress your own inferiority. Now, for a change, I have intercepted letters addressed to you.

LAURA: How chivalrous!

CAPTAIN: In keeping with the high opinion you have of me. From these letters it appears that for a long time now you've been setting my old friends against me, by spreading rumours about my mental condition. So successful have your efforts been that now scarcely one person from Colonel to kitchen-maid believes I am sane. The actual facts about my condition are these. My reason is, as you know, unaffected, and I am able to discharge my duties both as soldier and father. My emotions are still pretty well under control, but only so long as my will-power remains intact. And you have so gnawed and gnawed at my will that at any moment it may slip its cogs, and then the whole bag of tricks will go to pieces. I won't appeal to your feelings, because you haven't any—that is your strength. I appeal to your own interests.

LAURA: Go on.

CAPTAIN: By behaving in this way you have made me so full of suspicion that my judgment is fogged and my mind is beginning to stray. This means that the insanity you have been waiting for is on its way and may come at any moment. The question you now have to decide is whether it is more to your advantage for me to be well or ill. Consider. If I go to pieces, I shall have to leave the Service, and where will you be then? If I die, you get my life-insurance. But if I take my own life, you get nothing. It is therefore to your advantage that I should live my life out.

LAURA: Is this a trap?

CAPTAIN: Certainly. You can avoid it or stick your head in it.

LAURA: You say you'd kill yourself, but you never would.

CAPTAIN: Are you so sure? Do you think a man can go on living when he has nothing and nobody to live for?

LAURA: Then you give in?

CAPTAIN: No, I offer peace.

LAURA: On what terms?

CAPTAIN: That I may keep my reason. Free me from doubt and I will give up the fight.

LAURA: Doubt about what?

CAPTAIN: Bertha's parentage.

LAURA: Are there doubts about that?

CAPTAIN: Yes, for me there are, and it was you who roused them.

LAURA: I?

CAPTAIN: Yes. You dropped them like henbane in my ear, and circumstances encouraged them to grow. Free me from uncertainty. Tell me straight out it is so, and I will forgive you in advance.

LAURA: I can scarcely admit to guilt that isn't mine.

CAPTAIN: What can it matter to you, when you know I won't reveal it? Do you think any man would proclaim his shame from the housetops?

LAURA: If I say it isn't so, you still won't be certain, but if I say it is, you will believe me. You must want it to be true.

CAPTAIN: Strangely enough I do. Perhaps because the first supposition can't be proved, while the second can.

LAURA: Have you any grounds for suspicion?

CAPTAIN: Yes and no.

LAURA: I believe you want to make out I'm guilty, so you can get rid of me and have absolute control of the child. But you won't catch me in any such trap.

CAPTAIN: Do you think, if I were convinced of your guilt, I should want to take on another man's child?

LAURA: No, I'm sure you wouldn't. So evidently you were lying when you said you'd forgive me in advance.

CAPTAIN: (rising.) Laura, save me and my reason! You can't have understood what I was saying. If the child's not mine, I have no rights over her, nor do I want any. And that's how you'd like it, isn't it? But that's not all. You want complete power over the child, don't you, with me still there to support you both?

LAURA: Power, that's it. What's this whole life and death struggle for if not power?

CAPTAIN: For me, as I don't believe in a life to come, this child was my life after death, my conception of immortality —the only one, perhaps, that's valid. If you take her away, you cut my life short.

LAURA: Why didn't we separate sooner?

CAPTAIN: Because the child bound us together, but the bond became a chain. How was that? I never thought of this before, but now memories return, accusing, perhaps condemning. After two years of marriage we were still childless —you know best why. Then I was ill and almost died. One day, between bouts of fever, I heard voices in the next room. You and the lawyer were discussing the property I still owned then. He was explaining that as there were no children, you could not inherit, and he asked if by any chance you were pregnant. I did not hear your reply. I recovered and we had a child. Who is the father?

LAURA: You are.

CAPTAIN: No, I am not. There's a crime buried here that's beginning to stink. And what a fiendish crime! You women, who were so tender-hearted about freeing black slaves, kept the white ones. I have slaved for you, your child, your mother, your servants. I have sacrificed career and promotion. Tortured, beaten, sleepless—my hair has gone grey through the agony of mind you have inflicted on me. All this I have suffered in order that you might enjoy a care-free life and, when you were old, relive it in your child. This is the lowest form of theft, the cruellest slavery. I have had seventeen years of

penal servitude—and I was innocent. How can you make up to me for this?

LAURA: Now you really are mad.

CAPTAIN: (*sitting.*) So you hope. I have watched you trying to conceal your crime, but because I didn't understand I pitied you. I've soothed your conscience, thinking I was chasing away some nightmare. I've heard you crying out in your sleep without giving your words a second thought. But now . . . now! The other night—Bertha's birthday—comes back to me. I was still up in the early hours, reading, and you suddenly screamed as if someone were trying to strangle you. "Don't! Don't!" you cried. I knocked on the wall—I didn't want to hear any more. For a long time I have had vague suspicions. I did not want them confirmed. This is what I have suffered for you. What will you do for me?

LAURA: What can I do? Swear before God and all that I hold sacred that you are Bertha's father?

CAPTAIN: What good would that do? You have already said that a mother can and ought to commit any crime for her child. I implore you by the memory of the past, I implore you as ᴀ wounded man begs to be put out of his misery, tell me the truth. Can't you see I'm helpless as a child? Can't you hear me crying to my mother that I'm hurt? Forget I'm a man, a soldier whose word men—and even beasts—obey. I am nothing but a sick creature in need of pity. I renounce every vestige of power and only beg for mercy on my life.

LAURA: (*laying her hand on his forehead.*) What? You, a man, in tears?

CAPTAIN: Yes, a man in tears. Has not a man eyes? Has not a man hands, limbs, senses, opinions, passions? Is he not nourished by the same food as a woman, wounded by the same weapons, warmed and chilled by the same winter and sum-

mer? If you prick us, do we not bleed?
If you tickle us, do we not laugh? If you
poison us, do we not die? Why should
a man suffer in silence or a soldier hide
his tears? Because it's not manly? Why
isn't it manly?

LAURA: Weep, then, my child, and you
shall have your mother again. Remember,
it was as your second mother that I came
into your life. You were big and strong,
yet not fully a man. You were a giant
child who had come into the world too
soon, or perhaps an unwanted child.

CAPTAIN: That's true. My father and
mother had me against their will, and
therefore I was born without a will. That
is why, when you and I became one, I felt
I was completing myself—and that is why
you dominated. I—in the army the one to
command—became at home the one to
obey. I grew up at your side, looked up
to you as a superior being and listened
to you as if I were your foolish little boy.

LAURA: Yes, that's how it was, and I
loved you as if you were my little boy.
But didn't you see how, when your feelings changed and you came to me as a
lover, I was ashamed? The joy I felt in
your embraces was followed by such a
sense of guilt my very blood seemed
tainted. The mother became the mistress
—horrible!

CAPTAIN: I saw, but I didn't understand. I thought you despised my lack of
virility, so I tried to win you as a woman
by proving myself as a man.

LAURA: That was your mistake. The
mother was your friend, you see, but the
woman was your enemy. Sexual love is
conflict. And don't imagine I gave myself.
I didn't give. I only took what I meant
to take. Yet you did dominate me . . .
I felt it and wanted you to feel it.

CAPTAIN: You always dominated me.
You could hypnotise me when I was wide
awake, so that I neither saw nor heard,

but simply obeyed. You could give me a
raw potato and make me think it was a
peach; you could make me take your
ridiculous ideas for flashes of genius. You
could corrupt me—yes, make me do the
shabbiest things. You never had any real
intelligence, yet, instead of being guided
by me, you would take the reins into your
own hands. And when at last I woke to
the realisation that I had lost my integrity,
I wanted to blot out my humiliation by
some heroic action—some feat, some discovery—even by committing *hara-kiri*. I
wanted to go to war, but I couldn't. It was
then that I gave all my energies to science.
And now—now when I should be stretching out my hand to gather the fruit, you
chop off my arm. I'm robbed of my
laurels; I'm finished. A man cannot live
without repute.

LAURA: Can a woman?

CAPTAIN: Yes—she has her children,
but he has not . . . Yet you and I and
everyone else went on living, unconscious
as children, full of fancies and ideals and
illusions, until we woke up. Right—but
we woke topsy-turvy, and what's more,
we'd been woken by someone who was
talking in his own sleep. When women
are old and stop being women, they grow
beards on their chins. What do men grow,
I wonder, when they are old and stop
being men? In this false dawn, the birds
that crowed weren't cocks, they were
capons, and the hens that answered their
call were sexless, too. So when the sun
should have risen for us, we found ourselves back among the ruins in the full
moonlight, just as in the good old times.
Our light morning sleep had only been
troubled by fantastic dreams—there had
been no awakening.

LAURA: You should have been a writer,
you know.

CAPTAIN: Perhaps.

LAURA: But I'm sleepy now, so if you

have any more fantasies, keep them till to-morrow.

CAPTAIN: Just one thing more—a fact. Do you hate me?

LAURA: Sometimes—as a man.

CAPTAIN: It's like race-hatred. If it's true we are descended from the ape, it must have been from two different species. There's no likeness between us, is there?

LAURA: What are you getting at?

CAPTAIN: In this fight, one of us must go under.

LAURA: Which?

CAPTAIN: The weaker naturally.

LAURA: Then is the stronger in the right?

CAPTAIN: Bound to be as he has the power.

LAURA: Then I am in the right.

CAPTAIN: Why, what power have you?

LAURA: All I need. And it will be legal power to-morrow when I've put you under restraint.

CAPTAIN: Under restraint?

LAURA: Yes. Then I shall decide my child's future myself out of reach of your fantasies.

CAPTAIN: Who will pay for her if I'm not there?

LAURA: Your pension.

CAPTAIN: (*moving towards her menacingly.*) How can you have me put under restraint?

LAURA: (*producing a letter.*) By means of this letter, an attested copy of which is already in the hands of the authorities.

CAPTAIN: What letter?

LAURA: (*retreating.*) Your own. The one in which you told the doctor you were mad. (*He stares at her in silence.*) Now you have fulfilled the unfortunately necessary functions of father and bread-winner. You are no longer needed, and

you must go. You must go, now that you realise my wits are as strong as my will—you won't want to stay and acknowledge my superiority.

(*The* CAPTAIN *goes to the table, picks up the lighted lamp and throws it at* LAURA, *who escapes backward through the door.*)

ACT THREE

(*The same. The following evening. A new lamp, lighted, is on the table. The wall-papered door is barricaded with a chair. From the room above comes the sound of pacing footsteps. The* NURSE *stands listening, troubled. Enter* LAURA *from within.*)

LAURA: Did he give you the keys?

NURSE: Give? No, God help us, I took them from the coat Nöjd had out to brush.

LAURA: Then it's Nöjd who's on duty?

NURSE: Aye, it's Nöjd.

LAURA: Give me the keys.

NURSE: Here you are, but it's no better than stealing. Hark at him up there! To and fro, to and fro.

LAURA: Are you sure the door's safely bolted?

NURSE: It's bolted safe enough (*Weeps.*)

LAURA: (*opening the bureau and sitting down at it.*) Pull yourself together, Margaret. The only way we can protect ourselves is by keeping calm. (*A knock at the hall door.*) See who that is.

NURSE: (*opening door.*) It's Nöjd.

LAURA: Tell him to come in.

NÖJD: (*entering.*) Despatch from the Colonel.

LAURA: Give it to me. (*Reads.*) I see ∴ Nöjd, have you removed the cartridges from all the guns and pouches?

NÖJD: Yes, Ma'am, just as you said.

LAURA: Wait outside while I write to the Colonel.

(*Exit* NÖJD. LAURA *writes. Sound of sawing above.*)

NURSE: Listen, Madam. Whatever is he doing now?

LAURA: Do be quiet. I'm writing.

NURSE (*muttering.*) Lord have mercy on us! What will be the end of all this?

LAURA: (*holding out the note.*) Here you are. Give it to Nöjd. And, remember, my mother's to know nothing of all this.

(*Exit* NURSE *with note.* LAURA *opens the bureau drawers and takes out papers. Enter* PASTOR.)

PASTOR: My dear Laura! As you probably gathered, I have been out all day and only just got back. I hear you've been having a terrible time.

LAURA: Yes, brother, I've never been through such a night and day in all my life!

PASTOR: Well, I see you're looking none the worse for it.

LAURA: No, thank heaven, I wasn't hurt. But just think what might have happened!

PASTOR: Tell me all about it. I've only heard rumours. How did it begin?

LAURA: It began by him raving about not being Bertha's father, and ended by him throwing the lighted lamp in my face.

PASTOR: But this is appalling. He must be quite out of his mind. What in heaven's name are we to do?

LAURA: We must try to prevent further violence. The doctor has sent to the hospital for a strait-jacket. I have just written a note to the Colonel, and now I'm trying to get some idea of the state of our affairs, which Adolf has so shockingly mismanaged. (*Opens another drawer.*)

PASTOR: It's a miserable business altogether, but I always feared something of the kind might happen. When fire and water meet, there's bound to be an explosion. (*Looks in drawer.*) Whatever's all this?

LAURA: Look! This is where he's kept everything hidden.

PASTOR: Good heavens! Here's your old doll. And there's your christening cap . . . and Bertha's rattle . . . and your letters . . . and that locket . . . (*Wipes his eyes.*) He must have loved you very dearly, Laura. I never kept this kind of thing.

LAURA: I believe he did love me once, but time changes everything.

PASTOR: What's this imposing document? (*Examines it.*) The purchase of a grave! Well, better a grave than the asylum! Laura, be frank with me. Aren't you at all to blame?

LAURA: How can I be to blame because someone goes out of his mind?

PASTOR: We—ell! I will say no more. After all, blood's thicker than water.

LAURA: Meaning what, if I may ask?

PASTOR: (*gazing at her.*) O come now!

LAURA: What?

PASTOR: Come, come! You can scarcely deny that it would suit you down to the ground to have complete control of your daughter.

LAURA: I don't understand.

PASTOR: I can't help admiring you.

LAURA: Really?

PASTOR: And as for me—I shall be appointed guardian to that Freethinker whom, as you know, I always regarded as a tare among our wheat.

(LAURA *gives a quick laugh which she suppresses.*)

LAURA: You dare say that to me, his wife?

PASTOR: How strong-willed you are, Laura, how amazingly strong-willed! Like a fox in a trap that would gnaw off its own leg rather than be caught. Like a master-thief working alone, without even a conscience for accomplice. Look in the mirror! You daren't.

LAURA: I never use a mirror.

PASTOR: No. You daren't look at yourself. Let me see your hand. Not one telltale spot of blood, not a trace of that subtle poison. A little innocent murder that the law cannot touch. An unconscious crime. Unconscious? A stroke of genius that. Listen to him up there! Take care, Laura! If that man gets loose, he will saw you in pieces too.

LAURA: You must have a bad conscience to talk like that. Pin the guilt on me if you can.

PASTOR: I can't.

LAURA: You see? You can't and so—I am innocent. And now, you look after your charge and I'll take care of mine.

(*Enter* DOCTOR.)

Ah, here is the Doctor! (*Rises.*) I'm so glad to see you, Doctor. I know I can count on you to help me, although I'm afraid not much can be done now. You hear him up there. Are you convinced at last?

DOCTOR: I am convinced there has been an act of violence. But the question is— should that act of violence be regarded as an outbreak of temper or insanity?

PASTOR: But apart from this actual outbreak, you must admit that he suffers from fixed ideas.

DOCTOR: I have a notion, Pastor, that *your* ideas are even more fixed.

PASTOR: My firmly rooted convictions of spiritual . . .

DOCTOR: Convictions apart, it rests with you, Madam, to decide if your husband

is to be fined or imprisoned or sent to the asylum. How do you regard his conduct?

LAURA: I can't answer that now.

DOCTOR: Oh? Have you no—er—firmly rooted convictions of what would be best for the family? And you, Pastor?

PASTOR: There's bound to be a scandal either way. It's not easy to give an opinion.

LAURA: But if he were only fined for violence he could be violent again.

DOCTOR: And if he were sent to prison he would soon be out again. So it seems best for all parties that he should be treated as insane. Where is the nurse?

LAURA: Why?

DOCTOR: She must put the strait-jacket on the patient. Not at once, but after I have had a talk with him—and not then until I give the order. I have the—er— garment outside. (*Goes out to hall and returns with a large parcel.*) Kindly call the nurse.

(LAURA *rings. The* DOCTOR *begins to unpack the strait-jacket.*)

PASTOR: Dreadful! Dreadful!

(*Enter* NURSE.)

DOCTOR: Ah, Nurse! Now please pay attention. You see this jacket. When I give you the word I want you to slip it on the Captain from behind. So as to prevent any further violence, you understand. Now it has, you see, unusually long sleeves. That is to restrict his movements. These sleeves must be tied together behind his back. And now here are two straps with buckles, which afterwards you must fasten to the arm of a chair—or to whatever's easiest. Can you do this, do you think?

NURSE: No. Doctor, I can't. No, not that.

LAURA: Why not do it yourself, Doctor?

DOCTOR: Because the patient distrusts me. You, Madam, are the proper person, but I'm afraid he doesn't trust you either. (LAURA *grimaces.*) Perhaps you, Pastor . . .

PASTOR: I must beg to decline.

(*Enter* NÖJD.)

LAURA: Did you deliver my note?

NÖJD: Yes, Madam.

DOCTOR: Oh, it's you, Nöjd! You know the state of things here, don't you? You know the Captain has had a mental breakdown. You must help us look after the patient.

NÖJD: If there's aught I can do for Captain, he knows I'll do it.

DOCTOR: You are to put this jacket on him.

NURSE: He's not to touch him. Nöjd shan't hurt him. I'd rather do it myself, gently, gently. But Nöjd can wait outside and help me if need be—yes, that's what he'd best do.

(*A pounding on the paper-covered door.*)

DOCTOR: Here he is! (*To* NURSE.) Put the jacket on that chair under your shawl. And now go away, all of you, while the Pastor and I talk to him. That door won't hold long. Hurry!

NURSE: (*going out.*) Lord Jesus, help us!

(LAURA *shuts the bureau and follows the* NURSE. NÖJD *goes out to the hall. The paper-covered door bursts open, the lock broken and the chair hurled to the floor. The* CAPTAIN *comes out, carrying a pile of books.*)

CAPTAIN: (*putting the books on the table.*) Here it all is. You can read it in every one of these volumes. So I wasn't mad after all. (*Picks one up.*) Here it is in the Odyssey, Book I, page 6, line 215 in the Uppsala translation. Telemachus speaking to Athene: "My mother says I am Odysseus' son; but for myself I cannot tell. It's a wise child that knows its own father."* And that's the suspicion

* English translation E. V. Rieu. Penguin Classics.

Telemachus has about Penelope, the most virtuous of women. Fine state of affairs, eh? (*Takes up another book.*) And here we have the Prophet Ezekiel: "The fool saith, Lo, here is my father; but who can tell whose loins have engendered him?" That's clear enough. (*Picks up another.*) And what's this? A history of Russian literature by Merzlyakov. Alexander Pushkin, Russia's greatest poet, was mortally wounded—but more by the rumours of his wife's unfaithfulness than by the bullet he received in his breast at the duel. On his deathbed he swore she was innocent. Jackass! How could he swear any such thing? I *do* read my books, you see! Hullo, Jonas, are you here? And the Doctor, of course. Did I ever tell you what I said to the English lady who was deploring the habit Irishmen have of throwing lighted lamps in their wives' faces? "God, what women!" I said. "Women?" she stammered. "Of course," I replied. "When things get to such a pass that a man who has loved, has worshipped a woman, picks up a lighted lamp and flings it in her face, then you may be sure . . ."

PASTOR: Sure of what?

CAPTAIN: Nothing. You can never be sure of anything—you can only believe. That's right, isn't it, Jonas? One believes and so one is saved. Saved, indeed! No. One can be damned through believing. That's what I've learnt.

DOCTOR: But, Captain . . .

CAPTAIN: Hold your tongue! I don't want any chat from you. I don't want to hear you relaying all the gossip from in there like a telephone. In there—you know what I mean. Listen to me, Jonas. Do you imagine you're the father of your children? I seem to remember you had a tutor in the house, a pretty boy about whom there was quite a bit of gossip.

PASTOR: Take care, Adolf!

CAPTAIN: Feel under your wig and see if you don't find two little nobs. Upon my soul, he's turning pale! Well, well! It was only talk, of course, but my God, how they talked! But we married men are all figures of fun, every man Jack of us. Isn't that right, Doctor? What about your own marriage bed? Didn't you have a certain lieutenant in your house, eh? Wait now, let me guess. He was called . . . (*Whispers in the* DOCTOR's *ear.*) By Jove, he's turned pale too! But don't worry. She's dead and buried, so what was done can't be done again. As a matter of fact, I knew him, and he's now—look at me, Doctor—no, straight in the eyes! He is now a major of Dragoons. Good Lord, I believe *he* has horns too!

DOCTOR: (*angrily.*) Be so good as to change the subject, Captain.

CAPTAIN: See! As soon as I mention horns he wants to change the subject.

PASTOR: I suppose you know, brother-in-law, that you're not in your right mind?

CAPTAIN: Yes, I do know. But if I had the handling of your decorated heads, I should soon have you shut up too. I am mad. But how did I become mad? Doesn't that interest you? No, it doesn't interest anyone. (*Takes the photograph album from the table.*) Christ Jesus, there is my daughter! Mine? That's what we can never know. Shall I tell you what we should have to do so as to know? First marry, in order to be accepted by society, then immediately divorce; after that become lovers and finally adopt the children. That way one could at least be sure they were one's own adopted children. Eh? But what good's that to me? What good's anything now you have robbed me of my immortality? What can science or philosophy do for me when I have nothing left to live for? How can I live without honour? I grafted my right arm and half my brain and spinal cord on to another stem. I believed they would unite and grow into a single, more perfect tree. Then someone brought a knife and cut below the graft, so now I'm only half a tree. The other part, with my arm and half my brain, goes on growing. But I wither—I am dying, for it was the best part of myself I gave away. Let me die. Do what you like with me. I'm finished.

(*The* DOCTOR *and* PASTOR *whisper, then go out. The* CAPTAIN *sinks into a chair by the table.* BERTHA *enters.*)

BERTHA: (*going to him.*) Are you ill, Father?

CAPTAIN: (*looking up stupidly at word "Father."*) Me?

BERTHA: Do you know what you did? You threw a lamp at Mother.

CAPTAIN: Did I?

BERTHA: Yes. Supposing she'd been hurt!

CAPTAIN: Would that have mattered?

BERTHA: You're not my father if you talk like that.

CAPTAIN: What d'you say? Not your father? How d'you know? Who told you? Who is your father, then? Who?

BERTHA: Not you, anyway.

CAPTAIN: Anyone but me! Who then? Who? You seem well informed. Who told you? That I should live to hear my own child tell me to my face I am not her father! Do you realise you're insulting your mother by saying this? Don't you understand that, if it's true, *she* is disgraced?

BERTHA: You're not to say anything against Mother, I tell you!

CAPTAIN: Yes, all in league against me, just as you've always been.

BERTHA: Father!

CAPTAIN: Don't call me that again!

BERTHA: Father, Father!

CAPTAIN: (*drawing her to him.*) Bertha, my beloved child, yes, you *are* my child. Yes, yes, it must be so—it *is* so. All that was only a sick fancy—it came on the wind like an infection or a fever. Look at me!

Let me see my soul in your eyes . . . But I see *her* soul as well. You have two souls. You love me with one and hate me with the other. You must love me and only me. You must have only one soul or you'll have no peace—neither shall I. You must have only one mind, fruit of my mind. You must have only one will—mine!

BERTHA: No, no! I want to be myself.

CAPTAIN: Never! I am a cannibal, you see, and I'm going to eat you. Your mother wanted to eat me, but she didn't succeed. I am Saturn who devoured his children because it was foretold that otherwise they would devour him. To eat or to be eaten —that is the question. If I don't eat you, you will eat me—you've shown your teeth already. (*Goes to the rack.*) Don't be afraid, my darling child. I shan't hurt you. (*Takes down a revolver.*)

BERTHA: (*dodging away from him.*) Help! Mother, help! He wants to kill me!

NURSE: (*hurrying in.*) What in heaven's name are you doing, Mr. Adolf?

CAPTAIN: (*examining the revolver.*) Did you remove the cartridges?

NURSE: Well, I did just tidy them away, but sit down here and take it easy and I'll soon fetch them back.

(*She takes the* CAPTAIN *by the arm and leads him to a chair. He slumps down. She picks up the strait-jacket and goes behind the chair.* BERTHA *creeps out.*)

Mr. Adolf, do you remember when you were my dear little boy, and I used to tuck you up at night and say your prayers with you? And do you remember how I used to get up in the night to get you a drink when you were thirsty? And how, when you had bad dreams and couldn't go to sleep again, I'd light the candle and tell you pretty stories. Do you remember?

CAPTAIN: Go on talking, Margaret. It soothes my mind. Go on talking.

NURSE: Aye, that I will, but you listen carefully. D'you remember how once you took a great big kitchen knife to carve a boat with, and I came in and had to trick the knife away from you? You were such a silly little lad, one had to trick you, you never would believe what anyone did was for your own good . . . "Give me that snake," I said, "or else he'll bite you." And then, see, you let go of the knife. (*Takes the revolver from his hand.*) And then, too, when it was time for you to dress yourself, and you wouldn't. I had to coax you, and say you should have a golden coat and be dressed just like a prince. Then I took your little tunic, that was just made of green wool, and held it up in front of you and said: "In with your arms, now, both together." (*Gets the jacket on.*) And then I said: "Sit nice and still now, while I button it up behind." (*Ties the sleeves behind him.*) And then I said: "Up with you, and walk across the floor like a good boy, so Nurse can see how it fits." (*Leads him to the sofa.*) And then I said: "Now you must go to bed."

CAPTAIN: What's that? Go to bed, when I'd just been dressed? My God! What have you done to me? (*Tries to get free.*) Oh you fiendish woman, what devilish cunning! Who would have thought you had the brains for it? (*Lies down on the sofa.*) Bound, fleeced, outwitted and unable to die!

NURSE: Forgive me, Mr. Adolf, forgive me! I had to stop you killing the child.

CAPTAIN: Why didn't you let me kill her? If life's hell and death's heaven, and children belong to heaven?

NURSE: What do you know of the hereafter?

CAPTAIN: It's the only thing one does know. Of life one knows nothing. Oh, if one had known from the beginning!

NURSE: Humble your stubborn heart, Mr. Adolf, and cry to God for mercy! Even now it's not too late. It wasn't too late for the thief on the Cross, for Our Saviour said: "To-day shalt thou be with me in paradise."

CAPTAIN: Croaking for a corpse already, old crow? (*She takes her hymn-book from her pocket. He calls.*) Nöjd! Are you there, Nöjd?

(*Enter* NÖJD.)

Throw this women out of the house or she'll choke me to death with her hymn-book. Throw her out of the window, stuff her up the chimney, do what you like only get rid of her!

NÖJD: (*staring at the* NURSE.) God save you Captain—and that's from the bottom of my heart—but I can't do that, I just can't. If it were six men now, but a woman!

CAPTAIN: What? You can't manage one woman?

NÖJD: I could manage her all right, but there's something stops a man laying hands on a woman.

CAPTAIN: What is this something? Haven't they laid hands on me?

NÖJD: Yes, but I just can't do it, Sir. Same as if you was to tell me to hit Pastor. It's like religion, it's in your bones. I can't do it.

(*Enter* LAURA. *She signs to* NÖJD, *who goes out.*)

CAPTAIN: Omphale! Omphale! Playing with the club while Hercules spins your wool.

LAURA: (*approaching the sofa.*) Adolf, look at me! Do you believe I'm your enemy?

CAPTAIN: Yes, I do. I believe all you women are my enemies. My mother did not want me to come into the world because my birth would give her pain. She was my enemy. She robbed my embryo of nourishment, so I was born incomplete. My sister was my enemy when she made

me knuckle under to her. The first woman I took in my arms was my enemy. She gave me ten years of sickness in return for the love I gave her. When my daughter had to choose between you and me, she became my enemy. And you, you, my wife, have been my mortal enemy, for you have not let go your hold until there is no life left in me.

LAURA: But I didn't mean this to happen. I never really thought it out. I may have had some vague desire to get rid of you—you were in my way—and perhaps, if you see some plan in my actions, there was one, but I was unconscious of it. I have never given a thought to my actions —they simply ran along the rails you laid down. My conscience is clear, and before God I feel innocent, even if I'm not. You weighed me down like a stone, pressing and pressing till my heart tried to shake off its intolerable burden. That's how it's been, and if without meaning to I have brought you to this, I ask your forgiveness.

CAPTAIN: Very plausible, but how does that help me? And whose fault is it? Perhaps our cerebral marriage is to blame. In the old days one married a wife. Now one goes into partnership with a business woman or sets up house with a friend. Then one rapes the partner or violates the friend. What becomes of love, the healthy love of the senses? It dies of neglect. And what happens to the dividends from those love shares, payable to holder, when there's no joint account? Who is the holder when the crash comes? Who is the bodily father of the cerebral child?

LAURA: Your suspicions about our daughter are entirely unfounded.

CAPTAIN: That's the horror of it. If they had some foundation, there would at least be something to catch hold of, to cling to. Now there are only shadows, lurking in the undergrowth, peering out with grinning faces. It's like fighting with air, a mock battle with blank cartridges. Reality, however deadly, puts one on one's mettle, nerves body and soul for action, but as it is . . . my thoughts dissolve in fog, my brain grinds a void till it catches fire . . . Put a pillow under my head. Lay something over me. I'm cold. I'm terribly cold.

(LAURA *takes off her shawl and spreads it over him. Exit* NURSE.)

LAURA: Give me your hand, my dear.

CAPTAIN: My hand! Which you have bound behind my back. Omphale, Omphale! But I can feel your shawl soft against my mouth. It's warm and gentle like your arms and smells of vanilla like your hair when you were young. When you were young, Laura, and we used to walk in the birch woods. There were primroses and thrushes—lovely, lovely! Think how beautiful life was then—and what it has become! You did not want it to become like this, neither did I. Yet it has. Who then rules our lives?

LAURA: God.

CAPTAIN: The God of strife then—or nowadays the Goddess!

(*Enter* NURSE *with a pillow.*)

Take away this cat that's lying on me. Take it away! (NURSE *removes the shawl and puts the pillow under his head.*) Bring my uniform. Put my tunic over me. (*The* NURSE *takes the tunic from a peg and spreads it over him. To* LAURA.) Ah, my tough lion's-skin that you would take from me! Omphale! Omphale! You cunning woman, lover of peace and contriver of disarmament. Wake, Hercules, before they take away your club! You would trick us out of our armour, calling it tinsel. It was iron, I tell you, before it became tinsel. In the old days the smith forged the soldier's coat, now it is made by the needlewoman. Omphale! Omphale! Rude strength has fallen before treacherous weakness. Shame on you, woman of Satan, and a curse on all your sex! (*He raises himself to spit at her, but sinks back again.*) What sort of a pillow have you given me, Margaret? How hard and cold it is! So cold! Come and sit beside me on this chair. (*She does so.*) Yes, like that. Let me put my head on your lap. Ah, that's warmer! Lean over me so I can feel your breast. Oh how sweet it is to sleep upon a woman's breast, be she mother or mistress! But sweetest of all a mother's.

LAURA: Adolf, tell me, do you want to see your child?

CAPTAIN: My child? A man has no children. Only women have children. So the future is theirs, while we die childless. O God, who holds all children dear!

NURSE: Listen! He's praying to God.

CAPTAIN: No, to you, to put me to sleep. I'm tired, so tired. Goodnight, Margaret. "Blessed art thou among women."

(*He raises himself, then with a cry falls back on the* NURSE's *knees.*)

LAURA: (*at the door, calling.*) Doctor!

(*Enter* DOCTOR *and* PASTOR.)

Help him, Doctor—if it's not too late! Look, he has stopped breathing!

DOCTOR: (*feeling his pulse.*) It is a stroke.

PASTOR: Is he dead?

DOCTOR: No, he might still wake—but to what, who can say?

PASTOR: ". . . once to die, but after this the judgment."*

DOCTOR: No judgment—and no recriminations. You who believe that a God rules over human destiny must lay this to his charge.

NURSE: Ah Pastor, with his last breath he prayed to God!

PASTOR: (*To* LAURA.) Is this true?

* HEBREWS: ix, 27.

LAURA: It is true.

DOCTOR: If this be so, of which I am as poor a judge as of the cause of his illness, in any case my skill is at an end. Try yours now, Pastor.

LAURA: Is that all you have to say at this deathbed, Doctor?

DOCTOR: That is all. I know no more. Let him who knows more, speak.

(BERTHA *comes in and runs to* LAURA.)

BERTHA: Mother! Mother!

LAURA: My child! My own child!

PASTOR: Amen.

The Three Sisters

ANTON CHEKHOV

COMMENTARY

 Anton Chekhov (1860-1904) was born in Taganrog, South Russia, the son of a merchant who had been a serf. After a good early education, he enrolled in the University of Moscow, from which he graduated with a medical degree in 1884. He wrote his first full-length drama *Ivanov* in 1887. *The Sea Gull* (1895), *Uncle Vanya* (1899), *Three Sisters* (1900) and *The Cherry Orchard* (1903) are his other full-length plays. Chekhov also achieved fame as a writer of short stories, some of which he adapted as one-act plays. During his last years he was associated with the Moscow Art Theatre, working closely with the great director, Stanislavsky.

Mary McCarthy reports that Mme. Litvinoff, the English-born wife of a Soviet Russian ambassador to England, "remarked to newspaper reporters that *The Three Sisters* is an absurd play about three grown-up women who spend four acts not going to Moscow when they have the price of the ticket." ("The Russian Soul in Wartime," in *Sights and Spectacles* [New York, 1957].) No doubt the play is a study in futility; John Gassner has described Chekhov's work as "the tragedy of attrition."

The Three Sisters, however, ends on a note of hope in the salvation to be found in work. The progress of the classical tragic hero is toward a heightened self-awareness, a discovery of identity, a casting away of insulating illusions. At the end of the play, the three sisters know themselves and those around them much more honestly, much less romantically, as they give themselves over to their bland new lives, unseasoned now by fantasies.

The Three Sisters does not have a *single* tragic figure, although an argument might be sustained that any one of the sisters suffers more and learns more than the others. It is more a familial, a group tragedy, and the final tone is bitter and ironic, a tone perhaps more appropriate to modern tragicomedy than to that of Sophoclean tragedy. The play poses

sharply the issue of personal self-definition. The defeat of the sisters'
dream, the withering away of their historical gentility, their acceptance
of the inevitability of daily coping, the reversal of the aristocratic and
the vulgar roles, all add up to more than merely a sad or sardonic record.
Tragedy in the modern world may perhaps be found only in a form
of bleak comedy.

David Magarshack's discussion of the play, in his *Chekhov, The
Dramatist* (London, 1960), is valuable. The accounts of Chekhov's
differences of interpretation with Stanislavsky are relevant to the issue
of whether the text alone carries the full meaning of a play, or whether
a production shaped by a director and filtered through actors is better
able to carry that meaning. Robert Brustein's chapters on Chekhov in
The Theatre of Revolt (Boston, 1964) offers a close, original reading.
Bernard Shaw's *Heartbreak House* is a Shavian commentary, in the
form of a play, on Chekhov. Morris Freedman's essay, "Chekhov's
Morality of Work," in *The Moral Impulse* (Carbondale, 1967), provides
a larger perspective for this particular play.

Anton Chekhov

THE THREE SISTERS

Translated by Stark Young

CHARACTERS

PROZOROFF, ANDREI SERGEEVICH.
NATALIA IVANOVNA, *his fiancée, later his wife.*
OLGA ⎫
MASHA ⎬ *his sisters*
IRINA ⎭
KULYGIN, FYODOR ILYICH, *a high-school teacher,*
husband of Masha.
VERSHININ, ALEXANDER IGNATIEVICH, *Lieutenant*
Colonel, a battery Commander.
TUSENBACH, NIKOLAI LVOVICH, *Baron, Lieutenant.*
SOLYONY, VASILI VASILIEVICH, *Staff Captain.*
TCHEBUTYKIN, IVAN ROMANOVICH, *an Army Doctor.*
FEDOTIK, ALEXEI PETROVICH, *Second Lieutenant.*
RODAY, VLADIMIR KARLOVICH, *Second Lieutenant.*
FERAPONT, *porter of the District Board, an old man.*
ANFISA, *the nurse, an old woman of eighty.*

The action takes place in a provincial town in Russia.

ACT ONE

(*In the* PROZOROFFS' *house. A drawing room with columns beyond which a large room is seen. Midday: outside it is sunny and bright. The table in the dining room is being set for lunch.* OLGA, *in the blue uniform of a girls' high-school teacher, is busy correcting school papers, standing and walking to and fro;* MASHA, *in a black dress with her hat on her knees, sits and reads a book;* IRINA, *in a white dress, stands lost in thought.*)

OLGA: Father died just a year ago today, on the fifth of May—your saint's day, Irina. It was very cold then and snowing. I thought I could never live through it; you were lying in a dead faint. But now a year has passed and we can talk of it freely; you've a white dress on, your face is beaming. (*The clock strikes twelve*) And the clock was striking then too. (*A pause*) I remember as they carried Father along, the band was playing, and at the cemetery they fired a volley. He was a brigadier general; but at that there were very few people walking behind his coffin. It was raining, though, then. Heavy rain and snow.

IRINA: Why think of it?

(*Behind the columns in the dining room near the table,* BARON TUSENBACH, TCHEBUTYKIN *and* SOLYONY *appear.*)

OLGA: It's warm today. We can keep the windows wide open, but the birches haven't any leaves yet. Father was given his brigade and left Moscow with us eleven years ago, and I remember distinctly that early in May, at this very time, in Moscow everything is in bloom, it's warm, everything is bathed in sunshine. That's eleven years ago, but I remember it all as if we'd left there yesterday. Oh, God! I woke up this morning, saw a flood of light, saw the spring, and my heart leapt with joy. And I did long passionately to go home again.

TCHEBUTYKIN: The devil!

TUSENBACH: Of course, it's all rot.

(MASHA, *brooding over a book, softly whistles a song.*)

OLGA: Don't whistle, Masha. How can you do that! (*A pause*) I'm at the high school every day giving lessons till evening, that's why my head aches all the time and what thoughts I have might just as well belong to an old woman and be done with it. These four years I've been teaching in high school, I have felt my strength and youth going out of me day by day, drop by drop. And just one dream grows stronger and stronger. . . .

IRINA: To go to Moscow. Sell the house, wind up everything here and to Moscow.

OLGA: Yes! Soon to Moscow.

(TCHEBUTYKIN *and* TUSENBACH *laugh.*)

IRINA: Brother will be a professor very likely, but all the same he won't live here. The one thing that stops us is poor Masha.

OLGA: Masha will be coming to Moscow for the whole summer every year.

(MASHA *is softly whistling a song.*)

IRINA: God grant it all works out! (*Looking out of the window*) The weather is beautiful today. I don't know why my heart's so light! This morning I remembered it was my saint's day and suddenly felt happy, and remembered when I was a child and Mother was still alive. And such wonderful thoughts thrilled me; such thoughts!

OLGA: You look radiant today, lovelier than ever. And Masha is lovely too. Andrei would be good-looking if he hadn't got so heavy, it's not becoming to him. And I've grown older, a lot thinner; it must be because I get cross with the girls. Now that I'm free today and am here at home and my head's not aching, I feel younger than yesterday. I'm only twenty-eight. . . . It's all good, all God's will, but it seems to me if I had married and stayed at home the whole day long, it would have been better. (*A pause*) I'd have loved my husband.

TUSENBACH: (*To* SOLYONY) You talk such nonsense that I'm tired of listening to you. (*Entering the drawing room*) Forgot to tell you. Today you'll receive a call from our new Battery Commander Vershinin. (*Sitting down at the piano.*)

OLGA: Well, I'll be very glad of it.

IRINA: Is he old?

TUSENBACH: No, not very. Forty or forty-five at most. (*Playing softly*) He seems a nice chap. Not stupid, that's certain. Except that he talks a lot.

IRINA: Is he an interesting person?

TUSENBACH: Yes, quite, only there is a wife, a mother-in-law and two girls. What's more he's married for the second time. He pays calls and says everywhere that he has a wife and two girls. And he'll say so here. The wife is sort of half-crazy, wears long girlish braids, speaks only of lofty matters, philosophizes, and often tries to commit suicide, obviously to plague the husband. I'd have left such a woman long ago myself, but he puts up with her and merely complains.

SOLYONY: (*Entering the drawing room from the dining room with* TCHEBUTYKIN) With one hand I can lift only fifty pounds, but with both, one hundred eighty, or even two hundred pounds. From this I conclude that two men are not twice as strong as one, but three times, even more. . . .

TCHEBUTYKIN: (*Reading a newspaper as he comes in*) For falling hair . . . two ounces of naphthalene to half a bottle of spirits. . . . Dissolve and use daily. . . . (*Writing it down in his notebook*) Let's write it down! (*To* SOLYONY) And so, I tell you, a little cork is put in a bottle and through the cork there's a glass tube. . . . Then you take a pinch of plain ordinary alum . . .

IRINA: Ivan Romanovich, dear Ivan Romanovich!

TCHEBUTYKIN: What is it, my child, my sweet?

IRINA: Tell me, why am I so happy today? It's just as if I were going full sail, with the wide blue sky above me and great white birds floating there. Why is that? Why?

TCHEBUTYKIN: (*Kissing both her hands tenderly*) My white bird . . .

IRINA: This morning when I awoke and got up and bathed, it seemed all at once that everything in this world was clear to me and I knew how one must live. Dear Ivan Romanovich, I know everything. A man must do something, he must toil by the sweat of his brow, no matter who he is; and all the meaning and aim of his life, his happiness, his ecstasies must lie in this only. How good it is to be a workman who gets up at dawn and breaks stones in the street, or a shepherd, or a schoolmaster who teaches children, or an engineer on a railroad. My God! Next to being a man, it's better to be an ox, it's better to be a common horse, if only you do some work, than be a young woman who wakes up at twelve o'clock, has coffee in bed, and then dresses for two hours. . . . Oh, but that's dreadful! Just as on hot days one may have a craving for water, I have a craving for work. And if I don't get up early and go to work, give me up as a friend, Ivan Romanovich.

TCHEBUTYKIN: (*Tenderly*) I'll give you up, I'll give you up—

OLGA: Father trained us to get up at seven. Now Irina wakes at seven and lies there till at least nine thinking. And looking so serious! (*Laughing.*)

IRINA: You are used to thinking of me as a little girl, so it seems strange to you when I look serious. I'm twenty years old.

TUSENBACH: Longing for work. Oh my God, how I understand that! I have never worked in my life. I was born in Petersburg, cold, idle Petersburg, in a family that never knew any sort of work or worry. I remember when I came home from military school the footman pulled off my boots while I fidgeted and my mother looked adoringly at me, and was surprised when the others didn't look at me the same way. I was shielded from work. Though I doubt if they succeeded in shielding me, I doubt it! The time has come, something tremendous is hovering over us all, a vast, healing storm is gathering; it's coming, it's near already, and will soon clear our society of the laziness, the indifference, the prejudice against work, the rotten boredom. I'll work and in another twenty-five or thirty years, every man will be working. Every one!

TCHEBUTYKIN: I shan't work.

TUSENBACH: You don't count.

SOLYONY: Twenty-five years from now you won't even be on earth, thank God! In two or three years you'll die of distemper, or I'll forget myself and put a bullet in your forehead, my angel. (*Taking a phial of perfume from his pocket and sprinkling his chest and hands.*)

TCHEBUTYKIN: (*Laughing*) And I really never did anything. Since I left the University, I haven't lifted a finger, I've not read a single book even, but just read the newspapers. . . . (*Taking another newspaper out of his pocket*) Listen—I know from the newspapers that there was, let's say, a Dobrolyubov, but what he wrote about I don't know. God only knows. (*A knock is heard on the floor from the floor below*) Listen. . . . They are calling me from downstairs, somebody has come to see me. I'll be back right away. . . . Wait. . . . (*He leaves hurriedly, combing out his beard as he goes.*)

IRINA: He's up to something.

TUSENBACH: Yes. He left with a triumphant face, obviously he will now bring you a present.

IRINA: That's too bad.

OLGA: Yes, it's awful. He always does something childish.

MASHA: By the curved seashore a green oak, a golden chain upon that oak . . . a golden chain upon that oak. (*Getting up and singing softly.*)

OLGA: You are not very merry today, Masha.

(MASHA *sings as she puts on her hat.*)

OLGA: Where to?

MASHA: Home.

IRINA: That's strange. . . .

TUSENBACH: To leave a saint's day party!

MASHA: It's all the same. . . . I'll come this evening. Good-by, my pretty . . . (*Kissing* IRINA) I wish you once again good health and happiness. When father was alive, thirty or forty officers used to come to our birthday parties, it was good and noisy; but nowadays there's only a man and a half, and it's quiet as the desert. . . . I'm going. . . . I've got the blues today, I feel depressed, so don't listen to me. (*Laughing through her tears*) We'll talk later on, so good-by now, my dear, I'll go somewhere or other.

IRINA: (*Vexed*) Oh, you are such a . . .

OLGA: (*Tearfully*) I understand you, Masha.

SOLYONY: If a man philosophizes, it will be philosophy or sophistry; but if a woman philosophizes, or two women, it will be—like cracking your fingers.

MASHA: What are you trying to say, you terribly dreadful man?

SOLYONY: Nothing. Quick as a flash, the bear made a dash. . . . (*A pause.*)

MASHA: (*To* OLGA, *crossly*) Don't howl.

(ANFISA *enters, and after her,* FERAPONT *with a cake.*)

ANFISA: Here, little Father. Come in, your feet are clean. (*To* IRINA) From the District Board, from Mikhail Ivanovich Protopopov . . . a cake.

IRINA: Thank you. Thank him for me. (*Taking the cake.*)

FERAPONT: How's that?

IRINA: (*Louder*) Thank him for me.

OLGA: Nursey, give him some pie. Go on, Ferapont. They'll give you some pie.

FERAPONT: How's that?

ANFISA: Come on, little Father, Ferapont Spiridonich. Come on. . . . (*Goes out with* FERAPONT.)

MASHA: I don't like Protopopov, that Mikhail Potopich or Ivanovich. He should not be invited.

IRINA: I didn't do the inviting.

MASHA: That's fine!

(TCHEBUTYKIN *enters, behind him an* ORDERLY *with a silver samovar; there is a hum of astonishment and displeasure.*)

OLGA: (*Covering her face with her hands*) A samovar! This is terrible. (*Going to the table in the dining room.*)

IRINA: Darling Ivan Romanovich, what are you doing?

TUSENBACH: (*Laughing*) I told you so.

MASHA: Ivan Romanovich, you're simply shameless.

TCHEBUTYKIN: My darlings, my good little ones, you are all I have, to me you are everything that's most precious in the world. I'll soon be sixty, I'm an old man, a lonely worthless old man. . . . There is nothing good about me but this love for you, and if it weren't for you I'd long ago have stopped living in this world. . . . (*To* IRINA) My dear, my little child, I have known you since the day you were born. . . . I carried you in my arms. . . . I loved your dear mother. . . .

IRINA: But why such expensive presents!

TCHEBUTYKIN: (*Through his tears, angrily*) Expensive presents! . . . Why, you're completely . . . (*To the* ORDERLY) Carry the samovar in there. . . . (*Mimicking*) Expensive presents . . .

(*The* ORDERLY *carries the samovar into the dining room.*)

ANFISA: (*Passing through the drawing room*) My dears, there's a colonel, a stranger. He's already taken off his overcoat, children, and is coming in here. Irinushka, now be a nice, polite girl. (*As she goes out*) And it was time for lunch long ago. . . . Lord, have mercy! . . .

TUSENBACH: It must be Vershinin.

(VERSHININ *enters.*)

TUSENBACH: Lieutenant Colonel Vershinin!

VERSHININ: (*To* MASHA *and* IRINA) I have the honor to introduce myself: Vershinin. I'm very, very glad that at last I am in your house. How you've grown! Ay! Ay!

IRINA: Please sit down. We are delighted.

VERSHININ: (*Gaily*) How glad I am! How glad I am! But you are three sisters. I remember—three girls. Your faces I don't remember now, but your father, Colonel Prozoroff, had three little girls, I remember that perfectly, I saw them with my own eyes. How time does pass! Oh, oh, how time does pass!

TUSENBACH: Alexander Ignatievich is from Moscow.

IRINA: From Moscow. You are from Moscow?

VERSHININ: Yes, from there. Your father was a battery commander there, and I was an officer in the same brigade. (*To* MASHA) It seems to me now I do remember your face rather.

MASHA: And you I—No!

IRINA: Olya! Olya! (*Calling into the dining room*) Olya! Come here. (OLGA *comes in from the dining room*) Lieutenant Colonel Vershinin, it turns out, is from Moscow.

VERSHININ: You must be Olga Sergeevna, the eldest. . . . And you Maria. . . . And you Irina—the youngest. . . .

OLGA: You are from Moscow?

VERSHININ: Yes. I was at school in Moscow and began my service in Moscow, served there a long time, was finally assigned a battery here—moved here, as you see. I don't remember you, as a matter of fact, but only that you were three sisters. Your father is fresh in my memory; I can close my eyes now and see him as plain as life. I used to pay you calls in Moscow. . . .

OLGA: I thought I remembered everybody, and look, all of a sudden . . .

VERSHININ: My name is Alexander Ignatievich.

IRINA: Alexander Ignatievich, you are from Moscow. What a surprise!

OLGA: We are going to move there, you know.

IRINA: We think by autumn we'll be there. It's our native town, we were born there. . . . In Old Basmanny Street.

(*They both laugh delightedly.*)

MASHA: Unexpectedly we see a fellow countryman. (*Vivaciously*) Now I remember! Do you remember, Olya, at our house they used to say, "the lovesick major." You were a lieutenant then and in love with someone, and they all teased you for some reason as the lovesick major.

VERSHININ: (*Laughing*) That's right! That's right! The lovesick major. That was it!

MASHA: But you had only a mustache then. . . . Oh, how much older you look! (*Tearfully*) How much older you look!

VERSHININ: Yes, when they called me the lovesick major, I was still young, I was in love. Not so now.

OLGA: But you still haven't a single gray hair. You look older, but you are still not old.

VERSHININ: For all that, I'm in my forty-third year. Is it long since you left Moscow?

IRINA: Eleven years. But why are you crying, Masha, you little fool? (*Through her tears*) I'm starting to cry, too. . . .

MASHA: I'm all right. And in what street did you live?

VERSHININ: In Old Basmanny.

OLGA: And we lived there, too. . . .

VERSHININ: At one time I lived in Nemetzky Street. I used to walk from Nemetzky Street to the Red Barracks. There's a sullen-looking bridge on the way, and under the bridge you hear the water roaring. A lonely man feels sick at heart there. (*A pause*) But here, what a broad, what a superb river! A wonderful river!

OLGA: Yes, except that it's cold. It's cold here and there are mosquitoes. . . .

VERSHININ: How can you! You have such a fine, heathy Russian climate here. Woods, river . . . and birches too. Sweet, modest birches, of all trees I love them best. It's good to live here. And yet, strangely enough, the railway station is thirteen miles away. . . . And nobody knows why that is.

SOLYONY: But I know why it is. (*Everyone looks at him*) Because if the station were right here then 'twere not off there, and if it is off there, then it's not right here.

(*An awkward silence.*)

TUSENBACH: You're a joker, Vasili Vasilievich.

OLGA: Now I remember you too. I remember.

VERSHININ: I knew your mother.

TCHEBUTYKIN: She was a lovely woman . . . bless her soul!

IRINA: Mother is buried in Moscow.

OLGA: In the Novo Devichy. . . .

MASHA: Imagine, I'm already beginning to forget her face. Just as we won't be remembered either. They'll forget us.

VERSHININ: Yes. They'll forget us. Such is our fate, it can't be helped. What seems to us serious, significant, highly important—the time will come when it will be forgotten or seem unimportant. (*A pause*) And it's an interesting thing, we can't possibly tell now just what will be considered great, or important, and what pitiful, ridiculous. Didn't the discoveries of Copernicus or, let's say, Columbus, seem at first unnecessary, ridiculous, and some shallow nonsense written by a fool seem to be the truth? And it may be that our present life, to which we are so reconciled, will seem very strange some day, uncomfortable, stupid, not pure enough, perhaps even sinful. . . .

TUSENBACH: Who knows? Perhaps our life will be called superior and remembered with respect. Nowadays there are no tortures, no executions, no invasions, though, for all that, there's so much unhappiness!

SOLYONY: (*In a high-pitched voice*) Chick, chick, chick. . . . Don't feed the Baron grain, just let him philosophize.

TUSENBACH: Vasili Vasilievich, I beg you leave me alone. (*Sits at another place*) After all, it's tiresome.

SOLYONY: (*In a high-pitched voice*) Chick, chick, chick. . . .

TUSENBACH: (*To* VERSHININ) The unhappiness we see now, however, though there is still so much of it even now—bespeaks a certain moral regeneration that has already reached society. . . .

VERSHININ: Yes, yes, of course.

TCHEBUTYKIN: You just said, Baron, that they will call our present life superior; but, all the same, people are small. . . . (*Standing up*) Look how small I am. It would only be to console me if anybody called my life a superior, understandable thing.

(*Behind the scenes a violin plays.*)

MASHA: It's Andrei playing, our brother.

IRINA: He is the learned member of the family. It looks as if he'd be a professor. Father was a military man, but his son chose for himself a learned career.

MASHA: According to Father's wish.

OLGA: Today we teased him to death. It seems he's a bit in love.

IRINA: With a local girl. She'll be with us today, there's every chance of it.

MASHA: Oh, how she dresses! Not merely ugly and out of style but simply pitiful. Some sort of strange, loud, yellowish skirt with a vulgar fringe and a red blouse. And her cheeks are so scrubbed, scrubbed! Andrei isn't in love—I won't admit it, after all he has taste, he's simply teasing us, he's fooling. I heard yesterday that she is marrying Protopopov, the Chairman of the Board. And that's fine—(*At the side door*) Andrei, come here! Darling, just for a minute!

(ANDREI *enters.*)

OLGA: This is my brother, Andrei Sergeevich.

VERSHININ: Vershinin.

ANDREI: Prozoroff. (*He wipes his perspiring face*) You are our new Battery Commander?

OLGA: Can you imagine, Alexander Ignatievich is from Moscow.

ANDREI: Yes? Well, I congratulate you, now my little sisters won't give you any peace.

VERSHININ: I have already had time to tire your sisters out.

IRINA: Look at the frame Andrei gave me today! (*Showing the frame*) He made it himself.

VERSHININ: (*Looking at the frame and not knowing what to say*) Yes. . . . A thing . . .

IRINA: And the frame that's over the piano there, he made that, too.

(ANDREI *waves his hand as if disparagingly and moves away.*)

OLGA: He is not only our learned one, he also plays the violin and he saws various things out of wood. In sum he has a hand for anything. Andrei, don't go away! That's the way he does—he's always leaving us. Come here!

(MASHA *and* IRINA, *laughing, take him by the arms and lead him back.*)

MASHA: Come! Come!

ANDREI: Let me alone, please.

MASHA: How funny he is! Alexander Ignatievich used to be called the lovesick major and he didn't get a bit angry.

VERSHININ: Not a bit.

MASHA: And I want to call you the lovesick violinist!

IRINA: Or the lovesick professor! . . .

OLGA: He's in love! Andrusha's in love!

IRINA: (*Applauding*) Bravo, bravo! *Bis!* Andrushka is in love!

TCHEBUTYKIN: (*Comes up behind* ANDREI *and puts both arms around his waist*) For love alone did Nature put us in this world. (*Laughing. All the while he is holding a newspaper.*)

ANDREI: Well, that's enough, that's enough. . . . (*Wiping his face*) I haven't slept all night and now I'm not myself, as they say. Till four o'clock I read, then lay down, but nothing happened. I thought of this and of that, and then, of course, at the crack of dawn here the sun swarms into my bedroom. During the summer while I am here, I want to translate a certain book from English.

VERSHININ: And do you read English?

ANDREI: Yes. Our father—bless his soul! —loaded us down with education. It's ridiculous and stupid, but all the same I must admit that in a year after his death, I began to fill out and get fat like this, as if my body were freed from the load. Thanks to Father, my sisters and I know the French, German and English languages and Irina knows Italian too. But at what a cost!

MASHA: In this town, to know three languages is an unnecessary luxury. It isn't even a luxury, it's a sort of unnecessary appendage like a sixth finger. We know a lot that's useless.

VERSHININ: There we have it! (*Laughing*) You know a lot that is useless! It seems to me there's not and can't be a town so boring and dull that a clever, educated person would be unnecessary in it. Let's suppose that among the hundred thousand inhabitants of this town, which evidently is backward and crude, there are only three such people as you. It is obvious that you cannot triumph over the dark masses that surround you; in the course of your life you'll have to yield little by little and be lost in the crowd of a hundred thousand; life will stifle you, but just the same you'll still be there and not without influence; your kind, after you, will begin to appear, six, perhaps, then twelve, and so on, until finally your kind will get to be the majority. After two or three hundred years, life on earth will be unimaginably beautiful, wonderful. Man needs such a life, and if it is not here yet, he must anticipate it, wait, dream of it, be prepared for it, for it he must see and know more than his grandfather and father saw and knew. (*Laughing*) And you complain of knowing a lot that's useless.

MASHA: (*Taking off her hat*) I am staying for lunch.

IRINA: (*With a sigh*) Really all that should be written down. . . .

(ANDREI *is not to be seen, he has gone out unobserved.*)

TUSENBACH: After many years, you say, life on earth will be beautiful, wonderful. That's true. But to share it now, even from afar, we must prepare ourselves for it, must be doing something. . . .

VERSHININ: (*Getting up*) Yes. How many flowers you have! (*Looking around*) And a beautiful apartment. I envy you! And all my life I have hung around little apartments with two chairs, a sofa and a stove that always smokes. In my life I have lacked just such flowers . . . (*Rubbing his hands*) Well, nothing can be done about it!

TUSENBACH: Yes, one must work. You probably think the German is getting sentimental. But on my word of honor, I am Russian and don't even speak German. My father was Orthodox. . . .

(*A pause.*)

VERSHININ: (*Walking about the stage*) I often think: what might happen if we began life anew, and did it consciously? If one life, already lived through, had been, as it were the first draft, the other, the final copy! Then each of us, I think, would try above all things not to repeat himself, at least he would create for himself a different setting for his life, would arrange for himself an apartment such as this, with flowers, with a flood of light. . . . I have a wife and two girls; and, at that, the wife is a delicate lady, and so forth and so on, well, and if I were to

begin life anew, I would never marry. . . . No, no!

(KULYGIN *enters, in a schoolteacher's uniform.*)

KULYGIN: (*Going up to* IRINA) My dear sister, allow me to congratulate you on your saint's day and wish you sincerely, from my heart, health and all that could be wished for a girl of your age. And then to present this book to you as a gift. (*Giving her the book*) A history of our high school covering fifty years, written by me. A trifle of a book, written out of nothing else to do, but all the same you must read it. Good morning, gentlemen! (*To* VERSHININ) Kulygin, teacher in the local high school, County Councilor. (*To* IRINA) In this book you will find a list of all the graduates of our high school for the last fifty years. *Feci, quod potui, faciant meliora potentes.* (*He kisses* MASHA.)

IRINA: But you've already given me a book like that at Easter.

KULYGIN: (*Laughing*) It couldn't be! In that case give it back, or better still, give it to the Colonel. Take it, Colonel. Read it sometime when you are bored.

VERSHININ: Thank you. (*He is about to leave*) I am extremely glad I made your acquaintance. . . .

OLGA: You are leaving? No, no!

IRINA: Stay and lunch with us. Please.

OLGA: I beg you!

VERSHININ: (*Bowing*) It seems I've stumbled on to a saint's day party. Forgive me, I didn't know, didn't congratulate you. (*Goes with* OLGA *to the dining room.*)

KULYGIN: Today is Sunday, gentlemen, a day of rest, let us rest, let us be gay, each one according to his age and position. The rugs should be taken up for the summer and stored till winter. . . . Persian powder or naphthalene. . . . The Romans were healthy because they knew how to work, knew how to rest, they had *mens sana in corpore sano.* Their life flowed on according to fixed forms. Our director says: the principal thing in every life is its form. . . . That which loses its form ends itself—and it's the same with our everyday existence. (*Takes* MASHA *by the waist, laughing*) Masha loves me. My wife loves me. And the window curtains, too, together with the rugs. . . . Today, I am gay, in a splendid mood. Masha, at four o'clock today we are to be at the director's. There's a walk being arranged for the teachers and their families.

MASHA: I am not going.

KULYGIN: (*Aggrieved*) Dear Masha, why?

MASHA: Later on about that. . . . (*Angrily*) Oh, very well, I'll go, but just leave me alone, please. . . . (*Walks away.*)

KULYGIN: And then we'll spend the evening at the director's. In spite of his sickly state of health, this man tries above all else to be sociable. A superior, bright personality. A magnificent man. Yesterday, after the teacher's conference, he says to me: "I am tired, Fyodor Ilyich: I am tired!" (*Looks at the clock on the wall, then at his watch*) Your clock is seven minutes fast. Yes, he says, I am tired!

(*Behind the scene a violin is playing.*)

OLGA: Ladies and gentlemen, come to lunch, please! There's a meat-pie.

KULYGIN: Ah, my dear Olga, my dear! Yesterday, I worked from early morning till eleven o'clock in the evening, got tired and today I feel happy. (*Goes into the dining room and up to the table.*)

TCHEBUTYKIN: (*Puts the newspaper in his pocket, combs his beard*) A meat-pie? Splendid!

MASHA: (*To* TCHEBUTYKIN, *sternly*) Only, look out: nothing to drink today. Do you hear? Drinking's bad for you.

TCHEBUTYKIN: Oh, go on! I'm past all that. It is two years I've not been on a drunk. (*Impatiently*) Ah, old girl, isn't it all the same?

MASHA: All the same, don't you dare drink. Don't you dare. (*Angrily, but so that her husband doesn't hear*) The Devil take it, to be bored again all evening long at the director's.

TUSENBACH: I wouldn't go if I were in your place. It's very simple.

TCHEBUTYKIN: Don't go, dearie.

MASHA: Yes, don't go. . . . This curst, unbearable life . . . (*Going to the dining room.*)

TCHEBUTYKIN: (*Going with her*) Now!

SOLYONY: (*Going to the dining room*) Chick, chick, chick. . . .

TUSENBACH: That's enough, Vasili Vasilievich. Drop it!

SOLYONY: Chick, chick, chick. . . .

KULYGIN: (*Gaily*) Your health, Colonel! I am a pedagogue and here in this house I'm one of the family, Masha's husband. . . . She is kind, very kind. . . .

VERSHININ: I'll have some of that dark vodka. . . . (*Drinking*) Your health! (*To* OLGA) I feel so good in your house! . . . (*In the drawing room only* IRINA *and* TUSENBACH *are left.*)

IRINA: Masha is in a bad humor today. She got married at eighteen, when he seemed to her the most intelligent of men. But now it's not the same. He's the kindest but not the most intelligent.

OLGA: (*Impatiently*) Andrei, do come, after all!

ANDREI: (*Behind the scenes*) This minute. (*Enters and goes to the table.*)

TUSENBACH: What are you thinking about?

IRINA: This: I dislike and I'm afraid of that Solyony of yours. He talks nothing but nonsense. . . .

TUSENBACH: He is a strange person. I am both sorry for him and annoyed, but more sorry. It seems to me he's shy. . . . When the two of us are alone, he's very clever and gentle sometimes; but in company he is a crude fellow, a bully. Don't go away, let them get settled at the table. Let me be near you awhile. What are you thinking about? (*A pause*) You are twenty, I am not yet thirty. How many years there are left for us ahead, a long, long row of days, full of my love for you. . . .

IRINA: Nikolai Lvovich, don't talk to me of love.

TUSENBACH: (*Not listening*) I have a passionate thirst for life, struggle, work, and that thirst is mingled in my soul with love for you, Irina. And it's as though it were by some design that you are beautiful and life seems beautiful to me because of you. What are you thinking about?

IRINA: You say life is beautiful. Yes, but what if it only seems so! With us three sisters, life hasn't yet been beautiful, it has stifled us as weeds do grass. . . . I'm letting my tears fall. I shouldn't do that. . . . (*Quickly wiping her face, smiling*) We must do something, must work. That's why we are not happy and look at life so gloomily—we don't know anything about working. We come of people who despised work.

(NATALIA IVANOVNA *enters; she has a pink dress with a green belt.*)

NATASHA: Look, they are already sitting down to lunch. . . . I'm late. . . . (*She steals a glance at herself in the mirror and tidies herself up*) My hair seems to be all right. . . . (*Seeing* IRINA) Dear Irina Sergeevna, I congratulate you! (*Kissing her vigorously and long*) You have lots of guests, I really feel shy. . . . How do you do, Baron!

OLGA: (*Entering the living room*) Well, and here is Natalia Ivanovna. Good day, my dear. (*They kiss.*)

NATASHA: Congratulations on the saint's day. You have so much company, I feel awfully that . . .

OLGA: Never mind, it's just the family. (*In an undertone, alarmed*) You have on a green belt! My dear, that's not right!

NATASHA: Is it a sign of something?

OLGA: No, it just doesn't match . . . and somehow it looks odd—

NATASHA: (*In a tearful voice*) Yes? But it's not really green, it's more of a neutral color. (*Follows* OLGA *into the dining room.*)

(*In the dining room they are sitting down to lunch; there is not a soul in the living room.*)

KULYGIN: I wish you, Irina, a good fiancé! It's time you married.

TCHEBUTYKIN: Natalia Ivanovna, I wish you a fiancé too.

KULYGIN: Natalia Ivanovna already has a fiancé.

MASHA: (*Strikes her plate with her fork*) I'll take a little drink! What the . . . life is all roses, I'll risk it. . . .

KULYGIN: Your conduct gets C minus.

VERSHININ: And the liqueur tastes good. What's it made of?

SOLYONY: Cockroaches.

IRINA: (*In a tearful voice*) Phew! How disgusting! . . .

OLGA: For supper there will be roast turkey and apple pie. Thank the Lord, I'll be at home all day, and in the evening —at home. . . . Everybody must come this evening. . . .

VERSHININ: Allow me, too, to come this evening!

IRINA: Please do.

NATASHA: They are very informal.

TCHEBUTYKIN: For love alone did Nature put us in this world. (*Laughing.*)

ANDREI: (*Angrily*) Stop it, everybody! Aren't you tired of it?

(FEDOTIK *and* RODAY *enter with a big basket of flowers.*)

FEDOTIK: But say, they are already lunching.

RODAY: (*Talking loud and affectedly*) Lunching? Yes, already lunching. . . .

FEDOTIK: Wait a minute! (*Taking a snapshot*) One! Wait, just one more. . . . (*Taking another snapshot*) Two! Now, ready! (*They pick up the basket and go to the dining room, where they are greeted noisily.*)

RODAY: (*In a loud voice*) Congratulations, I wish you everything, everything! The weather today is charming, perfectly magnificent. Today, all morning long, I was walking with the high school boys. I teach gymnastics at the high school. . . .

FEDOTIK: You may move, Irina Sergeevna, you may! (*Taking a snapshot*) You look well today. (*Getting a top out of his pocket*) By the way, see this top. . . . It has an amazing sound. . . .

IRINA: How delightful!

MASHA: By the curved seashore a green oak, a golden chain upon that oak. . . . A golden chain upon that oak. . . . (*Tearfully*) Now, why do I say that? This phrase has stuck in my mind ever since morning. . . .

KULYGIN: Thirteen at the table!

RODAY: (*In a loud voice*) Could it really be, ladies and gentlemen, that you attach importance to these superstitions?

(*Laughing.*)

KULYGIN: Thirteen at the table shows that there are lovers here. It's not you, Ivan Romanovich by any chance? (*Laughter.*)

TCHEBUTYKIN: I am an old sinner, but why Natalia Ivanovna should be embarrassed I simply can't understand.

(*Loud laughter;* NATASHA *runs out from the dining room into the living room,* ANDREI *following her.*)

ANDREI: Come on, don't pay any attention to them! Wait. . . . Stop. . . . I beg you. . . .

NATASHA: I'm ashamed. . . . I don't know what it's all about and they are making fun of me. It was bad manners for me to leave the table just now, but I can't . . . I can't . . . (*Covers her face with her hands.*)

ANDREI: My dear, I beg you, I entreat you, don't be upset. I assure you they are only joking, they have kind hearts. My darling, my beautiful, they all are gentle, kind-hearted people and they love me and you. Come over here to the window, they can't see us here. . . .

(*He glances around.*)

NATASHA: I am so unused to being in society! . . .

ANDREI: Ah, youth, wonderful, beautiful youth! My dear, my darling, don't be so upset! . . . Believe me, believe . . . I feel so happy, my soul is full of love, ecstasy. . . . Oh, they can't see us! They can't see! Why, why I fell in love with you; when I fell in love. My dear, darling, pure one, be my wife! I love you, love . . . as nobody ever. . . . (*A kiss.*)

(*The* TWO OFFICERS *enter and seeing the pair kissing, stop in astonishment.*)

Curtain

ACT TWO

The setting is the same as in Act One. It is eight o'clock in the evening. Offstage faintly we hear an accordion, playing in the street. There are no lights.

(NATALIA IVANOVNA *enters in a dressing gown, with a candle; she comes in and stops at the door that leads into* ANDREI's *room.*)

NATASHA: Andrusha, what are you doing? Reading? It's nothing, I just . . . (*Goes and opens another door and after looking in, closes it*) If there's a light . . .

ANDREI: (*Enters with a book in his hand*) You what, Natasha?

NATASHA: Looking to see if there's a light. . . . Now it's Carnival week the servants are beside themselves, we have to look and look, so that nothing goes wrong. Last night at midnight, I passed through the dining room, and a candle was burning there. Who lighted it I couldn't find out. (*Putting down her candle*) What time is it?

ANDREI: (*Looking at his watch*) It's a quarter past eight.

NATASHA: And Olga and Irina not in yet. They haven't come in. Always working, poor girls! Olga at the Teachers' Council, Irina at the telegraph office. . . . (*Sighing*) This morning I say to your sister: "Spare yourself, I say, Irina darling." But she won't listen. Quarter past eight, you say? I am anxious for fear, our Bobik is not at all well. Why is he so cold? Yesterday he had fever, and today he is cold all over. . . . I am so anxious!

ANDREI: It's nothing, Natasha. The boy is all right.

NATASHA: Still it's better to put him on a diet. I'm anxious. And tonight, around ten o'clock, they said, the maskers will be here, it would be better if they didn't come, Andrusha.

ANDREI: Really, I don't know. But they were invited.

NATASHA: This morning the little fellow wakes up and looks at me and all at once he smiles; so he knew me. "Bobik," I say, "good morning! Good morning, dear!" And he laughs. Children understand, they understand perfectly. So, Andrusha, I'll tell them not to let the maskers in.

ANDREI: (*Indecisively*) But that's for my sisters to say, they are mistresses here.

NATASHA: And they too, I'll tell them. They are kind. . . . (*Going*) For supper I ordered some buttermilk. The doctor says, you're to have nothing but buttermilk or you'll never get any thinner. (*Stopping*) Bobik is cold. I'm afraid he may be cold in that room of his. We ought to—at least till warm weather comes—put him in a different room. For instance, Irina's room is just right for a child; it's dry and sunny too all day long. I must tell her that. For a while at least she could be in the same room with Olga. . . . She's not at home during the day anyhow, she only spends the night. . . . (*A pause*) Andrushanchik, why don't you say something?

ANDREI: I was just thinking—Besides there's nothing to talk about. . . .

NATASHA: Yes. . . . There's something I wanted to tell you. . . . Oh, yes. Ferapont has just come from the District Board, he's asking for you.

ANDREI: (*Yawning*) Call him in.

(NATASHA *goes out.* ANDREI, *bending over to the candle, which she has forgotten to take along, reads his book.* FERAPONT *enters; he is in a shabby old coat, with the collar turned up, a scarf over his ears.*)

ANDREI: Good evening, my good soul. What have you got to say?

FERAPONT: The Chairman has sent you a book and a paper of some kind. Here. . . . (*He gives the book and an envelope to* ANDREI.)

ANDREI: Thanks. Good! But why did you come so late? It's after eight now?

FERAPONT: How's that?

ANDREI: (*Louder*) I say you came late, it's now after eight.

FERAPONT: Exactly. I got here when it was still light, but they all wouldn't let me in. The master, they said, is busy. Well, it's like this. You're busy, very busy. I have nowhere to hurry to. (*Thinking that* ANDREI *is asking him something*) How's that?

ANDREI: Nothing. (*Examining the book*) Tomorrow is Friday, we haven't any school, but all the same I'll come, just to be doing something. It's tiresome at home. . . . (*A pause*) Dear Grandpa, how strangely it changes, how life deceives one! Today, out of boredom, out of nothing else to do, I picked up this book here —old university lectures, and I felt like laughing. . . . My God! I'm the secretary of the District Board, that board where Protopopov presides, I am the secretary and the very most I can hope for—is to be a member of the District Board! Me, a member of the local district board, I who dream every night that I'm a professor in Moscow University, a famous scholar whom this Russian land is proud of!

FERAPONT: I wouldn't know. Don't hear well. . . .

ANDREI: If you could hear well, I might not have talked to you. I must talk to somebody, but my wife doesn't understand me, and I am afraid of my sisters somehow, I'm afraid they will laugh at me, make me ashamed. . . . I don't drink, don't like bars; but with what pleasure I could be sitting right now in Moscow at Testoff's or in the Bolshoy Moscoffsky, my dear fellow.

FERAPONT: And in Moscow, so a contractor was saying the other day at the District Board, some merchants were eating bliny; one of them, it seems, ate forty blinies and died. It was either forty or fifty. I wouldn't remember.

ANDREI: You sit in Moscow in a huge room at a restaurant, you don't know anybody, and nobody knows you, but at the same time you don't feel like a stranger. . . . And here you know everybody and everybody knows you, but you are a stranger, a stranger. . . . A stranger and lonely.

FERAPONT: How's that? (*A pause*) And the same contractor was saying— maybe he was just lying—that a rope is stretched all the way across Moscow.

ANDREI: What for?

FERAPONT: I wouldn't know. The contractor said so.

ANDREI: Fiddlesticks. (*Reading*) Were you ever in Moscow?

FERAPONT: (*After a pause*) Never was. God didn't grant me that. (*A pause*) Shall I go?

ANDREI: You may go. Good-by. (FERAPONT *goes out*) Good-by. (*Reading*) Come tomorrow morning and get these papers. . . . Go. . . . (*A pause*) He's gone. (*A bell rings*) Yes, it's a business—(*Stretching and going slowly into his room.*)

(*Behind the scenes a nurse is singing, rocking a child.* MASHA *and* VERSHININ *enter conversing. In the dining room one of the maids is lighting a lamp and the candles.*)

MASHA: I don't know. (*A pause*) I don't know. Of course habit means a lot. For example, after Father's death it took us a long time to get used to not having orderlies in the house. But even apart from habit, I think, common justice makes me say it—in other places it may not be so, but in our town the most decent, the most honorable and well-brought-up people—are the military.

VERSHININ: I'm thirsty. I'd drink some tea.

MASHA: (*Glancing at the clock*) It will soon be here. They married me off when I was eighteen years old, and I was afraid of my husband because he was a teacher, and that was when I had barely finished my courses. He seemed to me terribly learned then, clever, and important. But now it's not the same, unfortunately.

VERSHININ: So—yes.

MASHA: I am not talking about my husband. I'm used to him, but among the civilians generally there are so many people who are crude and unfriendly and haven't any manners. Rudeness upsets me and offends me, I suffer when I see that a man is not fine enough, gentle enough, polite. When I happen to be among the teachers, my husband's colleagues, I'm simply miserable.

VERSHININ: Yes. . . . But it seems to me it's all the same whether they are civilian or military, they are equally uninteresting, at any rate in this town they are. It's all the same! If you listen to one of the local intelligentsia—civilian or military—what you hear is that he's worn out with his wife, worn out with his home, worn out with his estate, worn out with his horses. . . . A Russian is quite supremely given to lofty ways in thought, but will you tell me why it is that in life he strikes so low? Why?

MASHA: Why?

VERSHININ: Why is he worn out with his children, worn out with his wife? And why are the wife and the children worn out with him?

MASHA: You are not in a very good humor today.

VERSHININ: Perhaps. I haven't had any dinner today, nothing to eat since morning. One of my daughters is not very well, and when my girls are ailing, I am seized with anxiety, and my conscience torments me for their having such a mother. Oh, if you'd seen her today! What a miserable wretch! We began to quarrel at seven o'clock in the morning, and at nine I slammed the door and went out. (A pause) I never speak of it, and strangely enough I complain just to you. (Kissing her hand) Don't be angry with me. But for you alone, I'd not have anybody—nobody. . . .

(A pause.)

MASHA: What a noise in the stove! At home, just before Father died, it was howling in the chimney. There, just like that!

VERSHININ: Are you superstitious?

MASHA: Yes.

VERSHININ: That's strange. (Kissing her hand) You are a magnificent, wonderful woman. Magnificent, wonderful! It is dark here, but I see the sparkle of your eyes.

MASHA: (Moving to another chair) It's lighter here.

VERSHININ: I love, love, love. . . . Love your eyes, your gestures, I see them in my dreams. . . . Magnificent, wonderful woman!

MASHA: (Laughing quietly) When you talk to me like that, for some reason or other, I laugh, though I'm frightened. Don't do it again, I beg you. . . . (In a low voice) But talk, though, it's all the same to me. (Covering her face with her hands) It's all the same to me. They're coming here—talk about something else. . . .

(IRINA and TUSENBACH enter from the dining room.)

TUSENBACH: I have a triple name. I am called Tusenbach—Krone—Altschauer—but I am Russian, Orthodox, like you. There's very little German left in me, perhaps only this patience and stubbornness that I bore you with. I see you home every evening.

IRINA: I'm so tired!

TUSENBACH: And every day I'll come to the telegraph office and see you home,

I'll do that for ten, twenty, years, for as long as you don't drive me away. . . . (*Seeing* MASHA *and* VERSHININ, *delightedly*) It's you? Good evening.

IRINA: Here I am home at last. (*To* MASHA) Just now a lady came, telegraphed her brother in Saratov that her son died today, and couldn't remember the address at all. So she sent it without the address, simply to Saratov. She was crying. And I was rude to her for no reason whatever. "I haven't got time," I said. 'Twas so silly! Are the maskers coming tonight?

MASHA: Yes.

IRINA: (*She sits down in an armchair*) I must rest. I'm tired.

TUSENBACH: (*Smiling*) When you come back from your office, you seem so young, unhappy. . . .

(*A pause.*)

IRINA: I'm tired. No, I don't like the telegraphing, I don't like it.

MASHA: You are thinner. . . . (*She begins to whistle*) And look younger and your face begins to look like a little boy's.

TUSENBACH: That's from her hair.

IRINA: I must try and find another position, this one is not for me. What I wanted so, what I dreamed of, that's exactly what's not there. Work without poetry, without thoughts. . . . (*A knock on the floor*) The doctor is knocking. . . . (*To* TUSENBACH) Knock back, dear. . . . I can't. . . . I'm tired. . . .

(TUSENBACH *knocks on the floor.*)

IRINA: He'll come this minute. Something or other will have to be done about it. The doctor and our Andrei were at the club yesterday and lost again. They say Andrei lost two hundred roubles.

MASHA: (*Indifferently*) So what's there to do now?

IRINA: Two weeks ago he lost, in December he lost. If he'd lose everything soon, perhaps we'd go away from this town. Oh my Lord God, I dream of Moscow every night, I am like someone completely possessed. (*Laughing*) We are moving there in June and from now to June leaves still . . . February, March, April, May. . . . Almost half a year!

MASHA: The only thing is Natasha mustn't some way or other hear of his losses.

IRINA: It's all one to her, I imagine.

(TCHEBUTYKIN, *who has just got out of bed—he has been resting after dinner—enters the dining room combing his beard, then sits down at the table and takes a newspaper from his pocket.*)

MASHA: There he comes. . . . Has he paid anything on his apartment?

IRINA: (*Laughing*) No. Not a kopeck for eight months. He's forgotten it evidently.

MASHA: (*Laughing*) How importantly he sits!

(*Everybody laughs; a pause.*)

IRINA: Why are you so quiet, Alexander Ignatievich?

VERSHININ: I don't know. What I'd like is some tea. Half my life for a glass of tea! I've eaten nothing since morning. . . .

TCHEBUTYKIN: Irina Sergeevna!

IRINA: What do you want?

TCHEBUTYKIN: Please come here. *Venez ici!* (IRINA *goes and sits down at the table*) I can't do without you.

(IRINA *lays out the cards for patience.*)

VERSHININ: Well? If they are not giving us any tea, let's at least philosophize.

TUSENBACH: Yes, lets. What about?

VERSHININ: What about? Let's dream . . . for example, of the life that will come after us in two or three hundred years.

TUSENBACH: Well? After us they will fly in balloons, the style of coats will change, they will discover the sixth sense perhaps, and develop it; but life will remain quite the same, a difficult life, mysterious and happy. And after a thousand years, man will be sighing the same: "Ah, how hard it is to live!" and meanwhile, exactly the same as now, he will be afraid of death and not want to die.

VERSHININ: (*After a moment's thought*) How shall I put it? It seems to me everything on earth must change little by little and is already changing before our very eyes. In two or three hundred, eventually a thousand, years—it's not a matter of time—a new, happy life will come. We won't share in that life of course, but we are living for it now, working, well—suffering; we are creating it—and in that alone lies the purpose of our being and, if you like, our happiness.

(MASHA *laughs softly.*)

TUSENBACH: What are you laughing at?

MASHA: I don't know. All day today I've been laughing, ever since morning.

VERSHININ: I was graduated from the same school you were, but was not at the academy; I read a great deal, but don't know how to choose books, and read, perhaps, not at all what I should; and meanwhile the longer I live the more I want to know. My hair is turning gray, I'm almost an old man now, but I know very little, or, how very little! And yet it does seem to me that what's most important and real I do know, know solidly. And I'd so like to prove to you that there's no happiness, there should not be, and there won't be, for us. . . . We should only work and work, and happiness—that's the lot of our remote descendants. (*A pause*) Not I, but at least the descendants of my descendants.

(FEDOTIK *and* RODAY *appear in the dining room; they sit down and sing softly, strumming a guitar.*)

TUSENBACH: According to you, we are not even to dream of happiness! But what if I'm happy?

VERSHININ: No.

TUSENBACH: (*Throwing up his hands and laughing*) Obviously we don't understand each other. Well, how can I convince you?

(MASHA *laughs softly.*)

TUSENBACH: (*Holding up a finger to her*) Laugh! (*To* VERSHININ) Not only in two or three hundred but in a million years, even, life will be just the same as it was; it doesn't change, it stays constant, following its own laws, which are none of our affair, or which, at least you will never know. Birds of passage, cranes, for example, fly and fly, and no matter what thoughts, great or small, stray through their heads, they will fly just the same and not know why and where. They fly and will fly, no matter what philosophers spring up among them; and they may philosophize as much as they like so long as they fly. . . .

MASHA: Just the same, has it meaning?

TUSENBACH: Meaning. . . . Look, it's snowing. What meaning has that?

(*A pause.*)

MASHA: It seems to me a man must be a believer or must seek some belief, otherwise his life is empty, empty. . . . To live and not know why the cranes fly, why children are born, why there are stars in the sky. . . . Either he knows what he's living for, or it's all nonsense, waste.

VERSHININ: Yet it's a shame youth is gone. . . .

MASHA: Gogol says: It is boring to live in this world, gentlemen.

TUSENBACH: And I say: it is difficult to argue with you, gentlemen! Why you completely. . . .

TCHEBUTYKIN: (*Reading a newspaper*) Balzac was married in Berdichev. (IRINA *sings softly*) Really I'll put that in my book. (*Writing*) Balzac was married in Berdichev. (*Reading his newspaper.*)

IRINA: (*As she lays out cards for patience, musing*) Balzac was married in Berdichev.

TUSENBACH: The die is cast. You know, Maria Sergeevna, I have tendered my resignation.

MASHA: So I heard. And I don't see anything good about that. I don't like civilians.

TUSENBACH: Just the same . . . (*Getting up*) I'm not handsome, what sort of military man am I? Well, well, but all the same, however. . . . I shall work. For just one day in my life, work so that I come home in the evening, drop exhausted into bed and fall asleep right off. (*Going into the dining room*) Workmen must sleep soundly!

FEDOTIK: (*To* IRINA) I bought you some crayons on Moscoffsky Street, at Pyjokoff's, and this penknife.

IRINA: You are used to treating me as if I were little, but I'm grown up now. . . . (*She takes the crayons and the penknife, gaily*) How delightful!

FEDOTIK: And I bought a knife for myself. . . . Look here . . . a blade, and another blade, a third, this to pick the ears, these small scissors, this to clean the nails. . . .

RODAY: (*Talking very loud*) Doctor, what's your age?

TCHEBUTYKIN: Me? Thirty-two.

(*Laughter.*)

FEDOTIK: I'll now show you another game of patience. . . . (*Laying out cards for patience.*)

(*The samovar is brought:* ANFISA *is at the samovar; a little later* NATASHA *also comes in and hovers near the table;* SOLYONY *enters and after greetings, sits down at the table.*)

VERSHININ: But what a wind!

MASHA: Yes. I'm tired of winter. I've already forgotten what summer is like.

IRINA: It's coming out right, the patience, I see. We shall be in Moscow.

FEDOTIK: No, it's not coming out right. Look, the eight falls on the two of spades. (*Laughing*) So you will not be in Moscow.

TCHEBUTYKIN: (*Reading his newspaper*) Tsitsikar. Smallpox is raging here.

ANFISA: (*Approaching* MASHA) Masha, have some tea, little one. (*To* VERSHININ) If you please, Your Excellency. . . . Excuse me, dear sir, your name, your family name, I've forgotten. . . .

MASHA: Bring it here, Nurse. I'm not going there.

IRINA: Nurse!

ANFISA: I'm coming!

NATASHA: (*To* SOLYONY) Bobik understands beautifully. "Good morning," I say, "Bobik. Good morning, dear!" He gave me a special look somehow. You think I'm only a mother talking, but no, no, I assure you! That's an unusual child.

SOLYONY: If this child were mine, I would have fried him in a skillet and eaten him. (*He goes with his glass into the living room and sits down in the corner.*)

NATASHA: (*Covering her face with her hands*) Rude, ill-bred man!

MASHA: Happy is he who does not notice whether it's summer now or winter. If I were in Moscow, I think I should scorn the weather. . . .

VERSHININ: The other day I read the diary of a certain French Minister, written in prison. The Minister was convicted of fraud. With what rapture and delight, he mentions the birds he saw through the prison window and had never noticed before when he was a Minister. And now, of course, that he's released, it's the same as it was before, he doesn't notice the birds. Just as you won't notice Moscow when you live there. Happiness we have not and it does not exist, we only long for it.

TUSENBACH: (*Taking a box from the table*) But where's the candy?

IRINA: Solyony ate it all.

TUSENBACH: All of it?

ANFISA: (*Serving tea*) A letter for you, dear sir.

VERSHININ: For me? (*Taking the letter*) From my daughter. (*Reading*) Yes, of course. . . . Forgive me, Maria Sergeevna, I'll just slip out. Not any tea for me—(*Getting up very much disturbed*) These eternal messes. . . .

MASHA: What is it? Not a secret?

VERSHININ: (*In a low voice*) The wife has taken poison again. Got to go. I'll slip out, won't be seen. Terribly unpleasant, all this. (*Kissing* MASHA's *hand*) My dear, kind, good woman. . . . I'll slip out of here quietly. . . . (*He goes out.*)

ANFISA: Where is he going now? And I have poured his tea. . . . Such a . . .

MASHA: (*Losing her temper*) Let it be! Plaguing us around here, there's no rest from you. . . . (*Going to the table with her cup*) I am tired of you, old woman!

ANFISA: Why are you offended? Darling!

ANDREI'S VOICE: Anfisa!

ANFISA: (*Mocking him*) Anfisa! Sitting there. . . . (*She goes out.*)

MASHA: (*In the dining room at the table, angrily*) Do let me sit down! (*Musses up the cards on the table*) Lounging here with the cards. Drink your tea!

IRINA: You are spiteful, Masha.

MASHA: If I'm spiteful, don't talk to me. Don't touch me!

TCHEBUTYKIN: (*Laughing*) Don't touch her, don't touch. . . .

MASHA: You are sixty years old, and you are like a little boy, always prattling the devil knows what.

NATASHA: (*Sighing*) Dear Masha, why use such expressions in your conversation? With your beautiful looks you'd be, I'll tell you candidly, simply charming in a decent, well-bred society, if it weren't for these words of yours. *Je vous prie, pardonnez-moi, Marie, mais vous avez des manières un peu grossières.*

TUSENBACH: (*Suppressing a laugh*) Give me. . . . Give me. . . . Seems there's some cognac.

NATASHA: *Il paraît que mon Bobik déjà ne dort pas,* he's waked up. He doesn't seem to me very well today. I'm going to him, excuse me. . . . (*She goes out.*)

IRINA: And where's Alexander Ignatievich gone?

MASHA: Home. There's something extraordinary the matter with his wife again.

TUSENBACH: (*Going to* SOLYONY, *with a decanter of cognac*) You sit by yourself all the time, you are thinking of something—and there's no grasping what it is. Well, let's make peace. Let's drink some cognac. (*Drinking*) I'll have to play the piano all night tonight probably, play all kinds of trash. . . . Come what may!

SOLYONY: Why make peace? I have not quarreled with you.

TUSENBACH: You always give me a sort of feeling that something has happened between us. You are a strange character, we must admit.

SOLYONY: (*Declaiming*) I am strange, who isn't strange! Don't be angry, Aleko!

TUSENBACH: But why this Aleko. . . .

(*A pause.*)

SOLYONY: When I am alone with some-one I'm all right, I am like everybody else, but in company I am gloomy, shy and . . . talk all kinds of rot. Nevertheless, I am more honest and nobler than many, many others are. And I can prove it.

TUSENBACH: I often get sore at you, you are forever plaguing me when we are in company, but just the same you attract me somehow. Come what may, I'll get drunk today. Let's drink!

SOLYONY: Let's go. (*Drinking*) I've never had anything against you, Baron. But I have the disposition of Lermontov. (*In a low voice*) I even resemble Lermontov a little. . . . So they say. . . . (*Getting a bottle of perfume out of his pocket and pouring some of it over his hands.*)

TUSENBACH: I am sending in my resignation. *Basta!* For five years I kept pondering it and finally decided. I'm going to work.

SOLYONY: (*Declaiming*) Don't be angry, Aleko. . . . Forget, forget those dreams of yours. . . .

(*While they are talking,* ANDREI *comes in quietly with a book and sits down near a candle.*)

TUSENBACH: I'm going to work.

TCHEBUTYKIN: (*Going into the living room with* IRINA) And the refreshments were real Caucasian too: onion soup, and for the roast—tchehartma, meat.

SOLYONY: Tcheremsha is not meat at all, but a plant something like our onion.

TCHEBUTYKIN: No, my angel . . . Tchehartma is not onion but a mutton roast.

SOLYONY: And I tell you, tcheremsha —onion.

TCHEBUTYKIN: And I tell you, tche-hartma—mutton.

SOLYONY: And I tell you, tcheremsha —onion.

TCHEBUTYKIN: But why should I argue with you, you never were in the Caucasus, and never ate tchehartma.

SOLYONY: I haven't eaten it because I can't bear it. Tcheremsha smells exactly like garlic.

ANDREI: (*Imploringly*) That's enough, gentlemen! I beg you!

TUSENBACH: When are the maskers coming?

IRINA: They promised toward nine; which means, this minute.

TUSENBACH: (*Embracing* ANDREI. *Singing*) Oh, you porch, my porch, new porch of mine. . . .

ANDREI: (*Dancing and singing*) New porch of maple. . . .

TCHEBUTYKIN: (*Dancing*) Made of lattice!

(*Laughter.*)

TUSENBACH: (*Kissing* ANDREI) The Devil take it, let's have a drink! Andrusha, let us drink with you. And I'll go with you, Andrusha, to Moscow, to the university.

SOLYONY: To which one? In Moscow there are two universities.

ANDREI: In Moscow, there's one university.

SOLYONY: And I tell you—two.

ANDREI: Let there be three even. So much the better!

SOLYONY: In Moscow there are two universities! (*Disapproval and hisses*) In Moscow there are two universities: the old and the new. And if you don't want to listen, if my words irritate you, I can stop talking. I can even go to another room. . . . (*He goes out through one of the doors.*)

TUSENBACH: Bravo, bravo! (*Laughing*)

Ladies and gentlemen, begin, I am sitting down to play! Funny this Solyony. . . . (*Sitting down at the piano and playing a waltz.*)

MASHA: (*Waltzing by herself*) The Baron is drunk, the Baron is drunk, the Baron is drunk.

(NATASHA *enters.*)

NATASHA: (*To* TCHEBUTYKIN) Ivan Romanovich!

(*She says something to* TCHEBUTYKIN, *then goes out quietly.* TCHEBUTYKIN *touches* TUSENBACH *on the shoulder and whispers something to him.*)

IRINA: What is it?

TCHEBUTYKIN: It's time for us to go.

TUSENBACH: Good night. It's time to go.

IRINA: But look here—what about the maskers?

ANDREI: (*Embarrassed*) There won't be any maskers. Don't you see, my dear, Natasha says that Bobik isn't quite well, and therefore . . . In sum, I don't know, it's all the same to me, absolutely.

IRINA: (*Shrugging her shoulders*) Bobik not well!

MASHA: What of it! If they run us out, we must go. (*To* IRINA) It is not Bobik that's sick, but she herself is. . . . Here! (*Tapping her forehead*) Common creature!

(ANDREI *goes through the right door into his room.* TCHEBUTYKIN *follows him: in the dining room good-bys are being said.*)

FEDOTIK: What a pity! I counted on spending the evening, but if the child is sick, of course . . . Tomorrow I'll bring him some toys. . . .

RODAY: (*In a loud voice*) I purposely took a nap after dinner today, thought I would dance all night. Why, it's only nine o'clock now.

MASHA: Let's go out in the street: we'll talk things over there. We'll decide what's what.

(*Sounds of:* "Good-by! . . . Farewell!" *You can hear* TUSENBACH's *gay laughter. Everyone is gone.* ANFISA *and a maid clear the table, put out the lights. A nurse can be heard singing.* ANDREI *in his coat and hat and* TCHEBUTYKIN *enter quietly.*)

TCHEBUTYKIN: I've had no time to marry because life has flashed by me like lightning, and also because I was madly in love with your mother, who was married. . . .

ANDREI: One shouldn't marry. One shouldn't, it's boring.

TCHEBUTYKIN: That may be so, but the loneliness! You may philosophize as much as you please, but loneliness is a frightful thing, my boy. . . . Though as a matter of fact . . . of course it's absolutely all the same.

ANDREI: Let's go quick.

TCHEBUTYKIN: Why hurry? We have time.

ANDREI: I am afraid the wife might stop us.

TCHEBUTYKIN: Ah!

ANDREI: Today I shan't play, but just sit. I don't feel well. . . . What shall I do, Ivan Romanovich, for shortness of breath?

TCHEBUTYKIN: Why ask me? Don't remember, my boy. Don't know.

ANDREI: Let's go through the kitchen.

(*They go out. A ring, then another ring; voices are heard, laughter.* IRINA *enters.*)

IRINA: What is it?

ANFISA: (*In a whisper*) The maskers!

(*A ring.*)

IRINA: Tell them, Nursey, nobody's at home. They must excuse us.

(ANFISA *goes out.* IRINA *paces the room, thinking things over, she is perturbed.* SOLYONY *enters.*)

SOLYONY: (*In a quandary*) Nobody here. . . . But where are they all?

IRINA: Gone home.

SOLYONY: That's odd. Are you alone here?

IRINA: Alone. (*A pause*) Good-by.

SOLYONY: I behaved without enough restraint just now, tactlessly. But you are not like the rest of them, you are superior and pure, you can see the truth. . . . Only you alone can understand me. I love you, deeply, love you without end. . . .

IRINA: Good-by; Go away.

SOLYONY: I can't live without you. (*Following her*) Oh, my delight! (*Through his tears*) Oh, happiness! Such glorious, wonderful, marvelous eyes as I have never seen in any other woman. . . .

IRINA: (*Coldly*) Stop it, Vasili Vasili-evich!

SOLYONY: I'm speaking of love to you for the first time and it's as if I were not on earth but on another planet. (*Rubbing his forehead*) Well, it's all the same. Love is not to be forced, certainly. . . . But lucky rivals I cannot have. . . . Cannot. . . . I swear to you by all that's holy, I'll kill any rival. . . . Oh, wonderful creature!

(*NATASHA passes by with a candle.*)

NATASHA: (*Looks in at one door, then at another and passes by the door leading into her husband's room*) Andrei is there. Let him read. Excuse me, Vasili Vasili-evich, I didn't know you were here. I'm in my dressing gown.

SOLYONY: It's all the same to me. Good-by! (*He goes out.*)

NATASHA: And you are tired, my dear, poor girl! (*Kissing* IRINA) You should go to bed a little earlier.

IRINA: Is Bobik asleep?

NATASHA: Asleep. But not sound asleep. By the way, dear, I wanted to tell you, but you are never here, or else I haven't time. . . . In the nursery Bobik has now, seems to me it's cold and damp. And your room is so good for a child. My dear, my own, move in with Olya for a while!

IRINA: (*Not understanding*) Where?

(*A troika with bells is heard driving up to the house.*)

NATASHA: You and Olya will be in one room, for this little while, and your room will be for Bobik. He's such a darling, today I say to him: "Bobik, you are mine! Mine!" And he looks at me with his little eyes. (*A ring*) It must be Olga. How late she is!

(*A* MAID *comes and whispers in* NATASHA'S *ear.*)

NATASHA: Protopopov? What a queer man! Protopopov has come, he's asking me to go for a ride with him in a troika. (*Laughing*) How strange these men are . . . ! (*A ring*) Somebody's come out there. I might go ride for a quarter of an hour. . . . (*To the* MAID) Tell him right away—(*A ring*) There's a ring.'. . . . Olga must be here. (*She goes out.*)

(*The* MAID *runs out;* IRINA *sits there thinking.* KULYGIN, OLGA *enter, behind them* VERSHININ.)

KULYGIN: There you are! And they said there would be a party.

VERSHININ: Strange, I went away a while ago, half an hour ago, and they were expecting the maskers. . . .

IRINA: They have all gone.

KULYGIN: And Masha's gone? Where did she go? And why is Protopopov downstairs waiting in the troika? Who's he waiting for?

IRINA: Don't ask questions. . . . I'm tired.

KULYGIN: Well, Miss Caprice . . .

OLGA: The council has just finished. I'm exhausted. Our headmistress is ill, and I'm taking her place. My head, my head aches, my head . . . (*Sitting down*) Andrei lost two hundred roubles yesterday at cards. . . . The whole town is talking about it. . . .

KULYGIN: Yes, and I got tired at the council. (*He sits down.*)

VERSHININ: My wife decided just now to scare me, she almost poisoned herself. It all passed over and I'm happy, I'm easy now. . . . The order is we must leave here. So—let me wish you all well. Fyodor Ilyich, go somewhere with me. I can't stay at home, absolutely cannot. . . . Let's go!

KULYGIN: I'm tired. I'm not going. (*Rising*) I'm tired. Has the wife come home?

IRINA: She must have.

KULYGIN: (*Kissing* IRINA's *hand*) Good-by. Tomorrow and the day after I'll rest all day long. I wish you well. (*Going*) I'd like some tea very much. I counted on spending the evening in pleasant company and—o, *fallacem hominum spem!* Accusative case exclamatory. . . .

VERSHININ: Which means I'm going by myself. (*He goes out with* KULYGIN, *whistling.*)

OLGA: My head aches, my head . . . Andrei has lost . . . the whole town is talking. . . . I'll go lie down. . . . (*Starting out of the room*) Tomorrow I am free. . . . O Lord, how pleasant it is! Tomorrow is free, day after tomorrow is free. . . . My head aches, my head . . . (*She goes out.*)

IRINA: (*Alone*) They've all gone. There's nobody here.

(*In the street an accordion is heard, the* NURSE *sings a song.*)

NATASHA: (*With a fur coat and cap, passes through the dining room; behind her a* MAID) I'll be home in half an hour. I'll take just a little ride. (*She goes out.*)

IRINA: (*Left alone, dejected*) To Moscow! To Moscow! To Moscow!

Curtain

ACT THREE

(OLGA's *and* IRINA's *room. To the left and to the right are beds, with screens around them. It is going on three o'clock in the morning. Offstage they are ringing the firebell for a fire that began a long time back. Plainly no one in the house has gone to bed yet.* MASHA *lies on the sofa, she wears, as usual, a black dress.* OLGA *and* ANFISA *enter.*)

ANFISA: Sitting down there now under the staircase . . . I say—"If you please, come upstairs, as if," I say, "you could sit there like that!"—they are crying, "Daddy," they say, "we don't know where Daddy is. God forbid," they say, "he's burned!" They thought that up! And in the courtyard there are some people. . . . They are undressed too.

OLGA: (*Taking some dresses out of the closet*) Here, this gray one—take it. . . . And this one here. . . . The blouse too . . . And take the skirt, Nursey. . . . All Kirsanoffsky Street seems to be burned down. . . . Take this. . . . Take this. . . . (*Throws the dresses for her to catch*) The poor Vershinins were frightened. . . . Their house nearly burned up. They must spend the night here. . . . We can't let them go home. . . . At poor Fedotik's everything got burned, there's nothing left. . . .

ANFISA: You'll have to call Ferapont, Olyushka, or I can't carry . . .

OLGA: (*She rings*) Nobody answers. . . . (*Through the door*) Come here, whoever it is! (*Through the open door she sees a window glowing red with the fire; a fire brigade is heard passing the house*) How frightful! And how sickening! (FERAPONT *enters*) Here, take this and carry it downstairs. . . . Down there under the staircase are the young Kolotilin girls. . . . Give it to them. And give this. . . .

FERAPONT: Yes, miss. In the year '12, Moscow also burned. Oh my Lord God! The French were astonished.

OLGA: Go on, step along. . . .

FERAPONT: Yes, miss. (*He goes out.*)

OLGA: Nursey, dear, give everything away. We don't need anything. Give everything away! Nursey . . . I'm tired, I can barely stand on my feet. . . . The Vershinins shouldn't be allowed to go home. . . . The girls can sleep in the drawing room, and Alexander Ignatievich downstairs at the Baron's . . . Fedotik too at the Baron's, or let him stay with us in the dining room. . . . The doctor, as if he'd done it on purpose, is drunk, terribly drunk, and we mustn't send anyone to him. And Vershinin's wife too in the drawing room.

ANFISA: (*Wearily*) Olyushka, dear, don't you drive me away! Don't drive me away!

OLGA: You are talking nonsense, Nurse. Nobody's driving you away.

ANFISA: (*Laying her head on* OLGA'S *breast*) My own, my treasure, I do try, I work. . . . I'll get feeble and everybody will say: get out! And where will I go? Eighty years old. My eighty-second year. . . .

OLGA: You sit down a while, Nursey. . . . You are tired, poor thing. . . . (*Making her sit down*) Rest, my dear good old Nurse. You look so pale!

(NATASHA *enters.*)

NATASHA: They are saying it around that we must form right off a relief society for those who have been burnt out. Why not! It's a fine idea. We must be quick to help poor people, that's the duty of the rich. Bobik and Sofotchka have just gone to sleep, they sleep as if nothing had happened. There are so many people everywhere here that anywhere you go the house is full. There's influenza in town now, I'm afraid the children may catch it.

OLGA: (*Not listening to her*) In this room you don't see the fire, it's peaceful here. . . .

NATASHA: Yes. . . . I must be very much disheveled. (*In front of the mirror*) They say I have filled out. . . . And it isn't true! Not at all! And Masha's sleeping, exhausted . . . poor thing. . . . (*To* ANFISA, *coldly*) In my presence, don't you dare sit down! Get up! Get out of here! (ANFISA *goes out; a pause*) Why you keep this old woman I don't understand!

OLGA: (*Taken aback*) Excuse me, I don't understand either. . . .

NATASHA: For no reason at all she's here. She is a peasant, she should live in the country. . . . What a lot of pampering! I like in a house to have order. Useless people shouldn't be in a house. (*Stroking* OLGA'S *cheek*) Poor dear, you are tired! Our headmistress is tired. And when my Sofotchka grows up and enters high school, I shall be afraid of you.

OLGA: I shan't be the headmistress.

NATASHA: You will be elected, Olitchka, that's decided.

OLGA: I'll decline it. I can't, I've not the strength for it. (*Drinking some water*) You were so rude just now to Nurse. . . . Forgive me, I'm not in any condition to bear . . . It's getting all black before my eyes. . . .

NATASHA: (*Disturbed*) Forgive me, Olya, forgive me. . . . I didn't mean to distress you.

(MASHA *gets up, takes a pillow and goes out, angrily.*)

OLGA: Understand, my dear . . . perhaps we were brought up strangely, but I can't bear it. That kind of attitude depresses me, I get sick. . . . I'm just sick at heart!

NATASHA: Forgive me, forgive me. . . . (*Kissing her*)

OLGA: Every rudeness, even the slightest, even a word indelicately spoken, upsets me. . . .

NATASHA: I often talk too much, it's true, but you must agree, my dear, she might very well have lived in the country.

OLGA: She's been these thirty years with us.

NATASHA: But now, though, she can't do anything. It's either that I don't understand or else you don't want to understand me. She is not up to doing any sort of work, she just sleeps and sits.

OLGA: But let her sit.

NATASHA: (*Surprised*) How let her sit? She's a servant nevertheless. (*Tearfully*) I don't understand you, Olya. I have a nurse, have a wet nurse, we have a maid, a cook. . . . What do we have that old woman too for? What for?

(*Behind the scene the fire-alarm rings.*)

OLGA: I have aged ten years in this one night!

NATASHA: We must come to some sort of understanding, Olya. You are at high school, I'm at home; you have the teaching, I have the housekeeping. And if I say anything about the servants, I know what I'm saying. I know what I'm saying. . . . And by tomorrow there won't be this old thief here, this old hag. (*Stamping her foot*) This witch . . . Don't dare cross me! Don't you dare! (*Catching herself*) Really, if you don't move downstairs, we'll always be quarreling. It's terrible.

(KULYGIN *enters.*)

KULYGIN: Where is Masha? It's quite time to go home. The fire, they say, is subsiding. (*Stretching*) Burnt just one section of the town, in spite of the fact that there was a wind; at first it looked as if the whole town was on fire. (*Sitting down*) I'm tired out, Olitchka, my dear. . . . I often think if there hadn't been Masha, I'd have married you, Olitchka. You are so good. . . . I'm exhausted. (*Listening for something.*)

OLGA: What is it?

KULYGIN: As if on purpose, the doctor is drunk, he's terribly drunk. As if on purpose! (*Getting up*) There he is coming here, I imagine . . . Do you hear? Yes, coming . . . (*Laughing*) What a fellow, really . . . I'll hide. (*Going to the cupboard and standing in the corner*) Such a rascal!

OLGA: For two years he hasn't been drinking and here all of a sudden he's gone and got drunk. (*Following* NATASHA *to the back of the room.*)

(TCHEBUTYKIN *enters; without staggering, as if he were sober, he walks across the room, stops, looks around, then goes to the washstand and begins to wash his hands.*)

TCHEBUTYKIN: (*Crossly*) The Devil take all of 'em, take—They think I'm a doctor, know how to cure any sickness, but I know absolutely nothing, I've forgotten everything I ever knew, remember nothing, absolutely nothing. (OLGA *and* NATASHA *go out, unnoticed by him*) The Devil take it! Last Wednesday, I treated a woman at Zasip—she died, and I'm to blame for her dying. Yes . . . I knew a little something twenty-five years ago, but now I don't remember anything. Nothing. Perhaps I'm not even a man, but only give the appearance here of having hands and legs and a head; perhaps I don't even exist, and it only seems to me that I walk and eat and sleep. (*Crying*) Oh, that I didn't exist! (*No longer crying, crossly*)

The Devil knows . . . ! Three days ago there was a conversation at the club, they were talking about Shakespeare, Voltaire . . . I hadn't read them, hadn't read them at all, but I looked as if I had read them. And the others did too, just as I did. The banality of it! The meanness! And that woman I killed Wednesday came back to me . . . And everything came back to me, and it weighed on my soul, crooked, foul, disgusting . . . I went and got drunk. . . .

(IRINA, VERSHININ *and* TUSENBACH *enter;* TUSENBACH *wears civilian clothes, new and stylish.*)

IRINA: Let's sit here. Nobody's coming here.

VERSHININ: If it were not for the soldiers, the whole town would be burnt up. Brave boys! (*Rubbing his hands with pleasure*) Salt of the earth! Ah, what brave boys!

KULYGIN: What's the time, gentlemen?

TUSENBACH: Going on four by now. It's getting light.

IRINA: Everybody is sitting in the dining room, nobody is going out. And that Solyony of yours is sitting . . . (*To* TCHEBUTYKIN) Doctor, you should have gone to sleep.

TCHEBUTYKIN: Not at all . . . Thank you . . . (*Combing his beard.*)

KULYGIN: (*Laughing*) You got a little tipsy, Ivan Romanovich! (*Slapping him on the shoulder*) Bravo! *In vino veritas,* said the ancients.

TUSENBACH: They keep asking me to arrange a concert for the benefit of the refugees.

IRINA: Well, who is there to . . . ?

TUSENBACH: It could be arranged if we wanted to do it. Maria Sergeevna, in my opinion, plays the piano wonderfully.

KULYGIN: She does play wonderfully!

IRINA: She has forgotten how by now.

It's three years since she's played. . . . Or four.

TUSENBACH: Here in this town absolutely nobody understands music, not one soul; but I, I do understand it, and on my word of honor, I assure you that Maria Sergeevna plays magnificently, almost with genius.

KULYGIN: You are right, Baron. I love her very much, I love my Masha. She's sweet.

TUSENBACH: Think of being able to play so splendidly and at the same time know quite well that nobody, nobody, understands you!

KULYGIN: (*Sighing*) Yes. . . . But is it proper for her to take part in a concert? (*A pause*) Really, gentlemen, I don't know anything about that. Perhaps it would be a good thing. I must admit our director is a fine man, in fact, very fine, of the brainiest; but he has such views that . . . Of course, it's not his affair, but just the same, if you like, I might talk with him.

(TCHEBUTYKIN *is taking up a china clock in both hands and examining it.*)

VERSHININ: I got all covered with dirt at the fire—I'm not presentable. (*A pause*) Yesterday I heard in passing that they might transfer our brigade somewhere far away. Some say to the Kingdom of Poland, others—that it looks like Chita.

TUSENBACH: I heard that too. And so what? The town will be completely empty then.

IRINA: And we shall go away!

TCHEBUTYKIN: (*He drops the clock, shattering it.*) All to pieces!

(*A pause; everyone is distressed and embarrassed.*)

KULYGIN: (*Picks up the pieces*) To break such a precious thing—Oh, Ivan Romanovich, Ivan Romanovich! Minus zero to you for conduct.

IRINA: That clock was our dear mother's.

TCHEBUTYKIN: Perhaps . . . Mother's, then, mother's. Perhaps I didn't break it but only seemed to break it. Perhaps it only seems to us that we exist, and we don't really. I don't know anything, nobody knows anything. (*By the door*) What are you looking at? Natasha has an affair with Protopopov, and you don't see it. . . . There you sit and see nothing, and Natasha has an affair with Protopopov. . . . (*Singing*) How do you like swallowing that dose . . . ? (*He goes out.*)

VERSHININ: Yes. . . . (*Laughing*) How strange all this is at bottom! (*A pause*) When the fire began, I ran home fast; got there, looked . . . our house was unharmed and out of danger, but my two girls stood at the door in nothing but their underclothes, the mother wasn't there, people were scurrying about, horses running around, and dogs, and on my girls' faces was all that anxiety, terror, entreaty, who knows what; my heart was wrung when I saw those faces. My God, I thought, what more will these girls have to go through, in a long life! I grabbed them, ran and kept thinking one thing: What more will they have to live through in this world! (*Fire-alarm; a pause*) I came this way and the mother was here, shouting, angry.

(MASHA *enters with a pillow and sits down on the sofa.*)

VERSHININ: And while my girls were standing at the door in nothing but their underclothes and the street was red with the fire, the noise was terrible, I reflected that something like that used to happen when the enemy made a sudden raid, plundering and burning as they went. Meanwhile what a difference there is essentially between what is and what was! And a little more time will pass, some two or three hundred years, and they will look on this life of ours now with fear and derision, everything now will seem then to be all angles and heavy and most inconvenient and strange. Oh, what a life that will be, what a life! (*Laughing*) Forgive me, I'm philosophizing again. Allow me to continue, ladies and gentlemen. I'd like awfully to philosophize, now that I'm in such a mood for it. (*A pause*) It's as if everybody were asleep. And so I say: What a life it will be! You can just imagine. . . . Here in town there are only three of your kind now, but in coming generations there will be more, always more and more; a time will come when everything will veer to you, they will live like you, and then, too, later on you'll get antiquated, there'll be people springing up who are better than you. . . . (*Laughing*) I am in a most singular mood today. I want like the devil to live. . . . (*Singing*) Unto love all ages bow, its pangs are blest. . . .

MASHA: Tram-tum-tum. . . .

VERSHININ: Tum-tum . . .

MASHA: Tra-ra-ra?

VERSHININ: Tra-ta-ta. (*Laughing.*)

(FEDOTIK *enters.*)

FEDOTIK: (*Dancing*) Burnt out, burnt out! Absolutely everything!

(*Laughter.*)

IRINA: What sort of a joke is that? Is it all gone?

FEDOTIK: (*Laughing*) Absolutely everything. There's nothing left. And the guitar burned, and the photography outfit burned, and all my letters. . . . And I wanted to present you with a notebook . . . it burned up too.

(SOLYONY *enters.*)

IRINA: No. Please go away, Vasili Vasilievich. You can't come in here.

SOLYONY: But why is it the Baron can and I can't?

VERSHININ: We must go, really. How's the fire?

SOLYONY: They say it's subsiding. No, it's decidedly strange to me, why is it the Baron can and I can't? (*Taking out the perfume bottle and sprinkling himself.*)

VERSHININ: Tram-tum-tum.

MASHA: Tram-tum.

VERSHININ: (*Laughing, to* SOLYONY) Let's go to the dining room.

SOLYONY: Very well, I'll make a note of it so. This thought could be made more clear, but 'twould annoy the geese, I fear. . . . (*Looking at* TUSENBACH) Chick, chick, chick. . . . (*He goes out with* VERSHININ *and* FEDOTIK.)

IRINA: How that Solyony has smoked things up. (*With surprise*) The Baron is asleep! Baron! Baron!

TUSENBACH: (*Waking up*) I'm tired, however. . . . The brickyard. . . . I'm not saying this in my sleep, for it's a fact that I'll soon be going to the brickyard to start work. . . . It's already been discussed. (*To* IRINA, *tenderly*) You are so pale, beautiful, bewitching. . . . It seems to me your paleness brightens the dark air like light. . . . You are sad, you are not satisfied with life. . . . Oh, come along with me, let's go to work together!

MASHA: Nikolai Lvovich, do go on out of here!

TUSENBACH: (*Laughing*) You here? I didn't see you. (*Kissing* IRINA's *hand*) Good-by, I'm going. . . . I'm looking at you now and am reminded of how long ago once on your saint's day you were all so gay and happy, talking of the joy of work. . . . And what a happy life I dreamed of then! Where is it? (*Kissing her hand*) You have tears in your eyes. Go to bed. . . . It's getting light now . . . morning has begun. . . . If only it were granted me to give my life for you!

MASHA: Nikolai Lvovich, go on! Why, really, what . . .

TUSENBACH: I'm going. . . . (*He goes out.*)

MASHA: (*Lying down*) Are you asleep, Fyodor?

KULYGIN: Eh?

MASHA: You ought to go home.

KULYGIN: My darling Masha, my dear Masha. . . .

IRINA: She's tired. . . . You ought to let her rest, Fedya.

KULYGIN: I'm going right away. . . . My good wife, darling . . . I love you, my one and only. . . .

MASHA: (*Bored and cross*) Amo, amas, amat, amamus, amatis, amant.

KULYGIN: (*Laughing*) No, really, she's amazing. I've been married to you for seven years; but it seems as if we'd married only yesterday. Word of honor! No, really, you are an amazing woman. I am content, I am content, I am content!

MASHA: Bored, bored, bored. . . . (*She sits up, and speaks sitting*) It just won't go out of my head. . . . It's simply shocking. It's there like a nail in my head. I can't stay silent. I mean about Andrei. . . . He's mortgaged this house to the bank and his wife grabbed all the money, but the house belongs not just to him, but to the four of us! He ought to know that if he's a decent man.

KULYGIN: What do you care, Masha! Why should you? Andrusha is in debt all round, well, God reward him!

MASHA: Anyhow it's shocking. (*She lies back down.*)

KULYGIN: You and I are not poor. I work, I go to the high school, and then give private lessons. . . . I'm an honest man. Simple. . . . *Omnia mea mecum porto,* as they say.

MASHA: I don't need anything. But injustice makes me furious. (*A pause*) Go on, Fyodor!

KULYGIN: (*Kissing her*) You are tired,

rest about half an hour, and I'll sit and wait out there. Sleep. . . . (*Going*) I am content, I am content, I am content. (*He goes out.*)

IRINA: How small our Andrei has grown, how he has dried up and aged beside that woman! There was a time when he was preparing for a professorship, and yesterday he was bragging that at last he could become a member of the District Board. He a member of the board and Protopopov chairman. . . . The whole town's talking, is laughing, and he's the only one who knows nothing and sees nothing. And now, everybody has rushed off to the fire, but he sits there in his room and pays not the least attention to it. He just plays the violin. (*Nervously*) Oh, it's awful, awful, awful! (*Crying*) I can't, I can't bear any more! . . . I can't— I can't!

(OLGA *enters. She tidies up her dressing table.*)

IRINA: (*Sobbing aloud*) Cast me out, cast me out, I can't stand any more! . . .

OLGA: (*Alarmed*) What is it, what is it? Darling!

IRINA: (*Sobbing*) Where? Where is it all gone? Where is it? Oh, my God, my God! I've forgotten everything, I've forgotten . . . it's muddled in my head. . . . I don't remember what in Italian *window* is, or the ceiling there. . . . I'm forgetting everything, every day forgetting, and life slips away and will never return, never, we'll never go to Moscow. . . . I can see we'll never go.

OLGA: Darling, darling. . . .

IRINA: (*Restraining herself*) Oh, I'm miserable. . . . I can't work and won't work. I'm sick of it, sick of it! I was a telegraph operator, and now have a place with the Town Board, and hate and despise everything they give me to do. . . . I'm going on twenty-four and have already been working a long time, and my brain's drying up, I'm getting thin, losing my looks, getting old, and there's nothing, nothing—no satisfaction of any kind— and time is passing, and it all seems to be moving away from any real, beautiful life, all moving away farther and farther into some abyss. . . . I'm in despair, and how I'm alive, how it is I haven't killed myself, I can't understand. . . .

OLGA: Don't cry, my own little girl, don't cry. . . .

IRINA: I am not crying, not crying. . . . I'm sick of it. . . . Now look—I am not crying any more. I'm sick of it. . . . I'm sick of it!

OLGA: Darling, I'm telling you as a sister, as a friend, if you want my advice, marry the Baron!

(IRINA *weeps silently.*)

OLGA: Why, you respect him, you value him highly. It's true he's not good-looking, but he's so decent and clean. . . . Why, one doesn't marry for love but to do one's duty. At least, I think so, and I would marry without being in love. At any rate I'd marry anyone who proposed to me so long as he was an honorable man. I'd marry even an old man. . . .

IRINA: I kept expecting us to move to Moscow; there I'd meet my real beloved, I dreamed of him, loved him. But it turned out just foolishness, just foolishness! . . .

OLGA: (*Embracing her sister*) My dear, lovely sister, I understand it all; when Baron Nikolai Lvovich left the military service and came to see us in civilian clothes, he seemed to me so homely that I even cried. He asked, "Why are you crying?" How could I tell him! But if God should grant he married you, I'd be happy. Now, that's different, quite different!

(NATASHA *crosses the stage from the right door to the left, without speaking, a candle in her hand.*)

MASHA: (*Sitting up*) She walks as if she had been the one to start the fire.

OLGA: Masha, you are silly! The silliest one in our family is you. Forgive me, please.

(*A pause.*)

MASHA: I want to confess, my dear sisters. I'm tired in my soul. I'll confess to you and then to nobody else, never. . . . I'll say it this minute. (*Quietly*) It's my secret, but you must know everything. . . . I can't be silent. . . . (*A pause*) I love, love . . . I love that man. . . . You just saw him. . . . Well, there it is. In one word, I love Vershinin. . . .

OLGA: (*Going behind her screen*) Stop that. At any rate I'm not hearing.

MASHA: What is there to do about it? (*Clutching her head*) At first he seemed to me strange, then I felt sorry for him. . . . Then I began to love him . . . began to love him with his voice, his words, his misfortunes, his two girls. . . .

OLGA: (*Behind the screen*) I'm not hearing you at any rate. Whatever silly things you say, at any rate I'm not hearing you!

MASHA: Oh, Olya, you are silly. I love —such, that is to say, is my fate. That is to say my lot is such. . . . And he loves me. . . . All that is frightening. Yes? Is it wrong? (*Taking* IRINA *by the hand and drawing her to her*) Oh, my darling . . . how are we going to live our life, what's to become of us? . . . When one reads some novel, all this seems old and all of it so understandable, but when you fall in love yourself, you begin to see that nobody knows anything and everybody must decide for himself. . . . My darlings, my sisters. . . . I confessed to you, now I'll be silent. . . . I'll be now like Gogol's madman . . . silence . . . silence. . . .

(ANDREI *enters, followed by* FERAPONT.)

ANDREI: (*Annoyed*) What do you want? I don't understand.

FERAPONT: (*Standing in the door, impatiently*) Andrei Sergeevich, I have already told you ten times.

ANDREI: First, I am not Andrei Sergeevich to you but Your Excellency!

FERAPONT: The firemen, Your Excellentness, ask your permission to go to the river through your garden. As it is, they are driving round and round—it's pure punishment.

ANDREI: Very well. Tell them, very well. (FERAPONT *goes out*) That's enough of them. Where's Olga? (OLGA *comes out from behind the screen*) I've come to ask you to give me the key to the cupboard. I've lost mine. You have one of the little keys. (OLGA *gives him the key without speaking.* IRINA *goes behind her screen; a pause*) And what a tremendous fire! It's starting to die down now. The devil take it, that Ferapont's made me lose my temper. I said a stupid thing to him. . . . Your Excellency. . . . (*A pause*) But why are you silent, Olya? (*A pause*) It's high time to stop this silliness and stop pouting for no reason at all. . . . You are here, Masha, Irina's here, well, that's fine—let's have it out once and for all. What have you got against me? Now what?

OLGA: Let it rest, Andrusha. Tomorrow we'll have it out. (*Anxiously*) What a night of torment!

ANDREI: (*He is very much confused*) Don't be upset. I ask you absolutely in cold blood: what have you got against me? Speak right out.

VERSHININ'S VOICE: Tram-tum-tum!

MASHA: (*Rising, in a loud voice*) Tra-ta-ta! (*To* OLGA) Good-by Olya, God be with you! (*She goes behind the screen, kisses* IRINA) Sleep well. . . . Good-by, Andrei. Go on away, they are tired. . . . Tomorrow you will have it out. (*She goes out.*)

OLGA: Indeed, Andrusha, let's put it

off till tomorrow. . . . (*She goes behind her screen*) It's time to go to sleep.

ANDREI: I'll just say it and go. Right away. . . . In the first place, you have something against Natasha, my wife, and that I have noticed from the very day of my wedding. Natasha is a splendid, honest person, straightforward, and honorable—in my opinion. I love and respect my wife, understand, I respect her and demand that others respect her too. I repeat, she is an honest, honorable person, and all your dissatisfactions, excuse me, are simply caprices. . . . (*A pause*) In the second place, you seem to be angry because of the fact that I am not a professor, don't occupy myself with learning. But I serve in the Zemstvo, I am a member of the District Board, and this service of mine I consider just as sacred and lofty as service to learning. I'm a member of the District Board and I'm proud of it, if you want to know. . . . (*A pause*) In the third place, I have something else to say . . . : I mortgaged the house without asking your permission. . . . Of that I am guilty, yes, and ask you to forgive me. I was forced to it by debts. . . . Thirty-five thousand. . . . I don't play cards any more, gave it up long ago, but the chief thing I can say in my own justification, is that you—girls, as of the privileged sex, you receive a pension, while I didn't have . . . my earnings, so to speak. . . . (*A pause.*)

KULYGIN: (*At the door*) Masha not here? (*Perturbed*) But where is she? That's strange. . . . (*He goes out.*)

ANDREI: They don't listen. Natasha is a superior, honest person. (*Walks up and down the stage in silence, then stops*) When I married, I thought we should be happy . . . everybody happy . . . but, my God . . . ! (*Crying*) My dear sisters, darling sisters, don't believe me, don't believe . . . (*He goes out.*)

KULYGIN: (*At the door, anxiously*) Where is Masha? Masha's not here? What an astonishing business! (*He goes out.*)

(*Fire-alarm; the stage is empty.*)

IRINA: (*Behind the screen*) Olya! Who is that knocking on the floor?

OLGA: It's the doctor, Ivan Romanovich. He's drunk.

IRINA: What a torn-up night! (*A pause*) Olya! (*Looking out from behind the screen*) Did you hear? They are taking the brigade from us, transferring it somewhere far away.

OLGA: That's only a rumor.

IRINA: We'll be left alone then. . . . Olya!

OLGA: Well?

IRINA: Darling, precious, I respect, I value the Baron, he's a marvelous person, I'll marry him, I consent, only let's go to Moscow! I beg you, let's go! There's nothing in the world better than Moscow! Let's go, Olya! Let's go!

Curtain

ACT FOUR

(*An old garden in front of the* PROZOROFFS' *house. A long alley of fir trees, at the end of which a river is seen. On the other side of the river, a wood. To the right a terrace of the house and on it a table with bottles and glasses; you can see they have just been drinking champagne. Twelve o'clock noon. Now and then on their way from the street to the river, people cross the garden; four or five soldiers pass that way, walking fast.* TCHEBUTYKIN, *in an amiable mood, which does not leave him during the entire Act, sits in an easy chair, in the garden, waiting to be called; he wears a military cap and carries a stick.* IRINA, KULYGIN *with a decoration around his neck, with no mustache, and* TUSENBACH, *are standing on the terrace, saying good-by to* FEDOTIK *and* RODAY, *who are going down the steps; both officers are in campaign uniform.*)

TUSENBACH: (*Exchanging kisses with* FEDOTIK) You are a good fellow, we lived like good friends. (*Exchanging kisses with* RODAY) Once again. . . . Good-by, my dear boy. . . .

IRINA: Till we meet again.

FEDOTIK: It's not meet again, but good-by, we shall never meet again.

KULYGIN: Who knows! (*Wiping his eyes, smiling*) There, I'm beginning to cry too.

IRINA: Some day we'll run across each other.

FEDOTIK: In ten or fifteen years maybe? But by then we'll scarcely know each other, we'll greet each other coldly. . . . (*Taking a snapshot*) Stand still. . . . Once more, for the last time.

RODAY: (*Embracing* TUSENBACH) We won't meet again. . . . (*Kissing* IRINA's *hand*) Thank you for everything, for everything!

FEDOTIK: (*Vexed*) Oh, wait a little!

TUSENBACH: God grant we meet. Write us though. Without fail write.

RODAY: (*Casting a glance around the garden*) Good-by, trees! (*Shouting*) Yoo hoo! (*A pause*) Good-by, echo!

KULYGIN: I am afraid you'll marry there in Poland. . . . The Polish wife will embrace you and say: *"Kochany!"* (*Laughing*).

FEDOTIK: (*Looking at his watch*): There's less than an hour left. Out of our battery only Solyony is going on the barge, we are with the rank and file. Three battery divisions are going today, tomorrow three more—and quiet and peace will reign in the town. . . .

TUSENBACH: And terrible boredom.

RODAY: And where is Maria Sergeevna?

KULYGIN: Masha is in the garden.

FEDOTIK: We must say good-by to her.

RODAY: Good-by, I must go or I'll be crying. . . . (*He hurriedly embraces* TUSENBACH *and* KULYGIN, *kisses* IRINA's *hand*) It was fine living here.

FEDOTIK: (*To* KULYGIN) This is a memento for you. . . . A notebook with a pencil. . . . We'll go this way to the river. . . . (*They move off, both look back.*)

RODAY: (*Shouts*) Yoo hoo!

KULYGIN: (*Shouts*) Good-by!

(*At the rear of the stage* FEDOTIK *and* RODAY *meet* MASHA *and bid her good-by. She walks away with them.*)

IRINA: They are gone. . . . (*Sitting down on the bottom step of the terrace.*)

TCHEBUTYKIN: And forgot to say good-by to me.

IRINA: And what about you?

TCHEBUTYKIN: And I forgot too somehow. Anyway I'll soon see them, I'm leaving tomorrow. Yes. . . . One more short day is left. In a year they will retire me, I'll come back here and live out my little span near you. Just one short year is left before my pension. (*He puts one newspaper in his pocket and takes out another*) I'll come here to you and change my life from the very roots. I'll become so quiet, right—right-minded, respectable.

IRINA: And you really should change your life, dovey. You should somehow.

TCHEBUTYKIN: Yes, I feel so. (*Singing softly*) Ta-ra-ra-boom-de-aye. . . . Sit on a curb I may. . . .

KULYGIN: You're incorrigible, Ivan Romanovich! You're incorrigible!

TCHEBUTYKIN: Now then, if you'd only teach me! Then I'd be reformed.

IRINA: Fyodor has shaved off his mustache. I can't bear to look at him.

KULYGIN: Why not?

TCHEBUTYKIN: I could say what your physiognomy looks like now, but I can't.

KULYGIN: Well! It's the accepted thing, it is *modus vivendi*. Our director shaved off his mustache, and as soon as I became inspector, I shaved clean too. Nobody likes it, but that's all the same to me. I am content. I may be with a mustache, or without a mustache, but I'm equally content. . . . (*Sitting down.*)

(*At the rear of the stage* ANDREI *passes, wheeling a baby-carriage with a child asleep in it.*)

IRINA: Ivan Romanovich, my own darling, I am terribly disturbed. You were on the boulevard yesterday, tell me what happened there?

TCHEBUTYKIN: What happened? Nothing. Fiddlesticks. (*Reading the newspaper*) All the same!

KULYGIN: What they are saying is that Solyony and the Baron met yesterday on the boulevard near the theatre. . . .

TUSENBACH: Stop it! Well, what really. . . . (*With a wave of his hand he goes into the house.*)

KULYGIN: Near the theatre . . . Solyony began picking on the Baron, and he wouldn't tolerate it, he said something insulting. . . .

TCHEBUTYKIN: I don't know. It's all nonsense.

KULYGIN: In a certain theological seminary a teacher wrote on a composition paper, "Nonsense" and the pupil read "consensus"—thought it was written in Latin. (*Laughing*) Amazingly funny. It's said that Solyony is in love with Irina, and that he's begun to hate the Baron. . . . That's understandable. Irina is a very nice girl. She even resembles Masha, just as thoughtful. It's merely that you have a gentle character, Irina. Though Masha, too, has a very fine character. I love her, my Masha.

(*At the rear of the garden offstage:* "Yoo, hoo!")

IRINA: (*Shivering*) Somehow everything frightens me today. (*A pause*) I have everything all ready, after dinner I'm sending off my things. The Baron and I are getting married tomorrow, and tomorrow we are leaving for the brickyard, and day after tomorrow I'll be at the school, a new life is beginning. Somehow God will help me! When I passed my teacher's examination I cried for pure joy . . . so happy. (*A pause*) The cart will soon be here for my things. . . .

KULYGIN: That's all very well, only somehow it's not serious. Just ideas—and very little seriousness. However, I wish you luck with all my heart.

TCHEBUTYKIN: (*Tenderly*) My darling, my dear child. . . . My treasure. . . . You have gone far away. I can't catch up with you. I'm left behind, like a bird of passage that has grown old, that can't fly. Fly on, my dears, fly on and God be with you! (*A pause*) It's too bad, Fyodor Ilyich, you shaved off your mustache.

KULYGIN: That'll do from you! (*Sighing*) Well, today the officers are leaving and everything will go on again as of old. Whatever they may say, Masha is a good, honest woman and I love her very much and I am thankful for my fate. People's fate differs. . . . In the excise office here a certain Kozyroff works. He went to school with me, was expelled from the fifth class at high school because he just couldn't understand *ut consecutivum*. Now he is terribly poor, ill, and when we meet I say to him: "Greetings, *ut consecutivum!*" Yes, he says, that's it, *consecutivum* . . . and then coughs. . . . And here I am, all my life I've been successful, I am happy, I have the Order of Stanislav, Second Degree, and am teach-

ing others myself now that *ut consecutivum.* Of course, I am a clever man,
cleverer than many others, but happiness
doesn't consist in that. . . .

(*In the house they are playing "The
Maiden's Prayer" on the piano.*)

IRINA: And tomorrow evening I won't
be hearing that "Maiden's Prayer" any
more, and won't be meeting Protopopov.
. . . (*A pause*) And Protopopov is sitting
there in the drawing room now; he came
again today. . . .

KULYGIN: The headmistress has not
come yet?

IRINA: No. They have sent for her. If
only you knew how hard it is for me to
live here alone, without Olya. . . . She
lives at the high school; she's the headmistress, busy all day long with her duties,
and I'm alone, I am bored with nothing
to do, and the very room I live in is hateful. . . . So I have made up my mind:
If it isn't my lot to be in Moscow, then
let it be so. That's my lot. There's nothing
to be done. All is God's will, that's the
truth. Nikolai Lvovich proposed to me.
. . . Well, then? I thought it over and
made up my mind. He is a good man, it
is really amazing how good. . . . And
suddenly as if wings had grown on my
soul, I grew happier, relieved, and felt
once more the desire for work, work. . . .
Except that something happened yesterday,
there's something hidden that's hanging
over me. . . .

TCHEBUTYKIN: Consensus. Nonsense.

NATASHA: (*At the window*) The head
mistress!

KULYGIN: The headmistress has arrived.
Let's go. (*He goes with* IRINA *into the
house.*)

TCHEBUTYKIN: (*Reading the newspaper,
softly singing to himself*) Ta-ra-ra-boom-
de-aye. . . . Sit on the curb I may. . . .
(MASHA *approaches; in the background*
ANDREI *is seen pushing the baby-carriage.*)

MASHA: There he sits, all settled. . . .

TCHEBUTYKIN: And what?

MASHA: (*Sitting down*) Nothing. . . .
(*A pause*) Did you love my mother?

TCHEBUTYKIN: Very much.

MASHA: And did she love you?

TCHEBUTYKIN: (*After a pause*) That I
no longer remember.

MASHA: Is "mine" here? Our cook
Marfa used to talk about her policeman
like that: mine. Is "mine" here?

TCHEBUTYKIN: Not yet.

MASHA: When you get happiness in
snatches, in bits, and you lose it, like me,
then little by little you harden, you grow
bitter. (*Pointing to her breast*) Right here
I'm boiling. . . . (*Looking at her brother*
ANDREI *pushing the baby-carriage*) There's
Andrei, our little brother. . . . All our
hopes gone. . . . Once upon a time thousands of people were hoisting a bell, a
lot of effort and money were spent, and
then suddenly it fell and broke. Suddenly
for neither one reason nor another. The
same with Andrei.

ANDREI: And when will they finally
quiet down in the house? Such noise!

TCHEBUTYKIN: Soon. (*Looking at his
watch*) I have a very old watch, with
chimes. . . . (*Winding the watch; it
chimes*) The first, second, and fifth bat-
teries are going at one o'clock sharp. (*A
pause*) And I tomorrow.

ANDREI: For good?

TCHEBUTYKIN: I don't know. I might
return in a year. Though the devil knows
. . . it's all the same. . . .

(*Somewhere far off a harp and violin are
playing.*)

ANDREI: The town will be dead. As if
they had covered it with a cowl. (*A
pause*) Something happened yesterday
near the theatre; everybody is talking
about it, but I don't know what it was.

TCHEBUTYKIN: Nothing. Nonsense.

Solyony began to pick on the Baron and he lost his temper and insulted him, and it got finally to the point where Solyony had to challenge him to a duel. (*Looks at his watch*) It's time now, I believe. At half-past twelve, in the State forest there, the one we see from here, beyond the river. . . . Piff—paff. (*Laughing*) Solyony imagines he is Lermontov and even writes verses. Now jokes are jokes, but it is the third duel for him

MASHA: For whom?

TCHEBUTYKIN: For Solyony.

MASHA: And for the Baron?

TCHEBUTYKIN: What for the Baron?

(*A pause.*)

MASHA: I'm all confused in the head. All the same, I say it shouldn't be allowed. He might wound the Baron or even kill him.

TCHEBUTYKIN: The Baron is a good man but one baron more, one less— isn't it all the same? Let them! All the same! (*Beyond the garden there are shouts:* "Yoo hoo." *Answering the shout*) You can wait. (*To* MASHA) That's Skvortzoff shouting, the second. He's sitting in a boat.

(*A pause*)

ANDREI: To my mind either to engage in a duel or to be present at one even in the capacity of doctor, is simply immoral.

TCHEBUTYKIN: That only seems so. . . . We are not here, there is nothing in the world, we don't exist, but it only seems that we exist. . . . And isn't it all the same!

MASHA: Just like that . . . all day long they talk, talk. . . . (*Going*) To live in such a climate, be afraid it will snow any minute, and still to have these conversations—(*Stopping*) I'm not going into the house, I can't. . . . When Vershinin comes let me know—(*She goes down the alley*) And the birds of passage are flying

already. . . . (*Looking up*) Swans or geese. . . . My dear ones, my happy ones—! (*She goes out.*)

ANDREI: Our house will be empty. The officers will go, you will go, my sister will be married, and I'll be left alone in the house.

TCHEBUTYKIN: And your wife?

(FERAPONT *enters with some papers.*)

ANDREI: A wife is a wife. She is honest, decent, well—kind, but along with all that there's something in her that reduces her to the level of some sort of petty, blind, coarse animal. In any case, she's not a human being. I say this to you as to a friend, the only man I can open my soul to. I love Natasha, it's true, but at times she seems to me amazingly vulgar, and then I lose my wits, I don't understand, what for or why, I love her so or, at least, did love. . . .

TCHEBUTYKIN: (*Getting up*) Brother, I'm going away tomorrow, we may never see each other again, so here is my advice to you. You know, put on your hat, take a walking-stick in your hands and be off— Be off, and go, go without looking back. And the farther you get the better.

(SOLYONY *walks by at the rear of the stage with two officers; seeing* TCHEBUTYKIN *he turns toward him; the officers walk on.*)

SOLYONY: Doctor, it's time. Half-past twelve. (*Greeting* ANDREI.)

TCHEBUTYKIN: Directly. I've had enough of you all. (*To* ANDREI) If anybody asks for me, Andrusha, say that I —directly . . . (*Sighing*) Oho-ho-ho—

SOLYONY: (*Starting off with* TCHEBUTYKIN) Quick as a flash the bear made a dash—Why are you grunting, old man?

TCHEBUTYKIN: Get out!

SOLYONY: How's your health?

TCHEBUTYKIN: (*Angrily*) Smooth as butter.

SOLYONY: The old man is needlessly upset. I'll indulge myself a little, I'll only wing him like a snipe. (*Takes out the perfume and sprinkles it on his hands*) There, I've poured a whole bottle out today and they still smell. My hands smell of a corpse. (*A pause*) So . . . Do you remember the poem? "And, rebellious, he seeks the storm, as if in storms were peace." . . .

TCHEBUTYKIN: Yes. Quick as a flash, the bear made a dash! (*He goes out with* SOLYONY.)

(*Shouts are heard:* "Yoo hoo!" ANDREI *and* FERAPONT *enter.*)

FERAPONT: The papers to sign. . . .

ANDREI: (*Nervously*) Leave me alone! Leave me! I beg of you! (*He walks away with the baby-carriage.*)

FERAPONT: But that's what papers are for, so they can be signed. (*He goes to the rear of the stage.*)

(*Enter* IRINA *and* TUSENBACH, TUSENBACH *in a straw hat,* KULYGIN *crosses the stage, calling* "Ah-oo, Masha, Ah-oo.")

TUSENBACH: That seems to be the only man in town who's glad the officers are leaving.

IRINA: That's understandable. (*A pause*) Our town will be empty now.

TUSENBACH: Dear, I'll come right back.

IRINA: Where are you going?

TUSENBACH: I have to go to town, then . . . to see my comrades off.

IRINA: It's not true. . . . Nikolai, why are you so distraught today? (*A pause*) What happened yesterday near the theatre?

TUSENBACH: (*With an impatient gesture*) In an hour I'll be back and will be with you again. (*Kissing her hand*) My beloved. . . . (*Looking into her face*) It's five years now I've loved you, and somehow I can't get used to it, and you seem always more beautiful to me. What lovely, wonderful hair! What eyes! I'll take you away tomorrow, we will work, we'll be rich, my dreams will come true. You shall be happy. Only there is one thing, one thing: You don't love me.

IRINA: That's not in my power! I'll be your wife, faithful and obedient, but it's not love, what is there to do! (*Crying*) I have never been in love—not once in my life. Oh, I've dreamed so of love, I've dreamed of it a long time now, day and night, but my soul is like some fine piano that's locked and the key is lost. (*A pause*) You have a restless look.

TUSENBACH: I haven't slept all night. There is nothing in my life so terrible that it could frighten me, and only that lost key tortures my soul—won't let me sleep. Say something to me. (*A pause*) Say something to me. . . .

IRINA: What? What shall I say? What?

TUSENBACH: Something.

IRINA: That's enough! That's enough!

(*A pause.*)

TUSENBACH: What nothings sometimes in life, what foolish trifles will take on meaning suddenly, for no reason at all. You laugh at them as you've always done, you consider them nothings, and yet you go on and feel that you haven't the strength to stop. Oh, let's not talk about that! I feel gay. I see these firs, maples, birches now as if I were seeing them for the first time and they are all looking at me curiously and waiting. What beautiful trees and what a beautiful life there should be under them! (*A shout:* "Yoo hoo!") I must go. It's time. . . . There's a tree that's dead, but it still waves with the others in the wind. So it seems to me even if I die, I'll still share in life somehow or other. Good-by, my dearest. . . . (*Kissing her hands*) The papers you gave me are lying on my table, under the calendar.

IRINA: But I'm going with you.

TUSENBACH: (*Alarmed*) No, no! (*Going quickly, stopping in the alley*) Irina!

IRINA: What?

TUSENBACH: (*Not knowing what to say*) I didn't drink any coffee today. Tell them, so that they'll make me some. . . . (*He goes quickly out.*)

(IRINA *stands thinking, then goes to the rear of the stage and sits down in the swing.* ANDREI *comes in with the baby-carriage;* FERAPONT *appears.*)

FERAPONT: But Andrei Sergeevich, the papers aren't mine, they are official. I didn't think them up.

ANDREI: Oh, where is it, where is gone my past, when I was young and gay and clever, when my dreams and thoughts were full of grace, and the present and future bright with hope? Why is it that when we have barely begun to live we grow dull, gray, uninteresting, lazy, indifferent, useless, unhappy. . . . Our town has been in existence now for two hundred years, a hundred thousand people living in it, and there's not one who's not just like the others, not one that's outstanding either in the past or in the present, not one scholar, not one artist, not one who's even faintly remarkable, and would arouse envy or any passionate desire to imitate him. They just eat, drink, sleep, and then die. . . . Others are born and they, too, eat, drink, sleep and to keep from sinking into the torpor of boredom, vary their lives with foul gossip, vodka, cards, chicanery, and the wives deceive the husbands, while the husbands lie, pretend not to see anything, hear anything, and an unavoidably banal influence weighs on the children, and the divine spark dies in them and they become just as pitiful, identical corpses as their fathers and mothers were. . . . (*To* FERAPONT, *crossly*) What do you want?

FERAPONT: Hey? Papers to sign.

ANDREI: I've had enough of you.

FERAPONT: (*Handing over the paper*) Just now the doorman from the State Chamber was saying . . . It appears he says, this winter in Petersburg there was a frost of two hundred degrees.

ANDREI: The present is hateful, but on the other hand, when I think of the future —Oh, how good it is! I begin to feel so easy, so free; and in the distance a light dawns, I see freedom, I see how my children and I are freed from idleness, from kvass, from goose with cabbage, from naps after dinner, from despicable sloth. . . .

FERAPONT: Two thousand people were frozen, it appears. The people, they say, were horrified. It was either in Petersburg, or it was in Moscow, I can't remember.

ANDREI: (*Seized with a tender feeling*) My dear sisters, my wonderful sisters (*Tearfully*) Masha, my sister. . . .

NATASHA: (*In the window*) Who is it talking so loud out here? Is it you, Andrusha? You will wake up Sofie. *Il ne faut pas faire du bruit, la Sofie est dormie déjà. Vous êtes un ours.* (*Getting angry*) If you want to talk, give the carriage and child to somebody else. Ferapont, take the carriage from your master.

FERAPONT: Yes, ma'am. (*He takes the carriage.*)

ANDREI: (*Embarrassed*) I'm speaking low.

NATASHA: (*Behind the window, caressing her child*) Bobik! Mischievous Bobik! Naughty Bobik!

ANDREI: (*Glancing through the papers*) Very well, I'll look through them and sign what's necessary, and you can take them back to the Board. . . . (*He goes into the house, reading the papers;* FERAPONT *pushes the baby-carriage toward the rear of the garden.*)

NATASHA: (*Behind the window*) Bobik, what is your Mama's name? Darling, darling! And who is this? This is Aunt Olya. Say to Auntie: "How do you do, Olya!"

(*Some wandering musicians, a man and a girl, begin to play a violin and a harp;* VERSHININ, OLGA *and* ANFISA *emerge from the house, and listen quietly for a moment.* IRINA *joins them.*)

OLGA: Our garden's like a lot opening into several streets, they walk and drive through it. Nurse, give these musicians something!

ANFISA: (*Giving money to the musicians*) Good-by, my dear souls! (*The musicians bow and go away*) Hard lives they have! When you're full you don't play. (*To* IRINA) Good morning, Irisha! (*Kissing her*) M-m-m-m, child, how I live! How I live! At the high school in a Government apartment, with Olyushka—God has granted me that for my old age. Not since I was born, sinner that I am, have I lived so. . . . A large apartment, the Government's, and a whole room for me and a little bed. All the Government's. I wake up in the night and—Oh Lord, Mother of God, there's nobody happier than I am.

VERSHININ: (*Looking at his watch*) We are going now, Olga Sergeevna. It's time. (*A pause*) I wish you everything, everything. . . . Where's Maria Sergeevna?

IRINA: She's somewhere in the garden. I'll go look for her.

VERSHININ: Kindly, I'm in a hurry.

ANFISA: I'll go, too, and look for her. (*Calling*) Mashenka. Ah, oo-oo! (*Going away with* IRINA *to the rear of the garden*) Ah, oo-oo! Ah, oo-oo!

VERSHININ: Everything has its end. And here we are parting. (*Looking at his watch*) The town gave our company a sort of lunch, we drank champagne, the Mayor made a speech, I ate and listened, but in my heart I was here with you all—

(*Looking around the garden*) I've grown used to you. . . .

OLGA: Are we ever to see each other again?

VERSHININ: Most likely not. (*A pause*) My wife and my two girls are leaving here in about two months; please, if anything happens, if anything is needed. . . .

OLGA: Yes, yes, of course. Be sure of that. (*A pause*) By tomorrow there won't be an officer in town; it will all be a memory and for us, of course, a new life will begin. . . . (*A pause*) Everything turns out not as we'd like to have it. I didn't want to be a headmistress and yet I became one. Which means we are not to be in Moscow.

VERSHININ: Well. . . . Thank you for everything. Forgive me, if anything was not quite. . . . Much, much too much, I've talked—forgive me for that, too, don't bear me any grudge.

OLGA: (*Wiping her eyes*) Now why doesn't Masha come. . . .

VERSHININ: What else can I say to you as we part? What shall I philosophize about? . . . (*Laughing*) Life is difficult. It presents itself to many of us as blank and hopeless, and yet, one must admit, it gets always clearer and easier, and the day is not far off, apparently, when it will be wholly bright. (*Looking at his watch*) It's time for me to go, it's time! Once humanity was occupied with wars, filling its whole existence with marches, invasions, conquests, whereas now all of that is outlived, leaving behind it an enormous empty space which so far there is nothing to fill; humanity is searching passionately and, of course, will find it. Ah, if only it were quicker! (*A pause*) You know, if culture were added to industry and industry to culture. . . . (*Looking at his watch*) However, it's time for me. . . .

OLGA: There she comes.

(MASHA *enters.*)

VERSHININ: I came to say good-by. . . .

(OLGA *moves a little away so as not to disturb their farewell.*)

MASHA: (*Looking into his face*) Good-by. . . . (*A long kiss*)

OLGA: Now, now. . . .

(MASHA *sobs violently.*)

VERSHININ: Write to me. . . . Don't forget me! Let me go . . . it's time. . . . Olga Sergeevna, take her, I'm all ready—it's time . . . late— (*Deeply moved, he kisses* OLGA'S *hand, then embraces* MASHA *again and goes quickly out.*)

OLGA: There, Masha! Stop, darling! . . .

(KULYGIN *enters.*)

KULYGIN: (*Embarrassed*) No matter, let her cry, let her. . . . My good Masha, my kind Masha. . . . You are my wife and I am happy whatever happens. . . . I don't complain. . . . I don't make you a single reproach. And here's Olga to witness. . . . We'll begin to live again as we used to, and I won't say one word to you, not a breath. . . .

MASHA: (*Stifling her sobs*) By the curved seashore a green oak, a golden chain upon that oak. . . . A golden chain upon that oak. . . . I'm going out of my mind. . . . By the curved seashore . . . a green oak. . . .

OLGA: Be calm, Masha. . . . Be calm. . . . Give her some water.

MASHA: I am not crying any more.

KULYGIN: She is not crying now. . . . She's good. . . .

(*A shot is heard, faintly, from a distance.*)

MASHA: By the curved seashore a green oak, a golden chain upon that oak. . . . The cat's green . . . the oak's green. . . . I am mixing it up. . . . (*Taking a drink of water*) My life is a failure. I don't want anything now. I'll soon be calm. It's all the same. . . . What does it mean: "By the curved seashore"? Why does this word keep running through my head? My thoughts are all mixed up.

(IRINA *enters.*)

OLGA: Be calm, Masha. Now, that's a good girl. . . . Let's go in. . . .

MASHA: (*Angrily*) I'm not going in there. (*Sobbing, but checking herself at once*) I don't go in the house any more, so I won't do it now.

IRINA: Let's sit down together just quietly. Well, tomorrow I'm going away. . . .

(*A pause.*)

KULYGIN: In the third grade yesterday I took this mustache and beard from a boy, see— (*Putting on the mustache and beard*) I look like the German teacher. . . . (*Laughing*) Isn't that so? Funny, these boys. . . .

MASHA: Really you do look like your German.

OLGA: (*Laughing*) Yes.

(MASHA *weeps.*)

IRINA: There, Masha!

KULYGIN: A lot like. . . .

(NATASHA *enters.*)

NATASHA: (*To the maid*) What? Protopopov will sit with Sofotchka, Mikhail Ivanovich, and let Andrei Sergeevich wheel Bobik. There's so much bother with children. . . . (*To* IRINA) Irina, you are going away tomorrow—it's such a pity! Stay at least another week. (*Seeing* KULYGIN *she gives a shriek; he laughs and takes off the mustache and beard.*) Why, look at you, you scared me! (*To* IRINA) I am used to you and do you think parting with you will be easy for me? I'll give orders to put Andrei in your room, with his violin—let him saw away there!—and in his room we'll put Sofotchka. Marvelous, wonderful child! What a girl! Today she

looked at me with such eyes, and—
"Mama!"

KULYGIN: Beautiful child, that's true.

NATASHA: And so tomorrow I'll be all
alone here. (*Sighing*) First of all, I'll give
orders to chop down this alley of fir trees,
then this maple here. . . . In the evening
it looks so ugly. . . . (*To* IRINA) Dear, that
belt doesn't suit you at all. . . . It's in
very poor taste. You need something light.
. . . And I'll order flowers planted, everywhere, flowers, and there'll be a fragrance
. . . (*Severely*) What's a fork doing here
on the bench? (*She goes into the house, to
the maid.*) What's a fork doing here on
the bench, I'd like to know? (*Shouting*)
Shut up!

KULYGIN: She's off again!

(*Behind the scenes a band is playing a
march; everybody listens.*)

OLGA: They are leaving.

(TCHEBUTYKIN *enters.*)

MASHA: Our friends are going. Well,
then. . . . A pleasant journey to them!
(*To her husband*) We must go home.
. . . Where are my hat and cape?

KULYGIN: I carried them in the house
. . . I'll get them right away.

OLGA: Yes, now we can all go home.
It's time.

TCHEBUTYKIN: Olga Sergeevna!

OLGA: What? (*A pause*) What?

TCHEBUTYKIN: Nothing. . . . Don't
know how to tell you. . . . (*Whispering
in her ear*)

OLGA: (*Alarmed*) It's not possible!

TCHEBUTYKIN: Yes. . . . What a story.
. . . I'm tired, completely exhausted, don't
want to talk any more. (*Irritably*) However, it's all the same!

MASHA: What happened?

OLGA: (*Embracing* IRINA) It's a terrible
day today. . . . I don't know how to tell
you, my darling. . . .

IRINA: What? Say it quick. . . . What?
For God's sake! (*Crying.*)

TCHEBUTYKIN: The Baron was killed
just now in a duel.

IRINA: (*Weeping quietly*) I knew, I
knew. . . .

TCHEBUTYKIN: (*Sitting down on a
bench to the rear of the stage*) I'm tired.
. . . (*Taking a newspaper out of his
pocket*) Let them cry a little. . . . (*Singing softly*) Ta-ra-ra-boom-de-aye. . . . Sit
on a curb I may. . . . As if it weren't all
the same!

(*The three sisters stand with their arms
around one another.*)

MASHA: Oh, how the music is playing!
They are leaving us, one has gone entirely, entirely, forever. We'll be left alone
to begin our life over again. We must
live. . . . We must live. . . .

IRINA: (*Putting her head on* OLGA's
breast) The time will come when all will
know why all this is, what these sufferings are for, there will be no secrets—but
meanwhile we must live—must work, only
work! Tomorrow I'm going away alone,
I'll teach in the school and give my whole
life to those who need it perhaps. It's
autumn now; winter will soon come and
cover everything with snow, and I'll work,
work. . . .

OLGA: (*Embracing both her sisters*)
The music plays so gaily, bravely, and
one wants to live. Oh, Lord! Time will
pass and we shall be gone forever, they
will forget us, they will forget our faces,
voices, and how many of us there were,
but our sufferings will turn into joy for
those who will be living after us, happiness and peace will come on earth, and
they will remember with some gentle
word those who live now and will bless
them. Oh, dear sisters, our life isn't over
yet. We shall live! The music plays so
gaily, so joyously, and it looks as if a little

more and we shall know why we live, why we suffer. . . . If we only knew, if we only knew!

(*The music plays always softer and softer;* KULYGIN, *smiling and gay, brings the hat and cape,* ANDREI *is pushing the baby-carriage with Bobik in it.*)

TCHEBUTYKIN: (*Singing softy*) Ta-ra-ra-boom-de-aye. . . . Sit on a curb I may. . . . (*Reading the newspaper*) It's all the same! It's all the same!

OLGA: If we only knew, if we only knew!

Curtain

Henry IV

LUIGI PIRANDELLO

COMMENTARY

Luigi Pirandello (1867-1936) was born in Sicily. He attended the universities at Rome and Bonn, receiving a doctorate in philosophy. Two personal catastrophes marked his life: his family became penniless when their mines were flooded, and his wife went insane after the birth of their third child. He wrote and taught. As his literary reputation developed, he worked closely with the company producing his plays, directing them, casting roles, and moving socially in theatrical circles. His plays are based either on some distortion of nature, on some fantasticated rearrangement of familiar reality, as in *Six Characters in Search of an Author* (1922) and *It Is So! (If You Think So)* (1917), or on some entirely natural if somewhat bizarre situation, as in *Liolà* (1917), *Each in His Own Way* (1924), and *Henry IV* (1922). He was awarded the Nobel Prize in 1934.

Like so many playwrights before him, Pirandello is much concerned with the differences and the tensions between illusion and reality. In *Six Characters,* the father, one of the "characters," delivers extensive little essays on the subject, arguing, for example, that "characters" in a work, because they are "fixed" in a critical moment of their lives, are more "real" than real people, who are constantly changing in the course of *their* lives. *Henry IV,* thought by Pirandello himself and by critics to be his best play, is a sustained study of how illusion affects reality, is reciprocally affected by it, and of the resultant tragic result when the balance is disturbed.

Henry's madness is ambiguously controlled. Henry is the leading actor in a drama he is producing, writing, and directing; the larger drama has had a remote opening curtain and may have its final one only with Henry's death. He is perhaps no more mad and no more sane than anyone who takes himself seriously in a role he assumes. The tragedy is to be found as much in Henry's desperate need to survive through sustaining an elaborate illusion as in that sudden violent act when the illusion is momentarily pierced. His sustained masquerade, of course, suggests a nearly pathologcal need to keep his identity insulated from the present, real world.

Although *Henry IV* is a drama about drama, so to speak, do you think it would *play* better than it reads? The work of Pirandello poses this question with particular sharpness. Are there scenes here by which you might be bored on stage? Or might especially talky ones be improved when acted out?

Six Characters, as suggested, should be read for an extended presentation of many of Pirandello's ideas on the interrelation of illusion and reality. Critical studies are those by Domenico Vittorni (*The Drama of Luigi Pirandello* [London and Philadelphia, 1935]); Eric Bentley's chapter in *The Playwright as Thinker* (New York, 1946); Morris Freedman's "Moral Perspective in Pirandello," in *The Moral Impulse;* and *Luigi Pirandello: 1867-1936,* (Los Angeles, 1965) by Walter Starkie.

Luigi Pirandello

HENRY IV

(Enrico IV)

A TRAGEDY IN THREE ACTS

English Version by Edward Storer

CHARACTERS

HENRY IV

THE MARCHIONESS MATILDA SPINA

FRIDA, *her daughter*

CHARLES DI NOLLI, *the young*
  Marquis

BARON TITO BELCREDI

DOCTOR DIONYSIUS GENONI

HAROLD [FRANK]

LANDOLPH [LOLO]

ORDULPH [MOMO]

BERTHOLD [FINO]

} *The four private counsellors (The names in brackets are nicknames)*

JOHN, *the old waiter*

THE TWO VALETS IN COSTUME

A Solitary Villa in Italy in Our Own Time

ACT I

Salon in the villa, furnished and deco-rated so as to look exactly like the throne room of Henry IV in the royal residence at Goslar. Among the antique decorations there are two modern life-size portraits in oil painting. They are placed against the back wall, and mounted in a wooden stand that runs the whole length of the wall. (It is wide and protrudes, so that it is like a large bench.) One of the paintings is on the right; the other on the left of the throne, which is in the middle of the wall and divides the stand.

The Imperial chair and Baldachin.

The two portraits represent a lady and a gentleman, both young, dressed up in carnival costumes: one as "Henry IV," the other as the "Marchioness Matilda of Tuscany." Exits to right and left.

When the curtain goes up, the two valets jump down, as if surprised, from the stand on which they have been lying, and go and take their positions, as rigid as statues, on either side below the throne with their halberds in their hands. Soon after, from the second exit, right, enter HAROLD, LANDOLPH, ORDULPH *and* BERTHOLD, *young men employed by the* MARQUIS CHARLES DI NOLLI *to play the part of "Secret Counsellors at the court of 'Henry IV.'" They are, therefore, dressed like German knights of the XIth century.* BERTHOLD, *nicknamed Fino, is just entering on his duties for the first time. His companions are telling him what he has to do and amusing themselves at his expense. The scene is to be played rapidly and vivaciously.*

LANDOLPH: (*to* BERTHOLD *as if explaining.*) And this is the throne room.

HAROLD: At Goslar.

ORDULPH: Or at the castle in the Hartz, if you prefer.

HAROLD: Or at Wurms.

LANDOLPH: According as to what's doing, it jumps about with us, now here, now there.

ORDULPH: In Saxony.

HAROLD: In Lombardy.

LANDOLPH: On the Rhine.

ONE OF THE VALETS: (*without moving, just opening his lips.*) I say . . .

HAROLD: (*turning round.*) What is it?

FIRST VALET: (*like a statue.*) Is he coming in or not? (*He alludes to* HENRY IV.)

ORDULPH: No, no, he's asleep. You needn't worry.

SECOND VALET: (*releasing his pose, taking a long breath and going to lie down again on the stand.*) You might have told us at once.

FIRST VALET: (*going over to* HAROLD.) Have you got a match, please?

LANDOLPH: What? You can't smoke a pipe here, you know.

FIRST VALET: (*while* HAROLD *offers him a light.*) No; a cigarette. (*Lights his cigarette and lies down again on the stand.*)

BERTHOLD: (*who has been looking on in amazement, walking round the room, regarding the costumes of the others.*) I say . . . this room . . . these costumes . . . Which Henry IV is it? I don't quite get it. Is he Henry IV of France or not? (*At this* LANDOLPH, HAROLD, *and* ORDULPH, *burst out laughing.*)

LANDOLPH: (*still laughing; and pointing to* BERTHOLD *as if inviting the others to make fun of him.*) Henry of France he says: ha! ha!

ORDULPH: He thought it was the king of France!

HAROLD: Henry IV of Germany, my boy: the Salian dynasty!

ORDULPH: The great and tragic Emperor!

LANDOLPH: He of Canossa. Every day we carry on here the terrible war between Church and State, by Jove.

ORDULPH: The Empire against the Papacy!

HAROLD: Antipopes against the Pope!

LANDOLPH: Kings against anti-kings!

ORDULPH: War on the Saxons!

HAROLD: And all the rebels Princes!

LANDOLPH: Against the Emperor's own sons!

BERTHOLD: (*covering his head with his hands to protect himself against this avalanche of information.*) I understand! I understand! Naturally, I didn't get the idea at first. I'm right then: these aren't costumes of the XVIth century?

HAROLD: XVIth century be hanged!

ORDULPH: We're somewhere between a thousand and eleven hundred.

LANDOLPH: Work it out for yourself: if we are before Canossa on the 25th of January, 1071 . . .

BERTHOLD: (*more confused than ever.*) Oh my God! What a mess I've made of it!

ORDULPH: Well, just slightly, if you supposed you were at the French court.

BERTHOLD: All that historical stuff I've swatted up!

LANDOLPH: My dear boy, it's four hundred years earlier.

BERTHOLD: (*getting angry.*) Good Heavens! You ought to have told me it was Germany and not France. I can't tell you how many books I've read in the last fifteen days.

HAROLD: But I say, surely you knew that poor Tito was Adalbert of Bremen, here?

BERTHOLD: Not a damned bit!

LANDOLPH: Well, don't you see how it is? When Tito died, the Marquis Di Nolli . . .

BERTHOLD: Oh, it was he, was it? He might have told me.

HAROLD: Perhaps he thought you knew.

LANDOLPH: He didn't want to engage anyone else in substitution. He thought the remaining three of us would do. But *he* began to cry out: "With Adalbert driven away . . .": because, you see, he didn't imagine poor Tito was dead; but that, as Bishop Adalbert, the rival bishops of Cologne and Mayence had driven him off . . .

BERTHOLD: (*taking his head in his hand.*) But I don't know a word of what you're talking about.

ORDULPH: So much the worse for you, my boy!

HAROLD: But the trouble is that not even we know who you are.

BERTHOLD: What? Not even you? You don't know who I'm supposed to be?

ORDULPH: Hum! "Berthold."

BERTHOLD: But which Berthold? And why Berthold?

LANDOLPH: (*solemnly imitating* HENRY IV.) "They've driven Adalbert away from me. Well then, I want Berthold! I want Berthold!" That's what he said.

HAROLD: We three looked one another in the eyes: who's got to be Berthold?

ORDULPH: And so here you are, "Berthold," my dear fellow!

LANDOLPH: I'm afraid you will make a bit of a mess of it.

BERTHOLD: (*indignant, getting ready to go.*) Ah, no! Thanks very much, but I'm off! I'm out of this!

HAROLD: (*restraining him with the other two, amid laughter.*) Steady now! Don't get excited!

LANDOLPH: Cheer up, my dear fellow! We don't any of us kno· v who we are really. He's Harold; he's Ordulph; I'm Landolph! That's the way he calls us. We've got used to it. But who are we? Names of the period! Yours, too, is a name of the period: Berthold! Only one of us, poor Tito, had got a really decent part, as you can read in history: that of the Bishop of Bremen. He was just like a real bishop. Tito did it awfully well, poor chap!

HAROLD: Look at the study he put into it!

LANDOLPH: Why, he even ordered his Majesty about, opposed his views, guided and counselled him. We're "secret counsellors"—in a manner of speaking only; because it is written in history that Henry

IV was hated by the upper aristocracy for surrounding himself at court with young men of the bourgeoise.

ORDULPH: Us, that is.

LANDOLPH: Yes, small devoted vassals, a bit dissolute and very gay . . .

BERTHOLD: So I've got to be gay as well?

HAROLD: I should say so! Same as we are!

ORDULPH: And it isn't too easy, you know.

LANDOLPH: It's a pity; because the way we're got up, we could do a fine historical reconstruction. There's any amount of material in the story of Henry IV. But, as a matter of fact, we do nothing. We have the form without the content. We're worse than the real secret counsellors of Henry IV; because certainly no one had given them a part to play—at any rate, they didn't feel they had a part to play. It was their life. They looked after their own interests at the expense of others, sold investitures and—what not! We stop here in this magnificent court—for what? —Just doing nothing. We're like so many puppets hung on the wall, waiting for some one to come and move us or make us talk.

HAROLD: Ah, no, old sport, not quite that! We've got to give the proper answer, you know. There's trouble if he asks you something and you don't chip in with the cue.

LANDOLPH: Yes, that's true.

BERTHOLD: Don't rub it in too hard! How the devil am I to give him the proper answer, if I've swatted up Henry IV of France, and now he turns out to be Henry IV of Germany? (*The other three laugh.*)

HAROLD: You'd better start and prepare yourself at once.

ORDULPH: We'll help you out.

HAROLD: We've got any amount of books on the subject. A brief run through the main points will do to begin with.

ORDULPH: At any rate, you must have got some sort of general idea.

HAROLD: Look here! (*Turns him around and shows him the portrait of the Marchioness Matilda on the wall.*) Who's that?

BERTHOLD: (*looking at it.*) That? Well, the thing seems to me somewhat out of place, anyway: two modern paintings in the midst of all this respectable antiquity!

HAROLD: You're right! They weren't there in the beginning. There are two niches there behind the pictures. They were going to put up two statues in the style of the period. Then the places were covered with those canvases there.

LANDOLPH: (*interrupting and continuing.*) They would certainly be out of place if they really were paintings!

BERTHOLD: What are they, if they aren't paintings?

LANDOLPH: Go and touch them! Pictures all right . . . but for him! (*Makes a mysterious gesture to the right, alluding to* HENRY IV.) . . . who never touches them! . . .

BERTHOLD: No? What are they for him?

LANDOLPH: Well, I'm only supposing, you know; but I imagine I'm about right. They're images such as . . . well—such as a mirror might throw back. Do you understand? That one there represents himself, as he is in this throne room, which is all in the style of the period. What's there to marvel at? If we put you before a mirror, won't you see yourself, alive, but dressed up in ancient costume? Well, it's as if there were two mirrors there, which cast back living images in the midst of a world which, as you well see, when you have lived with us, comes to life too.

BERTHOLD: I say, look here . . . I've no particular desire to go mad here.

HAROLD: Go mad, be hanged! You'll have a fine time!

BERTHOLD: Tell me this: how have you all managed to become so learned?

LANDOLPH: My dear fellow, you can't go back over 800 years of history without picking up a bit of experience.

HAROLD: Come on! Come on! You'll see how quickly you get into it!

ORDULPH: You'll learn wisdom, too, at this school.

BERTHOLD: Well, for Heaven's sake, help me a bit! Give me the main lines, anyway.

HAROLD: Leave it to us. We'll do it all between us.

LANDOLPH: We'll put your wires on you and fix you up like a first-class marionette. Come along! (THEY *take him by the arm to lead him away.*)

BERTHOLD: (*stopping and looking at the portrait on the wall.*) Wait a minute! You haven't told me who that is. The Emperor's wife?

HAROLD: No! The Emperor's wife is Bertha of Susa, the sister of Amadeus II of Savoy.

ORDULPH: And the Emperor, who wants to be young with us, can't stand her, and wants to put her away.

LANDOLPH: That is his most ferocious enemy: Matilda, Marchioness of Tuscany.

BERTHOLD: Ah, I've got it: the one who gave hospitality to the Pope!

LANDOLPH: Exactly: at Canossa!

ORDULPH: Pope Gregory VII!

HAROLD: Our *bête noir!* Come on! come on! (*All four move toward the right to go out, when, from the left, the old servant* JOHN *enters in evening dress.*)

JOHN: (*quickly, anxiously.*) Hss! Hss! Frank! Lolo!

HAROLD: (*turning round.*) What is it?

BERTHOLD: (*marvelling at seeing a man in modern clothes enter the throne room.*) Oh! I say, this is a bit too much, this chap here!

LANDOLPH: A man of the XXth century, here! Oh, go away! (THEY *run over to him, pretending to menace him and throw him out.*)

ORDULPH: (*heroically.*) Messenger of Gregory VII, away!

HAROLD: Away! Away!

JOHN: (*annoyed, defending himself.*) Oh, stop it! Stop it, I tell you!

ORDULPH: No, you can't set foot here!

HAROLD: Out with him!

LANDOLPH: (*to* BERTHOLD.) Magic, you know! He's a demon conjured up by the Wizard of Rome! Out with your swords! (*Makes as if to draw a sword.*)

JOHN: (*shouting.*) Stop it, will you? Don't play the fool with me! The Marquis has arrived with some friends . . .

LANDOLPH: Good! Good! Are there ladies too?

ORDULPH: Old or young?

JOHN: There are two gentlemen.

HAROLD: But the ladies, the ladies, who are they?

JOHN: The Marchioness and her daughter.

LANDOLPH: (*surprised.*) What do you say?

ORDULPH: The Marchioness?

JOHN: The Marchioness! The Marchioness!

HAROLD: Who are the gentlemen?

JOHN: I don't know.

HAROLD: (*to* BERTHOLD.) They're coming to bring us a message from the Pope, do you see?

ORDULPH: All messengers of Gregory VII! What fun!

JOHN: Will you let me speak, or not?

HAROLD: Go on, then!

JOHN: One of the two gentlemen is a doctor, I fancy.

LANDOLPH: Oh, I see, one of the usual doctors.

HAROLD: Bravo Berthold, you'll bring us luck!

LANDOLPH: You wait and see how we'll manage this doctor!

BERTHOLD: It looks as if I were going to get into a nice mess right away.

JOHN: If the gentlemen would allow me to speak . . . they want to come here into the throne room.

LANDOLPH: (surprised.) What? She? The Marchioness here?

HAROLD: Then this is something quite different! No play-acting this time!

LANDOLPH: We'll have a real tragedy: that's what!

BERTHOLD: (curious.) Why? Why?

ORDULPH: (pointing to the portrait.) She is that person there, don't you understand?

LANDOLPH: The daughter is the fiancée of the Marquis. But what have they come for, I should like to know?

ORDULPH: If he sees her, there'll be trouble.

LANDOLPH: Perhaps he won't recognize her any more.

JOHN: You must keep him there, if he should wake up . . .

ORDULPH: Easier said than done, by Jove!

HAROLD: You know what he's like!

JOHN: —even by force, if necessary! Those are my orders. Go on! Go on!

HAROLD: Yes, because who knows if he hasn't already wakened up?

ORDULPH: Come on then!

LANDOLPH: (going towards JOHN with the others.) You'll tell us later what it all means.

JOHN: (shouting after them.) Close the door there, and hide the key! That other door too. (Pointing to the other door on right.)

JOHN: (to the TWO VALETS.) Be off, you two! There! (Pointing to exit right.) Close the door after you, and hide the key!

(The TWO VALETS go out by the first door on right. JOHN moves over to the left to show in: DONNA MATILDA SPINA, the young MARCHIONESS FRIDA, DR. DIONYSIUS GENONI, the BARON TITO BELCREDI and the young MARQUIS CHARLES DI NOLLI, who, as master of the house, enters last.

DONNA MATILDA SPINA is about 45, still handsome, although there are too patent signs of her attempts to remedy the ravages of time with make-up. Her head is thus rather like a Walkyrie. This facial make-up contrasts with her beautiful sad mouth. A widow for many years, she now has as her friend the BARON TITO BELCREDI, whom neither she nor anyone else takes seriously—at least so it would appear.

What TITO BELCREDI really is for her at bottom, he alone knows; and he is, therefore, entitled to laugh, if his friend feels the need of pretending not to know. He can always laugh at the jests which the beautiful Marchioness makes with the others at his expense. He is slim, prematurely gray, and younger than she is. His head is bird-like in shape. He would be a very vivacious person, if his ductile agility [which among other things makes him a redoubtable swordsman] were not enclosed in a sheath of Arab-like laziness, which is revealed in his strange, nasal drawn-out voice.

FRIDA, the daughter of the Marchioness is 19. She is sad; because her imperious and too beautiful mother puts her in the shade, and provokes facile gossip against her daughter as well as against herself.

Fortunately for her, she is engaged to the MARQUIS CHARLES DI NOLLI.

CHARLES DI NOLLI *is a stiff young man, very indulgent towards others, but sure of himself for what he amounts to in the world. He is worried about all the responsibilities which he believes weigh on him. He is dressed in deep mourning for the recent death of his mother.*

DR. DIONYSIUS GENONI *has a bold rubicund Satyr-like face, prominent eyes, a pointed beard [which is silvery and shiny] and elegant manners. He is nearly bald. All enter in a state of perturbation, almost as if afraid, and all [except DI NOLLI] looking curiously about the room. At first, they speak sotto voce.)*

DI NOLLI: (*To* JOHN.) Have you given the orders properly?

JOHN: Yes, my Lord; don't be anxious about that.

BELCREDI: Ah, magnificent! magnificent!

DOCTOR: How extremely interesting! Even in the surroundings his raving madness—is perfectly taken into account!

DONNA MATILDA: (*glancing round for her portrait, discovers it, and goes up close to it.*) Ah! Here it is! (*Going back to admire it, while mixed emotions stir within her.*) Yes . . . yes . . . (*Calls her daughter* FRIDA.)

FRIDA: Ah, your portrait!

DONNA MATILDA: No, no . . . look again; it's you, not I, there!

DI NOLLI: Yes, it's quite true. I told you so, I . . .

DONNA MATILDA: But I would never have believed it! (*Shaking as if with a chill.*) What a strange feeling it gives one! (*Then looking at her daughter.*) Frida, what's the matter? (*She pulls her to her side, and slips an arm round her waist.*) Come: don't you see yourself in me there?

FRIDA: Well, I really . . .

DONNA MATILDA: Don't you think so? Don't you, really? (*Turning to* BELCREDI.) Look at it, Tito! Speak up, man!

BELCREDI: (*without looking.*) Ah, no! I shan't look at it. For me, *a priori*, certainly not!

DONNA MATILDA: Stupid! You think you are paying me a compliment! (*Turning to* DOCTOR GENONI.) What do you say, Doctor? Do say something, please!

DOCTOR: (*makes a movement to go near to the picture.*)

BELCREDI: (*with his back turned, pretending to attract his attention secretly.*) —Hss! No, Doctor! For the love of Heaven, have nothing to do with it!

DOCTOR: (*getting bewildered and smiling.*) And why shouldn't I?

DONNA MATILDA: Don't listen to him! Come here! He's insufferable!

FRIDA: He acts the fool by profession, didn't you know that?

BELCREDI: (*to the* DOCTOR, *seeing him go over.*) Look at your feet, Doctor! Mind where you're going!

DOCTOR: Why?

BELCREDI: Be careful you don't put your foot in it!

DOCTOR: (*laughing feebly.*) No, no. After all, it seems to me there's no reason to be astonished at the fact that a daughter should resemble her mother!

BELCREDI: Hullo! Hullo! He's done it now; he's said it.

DONNA MATILDA: (*with exaggerated anger, advancing towards* BELCREDI.) What's the matter? What has he said? What has he done?

DOCTOR: (*candidly.*) Well, isn't it so?

BELCREDI: (*answering the* MARCHIONESS.) I said there was nothing to be astounded at—and you are astounded! And why so, then, if the thing is so simple and natural for you now?

DONNA MATILDA: (*still more angry.*) Fool! fool! It's just because it is so natural! Just because it isn't my daughter who is there. (*Pointing to the canvas.*) That is my portrait; and to find my daughter there instead of me fills me with astonishment, an astonishment which, I beg you to believe, is sincere. I forbid you to cast doubts on it.

FRIDA: (*slowly and wearily.*) My God! It's always like this . . . rows over nothing . . .

BELCREDI: (*also slowly, looking dejected, in accents of apology.*) I cast no doubt on anything! I noticed from the beginning that you haven't shared your mother's astonishment; or, if something did astonish you, it was because the likeness between you and the portrait seemed so strong.

DONNA MATILDA: Naturally! She cannot recognize herself in me as I was at her age; while I, there, can very well recognize myself in her as she is now!

DOCTOR: Quite right! Because a portrait is always there fixed in the twinkling of an eye: for the young lady something far away and without memories, while, for the Marchioness, it can bring back everything: movements, gestures, looks, smiles, a whole heap of things . . .

DONNA MATILDA: Exactly!

DOCTOR: (*continuing, turning towards her.*) Naturally enough, you can live all these old sensations again in your daughter.

DONNA MATILDA: He always spoils every innocent pleasure for me, every touch I have of spontaneous sentiment! He does it merely to annoy me.

DOCTOR: (*frightened at the disturbance he has caused, adopts a professorial tone.*) Likeness, dear Baron, is often the result of imponderable things. So one explains that . . .

BELCREDI: (*interrupting the discourse.*) Somebody will soon be finding a likeness between you and me, my dear Professor!

DI NOLLI: Oh! let's finish with this, please. (*Points to the two doors on the right, as a warning that there is someone there who may be listening.*) We've wasted too much time as it is!

FRIDA: As one might expect when *he's* present. (*Alludes to* BELCREDI.)

DI NOLLI: Enough! The Doctor is here; and we have come for a very serious purpose which you all know is important for me.

DOCTOR: Yes, that is so! But now, first of all, let's try to get some points down exactly. Excuse me, Marchioness, will you tell me why your portrait is here? Did you present it to him then?

DONNA MATILDA: No, not at all. How could I have given it to him? I was just like Frida then—and not even engaged. I gave it to him three or four years after the accident. I gave it to him because his mother wished it so much . . . (*Points to* DI NOLLI.)

DOCTOR: She was his sister? (*Alludes to* HENRY IV.)

DI NOLLI: Yes Doctor; and our coming here is a debt we pay to my mother who has been dead for more than a month. Instead of being here, she and I (*Indicating* FRIDA.) ought to be traveling together . . .

DOCTOR: . . . taking a cure of quite a different kind!

DI NOLLI: —Hum! Mother died in the firm conviction that her adored brother was just about to be cured.

DOCTOR: And can't you tell me, if you please, how she inferred this?

DI NOLLI: The conviction would appear to have derived from certain strange remarks which he made, a little before mother died.

DOCTOR: Oh, remarks! . . . Ah! . . . It would be extremely useful for me to have those remarks, word for word, if possible.

DI NOLLI: I can't remember them. I know that mother returned awfully upset from her last visit with him. On her deathbed, she made me promise that I would never neglect him, that I would have doctors see him, and examine him.

DOCTOR: Um! Um! Let me see! let me see! Sometimes very small reasons determine . . . and this portrait here then? . . .

DONNA MATILDA: For Heaven's sake, Doctor, don't attach excessive importance to this. It made an impression on me because I had not seen it for so many years!

DOCTOR: If you please, quietly, quietly . . .

DI NOLLI: —Well, yes, it must be about fifteen years ago.

DONNA MATILDA: More, more: eighteen!

DOCTOR: Forgive me, but you don't quite know what I'm trying to get at. I attach a very great importance to these two portraits . . . They were painted, naturally, prior to the famous—and most regrettable pageant, weren't they?

DONNA MATILDA: Of course!

DOCTOR: That is . . . when he was quite in his right mind—that's what I've been trying to say. Was it his suggestion that they should be painted?

DONNA MATILDA: Lots of the people who took part in the pageant had theirs done as a souvenir . . .

BELCREDI: I had mine done—as "Charles of Anjou!"

DONNA MATILDA: . . . as soon as the costumes were ready.

BELCREDI: As a matter of fact, it was proposed that the whole lot of us should be hung together in a gallery of the villa where the pageant took place. But in the end, everybody wanted to keep his own portrait.

DONNA MATILDA: And I gave him this portrait of me without very much regret . . . since his mother . . . (*Indicates* DI NOLLI.)

DOCTOR: You don't remember if it was he who asked for it?

DONNA MATILDA: Ah, that I don't remember . . . Maybe it was his sister, wanting to help out . . .

DOCTOR: One other thing: was it his idea, this pageant?

BELCREDI: (*at once.*) No, no, it was mine!

DOCTOR: If you please . . .

DONNA MATILDA: Don't listen to him! It was poor Belassi's idea.

BELCREDI: Belassi! What had he got to do with it?

DONNA MATILDA: Count Belassi, who died, poor fellow, two or three months after . . .

BELCREDI: But if Belassi wasn't there when . . .

DI NOLLI: Excuse me, Doctor; but is it really necessary to establish whose the original idea was?

DOCTOR: It would help me, certainly!

BELCREDI: I tell you the idea was mine! There's nothing to be proud of in it, seeing what the result's been. Look here, Doctor, it was like this. One evening, in the first days of November, I was looking at an illustrated German review in the club. I was merely glancing at the pictures, because I can't read German. There was a picture of the Kaiser, at some University town where he had been a student . . . I don't remember which.

DOCTOR: Bonn, Bonn!

BELCREDI: —You are right: Bonn! He was on horseback, dressed up in one of those ancient German student guild-costumes, followed by a procession of noble students, also in costume. The picture gave me the idea. Already someone at the club had spoken of a pageant for the forthcoming carnival. So I had the notion that each of us should choose for this Tower of Babel pageant to represent some character: a king, an emperor, a prince, with his queen, empress, or lady, alongside of him—and all on horseback. The suggestion was at once accepted.

DONNA MATILDA: I had my invitation from Belassi.

BELCREDI: Well, he wasn't speaking the truth! That's all I can say, if he told you the idea was his. He wasn't even at the club the evening I made the suggestion, just as he (*Meaning* HENRY IV.) wasn't there either.

DOCTOR: So he chose the character of Henry IV?

DONNA MATILDA: Because I . . . thinking of my name, and not giving the choice any importance, said I would be the Marchioness Matilda of Tuscany.

DOCTOR: I . . . don't understand the relation between the two.

DONNA MATILDA: —Neither did I, to begin with, when he said that in that case he would be at my feet like Henry IV at Canossa. I had heard of Canossa of course; but to tell the truth, I'd forgotten most of the story; and I remember I received a curious impression when I had to get up my part, and found that I was the faithful and zealous friend of Pope Gregory VII in deadly enmity with the Emperor of Germany. Then I understood why, since I had chosen to represent his implacable enemy, he wanted to be near me in the pageant as Henry IV.

DOCTOR: Ah, perhaps because . . .

BELCREDI: —Good Heavens, Doctor, because he was then paying furious court

to her! (*Indicates the* MARCHIONESS.) And she, naturally . . .

DONNA MATILDA: Naturally? Not naturally at all . . .

BELCREDI: (*pointing to her.*) She shouldn't stand him . . .

DONNA MATILDA: —No, that isn't true! I didn't dislike him. Not at all! But for me, when a man begins to want to be taken seriously, well . . .

BELCREDI: (*continuing for her.*) He gives you the clearest proof of his stupidity.

DONNA MATILDA: No, dear; not in this case; because he was never a fool like you.

BELCREDI: Anyway, I've never asked you to take me seriously.

DONNA MATILDA: Yes, I know. But with him one couldn't joke. (*Changing her tone and speaking to the* DOCTOR.) One of the many misfortunes which happen to us women, Doctor, is to see before us every now and again a pair of eyes glaring at us with a contained intense promise of eternal devotion. (*Bursts out laughing.*) There is nothing quite so funny. If men could only see themselves with that eternal look of fidelity in their faces! I've always thought it comic; then more even than now. But I want to make a confession—I can do so after twenty years or more. When I laughed at him then, it was partly out of fear. One might have almost believed a promise from those eyes of his. But it would have been very dangerous.

DOCTOR: (*with lively interest.*) Ah! ah! This is most interesting! Very dangerous, you say?

DONNA MATILDA: Yes, because he was very different from the others. And then, I am . . . well . . . what shall I say? . . . a little impatient of all that is pondered, or tedious. But I was too young then, and a woman. I had the bit between my teeth. It would have required more courage than I felt I possessed. So I laughed at him too—with remorse, to spite myself indeed; since I saw that my own laugh mingled with those of all the others— the other fools—who made fun of him.

BELCREDI: My own case, more or less!

DONNA MATILDA: You make people laugh at you, my dear, with your trick of always humiliating yourself. It was quite a different affair with him. There's a vast difference. And you—you know— people laugh in your face!

BELCREDI: Well, that's better than behind one's back!

DOCTOR: Let's get to the facts. He was then already somewhat exalted, if I understand rightly.

BELCREDI: Yes, but in a curious fashion, Doctor.

DOCTOR: How?

BELCREDI: Well, cold-bloodedly so to speak.

DONNA MATILDA: Not at all! It was like this, Doctor! He was a bit strange, certainly; but only because he was fond of life: eccentric, there!

BELCREDI: I don't say he simulated exaltation. On the contrary, he was often genuinely exalted. But I could swear, Doctor, that he saw himself at once in his own exaltation. Moreover, I'm certain it made him suffer. Sometimes he had the most comical fits of rage against himself.

DOCTOR: Yes?

DONNA MATILDA: That is true.

BELCREDI: (to DONNA MATILDA.) And why? (To the DOCTOR.) Evidently, because that immediate lucidity that comes from acting, assuming a part, at once put him out of key with his own feelings, which seemed to him not exactly false, but like something he was obliged to give the value there and then of—what shall I say—of an act of intelligence, to make

up for that sincere cordial warmth he felt lacking. So he improvised, exaggerated, let himself go, so as to distract and forget himself. He appeared inconstant, fatuous, and—yes—even ridiculous, sometimes.

DOCTOR: And may we say unsociable?

BELCREDI: No, not at all. He was famous for getting up things: *tableaux vivants,* dances, theatrical performances for charity: all for the fun of the thing, of course. He was a jolly good actor, you know!

DI NOLLI: Madness has made a superb actor of him.

BELCREDI: —Why, so he was even in the old days. When the accident happened, after the horse fell . . .

DOCTOR: Hit the back of his head, didn't he?

DONNA MATILDA: Oh, it was horrible! He was beside me! I saw him between the horse's hoofs! It was rearing!

BELCREDI: None of us thought it was anything serious at first. There was a stop in the pageant, a bit of disorder. People wanted to know what had happened. But they'd already taken him off to the villa.

DONNA MATILDA: There wasn't the least sign of a wound, not a drop of blood.

BELCREDI: We thought he had merely fainted.

DONNA MATILDA: But two hours afterwards . . .

BELCREDI: He reappeared in the drawing-room of the villa . . . that is what I wanted to say . . .

DONNA MATILDA: My God! What a face he had. I saw the whole thing at once!

BELCREDI: No, no! that isn't true. Nobody saw it, Doctor, believe me!

DONNA MATILDA: Doubtless, because you were all like mad folk.

BELCREDI: Everybody was pretending to act his part for a joke. It was a regular Babel.

DONNA MATILDA: And you can imagine, Doctor, what terror struck into us when we understood that he, on the contrary, was playing his part in deadly earnest . . .

DOCTOR: Oh, he was there too, was he?

BELCREDI: Of course! He came straight into the midst of us. We thought he'd quite recovered, and was pretending, fooling, like all the rest of us . . . only doing it rather better; because, as I say, he knew how to act.

DONNA MATILDA: Some of them began to hit him with their whips and fans and sticks.

BELCREDI: And then—as a king, he was armed, of course—he drew out his sword and menaced two or three of us . . . It was a terrible moment, I can assure you!

DONNA MATILDA: I shall never forget that scene—all our masked faces hideous and terrified gazing at him, at that terrible mask of his face, which was no longer a mask, but madness, madness personified.

BELCREDI: He was Henry IV, Henry IV in person, in a moment of fury.

DONNA MATILDA: He'd got into it all the detail and minute preparation of a month's careful study. And it all burned and blazed there in the terrible obsession which lit his face.

DOCTOR: Yes, that is quite natural, of course. The momentary obsession of a dilettante became fixed, owing to the fall and the damage to the brain.

BELCREDI: (*to* FRIDA *and* DI NOLLI.) You see the kind of jokes life can play on us. [*To* DI NOLLI.] You were four or five years old. [*To* FRIDA.] Your mother imagines you've taken her place there in that portrait; when, at the time, she had not the remotest idea that she would bring you into the world. My hair is already grey; and he—look at him— (*Points to portrait*)—ha! A smack on

the head, and he never moves again: Henry IV for ever!

DOCTOR: (*seeking to draw the attention of the others, looking learned and imposing.*)—Well, well, then it comes, we may say, to this . . .

(*Suddenly the first exit to right, the one nearest footlights, opens, and* BERTHOLD *enters all excited.*)

BERTHOLD: (*rushing in.*) I say! I say! (*Stops for a moment, arrested by the astonishment which his appearance has caused in the others.*)

FRIDA: (*running away terrified.*) Oh dear! oh dear! it's he, it's . . .

DONNA MATILDA: (*covering her face with her hands so as not to see.*) Is it, is it he?

DI NOLLI: No, no, what are you talking about? Be calm!

DOCTOR: Who is it then?

BELCREDI: One of our masqueraders.

DI NOLLI: He is one of the four youths we keep here to help him out in his madness . . .

BERTHOLD: I beg your pardon, Marquis . . .

DI NOLLI: Pardon be damned! I gave orders that the doors were to be closed, and that nobody should be allowed to enter.

BERTHOLD: Yes, sir, but I can't stand it any longer, and I ask you to let me go away this very minute.

DI NOLLI: Oh, you're the new valet, are you? You were supposed to begin this morning, weren't you?

BERTHOLD: Yes, sir, and I can't stand it, I can't bear it.

DONNA MATILDA: (*to* DI NOLLI *excitedly.*) What? Then he's not so calm as you said?

BERTHOLD: (*quickly.*) —No, no, my lady, it isn't he; it's my companions. You

say "help him out with his madness,"
Marquis; but they don't do anything of
the kind: They're the real madmen. I
come here for the first time, and instead
of helping me . . .

(LANDOLPH *and* HAROLD *come in from the
same door, but hesitate on the threshold.*)

LANDOLPH: Excuse me?

HAROLD: May I come in, my Lord?

DI NOLLI: Come in! What's the matter?
What are you all doing?

FRIDA: Oh God! I'm frightened! I'm
going to run away. (*Makes towards exit
at left.*)

DI NOLLI: (*restraining her at once.*)
No, no, Frida!

LANDOLPH: My Lord, this foot here . . .
(*Indicates* BERTHOLD.)

BERTHOLD: (*protesting.*) Ah, no thanks,
my friends, no thanks! I'm not stopping
here! I'm off!

LANDOLPH: What do you mean—you're
not stopping here?

HAROLD: He's ruined everything, my
Lord, running away in here!

LANDOLPH: He's made him quite mad.
We can't keep him in there any longer.
He's given orders that he's to be arrested;
and he wants to "judge" him at once
from the throne: What is to be done?

DI NOLLI: Shut the door, man! Shut the
door! Go and close that door! (LANDOLPH
goes over to close it.)

HAROLD: Ordulph alone, won't be able
to keep him there.

LANDOLPH: —My Lord, perhaps if we
could announce the visitors at once, it
would turn his thoughts. Have the gentlemen thought under what pretext they will
present themselves to him?

DI NOLLI: —It's all been arranged!
(*To the* DOCTOR.) If you, Doctor, think
it well to see him at once. . . .

FRIDA: I'm not coming! I'm not com-

ing! I'll keep out of this. You too, mother,
for Heaven's sake, come away with me!

DOCTOR: —I say . . . I suppose he's not
armed, is he?

DI NOLLI: —Nonsense! Of course not.
(*To* FRIDA.) Frida, you know this is childish of you. You wanted to come!

FRIDA: I didn't at all. It was mother's
idea.

DONNA MATILDA: And I'm quite ready
to see him. What are we going to do?

BELCREDI: Must we absolutely dress up
up in some fashion or other?

LANDOLPH: —Absolutely essential, in-
dispensable, sir. Alas! as you see . . .
(*Shows his costume*), there'd be awful
trouble if he saw you gentlemen in modern dress.

HAROLD: He would think it was some
diabolical masquerade.

DI NOLLI: As these men seem to be in
costume to you, so we appear to be in
costume to him, in these modern clothes
of ours.

LANDOLPH: It wouldn't matter so much
if he wouldn't suppose it to be the work
of his mortal enemy.

BELCREDI: Pope Gregory VII?

LANDOLPH: Precisely. He calls him "a
pagan."

BELCREDI: The Pope a pagan? Not bad
that!

LANDOLPH: —Yes, sir,—and a man who
calls up the dead! He accuses him of all
the diabolical arts. He's terribly afraid of
him.

DOCTOR: Persecution mania!

HAROLD: He'd be simply furious.

DI NOLLI: (*to* BELCREDI.) But there's
no need for you to be there, you know.
It's sufficient for the Doctor to see him.

DOCTOR: —What do you mean? . . .
I? Alone?

DI NOLLI: —But they are there. (*Indicates the three young men.*)

DOCTOR: I don't mean that . . . I mean if the Marchioness . . .

DONNA MATILDA: Of course. I mean to see him too, naturally. I want to see him again.

FRIDA: Oh, why, mother, why? Do come away with me, I implore you!

DONNA MATILDA: (*imperiously.*) Let me do as I wish! I came here for this purpose! (*To* LANDOLPH.) I shall be "Adelaide," the mother.

LANDOLPH: Excellent! The mother of the Empress Bertha. Good! It will be enough if her Ladyship wears the ducal crown and puts on a mantle that will hide her other clothes entirely. (*To* HAROLD.) Off you go, Harold!

HAROLD: Wait a moment! And this gentleman here? . . . (*Alludes to the* DOCTOR.)

DOCTOR: —Ah yes . . . we decided I was to be . . . the Bishop of Cluny, Hugh of Cluny!

HAROLD: The gentleman means the Abbot. Very good! Hugh of Cluny.

LANDOLPH: —He's often been here before!

DOCTOR: (*amazed.*) —What? Been here before?

LANDOLPH: —Don't be alarmed! I mean that it's an easily prepared disguise. . . .

HAROLD: We've made use of it on other occasions, you see!

DOCTOR: But . . .

LANDOLPH: Oh, no, there's no risk of his remembering. He pays more attention to the dress than to the person.

DONNA MATILDA: That's fortunate for me too then.

DI NOLLI: Frida, you and I'll get along. Come on, Tito!

BELCREDI: Ah no. If she (*Indicates the* MARCHIONESS.) stops here, so do I!

DONNA MATILDA: But I don't need you at all.

BELCREDI: You may not need me, but I should like to see him again myself. Mayn't I?

LANDOLPH: Well, perhaps it would be better if there were three.

HAROLD: How is the gentleman to be dressed then?

BELCREDI: Oh, try and find some easy costume for me.

LANDOLPH: (*to* HAROLD.) Hum! Yes . . . he'd better be from Cluny too.

BELCREDI: What do you mean—from Cluny?

LANDOLPH: A Benedictine's habit of the Abbey of Cluny. He can be in attendance on Monsignor. (*To* HAROLD.) Off you go! (*To* BERTHOLD.) And you too get away and keep out of sight all today. No, wait a bit! (*To* BERTHOLD.) You bring here the costumes he will give you. (*To* HAROLD.) You go at once and announce the visit of the "Duchess Adelaide" and "Monsignor Hugh of Cluny." Do you understand? (HAROLD *and* BERTHOLD *go off by the first door on the right.*)

DI NOLLI: We'll retire now. (*Goes off with* FRIDA, *left.*)

DOCTOR: Shall I be a *persona grata* to him, as Hugh of Cluny?

LANDOLPH: Oh, rather! Don't worry about that! Monsignor has always been received here with great respect. You too, my Lady, he will be glad to see. He never forgets that it was owing to the intercession of you two that he was admitted to the Castle of Canossa and the presence of Gregory VII, who didn't want to receive him.

BELCREDI: And what do I do?

LANDOLPH: You stand a little apart, respectfully: that's all.

DONNA MATILDA: (*irritated, nervous.*) You would do well to go away, you know.

BELCREDI: (*slowly, spitefully.*) How upset you seem! . . .

DONNA MATILDA: (*proudly.*) I am as I am. Leave me alone!

(BERTHOLD *comes in with the costumes.*)

LANDOLPH: (*seeing him enter.*) Ah, the costumes: here they are. This mantle is for the Marchioness . . .

DONNA MATILDA: Wait a minute! I'll take off my hat. (*Does so and gives it to* BERTHOLD.)

LANDOLPH: Put it down there! (*Then to* the MARCHIONESS, *while he offers to put the ducal crown on her head.*) Allow me!

DONNA MATILDA: Dear, dear! Isn't there a mirror here?

LANDOLPH: Yes, there's one there (*Points to the door on the left.*) If the Marchioness would rather put it on herself . . .

DONNA MATILDA: Yes, yes, that will be better. Give it to me! (*Takes up her hat and goes off with* BERTHOLD, *who carries the cloak and the crown.*)

BELCREDI: Well, I must say, I never thought I should be a Benedictine monk! By the way, this business must cost an awful lot of money.

THE DOCTOR: Like any other fantasy, naturally!

BELCREDI: Well, there's a fortune to go upon.

LANDOLPH: We have got there a whole wardrobe of costumes of the period, copied to perfection from old models. This is my special job. I get them from the best theatrical costumers. They cost lots of money. (DONNA MATILDA *re-enters, wearing mantle and crown.*)

BELCREDI: (*at once, in admiration.*) Oh magnificent! Oh, truly regal!

DONNA MATILDA: (*looking at* BELCREDI *and bursting out into laughter.*) Oh no, no! Take it off! You're impossible. You look like an ostrich dressed up as a monk.

BELCREDI: Well, how about the Doctor?

THE DOCTOR: I don't think I look so bad, do I?

DONNA MATILDA: No; the Doctor's all right . . . but you are too funny for words.

THE DOCTOR: Do you have many receptions here then?

LANDOLPH: It depends. He often gives orders that such and such a person appear before him. Then we have to find someone who will take the part. Women too . . .

DONNA MATILDA: (*hurt, but trying to hide the fact.*) Ah, women too?

LANDOLPH: Oh, yes; many at first.

BELCREDI: (*laughing.*) Oh, that's great! In costume, like the Marchioness?

LANDOLPH: Oh well, you know, women of the kind that lend themselves to . . .

BELCREDI: Ah, I see! (*Perfidiously to* the MARCHIONESS.) Look out, you know he's becoming dangerous for you.

(*The second door on the right opens, and* HAROLD *appears making first of all a discreet sign that all conversation should cease.*)

HAROLD: His Majesty, the Emperor!

(*The* TWO VALETS *enter first, and go and stand on either side of the throne. Then* HENRY IV *comes in between* ORDULPH *and* HAROLD, *who keep a little in the rear respectfully.*)

HENRY IV *is about 50 and very pale. The hair on the back of his head is already grey; over the temples and forehead it appears blond, owing to its having been tinted in an evident and puerile fashion. On his cheek bones he has two small, doll-like dabs of color, that stand out prominently against the rest of his tragic pallor. He is wearing a penitent's sack over his regal habit, as at Canossa. His eyes have a fixed look which is dreadful to see, and this expression is in strained contrast with the sackcloth.* ORDULPH *carries the Imperial crown;* HAROLD, *the sceptre with eagle, and the globe with the cross.*)

HENRY IV: (*bowing first to* DONNA MA-TILDA *and afterwards to the* DOCTOR.) My lady . . . Monsignor . . . (*Then he looks at* BELCREDI *and seems about to greet him too; when, suddenly, he turns to* LAN-DOLPH, *who has approached him, and asks him sotto voce and with diffidence.*) Is that Peter Damiani?

LANDOLPH: No, Sire. He is a monk from Cluny who is accompanying the Abbot.

HENRY IV: (*looks again at* BELCREDI *with increasing mistrust, and then noticing that he appears embarrassed and keeps glancing at* DONNA MATILDA *and the* DOC-TOR, *stands upright and cries out.*) No, it's Peter Damiani! It's no use, father, your looking at the Duchess. (*Then turning quickly to* DONNA MATILDA *and the* DOCTOR *as though to ward off a danger.*) I swear it! I swear that my heart is changed to-wards your daughter. I confess that if he (*Indicates* BELCREDI.) hadn't come to for-bid it in the name of Pope Alexander, I'd have repudiated her. Yes, yes, there were people ready to favour the repudiation: the Bishop of Mayence would have done it for a matter of one hundred and twenty farms. (*Looks at* LANDOLPH *a little per-plexed and adds.*) But I mustn't speak ill of the bishops at this moment! (*More humbly to* BELCREDI.) I am grateful to you, believe me, I am grateful to you for the hindrance you put in my way!—God knows, my life's been all made of humili-ations: my mother, Adalbert, Tribur, Gos-lar! And now this sackcloth you see me wearing! (*Changes tone suddenly and speaks like one who goes over his part in a parenthesis of astuteness.*) It doesn't matter: clarity of ideas, perspicacity, firm-ness and patience under adversity that's the thing. (*Then turning to all and speak-ing solemnly.*) I know how to make amend for the mistakes I have made; and I can humiliate myself even before you, Peter Damiani. (*Bows profoundly to him and remains curved. Then a suspicion is* born in him which he is obliged to utter in menacing tones, almost against his will.) Was it not perhaps you who started that obscene rumor that my holy mother had illicit relations with the Bishop of Au-gusta?

BELCREDI: (*since* HENRY IV *has his finger pointed at him.*) No, no, it wasn't I . . .

HENRY IV: (*straightening up.*) Not true, not true? Infamy! (*Looks at him and then adds.*) I didn't think you capable of it! (*Goes to the* DOCTOR *and plucks his sleeve, while winking at him knowingly.*) Always the same, Monsignor, those bishops, always the same!

HAROLD: (*softly, whispering as if to help out the doctor.*) Yes, yes, the rapacious bishops!

THE DOCTOR: (*to* HAROLD, *trying to keep it up.*) Ah, yes, those fellows . . . ah yes . . .

HENRY IV: Nothing satisfies them! I was a little boy, Monsignor . . . One passes the time, playing even, when, without knowing it, one is a king.—I was six years old; and they tore me away from my mother, and made use of me against her without my knowing anything about it . . . always profaning, always stealing, stealing! . . . One greedier than the other . . . Hanno worse than Stephen! Stephen worse than Hanno!

LANDOLPH: (*sotto voce, persuasively, to call his attention.*) Majesty!

HENRY IV: (*turning round quickly.*) Ah yes . . . this isn't the moment to speak ill of the bishops. But this infamy against my mother, Monsignor, is too much. (*Looks at the* MARCHIONESS *and grows tender.*) And I can't even weep for her, Lady . . . I appeal to you who have a mother's heart! She came here to see me from her convent a month ago . . . They had told me she was dead! (*Sustained pause full of feeling. Then smiling sadly.*)

I can't weep for her; because if you are here now and I am like this (*Shows the sackcloth he is wearing.*) it means I am twenty-six years old!

HAROLD: And that she is therefore alive, Majesty! . . .

ORDULPH: Still in her convent!

HENRY IV: (*looking at them.*) Ah yes! And I can postpone my grief to another time. (*Shows the* MARCHIONESS *almost with coquetry the tint he has given to his hair.*) Look! I am still fair . . . (*Then slowly as if in confidence.*) For you . . . there's no need! But little exterior details do help! A matter of time, Monsignor, do you understand me? (*Turns to the* MARCHIONESS *and notices her hair.*) Ah, but I see that you too, Duchess . . . Italian, eh? (*As much as to say "false"; but without any indignation, indeed rather with malicious admiration.*) Heaven forbid that I should show disgust or surprise! Nobody cares to recognize that obscure and fatal power which sets limits to our will. But I say, if one is born and one dies . . . Did you want to be born, Monsignor? I didn't! And in both cases, independently of our wills, so many things happen we would wish didn't happen, and to which we resign ourselves as best we can! . . .

DOCTOR: (*merely to make a remark, while studying* HENRY IV *carefully.*) Alas! Yes, alas!

HENRY IV: It's like this: When we are not resigned, out come our desires. A woman wants to be a man . . . an old man would be young again. Desires, ridiculous fixed ideas of course— But reflect! Monsignor, those other desires are not less ridiculous: I mean, those desires where the will is kept within the limits of the possible. Not one of us can lie or pretend. We're all fixed in good faith in a certain concept of ourselves. However, Monsignor, while you keep yourself in order, holding on with both your hands to your holy habit, there slips down from your sleeves,

there peels off from you like . . . like a serpent . . . something you don't notice: life, Monsignor! (*Turns to the* MARCHIONESS.) Has it never happened to you, my Lady, to find a different self in yourself? Have you always been the same? My God! One day . . . how was it, how was it you were able to commit this or that action? (*Fixes her so intently in the eyes as almost to make her blanch.*) Yes, that particular action, that very one: we understand each other! But don't be afraid: I shall reveal it to none. And you, Peter Damiani, how could you be a friend of that man? . . .

LANDOLPH: Majesty!

HENRY IV: (*at once.*) No, I won't name him! (*Turning to* BELCREDI.) What did you think of him? But we all of us cling tight to our conceptions of ourselves, just as he who is growing old dyes his hair. What does it matter that this dyed hair of mine isn't a reality for you, if it *is*, to some extent, for me?—you, you, my Lady, certainly don't dye your hair to deceive the others, nor even yourself; but only to cheat your own image a little before the looking-glass. I do it for a joke! You do it seriously! But I assure you that you too, Madam, are in masquerade, though it be in all seriousness; and I am not speaking of the venerable crown on your brows or the ducal mantle. I am speaking only of the memory you wish to fix in yourself of your fair complexion one day when it pleased you—or of your dark complexion, if you were dark: the fading image of your youth! For you, Peter Damiani, on the contrary, the memory of what you have been, of what you have done, seems to you a recognition of past realities that remain within you like a dream. I'm in the same case too: with so many inexplicable memories—like dreams! Ah! . . . There's nothing to marvel at in it, Peter Damiani! Tomorrow it will be the same thing with our life of today! (*Suddenly getting ex-*

cited and taking hold of his sackcloth.)
This sackcloth here . . . (*Beginning to
take it off with a gesture of almost ferocious joy while the* THREE VALETS *run
over to him, frightened, as if to prevent
his doing so.*) Ah, my God! (*Draws back
and throws off sackcloth.*) Tomorrow, at
Bressanone, twenty-seven German and
Lombard bishops will sign with me the
act of deposition of Gregory VII! No
Pope at all! Just a false monk!

ORDULPH: (*with the other three.*) Majesty! Majesty! In God's name! . . .

HAROLD: (*inviting him to put on the
sackcloth again.*) Listen to what he says,
Majesty!

LANDOLPH: Monsignor is here with the
Duchess to intercede in your favor. (*Make
secret signs to the* DOCTOR *to say something
at once.*)

DOCTOR: (*foolishly.*) Ah yes . . . yes
. . . we are here to intercede . . .

HENRY IV: (*repenting at once, almost
terrified, allowing the three to put on the
sackcloth again, and pulling it down over
him with his own hands.*) Pardon . . .
yes . . . yes . . . pardon, Monsignor: forgive me, my Lady . . . I swear to you I
feel the whole weight of the anathema.
(*Bends himself, takes his face between his
hands, as though waiting for something
to crush him. Then changing tone, but
without moving, says softly to* LANDOLPH,
HAROLD *and* ORDULPH.) But I don't know
why I cannot be humble before that man
there! (*Indicates* BELCREDI.)

LANDOLPH: (*sotto voce.*) But why, Majesty, do you insist on believing he is
Peter Damiani, when he isn't, at all?

HENRY IV: (*looking at him timorously.*)
He isn't Peter Damiani?

HAROLD: No, no, he is a poor monk,
Majesty.

HENRY IV: (*sadly with a touch of ex-
asperation.*) Ah! None of us can estimate

what we do when we do it from instinct
. . . You perhaps, Madam, can understand
me better than the others, since you are a
woman and a Duchess. This is a solemn
and decisive moment. I could, you know,
accept the assistance of the Lombardi bishops, arrest the Pope, lock him up here in
the castle, run to Rome and elect an anti-
Pope; offer alliance to Robert Guiscard—
and Gregory VII would be lost! I resist the
temptation; and, believe me, I am wise in
doing so. I feel the atmosphere of our
times and the majesty of one who knows
how to be what he ought to be! a Pope!
Do you feel inclined to laugh at me, seeing me like this? You would be foolish to
do so; for you don't understand the political wisdom which makes this penitent's
sack advisable. The parts may be changed
tomorrow. What would you do then?
Would you laugh to see the Pope a
prisoner? No! It would come to the same
thing: I dressed as a penitent, today; he,
as prisoner tomorrow! But woe to him
who doesn't know how to wear his mask,
be he king or Pope!—Perhaps he is a bit
too cruel! No! Yes, yes, maybe!—You remember, my Lady, how your daughter
Bertha, for whom, I repeat, my feelings
have changed (*Turns to* BELCREDI *and
shouts to his face as if he were being con-
tradicted by him.*)—yes, changed on account of the affection and devotion she
showed me in that terrible moment . . .
(*Then once again to the* MARCHIONESS.)
. . . you remember how she came with me,
my Lady, followed me like a beggar and
passed two nights out in the open, in the
snow? You are her mother! Doesn't this
touch your mother's heart? Doesn't this
urge you to pity, so that you will beg His
Holiness for pardon, beg him to receive
us?

DONNA MATILDA: (*trembling, with feeble
voice.*) Yes, yes, at once . . .

DOCTOR: It shall be done!

HENRY IV: And one thing more! (*Draws them in to listen to him.*) It isn't enough that he should receive me! You know he can do *everything—everything* I tell you! He can even call up the dead. (*Touches his chest.*) Behold me! Do you see me? There is no magic art unknown to him. Well, Monsignor, my Lady, my torment is really this: that whether here or there (*Pointing to his portrait almost in fear.*) I can't free myself from this magic. I am a penitent now, you see; and I swear to you I shall remain so until he receives me. But you two, when the excommunication is taken off, must ask the Pope to do this thing he can so easily do: to take me away from that; (*Indicating the portrait again.*) and let me live wholly and freely my miserable life. A man can't always be twenty-six, my Lady. I ask this of you for your daughter's sake too; that I may love her as she deserves to be loved, well disposed as I am now, all tender towards her for her pity. There: it's all there! I am in your hands! (*Bows.*) My Lady! Monsignor!

(*He goes off, bowing grandly, through the door by which he entered, leaving everyone stupefied, and the* MARCHIONESS *so profoundly touched, that no sooner has he gone than she breaks out into sobs and sits down almost fainting.*)

ACT II

Another room of the villa, adjoining the throne room. Its furniture is antique and severe. Principal exit at rear in the background. To the left, two windows looking on the garden. To the right, a door opening into the throne room.

Late afternoon of the same day.

DONNA MATILDA, *the* DOCTOR *and* BELCREDI *are on the stage engaged in conversation; but* DONNA MATILDA *stands to one side, evidently annoyed at what the other two are saying; although she cannot help listening, because, in her agitated state, everything interests her in spite of herself. The talk of the other two attracts her attention, because she instinctively feels the need for calm at the moment.*

BELCREDI: It may be as you say, Doctor, but that was my impression.

DOCTOR: I won't contradict you; but, believe me, it is only . . . an impression.

BELCREDI: Pardon me, but he even said so, and quite clearly (*Turning to the* MARCHIONESS.) Didn't he, Marchioness?

DONNA MATILDA: (*turning round.*) What did he say? . . . (*Then not agreeing.*) Oh yes . . . but not for the reason you think!

DOCTOR: He was alluding to the costumes we had slipped on . . . Your cloak (*Indicating the* MARCHIONESS.) our Benedictine habits . . . But all this is childish!

DONNA MATILDA: (*turning quickly, indignant.*) Childish? What do you mean, Doctor?

DOCTOR: From one point of view, it is —I beg you to let me say so, Marchioness! Yet, on the other hand, it is much more complicated than you can imagine.

DONNA MATILDA: To me, on the contrary, it is perfectly clear!

DOCTOR: (*with a smile of pity of the competent person towards those who do not understand.*) We must take into account the peculiar psychology of madmen; which, you must know, enables us to be certain that they observe things and can, for instance, easily detect people who are disguised; can in fact recognize the disguise and yet believe in it; just as children do, for whom disguise is both play and reality. That is why I used the word childish. But the thing is extremely complicated, inasmuch as he must be perfectly aware of being an image to himself and for himself—that image there, in fact! (*Alluding to the portrait in the throne room, and pointing to the left.*)

BELCREDI: That's what he said!

DOCTOR: Very well then— An image before which other images, ours, have appeared: understand? Now he, in his acute and perfectly lucid delirium, was able to detect at once a difference between his image and ours: that is, he saw that ours were make-believes. So he suspected us; because all madmen are armed with a special diffidence. But that's all there is to it! Our make-believe, built up all round his, did not seem pitiful to him. While his seemed all the more tragic to us, in that he, as if in defiance—understand?—and induced by his suspicion, wanted to show us up merely as a joke. That was also partly the case with him, in coming before us with painted cheeks and hair, and saying he had done it on purpose for a jest.

DONNA MATILDA: (*impatiently.*) No, it's not that, Doctor. It's not like that! It's not like that!

DOCTOR: Why isn't it, may I ask?

DONNA MATILDA: (*with decision but trembling.*) I am perfectly certain he recognized me!

DOCTOR: It's not possible . . . it's not possible!

BELCREDI: (*at the same time.*) Of course not!

DONNA MATILDA: (*more than ever determined, almost convulsively.*) I tell you, he recognized me! When he came close up to speak to me—looking in my eyes, right into my eyes—he recognized me!

BELCREDI: But he was talking of your daughter!

DONNA MATILDA: That's not true! He was talking of me! Of me!

BELCREDI: Yes, perhaps, when he said . . .

DONNA MATILDA: (*letting herself go.*) About my dyed hair! But didn't you notice that he added at once: "or the memory of your dark hair, if you were dark"? He remembered perfectly well that I was dark—then!

BELCREDI: Nonsense! Nonsense!

DONNA MATILDA: (*not listening to him, turning to the* DOCTOR.) My hair, Doctor, is really dark—like my daughter's! That's why he spoke of her.

BELCREDI: But he doesn't even know your daughter! He's never seen her!

DONNA MATILDA: Exactly! Oh, you never understand anything! By my daughter, stupid, he meant me—as I was then!

BELCREDI: Oh, this is catching! This is catching, this madness!

DONNA MATILDA: (*softly, with contempt.*) Fool!

BELCREDI: Excuse me, were you ever his wife? Your daughter is his wife—in his delirium: Bertha of Susa.

DONNA MATILDA: Exactly! Because I, no longer dark—as he remembered me—but *fair,* introduced myself as "Adelaide," the mother. My daughter doesn't exist for him: he's never seen her—you said so yourself! So how can he know whether she's fair or dark?

BELCREDI: But he said dark, speaking generally, just as anyone who wants to recall, whether fair or dark, a memory of youth in the color of the hair! And you, as usual, begin to imagine things! Doctor, you said I ought not to have come! It's she who ought not to have come!

DONNA MATILDA: (*upset for a moment by* BELCREDI's *remark, recovers herself. Then with a touch of anger, because doubtful.*) No, no . . . he spoke of me . . . He spoke all the time to me, with me, of me . . .

BELCREDI: That's not bad! He didn't leave me a moment's breathing space; and you say he was talking all the time to you? Unless you think he was alluding to you too, when he was talking to Peter Damiani!

DONNA MATILDA: (*defiantly, almost exceeding the limits of courteous discussion.*) Who knows? Can you tell me why, from the outset, he showed a strong dislike for you, for you alone? (*From the tone of the question, the expected answer must almost explicitly be: "because he understands you are my lover."* BELCREDI *feels this so well that he remains silent and can say nothing.*)

DOCTOR: The reason may also be found in the fact that only the visit of the Duchess Adelaide and the Abbot of Cluny was announced to him. Finding a third person present, who had not been announced, at once his suspicions . . .

BELCREDI: Yes, exactly! His suspicion made him see an enemy in me: Peter Damiani! But she's got it into her head, that he recognized her . . .

DONNA MATILDA: There's no doubt about it! I could see it from his eyes, doctor. You know, there's a way of looking that leaves no doubt whatever . . . Perhaps it was only for an instant, but I am sure!

DOCTOR: It is not impossible: a lucid moment . . .

DONNA MATILDA: Yes, perhaps . . . And then his speech seemed to me full of regret for his and my youth—for the horrible thing that happened to him, that has held him in that disguise from which he has never been able to free himself, and from which he longs to be free—he said so himself!

BELCREDI: Yes, so as to be able to make love to your daughter, or you, as you believe—having been touched by your pity.

DONNA MATILDA: Which is very great, I would ask you to believe.

BELCREDI: As one can see, Marchioness; so much so that a miracle-worker might expect a miracle from it!

DOCTOR: Will you let me speak? I don't work miracles, because I am a doctor and not a miracle-worker. I listened very intently to all he said; and I repeat that that certain analogical elasticity, common to all systematized delirium, is evidently with him much . . . what shall I say?—much relaxed! The elements, that is, of his delirium no longer hold together. It seems to me he has lost the equilibrium of his second personality and sudden recollections drag him—and this is very comforting—not from a state of incipient apathy, but rather from a morbid inclination to reflective melancholy, which shows a . . . a very considerable cerebral activity. Very comforting, I repeat! Now if, by this violent trick we've planned . . .

DONNA MATILDA: (*turning to the window, in the tone of a sick person complaining.*) But how is it that the motor has not returned? It's three hours and a half since . . .

DOCTOR: What do you say?

DONNA MATILDA: The motor, Doctor! It's more than three hours and a half . . .

DOCTOR: (*taking out his watch and looking at it.*) Yes, more than four hours, by this!

DONNA MATILDA: It could have reached here an hour ago at least! But, as usual . . .

BELCREDI: Perhaps they can't find the dress . . .

DONNA MATILDA: But I explained exactly where it was! (*Impatiently.*) And Frida . . . where is Frida?

BELCREDI: (*looking out of the window.*) Perhaps she is in the garden with Charles . . .

DOCTOR: He'll talk her out of her fright.

BELCREDI: She's not afraid, Doctor; don't you believe it: the thing bores her rather . . .

DONNA MATILDA: Just don't ask anything of her! I know what she's like.

DOCTOR: Let's wait patiently. Anyhow, it will soon be over, and it has to be in the evening . . . It will only be the matter of a moment! If we can succeed in rousing him, as I was saying, and in breaking at one go the threads—already slack—which still bind him to this fiction of his, giving him back what he himself asks for—you remember, he said: "one cannot always be twenty-six years old, madam!" if we can give him freedom from this torment, which even *he* feels is a torment, then if he is able to recover at one bound the sensation of the distance of time . . .

BELCREDI: (*quickly.*) He'll be cured! (*Then emphatically with irony.*) We'll pull him out of it all!

DOCTOR: Yes, we may hope to set him going again, like a watch which has stopped at a certain hour . . . just as if we had our watches in our hands and were waiting for that other watch to go again.—A shake—so—and let's hope it'll tell the time again after its long stop. (*At this point the* MARQUIS CHARLES DI NOLLI *enters from the principal entrance.*)

DONNA MATILDA: Oh, Charles! . . . And Frida? Where is she?

DI NOLLI: She'll be here in a moment.

DOCTOR: Has the motor arrived?

DI NOLLI: Yes.

DONNA MATILDA: Yes? Has the dress come?

DI NOLLI: It's been here some time.

DOCTOR: Good! Good!

DONNA MATILDA: (*trembling.*) Where is she? Where's Frida?

DI NOLLI: (*shrugging his shoulders and smiling sadly, like one lending himself unwillingly to an untimely joke.*) You'll see, you'll see! . . . (*Pointing towards the hall.*) Here she is! . . . (BERTHOLD *appears at the threshold of the hall, and announces with solemnity.*)

BERTHOLD: Her Highness the Countess Matilda of Canossa! (FRIDA *enters, magnificent and beautiful, arrayed in the robes of her mother as "Countess Matilda of Tuscany," so that she is a living copy of the portrait in the throne room.*)

FRIDA: (*passing* BERTHOLD, *who is bowing, says to him with disdain.*) Of Tuscany, of Tuscany! Canossa is just one of my castles!

BELCREDI: (*in admiration.*) Look! Look! She seems another person . . .

DONNA MATILDA: One would say it were I! Look!—Why, Frida, look! She's exactly my portrait, alive!

DOCTOR: Yes, yes . . . Perfect! Perfect! The portrait, to the life.

BELCREDI: Yes, there's no question about it. She *is* the portrait! Magnificent!

FRIDA: Don't make me laugh, or I shall burst! I say, mother, what a tiny waist you had? I had to squeeze so to get into this!

DONNA MATILDA: (*arranging her dress a little.*) Wait! . . . Keep still . . . These pleats . . . is it really so tight?

FRIDA: I'm suffocating! I implore you, to be quick! . . .

DOCTOR: But we must wait till it's evening!

FRIDA: No, no, I can't hold out till evening!

DONNA MATILDA: Why did you put it on so soon?

FRIDA: The moment I saw it, the temptation was irresistible . . .

DONNA MATILDA: At least you could have called me, or have had someone help you! It's still all crumpled.

FRIDA: So I saw, mother; but they are old creases; they won't come out.

DOCTOR: It doesn't matter, Marchioness!

The illusion is perfect. (*Then coming nearer and asking her to come in front of her daughter, without hiding her.*) If you please, stay there, there . . . at a certain distance . . . now a little more forward . . .

BELCREDI: For the feeling of the distance of time . . .

DONNA MATILDA: (*slightly turning to him.*) Twenty years after! A disaster! A tragedy!

BELCREDI: Now don't let's exaggerate!

DOCTOR: (*embarrassed, trying to save the situation.*) No, no! I meant the dress . . . so as to see . . . You know . . .

BELCREDI: (*laughing.*) Oh, as for the dress, Doctor, it isn't a matter of twenty years! It's eight hundred! An abyss! Do you really want to shove him across it (*Pointing first to* FRIDA *and then to* MARCHIONESS.) from there to here? But you'll have to pick him up in pieces with a basket! Just think now: for us it is a matter of twenty years, a couple of dresses, and a masquerade. But, if, as you say, Doctor, time has stopped for and around him: if he lives there (*Pointing to* FRIDA.) with her, eight hundred years ago . . . I repeat: the giddiness of the jump will be such, that finding himself suddenly among us . . . (*The* DOCTOR *shakes his head in dissent.*) You don't think so?

DOCTOR: No, because life, my dear baron, can take up its rhythms. This—our life —will at once become real also to him; and will pull him up directly, wresting from him suddenly the illusion, and showing him that the eight hundred years, as you say, are only twenty! It will be like one of those tricks, such as the leap into space, for instance, of the Masonic rite, which appears to be heaven knows how far, and is only a step down the stairs.

BELCREDI: Ah! An idea! Yes! Look at Frida and the Marchioness, doctor! Which is more advanced in time? We old people

Doctor! The young ones think they are more ahead; but it isn't true: we are more ahead, because time belongs to us more than to them.

DOCTOR: If the past didn't alienate us . . .

BELCREDI: It doesn't matter at all! How does it alienate us? They (*Pointing to* FRIDA *and* DI NOLLI.) have still to do what we have accomplished, Doctor: to grow old, doing the same foolish things, more or less, as we did . . . This is the illusion: that one comes forward through a door to life. It isn't so! As soon as one is born, one starts dying; therefore, he who started first is the most advanced of all. The youngest of us is father Adam! Look there: (*Pointing to* FRIDA.) eight hundred years younger than all of us—the Countess Matilda of Tuscany. (*He makes her a deep bow.*)

DI NOLLI: I say, Tito, don't start joking.

BELCREDI: Oh, you think I am joking? . . .

DI NOLLI: Of course, of course . . . all the time.

BELCREDI: Impossible! I've even dressed up as a Benedictine . . .

DI NOLLI: Yes, but for a serious purpose.

BELCREDI: Well, exactly. If it has been serious for the others . . . for Frida, now, for instance. (*Then turning to the* DOCTOR.) I swear, Doctor, I don't yet understand what you want to do.

DOCTOR: (*annoyed.*) You'll see! Let me do as I wish . . . At present you see the Marchioness still dressed as . . .

BELCREDI: Oh, she also . . . has to masquerade?

DOCTOR: Of course! of course! In another dress that's in there ready to be used when it comes into his head he sees the Countess Matilda of Canossa before him.

FRIDA: (*while talking quietly to* DI NOLLI *notices the doctor's mistake.*) Of Tuscany, of Tuscany!

DOCTOR: It's all the same!

BELCREDI: Oh, I see! He'll be faced by two of them . . .

DOCTOR: Two, precisely! And then . . .

FRIDA: (*calling him aside.*) Come here, doctor! Listen!

DOCTOR: Here I am! (*Goes near the two young people and pretends to give some explanations to them.*)

BELCREDI: (*softly to* DONNA MATILDA.) I say, this is getting rather strong, you know!

DONNA MATILDA: (*looking him firmly in the face.*) What?

BELCREDI: Does it really interest you as much as all that—to make you willing to take part in . . . ? For a woman this is simply enormous! . . .

DONNA MATILDA: Yes, for an ordinary woman.

BELCREDI: Oh, no, my dear, for all women,—in a question like this! It's an abnegation.

DONNA MATILDA: I owe it to him.

BELCREDI: Don't lie! You know well enough it's not hurting you!

DONNA MATILDA: Well, then, where does the abnegation come in?

BELCREDI: Just enough to prevent you losing caste in other people's eyes—and just enough to offend me! . . .

DONNA MATILDA: But who is worrying about you now?

DI NOLLI: (*coming forward.*) It's all right. It's all right. That's what we'll do! (*Turning towards* BERTHOLD.) Here you, go and call one of those fellows!

BERTHOLD: At once! (*Exit.*)

DONNA MATILDA: But first of all we've got to pretend that we are going away.

DI NOLLI: Exactly! I'll see to that . . . (*To* BELCREDI.) you don't mind staying here?

BELCREDI: (*ironically.*) Oh, no, I don't mind, I don't mind! . . .

DI NOLLI: We must look out not to make him suspicious again, you know.

BELCREDI: Oh, Lord! *He* doesn't amount to anything!

DOCTOR: He must believe absolutely that we've gone away. (LANDOLPH followed *by* BERTHOLD *enters from the right.*)

LANDOLPH: May I come in?

DI NOLLI: Come in! Come in! I say— your name's Lolo, isn't it?

LANDOLPH: Lolo, or Landolph, just as you like!

DI NOLLI: Well, look here: the Doctor and the Marchioness are leaving, at once.

LANDOLPH: Very well. All we've got to say is that they have been able to obtain the permission for the reception from His Holiness. He's in there in his own apartments repenting of all he said—and in an awful state to have the pardon! Would you mind coming a minute? . . . If you would, just for a minute . . . put on the dress again . . .

DOCTOR: Why, of course, with pleasure . . .

LANDOLPH: Might I be allowed to make a suggestion? Why not add that the Marchioness of Tuscany has interceded with the Pope that he should be received?

DONNA MATILDA: You see, he has recognized me!

LANDOLPH: Forgive me . . . I don't know my history very well. I am sure you gentlemen know it much better! But I thought it was believed that Henry IV had a secret passion for the Marchioness of Tuscany.

DONNA MATILDA: (*at once.*) Nothing of the kind! Nothing of the kind!

LANDOLPH: That's what I thought! But he says he's loved her . . . he's always saying it . . . And now he fears that her indignation for this secret love of his will work him harm with the Pope.

BELCREDI: We must let him understand that this aversion no longer exists.

LANDOLPH: Exactly! Of course!

DONNA MATILDA: (*to* BELCREDI.) History says—I don't know whether you know it or not—that the Pope gave way to the supplications of the Marchioness Matilda and the Abbot of Cluny. And I may say, my dear Belcredi, that I intended to take advantage of this fact—at the time of the pageant—to show him my feelings were not so hostile to him as he supposed.

BELCREDI: You are most faithful to history, Marchioness . . .

LANDOLPH: Well then, the Marchioness could spare herself a double disguise and present herself with Monsignor (*Indicating the* DOCTOR.) as the Marchioness of Tuscany.

DOCTOR: (*quickly, energetically.*) No, no! That won't do at all. It would ruin everything. The impression from the confrontation must be a sudden one, give a shock! No, no, Marchioness, you will appear again as the Duchess Adelaide, the mother of the Empress. And then we'll go away. This is most necessary: that he should know we've gone away. Come on! Don't let's waste any more time! There's a lot to prepare.

(*Exeunt the* DOCTOR, DONNA MATILDA, *and* LANDOLPH, *right.*)

FRIDA: I am beginning to feel afraid again.

DI NOLLI: Again, Frida?

FRIDA: It would have been better if I had seen him before.

DI NOLLI: There's nothing to be frightened of, really.

FRIDA: He isn't furious, is he?

DI NOLLI: Of course not! he's quite calm.

BELCREDI: (*with ironic sentimental affectation.*) Melancholy! Didn't you hear that he loves you?

FRIDA: Thanks! That's just why I am afraid.

BELCREDI: He won't do you any harm.

DI NOLLI: It'll only last a minute . . .

FRIDA: Yes, but there in the dark with him . . .

DI NOLLI: Only for a moment; and I will be near you, and all the others behind the door ready to run in. As soon as you see your mother, your part will be finished . . .

BELCREDI: I'm afraid of a different thing: that we're wasting our time . . .

DI NOLLI: Don't begin again! The remedy seems a sound one to me.

FRIDA: I think so too! I feel it! I'm all trembling!

BELCREDI: But, mad people, my dear friends—though they don't know it, alas —have this felicity which we don't take into account . . .

DI NOLLI: (*interrupting, annoyed.*) What felicity? Nonsense!

BELCREDI: (*forcefully.*) They don't reason!

DI NOLLI: What's reasoning got to do with it, anyway?

BELCREDI: Don't you call it reasoning that he will have to do—according to us —when he sees her (*Indicates* FRIDA.) and her mother? We've reasoned it all out, surely!

DI NOLLI: Nothing of the kind: no reasoning at all! We put before him a double image of his own fantasy, or fiction, as the doctor says.

BELCREDI: (*suddenly.*) I say, I've never understood why they take degrees in medicine.

DI NOLLI: (*amazed.*) Who?

BELCREDI: The alienists!

DI NOLLI: What ought they to take degrees in, then?

FRIDA: If they are alienists, in what else should they take degrees?

BELCREDI: In law, of course! All a matter of talk! The more they talk, the more highly they are considered. "Analogous elasticity," "the sensation of distance in time!" And the first thing they tell you is that they don't work miracles —when a miracle's just what is wanted! But they know that the more they say they are not miracle-workers, the more folk believe in their seriousness!

BERTHOLD: (*who has been looking through the keyhole of the door on right.*) There they are! There they are! They're coming in here.

DI NOLLI: Are they?

BERTHOLD: He wants to come with them . . . Yes! . . . He's coming too!

DI NOLLI: Let's get away, then! Let's get away, at once! (*To* BERTHOLD.) You stop here!

BERTHOLD: Must I?

(*Without answering him,* DI NOLLI, FRIDA, *and* BELCREDI *go out by the main exit, leaving* BERTHOLD *surprised. The door on the right opens, and* LANDOLPH *enters first, bowing. Then* DONNA MATILDA *comes in, with mantle and ducal crown as in the first act; also the* DOCTOR *as the* ABBOT OF CLUNY. HENRY IV *is among them in royal dress.* ORDULPH *and* HAROLD *enter last of all.*)

HENRY IV: (*following up what he has been saying in the other room.*) And now I will ask you a question: how can I be astute, if you think me obstinate?

DOCTOR: No, no, not obstinate!

HENRY IV: (*smiling, pleased.*) Then you think me really astute?

DOCTOR: No, no, neither obstinate, nor astute.

HENRY IV: (*with benevolent irony.*) Monsignor, if obstinacy is not a vice which can go with astuteness, I hoped that in denying me the former, you would at least allow me a little of the latter. I can assure you I have great need of it. But if you want to keep it all for yourself . . .

DOCTOR: I? I? Do I seem astute to you?

HENRY IV: No. Monsignor! What do you say? Not in the least! Perhaps in this case, I may seem a little obstinate to you (*Cutting short to speak to* DONNA MATILDA.) With your permission: a word in confidence to the Duchess. (*Leads her aside and asks her very earnestly.*) Is your daughter really dear to you?

DONNA MATILDA: (*dismayed.*) Why, yes, certainly . . .

HENRY IV: Do you wish me to compensate her with all my love, with all my devotion, for the grave wrongs I have done her—though you must not believe all the stories my enemies tell about my dissoluteness!

DONNA MATILDA: No, no, I don't believe them. I never have believed such stories.

HENRY IV: Well, then are you willing?

DONNA MATILDA: (*confused.*) What?

HENRY IV: That I return to love your daughter again? (*Looks at her and adds, in a mysterious tone of warning.*) You mustn't be a friend of the Marchioness of Tuscany!

DONNA MATILDA: I tell you again that she has begged and tried not less than ourselves to obtain your pardon . . .

HENRY IV: (*softly, but excitedly.*) Don't tell me that! Dont' say that to me! Don't you see the effect it has on me, my Lady?

DONNA MATILDA: (*looks at him; then very softly as if in confidence.*) You love her still?

HENRY IV: (*puzzled.*) Still? Still, you

say? You know, then? But nobody knows!
Nobody must know!

DONNA MATILDA: But perhaps she
knows, if she has begged so hard for you!

HENRY IV: (*looks at her and says.*) And
you love your daughter? (*Brief pause. He
turns to the* DOCTOR *with laughing accents.*) Ah, Monsignor, it's strange how
little I think of my wife! It may be a sin,
but I swear to you that I hardly feel her
at all in my heart. What is stranger is
that her own mother scarcely feels her in
her heart. Confess, my Lady, that she
amounts to very little for you. (*Turning
to* DOCTOR.) She talks to me of that other
woman, insistently, insistently, I don't
know why! . . .

LANDOLPH: (*humbly.*) Maybe, Majesty, it is to disabuse you of some ideas
you have had about the Marchioness of
Tuscany. (*Then, dismayed at having allowed himself this observaiton, adds.*) I
mean just now, of course . . .

HENRY IV: You too maintain that she
has been friendly to me?

LANDOLPH: Yes, at the moment, Majesty.

DONNA MATILDA: Exactly! Exactly! . . .

HENRY IV: I understand. That is to say,
you don't believe I love her. I see! I see!
Nobody's ever believed it, nobody's ever
thought it. Better so, then! But enough,
enough! (*Turns to the* DOCTOR *with
changed expression.*) Monsignor, you see?
The reasons the Pope has had for revok-
ing the excommunication have got nothing at all to do with the reasons for which
he excommunicated me originally. Tell
Pope Gregory we shall meet again at
Brixen. And you, Madame, should you
chance to meet your daughter in the courtyard of the castle of your friend the Marchioness, ask her to visit me. We shall see
if I succeed in keeping her close beside me
as wife and Empress. Many women have

presented themselves here already assur-
ing me that they were she. And I thought
to have her—yes, I tried sometimes—
there's no shame in it, with one's wife!—
But when they said they were Bertha, and
they were from Susa, all of them—I can't
think why—started laughing! (*Confidentially.*) Understand?—in bed—I undressed
—so did she—yes, by God, undressed—
a man and a woman—it's natural after all!
Like that, we don't bother much about
who we are. And one's dress is like a
phantom that hovers always near one.
Oh, Monsignor, phantoms in general are
nothing more than trifling disorders of
the spirit: images we cannot contain
within the bounds of sleep. They reveal
themselves even when we are awake, and
they frighten us. I . . . ah . . . I am always
afraid when, at night time, I see disordered images before me. Sometimes I
am even afraid of my own blood pulsing
loudly in my arteries in the silence of
night, like the sound of a distant step in
a lonely corridor! . . . But, forgive me! I
have kept you standing too long already.
I thank you, my Lady, I thank you, Monsignor. (DONNA MATILDA *and the* DOCTOR
go off bowing. As soon as they have gone,
HENRY IV *suddenly changes his tone.*)
Buffoons, buffoons! One can play any
tune on them! And that other fellow . . .
Pietro Damiani! . . . Caught him out perfectly! He's afraid to appear before me
again. (*Moves up and down excitedly
while saying this; then sees* BERTHOLD,
*and points him out to the other three
valets.*) Oh, look at this imbecile watching me with his mouth wide open!
(*Shakes him.*) Don't you understand?
Don't you see, idiot, how I treat them,
how I play the fool with them, make
them appear before me just as I wish?
Miserable, frightened clowns that they
are! And you (*Addressing the* VALETS.) are
amazed that I tear off their ridiculous
masks now, just as if it wasn't I who had

made them mask themselves to satisfy this taste of mine for playing the madman!

LANDOLPH—HAROLD—ORDULPH (*bewildered, looking at one another.*) What? What does he say? What?

HENRY IV: (*answers them imperiously.*) Enough! enough! Let's stop it. I'm tired of it. (*Then as if the thought left him no peace.*) By God! The impudence! To come here along with her lover! . . . And pretending to do it out of pity! So as not to infuriate a poor devil already out of the world, out of time, out of life! If I hadn't been supposed to be done out of pity, one can well imagine that fellow wouldn't have allowed it. Those people expect others to behave as they wish all the time. And, of course, there's nothing arrogant in that! Oh, no! Oh, no! It's merely their way of thinking, of feeling, of seeing. Everybody has his own way of thinking; you fellows, too. Yours is that of a flock of sheep—miserable, feeble, uncertain . . . But those others take advantage of this and make you accept their way of thinking; or, at least, they suppose they do; because, after all, what do they succeed in imposing on you? Words, words which anyone can interpret in his own manner! That's the way public opinion is formed! And it's a bad look out for a man who finds himself labelled one day with one of these words which everyone repeats; for example, "madman," or "imbecile." Don't you think it is rather hard for a man to keep quiet, when he knows that there is a fellow going about trying to persuade everybody that he is as he sees him, trying to fix him in other people's opinion as a "madman"—according to him? Now I am talking seriously! Before I hurt my head, falling from my horse . . . (*Stops suddenly, noticing the dismay of the four young men.*) What's the matter with you? (*Imitates their amazed looks.*) What? Am I, or am I not, mad?

Oh, yes! I'm mad all right! (*He becomes terrible.*) Well, then, by God, down on your knees, down on your knees! (*Makes them go down on their knees one by one.*) I order you to go down on your knees before me! And touch the ground three times with your foreheads! Down, down! That's the way you've got to be before madmen! (*Then annoyed with their facile humiliation.*) Get up, sheep! You obeyed me didn't you? You might have put the strait jacket on me! . . . Crush a man with the weight of a word—it's nothing—a fly! all our life is crushed by the weight of words: the weight of the dead. Look at me here: can you really suppose that Henry IV is still alive? All the same, I speak, and order you live men about! Do you think it's a joke that the dead continue to live?—Yes, *here* it's a joke! But get out into the live world!—Ah, you say: what a beautiful sunrise—for us! All time is before us! Dawn! We will do what we like with this day—. Ah, yes! To Hell with tradition, the old conventions! Well, go on! You will do nothing but repeat the old, old words, while you imagine you are living! (*Goes up to* BERTHOLD *who has now become quite stupid.*) You don't understand a word of this, do you? What's your name?

BERTHOLD: I? . . . What? . . . Berthold . . .

HENRY IV: Poor Berthold! What's your name here?

BERTHOLD: I . . . I . . . my name is Fino.

HENRY IV: (*feeling the warning and critical glances of the others, turns to them to reduce them to silence.*) Fino?

BERTHOLD: Fino Pagliuca, sire.

HENRY IV: (*turning to* LANDOLPH.) I've heard you call each other by your nicknames often enough! Your name is Lolo, isn't it?

LANDOLPH: Yes, sire . . . (*Then with a sense of immense joy.*) Oh Lord! Oh Lord! Then he is not mad . . .

HENRY IV: (*brusquely.*) What?

LANDOLPH: (*hesitating.*) No . . . I said . . .

HENRY IV: Not mad, any more. No. Don't you see? We're having a joke on those that think I am mad! (*To* HAROLD.) I say, boy, your name's Franco . . . (*To* ORDULPH.) And yours . . .

ORDULPH: Momo.

HENRY IV: Momo, Momo . . . A nice name that!

LANDOLPH: So he isn't . . .

HENRY IV: What are you talking about? Of course not! Let's have a jolly, good laugh! . . . (*Laughs.*) Ah! . . . Ah! . . . Ah! . . .

LANDOLPH—HAROLD—ORDULPH: (*looking at each other half happy and half dismayed.*) Then he's cured . . . he's all right! . . .

HENRY IV: Silence! Silence! . . . (*To* BERTHOLD.) Why don't you laugh? Are you offended? I didn't mean it especially for you. It's convenient for everybody to insist that certain people are mad, so they can be shut up. Do you know why? Because it's impossible to hear them speak! What shall I say of these people who've just gone away? That one is a whore, another a libertine, another a swindler . . . don't you think so? You can't believe a word he says . . . don't you think so?— By the way, they all listen to me terrified. And why are they terrified, if what I say isn't true? Of course, you can't believe what madmen say—yet, at the same time, they stand there with their eyes wide open with terror!—Why? Tell me, tell me, why?—You see I'm quite calm now!

BERTHOLD: But, perhaps, they think that . . .

HENRY IV: No, no, my dear fellow! Look me well in the eyes! . . . I don't say that it's true—nothing is true, Berthold! But . . . look me in the eyes!

BERTHOLD: Well . . .

HENRY IV: You see? You see? . . . You have terror in your own eyes now because I seem mad to you! There's the proof of it! (*Laughs.*)

LANDOLPH: (*coming forward in the name of the others, exasperated.*) What proof?

HENRY IV: Your being so dismayed because now I seem again mad to you. You have thought me mad up to now, haven't you? You feel that this dismay of yours can become terror too—something to dash away the ground from under your feet and deprive you of the air you breathe! Do you know what it means to find yourselves face to face with a madman—with one who shakes the foundations of all you have built up in yourselves, your logic, the logic of all your constructions? Madmen, lucky folk! construct without logic, or rather with a logic that flies likes a feather. Voluble! Voluble! Today like this and tomorrow—who knows? You say: "This cannot be"; but for them everything can be. You say: "This isn't true!" And why? Because it doesn't seem true to you, or you, or you . . . (*Indicates the three of them in succession.*) . . . and to a hundred thousand others! One must see what seems true to these hundred thousand others who are not supposed to be mad! What a magnificent spectacle they afford, when they reason! What flowers of logic they scatter! I know that when I was a child, I thought the moon in the pond was real. How many things I thought real! I believed everything I was told—and I was happy! Because it's a terrible thing if you don't hold on to that which seems true to you today—to that which will seem true to you tomorrow, even if it is the opposite of that which seemed true to you yesterday. I would never wish you to think, as I have done, on this horrible thing which really drives one mad: that if you were beside another and looking into his eyes—as I one day looked into somebody's eyes—you might as well be a beggar before a door never to be opened to you; for he who does enter there will never be you, but someone unknown to you with his own different and impenetrable world . . . (*Long pause. Darkness gathers in the room, increasing the sense of strangeness and consternation in which the four young men are involved.* HENRY IV *remains aloof, pondering on the misery which is not only his, but everybody's. Then he pulls himself up, and says in an ordinary tone.*) It's getting dark here . . .

ORDULPH: Shall I go for a lamp?

HENRY IV: (*ironically.*) The lamp, yes the lamp! . . . Do you suppose I don't know that as soon as I turn my back with my oil lamp to go to bed, you turn on the electric light for yourselves, here, and even there, in the throne room? I pretend not to see it!

ORDULPH: Well, then, shall I turn it on now?

HENRY IV: No, it would blind me! I want my lamp!

ORDULPH: It's ready here behind the door. (*Goes to the main exit, opens the door, goes out for a moment, and returns with an ancient lamp which is held by a ring at the top.*)

HENRY IV: Ah, a little light! Sit there around the table, no, not like that; in an elegant, easy manner! . . . (*To* HAROLD.) Yes, you, like that! (*Poses him.*) (*Then to* BERTHOLD.) You, so! . . . and I, here! (*Sits opposite them.*) We could do with a little decorative moonlight. It's very useful for us, the moonlight. I feel a real necessity for it, and pass a lot of time look-ing up at the moon from my window. Who would think, to look at her that she knows that eight hundred years have passed, and that I, seated at the window, cannot really be Henry IV gazing at the moon like any poor devil? But, look, look! See what a magnificent night scene we have here: the emperor surrounded by his faithful counsellors! . . . How do you like it?

LANDOLPH: (*softly to* HAROLD, *so as not to break the enchantment.*) And to think it wasn't true! . . .

HENRY IV: True? What wasn't true?

LANDOLPH: (*timidly as if to excuse himself.*) No . . . I mean . . . I was saying this morning to him (*Indicates* BERTHOLD.) —he has just entered on service here— I was saying: what a pity that dressed like this and with so many beautiful costumes in the wardrobe . . . and with a room like that . . . (*Indicates the throne room.*)

HENRY IV: Well? what's the pity?

LANDOLPH: Well . . . that we didn't know . . .

HENRY IV: That it was all done in jest, this comedy?

LANDOLPH: Because we thought that . . .

HAROLD: (*coming to his assistance.*) Yes . . . that it was done seriously!

HENRY IV: What do you say? doesn't it seem serious to you?

LANDOLPH: But if you say that . . .

HENRY IV: I say that—you are fools! You ought to have known how to create a fantasy for yourselves, not to act it for me, or anyone coming to see me; but naturally, simply, day by day, before nobody, feeling yourselves alive in the history of the eleventh century, here at the court of your emperor, Henry IV! You, Ordulph (*Taking him by the arm.*), alive in the castle of Goslar, waking up in the morning, getting out of bed, and entering straightway into the dream, clothing yourself in the dream that would be no more a dream, because you would have lived it, felt it all alive in you. You would have drunk it in with the air you breathed; yet knowing all the time that it was a dream, so you could better enjoy the privilege afforded you of having to do nothing else but live this dream, this far off and yet actual dream! And to think that at a distance of eight centuries from this remote age of ours, so colored and so sepulchral, the men of the twentieth century are torturing themselves in ceaseless anxiety to know how their fates and fortunes will work out! Whereas you are already in history with me . . .

LANDOLPH: Yes, yes, very good!

HENRY IV: . . . Everything determined, everything settled!

ORDULPH: Yes, yes!

HENRY IV: And sad as is my lot, hideous as some of the events are, bitter the struggles and troublous the time—still all history! All history that cannot change, understand? All fixed for ever! And you could have admired at your ease how every effect followed obediently its cause with perfect logic, how every event took place precisely and coherently in each minute particular! The pleasure, the pleasure of history, in fact, which is so great, was yours.

LANDOLPH: Beautiful, beautiful!

HENRY IV: Beautiful, but it's finished! Now that you know, I could not do it any more! (*Takes his lamp to go to bed.*) Neither could you, if up to now you haven't understood the reason of it! I am sick of it now. (*Almost to himself with violent contained rage.*) By God, I'll make her sorry she came here! Dressed herself up as a mother-in-law for me . . . ! And he as an abbot . . . ! And they bring a doctor with them to study me . . . ! Who

knows if they don't hope to cure me? . . . Clowns . . . ! I'd like to smack one of them at least in the face: yes, that one—a famous swordsman, they say! . . . He'll kill me . . . Well, we'll see, we'll see! . . . (*A knock at the door.*) Who is it?

THE VOICE OF JOHN: Deo Gratias!

HAROLD: (*very pleased at the chance for another joke.*) Oh, it's John, it's old John, who comes every night to play the monk.

ORDULPH: (*rubbing his hands.*) Yes, yes! Let's make him do it!

HENRY IV: (*at once, severely.*) Fool, why? Just to play a joke on a poor old man who does it for love of me?

LANDOLPH: (*to* ORDULPH). It has to be as if it were true.

HENRY IV: Exactly, as if true! Because, only so, truth is not a jest. (*Opens the door and admits* JOHN *dressed as a humble friar with a roll of parchment under his arm.*) Come in, come in, father! (*Then assuming a tone of tragic gravity and deep resentment.*) All the documents of my life and reign favorable to me were destroyed deliberately by my enemies. One only has escaped destruction, this, my life, written by a humble monk who is devoted to me. And you would laugh at him! (*Turns affectionately to* JOHN, *and invites him to sit down at the table.*) Sit down, father, sit down! Have the lamp near you! (*Puts the lamp near him.*) Write! Write!

JOHN: (*opens the parchment and prepares to write from dictation*.) I am ready, your majesty!

HENRY IV: (*dictating.*) "The decree of peace proclaimed at Mayence helped the poor and the good, while it damaged the powerful and the bad. (*Curtain begins to fall.*) It brought wealth to the former, hunger and misery to the latter . . ."

Curtain.

ACT III

The throne room so dark that the wall at the bottom is hardly seen. The canvases of the two portraits have been taken away; and, within their frames, FRIDA, *dressed as the "Marchioness of Tuscany" and* CHARLES DI NOLLI, *as "Henry IV," have taken the exact positions of the portraits.*

For a moment, after the raising of curtain, the stage is empty. Then the door on the left opens; and HENRY IV, *holding the lamp by the ring on top of it, enters. He looks back to speak to the four young men, who, with* JOHN, *are presumably in the adjoining hall, as at the end of the second act.*

HENRY IV: No, stay where you are, stay where you are. I shall manage all right by myself. Good night! (*Closes the door and walks, very sad and tired, across the hall towards the second door on the right, which leads into his apartments.*)

FRIDA: (*as soon as she sees that he has just passed the throne, whispers from the niche like one who is on the point of fainting away with fright.*) Henry . . .

HENRY IV: (*Stopping at the voice, as if someone had stabbed him traitorously in the back, turns a terror-stricken face towards the wall at the bottom of the room; raising an arm instinctively, as if to defend himself and ward off a blow.*) Who is calling me? (*It is not a question, but an exclamation vibrating with terror, which does not expect a reply from the darkness and the terrible silence of the hall, which suddenly fills him with the suspicion that he is really mad.*)

FRIDA: (*at his shudder of terror, is herself not less frightened at the part she is playing, and repeats a little more loudly.*) Henry! . . . (*But, although she wishes to act the part as they have given it to her, she stretches her head a little out of the frame towards the other frame.*)

HENRY IV: (*gives a dreadful cry; lets the lamp fall from his hands to cover his head with his arms, and makes a movement as if to run away.*)

FRIDA: (*jumping from the frame on to the stand and shouting like a mad woman.*) Henry! . . . Henry! . . . I'm afraid! . . . I'm terrified! . . .

(*And while* DI NOLLI *jumps in turn on to the stand and thence to the floor and runs to* FRIDA *who, on the verge of fainting, continues to cry out, the* DOCTOR, DONNA MATILDA, *also dressed as "Matilda of Tuscany,"* TITO BELCREDI, LANDOLPH, BERTHOLD *and* JOHN *enter the hall from the doors on the right and on the left. One of them turns on the light: a strange light coming from lamps hidden in the ceiling so that only the upper part of the stage is well lighted. The others without taking notice of* HENRY IV, *who looks on astonished by the unexpected inrush, after the moment of terror which still causes him to tremble, run anxiously to support and comfort the still shaking* FRIDA, *who is moaning in the arms of her fiancé. All are speaking at the same time.*)

DI NOLLI: No, no, Frida . . . Here I am . . . I am beside you!

DOCTOR: (*coming with the others.*) Enough! Enough! There's nothing more to be done! . . .

DONNA MATILDA: He is cured, Frida. Look! He is cured! Don't you see?

DI NOLLI: (*astonished.*) Cured?

BELCREDI: It was only for fun! Be calm!

FRIDA: No! I am afraid! I am afraid!

DONNA MATILDA: Afraid of what? Look at him! He was never mad at all! . . .

DI NOLLI: That isn't true! What are you saying? Cured?

DOCTOR: It appears so. I should say so . . .

BELCREDI: Yes, yes! They have told us so. (*Pointing to the four young men.*)

DONNA MATILDA: Yes, for a long time!

He has confided in them, told them the truth!

DI NOLLI: (*now more indignant than astonished.*) But what does it mean? If, up to a short time ago . . . ?

BELCREDI: Hum! He was acting, to take you in and also us, who in good faith . . .

DI NOLLI: Is it possible? To deceive his sister, also, right up to the time of her death?

HENRY IV: (*remains apart, peering at one and now at the other under the accusation and the mockery of what all believe to be a cruel joke of his, which is now revealed. He has shown by the flashing of his eyes that he is meditating a revenge, which his violent contempt prevents him from defining clearly, as yet. Stung to the quick and with a clear idea of accepting the fiction they have insidiously worked up as true, he bursts forth at this point.*) Go on, I say! Go on!

DI NOLLI: (*astonished at the cry.*) Go on! What do you mean?

HENRY IV: It isn't *your* sister only that is dead!

DI NOLLI: My sister? Yours, I say, whom you compelled up to the last moment, to present herself here as your mother Agnes!

HENRY IV: And was she not *your* mother?

DI NOLLI: My mother? Certainly my mother!

HENRY IV: But your mother is dead for me, *old and far away!* You have just got down now from there. (*Pointing to the frame from which he jumped down.*) And how do you know whether I have not wept her long in secret, dressed even as I am?

DONNA MATILDA: (*dismayed, looking at the others.*) What does he say? (*Much impressed, observing him.*) Quietly! quietly, for Heaven's sake!

HENRY IV: What do I say? I ask all of you if Agnes was not the mother of Henry IV? (*Turns to* FRIDA *as if she were really the "Marchioness of Tuscany."*) You, Marchioness, it seems to me, ought to know.

FRIDA: (*still frightened, draws closer to* DI NOLLI.) No, no, I don't know. Not I!

DOCTOR: It's the madness returning. . . . Quiet now, everybody!

BELCREDI: (*indignant.*) Madness indeed, Doctor! He's acting again! . . .

HENRY IV: (*suddenly.*) I? You have emptied those two frames over there, and he stands before my eyes as Henry IV . . .

BELCREDI: We've had enough of this joke now.

HENRY IV: Who said joke?

DOCTOR: (*loudly to* BELCREDI.) Don't excite him, for the love of God!

BELCREDI: (*without lending an ear to him, but speaking louder.*) But they have said so (*Pointing again to the four young men.*), they, they!

HENRY IV: (*turning round and looking at them.*) You? Did you say it was all a joke?

LANDOLPH: (*timid and embarrassed.*) No . . . really we said that you were cured.

BELCREDI: Look here! Enough of this! (*To* DONNA MATILDA.) Doesn't it seem to you that the sight of him, (*Pointing to* DI NOLLI.) Marchioness, and that of your daughter dressed so, is becoming an intolerable puerility?

DONNA MATILDA: Oh, be quiet! What does the dress matter, if he is cured?

HENRY IV: Cured, yes! I am cured! (*To* BELCREDI.) ah, but not to let it end this way all at once, as you suppose! (*Attacks him.*) Do you know that for twenty years nobody has ever dared to appear before me here like you and that gentleman? (*Pointing to the* DOCTOR.)

BELCREDI: Of course I know it. As a matter of fact, I too appeared before you this morning dressed . . .

HENRY IV: As a monk, yes!

BELCREDI: And you took me for Peter Damiani! And I didn't even laugh, believing, in fact, that . . .

HENRY IV: That I was mad! Does it make you laugh seeing her like that, now that I am cured? And yet you might have remembered that in my eyes her appearance now . . . (*Interrupts himself with a gesture of contempt.*) Ah! (*Suddenly turns to the* DOCTOR.) You are a doctor, aren't you?

DOCTOR: Yes.

HENRY IV: And you also took part in dressing her up as the Marchioness of Tuscany? To prepare a counter-joke for me here, eh?

DONNA MATILDA: (*impetuously.*) No, no! What do you say? It was done for you! I did it for your sake.

DOCTOR: (*quickly.*) To attempt, to try, not knowing . . .

HENRY IV: (*cutting him short.*) I understand. I say counter-joke, in this case (*Indicates* BELCREDI.) because he believes that I have been carrying on a jest . . .

BELCREDI: But excuse me, what do you mean? You say yourself you are cured.

HENRY IV: Let me speak! (*To the* DOCTOR.) Do you know, Doctor, that for a moment you ran the risk of making me mad again? By God, to make the portraits speak; to make them jump alive out of their frames . . .

DOCTOR: But you saw that all of us ran in at once, as soon as they told us . . .

HENRY IV: Certainly! (*Contemplates* FRIDA *and* DI NOLLI, *and then looks at the* MARCHIONESS, *and finally at his own costume.*) The combination is very beautiful . . . Two couples . . . Very good, very

good, Doctor! For a madman, not bad! . . . (*With a slight wave of his hand to* BELCREDI.) It seems to him now to be a carnival out of season, eh? (*Turns to look at him.*) We'll get rid now of this masquerade costume of mine, so that I may come away with you. What do you say?

BELCREDI: With me? With us?

HENRY IV: Where shall we go? To the Club? In dress coats and with white ties? Or shall both of us go to the Marchioness' house?

BELCREDI: Wherever you like! Do you want to remain here still, to continue— alone—what was nothing but the unfortunate joke of a day of carnival? It is really incredible, incredible how you have been able to do all this, freed from the disaster that befell you!

HENRY IV: Yes, you see how it was! The fact is that falling from my horse and striking my head as I did, I was really mad for I know not how long . . .

DOCTOR: Ah! Did it last long?

HENRY IV: (*very quickly to the* DOCTOR.) Yes, Doctor, a long time! I think it must have been about twelve years. (*Then suddenly turning to speak to* BELCREDI.) Thus I saw nothing, my dear fellow, of all that, after that day of carnival, happened for you but not for me: how things changed, how my friends deceived me, how my place was taken by another, and all the rest of it! And suppose my place had been taken in the heart of the woman I loved? . . . And how should I know who was dead or who had disappeared? . . . All this, you know, wasn't exactly a jest for me, as it seems to you . . .

BELCREDI: No, no! I don't mean that if you please. I mean after . . .

HENRY IV: Ah, yes? After? One day (*Stops and addresses the* DOCTOR.)—A most interesting case, Doctor! Study me well! Study me carefully! (*Trembles while speaking.*) All by itself, who knows how, one day the trouble here (*Touches his forehead.*) mended. Little by little, I open my eyes, and at first I don't know whether I am asleep or awake. Then I know I am awake. I touch this thing and that; I see clearly again . . . Ah!—then, as *he* says (*Alludes to* BELCREDI.) away, away with this masquerade, this incubus! Let's open the windows, breathe life once again! Away! Away! Let's run out! (*Suddenly pulling himself up.*) But where? And to do what? To show myself to all, secretly, as Henry IV, not like this, but arm in arm with you, among my dear friends?

BELCREDI: What are you saying?

DONNA MATILDA: Who could think it? It's not to be imagined. It was an accident.

HENRY IV: They all said I was mad before. (*To* BELCREDI.) And you know it! You were more ferocious than any one against those who tried to defend me.

BELCREDI: Oh, that was only a joke!

HENRY IV: Look at my hair! (*Shows him the hair on the nape of his neck.*)

BELCREDI: But mine is grey too!

HENRY IV: Yes, with this difference: that mine went grey here, as Henry IV, do you understand? And I never knew it! I perceived it all of a sudden, one day, when I opened my eyes; and I was terrified because I understood at once that not only had my hair gone grey, but that I was all grey, inside; that everything had fallen to pieces, that everything was finished; and I was going to arrive, hungry as a wolf, at a banquet which had already been cleared away . . .

BELCREDI: Yes, but, what about the others? . . .

HENRY IV: (*quickly.*) Ah, yes, I know! They couldn't wait until I was cured, not even those, who, behind my back, pricked my saddled horse till it bled. . . .

DI NOLLI: (*agitated.*) What, what?

HENRY IV: Yes, treacherously, to make it rear and cause me to fall.

DONNA MATILDA: (*quickly, in horror.*) This is the first time I knew that.

HENRY IV: That was also a joke, probably!

DONNA MATILDA: But who did it? Who was behind us, then?

HENRY IV: It doesn't matter who it was. All those that went on feasting and were ready to leave me their scrapings, Marchioness, of miserable pity, or some dirty remnant of remorse in the filthy plate! Thanks! (*Turning quickly to the* DOCTOR.) Now, Doctor, the case must be absolutely new in the history of madness; I preferred to remain mad—since I found everything ready and at my disposal for this new exquisite fantasy. I would live it—this madness of mine—with the most lucid consciousness; and thus revenge myself on the brutality of a stone which had dinted my head. The solitude—this solitude—squalid and empty as it appeared to me when I opened my eyes again— I determined to deck it out with all the colors and splendors of that far off day of carnival, when you (*Looks at* DONNA MATILDA *and points* FRIDA *out to her.*) —when you, Marchioness, triumphed. So I would oblige all those who were around me to follow, by God, at my orders that famous pageant which had been—for you and not for me—the jest of a day. I would make it become—for ever—no more a joke but a reality, the reality of a real madness: here, all in masquerade, with throne room, and these my four secret counsellors: secret and, of course, traitors. (*He turns quickly towards them.*) I should like to know what you have gained by revealing the fact that I was cured! If I am cured, there's no longer any need of you, and you will be discharged! To give anyone one's confidence . . . that is really the act of a madman. But now I accuse you in my turn. (*Turning to the others.*) Do you know? They thought (*Alludes to the* VALETS.) they could make fun of me too with you. (*Bursts out laughing. The others laugh, but shamefacedly, except* DONNA MATILDA.)

BELCREDI: (*to* DI NOLLI.) Well, imagine that . . . That's not bad . . .

DI NOLLI: (*to the* FOUR YOUNG MEN.) You?

HENRY IV: We must pardon them. This dress (*Plucking his dress.*) which is for me the evident, voluntary caricature of that other continuous, everlasting masquerade, of which we are the involuntary puppets (*Indicates* BELCREDI.), when, without knowing it, we mask ourselves with that which we appear to be . . . ah, that dress of theirs, this masquerade of theirs, of course, we must forgive it them, since they do not yet see it is identical with themselves . . . (*Turning again to* BELCREDI.) You know, it is quite easy to get accustomed to it. One walks about as a tragic character, just as if it were nothing . . . (*Imitates the tragic manner.*) in a room like this . . . Look here, doctor! I remember a priest, certainly Irish, a nice-looking priest, who was sleeping in the sun one November day, with his arm on the corner of the bench of a public garden. He was lost in the golden delight of the mild sunny air which must have seemed for him almost summery. One may be sure that in that moment he did not know any more that he was a priest, or even where he was. He was dreaming . . . A little boy passed with a flower in his hand. He touched the priest with it here on the neck. I saw him open his laughing eyes, while all his mouth smiled with the beauty of his dream. He was forgetful of everything . . . But all at once, he pulled himself together, and stretched out his priest's cassock; and there came back to his eyes the same seriousness which you have seen in mine; because the Irish

priests defend the seriousness of their Catholic faith with the same zeal with which I defend the sacred rights of hereditary monarchy! I am cured, gentlemen: because I can act the madman to perfection, here; and I do it very quietly, I'm only sorry for you that have to live your madness so agitatedly, without knowing it or seeing it.

BELCREDI: It comes to this, then, that it is we who are mad. That's what it is!

HENRY IV: (*containing his irritation.*) But if you weren't mad, both you and she (*Indicating the* MARCHIONESS.) would you have come here to see me?

BELCREDI: To tell the truth, I came here believing that you were the madman.

HENRY IV: (*suddenly indicating the* MARCHIONESS.) And she?

BELCREDI: Ah, as for her . . . I can't say. I see she is all fascinated by your words, by this *conscious* madness of yours. (*Turns to her.*) Dressed as you are (*Speaking to her.*), you could even remain here to live it out, Marchioness.

DONNA MATILDA: You are insolent!

HENRY IV: (*conciliatingly.*) No, Marchioness, what he means to say is that the miracle would be complete, according to him, with you here, who—as the Marchioness of Tuscany, you well know,—could not be my friend, save, as at Canossa, to give me a little pity . . .

BELCREDI: Or even more than a little! She said so herself!

HENRY IV: (*to the* MARCHIONESS, *continuing.*) And even, shall we say, a little remorse! . . .

BELCREDI: Yes, that too she has admitted.

DONNA MATILDA: (*angry.*) Now look here . . .

HENRY IV: (*quickly, to placate her.*) Don't bother about him! Don't mind him! Let him go on infuriating me—though the Doctor's told him not to. (*Turns to* BELCREDI.) But do you suppose I am going to trouble myself any more about what happened between us—the share you had in my misfortune with her (*Indicates the* MARCHIONESS *to him and pointing* BELCREDI *out to her.*) the part he has now in your life? This is my life! Quite a different thing from your life! Your life, the life in which you have grown old—I have not lived that life. (*To* DONNA MATILDA.) Was this what you wanted to show me with this sacrifice of yours, dressing yourself up like this, according to the Doctor's idea? Excellently done, Doctor! Oh, an excellent idea:—"As we were then, eh? and as we are now?" But I am not a madman according to your way of thinking, Doctor. I know very well that that man there (*Indicates* DI NOLLI.) cannot be me; because I am Henry IV, and have been, these twenty years, cast in this eternal masquerade. She has lived these years! (*Indicates the* MARCHIONESS.) She has enjoyed them and has become—look at her! —a woman I can no longer recognize. It is so that I knew her! (*Points to* FRIDA *and draws near her.*) This is the Marchioness I know, always this one! . . . You seem a lot of children to be so easily frightened by me . . . (*To* FRIDA.) And you're frightened too, little girl, aren't you, by the jest that they made you take part in —though they didn't understand it wouldn't be the jest they meant it to be, for me? Oh miracle of miracles! Prodigy of prodigies! The dream alive in you! More than alive in you! It was an image that wavered there and they've made you come to life! Oh, mine! You're mine, mine, mine, in my own right! (HE *holds her in his arms, laughing like a madman, while all stand still terrified. Then as they advance to tear* FRIDA *from his arms, he* becomes *furious, terrible and cries imperiously to his* VALETS.) Hold them! Hold them! I order you to hold them!

(*The* FOUR YOUNG MEN *amazed, yet fascinated, move to execute his orders, automatically, and seize* DI NOLLI, *the* DOCTOR, *and* BELCREDI.)

BELCREDI: (*freeing himself.*) Leave her alone! Leave her alone! You're no madman!

HENRY IV: (*in a flash draws the sword from the side of* LANDOLPH, *who is close to him.*) I'm not mad, eh! Take that, you! . . . (*Drives sword into him. A cry of horror goes up. All rush over to assist* BELCREDI, *crying out together.*)

DI NOLLI: Has he wounded you?

BERTHOLD: Yes, yes, seriously!

DOCTOR: I told you so!

FRIDA: Oh God, oh God!

DI NOLLI: Frida, come here!

DONNA MATILDA: He's mad, mad!

DI NOLLI: Hold him!

BELCREDI: (*while* THEY *take him away by the left exit,* HE *protests as he is borne out.*) No, no, you're not mad! You're not mad. He's not mad!

(THEY *go out by the left amid cries and excitement. After a moment, one hears a still sharper, more piercing cry from* DONNA MATILDA, *and then, silence.*)

HENRY IV: (*who has remained on the stage between* LANDOLPH, HAROLD *and* ORDULPH, *with his eyes almost starting out of his head, terrified by the life of his own masquerade which has driven him to crime.*) Now, yes. . . . we'll have to (*Calls his* VALETS *around him as if to protect him.*) here we are . . . together . . . for ever!

Curtain.

Desire Under the Elms

EUGENE O'NEILL

COMMENTARY

 Eugene O'Neill (1888-1953) was born in a Broadway hotel in New York, the son of a financially very successful actor, James O'Neill. He toured the country with his parents, who periodically enrolled him in Roman Catholic schools. He left Princeton in his freshman year, never to return, and launched on a series of short-lived careers. While hospitalized with tuberculosis, he became interested in Greek tragedy and the plays of Strindberg. In 1920, he wrote his first full-length play, and in 1936 he received the Nobel Prize. Critics place him with the great American and European writers.

Desire Under the Elms (1924) is characteristic of O'Neill's tragedy. Like his last, posthumously published play, *Long Day's Journey Into Night* (finished 1941; published 1956), it records the conflict between a strong, domineering father and his sons. In spite of a certain melodramatic excess in speech and obviousness in symbolism, it rises above any limitations. Its intensity and seriousness remain large and finally impervious to obvious parody. O'Neill makes the American and puritan context of his tragedy as haunting, as affecting, as Faulkner's landscape is, or Hawthorne's or Melville's. One of O'Neill's unfulfilled ambitions was to write a sustained, massive dramatic saga modeled on ancient precedent but rooted firmly in American soil.

Desire Under the Elms opposes the passion of a fixed idea—the wish to have a suitable heir for the farm-land Ephraim has enriched, virtually with his own hands—against the passion of feeling—the love between Eben and Abbie. In this aspect, the play derives from Racine and from Euripides and is to be compared with Lorca. It may thus be read as a play whose central character is a heroine rather than a hero.

But the play suggests another and even darker dimension, the destructive effects of excessive self-discipline. The monomania of the father here is akin to that of Strindberg's *Father*. Ephraim Cabot sees himself as more than human; he equates his loneliness with the loneliness of God.

His son Eben, seemingly intent at first on shaping himself in the image of his father, is finally softened by his human needs. The heroism of Eben is of a different texture and of a different order from that of Ephraim, and the question arises as to whose tragedy the play records, the son's or the father's.

How do you feel about O'Neill's attempt to record the regional speech peculiarities of the characters? What is the relation between the dialect on the page and a stage production? What obvious problems would be raised or resolved in a production?

Long Day's Journey is itself one of the more revealing commentaries on *Desire Under the Elms;* perhaps the best approach to the analysis of an O'Neill play is through another one since he eludes comfortable critical formulation: Eric Bentley wrote a famous, widely anthologized essay called "Trying to Like O'Neill" (originally in *Kenyon Review,* July 1952, no. 172, pp. 476-92). General critical articles and individual essays and reviews have been collected in recent years in the volumes edited by John Gassner (Englewood Cliffs, N. J., 1964) and Jordan Y. Miller (Chicago, 1965), and in the one by Oscar Cargill, N. Bryllion Fagin, and William J. Fisher (New York, 1961). Among the more notable are the essays by Lionel Trilling, John Henry Raleigh, and Joseph Wood Krutch. Raleigh's book on O'Neill (Carbondale, Illinois, 1965) is a full critical consideration; the fullest biographical study is that by Arthur and Barbara Gelb (New York, 1962). Robert Brustein's chapter on O'Neill in his *The Theatre of Revolt* (Boston, 1964) relates the playwright to recent developments in the theatre.

Eugene O'Neill

DESIRE UNDER THE ELMS

CHARACTERS

EPHRAIM CABOT
SIMEON ⎫
PETER ⎬ *His sons*
EBEN ⎭
ABBIE PUTNAM

*Young Girl, Two Farmers, The Fiddler, A Sheriff, and other folk from
the neighboring farms.*

The action of the entire play takes place in, and immediately outside of,
the Cabot farmhouse in New England, in the year 1850. The south end
of the house faces front to a stone wall with a wooden gate at center
opening on a country road. The house is in good condition but in need of
paint. Its walls are a sickly grayish, the green of the shutters faded. Two
enormous elms are on each side of the house. They bend their trailing
branches down over the roof. They appear to protect and at the same
time subdue. There is a sinister maternity in their aspect, a crushing,
jealous absorption. They have developed from their intimate contact with
the life of man in the house an appalling humaneness. They brood op-
pressively over the house. They are like exhausted women resting their
sagging breasts and hands and hair on its roof, and when it rains their
tears trickle down monotonously and rot on the shingles.

There is a path running from the gate around the right corner of the
house to the front door. A narrow porch is on this side. The end wall
facing us has two windows in its upper story, two larger ones on the floor
below. The two upper are those of the father's bedroom and that of the
brothers. On the left, ground floor, is the kitchen—on the right, the
parlor, the shades of which are always drawn down.

PART ONE
Scene One

Exterior of the farmhouse. It is sunset of a day at the beginning of summer in the year 1850. There is no wind and everything is still. The sky above the roof is suffused with deep colors, the green of the elms glows, but the house is in shadow, seeming pale and washed out by contrast.

A door opens and EBEN CABOT *comes to the end of the porch and stands looking down the road to the right. He has a large bell in his hand and this he swings mechanically, awakening a deafening clangor. Then he puts his hands on his hips and stares up at the sky. He sighs with a puzzled awe and blurts out with halting appreciation.*

EBEN: God! Purty! (*His eyes fall and he stares about him frowningly. He is twenty-five, tall and sinewy. His face is well-formed, good-looking, but its expression is resentful and defensive. His defiant, dark eyes remind one of a wild animal's in captivity. Each day is a cage in which he finds himself trapped but inwardly unsubdued. There is a fierce repressed vitality about him. He has black hair, mustache, a thin curly trace of beard. He is dressed in rough farm clothes.*

He spits on the ground with intense disgust, turns and goes back into the house.

SIMEON *and* PETER *come in from their work in the fields. They are tall men, much older than their half-brother [*SIMEON *is thirty-nine and* PETER *thirty-seven], built on a squarer, simpler model, fleshier in body, more bovine and homelier in face, shrewder and more practical. Their shoulders stoop a bit from years of farm work. They clump heavily along in their clumsy thick-soled boots caked with earth. Their clothes, their faces, hands,* bare arms and throats are earth-stained. They smell of earth. They stand together for a moment in front of the house and, as if with the one impulse, stare dumbly up at the sky, leaning on their hoes. Their faces have a compressed, unresigned expression. As they look upward, this softens.*)

SIMEON: (*grudgingly*) Purty.

PETER: Ay-eh.

SIMEON: (*suddenly*) Eighteen years ago.

PETER: What?

SIMEON: Jenn. My woman. She died.

PETER: I'd fergot.

SIMEON: I rec'lect—now an' agin. Makes it lonesome. She'd hair long's a hoss' tail—an' yaller like gold!

PETER: Waal—she's gone. (*This with indifferent finality—then after a pause*) They's gold in the West, Sim.

SIMEON: (*still under the influence of sunset—vaguely*) In the sky!

PETER: Waal—in a manner o' speakin' —thar's the promise. (*Growing excited*) Gold in the sky—in the West—Golden Gate—Californi-a!—Goldest West!—fields o' gold!

SIMEON: (*excited in his turn*) Fortunes layin' just atop o' the ground waitin' t' be picked! Solomon's mines, they says! (*For a moment they continue looking up at the sky—then their eyes drop*).

PETER: (*with sardonic bitterness*) Here —it's stones atop o' the ground—stones atop o' stones—makin' stone walls—year atop o' year—him 'n' yew 'n' me 'n' then Eben—makin' stone walls fur him to fence us in!

SIMEON: We've wuked. Give our strength. Give our years. Plowed 'em under in the ground,—(*he stamps rebelliously*)—rottin'—makin' soil for his crops! (*A pause*) Waal—the farm pays good for hereabouts.

PETER: If we plowed in Californi-a, they'd be lumps o' gold in the furrow!

SIMEON: Californi-a's t'other side o' earth, a'most. We got t' calc'late—

PETER: (*after a pause*) 'Twould be hard fur me, too, to give up what we've 'arned here by our sweat. (*A pause.* EBEN *sticks his head out of the dining-room window, listening*).

SIMEON: Ay-eh. (*A pause*) Mebbe—he'll die soon.

PETER: (*doubtfully*) Mebbe.

SIMEON: Mebbe—fur all we knows—he's dead now.

PETER: Ye'd need proof.

SIMEON: He's been gone two months—with no word.

PETER: Left us in the fields an evenin' like this. Hitched up an' druv off into the West. That's plum onnateral. He hain't never been off this farm 'ceptin' t' the village in thirty year or more, not since he married Eben's maw. (*A pause. Shrewdly*) I calc'late we might git him declared crazy by the court.

SIMEON: He skinned 'em too slick. He got the best o' all on 'em. They'd never b'lieve him crazy. (*A pause*) We got t' wait—till he's under ground.

EBEN: (*with a sardonic chuckle*) Honor thy father! (*They turn, startled, and stare at him. He grins, then scowls*) I pray he's died. (*They stare at him. He continues matter-of-factly*) Supper's ready.

SIMEON *and* PETER: (*together*) Ay-eh.

EBEN: (*gazing up at the sky*) Sun's downin' purty.

SIMEON *and* PETER: (*together*) Ay-eh. They's gold in the West.

EBEN: Ay-eh. (*Pointing*) Yonder atop o' the hill pasture, ye mean?

SIMEON *and* PETER: (*together*) In Californi-a!

EBEN: Hunh? (*Stares at them indifferently for a second, then drawls*) Waal—supper's gettin' cold. (*He turns back into kitchen*).

SIMEON: (*startled—smacks his lips*) I air hungry!

PETER: (*sniffing*) I smells bacon!

SIMEON: (*with hungry appreciation*) Bacon's good!

PETER: (*in same tone*) Bacon's bacon! (*They turn, shouldering each other, their bodies bumping and rubbing together as they hurry clumsily to their food, like two friendly oxen toward their evening meal. They disappear around the right corner of house and can be heard entering the door.*)

CURTAIN

Scene Two

The color fades from the sky. Twilight begins. The interior of the kitchen is now visible. A pine table is at center, a cookstove in the right rear corner, four rough wooden chairs, a tallow candle on the table. In the middle of the rear wall is fastened a big advertising poster with a ship in full sail and the word "California" in big letters. Kitchen utensils hang from nails. Everything is neat and in order but the atmosphere is of a men's camp kitchen rather than that of a home.

Places for three are laid. EBEN *takes boiled potatoes and bacon from the stove and puts them on the table, also a loaf of bread and a crock of water.* SIMEON *and* PETER *shoulder in, slump down in their chairs without a word.* EBEN *joins them. The three eat in silence for a moment, the two elder as naturally unrestrained as beasts of the field,* EBEN *picking at his food without appetite, glancing at them with a tolerant dislike.*

SIMEON: (*suddenly turns to* EBEN) Looky here! Ye'd oughtn't t' said that, Eben.

PETER: 'Twa'n't righteous.

EBEN: What?

SIMEON: Ye prayed he'd died.

EBEN: Waal—don't yew pray it? (*A pause*).

PETER: He's our Paw.

EBEN: (*violently*) Not mine!

SIMEON: (*dryly*) Ye'd not let no one else say that about yer Maw! Ha! (*He gives one abrupt sardonic guffaw.* PETER *grins*).

EBEN: (*very pale*) I meant—I hain't his'n—I hain't like him—he hain't me!

PETER: (*dryly*) Wait till ye've growed his age!

EBEN: (*intensely*) I'm Maw—every drop o' blood! (*A pause. They stare at him with indifferent curiosity*).

PETER: (*reminiscently*) She was good t' Sim 'n' me. A good step-maw's scurse.

SIMEON: She was good t' everyone.

EBEN: (*greatly moved, gets to his feet and makes an awkward bow to each of them—stammering*) I be thankful t' ye. I'm her—her heir. (*He sits down in confusion*).

PETER: (*after a pause—judicially*) She was good even t' him.

EBEN: (*fiercely*) An' fur thanks he killed her!

SIMEON: (*after a pause*) No one never kills nobody. It's allus some thin'. That's the murderer.

EBEN: Didn't he slave Maw t' death?

PETER: He's slaved himself t' death. He's slaved Sim 'n' me 'n' yew t' death—on'y none o' us hain't died—yit.

SIMEON: It's somethin'—drivin' him—t' drive us!

EBEN: (*vengefully*) Waal—I hold him t' jedgment! (*Then scornfully*) Somethin'! What's somethin'?

SIMEON: Dunno.

EBEN: (*sardonically*) What's drivin' yew to Californi-a' mebbe? (*They look at him in surprise*) Oh, I've heerd ye! (*Then, after a pause*) But ye'll never go t' the gold fields!

PETER: (*assertively*) Mebbe!

EBEN: Whar'll ye git the money?

PETER: We kin walk. It's an a'mighty ways—Californi-a—but if yew was t' put all the steps we've walked on this farm end t' end we'd be in the moon!

EBEN: The Injuns'll skulp ye on the plains.

SIMEON: (*with grim humor*) We'll mebbe make 'em pay a hair fur a hair!

EBEN: (*decisively*) But t'aint that. Ye won't never go because ye'll wait here fur yer share o' the farm, thinkin' allus he'll die soon.

SIMEON: (*after a pause*) We've a right.

PETER: Two-thirds belong t' us.

EBEN: (*jumping to his feet*) Ye've no right! She wa'n't yewr Maw! It was her farm! Didn't he steal it from her? She's dead. It's my farm.

SIMEON: (*sardonically*) Tell that t' Paw —when he comes! I'll bet ye a dollar he'll laugh—fur once in his life. Ha! (*He laughs himself in one single mirthless bark.*)

PETER: (*amused in turn, echoes his brother*) Ha!

SIMEON: (*after a pause*) What've ye got held agin us, Eben? Year arter year it's skulked in yer eye—somethin'.

PETER: Ay-eh.

EBEN: Ay-eh. They's somethin'. (*Suddenly exploding*) Why didn't ye never stand between him 'n' my Maw when he was slavin' her to her grave—t' pay her back fur the kindness she done t' yew?

(There is a long pause. They stare at him in surprise).

SIMEON: Waal—the stock's got t' be watered.

PETER: 'R they was woodin' t' do.

SIMEON: 'R plowin'.

PETER: 'R hayin'.

SIMEON: 'R spreadin' manure.

PETER: 'R weedin'.

SIMEON: 'R prunin'.

PETER: 'R milkin'.

EBEN: *(breaking in harshly)* An' makin' walls—stone atop o' stone—makin' walls till yer heart's a stone ye heft up out o' the way o' growth onto a stone wall t' wall in yer heart!

SIMEON: *(matter-of-factly)* We never had no time t' meddle.

PETER: *(to EBEN)* Yew was fifteen afore yer Maw died—an' big fur yer age. Why didn't ye never do nothin'?

EBEN: *(harshly)* They was chores t' do, wa'nt they? *(A pause—then slowly)* It was on'y arter she died I come to think o' it. Me cookin'—doin' her work—that made me know her, suffer her sufferin' —she'd come back t' help—come back t' bile potatoes—come back t' fry bacon— come back t' bake biscuits—come back all cramped up t' shake the fire, an' carry ashes, her eyes weepin' an' bloody with smoke an' cinders same's they used t' be. She still comes back—stands by the stove thar in the evenin'—she can't find it nateral sleepin' an' restin' in peace. She can't git used t' bein' free—even in her grave.

SIMEON: She never complained none.

EBEN: She'd got too tired. She'd got too used t' bein' too tired. That was what he done. *(With vengeful passion)* An' sooner'r later, I'll meddle. I'll say the thin's I didn't say then t' him! I'll yell 'em at the top o' my lungs. I'll see t' it my Maw gits some rest an' sleep in her grave! *(He sits down again, relapsing into a brooding silence. They look at him with a queer indifferent curiosity.)*

PETER: *(after a pause)* Whar in tarnation d'ye s'pose he went, Sim?

SIMEON: Dunno. He druv off in the buggy, all spick an' span, with the mare all breshed an' shiny, druv off clackin' his tongue an' wavin' his whip. I remember it right well. I was finishin' plowin', it was spring an' May an' sunset, an' gold in the West, an' he druv off into it. I yells "Whar ye goin', Paw?" an' he hauls up by the stone wall a jiffy. His old snake's eyes was glitterin' in the sun like he'd been drinkin' a jugful an' he says with a mule's grin: "Don't ye run away till I come back!"

PETER: Wonder if he knowed we was wantin' fur Californi-a?

SIMEON: Mebbe. I didn't say nothin' and he says, lookin' kinder queer an' sick: "I been hearin' the hens cluckin' an' the roosters crowin' all the durn day. I been listenin' t' the cows lowin' an' everythin' else kickin' up till I can't stand it no more. It's spring an' I'm feelin' damned," he says. "Damned like an old bare hickory tree fit on'y fur burnin'," he says. An' then I calc'late I must've looked a mite hopeful, fur he adds real spry and vicious: "But don't git no fool idee I'm dead. I've sworn t' live a hundred an' I'll do it, if on'y t' spite yer sinful greed! An' now I'm ridin' out t' learn God's message t' me in the spring, like the prophets done. An' yew git back t' yer plowin'," he says. An' he druv off singin' a hymn. I thought he was drunk—'r I'd stopped him goin'.

EBEN: *(scornfully)* No, ye wouldn't! Ye're scared o' him. He's stronger—inside —than both o' ye put together!

PETER: *(sardonically)* An' yew—be yew Samson?

EBEN: I'm gittin' stronger. I kin feel it growin' in me—growin' an' growin'—till it'll bust out—! (*He gets up and puts on his coat and a hat. They watch him, gradually breaking into grins.* EBEN *avoids their eyes sheepishly*) I'm goin' out fur a spell—up the road.

PETER: T' the village?

SIMEON: T' the village?

SIMEON: T' see Minnie?

EBEN: (*defiantly*) Ay-eh?

PETER: (*jeeringly*) The Scarlet Woman!

SIMEON: Lust—that's what's growin' in ye!

EBEN: Waal—she's purty!

PETER: She's been purty fur twenty year!

SIMEON: A new coat o' paint'll make a heifer out of forty.

EBEN: She hain't forty!

PETER: If she hain't, she's teeterin on the edge.

EBEN: (*desperately*) What d'yew know—

PETER: All they is . . . Sim knew her—an' then me arter—

SIMEON: An' Paw kin tell yew somethin' too! He was fust!

EBEN: D'ye mean t' say he . . . ?

SIMEON: (*with a grin*) Ay-eh! We air his heirs in everythin'!

EBEN: (*intensely*) That's more to it! That grows on it! It'll bust soon! (*Then violently*) I'll go smash my fist in her face! (*He pulls open the door in rear violently*).

SIMEON: (*with a wink at* PETER—*drawling*) Mebbe—but the night's wa'm —purty—by the time ye git thar mebbe ye'll kiss her instead!

PETER: Sart'n he will! (*They both roar with coarse laughter.* EBEN *rushes out and slams the door—then the outside front door—comes around the corner of the house and stands still by the gate, staring up at the sky.*)

SIMEON: (*looking after him*) Like his Paw.

PETER: Dead spit an' image!

SIMEON: Dog'll eat dog!

PETER: Ay-eh. (*Pause. With yearning*) Mebbe a year from now we'll be in Californi-a.

SIMEON: Ay-eh. (*A pause. Both yawn*) Let's git t' bed. (*He blows out the candle. They go out door in rear.* EBEN *stretches his arms up to the sky—rebelliously*).

EBEN: Waal—thar's a star, an' somewhar's they's him, an' here's me, an' thar's Min up the road—in the same night. What if I does kiss her? She's like t'night, she's soft 'n' wa'm, her eyes kin wink like a star, her mouth's wa'm, her arms're wa'm, she smells like a wa'm plowed field, she's purty . . . Ay-eh! By God A'mighty she's purty, an' I don't give a damn how many sins she's sinned afore mine or who she's sinned 'em with, my sin's as purty as any one of 'em! (*He strides off down the road to the left*).

CURTAIN

SCENE THREE

It is pitch darkness just before dawn. EBEN *comes in from the left and goes around to the porch, feeling his way, chuckling bitterly and cursing half-aloud to himself.*

EBEN: The cussed old miser! (*He can be heard going in the front door. There is a pause as he goes upstairs, then a loud knock on the bedroom door of the brothers*) Wake up!

SIMEON: (*startedly*) Who's thar?

EBEN: (*pushing open the door and coming in, a lighted candle in his hand. The bedroom of the brothers is revealed. Its ceiling is the sloping roof. They can stand upright only close to the center dividing wall of the upstairs.* SIMEON *and* PETER *are in a double bed, front.* EBEN's *cot is to the rear.* EBEN *has a mixture of silly grin and vicious scowl on his face*) I be!

PETER: (*angrily*) What in hell's-fire . . . ?

EBEN: I got news fur ye! Ha! (*He gives one abrupt sardonic guffaw*).

SIMEON: (*angrily*) Couldn't ye hold it 'til we'd got our sleep?

EBEN: It's nigh sunup. (*Then explosively*) He's gone an' married agen!

SIMEON *and* PETER (*explosively*) Paw?

EBEN: Got himself hitched to a female 'bout thirty-five—an' purty, they says . . .

SIMEON: (*aghast*) It's a durn lie!

PETER: Who says?

SIMEON: They been stringin' ye!

EBEN: Think I'm a dunce, do ye? The hull village says. The preacher from New Dover, he brung the news—told it t' our preacher—New Dover, that's whar the old loon got himself hitched—that's whar the woman lived—

PETER: (*no longer doubting—stunned*) Waal . . . !

SIMEON: (*the same*) Waal . . . !

EBEN: (*sitting down on a bed—with vicious hatred*) Ain't he a devil out o' hell? It's jest t' spite us—the damned old mule!

PETER: (*after a pause*) Everythin'll go t' her now.

SIMEON: Ay-eh. (*A pause—dully*) Waal —if it's done—

PETER: It's done us. (*Pause—then persuasively*) They's gold in the fields o' Californi-a, Sim. No good a-staying' here now.

SIMEON: Jest what I was a-thinkin'. (*Then with decision*) S'well fust's last. Let's light out and git this mornin'.

PETER: Suits me.

EBEN: Ye must like walkin'.

SIMEON: (*sardonically*) If ye'd grow wings on us we'd fly thar!

EBEN: Ye'd like ridin' better—on a boat, wouldn't ye? (*Fumbles in his pocket and takes out a crumpled sheet of foolscap*) Waal, if ye sign this ye kin ride on a boat. I've had it writ out an' ready in case ye'd ever go. It says fur three hundred dollars t' each ye agree yewr shares o' the farm is sold t' me. (*They look suspiciously at the paper. A pause*).

SIMEON: (*wonderingly*) But if he's hitched agen—

PETER: An' whar'd yew kit that sum o' money, anyways?

EBEN: (*cunningly*) I know whar it's hid. I been waitin'—Maw told me. She knew whar it lay fur years, but she was waitin' . . . It's her'n—the money he hoarded from her farm an' hid from Maw. It's my money by rights now.

PETER: Whar's it hid?

EBEN: (*cunningly*) Whar yew won't never find it without me. Maw spied on him—'r she'd never knowed. (*A pause. They look at him suspiciously, and he at them*) Waal, is it fa'r trade?

SIMEON: Dunno.

PETER: Dunno.

SIMEON: (*looking at window*) Sky's grain'.

PETER: Ye better start the fire, Eben.

SIMEON: An' fix some vittles.

EBEN: Ay-eh. (*Then with a forced jocular heartiness*) I'll git ye a good one. If ye're startin' t' hoof it t' Californi-a ye'll need somethin' that'll stick t' yer ribs. (*He turns to the door, adding meaningly*) But ye kin ride on a boat if ye'll swap. (*He stops at the door and pauses. They stare at him*).

SIMEON: (*suspiciously*) Whar was ye all night?

EBEN: (*defiantly*) Up t' Min's. (*Then slowly*) Walkin' thar, fust, I felt 's if I'd kiss her; then I got a-thinkin' o' what ye'd said o' him an' her an' I says, I'll bust her nose fur that! Then I got t' the village an' heerd the news an' I got madder'n hell an' run all the way t' Min's not knowin' what I'd do— (*He pauses—then sheepishly but more defiantly*) Waal—when I seen her, I didn't hit her—nor I didn't kiss her nuther —I begun t' beller like a calf an' cuss at the same time, I was so durn mad—an' she got scared—an' I jest grabbed holt an' tuk her! (*Proudly*) Yes, sirree! I tuk her. She may've been his'n—an' your'n, too—but she's mine now!

SIMEON: (*dryly*) In love, air yew?

EBEN: (*with lofty scorn*) Love! I don't take no stock in sech slop!

PETER: (*winking at* SIMEON) Mebbe Eben's aimin' t' marry, too.

SIMEON: Min'd make a true faithful he'pmeet! (*They snicker*).

EBEN: What do I care fur her—'ceptin' she's round an' wa'm? The p'int is she was his'n—an' now she b'longs t' me! (*He goes to the door—then turns—rebelliously*) An' Min hain't sech a bad un. They's worse'n Min in the world, I'll bet ye! Wait'll we see this cow the Old Man's hitched t'! She'll beat Min, I got a notion! (*He starts to go out*).

SIMEON: (*suddenly*) Mebbe ye'll try t' make her your'n, too?

PETER: Ha! (*He gives a sardonic laugh of relish at this idea*).

EBEN: (*spitting with disgust*) Her— here—sleepin' with him—stealin' my Maw's farm! I'd as soon pet a skunk 'r kiss a snake! (*He goes out. The two stare after him suspiciously. A pause. They listen to his steps receding*).

PETER: He's startin' the fire.

SIMEON: I'd like t' ride t' Californi-a— but—

PETER: Min might o' put some scheme in his head.

SIMEON: Mebbe it's all a lie 'bout Paw marryin'. We'd best wait an' see the bride.

PETER: An' don't sign nothin' till we does!

SIMEON: Nor till we've tested it's good money! (*Then with a grin*) But if Paw's hitched we'd be sellin' Eben somethin' we'd never git nohow!

PETER: We'll wait an' see. (*Then with sudden vindictive anger*) An' till he comes, let's yew 'n' me not wuk a lick, let Eben tend to thin's if he's a mind t', let's us jest sleep an' eat an' drink likker an' let the hull damned farm go t' blazes!

SIMEON: (*excitedly*) By God, we've 'arned a rest! We'll play rich fur a change. I hain't a-goin to stir outa bed till breakfast's ready.

PETER: An' on the table!

SIMEON: (*after a pause—thoughtfully*) What d'ye calc'late she'll be like—our new Maw? Like Eben thinks?

PETER: More'n likely.

SIMEON: (*vindictively*) Waal—I hope she's a she-devil that'll make him wish he was dead an' livin' in the pit o' hell fur comfort!

PETER: (*fervently*) Amen!

SIMEON: (*imitating his father's voice*) "I'm ridin' out t' learn God's message t' me in the spring like the prophets done," he says. I'll bet right then an' thar he knew plumb well he was goin' whorin', the stinkin' old hypocrite!

CURTAIN

SCENE FOUR

Same as Scene Two—shows the interior of the kitchen with a lighted candle on table. It is gray dawn outside. SIMEON *and* PETER *are just finishing their breakfast.* EBEN *sits before his plate of untouched food, brooding frowningly.*

PETER: (*glancing at him rather irritably*) Lookin' gum don't help none.

SIMEON: (*sarcastically*) Sorrowin' over his lust o' the flesh!

PETER: (*with a grin*) Was she yer fust?

EBEN: (*angrily*) None o' yer business. (*A pause*) I was thinkin' o' him. I got a notion he's gittin near—I kin feel him comin' on like yew kin feel malaria chill afore it takes ye.

PETER: It's too early yet.

SIMEON: Dunno. He'd like t' catch us nappin'—jest t' have somethin' t' hoss us 'round over.

PETER: (*mechanically gets to his feet. SIMEON does the same*) Waal—let's git t' wuk. (*They both plod mechanically toward the door before they realize. Then they stop short*).

SIMEON: (*grinning*) Ye're a cussed fool, Pete—and I be wuss! Let him see we hain't wukin'! We don't give a durn!

PETER: (*as they go back to the table*) Not a damned durn! It'll serve t' show him we're done with him. (*They sit down again.* EBEN *stares from one to the other with surprise*).

SIMEON: (*grins at him*) We're aimin' t' start bein' lilies o' the field.

PETER: Nary a toil 'r spin 'r lick o' wuk do we put in!

SIMEON: Ye're sole owner—till he comes —that's what ye wanted. Waal, ye got t' be sole hand, too.

PETER: The cows air bellerin'. Ye better hustle at the milkin'.

EBEN: (*with excited joy*) Ye mean ye'll sign the paper?

SIMEON: (*dryly*) Mebbe.

PETER: Mebbe.

SIMEON: We're considerin'. (*Peremptorily*) Ye better git t' wuk.

EBEN: (*with queer excitement*) It's Maw's farm agen! It's my farm! Them's

my cows! I'll milk my durn fingers off fur cows o' mine! (*He goes out door in rear, they stare after him indifferently*).

SIMEON: Like his Paw.

PETER: Dead spit 'n' image!

SIMEON: Waal—let dog eat dog! (EBEN *comes out of front door and around the corner of the house. Thy sky is beginning to grow flushed with sunrise.* EBEN *stops by the gate and stares around him with glowing, possessive eyes. He takes in the whole farm with his embracing glance of desire*).

EBEN: It's purty! It's damned purty! It's mine! (*He suddenly throws his head back boldly and glares with hard, defiant eyes at the sky*) Mine, d'ye hear? Mine! (*He turns and walks quickly off left, rear, toward the barn. The two brothers light their pipes*).

SIMEON: (*putting his muddy boots up on the table, tilting back his chair, and puffing defiantly*) Waal—this air solid comfort—fur once.

PETER: Ay-eh. (*He follows suit. A pause. Unconsciously they both sigh.*)

SIMEON: (*suddenly*) He never was much o' a hand at milkin', Eben wa'nt.

PETER: (*with a snort*) His hands air like hoofs! (*A pause*).

SIMEON: Reach down the jug thar! Let's take a swaller. I'm feelin' kind o' low.

PETER: Good idee! (*He does so—gets two glasses—they pour out drinks of whisky*) Here's t' the gold in Californi-a!

SIMEON: An' luck t' find it! (*They drink—puff resolutely—sigh—take their feet down from the table*).

PETER: Likker don't 'pear t' sot right.

SIMEON: We hain't used t' it this early. (*A pause. They become very restless*).

PETER: Gittin' close in this kitchen.

SIMEON: (*with immense relief*) Let's git a breath o' air. (*They arise briskly and go out rear—appear around house and stop by the gate. They stare up at the sky with a numbed appreciation).*

PETER: Purty!

SIMEON: Ay-eh. Gold's t' the East now.

PETER: Sun's startin' with us fur the Golden West.

SIMEON: (*staring around the farm, his compressed face tightened, unable to conceal his emotion*) Waal—it's our last mornin'—mebbe.

PETER: (*the same*) Ay-eh.

SIMEON: (*stamps his foot on the earth and addresses it desperately*) Waal—ye've thirty year o' me buried in ye—spread out over ye—blood an' bone an' sweat—rotted away—fertilizin' ye—richin' yer soul—prime manure, by God, that's what I been t' ye!

PETER: Ay-eh! An' me!

SIMEON: An' yew, Peter. (*He sighs—then spits*) Waal—no use'n cryin' over spilt milk.

PETER: They's gold in the West—an' freedom, mebbe. We been slaves t' stone walls here.

SIMEON: (*defiantly*) We hain't nobody's slaves from this out—nor no thin's slaves nuther. (*A pause—restlessly*) Speakin' o' milk, wonder how Eben's managin'?

PETER: I s'pose he's managin'.

SIMEON: Mebbe we'd ought t' help—this once.

PETER: Mebbe. The cows knows us.

SIMEON: An' likes us. They don't know him much.

PETER: An' the hosses, an' pigs, an' chickens. They don't know him much.

SIMEON: They knows us like brothers—an' likes us! (*Proudly*). Hain't we raised 'em t' be fust-rate, number one prize stock?

PETER: We hain't—not no more.

SIMEON: (*dully*) I was fergittin'. (*Then resignedly*) Waal, let's go help Eben a spell an' git waked up.

PETER: Suits me. (*They are starting off down left, rear, for the barn when* EBEN *appears from there hurrying toward them, his face excited*).

EBEN: (*breathlessly*) Waal—thar they be! The old mule an' the bride! I seen 'em from the barn down below at the turnin'.

PETER: How could ye tell that far?

EBEN: Hain't I as far-sight as he's near-sight? Don't I know the mare 'n' buggy, an' two people settin' in it? Who else . . . ? An' I tell ye I kin feel 'em a-comin', too! (*He squirms as if he had the itch*).

PETER: (*beginning to be angry*) Waal —let him do his own unhitchin'!

SIMEON: (*angry in his turn*) Let's hustle in an' git our bundles an' be a-goin' as he's a-comin'. I don't want never t' step inside the door agen arter he's back. (*They both start back around the corner of the house.* EBEN *follows them*).

EBEN: (*anxiously*) Will ye sign it afore ye go?

PETER: Let's see the color o' the old skinflint's money an' we'll sign. (*They disappear left. The two brothers clump upstairs to get their bundles.* EBEN *appears in the kitchen, runs to window, peers out, comes back and pulls up a strip of flooring in under stove, takes out a canvas bag and puts it on table, then sets the floorboard back in place. The two brothers appear a moment after. They carry old carpetbags*).

EBEN: (*puts his hand on bag guardingly*) Have ye signed?

SIMEON: (*shows paper in his hand*) Ay-eh. (*Greedily*) Be that the money?

EBEN: (*opens bag and pours out pile of twenty-dollar gold pieces*) Twenty-dollar pieces—thirty of 'em. Count 'em.

(*Peter does, so arranging them in stacks of five, biting one or two to test them*).

PETER: Six hundred. (*He puts them in bag and puts it inside his shirt carefully*).

SIMEON: (*handing paper to* EBEN) Har ye be.

EBEN: (*after a glance, folds it carefully and hides it under his shirt—gratefully*) Thank yew.

PETER: Thank yew fur the ride.

SIMEON: We'll send ye a lump o' gold fur Christmas. (*A pause.* EBEN *stares at them and they at him*).

PETER: (*awkwardly*) Waal—we're a-goin'.

SIMEON: Comin' out t' the yard?

EBEN: No, I'm waitin' in here a spell. (*Another silence. The brothers edge awkwardly to door in rear—then turn and stand*).

SIMEON: Waal—good-by.

PETER: Good-by.

EBEN: Good-by. (*They go out. He sits down at the table, faces the stove and pulls out the paper. He looks from it to the stove. His face, lighted up by the shaft of sunlight from the window, has an expression of trance. His lips move. The two brothers come out to the gate*).

PETER: (*looking off toward barn*) Thar he be—unhitchin'.

SIMEON: (*with a chuckle*) I'll bet ye he's riled!

PETER: An' thar she be.

SIMEON: Let's wait 'n' see what our new Maw looks like.

PETER: (*with a grin*) An' give him our partin' cuss!

SIMEON: (*grinning*) I feel like raisin' fun. I feel light in my head an' feet.

PETER: Me, too. I feel like laffin' till I'd split up the middle.

SIMEON: Reckon its the likker?

PETER: No. My feet feel itchin' t' walk an' walk—an' jump high over thin's—an'. . . .

SIMEON: Dance? (*A pause*).

PETER: (*puzzled*) It's plumb onnateral.

SIMEON: (*a light coming over his face*) I calc'late it's 'cause school's out. It's holiday. Fur once we're free!

PETER: (*dazedly*) Free?

SIMEON: The halter's broke—the harness is busted—the fence bars is down—the stone walls air crumblin' an' tumblin'! We'll be kickin' up an' tearin' away down the road!

PETER: (*drawing a deep breath—oratorically*) Anybody that wants this stinkin' old rock-pile of a farm kin hev it. T'ain't our'n, no sirree!

SIMEON: (*takes the gate off its hinges and puts it under his arm*) We 'harby 'bolishes shet gates, an' open gates, an' all gates, by thunder!

PETER: We'll take it with us fur luck an' let 'er sail free down some river.

SIMEON: (*as a sound of voices comes from left, rear*) Har they comes! (*The two brothers congeal into two stiff, grim-visaged statues.* EPHRAIM CABOT *and* ABBIE PUTNAM *come in.* CABOT *is seventy-five, tall and gaunt, with great, wiry, concentrated power, but stoop-shouldered from toil. His face is as hard as if it were hewn out of a boulder, yet there is a weakness in it, a petty pride in its own narrow strength. His eyes are small, close together, and extremely near-sighted, blinking continually in the effort to focus on objects, their stare having a straining, ingrowing quality. He is dressed in his dismal black Sunday suit.* ABBIE *is thirty-five, buxom, full of vitality. Her round face is pretty but marred by its rather gross sensuality. There is strength and obstinacy in her jaw, a hard determination in her eyes, and about her whole personality the same unsettled, untamed, desperate quality which is so apparent in Eben).*

CABOT: (*as they enter—a queer strangled emotion in his dry cracking voice*) Har we be t' hum, Abbie.

ABBIE: (*with lust for the world*) Hum! (*Her eyes gloating on the house without seeming to see the two stiff figures at the gate*) It's purty—purty! I can't b'lieve it's r'ally mine.

CABOT: (*sharply*) Yewr'n? Mine! (*He stares at her penetratingly, she stares back. He adds relentingly*) Our'n—mebbe! It was lonesome too long. I was growin' old in the spring. A hum's got t' hev a woman.

ABBIE: (*her voice taking possession*) A woman's got t' hev a hum!

CABOT: (*nodding uncertainly*) Ay-eh. (*Then irritably*) Whar be they? Ain't thar nobody about—'r wukin'—'r nothin'?

ABBIE: (*sees the brothers. She returns their stare of cold appraising contempt with interest—slowly*) Thar's two men loafin' at the gate an' starin' at me like a couple o' strayed hogs.

CABOT: (*straining his eyes*) I kin see 'em—but I can't make out. . . .

SIMEON: It's Simeon.

PETER: It's Peter.

CABOT: (*exploding*) Why haint't ye wukin'?

SIMEON: (*dryly*) We're waitin' t' welcome ye hum—yew an' the bride!

CABOT: (*confusedly*) Huh? Waal—this be yer new Maw, boys. (*She stares at them and they at her*).

SIMEON: (*turns away and spits contemptuously*) I see her!

PETER: (*spits also*) An' I see her!

ABBIE: (*with the conqueror's conscious superiority*) I'll go in an' look at my house. (*She goes slowly around to porch.*)

SIMEON: (*with a snort*) Her house!

PETER: (*calls after her*) Ye'll find Eben inside. Ye better not tell him it's *yewr* house.

ABBIE: (*mouthing the name*) Eben. (*Then quietly*) I'll tell Eben.

CABOT: (*with a contemptuous sneer*) Ye needn't heed Eben. Eben's a dumb fool—like his Maw—soft an' simple!

SIMEON: (*with his sardonic burst of laughter*) Ha! Eben's a chip o' yew—spit 'n' image—hard 'n' bitter's a hickory tree! Dog'll eat dog. He'll eat ye yet, old man!

CABOT: (*commandingly*) Ye git t' wuk!

SIMEON: (*as ABBIE disappears in house —winks at PETER and says tauntingly*) So that thar's our new Maw, be it? Whar in hell did ye dig her up? (*He and PETER laugh*).

PETER: Ha! Ye'd better turn her in the pen with the other sows. (*They laugh uproariously, slapping their thighs*).

CABOT: (*so amazed at their effrontery that he stutters in confusion*) Simeon! Peter! What's come over ye? Air ye drunk?

SIMEON: We're free, old man—free o' yew an' the hull damned farm! (*They grow more and more hilarious and excited*).

PETER: An' we're startin' out fur the gold fields o' Californi-a!

SIMEON: Ye kin take this place an' burn it!

PETER: An' bury it—fur all we cares!

SIMEON: We're free, old man! (*He cuts a caper*).

PETER: Free! (*He gives a kick in the air*).

SIMEONS (*in a frenzy*) Whoop!

PETER: Whoop! (*They do an absurd Indian war dance about the old man who is petrified between rage and the fear that they are insane*).

SIMEON: We're free as Injuns! Lucky we don't skulp ye!

PETER: An' burn yer barn an' kill the stock!

SIMEON: An' rape yer new woman! Whoop! (*He and* PETER *stop their dance, holding their sides, rocking with wild laughter.*)

CABOT: (*edging away*) Lust fur gold—fur the sinful, easy gold o' Californi-a! It's made ye mad!

SIMEON: (*tauntingly*) Wouldn't ye like us to send ye back some sinful gold, ye old sinner?

PETER: They's gold besides what's in Californi-a! (*He retreats back beyond the vision of the old man and takes the bag of money and flaunts it in the air above his head, laughing*).

SIMEON: And sinfuller, too!

PETER: We'll be voyagin' on the sea! Whoop! (*He leaps up and down*).

SIMEON: Livin' free! Whoop! (*He leaps in turn*).

CABOT: (*suddenly roaring with rage*) My cuss on ye!

SIMEON: Take our'n in trade fur it! Whoop!

CABOT: I'll hev ye both chained up in the asylum!

PETER: Ye old skinflint! Good-by!

SIMEON: Ye old blood sucker! Good-by!

CABOT: Go afore I . . . !

PETER: Whoop! (*He picks a stone from the road.* SIMEON *does the same*).

SIMEON: Maw'll be in the parlor.

PETER: Ay-eh! One! Two!

CABOT: (*frightened*) What air ye . . . ?

PETER: Three! (*They both throw, the stones hitting the parlor window with a crash of glass, tearing the shade*).

SIMEON: Whoop!

PETER: Whoop!

CABOT: (*in a fury now, rushing toward them*) If I kin lay hands on ye—I'll break yer bones fur ye! (*But they beat a capering retreat before him,* SIMEON *with the gate still under his arm.* CABOT *comes back, panting with impotent rage. Their voices as they go off take up the song of the gold-seekers to the old tune of "Oh, Susannah!"*)

"I jumped aboard the Liza ship,
And traveled on the sea,
And every time I thought of home
I wished it wasn't me!
Oh! Californi-a,
That's the land fur me!
I'm off to Californi-a!
With my wash bowl on my knee."

(*In the meantime, the window of the upper bedroom on right is raised and* ABBIE *sticks her head out. She looks down at* CABOT—*with a sigh of relief*).

ABBIE: Waal—that's the last o' them two, hain't it? (*He doesn't answer. Then in possessive tones*) This here's a nice bedroom, Ephraim. It's a r'al nice bed. Is it my room, Ephraim?

CABOT: (*grimly—without looking up*) Our'n! (*She cannot control a grimace of aversion and pulls back her head slowly and shuts the window. A sudden horrible thought seems to enter* CABOT's *head*) They been up to somethin'! Mebbe—mebbe they've pizend the stock—'r somethin'! (*He almost runs off down toward the barn. A moment later the kitchen door is slowly pushed open and* ABBIE *enters. For a moment she stands looking at* EBEN. *He does not notice her at first. Her eyes take him in penetratingly with a calculating appraisal of his strength as against hers. But under this her desire is dimly awakened by his youth and good looks. Suddenly he becomes conscious of her presence and looks up. Their eyes meet. He leaps to his feet, glowering at her speechlessly*).

ABBIE: (*in her most seductive tones which she uses all through this scene*) Be you—Eben? I'm Abbie—(*She laughs*) I mean, I'm yer new Maw.

EBEN: (*viciously*) No, damn ye!

ABBIE: (*as if she hadn't heard—with a queer smile*) Yer Paw's spoke a lot o' yew. . . .

EBEN: Ha!

ABBIE: Ye mustn't mind him. He's an old man. (*A long pause. They stare at each other*) I don't want t' pretend playin' Maw t' ye, Eben. (*Admiringly*) Ye're too big an' too strong fur that. I want t' be frens with ye. Mebbe with me fur a fren ye'd find ye'd like livin' here better. I kin make it easy fur ye with him, mebbe. (*With a scornful sense of power*) I calc'-late I kin git him t' do most anythin' fur me.

EBEN: (*with bitter scorn*) Ha! (*They stare again, EBEN obscurely moved, physically attracted to her—in forced stilted tones*) Yew kin go t' the devil!

ABBIE: (*calmly*) If cussin' me does ye good, cuss all ye've a mind t'. I'm all pre-pared t' have ye agin me—at fust. I don't blame ye nuther. I'd feel the same at any stranger comin' t' take my Maw's place. (*He shudders. She is watching him care-fully*) Yew must've cared a lot fur yewr Maw, didn't ye? My Maw died afore I'd growed. I don't remember her none. (*A pause*) But yew won't hate me long, Eben. I'm not the wust in the world—an' yew an' me've got a lot in common. I kin tell that by lookin' at ye. Waal—I've had a hard life, too—oceans o' trouble an' nuthin' but wuk fur reward. I was a orphan early an' had t' wuk fur others in other folks' hums. Then I married an' he turned out a drunken spreer an' so he had to wuk fur others an' me too agen in other folks' hums, an' the baby died, an' my husband got sick an' died too, an' I was glad sayin' now I'm free fur once, on'y I diskivered right away all I was free fur was t' wuk agen in other folks' hums, doin' other folks' wuk till I'd most give up hope o' ever doin' my own wuk in my own hum, an' then your Paw come. . . . (*CABOT appears returning from the barn. He comes to the gate and looks down the road the brothers have gone. A faint strain of their retreating voices is heard: "Oh, Californi-a! That's the place for me." He stands glowering, his fist clenched, his face grim with rage*).

EBEN: (*fighting against his growing at-traction and sympathy—harshly*) An' bought yew—like a harlot! (*She is stung and flushes angrily. She has been sincerely moved by the recital of her troubles. He adds furiously*) An' the price he's payin' ye—this farm—was my Maw's, damn ye! —an' mine now!

ABBIE: (*with a cool laugh of confi-dence*) Yewr'n? We'll see 'bout that! (*Then strongly*) Waal—what if I did need a hum? What else'd I marry an old man like him fur?

EBEN: (*maliciously*) I'll tell him ye said that!

ABBIE: (*smiling*) I'll say ye're lyin' a-purpose—an' he'll drive ye off the place!

EBEN: Ye devil!

ABBIE: (*defying him*) This be my farm —this be my hum—this be my kitchen—!

EBEN: (*furiously, as if he were going to attack her*) Shut up, damn ye!

ABBIE: (*walks up to him—a queer coarse expression of desire in her face and body—slowly*) An' upstairs—that be my bedroom—an' my bed! (*He stares into her eyes, terribly confused and torn. She adds softly*) I hain't bad nor mean— 'ceptin' fur an enemy—but I got t' fight fur what's due me out o' life, if I ever 'spect t' git it. (*Then putting her hand on his arm—seductively*) Let's yew 'n' me be frens, Eben.

EBEN: (*stupidly—as if hynotized*) Ay-eh. (*Then furiously flinging off her arm*)

No, ye durned old witch! I hate ye! (*He rushes out the door*).

ABBIE: (*looks after him smiling satisfiedly—then half to herself, mouthing the word*) Eben's nice. (*She looks at the table, proudly*) I'll wash up *my* dishes now. (EBEN *appears outside, slamming the door behind him. He comes around corner, stops on seeing his father, and stands staring at him with hate*).

CABOT: (*raising his arms to heaven in the fury he can no longer control*) Lord God o' Hosts, smite the undutiful sons with Thy wust cuss!

EBEN: (*breaking in violently*) Yew 'n' yewr God! Allus cussin' folks—allus naggin' 'em!

CABOT: (*oblivious to him—summoningly*) God o' the old! God o' the lonesome!

EBEN: (*mockingly*) Naggin' His sheep t' sin! T' hell with yewr God! (CABOT *turns. He and* EBEN *glower at each other*).

CABOT: (*harshly*) So it's yew. I might've knowed it. (*Shaking his finger threateningly at him*) Blasphemin' fool! (*Then quickly*) Why hain't ye t' wuk?

EBEN: Why hain't yew? They've went. I can't wuk it all alone.

CABOT: (*contemptuously*) Nor noways! I'm wuth ten o' ye yit, old's I be! Ye'll never be more'n half a man! (*Then, matter-of-factly*) Waal—let's git t' the barn. (*They go. A last faint note of the "Californi-a" song is heard from the distance.* ABBIE *is washing her dishes*).

CURTAIN

PART TWO
SCENE ONE

The exterior of the farmhouse, as in Part One—a hot Sunday afternoon two months later. ABBIE, *dressed in her best, is discovered sitting in a rocker at the end of the porch. She rocks listlessly, enervated by the heat, staring in front of her with bored, half-closed eyes.*

EBEN *sticks his head out of his bedroom window. He looks around furtively and tries to see—or hear—if anyone is on the porch, but although he has been careful to make no noise,* ABBIE *has sensed his movement. She stops rocking, her face grows animated and eager, she waits attentively.* EBEN *seems to feel her presence, he scowls back his thoughts of her and spits with exaggerated disdain—then withdraws back into the room.* ABBIE *waits, holding her breath as she listens with passionate eagerness for every sound within the house.*

EBEN *comes out. Their eyes meet. His falter, he is confused, he turns away and slams the door resentfully. At this gesture,* ABBIE *laughs tantalizingly, amused but at the same time piqued and irritated. He scowls, strides off the porch to the path and starts to walk past her to the road with a grand swagger of ignoring her existence. He is dressed in his store suit, spruced up, his face shines from soap and water.* ABBIE *leans forward on her chair, her eyes hard and angry now, and, as he passes her, gives a sneering, taunting chuckle.*

EBEN: (*stung—turns on her furiously*) What air yew cacklin' about?

ABBIE: (*triumphant*) Yew!

EBEN: What about me?

ABBIE: Ye look all slicked up like a prize bull.

EBEN: (*with a sneer*) Waal—ye hain't so durned purty yerself, be ye? (*They stare into each other's eyes, his held by hers in spite of himself, hers glowingly possessive. Their physical attraction becomes a palpable force quivering in the hot air*).

ABBIE: (*softly*) Ye don't mean that, Eben. Ye may think ye mean it, mebbe, but ye don't. Ye can't. It's agin nature,

Eben. Ye been fightin' yer nature ever since the day I come—tryin' t' tell yerself I hain't purty t'ye. (*She laughs a low humid laugh without taking her eyes from his. A pause—her body squirms desirously — she murmurs languorously*) Hain't the sun strong an' hot? Ye kin feel it burnin' into the earth—Nature—makin' thin's grow—bigger 'n' bigger—burnin' inside ye—makin' ye want t' grow—into somethin' else—till ye're jined with it— an' it's your'n—but it owns ye, too—an' makes ye grow bigger—like a tree—like them elums— (*She laughs again softly, holding his eyes. He takes a step toward her, compelled against his will*) Nature'll beat ye, Eben. Ye might's well own up t' it fust 's last.

EBEN: (*trying to break from her spell —confusedly*) If Paw'd hear ye goin' on. . . . (*Resentfully*) But ye've made such a damned idjit out o' the old devil . . . ! (ABBIE *laughs*).

ABBIE: Waal—hain't it easier fur yew with him changed softer?

EBEN: (*defiantly*) No. I'm fightin' him —fightin' yew—fightin' fur Maw's rights t' her hum! (*This breaks her spell for him. He glowers at her*) An' I'm onto ye. Ye hain't foolin' me a mite. Ye're aimin' t' swaller up everythin' an' make it your'n. Waal, you'll find I'm a heap sight bigger hunk nor yew kin chew! (*He turns from her with a sneer*).

ABBIE: (*trying to regain her ascendancy —seductively*) Eben!

EBEN: Leave me be! (*He starts to walk away*).

ABBIE: (*more commandingly*) Eben!

EBEN: (*stops—resentfully*) What d'ye want?

ABBIE: (*trying to conceal a growing excitement*) Whar air ye goin'?

EBEN: (*with malicious nonchalance*) Oh—up the road a spell.

ABBIE: T' the village?

EBEN: (*airily*) Mebbe.

ABBIE: (*excitedly*) T' see that Min, I s'pose?

EBEN: Mebbe.

ABBIE: (*weakly*) What d'ye want t' waste time on her fur?

EBEN: (*revenging himself now—grinning at her*) Ye can't beat Nature, didn't ye say? (*He laughs and again starts to walk away*).

ABBIE: (*bursting out*) An ugly old hake!

EBEN: (*with a tantalizing sneer*) She's purtier'n yew be!

ABBIE: That every withless drunk in the country has. . . .

EBEN: (*tauntingly*) Mebbe—but she's better'n yew. She owns up fa'r 'n' squar' t' her doin's.

ABBIE: (*furiously*) Don't ye dare compare. . . .

EBEN: She don't go sneakin' an' stealin' —what's mine.

ABBIE: (*savagely seizing on his weak point*) Your'n? Yew mean—my farm?

EBEN: I mean the farm yew sold yerself fur like any other old whore—my farm!

ABBIE: (*stung—fiercely*) Ye'll never live t' see the day when even a stinkin' weed on it 'll belong t' ye! (*Then in a scream*) Git out o' my sight! Go on t' yer slut— disgracin' yer Paw 'n' me! I'll git yer Paw t' horsewhip ye off the place if I want t'! Ye're only livin' here 'cause I tolerate ye! Git along! I hate the sight o' ye! (*She stops panting and glaring at him*).

EBEN: (*returning her glance in kind*) An' I hate the sight o' yew! (*He turns and strides off up the road. She follows his retreating figure with concentrated hate. Old* CABOT *appears coming up from the barn. The hard, grim expression of his face has changed. He seems in some queer way softened, mellowed. His eyes have taken on a strange, incongruous dreamy quality. Yet there is not hint of physical weakness about him—rather he looks more robust and younger.* ABBIE *sees him and turns away quickly with unconcealed aversion. He comes slowly up to her).*

CABOT: (*mildly*) War yew an' Eben quarrelin' agen?

ABBIE: (*shortly*) No.

CABOT: Ye was talkin' a'mighty loud. (*He sits down on the edge of porch*).

ABBIE: (*snappishly*) If ye heerd us they hain't no need askin' questions.

CABOT: I didn't hear what ye said.

ABBIE: (*relieved*) Waal—it wa'n't nothin' t' speak on.

CABOT: (*after a pause*) Eben's queer.

ABBIE: (*bitterly*) He's the dead spit 'n' image o' yew!

CABOT: (*queerly interested*) D'ye think so, Abbie? (*After a pause, ruminatingly*) Me 'n' Eben's allus fit 'n' fit. I never could b'ar him noways. He's so thunderin' soft —like his Maw.

ABBIE: (*scornfully*) Ay-eh! 'Bout as soft as yew be!

CABOT: (*as if he hadn't heard*) Mebbe I been too hard on him.

ABBIE: (*jeeringly*) Waal—ye're gittin' soft now—soft as slop! That's what Eben was sayin'.

CABOT: (*his face instantly grim and ominous*) Eben was sayin'? Waal, he'd best not do nothin' t' try me 'r he'll soon diskiver. . . . (*A pause. She keeps her face turned away. His gradually softens. He stares up at the sky*) Purty, hain't it?

ABBIE: (*crossly*) I don't see nothin' purty.

CABOT: The sky. Feels like a wa'm field up thar.

ABBIE: (*sarcastically*) Air yew aimin' t' buy up over the farm too? (*She snickers contemptuously*).

CABOT: (*strangely*) I'd like t' own my place up thar. (*A pause*) I'm gittin' old,

Abbie. I'm gittin' ripe on the bough. (*A pause. She stares at him mystified. He goes on*) It's allus lonesome cold in the house—even when it's bilin' hot outside. Hain't yew noticed?

ABBIE: No.

CABOT: It's wa'm down t'the barn—nice smellin' an' warm—with the cows. (*A pause*) Cows is queer.

ABBIE: Like yew?

CABOT: Like Eben. (*A pause*) I'm gittin' t' feel resigned t' Eben—jest as I got t' feel 'bout his Maw. I'm gittin' t' learn to b'ar his softness—jest like her'n. I calc'late I c'd a'most take t' him—if he wa'n't sech a dumb fool! (*A pause*) I s'pose it's old age a-creepin' in my bones.

ABBIE: (*indifferently*) Waal—ye hain't dead yet.

CABOT: (*roused*) No, I hain't, yew bet —not by a hell of a sight—I'm sound 'n' tough as hickory! (*Then moodily*) But arter three score and ten the Lord warns ye t' prepare. (*A pause*) That's why Eben's come in my head. Now that his cussed sinful brothers is gone their path t' hell, they's no one left but Eben.

ABBIE: (*resentfully*) They's me, hain't they? (*Agitatedly*) What's all this sudden likin' ye've tuk to Eben? Why don't ye say nothin' 'bout me? Hain't I yer lawful wife?

CABOT: (*simply*) Ay-eh. Ye be. (*A pause—he stares at her desirously—his eyes grow avid—then with a sudden movement he seizes her hands and squeezes them, declaiming in a queer camp-meeting preacher's tempo*) Yew air my Rose o' Sharon! Behold, yew air fair; yer eyes air doves; yer lips air like scarlet; yer two breasts air like two fawns; yer navel be like a round goblet; yer belly be like a heap o' wheat. . . . (*He covers her hand with kisses. She does not seem to notice. She stares before her with hard angry eyes*).

ABBIE: (*jerking her hands away—harshly*) So ye're plannin' t' leave the farm t' Eben, air ye?

CABOT: (*dazedly*) Leave . . . ? (*Then with resentful obstinacy*) I hain't a-givin' it t' no one!

ABBIE: (*remorselessly*) Ye can't take it with ye.

CABOT: (*thinks a moment—then reluctantly*) No, I calc'late not. (*After a pause—with a strange passion*) But if I could, I would, by the Etarnal! 'R if I could, in my dyin' hour, I'd set it afire an' watch it burn—this house an' every ear o' corn an' every tree down t' the last blade o' hay! I'd sit an' know it was all a-dying with me an' no one else'd ever own what was mine, what I'd made out o' nothin' with my own sweat 'n' blood! (*A pause—then he adds with a queer affection*) 'Ceptin' the cows. Them I'd turn free.

ABBIE: (*harshly*) An' me?

CABOT: (*with a queer smile*) Ye'd be turned free, too.

ABBIE: (*furiously*) So that's the thanks I git fur marryin' ye—t' have ye change kind to Eben who hates ye, an' talk o' turnin' me out in the road.

CABOT: (*hastily*) Abbie! Ye know I wa'n't. . . .

ABBIE: (*vengefully*) Just let me tell ye a thing or two 'bout Eben! Whar's he gone? T' see that harlot, Min! I tried fur t' stop him. Disgracin' yew an' me—on the Sabbath, too!

CABOT: (*rather guiltily*) He's a sinner—nateral-born. It's lust eatin' his heart.

ABBIE: (*enraged beyond endurance—wildly vindictive*) An' his lust fur me! Kin ye find excuses fur that?

CABOT: (*stares at her—after a dead pause*) Lust—fur yew?

ABBIE: (*defiantly*) He was tryin t' make love t' me—when ye heerd us quarrelin'.

CABOT: (*stares at her—then a terrible expression of rage comes over his face—he springs to his feet shaking all over*) By the A'mighty God—I'll end him!

ABBIE: (*frightened now for* EBEN) No! Don't ye!

CABOT: (*violently*) I'll git the shotgun an' blow his soft brains t' the top o' them elums!

ABBIE: (*throwing her arms around him*) No, Ephraim!

CABOT: (*pushing her away violently*) I will, by God!

ABBIE: (*in a quieting tone*) Listen, Ephraim. 'Twa'n't nothin' bad—on'y a boy's foolin'—'twa'n't meant serious—jest jokin' an' teasin'. . . .

CABOT: Then why did ye say—lust?

ABBIE: It must hev sounded wusser'n I meant. An' I was mad at thinkin'—ye'd leave him the farm.

CABOT: (*quieter but still grim and cruel*) Waal then, I'll horsewhip him off the place if that much'll content ye.

ABBIE: (*reaching out and taking his hand*) No. Don't think o' me! Ye mustn't drive him off. 'Tain't sensible. Who'll ye get to help ye on the farm? They's no one hereabouts.

CABOT: (*considers this—then nodding his appreciation*) Ye got a head on ye. (*Then irritably*) Waal, let him stay. (*He sits down on the edge of the porch. She sits beside him. He murmurs contemptuously*) I oughn't t' git riled so—at that 'ere fool calf. (*A pause*) But har's the p'int. What son o' mine'll keep on here t' the farm—when the Lord does call me? Simeon 'n' Peter air gone t' hell—an' Eben's follerin' 'em.

ABBIE: They's me.

CABOT: Ye're on'y a woman.

ABBIE: I'm yewr wife.

CABOT: That hain't me. A son is me—

my blood—mine. Mine ought t' git mine. An' then it's still mine—even though I be six foot under. D'ye see?

ABBIE: (*giving him a look of hatred*) Ay-eh. I see. (*She becomes very thoughtful, her face growing shrewd, her eyes studying* CABOT *craftily*).

CABOT: I'm gittin' old—ripe on the bough. (*Then with a sudden forced reassurance*) Not but what I hain't a hard nut t' crack even yet—an' fur many a year t' come! By the Etarnal, I kin break most o' the young fellers' backs at any kind o' work any day o' the year!

ABBIE: (*suddenly*) Mebbe the Lord'll give *us* a son.

CABOT: (*turns and stares at her eagerly*) Ye mean—a son—t' me 'n' yew?

ABBIE: (*with a cajoling smile*) Ye're a strong man yet, hain't ye? 'Tain't noways impossible, be it? We know that. Why d'ye stare so? Hain't ye never thought o' that afore? I been thinkin' o' it all along. Ay-eh—an' I been prayin' it'd happen, too.

CABOT: (*his face growing full of joyous pride and a sort of religious ecstasy*) Ye been prayin', Abbie?—fur a son?—t' us?

ABBIE: Ay-eh. (*With a grim resolution*) I want a son now.

CABOT: (*excitedly clutching both of her hands in his*) It'd be the blessin' o' God, Abbie—the blessin' o' God A'mighty on me—in my old age—in my lonesomeness! They hain't nothin' I wouldn't do fur ye then, Abbie. Ye'd hev on'y t' ask it—anythin' ye a mind t'!

ABBIE: (*interrupting*) Would ye will the farm t' me then—t' me an' it . . . ?

CABOT: (*vehemently*) I'd do anythin' ye axed, I tell ye! I swar it! May I be everlastin' damned t' hell if I wouldn't! (*He sinks to his knees pulling her down with him. He trembles all over with the fervor of his hopes*) Pray t' the Lord agen, Abbie.

It's the Sabbath! I'll jine ye! Two prayers air better nor one. "An' God hearkened unto Rachel"! An' God hearkened unto Abbie! Pray, Abbie! Pray fur him to hearken! (*He bows his head, mumbling. She pretends to do likewise but gives him a side glance of scorn and triumph*).

CURTAIN

SCENE TWO

About eight in the evening. The interior of the two bedrooms on the top floor is shown. EBEN *is sitting on the side of his bed in the room on the left. On account of the heat he has taken off everything but his undershirt and pants. His feet are bare. He faces front, brooding moodily, his chin propped on his hands, a desperate expression on his face.*

In the other room CABOT *and* ABBIE *are sitting side by side on the edge of their bed, an old four-poster with feather mattress. He is in his night shirt, she in her nightdress. He is still in the queer, excited mood into which the notion of a son has thrown him. Both rooms are lighted dimly and flickeringly by tallow candles.*

CABOT: The farm needs a son.

ABBIE: I need a son.

CABOT: Ay-eh. Sometimes ye air the farm an' sometimes the farm be yew. That's why I clove t' ye in my lonesomeness. (*A pause. He pounds his knee with his fist.*) Me an' the farm has got t' beget a son!

ABBIE: Ye'd best go t' sleep. Ye're gittin' thin's all mixed.

CABOT: (*with an impatient gesture*) No, I hain't. My mind's clear's a well. Ye don't know me, that's it. (*He stares hopelessly at the floor*).

ABBIE: (*indifferently*) Mebbe. (*In the next room* EBEN *gets up and paces up and down distractedly.* ABBIE *hears him. Her eyes fasten on the intervening wall with concentrated attention.* EBEN *stops and stares. Their hot glances seem to meet through the wall. Unconsciously he stretches out his arms for her and she half rises. Then aware, he mutters a curse at himself and flings himself face downward on the bed, his clenched fists above his head, his face buried in the pillow.* ABBIE *relaxes with a faint sigh but her eyes remain fixed on the wall; she listens with all her attention for some movement from* EBEN).

CABOT: (*suddenly raises his head and looks at her—scornfully*) Will ye ever know me—'r will any man 'r woman? (*Shaking his head*) No. I calc'late 't wa'n't t' be. (*He turns away.* ABBIE *looks at the wall. Then, evidently unable to keep silent about his thoughts without looking at his wife, he puts out his hand and clutches her knee. She starts violently, looks at him, sees he is not watching her, concentrates again on the wall and pays no attention to what he says*) Listen, Abbie. When I come here fifty odd year ago—I was jest twenty an' the strongest an' hardest ye ever seen—ten times as strong an' fifty times as hard as Eben. Waal—this place was nothin' but fields o' stones. Folks laughed when I tuk it. They couldn't know what I knowed. When ye kin make corn sprout out o' stones, God's livin' in yew! They wa'n't strong enuf fur that! They reckoned God was easy. They laughed. They don't laugh no more. Some died hereabouts. Some went West an' died. They're all under ground—fur follerin' arter an easy God. God hain't easy. (*He shakes his head slowly*) An' I growed hard. Folks kept allus sayin' he's a hard man like 'twas sinful t' be hard, so's at last I said back at 'em: Waal then, by thunder, ye'll git me hard an' see how ye like it! (*Then suddenly*) But I give in t' weakness once. 'Twas arter I'd been here two year. I got weak—despairful—they was so many stones. They was a party

leavin', givin' up, goin' West. I jined 'em. We tracked on 'n on. We come t' broad medders, plains, whar the soil was black an' rich as gold. Nary a stone. Easy. Ye'd on'y to plow an' sow an' then set an' smoke yer pipe an' watch thin's grow. I could o' been a rich man—but somethin' in me fit me an' fit me—the voice o' God sayin': "This hain't wuth nothin' t' Me. Git ye back t' hum!" I got afeerd o' that voice an' I lit out back t' hum here, leavin' my claim an' crops t' whoever'd a mind t' take 'em. Ay-eh. I actoolly give up what was rightful mine! God's hard, not easy! God's in the stones! Build my church on a rock—out o' stones an' I'll be in them! That's what He meant t' Peter! (*He sighs heavily—a pause*) Stones. I picked 'em up an' piled 'em into walls. Ye kin read the years o' my life in them walls, every day a hefted stone, climbin' over the hills up and down, fencin' in the fields that was mine, whar I'd made thin's grow out o' nothin'—like the will o' God, like the servant o' His hand. It wa'n't easy. It was hard an' He made me hard fur it. (*He pauses*) All the time I kept gittin' lonesomer. I tuk a wife. She bore Simeon an' Peter. She was a good woman. She wuked hard. We was married twenty year. She never knowed me. She helped but she never knowed what she was helpin'. I was allus lonesome. She died. After that it wa'n't so lonesome fur a spell. (*A pause*) I lost count o' the years. I had no time t' fool away countin' 'em. Sim an' Peter helped. The farm growed. It was all mine! When I thought o' that I didn't feel lonesome. (*A pause*) But ye can't hitch yer mind t' one thin' day an' night. I tuk another wife—Eben's Maw. Her folks was contestin' me at law over my deeds t' the farm—my farm! That's why Eben keeps a-talkin' his fool talk o' this bein' his Maw's farm. She bore Eben. She was purty—but soft. She tried t' be hard. She couldn't. She never knowed me nor nothin'. It was lonesomer 'n hell with her. After a matter o' sixteen odd years, she died. (*A pause*) I lived with the boys. They hated me 'cause I was hard. I hated them —'cause they was soft. They coveted the farm without knowin' what it meant. It made me bitter 'n wormwood. It aged me—them coveting what I'd made fur mine. Then this spring the call come—the voice o' God cryin' in my wilderness, in my lonesomeness—t' go out an' seek an' find! (*Turning to her with strange passion*) I sought ye an' I found ye! Yew air my Rose o' Sharon! Yer eyes air like. . . . (*She has turned a blank face, resentful eyes to his. He stares at her for a moment —then harshly*) Air ye any the wiser fur all I've told ye?

ABBIE: (*confusedly*) Mebbe.

CABOT: (*pushing her away from him— angrily*) Ye don't know nothin'—nor never will. If ye don't hev a son t' redeem ye. . . . (*This in a tone of cold threat*).

ABBIE: (*resentfully*) I've prayed, hain't I?

CABOT: (*bitterly*) Pray agen—fur understandin'!

ABBIE: (*a veiled threat in her tone*) Ye'll have a son out o' me, I promise ye.

CABOT: How kin ye promise?

ABBIE: I got second-sight mebbe. I kin foretell. (*She gives a queer smile*).

CABOT: I believe ye have. Ye give me the chills sometimes. (*He shivers*) It's cold in this house. It's oneasy. They's thin's pokin' about in the dark—in the corners. (*He pulls on his trousers, tucking in his night shirt, and pulls on his boots*).

ABBIE: (*surprised*) Whar air ye goin'?

CABOT: (*queerly*) Down whar it's restful—whar it's warm down t' the barn. (*Bitterly*) I kin talk t' the cows. They know. They know the farm an' me. They'll give me peace. (*He turns to go out the door*).

ABBIE: (*a bit frightenedly*) Air ye ailin' tonight, Ephraim?

CABOT: Growin'. Growin' ripe on the bough. (*He turns and goes, his boots clumping down the stairs.* EBEN *sits up with a start, listening.* ABBIE *is conscious of his movement and stares at the wall.* CABOT *comes out of the house around the corner and stands by the gate, blinking at the sky. He stretches up his hands in a tortured gesture*) God A'mighty, call from the dark! (*He listens as if expecting an answer. Then his arms drop, he shakes his head and plods off toward the barn.* EBEN *and* ABBIE *stare at each other through the wall.* EBEN *sighs heavily and* ABBIE *echoes it. Both become terribly nervous, uneasy. Finally* ABBIE *gets up and listens, her ear to the wall. He acts as if he saw every move she was making, he becomes resolutely still. She seems driven into a decision—goes out the door in rear determinedly. His eyes follow her. Then as the door of his room is opened softly, he turns away, waits in an attitude of strained fixity.* ABBIE *stands for a second staring at him, her eyes burning with desire. Then with a little cry she runs over and throws her arms about his neck, she pulls his head back and covers his mouth with kisses. At first, he submits dumbly; then he puts his arms about her neck and returns her kisses, but finally, suddenly aware of his hatred, he hurls her away from him, springing to his feet. They stand speechless and breathless, panting like two animals*).

ABBIE: (*at last—painfully*) Ye shouldn't, Eben—ye shouldn't—I'd make ye happy!

EBEN: (*harshly*) I don't want t' be happy—from yew!

ABBIE: (*helplessly*) Ye do, Eben! Ye do! Why d'ye lie?

EBEN: (*viciously*) I don't take t'ye, I tell ye! I hate the sight o' ye!

ABBIE: (*with an uncertain troubled laugh*) Waal, I kissed ye anyways—an' ye kissed back—yer lips was burnin'—ye can't lie 'bout that! (*Intensely*) If ye don't care, why did ye kiss me back—why was yer lips burnin'?

EBEN: (*wiping his mouth*) It was like pizen on 'em. (*Then tauntingly*) When I kissed ye back, mebbe I thought 'was someone else.

ABBIE: (*wildly*) Min?

EBEN: Mebbe.

ABBIE: (*torturedly*) Did ye go t' see see her? Did ye r'ally go? I thought ye mightn't. Is that why ye throwed me off jest now?

EBEN: (*sneeringly*) What if it be?

ABBIE: (*raging*) Then ye're a dog, Eben Cabot!

EBEN: (*threateningly*) Ye can't talk that way t' me!

ABBIE: (*with a shrill laugh*) Can't I? Did ye think I was in love with ye—a weak thin' like yew? Not much! I on'y wanted ye fur a purpose o' my own—an' I'll hev ye fur it yet 'cause I'm stronger'n yew be!

EBEN: (*resentfully*) I knowed well it was on'y part o' yer plan t' swaller everythin'!

ABBIE: (*tauntingly*) Mebbe!

EBEN: (*furious*) Git out o' my room!

ABBIE: This air my room an' ye're on'y hired help!

EBEN: (*threateningly*) Git out afore I murder ye!

ABBIE: (*quite confident now*) I hain't a mite afeerd. Ye want me, don't ye? Yes, ye do! An' yer Paw's son'll never kill what he wants! Look at yer eyes! They's lust fur me in 'em, burnin' 'em up! Look at yer lips now! They're tremblin' an' longin' t' kiss me, an' yer teeth t' bite! (*He is watching her now with a horrible fascination. She laughs a crazy triumphant laugh*) I'm a-goin' t' make all o' this hum my hum! They's one room hain't mine yet, but it's a-goin' t' be tonight. I'm a-goin' down now an' light up! (*She makes him a mocking bow*) Won't ye come courtin' me in the best parlor, Mister Cabot?

EBEN: (*staring at her—horribly confused—dully*) Don't ye dare! It hain't been opened since Maw died an' was laid out thar! Don't ye . . . ! (*But her eyes are fixed on his so burningly that his will seems to wither before hers. He stands swaying toward her helplessly*).

ABBIE: (*holding his eyes and putting all her will into her words as she backs out the door*) I'll expect ye afore long, Eben.

EBEN: (*stares after her for a while, walking toward the door. A light appears in the parlor window. He murmurs*) In the parlor? (*This seems to arouse connotations for he comes back and puts on his white shirt, collar, half ties the tie mechanically, puts on coat, takes his hat, stands barefooted looking about him in bewilderment, mutters wonderingly*) Maw! Whar air yew? (*Then goes slowly toward the door in rear*).

CURTAIN

SCENE THREE

A few minutes later. The interior of the parlor is shown. A grim, repressed room like a tomb in which the family has been interred alive. ABBIE *sits on the edge of the horsehair sofa. She has lighted all the candles and the room is revealed in all its preserved ugliness. A change has come over the woman. She looks awed and frightened now, ready to run away.*

The door is opened and EBEN *appears. His face wears an expression of obsessed confusion. He stands staring at her, his arms hanging disjointedly from his shoulders, his feet bare, his hat in his hand.*

ABBIE: (*after a pause—with a nervous, formal politeness*) Won't ye set?

EBEN: (*dully*) Ay-eh. (*Mechanically he*

places his hat carefully on the floor near the door and sits stiffly beside her on the edge of the sofa. A pause. They both remain rigid, looking straight ahead with eyes full of fear).

ABBIE: When I fust come in—in the dark—they seemed somethin' here.

EBEN: (*simply*) Maw.

ABBIE: I kin still feel—somethin'. . . .

EBEN: It's Maw.

ABBIE: At fust I was feered o' it. I wanted t' yell an' run. Now—since yew come—seems like it's growin' soft an' kind t' me. (*Addressing the air—queerly*) Thank yew.

EBEN: Maw allus loved me.

ABBIE: Mebbe it knows I love yew, too. Mebbe that makes it kind t' me.

EBEN: (*dully*) I dunno. I should think she'd hate ye.

ABBIE: (*with certainty*) No. I kin feel it don't—not no more.

EBEN: Hate ye fur stealin' her place—here in her hum—settin' in her parlor whar she was laid— (*He suddenly stops, staring stupidly before him*).

ABBIE: What is it, Eben?

EBEN: (*in a whisper*) Seems like Maw didn't want me t' remind ye.

ABBIE: (*excitedly*) I knowed, Eben! It's kind t' me! It don't b'ar me no grudges fur what I never knowed an' couldn't help!

EBEN: Maw b'ars him a grudge.

ABBIE: Waal, so does all o' us.

EBEN: Ay-eh. (*With passion*) I does, by God!

ABBIE: (*taking one of his hands in hers and patting it*) Thar! Don't git riled thinkin' o' him. Think o' yer Maw who's kind t' us. Tell me about yer Maw, Eben.

EBEN: They hain't nothin' much. She was kind. She was good.

ABBIE: (*putting one arm over his shoulder. He does not seem to notice—passionately*) I'll be kind an' good t' ye!

EBEN: Sometimes she used t' sing fur me.

ABBIE: I'll sing fur ye!

EBEN: This was her hum. This was her farm.

ABBIE: This is my hum! This is my farm!

EBEN: He married her t' steal 'em. She was soft an' easy. He couldn't 'preciate her.

ABBIE: He can't 'preciate me!

EBEN: He murdered her with his hardness.

ABBIE: He's murderin' me!

EBEN: She died (*A pause*) Sometimes she used to sing fur me. (*He bursts into a fit of sobbing*).

ABBIE: (*both her arms around him—with wild passion*) I'll sing fur ye! I'll die fur ye! (*In spite of her overwhelming desire for him, there is a sincere maternal love in her manner and voice—a horribly frank mixture of lust and mother love*) Don't cry, Eben! I'll take yer Maw's place! I'll be everythin' she was t' ye! Let me kiss ye, Eben! (*She pulls his head around. He makes a bewildered pretense of resistance. She is tender*) Don't be afeered! I'll kiss ye pure, Eben—same 's if I was a Maw t' ye—an' ye kin kiss me back 's if yew was my son—my boy—sayin' goodnight t' me! Kiss me, Eben. (*They kiss in restrained fashion. Then suddenly wild passion overcomes her. She kisses him lustfully again and again and he flings his arms about her and returns her kisses. Suddenly, as in the bedroom, he frees himself from her violently and springs to his feet. He is trembling all over, in a strange state of terror. ABBIE strains her arms toward him with fierce pleading*) Don't ye leave me, Eben! Can't ye see it hain't enuf—lovin' ye like a Maw—can't ye see

it's got t' be that an' more—much more
—a hundred times more—fur me t' be
happy—fur yew t' be happy?

EBEN: (*to the presence he feels in the
room*) Maw! Maw! What d'ye want?
What air ye tellin' me?

ABBIE: She's tellin' ye t' love me. She
knows I love ye an' I'll be good t' ye.
Can't ye feel it? Don't ye know? She's
tellin' ye t' love me, Eben!

EBEN: Ay-eh. I feel—mebbe she—but
—I can't figger out—why—when ye've
stole her place—here in her hum—in the
parlor whar she was—

ABBIE: (*fiercely*) She knows I love ye!

EBEN: (*his face suddenly lighting up
with a fierce, triumphant grin*) I see it!
I see why. It's her vengeance on him—
so's she kin rest quiet in her grave!

ABBIE: (*wildly*) Vengeance o' God on
the hull o' us! What d'we give a durn?
I love ye, Eben! God knows I love ye!
(*She stretches out her arms for him*).

EBEN: (*throws himself on his knees
beside the sofa and grabs her in his arms
—releasing all his pent-up passion*) An'
I love yew, Abbie!—now I kin say it! I
been dyin' fur want o' ye—every hour
since ye come! I love ye! (*Their lips meet
in a fierce, bruising kiss*).

CURTAIN

SCENE FOUR

*Exterior of the farmhouse. It is just
dawn. The front door at right is opened
and* EBEN *comes out and walks around to
the gate. He is dressed in his working
clothes. He seems changed. His face wears
a bold and confident expression, he is
grinning to himself with evident satisfaction. As he gets near the gate, the
window of the parlor is heard opening and
the shutters are flung back and* ABBIE
sticks her head out. Her hair tumbles
*over her shoulders in disarray, her face
is flushed, she looks at* EBEN *with tender,
languorous eyes and calls softly.*

ABBIE: Eben. (*As he turns—playfully*)
Jest one more kiss afore ye go. I'm goin'
to miss ye fearful all day.

EBEN: An' me yew, ye kin bet! (*He
goes to her. They kiss several times. He
draws away, laughingly*) Thar. That's
enuf, hain't it? Ye won't hev none left fur
next time.

ABBIE: I got a million o' 'em left fur
yew! (*Then a bit anxiously*) D'ye r'ally
love me, Eben?

EBEN: (*emphatically*) I like ye better'n
any gal I ever knowed! That's gospel!

ABBIE: Likin' hain't lovin'.

EBEN: Waal then—I love ye. Now air
yew satisfied?

ABBIE: Ay-eh, I be. (*She smiles at him
adoringly*).

EBEN: I better git t' the barn. The old
critter's liable t' suspicion an' come
sneakin' up.

ABBIE: (*with a confident laugh*) Let
him! I kin allus pull the wool over his
eyes. I'm goin' t' leave the shutters open
and let in the sun 'n' air. This room's
been dead long enuf. Now it's goin' t' be
my room!

EBEN: (*frowning*) Ay-eh.

ABBIE: (*hastily*) I meant—our room.

EBEN: Ay-eh.

ABBIE: We made it our'n last night,
didn't we? We give it life—our lovin' did.
(*A pause*).

EBEN: (*with a strange look*) Maw's
gone back t' her grave. She kin sleep now.

ABBIE: May she rest in peace! (*Then
tenderly rebuking*) Ye oughtn't t' talk o'
sad thin's—this mornin'.

EBEN: It jest come up in my mind o' itself.

ABBIE: Don't let it. (*He doesn't answer.*

She yawns) Waal, I'm a-goin' t' steal a wink o' sleep. I'll tell the Old Man I hain't feelin' pert. Let him git his own vittles.

EBEN: I see him comin' from the barn. Ye better look smart an' git upstairs.

ABBIE: Ay-eh. Good-by. Don't ferget me. (*She throws him a kiss. He grins— then squares his shoulders and awaits his father confidently.* CABOT *walks slowly up from the left, staring up at the sky with a vague face*).

EBEN: (*jovially*) Mornin', Paw. Star-gazin' in daylight?

CABOT: Purty, hain't it?

EBEN: (*looking around him posses-sively*) It's a durned purty farm.

CABOT: I mean the sky.

EBEN: (*grinning*) How d'ye know? Them eyes o' your'n can't see that fur. (*This tickles his humor and he slaps his thigh and laughs*) Ho-ho! That's a good un!

CABOT: (*grimly sarcastic*) Ye're feelin' right chipper, hain't ye? Whar'd ye steal the likker?

EBEN: (*good-naturedly*) 'Tain't likker. Jest life. (*Suddenly holding out his hand —soberly*) Yew 'n' me is quits. Let's shake hands.

CABOT: (*suspiciously*) What's come over ye?

EBEN: Then don't. Mebbe it's jest as well. (*A moment's pause*) What's come over me? (*Queerly*) Didn't ye feel her passin'—goin' back t' her grave?

CABOT: (*dully*) Who?

EBEN: Maw. She kin rest now an' sleep content. She's quit with ye.

CABOT: (*confusedly*) I rested. I slept good—down with the cows. They know how t' sleep. They're teachin' me.

EBEN: (*suddenly jovial again*) Good fur the cows! Waal—ye better git t' work.

CABOT: (*grimly amused*) Air ye bossin' me, ye calf?

EBEN: (*beginning to laugh*) Ay-eh! I'm bossin' yew! Ha-ha-ha! See how ye like it! Ha-ha-ha! I'm the prize rooster o' this roost. Ha-ha-ha! (*He goes off toward the barn laughing*).

CABOT: (*looks after him with scornful pity*) Soft-headed. Like his Maw. Dead spit 'n' image. No hope in him! (*He spits with contemptuous disgust*) A born fool! (*Then matter-of-factly*) Waal—I'm gittin' peckish. (*He goes toward door*).

CURTAIN

PART THREE
SCENE ONE

A night in late spring the following year. The kitchen and the two bedrooms up-stairs are shown. The two bedrooms are dimly lighted by a tallow candle in each. EBEN *is sitting on the side of the bed in his room, his chin propped on his fists, his face a study of the struggle he is making to understand his conflicting emotions. The noisy laughter and music from below where a kitchen dance is in progress annoy and distract him. He scowls at the floor.*

In the next room a cradle stands beside the double bed.

In the kitchen all is festivity. The stove has been taken down to give more room to the dancers. The chairs, with wooden benches added, have been pushed back against the walls. On these are seated, squeezed in tight against one another, farmers and their wives and their young folks of both sexes from the neighboring farms. They are all chattering and laugh-ing loudly. They evidently have some secret joke in common. There is no end of winking, of nudging, of meaning nods of the head toward CABOT *who, in a state of extreme hilarious excitement increased by the amount he has drunk, is standing near the rear door where there is a small keg of whisky and serving drinks to all the men. In the left corner, front, dividing the attention with her husband,* ABBIE *is sitting in a rocking chair, a shawl wrapped about her shoulders. She is very pale, her face is thin and drawn, her eyes are fixed anxiously on the open door in rear as if waiting for someone.*

The musician is tuning up his fiddle, seated in the far right corner. He is a lanky young fellow with a long, weak face. His pale eyes blink incessantly and he grins about him slyly with a greedy malice.

ABBIE: (*suddenly turning to a young girl on her right*) Whar's Eben?

YOUNG GIRL: (*eying her scornfully*) I dunno, Mrs. Cabot. I hain't seen Eben in ages. (*Meaningly*) Seems like he's spent most o' his time t' hum since yew come.

ABBIE: (*vaguely*) I tuk his Maw's place.

YOUNG GIRL: Ay-eh. So I've heerd. (*She turns away to retail this bit of gossip to her mother sitting next to her.* ABBIE *turns to her left to a big stoutish middle-aged man whose flushed face and starting eyes show the amount of "likker" he has consumed.*)

ABBIE: Ye hain't seen Eben, hev ye?

MAN: No, I hain't. (*Then he adds with a wink*) If yew hain't, who would?

ABBIE: He's the best dancer in the county. He'd ought t' come an' dance.

MAN: (*with a wink*) Mebbe he's doin' the dutiful an' walkin' the kid t' sleep. It's a boy, hain't it?

ABBIE: (*nodding vaguely*) Ay-eh—born two weeks back—purty's a picter.

MAN: They all is—t' their Maws. (*Then in a whisper, with a nudge and a leer*) Listen, Abbie—if ye ever git tired o' Eben, remember me! Don't fergit now! (*He looks at her uncomprehending face for a*

second—then grunts disgustedly*) Waal—guess I'll likker agin. (*He goes over and joins* CABOT *who is arguing noisily with an old farmer over cows. They all drink*).

ABBIE: (*this time appealing to nobody in particular*) Wonder what Eben's a-doin'? (*Her remark is repeated down the line with many a guffaw and titter until it reaches the fiddler. He fastens his blinking eyes on* ABBIE).

FIDDLER: (*raising his voice*) Bet I kin tell ye, Abbie, what Eben's doin'! He's down t' the church offerin' up prayers o' thanksgivin'. (*They all titter expectantly*).

A MAN: What fur? (*Another titter*).

FIDDLER: 'Cause unto him a— (*He hesitates just long enough*) brother is born! (*A roar of laughter. They all look from* ABBIE *to* CABOT. *She is oblivious, staring at the door.* CABOT, *although he hasn't heard the words, is irritated by the laughter and steps forward, glaring about him. There is an immediate silence*).

CABOT: What're ye all bleatin' about —like a flock o' goats? Why don't ye dance, damn ye? I axed ye here t' dance —t' eat, drink an' be merry—an' thar ye set cacklin' like a lot o' wet hens with the pip! Ye've swilled my likker an' guzzled my vittles like hogs, hain't ye? Then dance fur me, can't ye? That's fa'r an' squar', hain't it? (*A grumble of resentment goes around but they are all evidently in too much awe of him to express it openly*).

FIDDLER: (*slyly*) We're waitin' fur Eben. (*A suppressed laugh*).

CABOT: (*with a fierce exultation*) T'hell with Eben! Eben's done fur now! I got a new son! (*His mood switching with drunken suddenness*) But ye needn't t' laugh at Eben, none o' ye! He's my blood, if he be a dumb fool. He's better nor any o' yew. He kin do a day's work a'most up t' what I kin—an' that'd put any o' yew pore critters t' shame!

FIDDLER: An' he kin do a good night's work too! (*A roar of laughter*).

CABOT: Laugh, ye damn fools! Ye're right jist the same, Fiddler. He kin work day an' night too, like I kin, if need be!

OLD FARMER: (*from behind the keg where he is weaving drunkenly back and forth—with great simplicity*) They hain't many t' touch ye, Ephraim—a son at seventy-six. That's a hard man fur ye! I be on'y sixty-eight an' I couldn't do it. (*A roar of laughter in which* CABOT *joins uproariously*).

CABOT: (*slapping him on the back*) I'm sorry fur ye, Hi. I'd never suspicion sech weakness from a boy like yew!

OLD FARMER: An' I never reckoned yew had it in ye nuther, Ephraim. (*There is another laugh*).

CABOT: (*suddenly grim*) I got a lot in me—a hell of a lot—folks don't know on. (*Turning to the fiddler*) Fiddle 'er up, durn ye! Give 'em somethin' t' dance t'! What air ye, an ornament? Hain't this a celebration? Then grease yer elbow an' go it!

FIDDLER: (*seizes a drink which the* OLD FARMER *holds out to him and downs it*) Here goes! (*He starts to fiddle "Lady of the Lake." Four young fellows and four girls form in two lines and dance a square dance. The* FIDDLER *shouts directions for the different movements, keeping his words in the rhythm of the music and interspersing them with jocular personal remarks to the dancers themselves. The people seated along the walls stamp their feet and clap their hands in unison.* CABOT *is especially active in this respect. Only* ABBIE *remains apathetic, staring at the door as if she were alone in a silent room*).

FIDDLER: Swing your partner t' the right! That's it, Jim! Give her a b'ar hug! Her Maw hain't lookin'. (*Laughter*) Change partners! That suits ye, don't it,

Essie, now ye got Reub afore ye? Look at her redden up, will ye? Waal, life is short an' so's love, as the feller says. (*Laughter*).

CABOT: (*excitedly, stamping his foot*) Go it, boys! Go it, gals!

FIDDLER: (*with a wink at the others*) Ye're the spryest seventy-six ever I sees, Ephraim! Now if ye'd on'y good eyesight . . . ! (*Suppressed laughter. He gives* CABOT *no chance to retort but roars*) Promenade! Ye're walkin' like a bride down the aisle, Sarah! Waal, while they's life they's allus hope, I've heerd tell. Swing your partner to the left! Gosh A'mighty, look at Johnny Cook high-steppin'! They hain't goin' t'be much strength left fur howin' in the corn lot t'morrow. (*Laughter*).

CABOT: Go it! Go it! (*Then suddenly, unable to restrain himself any longer, he prances into the midst of the dancers, scattering them, waving his arms about wildly*) Ye're all hoofs! Git out o' my road! Give me room! I'll show ye dancin'. Ye're all too soft! (*He pushes them roughly away. They crowd back toward the walls, muttering, looking at him resentfully*).

FIDDLER: (*jeeringly*) Go it, Ephraim! Go it! (*He starts "Pop Goes the Weasel," increasing the tempo with every verse until at the end he is fiddling crazily as fast as he can go*).

CABOT: (*starts to dance, which he does very well and with tremendous vigor. Then he begins to improvise, cuts incredibly grotesque capers, leaping up and cracking his heels together, prancing around in a circle with body bent in an Indian war dance, then suddenly straightening up and kicking as high as he can with both legs. He is like a monkey on a string. And all the while he intersperses his antics with shouts and derisive comments*) Whoop! Here's dancin' fur ye! Whoop! See that! Seventy-six, if I'm a day! Hard as iron yet! Beatin' the young 'uns like I allus done! Look at me! I'd invite ye t' dance on my hundredth birthday on'y ye'll all be dead by then. Ye're a sickly generation! Yer hearts air pink, not red! Yer veins is full o' mud an' water! I be the on'y man in the county! Whoop! See that! I'm a Injun! I've killed Injuns in the West afore ye was born—an' skulped 'em too! They's a arrer wound on my backside I c'd show ye! The hull tribe chased me. I outrun 'em all—with the arrer stuck in me! An' I tuk vengeance on 'em. Ten eyes fur an eye, that was my motter! Whoop! Look at me! I kin kick the ceilin' off the room! Whoop!

FIDDLER: (*stops playing—exhaustedly*) God A'mighty, I got enuf. Ye got the devil's strength in ye.

CABOT: (*delightedly*) Did I beat yew, too? Wa'al, ye played smart. Hev a swig. (*He pours whisky for himself and* FIDDLER. *They drink. The others watch* CABOT *silently with cold, hostile eyes. There is a dead pause. The* FIDDLER *rests.* CABOT *leans against the keg, panting, glaring around him confusedly. In the room above,* EBEN *gets to his feet and tiptoes out the door in rear, appearing a moment later in the other bedroom. He moves silently, even frightenedly, toward the cradle and stands there looking down at the baby. His face is as vague as his reactions are confused, but there is a trace of tenderness, of interested discovery. At the same moment that he reaches the cradle,* ABBIE *seems to sense something. She gets up weakly and goes to* CABOT).

ABBIE: I'm goin' up t' the baby.

CABOT: (*with real solicitation*) Air ye able fur the stairs? D'ye want me t' help ye, Abbie?

ABBIE: No. I'm able. I'll be down agen soon.

CABOT: Don't ye git wore out! He needs ye, remember—our son does! (*He grins affectionately, patting her on the back. She shrinks from his touch*).

ABBIE: (*dully*) Don't—tech me. I'm goin'—up. (*She goes.* CABOT *looks after her. A whisper goes around the room.* CABOT *turns. It ceases. He wipes his forehead streaming with sweat. He is breathing pantingly*).

CABOT: I'm a-goin' out t' git fresh air. I'm feelin' a mite dizzy. Fiddle up thar! Dance, all o' ye! Here's likker fur them as wants it. Enjoy yerselves. I'll be back. (*He goes, closing the door behind him*).

FIDDLER: (*sarcastically*) Don't hurry none on our acount! (*A suppressed laugh. He imitates* ABBIE) Whar's Eben? (*More laughter*).

A WOMAN: (*loudly*) What's happened in this house is plain as the nose on yer face! (ABBIE *appears in the doorway upstairs and stands looking in surprise and adoration at* EBEN *who does not see her*).

A MAN: Ssshh! He's li-able t' be listenin' at the door. That'd be like him. (*Their voices die to an intensive whispering. Their faces are concentrated on this gossip. A noise as of dead leaves in the wind comes from the room.* CABOT *has come out from the porch and stands by the gate, leaning on it, staring at the sky blinkingly.* ABBIE *comes across the room silently.* EBEN *does not notice her until quite near*).

EBEN: (*starting*) Abbie!

ABBIE: Ssshh! (*She throws her arms around him. They kiss—then bend over the cradle together*) Ain't he purty?—dead spit 'n' image o' yew!

EBEN: (*pleased*) Air he? I can't tell none.

ABBIE: E-zackly like!

EBEN: (*frowningly*) I don't like this. I don't like lettin' on what's mine's his'n. I been doin' that all my life. I'm gittin' t' the end o' b'arin' it!

ABBIE: (*putting her finger on his lips*)

We're doin' the best we kin. We got t' wait. Somethin's bound t' happen. (*She puts her arms around him*) I got t' go back.

EBEN: I'm goin' out. I can't b'ar it with the fiddle playin' an' the laughin'.

ABBIE: Don't git feelin' low. I love ye, Eben. Kiss me. (*He kisses her. They remain in each other's arms*).

CABOT: (*at the gate, confusedly*) Even the music can't drive it out—somethin'. Ye kin feel it droppin' off the elums, climbin' up the roof, sneakin' down the chimney, pokin' in the corners! They's no peace in houses, they's no rest livin' with folks. Somethin's always livin' with ye. (*With a deep sigh*) I'll go t' the barn an' rest a spell. (*He goes wearily toward the barn*).

FIDDLER: (*tuning up*) Let's celebrate the old skunk gittin' fooled! We kin have some fun now he's went. (*He starts to fiddle "Turkey in the Straw." There is real merriment now. The young folks get up to dance*).

CURTAIN

Scene Two

*A half-hour later—Exterior—*EBEN *is standing by the gate looking up at the sky, an expression of dumb pain bewildered by itself on his face.* CABOT *appears, returning from the barn, walking wearily, his eyes on the ground. He sees* EBEN *and his whole mood immediately changes. He becomes excited, a cruel, triumphant grin comes to his lips, he strides up and slaps* EBEN *on the back. From within comes the whining of the fiddle and the noise of stamping feet and laughing voices.*

CABOT: So har ye be!

EBEN: (*startled, stares at him with hatred for a moment—then dully*) Ay-eh.

CABOT: (*surveying him jeeringly*) Why hain't ye been in t' dance? They was all axin' fur ye.

EBEN: Let 'em ax!

CABOT: They's a hull passel o' purty gals.

EBEN: T' hell with 'em!

CABOT: Ye'd ought t' be marryin' one o' 'em soon.

EBEN: I hain't marryin' no one.

CABOT: Ye might 'arn a share o' a farm that way.

EBEN: (*with a sneer*) Like yew did, ye mean? I hain't that kind.

CABOT: (*stung*) Ye lie! 'Twas yer Maw's folks aimed t' steal my farm from me.

EBEN: Other folks don't say so. (*After a pause—defiantly*) An' I got a farm, anyways!

CABOT: (*derisively*) Whar?

EBEN: (*stamps a foot on the ground*) Har!

CABOT: (*throws his head back and laughs coarsely*) Ho-ho! Ye hev, hev ye? Waal, that's a good un!

EBEN: (*controlling himself—grimly*) Ye'll see!

CABOT: (*stares at him suspiciously, trying to make him out—a pause—then with scornful confidence*) Ay-eh. I'll see. So'll ye. It's ye that's blind—blind as a mole underground. (EBEN *suddenly laughs, one short sardonic bark: "Ha." A pause.* CABOT *peers at him with renewed suspicion*) Whar air ye hawin' 'bout? (EBEN *turns away without answering.* CABOT *grows angry*) God A'mighty, yew air a dumb dunce! They's nothin' in that thick skull o' your'n but noise—like a empty keg it be! (EBEN *doesn't seem to hear.* CABOT's *rage grows*) Yewr farm! God A'mighty! If ye wa'n't a born donkey ye'd know ye'll never own stick nor stone on it, specially now arter him bein' born. It's his'n, I tell ye—his'n arter I die—but I'll live a hundred jest t' fool ye all—an' he'll be growed then—yewr age a'most! (EBEN *laughs again his sardonic "Ha." This drives* CABOT *into a fury*) Ha? Ye think ye kin git 'round that someways, do ye? Waal, it'll be her'n, too—Abbie's—ye won't git 'round her—she knows yer tricks—she'll be too much fur ye—she wants the farm her'n—she was afeerd o' ye—she told me ye was sneakin' 'round tryin' t' make love t' her t' git her on yer side . . . ye . . . ye mad fool, ye! (*He raises his clenched fists threateningly*).

EBEN: (*is confronting him choking with rage*) Ye lie, ye old skunk! Abbie never said no sech thing!

CABOT: (*suddenly triumphant when he sees how shaken* EBEN *is*) She did. An' I says, I'll blow his brains t' the top o' them elums—an' she says no, that ain't sense, who'll ye git t' help ye on the farm in his place—an' then she says yew'n me ought t' have a son—I know we kin, she says—an' I says, if we do, ye kin have anythin' I've got ye've a mind t'. An' she says, I wants Eben cut off so's this farm'll be mine when ye die! (*With terrible gloating*) An' that's what's happened, hain't it? An' the farm's her'n! An' the dust o' the road—that's your'n! Ha! Now who's hawin'?

EBEN: (*has been listening, petrified with grief and rage—suddenly laughs wildly and brokenly*) Ha-ha-ha! So that's her sneakin' game—all along!—like I suspicioned at fust—t' swaller it all—an' me, too . . . ! (*Madly*) I'll murder her! (*He springs toward the porch but* CABOT *is quicker and gets in between*).

CABOT: No, ye don't!

EBEN: Git out o' my road! (*He tries to throw* CABOT *aside. They grapple in what becomes immediately a murderous struggle. The old man's concentrated strength is too much for* EBEN. CABOT *gets*

one hand on his throat and presses him back across the stone well. At the same moment,* ABBIE *comes out on the porch. With a stifled cry she runs toward them*).

ABBIE: Eben! Ephraim! (*She tugs at the hand on* EBEN'S *throat*) Let go, Ephraim! Ye're chokin' him!

CABOT: (*removes his hand and flings* EBEN *sideways full length on the grass, gasping and choking. With a cry,* ABBIE *kneels beside him, trying to take his head on her lap, but he pushes her away.* CABOT *stands looking down with fierce triumph*) Ye needn't t've fret, Abbie, I wa'n't aimin' t' kill him. He hain't wuth hangin' fur—not by a hell of a sight! (*More and more triumphantly*) Seventy-six an' him not thirty yit—an' look whar he be fur thinkin' his Paw was easy! No, by God, I hain't easy! An' him upstairs, I'll raise him t' be like me! (*He turns to leave them*) I'm goin' in an' dance!—sing an' celebrate! (*He walks to the porch—then turns with a great grin*) I don't calc'late it's left in him, but if he gits pesky, Abbie, ye jest sing out. I'll come a-runnin' an' by the Etarnal, I'll put him across my knee an' birch him! Ha-ha-ha! (*He goes into the house laughing. A moment later his loud "whoop" is heard*).

ABBIE: (*tenderly*) Eben. Air ye hurt? (*She tries to kiss him but he pushes her violently away and struggles to a sitting position*).

EBEN: (*gaspingly*) T' hell—with ye!

ABBIE: (*not believing her ears*) It's me, Eben—Abbie—don't ye know me?

EBEN: (*glowering at her with hatred*) Ay-eh—I know ye—now! (*He suddenly breaks down, sobbing weakly*).

ABBIE: (*fearfully*) Eben—what's happened t' ye—why did ye look at me 's if ye hated me?

EBEN: (*violently, between sobs and*

gasps) I do hate ye! Ye're a whore—a damn trickin' whore!

ABBIE: (*shrinking back horrified*) Eben! Ye don't know what ye're sayin'!

EBEN: (*scrambling to his feet and following her—accusingly*) Ye're nothin' but a stinkin' passel o' lies! Ye've been lyin' t' me every word ye spoke, day an' night, since we fust—done it. Ye've kept sayin' ye loved me. . . .

ABBIE: (*frantically*) I do love ye! (*She takes his hand but he flings hers away*).

EBEN: (*unheeding*) Ye've made a fool o' me—a sick, dumb fool—a-purpose! Ye've been on'y playin' yer sneakin', stealin' game all along—gittin' me t' lie with ye so's ye'd hev a son he'd think was his'n, an' makin' him promise he'd give ye the farm and let me eat dust, if ye did git him a son! (*Staring at her with anguished, bewildered eyes*) They must be a devil livin' in ye! T'ain't human t' be as bad as that be!

ABBIE: (*stunned-dully*) He told yew . . . ?

EBEN: Hain't it true? It hain't no good in yew lyin'.

ABBIE: (*pleadingly*) Eben, listen—ye must listen—it was long ago—afore we done nothin'—yew was scornin' me—goin' t' see Min—when I was lovin' ye—an' I said it t' him t' git vengeance on ye!

EBEN: (*unheedingly. With tortured passion*) I wish ye was dead! I wish I was dead along with ye afore this come! (*Ragingly*) But I'll git my vengeance too! I'll pray Maw t' come back t' help me—t' put her cuss on yew an' him!

ABBIE: (*brokenly*) Don't ye, Eben! Don't ye! (*She throws herself on her knees before him, weeping*) I didn't mean t' do bad t' ye! Fergive me, won't ye?

EBEN: (*not seeming to hear her—fiercely*) I'll git squar' with the old skunk —an' yew! I'll tell him the truth 'bout the son he's so proud o'! Then I'll leave ye here t' pizen each other—with Maw comin' out o' her grave at nights—an' I'll go t' the gold fields o' Californi-a whar Sim an' Peter be!

ABBIE: (*terrified*) Ye won't—leave me? Ye can't!

EBEN: (*with fierce determination*) I'm a-goin', I tell ye! I'll git rich thar an' come back an' fight him fur the farm he stole— an' I'll kick ye both out in the road—t' beg an' sleep in the woods—an' yer son along with ye—t' starve an' die! (*He is hysterical at the end*).

ABBIE: (*with a shudder—humbly*) He's yewr son, too, Eben.

EBEN: (*torturedly*) I wish he never was born! I wish he'd die this minit! I wish I'd never sot eyes on him! It's him— yew havin' him—a-purpose t' steal—that's changed everythin'!

ABBIE: (*gently*) Did ye believe I loved ye—afore he come?

EBEN: Ay-eh—like a dumb ox!

ABBIE: An' ye don't believe no more?

EBEN: B'lieve a lyin' thief! Ha!

ABBIE: (*shudders—then humbly*) An' did ye r'ally love me afore?

EBEN: (*brokenly*) Ay-eh—an' ye was trickin' me!

ABBIE: An ye' don't love me now!

EBEN: (*violently*) I hate ye, I tell ye!

ABBIE: An' ye're truly goin' West— goin' t' leave me—all account o' him being born?

EBEN: I'm a-goin' in the mornin'—or may God strike me t' hell!

ABBIE: (*after a pause—with a dreadful cold intensity—slowly*) If that's what his comin 's done t' me—killin' yewr love— takin' yew away—my on'y joy—the on'y joy I ever knowed—like heaven t' me— purtier'n heaven—then I hate him, too, even if I be his Maw!

EBEN: (*bitterly*) Lies! Ye love him! He'll steal the farm fur ye! (*Brokenly*) But t'ain't the farm so much—not no more—it's yew foolin' me—gittin' me t' love ye—lyin' yew loved me—jest t' git a son t' steal!

ABBIE: (*distractedly*) He won't steal! I'd kill him fust! I do love ye! I'll prove t' ye . . . !

EBEN: (*harshly*) T'ain't no use lyin' no more. I'm deaf t' ye! (*He turns away*) I hain't seein' ye agen. Good-by!

ABBIE: (*pale with anguish*) Hain't ye even goin' t' kiss me—not once—arter all we loved?

EBEN: (*in a hard voice*) I hain't wantin' t' kiss ye never agen! I'm wantin' t' forgit I ever sot eyes on ye!

ABBIE: Eben!—ye mustn't—wait a spell —I want t' tell ye. . . .

EBEN: I'm a-goin' in t' git drunk. I'm a-goin' t' dance.

ABBIE: (*clinging to his arm—with passionate earnestness*) If I could make it—'s if he'd never come up between us—if I could prove t' ye I wa'n't schemin' t' steal from ye—so's everythin' could be jest the same with us, lovin' each other jest the same, kissin' an' happy the same's we've been happy afore he come—if I could do it—ye'd love me agen, wouldn't ye? Ye'd kiss me agen? Ye wouldn't never leave me, would ye?

EBEN: (*moved*) I calc'late not. (*Then shaking her hand off his arm—with a bitter smile*) But ye hain't God, be ye?

ABBIE: (*exultantly*) Remember ye've promised! (*Then with strange intensity*) Mebbe I kin take back one thin' God does!

EBEN: (*peering at her*) Ye're gittin' cracked, hain't ye? (*Then going towards door*) I'm a-goin' t' dance.

ABBIE: (*calls after him intensely*) I'll prove t' ye! I'll prove I love ye better'n. . . . (*He goes in the door, not seeming to hear. She remains standing where she is, looking after him—then she finishes desperately*) Better'n everythin' else in the world!

CURTAIN

SCENE THREE

Just before dawn in the morning—shows the kitchen and CABOT's *bedroom. In the kitchen, by the light of a tallow candle on the table,* EBEN *is sitting, his chin propped on his hands, his drawn face blank and expressionless. His carpetbag is on the floor beside him. In the bedroom, dimly lighted by a small whale-oil lamp,* CABOT *lies asleep.* ABBIE *is bending over the cradle, listening, her face full of terror yet with an undercurrent of desperate triumph. Suddenly, she breaks down and sobs, appears about to throw herself on her knees beside the cradle; but the old man turns restlessly, groaning in his sleep, and she controls herself, and, shrinking away from the cradle with a gesture of horror, backs swiftly toward the door in rear and goes out. A moment later she comes into the kitchen and, running to* EBEN, *flings her arms about his neck and kisses him wildly. He hardens himself, he remains unmoved and cold, he keeps his eyes straight ahead.*

ABBIE: (*hysterically*) I done it, Eben! I told ye I'd do it! I've proved I love ye— better'n everythin'—so's ye can't never doubt me no more!

EBEN: (*dully*) Whatever ye done, it hain't no good now.

ABBIE: (*wildly*) Don't ye say that! Kiss me, Eben, won't ye? I need ye t' kiss me arter what I done! I need ye t' say ye love me!

EBEN: (*kisses her without emotion— dully*) That's fur good-by. I'm a-goin' soon.

ABBIE: No! No! Ye won't go—not now!

EBEN: (*going on with his own thoughts*) I been a-thinkin'—an' I hain't goin' t' tell Paw nothin'. I'll leave Maw t' take vengeance on ye. If I told him, the old skunk'd jest be stinkin' mean enuf to take it out on that baby. (*His voice showing emotion in spite of him*) An' I don't want nothin' bad t' happen t' him. He hain't t' blame fur yew. (*He adds with a certain queer pride*) An' he looks like me! An' by God, he's mine! An' some day I'll be a-comin' back an' . . . !

ABBIE: (*too absorbed in her own thoughts to listen to him—pleadingly*) They's no cause fur ye t' go now—they's no sense—it's all the same's it was—they's nothin' come b'tween us now—arter what I done!

EBEN: (*something in her voice arouses him. He stares at her a bit frightenedly*) Ye look mad, Abbie. What did ye do?

ABBIE: I—I killed him, Eben.

EBEN: (*amazed*) Ye killed him?

ABBIE: (*dully*) Ay-eh.

EBEN: (*recovering from his astonishment—savagely*) An' serves him right! But we got t' do somethin' quick t' make it look 's if the old skunk'd killed himself when he was drunk. We kin prove by 'em all how drunk he got.

ABBIE: (*wildly*) No! No! Not him! (*Laughing distractedly*) But that's what I ought t' done, hain't it? I oughter killed him instead! Why didn't ye tell me?

EBEN: (*appalled*) Instead? What d'ye mean?

ABBIE: Not him.

EBEN: (*his face grown ghastly*) Not—not that baby!

ABBIE: (*dully*) Ay-eh?

EBEN: (*falls to his knees as if he'd been struck—his voice trembling with horror*) Oh, God A'mighty! A'mighty God! Maw, whar was ye, why didn't ye stop her?

ABBIE: (*simply*) She went back t' her grave that night we fust done it, remember? I hain't felt her about since. (*A pause. EBEN hides his head in his hands, trembling all over as if he had the ague. She goes on dully*) I left the piller over his little face. Then he killed himself. He stopped breathin'. (*She begins to weep softly*).

EBEN: (*rage beginning to mingle with grief*) He looked like me. He was mine, damn ye!

ABBIE: (*slowly and brokenly*) I didn't want t' do it. I hated myself fur doin' it. I loved him. He was so purty—dead spit 'n' image o' yew. But I loved yew more—an' yew was goin' away—far off whar I'd never see ye agen, never kiss ye, never feel ye pressed agin me agen—an' ye said ye hated me fur havin' him—ye said ye hated him an' wished he was dead—ye said if it hadn't been fur him comin' it'd be the same's afore between us.

EBEN: (*unable to endure this, springs to his feet in a fury, threatening her, his twitching fingers seeming to reach out for her throat*) Ye lie! I never said—I never dreamed ye'd—I'd cut off my head afore I'd hurt his finger!

ABBIE: (*piteously, sinking on her knees*) Eben, don't ye look at me like that—hatin' me—not after what I done fur ye—fur us—so's we could be happy agen—

EBEN: (*furiously now*) Shut up, or I'll kill ye! I see yer game now—the same old sneakin' trick—ye're aimin' t' blame me fur the murder ye done!

ABBIE: (*moaning—putting her hands over her ears*) Don't ye, Eben! Don't ye! (*She grasps his legs*).

EBEN: (*his mood suddenly changing to horror, shrinks away from her*) Don't ye tech me! Ye're pizen! How could ye—t' murder a pore little critter— Ye must've swapped yer soul t' hell! (*Suddenly rag-*

ing) Ha! I kin see why ye done it! Not the lies ye jest told—but 'cause ye wanted t' steal agen—steal the last thin' ye'd left me—my part o' him—no, the hull o' him —ye saw he looked like me—ye knowed he was all mine—an' ye couldn't b'ar it —I know ye! Ye killed him fur bein' mine! (*All this has driven him almost insane. He makes a rush past her for the door—then turns—shaking both fists at her, violently*) But I'll take vengeance now! I'll git the Sheriff! I'll tell him everythin'! Then I'll sing "I'm off to Californi-a!" an' go—gold—Golden Gate— gold sun—fields o' gold in the West! (*This last he half shouts, half croons incoherently, suddenly breaking off passionately*) I'm a-goin' fur the Sheriff t' come an' git ye! I want ye tuk away, locked up from me! I can't stand t' luk at ye! Murderer an' thief 'r not, ye still tempt me! I'll give ye up t' the Sheriff (*He turns and runs out, around the corner of house, panting and sobbing, and breaks into a swerving sprint down the road*).

ABBIE: (*struggling to her feet, runs to the door, calling after him*) I love ye, Eben! I love ye! (*She stops at the door weakly, swaying, about to fall*) I don't care what ye do—if ye'll on'y love me agen—(*She falls limply to the floor in a faint*).

CURTAIN

Scene Four

About an hour later. Same as Scene Three. Shows the kitchen and CABOT's *bedroom. It is after dawn. The sky is brilliant with the sunrise. In the kitchen,* ABBIE *sits at the table, her body limp and exhausted, her head bowed down over her arms, her face hidden. Upstairs,* CABOT *is still asleep but awakens with a start. He looks toward the window and gives a snort of surprise and irritation—throws back the covers*

and begins hurriedly pulling on his clothes. Without looking behind him, he begins talking to ABBIE *whom he supposes beside him.*

CABOT: Thunder 'n' lightin', Abbie! I hain't slept this late in fifty year! Looks 's if the sun was full riz a'most. Must've been the dancin' an' likker. Must be gittin' old. I hope Eben's t' wuk. Ye might've tuk the trouble t' rouse me, Abbie. (*He turns—sees no one there—surprised*) Waal —whar air she? Gittin' vittles, I calc'late. (*He tiptoes to the cradle and peers down —proudly*) Mornin' sonny. Purty's a picture! Sleepin' sound. He don't beller all night like most o' 'em. (*He goes quietly out the door in rear—a few moments later enters kitchen—sees* ABBIE—*with satisfaction*) So thar ye be. Ye got any vittles cooked?

ABBIE: (*without moving*) No.

CABOT: (*coming to her, almost sympathetically*) Ye feelin' sick?

ABBIE: No.

CABOT: (*pats her on shoulder. She shudders*) Ye'd best lie down a spell. (*Half jocularly*) Yer son'll be needin' ye soon. He'd ought t' wake up with a gnashin' appetite, the sound way he's sleepin'.

ABBIE: (*shudders—then in a dead voice*) He hain't never goin' t' wake up.

CABOT: (*jokingly*) Takes after me this mornin'. I hain't slept so late in . . .

ABBIE: He's dead.

CABOT: (*stares at her—bewilderedly*) What. . . .

ABBIE: I killed him.

CABOT: (*stepping back from her— aghast*) Air ye drunk— 'r crazy—'r . . . !

ABBIE: (*suddenly lifts her head and turns on him—wildly*) I killed him, I tell ye! I smothered him. Go up an' see if ye don't b'lieve me! (*CABOT stares at her a second, then bolts out the rear door—can be heard bounding up the stairs—and rushes into the bedroom and over to the cradle.* ABBIE *has sunk back lifelessly into her former position.* CABOT *puts his hand down on the body in the crib. An expression of fear and horror comes over his face).*

CABOT: (*shrinking away—tremblingly*) God A'mighty! God A'mighty. (*He stumbles out the door—in a short while returns to the kitchen—comes to* ABBIE, *the stunned expression still on his face—hoarsely*) Why did ye do it? Why? (*As she doesn't answer, he grabs her violently by the shoulder and shakes her*) I ax ye why ye done it! Ye'd better tell me 'r . . . !

ABBIE: (*gives him a furious push which sends him staggering back and springs to her feet—with wild rage and hatred*) Don't ye dare tech me! What right hev ye t' question me 'bout him? He wa'n't yewr son! Think I'd have a son by yew? I'd die fust! I hate the sight o' ye an' allus did! It's yew I should've murdered, if I'd had good sense! I hate ye! I love Eben. I did from the fust. An' he was Eben's son— mine an' Eben's—not your'n!

CABOT: (*stands looking at her dazedly— a pause—finding his words with an effort —dully*) That was it—what I felt—pokin' round the corners—while ye lied—holdin' yerself from me—sayin' ye'd already conceived— (*He lapses into crushed silence —then with a strange emotion*) He's dead, sart'n. I felt his heart. Pore little critter! (*He blinks back one tear, wiping his sleeve across his nose*).

ABBIE: (*hysterically*) Don't ye! Don't ye! (*she sobs unrestrainedly*).

CABOT: (*with a concentrated effort that stiffens his body into a rigid line and hardens his face into a stony mask— through his teeth to himself*) I got t' be— like a stone—a rock o' jedgment! (*A pause. He gets complete control over himself—harshly*) If he was Eben's, I be glad

he air gone! An' mebbe I suspicioned it all along. I felt they was somethin' onnateral —somewhars—the house got so lonesome —an' cold—drivin' me down t' the barn— t' the beasts o' the field. . . . Ay-eh. I must've suspicioned—somethin'. Ye didn't fool me—not altogether, leastways—I'm too old a bird—growin' ripe on the bough. . . . (*He becomes aware he is wandering, straightens again, looks at* ABBIE *with a cruel grin*) So ye'd like t' hev murdered me 'stead o' him, would ye? Waal, I'll live to a hundred! I'll live t' see ye hung! I'll deliver ye up t' the jedgment o' God an' the law! I'll git the Sheriff now. (*Starts for the door*).

ABBIE: (*dully*) Ye needn't. Eben's gone fur him.

CABOT: (*amazed*) Eben—gone for the Sheriff?

ABBIE: Ay-eh.

CABOT: T' inform agen ye?

ABBIE: Ay-eh.

CABOT: (*considers this—a pause—then in a hard voice*) Waal, I'm thankful fur him savin' me the trouble. I'll git t' wuk. (*He goes to the door—then turns—in a voice full of strange emotion*) He'd ought t' been my son, Abbie. Ye'd ought t' loved me. I'm a man. If ye'd loved me, I'd never told no Sheriff on ye no matter what ye did, if they was t' brile me alive!

ABBIE: (*defensively*) They's more to it nor yew know, makes him tell.

CABOT: (*dryly*) Fur yewr sake, I hope they be. (*He goes out—comes around to the gate—stares up at the sky. His control relaxes. For a moment he is old and weary. He murmurs despairingly*) God A'mighty, I be lonesomer'n ever! (*He hears running footsteps from the left, immediately is himself again.* EBEN *runs in, panting exhaustedly, wild-eyed and mad looking. He lurches through the gate.* CABOT *grabs him by the shoulder.* EBEN *stares at him dumbly*) Did ye tell the Sheriff?

EBEN: (*nodding stupidly*) Ay-eh.

CABOT: (*gives him a push away that sends him sprawling—laughing with withering contempt*) Good fur ye! A prime chip o' yer Maw ye be! (*He goes toward the barn, laughing harshly.* EBEN *scrambles to his feet. Suddenly* CABOT *turns —grimly threatening*) Git off this farm when the Sheriff takes her—or, by God, he'll have t' come back an' git me fur murder, too! (*He stalks off.* EBEN *does not appear to have heard him. He runs to the door and comes into the kitchen.* ABBIE *looks up with a cry of anguished joy.* EBEN *stumbles over and throws himself on his knees beside her—sobbing brokenly*).

EBEN: Fergive me!

ABBIE: (*happily*) Eben! (*She kisses him and pulls his head over against her breast*).

EBEN: I love ye! Fergive me!

ABBIE: (*ecstatically*) I'd fergive ye all the sins in hell fur sayin' that! (*She kisses his head, pressing it to her with a fierce passion of possession*).

EBEN: (*brokenly*) But I told the Sheriff. He's comin' fur ye!

ABBIE: I kin b'ar what happens' t' me —now!

EBEN: I woke him up. I told him. He says, wait 'til I git dressed. I was waiting. I got to thinkin' o' yew. I got to thinkin' how I'd loved ye. It hurt like somethin' was bustin' in my chest an' head. I got t' cryin'. I knowed sudden I loved ye yet, an' allus would love ye!

ABBIE: (*caressing his hair—tenderly*) My boy, hain't ye?

EBEN: I begun t' run back. I cut across the fields an' through the woods. I thought ye might have time t' run away—with me—an' . . .

ABBIE: (*shaking her head*) I got t' take my punishment—t' pay fur my sin.

EBEN: Then I want t' share it with ye.

ABBIE: Ye didn't do nothin'.

EBEN: I put it in yer head. I wisht he was dead! I as much as urged ye t' do it!

ABBIE: No. It was me alone!

EBEN: I'm as guilty as yew be! He was the child o' our sin.

ABBIE: (*lifting her head as if defying God*) I don't repent that sin! I hain't askin' God t' fergive that!

EBEN: Nor me—but it led up t' the other—an' the murder ye did, ye did 'count o' me—an' it's my murder, too, I'll tell the Sheriff—an' if ye deny it, I'll say we planned it t'gether—an' they'll all b'lieve me, fur they suspicion everythin' we've done, an' it'll seem likely an' true to 'em. An' it is true—way down. I did help ye—somehow.

ABBIE: (*laying her head on his—sobbing*) No! I don't want yew t' suffer!

EBEN: I got t' pay fur my part o' the sin! An' I'd suffer wust leavin' ye, goin' West, thinkin' o' ye day an' night, bein' out when yew was in— (*Lowering his voice*) 'r bein' alive when yew was dead. (*A pause*) I want t' share with ye, Abbie —prison 'r death 'r hell 'r anythin'! (*He looks into her eyes and forces a trembling smile*) If I'm sharin' with ye, I won't feel lonesome, leastways.

ABBIE: (*weakly*) Eben! I won't let ye! I can't let ye!

EBEN: (*kissing her—tenderly*) Ye can't he'p yerself. I got ye beat fur once!

ABBIE: (*forcing a smile—adoringly*) I hain't beat—s'long's I got ye!

EBEN: (*hears the sound of feet outside*) Ssshh! Listen! They've come t' take us!

ABBIE: No, it's him. Don't give him no chance to fight ye, Eben. Don't say nothin' —no matter what he says. An' I won't neither. (*It is* CABOT. *He comes up from the barn in a great state of excitement and strides into the house and then into the kitchen.* EBEN *is kneeling beside* ABBIE, *his arm around her, hers around him. They stare straight ahead*).

CABOT: (*stares at them, his face hard. A long pause—vindictively*) Ye make a slick pair o' murderin' turtle doves! Ye'd ought t' be both hung on the same limb an' left thar t' swing in the breeze an' rot —a warnin' t' old fools like me t' b'ar their lonesomeness alone—an' fur young fools like ye t' hobble their lust. (*A pause. The excitment returns to his face, his eyes snap, he looks a bit crazy*) I couldn't work today. I couldn't take no interest. T' hell with the farm! I'm leavin' it! I've turned the cows an' other stock loose! I've druv 'em into the woods whar they kin be free! By freein' 'em, I'm freein' myself! I'm quittin' here today! I'll set fire t' house an' barn an' watch 'em burn, an' I'll leave yer Maw t' haunt the ashes, an' I'll will the fields back t' God, so that nothin' human kin never touch 'em! I'll be a-goin' to Californi-a—t' jine Simeon an' Peter— true sons o 'mine if they be dumb fools— an' the Cabots'll find Solomon's Mines t'gether! (*He suddenly cuts a mad caper*) Whoop! What was the song they sung? "Oh, Californi-a! That's the land fur me." (*He sings this—then gets on his knees by the floor-board under which the money was hid*) An' I'll sail thar on one o' the finest clippers I kin find! I've got the money! Pity ye didn't know whar this was hidden so's ye could steal. . . . (*He has pulled up the board. He stares—feels— stares again. A pause of dead silence. He slowly turns, slumping into a sitting position on the floor, his eyes like those of a dead fish, his face the sickly green of an attack of nausea. He swallows painfully several times—forces a weak smile at last*) So—ye did steal it!

EBEN: (*emotionlessly*) I swapped it t' Sim an' Peter fur their share o' the farm —t' pay their passage t' Californi-a.

CABOT: (*with one sardonic*) Ha! (*He begins to recover. Gets slowly to his feet —strangely*) I calc'late God give it to 'em —not yew! God's hard, not easy! Mebbe they's easy gold in the West but it hain't God's gold. It hain't fur me. I kin hear His voice warnin' me agen t' be hard an' stay on my farm. I kin see his hand usin' Eben t' steal t' keep me from weakness. I kin feel I be in the palm o' His hand, His fingers guidin' me. (*A pause—then he mutters sadly*) It's a-goin' t' be lonesomer now than ever it war afore—an' I'm gittin' old, Lord—ripe on the bough. . . . (*Then stiffening*) Waal—what d'ye want? God's lonesome, hain't He? God's hard an' lonesome! (*A pause. The Sheriff with two men comes up the road from the left. They move cautiously to the door. The Sheriff knocks on it with the butt of his pistol*).

SHERIFF: Open in the name o' the law! (*They start*).

CABOT: They've come fur ye. (*He goes to the rear door*) Come in, Jim! (*The three men enter.* CABOT *meets them in doorway*) Jest a minit, Jim. I got 'em safe here. (*The Sheriff nods. He and his companions remain in the doorway*).

EBEN: (*suddenly calls*) I lied this mornin' Jim. I helped her to do it. Ye kin take me, too.

ABBIE: (*brokenly*) No!

CABOT: Take 'em both. (*He comes forward—stares at* EBEN *with a trace of grudging admiration*) Purty good—fur yew! Waal, I got t' round up the stock. Good-by.

EBEN: Good-by.

ABBIE: Good-by. (CABOT *turns and strides past the men—comes out and around the corner of the house, his shoul-*

ders squared, his face stony, and stalks grimly toward the barn. In the meantime the Sheriff and men have come into the room).

SHERIFF: (*embarrassedly*) Wall—we'd best start.

ABBIE: Wait. (*Turns to* EBEN) I love ye, Eben.

EBEN: I love ye, Abbie. (*They kiss. The three men grin and shuffle embarrassedly.* EBEN *takes* ABBIE's *hand. They go out the door in rear, the men following, and come from the house, walking hand in hand to the gate.* EBEN *stops there and points to the sunrise sky*) Sun's a-rizin'. Purty, hain't it?

ABBIE: Ay-eh. (*They both stand for a moment looking up raptly in attitudes strangely aloof and devout*).

SHERIFF: (*looking around at the farm enviously—to his companion*) It's a jim-dandy farm, no denyin'. Wished I owned it!

CURTAIN

Yerma

FEDERICO GARCÍA LORCA

COMMENTARY

Federico García Lorca (1899-1936) was born near Granada, in Andalusia, Spain, home of Pablo Picasso, the artist, and Manuel de Falla, the composer. He attended the University of Granada, to study law and literature, but he began early to write poetry and plays. He was associated with the advanced guard of Spanish artists from the beginning of his career. He studied music with de Falla and worked with him on a ballet. Salvador Dali, the famous surrealist painter, designed settings for an early Lorca play. After living a year in New York's Harlem, Lorca wrote *Poet in New York*, which established his international reputation as a poet. His three great tragedies, each about rural life, were *Blood Wedding* (1933), *Yerma* (1934), and *The House of Bernarda Alba* (1936). He was executed, for reasons that have never become clear, by Fascist rebels early in the Spanish Civil War.

Unlike his other two tragedies, which revolve around the fates of families, *Yerma* concentrates on a single woman. The word "Yerma" means "barren" in Spanish. From the play we are to infer that Yerma's husband, Juan, is responsible for her infertility, yet Yerma's obsessive urge for motherhood is almost pathological and possibly self-defeating. Like some Freudian overstatement, her obsession may actually mask a simple fear of fertility. Like the classically defined tragic hero, then, she may be understood as carrying within herself, with classical tragic irony, the seed of her fall.

Yerma moves relentlessly toward the crisis. In the course of her descent, she reveals an underlying frigidity; her wish to become a mother seems more intellectual than instinctual, an *idea* that possesses her rather than an emotion. She is paralyzed by the society in which she moves, by an "honor" that is determined for her from the outside. If she should attempt to fulfill her need outside the limits of honor, she would violate her own powerful sense of the proper. She is to be compared with such heroines who do act in violation of the social code, like Medea or

Clytemnestra, as well as with Phaedra, who does not so act but passionately wishes to.

Lorca's work has the spare quality of poetry or, possibly, of the scenario for ballet. What hints or undertones do you sense in the text? Should these be left as felt reverberations, or should they be made explicit? How do you imagine that the nature of Lorca's art might be changed in production? How might your sympathies with Yerma or with Juan be affected by seeing particular actors in the roles? Would Lorca's text support varying interpretations of the leading characters?

A full discussion of *Yerma* may be found in Edwin Honig's *García Lorca* (Norfolk, Conn., 1963). See also Warren Carrier's "Poetry in the Drama of Lorca," *Drama Survey,* vol. 2 (Winter, 1963), pp. 297-304, and Morris Freedman's "Lorca's Three Tragedies and the Morality of Passion," in *The Moral Impulse* (Carbondale, 1967).

Federico García Lorca

YERMA

A TRAGIC POEM IN THREE ACTS
AND SIX SCENES
(1934)

Translated by James Graham-Luján and Richard L. O'Connell

CHARACTERS

YERMA	FIRST YOUNG GIRL
MARIA	SECOND YOUNG GIRL
JUAN	THE FEMALE MASK
VICTOR	THE MALE MASK
PAGAN CRONE	FIRST SISTER-IN-LAW
DOLORES	SECOND SISTER-IN-LAW
FIRST LAUNDRESS	FIRST WOMAN
SECOND LAUNDRESS	SECOND WOMAN
THIRD LAUNDRESS	THE CHILD
FOURTH LAUNDRESS	FIRST MAN
FIFTH LAUNDRESS	SECOND MAN
SIXTH LAUNDRESS	THIRD MAN

ACT ONE
SCENE 1

When the curtain rises YERMA *is asleep with an embroidery frame at her feet. The stage is in the strange light of a dream. A shepherd enters on tiptoe looking fixedly at* YERMA. *He leads by the hand a* CHILD *dressed in white. The clock sounds. When the shepherd leaves, the light changes into the happy brightness of a spring morning.* YERMA *awakes.*

VOICE: (*within, singing.*)
   For the nursey, nursey, nursey,
   For the little nurse we'll make
   A tiny hut out in the fields
   And there we'll shelter take.

YERMA: Juan, do you hear me? Juan!

JUAN: Coming.

YERMA: It's time now.

JUAN: Did the oxen go by?

YERMA: They've already gone.

JUAN: See you later.

   (*He starts to leave.*)

YERMA: Won't you have a glass of milk?

JUAN: What for?

YERMA: You work a lot and your body's not strong enough for it.

JUAN: When men grow thin they get strong as steel.

YERMA: But not you. You were different when we were first married. Now you've got a face as white as though the sun had never shone on it. I'd like to see you go to the river and swim or climb up on the roof when the rain beats down on our house. Twenty-four months we've been married and you only get sadder, thinner, as if you were growing backwards.

JUAN: Are you finished?

YERMA: (*rising*) Don't take it wrong. If I were sick I'd like you to take care of me. "My wife's sick. I'm going to butcher this lamb and cook her a good meat dish." "My wife's sick. I'm going to save this chicken-fat to relieve her chest; I'm going to take her this sheepskin to protect her feet from the snow." That's the way I am. That's why I take care of you.

JUAN: I'm grateful.

YERMA: But you don't let me take care of you.

JUAN: Because there's nothing wrong with me. All these things are just your imagination. I work hard. Each year I'll get older.

YERMA: Each year. You and I will just go on here each year . . .

JUAN: (*smiling.*) Why, of course. And very peacefully. Our work goes well, we've no children to worry about.

YERMA: We've no children. . . . Juan!

JUAN: What is it?

YERMA: I love you, don't I?

JUAN: Yes, you love me.

YERMA: I know girls who trembled and cried before getting into bed with their husbands. Did I cry the first time I went to bed with you? Didn't I sing as I turned back the fine linen bed-clothes? And didn't I tell you, "These bed-clothes smell of apples!"

JUAN: That's what you said!

YERMA: My mother cried because I wasn't sorry to leave her. And that's true! No one ever got married with more happiness. And yet . . .

JUAN: Hush! I have a hard enough job hearing all the time that I'm . . .

YERMA: No. Don't tell me what they say. I can see with my own eyes that that isn't so. The rain just by the force of its falling on the stones softens them and makes weeds grow—weeds which people say aren't good for anything. "Weeds aren't good for anything," yet I see them plainly enough—moving their yellow flowers in the wind.

JUAN: We've got to wait!

YERMA: Yes; loving each other.

(YERMA *embraces and kisses her husband. She takes the initiative.*)

JUAN: If you need anything, tell me, and I'll bring it to you. You know well enough I don't like you to be going out.

YERMA: I never go out.

JUAN: You're better off here.

YERMA: Yes.

JUAN: The street's for people with nothing to do.

YERMA: (*darkly.*) Of course.

(*The husband leaves.* YERMA *walks toward her sewing. She passes her hand over her belly, lifts her arms in a beautiful sigh, and sits down to sew.*)

YERMA:
From where do you come, my love, my baby?
"From the mountains of icy cold."
What do you lack, sweet love, my baby?
"The woven warmth in your dress."

(*She threads the needle.*)

Let the branches tremble in the sun
and the fountains leap all around!

(*As if she spoke to a child.*)

In the courtyard the dog barks,
In the trees the wind sings.
The oxen low for the ox-herd,
and the moon curls up my hair.
What want you, boy, from so far away?

(*Pause.*)

"The mountains white upon your chest."
Let the branches tremble in the sun
and the fountains leap all around!

(*Sewing.*)

I shall say to you, child, yes,
for you I'll torn and broken be.
How painful is this belly now,
where first you shall be cradled!
When, boy, when will you come to me?

(*Pause.*)

"When sweet your flesh of jasmine smells."
Let the branches tremble in the sun
and the fountains leap all around!

(YERMA *continues singing.* MARÍA *enters through the door carrying a bundle of clothes.*)

YERMA: Where are you coming from?

MARIA: From the store.

YERMA: From the store so early?

MARIA: For what I wanted, I'd have waited at the door till they opened. Can't you guess what I bought?

YERMA: You probably bought some coffee for breakfast; sugar, bread.

MARIA: No. I bought laces, three lengths of linen, ribbons, and colored wool to make tassels. My husband had the money and he gave it to me without my even asking for it.

YERMA: You're going to make a blouse?

MARIA: No, it's because . . . Can't you guess?

YERMA: What?

MARIA: Because . . . well . . . it's here now!

(*She lowers her head.* YERMA *rises and looks at her in admiration.*)

YERMA: In just five months!

MARIA: Yes.

YERMA: You can tell it's there?

MARIA: Naturally.

YERMA: (*with curiosity.*) But, how does it make you feel?

MARIA: I don't know. Sad; upset.

YERMA: Sad? Upset?

(*Holding her.*)

But . . . when did he come? Tell me about it. You weren't expecting him.

MARIA: No, I wasn't expecting him.

YERMA: Why, you might have been singing; yes? I sing. You . . . tell me . . .

MARIA: Don't ask me about it. Have you ever held a live bird pressed in your hand?

YERMA: Yes.

MARIA: Well—the same way—but more in your blood.

YERMA: How beautiful!

(*She looks at her, beside herself.*)

MARIA: I'm confused. I don't know anything.

YERMA: About what?

MARIA: About what I must do. I'll ask my mother.

YERMA: What for? She's old now and she'll have forgotten about these things. Don't walk very much, and when you breathe, breathe as softly as if you had a rose between your teeth.

MARIA: You know, they say that later he kicks you gently with his little legs.

YERMA: And that's when you love him best, when you can really say: "*My* child!"

MARIA: In the midst of all this, I feel ashamed.

YERMA: What has your husband said about it?

MARIA: Nothing.

YERMA: Does he love you a lot?

MARIA: He doesn't tell me so, but when he's close to me his eyes tremble like two green leaves.

YERMA: Did he know that you were . . . ?

MARIA: Yes.

YERMA: But, how did he know it?

MARIA: I don't know. But on our wedding night he kept telling me about it with his mouth pressed against my cheek; so that now it seems to me my child is a dove of fire he made slip in through my ear.

YERMA: Oh, how lucky you are!

MARIA: But you know more about these things than I do.

YERMA: And what good does it do me?

MARIA: That's true! Why should it be like that? Out of all the brides of your time you're the only one who . . .

YERMA: That's the way it is. Of course, there's still time. Helena was three years, and long ago some in my mother's time were much longer, but two years and twenty days—like me—is too long to wait. I don't think it's right for me to burn myself out here. Many nights I go out barefooted to the patio to walk on the ground. I don't know why I do it. If I keep on like this, I'll end by turning bad.

MARIA: But look here, you infant, you're talking as if you were an old woman. You listen to me, now! No one can complain about these things. A sister of my mother's had one after fourteen years, and you should have seen what a beautiful child that was!

YERMA: (*eagerly.*) What was he like?

MARIA: He used to bellow like a little bull, as loud as a thousand locusts all buzzing at once, and wet us, and pull our braids; and when he was four months old he scratched our faces all over.

YERMA: (*laughing.*) But those things don't hurt.

MARIA: Let me tell you—

YERMA: Bah! I've seen my sister nurse her child with her breasts full of scratches. It gave her great pain, but it was a fresh pain—good, and necessary for health.

MARIA: They say one suffers a lot with children.

YERMA: That's a lie. That's what weak, complaining mothers say. What do they have them for? Having a child is no bouquet of roses. We must suffer to see them grow. I sometimes think half our blood must go. But that's good, healthy, beautiful. Every woman has blood for four or five children, and when she doesn't have them it turns to poison . . . as it will in me.

MARIA: I don't know what's the matter with me.

YERMA: I've always heard it said that you're frightened the first time.

MARIA: (*timidly.*) We'll see. You know, you sew so well that . . .

YERMA: (*taking the bundle.*) Give it here. I'll cut you two little dresses. And this . . . ?

MARIA: For diapers.

YERMA: (*she sits down*) All right.

MARIA: Well . . . See you later.

(*As she comes near,* YERMA *lovingly presses her hands against her belly.*)

YERMA: Don't run on the cobblestones.

MARIA: Good-bye.

(*She kisses her and leaves.*)

YERMA: Come back soon.

(YERMA *is in the same attitude as at the beginning of the scene. She takes her scissors and starts to cut.* VICTOR *enters.*)

Hello, Victor.

VICTOR: (*he is deep looking and has a firm gravity about him.*) Where's Juan?

YERMA: Out in the fields.

VICTOR: What's that you're sewing?

YERMA: I'm cutting some diapers.

VICTOR: (*smiling.*) Well, now!

YERMA: (*laughs.*) I'm going to border them with lace.

VICTOR: If it's a girl, you give her your name.

YERMA: (*trembling.*) How's that?

VICTOR: I'm happy for you.

YERMA: (*almost choking.*) No . . . they aren't for me. They're for María's child.

VICTOR: Well then, let's see if her example will encourage you. This house needs a child in it.

YERMA: (*with anguish.*) Needs one!

VICTOR: Well, get along with it. Tell your husband to think less about his work. He wants to make money and he will, but who's he going to leave it to when he dies? I'm going out with my sheep. Tell Juan to take out the two he bought from me, and about this other thing—try harder!

(*He leaves, smiling.*)

YERMA: (*passionately.*) That's it! Try . . . !

I shall say to you, child, yes,
for you I'll torn and broken be.
How painful is this belly now,
where first you shall be cradled!
When, child, when will you come to me?

(YERMA, *who has risen thoughtfully, goes to the place where* VICTOR *stood, and breathes deeply—like one who breathes mountain air. Then she goes to the other side of the room as if looking for something, and after that sits down and takes up the sewing again. She begins to sew. Her eyes remain fixed on one point.*)

CURTAIN

ACT ONE
SCENE 2

(*A field.* YERMA *enters carrying a basket. The* FIRST OLD WOMAN *enters.*)

YERMA: Good morning!

FIRST OLD WOMAN: Good morning to a beautiful girl! Where are you going?

YERMA: I've just come from taking dinner to my husband who's working in the olive groves.

FIRST OLD WOMAN: Have you been married very long?

YERMA: Three years.

FIRST OLD WOMAN: Do you have any children?

YERMA: No.

FIRST OLD WOMAN: Bah! You'll have them!

YERMA: (*eagerly.*) Do you think so?

FIRST OLD WOMAN: Well, why not?

(*She sits down.*)

I, too, have just taken my husband his food. He's old. He still has to work. I have nine children, like nine golden suns, but since not one of them is a girl, here you have me going from one side to the other.

YERMA: You live on the other side of the river?

FIRST OLD WOMAN: Yes. In the mills. What family are you from?

YERMA: I'm Enrique the shepherd's daughter.

FIRST OLD WOMAN: Ah! Enrique the shepherd. I knew him. Good people. Get up, sweat, eat some bread and die. No playing, no nothing. The fairs for somebody else. Silent creatures. I could have married an uncle of yours, but then . . . ! I've been a woman with her skirts to the wind. I've run like an arrow to melon cuttings, to parties, to sugar cakes. Many times at dawn I've rushed to the door thinking I heard the music of guitars going along and coming nearer, but it was only the wind.

(*She laughs.*)

You'll laugh at me. I've had two husbands, fourteen children—five of them dead—and yet I'm not sad, and I'd like to live much longer. That's what I say! The fig trees, how they last! The houses, how they last! And only we poor bedeviled women turn to dust for any reason.

YERMA: I'd like to ask you a question.

FIRST OLD WOMAN: Let's see.

(*She looks at her.*)

I know what you're going to ask me, and there's not a word you can say about those things.

(*She rises.*)

YERMA: (*holding her.*) But, why not? Hearing you talk has given me confidence. For some time I've been wanting to talk about it with an older woman—because I want to find out. Yes, you can tell me—

FIRST OLD WOMAN: Tell you what?

YERMA: (*lowering her voice.*) What you already know. Why am I childless? Must I be left in the prime of my life taking care of little birds, or putting up tiny pleated curtains at my little windows? No. You've got to tell me what to do, for I'll do anything you tell me—even to sticking needles in the weakest part of my eyes.

FIRST OLD WOMAN: Me, tell you? I don't know anything about it. I laid down face up and began to sing. Children came like water. Oh, who can say this body we've got isn't beautiful? You take a step and at the end of the street a horse whinnies. Ay-y-y! Leave me alone, girl; don't make me talk. I have a lot of ideas I don't want to tell you about.

YERMA: Why not? I never talk about anything else with my husband!

FIRST OLD WOMAN: Listen: Does your husband please you?

YERMA: What?

FIRST OLD WOMAN: I mean—do you really love him? Do you long to be with him?

YERMA: I don't know.

FIRST OLD WOMAN: Don't you tremble when he comes near you? Don't you feel something like a dream when he brings his lips close to yours? Tell me.

YERMA: No. I've never noticed it.

FIRST OLD WOMAN: Never? Not even when you've danced?

YERMA: (*remembering.*) Perhaps . . . one time . . . with Victor . . .

FIRST OLD WOMAN: Go on.

YERMA: He took me by the waist and I couldn't say a word to him, because I couldn't talk. Another time this same Victor, when I was fourteen years old— he was a husky boy—took me in his arms to leap a ditch and I started shaking so hard my teeth chattered. But I've always been shy.

FIRST OLD WOMAN: But with your husband . . . ?

YERMA: My husband's something else. My father gave him to me and I took him. With happiness. That's the plain truth. Why, from the first day I was engaged to him I thought about . . . our children. And I could see myself in his eyes. Yes, but it was to see myself reflected very small, very manageable, as if I were my own daughter.

FIRST OLD WOMAN: It was just the opposite with me. Maybe that's why you haven't had a child yet. Men have got to give us pleasure, girl. They've got to take down our hair and let us drink water out of their mouths. So runs the world.

YERMA: Your world, but not mine. I think about a lot of things, a lot, and I'm sure that the things I think about will come true in my son. I gave myself over to my husband for his sake, and I go on giving to see if he'll be born—but never just for pleasure.

FIRST OLD WOMAN: And the only result is—you're empty!

YERMA: No, not empty, because I'm filling up with hate. Tell me; is it my fault? In a man do you have to look for only the man, nothing more? Then, what are you going to think when he lets you lie in bed looking at the ceiling with sad eyes, and he turns over and goes to sleep? Should I go on thinking of him or what can come shining out of my breast? I don't know; but you tell me—out of charity!

(*She kneels.*)

FIRST OLD WOMAN: Oh, what an open flower! What a beautiful creature you are. You leave me alone. Don't make me say any more. I don't want to talk with you any more. These are matters of honor.

And I don't burn anyone's honor. You'll find out. But you certainly ought to be less innocent.

YERMA: (*sadly.*) Girls like me who grow up in the country have all doors closed to them. Everything becomes halfwords, gestures, because all these things, they say, must not be talked about. And you, too; you, too, stop talking and go off with the air of a doctor—knowing everything, but keeping it from one who dies of thirst.

FIRST OLD WOMAN: To any other calm woman, I could speak; not to you. I'm an old woman and I know what I'm saying.

YERMA: Then, God help me.

FIRST OLD WOMAN: Not God; I've never liked God. When will people realize he doesn't exist? Men are the ones who'll have to help you.

YERMA: But, why do you tell me that? Why?

FIRST OLD WOMAN: (*leaving.*) Though there should be a God, even a tiny one, to send his lightning against those men of rotted seed who make puddles out of the happiness of the fields.

YERMA: I don't know what you're trying to tell me.

FIRST OLD WOMAN: Well, I know what I'm trying to say. Don't you be unhappy. Hope for the best. You're still very young. What do you want me to do?

(*She leaves.* TWO GIRLS *appear.*)

FIRST GIRL: Everywhere we go we meet people.

YERMA: With all the work, the men have to be in the olive groves, and we must take them their food. No one's left at home but the old people.

SECOND GIRL: Are you on your way back to the village?

YERMA: I'm going that way.

FIRST GIRL: I'm in a great hurry. I left

my baby asleep and there's no one in the house.

YERMA: Then hurry up, woman. You can't leave babies alone like that. Are there any pigs at your place?

FIRST GIRL: No. But you're right. I'm going right away.

YERMA: Go on. That's how things happen. Surely you've locked him in?

FIRST GIRL: Naturally.

YERMA: Yes, but even so, we don't realize what a tiny child is. The thing that seems most harmless to us might finish him off. A little needle. A swallow of water.

FIRST GIRL: You're right. I'm on my way. I just don't think of those things.

YERMA: Get along now!

SECOND GIRL: If you had four or five, you wouldn't talk like that.

YERMA: Why not? Even if I had forty.

SECOND GIRL: Anyway, you and I, not having any, live more peacefully.

YERMA: Not I.

SECOND GIRL: I do. What a bother! My mother, on the other hand, does nothing but give me herbs so I'll have them, and in October we're going to the saint who, they say, gives them to women who ask for them eagerly. My mother will ask for them, not I.

YERMA: They, why did you marry?

SECOND GIRL: Because, they married me off. They get everyone married. If we keep on like this, the only unmarried ones will be the little girls. Well, anyway, you really get married long before you go to the church. But the old women keep worrying about all these things. I'm nineteen and I don't like to cook or do washing. Well, now I have to spend the whole day doing what I don't like to do. And all for what? We did the same things as sweethearts that we do now. It's all just the old folks' silly ideas.

YERMA: Be quiet; don't talk that way.

SECOND GIRL: You'll be calling me crazy, too. That crazy girl—that crazy girl!

(*She laughs.*)

I'll tell you the only thing I've learned from life: everybody's stuck inside their house doing what they don't like to do. How much better it is out in the streets. Sometimes I go to the arroyo, sometimes I climb up and ring the bells, or again I might just take a drink of anisette.

YERMA: You're only a child.

SECOND GIRL: Why, yes—but I'm not crazy.

(*She laughs.*)

YERMA: Doesn't your mother live at the topmost door in the village?

SECOND GIRL: Yes.

YERMA: In the last house?

SECOND GIRL: Yes.

YERMA: What's her name?

SECOND GIRL: Dolores. Why do you ask?

YERMA: Oh, nothing.

SECOND GIRL: You wouldn't be asking because of . . . ?

YERMA: I don't know . . . people say . . .

SECOND GIRL: Well, that's up to you. Look, I'm going to take my husband his food.

(*She laughs.*)

That's something to see! Too bad I can't say my sweetheart, isn't it?

(*She laughs.*)

Here comes that crazy girl!

(*She leaves, laughing happily.*)

Good-bye!

VICTOR'S VOICE: (*singing.*)
Why, shepherd, sleep alone?
Why, shepherd, sleep alone?
On my wool-quilt deep
you'd finer sleep.
Why, shepherd, sleep alone?

YERMA: (*listening.*)
Why, shepherd, sleep alone?
On my wool-quilt deep
you'd finer sleep.
Your quilt of shadowed stone,
    shepherd,
and your shirt of frost,
    shepherd,
gray rushes of the winter
on the night-tide of your bed.
The oak-roots weave their needles,
    shepherd,
Beneath your pillow silently,
    shepherd,
and if you hear a woman's voice
it's the torn voice of the stream.
    Shepherd, shepherd.
What does the hillside want of you,
    Shepherd?
Hillside of bitter weeds.
What child is killing you?
The thorn the broom-tree bore!

(*She starts to leave and meets* VICTOR *as he enters.*)

VICTOR: (*happily.*) Where is all this beauty going?

YERMA: Was that you singing?

VICTOR: Yes.

YERMA: How well you sing! I'd never heard you.

VICTOR: No?

YERMA: And what a vibrant voice! It's like a stream of water that fills your mouth.

VICTOR: I'm always happy.

YERMA: That's true.

VICTOR: Just as you're sad.

YERMA: I'm not usually sad, but I have reason to be.

VICTOR: And your husband's sadder than you.

YERMA: He is, yes. It's his character—dry.

VICTOR: He was always like that.

(*Pause.* YERMA *is seated.*)

Did you take his supper to him?

YERMA: Yes.

(*She looks at him. Pause.*)

What have you here?

(*She points to his face.*)

VICTOR: Where?

YERMA: (*she rises and stands near* VICTOR.) Here . . . on your cheek. Like a burn.

VICTOR: It's nothing.

YERMA: It looked like one to me.

(*Pause.*)

VICTOR: It must be the sun . . .

YERMA: Perhaps . . .

(*Pause. The silence is accentuated and without the slightest gesture, a struggle between the two begins.*)

YERMA: (*trembling.*) Do you hear that?

VICTOR: What?

YERMA: Don't you hear a crying?

VICTOR: (*listening.*) No.

YERMA: I thought I heard a child crying.

VICTOR: Yes?

YERMA: Very near. And he cried as though drowning.

VICTOR: There are always a lot of children around here who come to steal fruit.

YERMA: No, it's the voice of a small child.

(*Pause.*)

VICTOR: I don't hear anything.

YERMA: I probably just imagined it.

(*She looks at him fixedly.* VICTOR *also looks at her, then slowly shifts his gaze as if afraid.* JUAN *enters.*)

JUAN: Still here? What are you doing here?

YERMA: I was talking.

VICTOR: Salud!

(*He leaves.*)

JUAN: You should be at home.

YERMA: I was delayed.

JUAN: I don't see what kept you.

YERMA: I heard the birds sing.

JUAN: That's all very well. But this is just the way to give people something to talk about.

YERMA: (*strongly.*) Juan, what can you be thinking?

JUAN: I don't say it because of you. I say it because of other people.

YERMA: Other people be damned!

JUAN: Don't curse. That's ugly in a woman.

YERMA: I wish I were a woman.

JUAN: Let's stop talking. You go home.

(*Pause.*)

YERMA: All right. Shall I expect you?

JUAN: No. I'll be busy all night with the irrigating. There's very little water; it's mine till sun-up, and I've got to guard it from thieves. You go to bed and sleep.

YERMA: (*dramatically.*) I'll sleep.

(*She leaves.*)

CURTAIN

ACT TWO

SCENE 1

A fast flowing mountain stream where the village women wash their clothes. The laundresses are arranged at various levels. Song before the curtain rises.

SONG

Here in this icy current
let me wash your lace,
just like a glowing jasmine.
is your laughing face.

FIRST LAUNDRESS: I don't like to be talking.

SECOND LAUNDRESS: Well, we talk here.

FOURTH LAUNDRESS: And there's no harm in it.

FIFTH LAUNDRESS: Whoever wants a good name, let her earn it.

FOURTH LAUNDRESS:
I planted thyme,
I watched it grow.
Who wants a good name
Must live just so.

(*They laugh.*)

FIFTH LAUNDRESS: That's the way we talk.

FIRST LAUNDRESS: But we never really know anything for certain.

FOURTH LAUNDRESS: Well, it's certain enough that her husband's brought his two sisters to live with them.

FIFTH LAUNDRESS: The old maids?

FOURTH LAUNDRESS: Yes. They used to watch the church, and now they watch their sister-in-law. I wouldn't be able to live with them.

FIRST LAUNDRESS: Why not?

FOURTH LAUNDRESS: They'd give me the creeps. They're like those big leaves that quickly spring up over graves. They're smeared with wax. They grow inwards. I figure they must fry their food with lamp oil.

THIRD LAUNDRESS: And they're in the house now?

FOURTH LAUNDRESS: Since yesterday. Her husband's going back to his fields again now.

FIRST LAUNDRESS: But can't anyone find out what happened?

FIFTH LAUNDRESS: She spent the night before last sitting on her doorstep—in spite of the cold.

FIRST LAUNDRESS: But why?

FOURTH LAUNDRESS: It's hard work for her to stay in the house.

FIFTH LAUNDRESS: That's the way those mannish creatures are. When they could be making lace, or apple cakes, they like to climb up on the roof, or go wade barefoot in the river.

FIRST LAUNDRESS: Who are you to be talking like that? She hasn't any children but that's not her fault.

FOURTH LAUNDRESS: The one who wants children, has them. These spoiled, lazy and soft girls aren't up to having a wrinkled belly.

(*They laugh.*)

THIRD LAUNDRESS: And they dash face powder and rouge on themselves, and pin on sprigs of oleander, and go looking for some man who's not their husband.

FIFTH LAUNDRESS: Nothing could be truer!

FIRST LAUNDRESS: But have you seen her with anybody?

FOURTH LAUNDRESS: We haven't, but other people have.

FIRST LAUNDRESS: Always other people!

FIFTH LAUNDRESS: On two separate occasions, they say.

SECOND LAUNDRESS: And what were they doing?

FOURTH LAUNDRESS: Talking.

FIRST LAUNDRESS: Talking's no sin.

FOURTH LAUNDRESS: In this world just a glance can be something. My mother always said that. A woman looking at roses isn't the same thing as a woman looking at a man's thighs. And she looks at him.

FIRST LAUNDRESS: But at whom?

FOURTH LAUNDRESS: Someone. Haven't you heard? You find out for yourself. Do you want me to say it louder?

(*Laughter.*)

And when she's not looking at him—when she's alone, when he's not right in front of her—she carries his picture—in her eyes.

FIRST LAUNDRESS: That's a lie!

(*There is excitement.*)

FIFTH LAUNDRESS: But what about her husband?

THIRD LAUNDRESS: Her husband acts like a deaf man. Just stands around blankly—like a lizard taking the sun.

(*Laughter.*)

FIRST LAUNDRESS: All this would take care of itself if they had children.

SECOND LAUNDRESS: All this comes of people not being content with their lot.

FOURTH LAUNDRESS: Every passing hour makes the hell in that house worse. She and her sisters-in-law, never opening their lips, scrub the walls all day, polish the copper, clean the windows with steam, and oil the floors: but the more that house shines, the more it seethes inside.

FIRST LAUNDRESS: It's all his fault; his. When a man doesn't give children, he's got to take care of his wife.

FOURTH LAUNDRESS: It's her fault—because she's got a tongue hard as flint.

FIRST LAUNDRESS: What devil's got into your hair that makes you talk that way?

FOURTH LAUNDRESS: Well! Who gave your tongue permission to give me advice?

SECOND LAUNDRESS: Quiet, you two!

FIRST LAUNDRESS: I'd like to string all these clacking tongues on a knitting needle.

SECOND LAUNDRESS: Quiet, you!

FOURTH LAUNDRESS: And I the nipples of all hypocrites.

SECOND LAUNDRESS: Hush up! Can't you see? Here come the sisters-in-law.

(*There is whispering. Yerma's two sisters-in-law enter. They are dressed in mourning. In the silence, they start their washing. Sheep bells are heard.*)

FIRST LAUNDRESS: Are the shepherds leaving already?

THIRD LAUNDRESS: Yes, all the flocks leave today.

FOURTH LAUNDRESS: (*taking a deep breath*.) I like the smell of sheep.

THIRD LAUNDRESS: You do?

FOURTH LAUNDRESS: Yes. And why not? The smell of what's ours. Just as I like the smell of the red mud this river carries in the winter.

THIRD LAUNDRESS: Whims!

FIFTH LAUNDRESS: (*looking*.) All the flocks are leaving together.

FOURTH LAUNDRESS: It's a flood of wool. They sweep everything along. If the green wheat had eyes it'd tremble to see them coming.

THIRD LAUNDRESS: Look how they run! What a band of devils!

FIRST LAUNDRESS: They're all out now, not a flock is missing.

FOURTH LAUNDRESS: Let's see. No . . . Yes, yes. One is missing.

FIFTH LAUNDRESS: Which one?

FOURTH LAUNDRESS: Victor's.

(*The two* SISTERS-IN-LAW *sit up and look at each other*.)

FOURTH LAUNDRESS: *singing*.
Here in this icy current
let me wash your lace.
Just like a glowing jasmine
is your laughing face.
I would like to live
within the tiny snowstorm
that the jasmines give.

FIRST LAUNDRESS:
Alas for the barren wife!
Alas for her whose breasts are sand!

FIFTH LAUNDRESS:
Tell me if your husband
has fertile seed
so water through your clothes
will sing indeed.

FOURTH LAUNDRESS:
Your petticoat to me
is silvery boat and breeze
that sweep along the sea.

FIRST LAUNDRESS:
These clothes that are my baby's
I wash here in the stream
to teach the stream a lesson
how crystal-like to gleam.

SECOND LAUNDRESS:
Down the hillside he comes
at lunchtime to me,
my husband with one rose
and I give him three.

FIFTH LAUNDRESS:
Through meadows at dusk comes
my husband to eat.
To live coals he brings me
I give myrtle sweet.

FOURTH LAUNDRESS:
Through night skies he comes,
my husband, to bed.
I, like red gillyflowers,
he, a gillyflower red.

FIRST LAUNDRESS:
And flower to flower must be wed
when summer dries the reaper's blood so
    red.

FOURTH LAUNDRESS:
And wombs be opened to birds without
    sleep
when winter tries the door and cold's to
    keep.

FIRST LAUNDRESS:
The bedclothes must receive our tears,

FOURTH LAUNDRESS:
But we must sing in bed!

FIFTH LAUNDRESS:
When the husband comes
to bring the wreath and bread.

FOURTH LAUNDRESS:
Because our arms must intertwine.

SECOND LAUNDRESS:
Because in our throats the light is rent.

FOURTH LAUNDRESS:
Because the leaf-stem becomes fine.

FIRST LAUNDRESS:
And the hill is covered with a breeze's tent.

SIXTH LAUNDRESS: (*appearing at the top-most part of the swiftly flowing stream.*)
So that a child may weld
white crystals in the dawn.

FIRST LAUNDRESS:
And in our waists be held
torn stems of coral tree.

SIXTH LAUNDRESS:
So that oarsmen there will be
in the waters of the sea.

FIRST LAUNDRESS:
A tiny child, one.

SECOND LAUNDRESS:
And when the doves stretch wing and beak

THIRD LAUNDRESS:
an infant weeps, a son.

FOURTH LAUNDRESS:
And men push ever forward
like stags by wounds made weak.

FIFTH LAUNDRESS:
Joy, joy, joy!
of the swollen womb beneath the dress!

SECOND LAUNDRESS:
Joy, joy, joy!
The waist can miracles possess!

FIRST LAUNDRESS:
But, alas for the barren wife!
Alas for her whose breasts are sand!

THIRD LAUNDRESS:
Let her shine out resplendent!

FOURTH LAUNDRESS:
Let her run!

FIFTH LAUNDRESS:
And shine out resplendent again!

FIRST LAUNDRESS:
Let her sing!

SECOND LAUNDRESS:
Let her hide!

FIRST LAUNDRESS:
And sing once more.

SECOND LAUNDRESS:
Of whiteness like the dawn's
my baby's clean clothes store.

FIRST AND SECOND LAUNDRESS: (*they sing together.*)
Here in this icy current
let me wash your lace.
Just like a glowing jasmine
is your laughing face.
Ha! Ha! Ha!

(*They move the clothes in rhythm and beat them.*)

CURTAIN

ACT TWO
SCENE 2

(*Yerma's house. It is twilight.* JUAN *is seated. The two Sisters-in-law are standing.*)

JUAN: You say she went out a little while ago?

(*The* OLDER SISTER *answers with a nod.*)

She's probably at the fountain. But you've known all along I don't like her to go out alone.

(*Pause.*)

You can set the table.

(*The* YOUNGER SISTER *enters.*)

The bread I eat is hard enough earned!

(*To his* SISTER.)

I had a hard day yesterday. I was pruning the apple trees, and when evening fell I started to wonder why I should put so much into my work if I can't even lift an apple to my mouth. I'm tired.

(*He passes his hand over his face. Pause.*)

That woman's still not here. One of you should go out with her. That's why you're here eating at my table and drinking my wine. My life's in the fields, but my honor's here. And my honor is yours too.

(*The* SISTER *bows her head.*)

Don't take that wrong.

(YERMA *enters carrying two pitchers. She stands at the door.*)

Have you been to the fountain?

YERMA: So we'd have fresh water for supper.

(*The other* SISTER *enters.*)

How are the fields?

JUAN: Yesterday I pruned the trees.

(YERMA *sets the pitcher down. Pause.*)

YERMA: Are you going to stay in?

JUAN: I have to watch the flocks. You know that's an owner's duty.

YERMA: I know it very well. Don't repeat it.

JUAN: Each man has his life to lead.

YERMA: And each woman hers. I'm not asking you to stay. I have everything I need here. Your sisters guard me well. Soft bread and cheese and roast lamb I eat here, and in the field your cattle eat grass softened with dew. I think you can live in peace.

JUAN: In order to live in peace, one must be contented.

YERMA: And you're not?

JUAN: No, I'm not.

YERMA: Don't say what you started to.

JUAN: Don't you know my way of thinking? The sheep in the fold and women at home. You go out too much. Haven't you always heard me say that?

YERMA: Justly. Women in their homes. When those homes aren't tombs. When the chairs break and the linen sheets wear out with use. But not here. Each night, when I go to bed, I find my bed newer, more shining—as if it had just been brought from the city.

JUAN: You yourself realize that I've a right to complain. That I have reasons to be on the alert!

YERMA: Alert? For what? I don't offend you in any way. I live obedient to you, and what I suffer I keep close in my flesh. And every day that passes will be worse. Let's be quiet now. I'll learn to bear my cross as best I can, but don't ask me for anything. If I could suddenly turn into an old woman and have a mouth like a withered flower, I could smile and share my life with you. But now—now you leave me alone with my thorns.

JUAN: You speak in a way I don't understand. I don't deprive you of anything. I send to nearby towns for the things you like. I have my faults, but I want peace and quiet with you. I want to be sleeping out in the fields—thinking that you're sleeping too.

YERMA: But I don't sleep. I can't sleep.

JUAN: Is it because you need something? Tell me. Answer me!

YERMA: (*deliberately, looking fixedly at her husband.*) Yes, I need something.

(*Pause.*)

JUAN: Always the same thing. It's more than five years. I've almost forgotten about it.

YERMA: But I'm not you. Men get other things out of life: their cattle, trees, conversations, but women have only their children and the care of their children.

JUAN: Everybody's not the same way. Why don't you bring one of your brother's children here? I don't oppose that.

YERMA: I don't want to take care of somebody else's children. I think my arms would freeze from holding them.

JUAN: You brood on this one idea till you're half crazy—instead of thinking about something else—and you persist in running your head against a stone.

YERMA: A stone, yes; and its shameful that it is a stone, because it ought to be a basket of flowers and sweet scents.

JUAN: At your side one feels nothing but uneasiness, dissatisfaction. As a last resort, you should resign yourself.

YERMA: I didn't come to these four walls to resign myself. When a cloth binds my head so my mouth won't drop open, and my hands are tied tight in my coffin —then, then I'll resign myself!

JUAN: Well then, what do you want to do?

YERMA: I want to drink water and there's neither water nor a glass. I want to go up the mountain, and I have no feet. I want to embroider skirts and I can't find thread.

JUAN: What's happened is that you're not a real woman, and you're trying to ruin a man who has no choice in the matter.

YERMA: I don't know what I am. Let me walk around; get myself in hand again. I have in no way failed you.

JUAN: I don't like people to be pointing me out. That's why I want to see this door closed and each person in his house.

(*The* FIRST SISTER *enters slowly and walks toward some shelves.*)

YERMA: It's no sin to talk with people.

JUAN: But it can seem one.

(*The other* SISTER *enters and goes toward the water jars, from one of which she fills a pitcher.*)

JUAN: (*lowering his voice.*) I'm not strong enough for this sort of thing. When people talk to you, shut your mouth and remember you're a married woman.

YERMA: (*with surprise.*) Married!

JUAN: And that families have honor. And that honor is a burden that rests on all.

(*The* SISTER *leaves slowly with the pitcher.*)

But that it's both dark and weak in the same channels of the blood.

(*The other* SISTER *leaves with a platter in almost a processional manner. Pause.*)

Forgive me.

(YERMA *looks at her husband. He raises his head and his glance catches hers.*)

Even though you look at me so that I oughtn't to say to you: "Forgive me," but force you to obey me, lock you up, because that's what I'm the husband for.

(*The two* SISTERS *appear at the door.*)

YERMA: I beg you not to talk about it. Let the matter rest.

JUAN: Let's go eat.

(*The two* SISTERS *leave.*)

Did you hear me?

YERMA: (*sweetly.*) You eat with your sisters. I'm not hungry yet.

JUAN: As you wish.

(*He leaves.*)

YERMA: (*as though dreaming.*)
Oh, what a field of sorrow!
Oh, this is a door to beauty closed:
to beg a son to suffer, and for the wind
to offer dahlias of a sleeping moon!
These two teeming springs I have
of warm milk are in the closeness
of my flesh two rhythms of a horse's gal-
lop,
to make vibrate the branch of my anguish.
Oh, breasts, blind beneath my clothes!
Oh, doves with neither eyes nor whiteness!
Oh, what pain of imprisoned blood
is nailing wasps at my brain's base!
But you must come, sweet love, my baby,
because water gives salt, the earth fruit,
and our wombs guard tender infants,
just as a cloud is sweet with rain.

(*She looks toward the door.*)

María! Why do you hurry past my door so?

MARIA: (*she enters with a child in her arms.*) I hurry by whenever I have the child—since you always weep!

YERMA: Yes, you're right.

(*She takes the child and sits down.*)

MARIA: It makes me sad that you're envious.

YERMA: It's not envy I feel—it's poverty.

MARIA: Don't you complain.

YERMA: How can I help complaining when I see you and the other women full of flowers from within, and then see myself useless in the midst of so much beauty!

MARIA: But you have other things. If you'd listen to me you'd be happy.

YERMA: A farm woman who bears no children is useless—like a handful of thorns—and even bad—even though I may be a part of this wasteland abandoned by the hand of God.

(MARÍA *makes a gesture as if to take the child.*)

Take him. He's happier with you. I guess I don't have a mother's hands.

MARIA: Why do you say that?

YERMA: (*she rises.*) Because I'm tired. Because I'm tired of having them, and not being able to use them on something of my own. For I'm hurt, hurt and humiliated beyond endurance, seeing the wheat ripening, the fountains never ceasing to give water, the sheep bearing hundreds of lambs, the she-dogs; until it seems that the whole countryside rises to show me its tender sleeping young, while I feel two hammer-blows here, instead of the mouth of my child.

MARIA: I don't like you to talk that way.

YERMA: You women who have children can't think about us who don't! You stay always fresh, with no idea of it, just as anyone swimming in fresh water has no idea of thirst.

MARIA: I don't want to tell you again what I've always said.

YERMA: Each time I have more desire and less hope.

MARIA: That's very bad.

YERMA: I'll end up believing I'm my own son. Many nights I go down to feed the oxen—which I never did before, because no woman does it—and when I pass through the darkness of the shed my footsteps sound to me like the footsteps of a man.

MARIA: Each one of us reasons things out for herself.

YERMA: And in spite of all, I go on hoping in myself. You see how I live!

MARIA: How are your sisters-in-law?

YERMA: Dead may I be, and without a shroud, if ever I speak a word to them.

MARIA: And your husband?

YERMA: They are three against me.

MARIA: What do they think about it?

YERMA: The wildest imaginings; like all people who don't have clear consciences. They think I like another man. They don't know that even if I should like another man, to those of my kind, honor comes first. They're stones in my path, but they don't know that I can be, if I want to, an arroyo's rushing water and sweep them away.

(*One* SISTER *enters and leaves carrying a piece of bread.*)

MARIA: Even so, I think your husband still loves you.

YERMA: My husband gives me bread and a house.

MARIA: What troubles you have to go through! What troubles! But remember the wounds of Our Lord.

(*They are at the door.*)

YERMA: (*looking at the child.*) He's awake now.

MARIA: In a little while he'll start to sing.

YERMA: The same eyes as yours. Did you know that? Have you noticed them?

(*Weeping.*)

His eyes are the same as yours!

(YERMA *pushes* MARÍA *gently and she leaves silently.* YERMA *walks toward the door through which her husband left.*)

SECOND GIRL: Sst!

YERMA: (*turning.*) What?

SECOND GIRL: I waited till she left. My mother's expecting you.

YERMA: Is she alone?

SECOND GIRL: With two neighbors.

YERMA: Tell them to wait a little.

SECOND GIRL: But, are you really going to go? Aren't you afraid?

YERMA: I'm going to go.

SECOND GIRL: That's up to you!

YERMA: Tell them to wait for me even if it's late!

(VICTOR *enters.*)

VICTOR: Is Juan here?

YERMA: Yes.

SECOND GIRL: (*acting the accomplice.*) Well then, I'll bring the blouse later.

YERMA: Whenever you like.

(*The* GIRL *leaves.*)

Sit down.

VICTOR: I'm all right like this.

YERMA: (*calling.*) Juan!

VICTOR: I've come to say good-bye.

(*He trembles a little, but his composure returns.*)

YERMA: Are you going with your brothers?

VICTOR: That's what my father wants.

YERMA: He must be old now.

VICTOR: Yes. Very old.

(*Pause.*)

YERMA: You're right to change fields.

VICTOR: All fields are alike.

YERMA: No. I'd like to go very far away.

VICTOR: It's all the same. The same sheep have the same wool.

YERMA: For men, yes; but it's a different thing with women. I never heard a man eating say, "How good these apples are!" You go to what's yours without bothering over trifles. But for myself, I can say I've grown to hate the water from these wells.

VICTOR: That may be.

(*The stage is in a soft shadow.*)

YERMA: Victor.

VICTOR: Yes?

YERMA: Why are you going away? The people here like you.

VICTOR: I've behaved myself.

(*Pause.*)

YERMA: You always behave yourself. When you were a boy, you carried me once in your arms, do you remember that? One never knows what's going to happen.

VICTOR: Everything changes.

YERMA: Some things never change. There are things shut up behind walls that can't change because nobody hears them.

VICTOR: That's how things are.

(*The* SECOND SISTER *appears and goes slowly toward the door, where she remains fixed, illuminated by the last light of evening.*)

YERMA: But if they came out suddenly and shrieked, they'd fill the world.

VICTOR: Nothing would be gained. The ditch in its place, the sheep in fold, the moon in the sky, and the man with his plow.

YERMA: The great pity is we don't profit from the experience of our elders!

(*The long and melancholy sound of the shepherds' conchshell horns is heard.*)

VICTOR: The flocks.

JUAN: (*enters.*) Are you on your way?

VICTOR: Yes. I want to get through the pass before daybreak.

JUAN: Have you any complaints to make against me?

VICTOR: No. You paid me a good price.

JUAN: (*to* YERMA.) I bought his sheep.

YERMA: You did?

VICTOR: (*to* YERMA.) They're yours.

YERMA: I didn't know that.

JUAN: (*satisfied.*) Well, it's so.

VICTOR: Your husband will see his lands overflowing.

YERMA: The harvest comes to the worker who seeks it.

(*The* SISTER *who was at the door leaves and goes into another room.*)

JUAN: Now we haven't any place to put so many sheep.

YERMA: (*darkly.*) The earth is large.

(*Pauses.*)

JUAN: We'll go together as far as the arroyo.

VICTOR: I wish this house the greatest possible happiness.

(*He gives* YERMA *his hand.*)

YERMA: May God hear you! Salud!

(VICTOR *is about to leave, but, at an imperceptible movement from* YERMA, *he turns.*)

VICTOR: Did you say something?

YERMA: Salud, I said.

VICTOR: Thank you.

(*They leave.* YERMA *stands, anguished, looking at her hand that she gave to* VICTOR. *She goes quickly to the left and takes up a shawl.*)

SECOND GIRL: (*silently, covering her hand.*) Come, let's go.

YERMA: Come.

(*They leave cautiously. The stage is almost in darkness. The* FIRST SISTER *enters with a lamp that must not give the stage any light other than its own. She goes to one side of the stage looking for* YERMA. *The shepherds' conchshell horns sound.*)

SISTER-IN-LAW, *in a low voice.* Yerma!

(*The other* SISTER *enters. They look at each other and go toward the door.*)

SECOND SISTER-IN-LAW: (*louder.*) Yerma!

FIRST SISTER-IN-LAW: (*going to the door, and in an imperious voice.*) Yerma!

(*The bells and horns of the shepherds are heard. The stage is quite dark.*)

CURTAIN

ACT THREE
SCENE 1

(*The house of* DOLORES, *the sorceress. Day is breaking. Enter* YERMA *with* DOLORES *and two* OLD WOMEN.)

DOLORES: You've been brave.

FIRST OLD WOMAN: There's no force in the world like desire.

SECOND OLD WOMAN: But the cemetery was terribly dark.

DOLORES: Many times I've said these prayers in the cemetery with women who wanted to have a child, and they've all been afraid. All except you.

YERMA: I came because I want a child. I don't believe you're a deceitful woman.

DOLORES: I'm not. May my mouth fill with ants, like the mouths of the dead, if ever I've lied. The last time, I said the prayers with a beggar woman who'd been dry longer than you, and her womb sweetened so beautifully that she had two children down there at the river because there wasn't time to get to the village—and she carried them herself in a diaper for me to take care of.

YERMA: And she was able to walk from the river?

DOLORES: She came; her skirts and shoes drenched with blood—but her face shining.

YERMA: And nothing happened to her?

DOLORES: What could happen to her? God is God.

YERMA: Naturally, God is God. Nothing could happen to her. Just pick up her babies and wash them in fresh water. Animals lick them, don't they? I know a son of my own wouldn't make me sick. I have an idea that women who've recently given birth are as though illumined from within and the children sleep hours and hours on them, hearing that stream of warm milk filling the breasts for them to suckle, for them to play in until they don't want any more, until they lift their heads, "just a little more, child . . ."—and their faces and chests are covered with the white drops.

DOLORES: You'll have a child now. I can assure you, you will.

YERMA: I'll have one because I must. Or I don't understand the world. Sometimes, when I feel certain I'll never, ever . . . a tide of fire sweeps up through me from my feet and everything seems empty; and the men walking in the streets, the cattle, and the stones, all seem to be made of cotton. And I ask myself: "Why are they put here?"

FIRST OLD WOMAN: It's all right for a married woman to want children, of course, but if she doesn't have them, why this hungering for them? The important thing in life is to let the years carry us along. I'm not criticizing you. You see how I've helped at the prayers. But what land do you expect to give your son, or what happiness, or what silver chair.

YERMA: I'm not thinking about tomorrow; I'm thinking about today. You're old and you see things now like a book already read. I'm thinking how thirsty I am, and how I don't have any freedom. I want to hold my son in my arms so I'll sleep peacefully. Listen closely, and don't be frightened by what I say: even if I knew my son was later going to torture me and hate me and drag me through the streets by the hair, I'd still be happy at his birth, because it's much better to weep for a live man who stabs us than for this ghost sitting year after year upon my heart.

FIRST OLD WOMAN: You're much to young to listen to advice. But while you wait for God's grace, you ought to take refuge in your husband's love.

YERMA: Ah! You've put your finger in the deepest wound in my flesh!

DOLORES: Your husband's a good man.

YERMA: (she rises.) He's good! He's good! But what of it? I wish he were bad. But, no. He goes out with his sheep over his trails, and counts his money at night. When he covers me, he's doing his duty, but I feel a waist cold as a corpse's, and I, who've always hated passionate women, would like to be at that instant a mountain of fire.

DOLORES: Yerma!

YERMA: I'm not a shameless married woman, but I know that children are born of a man and a woman. Oh, if only I could have them by myself!

DOLORES: Remember, your husband suffers, too.

YERMA: He doesn't suffer. The trouble is, he doesn't want children!

FIRST OLD WOMAN: Don't say that!

YERMA: I can tell that in his glance, and, since he doesn't want them, he doesn't give them to me. I don't love him; I don't love him, and yet he's my only salvation. By honor and by blood. My only salvation.

FIRST OLD WOMAN: (*with fear.*) Day will soon be breaking. You ought to go home.

DOLORES: Before you know it, the flocks will be out, and it wouldn't do for you to be seen alone.

YERMA: I needed this relief. How many times do I repeat the prayers?

DOLORES: The laurel prayer, twice; and at noon, St. Anne's prayer. When you feel pregnant, bring me the bushel of wheat you promised me.

FIRST OLD WOMAN: It's starting to lighten over the hills already. Go.

DOLORES: They'll soon start opening the big street doors; you'd best go around by the ditch.

YERMA: (*discouraged.*) I don't know why I came!

DOLORES: Are you sorry?

YERMA: No!

DOLORES: (*disturbed.*) If you're afraid, I'll go with you to the corner.

FIRST OLD WOMAN: (*uneasily.*) It'll just be daylight when you reach home.

(*Voices are heard.*)

DOLORES: Quiet!

(*They listen.*)

FIRST OLD WOMAN: It's nobody. God go with you.

(YERMA *starts toward the door, but at this moment a knock is heard. The three women are standing.*)

DOLORES: Who is it?

VOICE: It's me.

YERMA: Open the door.

(DOLORES *is reluctant.*)

Will you open or not?

(*Whispering is heard.* JUAN *enters with the two* SISTERS.)

SECOND SISTER-IN-LAW: Here she is.

YERMA: Here I am.

JUAN: What are you doing in this place? If I could shout I'd wake up the whole village so they'd see where the good name of my house has gone to; but I have to swallow everything and keep quiet—because you're my wife.

YERMA: I too would shout, if I could, so that even the dead would rise and see the innocence that covers me.

JUAN: No, don't tell me that! I can stand everything but that. You deceive me; you trick me, and since I'm a man who works in the fields, I'm no match for your cleverness.

DOLORES: Juan!

JUAN: You, not a word out of you!

DOLORES: (*strongly.*) Your wife has done nothing wrong.

JUAN: She's been doing it from the very day of the wedding. Looking at me with two needles, passing wakeful nights with her eyes open at my side, and filling my pillows with evil sighs.

YERMA: Be quiet!

JUAN: And I can't stand any more. Because one would have to be made of iron to put up with a woman who wants to stick her fingers into your heart and who goes out of her house at night. In search of what? Tell me! There aren't any flowers to pick in the streets.

YERMA: I won't let you say another word. Not one word more. You and your people imagine you're the only ones who look out for honor, and you don't realize my people have never had anything to conceal. Come on now. Come near and smell my clothes. Come close! See if you can find an odor that's not yours, that's not from your body. Stand me naked in the middle of the square and spit on me. Do what you want with me, since I'm your wife, but take care not to set a man's name in my breast.

JUAN: I'm not the one who sets it there.

You do it by your conduct, and the town's beginning to say so. It's beginning to say it openly. When I come on a group, they all fall silent; when I go to weigh the flour, they all fall silent, and even at night, in the fields, when I awaken, it seems to me that the branches of the trees become silent too.

YERMA: I don't know why the evil winds that soil the wheat begin—but look you and see if the wheat is good!

JUAN: Nor do I know what a woman is looking for outside her house at all hours.

YERMA: (*bursting out, embracing her husband.*) I'm looking for you. I'm looking for you. It's you I look for day and night without finding a shade where to draw breath. It's your blood and help I want.

JUAN: Stay away from me.

YERMA: Don't put me away—love me!

JUAN: Get away!

YERMA: Look how I'm left alone! As if the moon searched for herself in the sky. Look at me!

(*She looks at him.*)

JUAN: (*he looks at her and draws away roughly.*) Let me be—once and for all!

DOLORES: Juan!

(YERMA *falls to the floor.*)

YERMA: (*loudly.*) When I went out looking for my flowers, I ran into a wall. Ay-y-y! Ay-y-y! It's against that wall I'll break my head.

JUAN: Be quiet. Let's go.

DOLORES: Good God!

YERMA: (*shouting.*) Cursed be my father who left me his blood of a father of a hundred sons. Cursed be my blood that searches for them, knocking against walls.

JUAN: I told you to be quiet!

DOLORES: People are coming! Speak lower.

YERMA: I don't care. At least let my voice go free, now that I'm entering the darkest part of the pit.

(*She rises.*)

At least let this beautiful thing come out of my body and fill the air.

(*Voices are heard.*)

DOLORES: They're going to pass by here.

JUAN: Silence.

YERMA: That's it! That's it! Silence. Never fear.

JUAN: Let's go. Quick!

YERMA: That's it! That's it! And it's no use for me to wring my hands! It's one thing to wish with one's head . . .

JUAN: Be still!

YERMA: (*low.*) It's one thing to wish with one's head and another for the body —cursed be the body!—not to respond. It's written, and I'm not going to raise my arms against the sea. That's it! Let my mouth be struck dumb!

(*She leaves.*)

QUICK CURTAIN

ACT THREE
SCENE 2

(*Environs of a hermitage high in the mountains. Downstage are the wheels of a cart and some canvas forming the rustic tent where* YERMA *is. Some women enter carrying offerings for the shrine. They are barefoot. The happy* OLD WOMAN *of the first act is on the stage.*)

SONG

(*Heard while the curtain is still closed.*)

You I never could see
when you were fancy free,
but now that you're a wife
I'll find you, yes,

and take off your dress,
you, pilgrim and a wife
when night is dark all 'round,
when midnight starts to sound.

OLD WOMAN: (*lazily.*) Have you already drunk the holy water?

FIRST WOMAN: Yes.

OLD WOMAN: Now let's see this saint work.

FIRST WOMAN: We believe in him.

OLD WOMAN: You come to ask the saint for children, and it just happens that every year more single men come on this pilgrimage too; what's going on here?

(*She laughs.*)

FIRST WOMAN: Why do you come here if you don't believe in him?

OLD WOMAN: To see what goes on. I'm just crazy to see what goes on. And to watch out for my son. Last year two men killed themselves over a barren wife, and I want to be on guard. And lastly, I come because I feel like it.

FIRST WOMAN: May God forgive you!

(*She leaves.*)

OLD WOMAN: (*sarcastically.*) May He forgive you.

(*She leaves.* MARÍA *enters with the* FIRST GIRL.)

FIRST GIRL: Did she come?

MARIA: There's her cart. It was hard work to make them come. She's been a month without getting up from her chair. I'm afraid of her. She has some idea I don't understand, but it's a bad idea.

FIRST GIRL: I came with my sister. She's been coming here eight years in vain.

MARIA: The one who's meant to have children, has them.

FIRST GIRL: That's what I say.

(*Voices are heard.*)

MARIA: I've never liked these pilgrim-ages. Let's get down to the farms where there are some people around.

FIRST GIRL: Last year, when it got dark, some young men pinched my sister's breasts.

MARIA: For four leagues 'round nothing is heard but these terrible stories.

FIRST GIRL: I saw more than forty barrels of wine back of the hermitage.

MARIA: A river of single men comes down these mountains.

(*They leave. Voices are heard.* YERMA *enters with six* WOMEN *who are going to the chapel. They are barefooted and carry decorated candles. Night begins to fall.*)

MARIA:
Lord, make blossom the rose,
leave not my rose in shadow.

SECOND WOMAN:
Upon her barren flesh
make blossom the yellow rose.

MARIA:
And in your servants' wombs
the dark flame of the earth.

CHORUS OF WOMEN:
Lord, make blossom the rose,
leave not my rose in shadow.

(*They kneel.*)

YERMA:
The sky must have such gardens
with rose trees of its joy,
between the rose and the rose,
one rose of all the wonder.
Bright flash of dawn appears,
and an archangel guards,
his wings like storms outspread,
his eyes like agonies.
While sweet about its leaves
the streams of warm milk play,
play and wet the faces
of the tranquil stars.
Lord, make your rose tree bloom
upon my barren flesh.

(*They rise.*)

SECOND WOMAN:
  Lord, with your own hand soothe
  the thorns upon her cheek.

YERMA:
  Hark to me, penitent
  in holy pilgrimage.
  Open your rose in my flesh
  though thousand thorns it have.

CHORUS OF WOMEN:
  Lord, make blossom the rose,
  leave not my rose in shadow.

YERMA:
  Upon my barren flesh
  one rose of all the wonder.

(They leave.)

(GIRLS *running with long garlands in their hands appear from the left. On the right, three others, looking backward. On the stage there is something like a crescendo of voices and harness bells, and bellringers' collars. Higher up appear the* SEVEN GIRLS *who wave the garlands toward the left. The noise increases and the two traditional* MASKS *appear. One is* MALE *and the other* FEMALE. *They carry large masks. They are not in any fashion grotesque, but of great beauty and with a feeling of pure earth. The* FEMALE *shakes a collar of large bells. The back of the stage fills with people who shout and comment on the dance. It has grown quite dark.)*

CHILDREN: The devil and his wife! The devil and his wife!

FEMALE:
In the wilderness stream
the sad wife was bathing.
About her body crept
the little water snails.
The sand upon the banks,
and the little morning breeze
made her laughter sparkle
and her shoulders shiver.
Ah, how naked stood
the maiden in the stream!

BOY:
Ah, how the maiden wept!

FIRST MAN:
Oh, wife bereft of love
in the wind and water!

SECOND MAN:
Let her say for whom she longs!

FIRST MAN:
Let her say for whom she waits!

SECOND MAN:
Ah, with her withered womb
and her color shattered!

FEMALE:
When night-tide falls I'll tell,
when night-tide glowing falls.
In the night-tide of the pilgrimage
I'll tear my ruffled skirt.

BOY:
Then quickly night-tide fell.
Oh, how the night was falling!
See how dark becomes
the mountain waterfall.

(Guitars begin to sound.)

MALE: *(he rises and shakes the horn.)*
Ah, how white
the sorrowing wife!
Ah, how she sighs beneath the branches!
Poppy and carnation you'll later be
when the male spreads out his cape.

(He approaches.)

If you come to the pilgrimage
to pray your womb may flower
don't wear a mourning veil
but a gown of fine Dutch linen.
Walk alone along the walls
where fig trees thickest grow
and bear my earthly body
until the white dawn wails.
Ah, how she shines!
How she was shining,
ah, how the sad wife sways!

FEMALE:
Ah, let love place on her
wreathes and coronets,

let darts of brightest gold
be fastened in her breast.

MALE:
Seven times she wept
and nine she rose,
fifteen times they joined
jasmines with oranges.

THIRD MAN:
Strike her now with the horn!

SECOND MAN:
With both the rose and the dance!

FIRST MAN:
Ah, how the wife is swaying!

MALE:
In this pilgrimage
the man commands always.
Husbands are bulls.
The man commands always
and women are flowers,
for him who wins them.

BOY:
Strike her now with the wind!

SECOND MAN:
Strike her now with the branch!

MALE:
Come and see the splendor
of the wife washed clean!

FIRST MAN:
Like a reed she curves.

MEN:
Let young girls draw away!

MALE:
Let the dance burn.
And the shining body
of the immaculate wife.

(*They disappear dancing amidst smiles
and the sound of beating palms. They
sing.*)

The sky must have such gardens
with rose trees of its joy,
between the rose and the rose
one rose of all the wonder.

(TWO GIRLS *pass again, shouting. The
happy* OLD WOMAN *enters.*)

OLD WOMAN: Let's see if you'll let us
sleep now. But pretty soon it'll be something else.

(YERMA *enters.*)

You.

(YERMA *is downcast and does not speak.*)
Tell me, what did you come here for?

YERMA: I don't know.

OLD WOMAN: Aren't you sure yet?
Where's your husband?

(YERMA *gives signs of fatigue and acts like
a person whose head is bursting with a
fixed idea.*)

YERMA: He's there.

OLD WOMAN: What's he doing?

YERMA: Drinking.

(*Pause. Putting her hands to her forehead.*)

Ay-y-y!

OLD WOMAN: Ay-y, ay-y! Less "ay!" and
more spirit. I couldn't tell you anything
before, but now I can.

YERMA: What can you tell me that I
don't know already?

OLD WOMAN: What can no longer be
hushed up. What shouts from all the roof-
tops. The fault is your husband's. Do you
hear? He can cut off my hands if it isn't.
Neither his father, nor his grandfather,
nor his great-grandfather behaved like
men of good blood. For them to have a
son heaven and earth had to meet—because they're nothing but spit. But not
your people. You have brothers and cousins for a hundred miles around. Just see
what a curse has fallen on your loveliness.

YERMA: A curse. A puddle of poison
on the wheat heads.

OLD WOMAN: But you have feet to leave
your house.

YERMA: To leave?

OLD WOMAN: When I saw you in the
pilgrimage, my heart gave a start. Women

come here to know new men. And the saint performs the miracle. My son's there behind the chapel waiting for me. My house needs a woman. Go with him and the three of us will live together. My son's made of blood. Like me. If you come to my house, there'll still be the odor of cradles. The ashes from your bedcovers will be bread and salt for your children. Come, don't you worry about what people will say. And as for your husband, in my house there are stout hearts and strong weapons to keep him from even crossing the street.

YERMA: Hush, hush! It's not that. I'd never do it. I can't just go out looking for someone. Do you imagine I could know another man? Where would that leave my honor? Water can't run uphill, nor does the full moon rise at noonday. On the road I've started, I'll stay. Did you really think I could submit to another man? That I could go asking for what's mine, like a slave? Look at me, so you'll know me and never speak to me again. I'm not looking for anyone.

OLD WOMAN: When one's thirsty, one's grateful for water.

YERMA: I'm like a dry field where a thousand pairs of oxen plow, and you offer me a little glass of well water. Mine is a sorrow already beyond the flesh.

OLD WOMAN: (strongly.) Then stay that way—if you want to! Like the thistles in a dry field, pinched, barren!

YERMA: (strongly.) Barren, yes, I know it! Barren! You don't have to throw it in my face. Nor come to amuse yourself, as youngsters do, in the suffering of a tiny animal. Ever since I married, I've been avoiding that word, and this is the first time I've heard it, the first time it's been said to my face. The first time I see it's the truth.

OLD WOMAN: You make me feel no pity. None. I'll find another woman for my boy.

(She leaves. A great chorus is heard distantly, sung by the pilgrims. YERMA goes toward the cart, and from behind it her husband appears.)

YERMA: Were you there all the time?

JUAN: I was.

YERMA: Spying?

JUAN: Spying.

YERMA: And you heard?

JUAN: Yes.

YERMA: And so? Leave me and go to the singing.

(She sits on the canvases.)

JUAN: It's time I spoke, too.

YERMA: Speak!

JUAN: And complained.

YERMA: About what?

JUAN: I have a bitterness in my throat.

YERMA: And I in my bones.

JUAN: This is the last time I'll put up with your continual lament for dark things, outside of life—for things in the air.

YERMA: (with dramatic surprise.) Outside of life, you say? In the air, you say?

JUAN: For things that haven't happened and that neither you nor I can control.

YERMA: (violently.) Go on! Go on!

JUAN: For things that don't matter to me. You hear that? That don't matter to me. Now I'm forced to tell you. What matters to me is what I can hold in my hands. What my eyes can see.

YERMA: (rising to her knees, desperately.) Yes, yes. That's what I wanted to hear from your lips . . . the truth isn't felt when it's inside us, but how great it is, how it shouts when it comes out and raises its arms! It doesn't matter to him! Now I've heard it!

JUAN: (coming near her.) Tell yourself it had to happen like this. Listen to me.

(He embraces her to help her rise.)

Many women would be glad to have your life. Without children life is sweeter. I am happy not having them. It's not your fault.

YERMA: Then what did you want with me?

JUAN: Yourself!

YERMA: *(excitedly.)* True! You wanted a home, ease, and a woman. But nothing more. Is what I say true?

JUAN: It's true. Like everyone.

YERMA: And what about the rest? What about your son?

JUAN: *(strongly.)* Didn't you hear me say I don't care? Don't ask me any more about it! Do I have to shout in your ear so you'll understand and perhaps live in peace now!

YERMA: And you never thought about it, even when you saw I wanted one?

JUAN: Never.

(Both are on the ground.)

YERMA: And I'm not to hope for one?

JUAN: No.

YERMA: Nor you?

JUAN: Nor I. Resign yourself!

YERMA: Barren!

JUAN: And live in peace. You and I —happily, peacefully. Embrace me!

(He embraces her.)

YERMA: What are you looking for?

JUAN: You. In the moonlight you're beautiful.

YERMA: You want me as you sometimes want a pigeon to eat.

JUAN: Kiss me . . . like this.

YERMA: That I'll never do. Never.

(YERMA gives a shriek and seizes her husband by the throat. He falls backward. She chokes him until he dies. The chorus of the pilgrimage begins.)

YERMA: Barren, barren, but sure. Now I really know it for sure. And alone.

(She rises. People begin to gather.)

Now I'll sleep without startling myself awake, anxious to see if I feel in my blood another new blood. My body dry forever! What do you want? Don't come near me, because I've killed my son. I myself have killed my son!

(A group that remains in the background, gathers. The chorus of the pilgrimage is heard.)

CURTAIN

Corruption in the Palace of Justice

UGO BETTI

COMMENTARY

 Ugo Betti (1892-1953) was born in Italy. Although essentially a traditional playwright, showing the influence of Chekhov and Ibsen as well
as of his fellow-countryman, Pirandello, his plays are peculiarly current
in their preoccupation with the moral problems of modern man in a
political context. In his emphasis on man's responsibility to define and
then choose between good and evil, not as these may be abstractly conceived but as they are specifically embodied in human affairs, Betti is
dramatically reflecting the modern philosophical and religious concern
with ethics and morals. His thematic concerns place him in the company
of such philosophical writers as Camus and Sartre.

The title of his tragedy, *Corruption in the Palace of Justice* (1949),
establishes the inherently paradoxical character of his drama: "corruption" and "justice" are necessarily antithetical. The paradox is more
subtle, however, and less purely philosophical; it is, ultimately, the
source of the tragedy here, for as the play demonstrates, justice can only
be administered by human beings and for human beings. Not even the
palace of justice itself can be quarantined from the corrupting effects
of daily mortality.

The play offers a chance to reflect on the tension between "document" and "drama." How would an in-depth magazine article on
the events of *Corruption in the Palace of Justice* differ from the play?
How would one be more or less "truthful" than the other? Would a
transcript of a court trial be more or less "dramatic" than the trial itself?
What are the significant differences between a tape-recording of a trial
and a play based on that trial?

Betti's essay, "Religion and the Theatre," in *The Modern Theatre*,
edited by Robert W. Corrigan (New York, 1964), as well as much general writing on contemporary ethical and religious problems, provide the

best context for considering Betti's particular intellectual contemporaneity. Corrigan's introduction to *The New Theatre of Europe* (New York, 1962) relates Betti's achievement in modern tragedy to the attempts of others; Corrigan's introductions in *Masterpieces of the Modern Theatre* (New York, 1967) are also valuable.

Ugo Betti

CORRUPTION IN THE PALACE OF JUSTICE

Translated by Henry Reed

PEOPLE IN THE PLAY

VANAN, *President of the Court*   BATA, *a judge*
ELENA, *his daughter*   MAVERI, *a judge*
ERZI, *Investigating Counsellor*   PERSIUS, *a judge*
CROZ, *Chief Justice*   MALGAI, *a record clerk*
CUST, *a judge*   A NURSE
And a number of officials, porters, bystanders.

The time is the present.

*The action takes place in a foreign city. The scene is the same through-
out: a large severe room in the Palace of Justice.*

ACT ONE

The room is empty. MALGAI, *the record
clerk, enters, pushing a wheeled basket.
He goes round the tables, which are piled
high with documents; some of these he
selects and throws into the basket, after
checking their dates against certain papers
in his hand. He hums to himself.*

(*A* STRANGER *appears in the doorway.*)

STRANGER: I wonder if you could tell
me where I can find Chief Justice Croz's
office?

MALGAI: Will you ask the porter, sir?
There's a porter for that purpose.

STRANGER: I'm sorry but I haven't been
able to find any porters.

MALGAI: Well, you can't expect them to

Ugo Betti, *Corruption in the Palace of Justice*, trans. Henry Reed. By permission of Ninon Tallon
Karlweis, exclusive agent for the play, 250 East 65th Street, New York, New York 10021.

be here before they have to clock in, can you? Oh, it's no good looking at me; I'm one of the old brigade. What do you want to see Chief Justice Croz for?

STRANGER: I have to speak to him.

MALGAI: Well, that would be fine, sir, only unfortunately poor Mr. Croz is dying. Has been for months. He doesn't come to the office any more. It has to be something very special to bring Mr. Croz here, and even then they almost have to carry him.

STRANGER: All the same I think he will come this morning.

MALGAI: (*Glancing at him.*) Ah. (*Cautiously.*) Is there a judges' meeting perhaps?

STRANGER: I fancy we shall see them all here.

MALGAI: Ah. (*His tone has changed slightly.*) Well . . . If you want to get to Chief Justice Croz's office, you go down the corridor to the end, then to the right, then to the right again. . . . But if you don't mind my saying so, I think you'd do best to wait for him in here.

STRANGER: In here?

MALGAI: Yes, you'll hear his cane. You can always hear him when he comes up the corridor: he has to use a cane nowadays. If there *is* a sitting, they'll all have to come in here: this is the council chamber for the division. (*He points to a seat near the door.*) You can sit down if you wish.

STRANGER: Thank you. (*He sits.*)

MALGAI: (*Throwing another glance at the visitor, as he goes on with his work.*) A huge building, this, isn't it? The place is just one great maze. We even get tourists in looking at it. In admiration. (*He drops his voice slightly.*) At the moment, unfortunately, the smell about the place isn't quite as sweet as it might be. I suppose it must be a dead rat or something, under one of the floorboards. What do you

think about it all, sir? I don't know if you saw last night's papers?

STRANGER: Yes.

MALGAI: Well, it's no business of mine, of course, but I think there's something of a storm blowing up. There's thunder in the air.

STRANGER: Are you one of the clerks?

MALGAI: No, sir. I'm what you might call the gravedigger. This (*He smacks the side of the trolley.*) is the hearse; and these (*He waves the papers in his hand.*) are the death certificates; and these (*He taps the bundles of documents.*) are the bodies.

STRANGER: And the graveyard?

MALGAI: (*Pointing to a door.*) Through there. The Archives. A quiet, shady little spot; I take all this stuff in there and see it gets decent burial.

STRANGER: Are you one of the record clerks?

MALGAI: The undertaker I always call myself. When I think of all the sweat, and all the money and tears, that have gone into even the silliest little bundle of these things here! Well, well . . . (*He drops a bundle into the trolley, and takes up another one.*) I stick a great big number on them, and register them in a great big book, so that people can pretend to believe they'll go on being important per secula et seculorum, and they can always take the thing up again . . .

STRANGER: While actually the only things really concerned about your graveyard are the mice and the grubs?

MALGAI: No, it's not the mice and the grubs, sir. It's the interested parties themselves: they get bored after a time, and turn their minds to other things. It's surprising how easily people *do* get bored and turn to other things.

(*A newcomer has entered, looking very worried.* MALGAI *turns to him solicitously.*)

MALGAI: Oh, good morning, Judge Bata.

BATA: (*As he enters.*) Good morning, my dear fellow, good morning. (*Taking him aside, and whispering.*) Have you heard?

MALGAI: (*Anxiously.*) What?

BATA: You didn't come past the secretary's office this morning?

MALGAI: No, I never go round that way.

BATA: (*Cautiously.*) I came past the door a few moments ago; there's an official posted outside it: rather important-looking.

MALGAI: An official?

BATA: Yes, a sort of policeman. He politely told us we couldn't go in.

MALGAI: Not even the judges?

BATA: He was stopping everyone.

MALGAI: What . . . what for?

BATA: Well, I was wondering if *you* . . .

MALGAI: No, sir, I haven't the foggiest.

BATA: You've no idea . . . what it's all about . . . ?

MALGAI: Good gracious, no! They'd never tell *me*. I expect it's just some new piece of nonsense they've—.

BATA: (*Trying to pooh-pooh the matter.*) Oh yes, yes, of course it is, but I do think they might have mentioned it to the magistrates.

MALGAI: Of course, sir! Naturally. I hear there's a special meeting of the division today.

BATA: Yes, it's all very odd. It's taken us all by surprise rather.

(*The other judges are entering:* PERSIUS, MAVERI, *and, shortly after,* CUST.)

PERSIUS: (*As he approaches.*) Well, what is it all about?

BATA: (*Pointing to the archivist, who backs respectfully away.*) *He* doesn't seem to know either.

MAVERI: (*Cautiously.*) I think it's just a mistake; some order must have been misunderstood.

PERSIUS: (*Unconvinced.*) Yes, quite. A mistake.

MAVERI: A misunderstanding. (*A brief silence.*)

BATA: (*To* PERSIUS, *suddenly.*) My dear Persius, you yourself can bear me out, can't you? I've been saying it for months; there are a lot of things need clearing up in here, we need more light and air in the place. The air in these courts is becoming too thick to breathe. I've said that again and again, haven't I? Haven't I?

PERSIUS: My dear fellow, you don't think you're the only one, do you?

MAVERI: Lots of people have been saying so.

CUST: We've said so, too: all of us.

MAVERI: A man with a clear conscience has nothing to fear from the light; nothing at all.

BATA: It's important to realize of course that it may have all just blown up out of nothing. People thrive on scandal. The law courts are always a hive of discontented murmuring. Someone starts spreading scandal about the place, someone else joins in, and by the next day there are ten or twenty of them, buzz- buzz- buzzing their heads off. It's like gangrene spreading.

MAVERI: And the newspapers too: you can't trust any of them.

PERSIUS: And the politicians: party intrigues the whole time. I can't help feeling the whole thing is a deliberate plot.

BATA: But it's the city itself, more than anything, surely? This filthy, diseased city. I never thought people could be so evil, so nasty.

PERSIUS: Yes, just listen to them talking: there isn't a word of truth in anything they say.

MAVERI: Not to mention the women.

BATA: Yes, the place is just a dungheap. The odd thing is to find them screaming with indignation because right in the middle of their own stink there should be a building where the atmosphere isn't (shall I say?) quite as fragrant as it might be. In fact, the magistrates' crime . . . is simply that they're a little too like the man in the street.

PERSIUS: (*Acidly.*) My dear friend and colleague, I never think one ought to generalize too readily. I don't think I personally bear the remotest resemblance to a dungheap.

BATA: Neither do I; the very idea.

PERSIUS: As far as I personally am concerned, I'm in the fortunate position of being able to say that I've never even *met* this man called Ludvi-Pol, never. I've never even seen him.

BATA: You sound rather as if your colleagues were less fortunate—what? As if some of us were in danger of being compromised in some way.

PERSIUS: (*Diplomatically.*) *Did* I say that? Nonsense. I always aim at saying precisely what I mean. And if any of our colleagues *have* been off their feed lately, and *have* been having bad nights, well, I'm not one of them, that's all. There are times when every man has to look out for himself. This is one of them. Don't *you* think so, Cust?

BATA: (*Spitefully.*) We all know that, my dear friend, we all know that. Some of our colleagues seem to have been very busy pulling strings and turning wheels these last few weeks. There seems to have been a good deal of angry fist-shaking about the place.

PERSIUS: (*Sarcastically.*) Maybe, but the impression I have is that a lot of people in danger are trying to cling to one another as hard as they can. One notices that certain of one's colleagues have become very friendly all of a sudden. They keep trying to get into conversation with one the whole time. You find them waiting behind for you, so that you can leave the place together. They are all clutching at each other. Unfortunately, I'm always in a hurry. I'm always going in a different direction. I never know anything. I'm made of stone, dear friend. Oh, incidentally, Cust, I wanted to ask you something . . . (*Rather ostentatiously, he draws* CUST *apart.*)

BATA: (*To* MAVERI.) Did you hear that? In any case, I don't quite see why it's suddenly become so very important whether people have or haven't known Ludvi-Pol. It rather looks—it rather *looks* now as if Ludvi-Pol had been put out of business. Though up to yesterday . . .

MAVERI: He was better respected than a cabinet minister!

BATA: One knows of course that these men are just like spiders; what keeps them going is precisely the web of relationships they so skilfully spin all around them. It stands to reason that a lot of people come into contact with them. It may be perfectly true that our dear friend Persius there has never met Ludvi-Pol; he still may have met one of his agents. (*He drops his voice.*) And considering what went on just before Persius was last promoted, he'd better not try being too self-righteous.

MAVERI: (*Dropping his voice.*) Persius feels he's in a strong position.

BATA: Oh, does he? Why?

MAVERI: Important contacts.

BATA: Very likely; he's a born toady.

MAVERI: And now he's trying to suck up to Cust; as one might expect.

BATA: Oh. Why?

MAVERI: Cust! Our rising star.

BATA: Cust?

MAVERI: Cust. A very able man; and not overburdened with scruples, I imagine.

BATA: But what about the great Vanan?

MAVERI: Done for. A corpse.

BATA: Are you sure? Oh dear, it's very difficult trying to steer one's way, isn't it? One person's up and another's down, the whole time. You can never be sure what's going on. (*Looking thoughtfully at* CUST.) I've always been on very good terms with Cust, myself, of course.

MAVERI: Really? I thought he seemed rather offhand with you, just now.

BATA: (*Disturbed.*) Cust? With me?

MAVERI: I expect it's only his way.

BATA: I've always said that he was really one of the best people in this place . . . (*Seeing that* MAVERI *is also about to join* CUST *and* PERSIUS.) Look, my dear Maveri, there's something I've been wanting to say to you for a long time. You *are* related to President Tomisco, aren't you?

MAVERI: (*Warily.*) Well, it's a . . . very *distant* relationship. Why?

BATA: (*Beaming sunnily.*) I was with President Tomisco for a time, you know, just when I was starting my career. A most admirable person. Influential. I'd so much like to meet him again sometime. Perhaps you'll be so good as to give him my kind regards, when next you . . .

MAVERI: (*Evasively.*) I hardly ever see him, you know, hardly ever.

BATA: (*Amiably.*) Dear colleague, please don't think that I'm trying to steal a march on you; please don't think that. On the contrary. If there's any way in which *I* can help *you*. . . . I have the greatest admiration for you, as you know.

MAVERI: So have I. For you, I mean.

BATA: Thank you. Sometimes . . . if two people are willing to stick together, they can . . . well, back each other up, stand by each other, as it were. It would

be dreadful to have enemies at a time like this!

MAVERI: (*Cautiously.*) Dreadful! But I hope . . .

BATA: One never knows, dear colleague. One can sometimes be betrayed by the very last person one expects it from. Well, of course, it's not for me to say.

MAVERI: What do you mean . . . ?

BATA: Well, you know how it is: one's colleagues . . . sometimes talk rather inconsiderately; I don't say they mean any harm, but . . .

MAVERI: Have you . . . heard anyone say anything about me?

BATA: Oh no, no. But the other night . . . Oh, it was just nonsense of course. But old Hill was in here, you know . . . (*He breaks off, and listens.*) Croz is coming.

(*A cane is heard in the corridor. This sound produces a rapid change in everyone present. The groups break up. Expressions change.*)

(CROZ *enters, leaning heavily on one side on his cane, and on the other on a manservant. His appearance reveals extreme physical prostration and at the same time a malignant energy: a quiver of the head gives him the appearance of continuously approving or disapproving of something. He advances half way across the room; here he halts for a few moments in order to draw breath, his eyes closed. He turns to the manservant without looking at him.*)

CROZ: Come back and fetch me later. That is, unless I die in the meantime. (*The manservant bows slightly and goes out.* CROZ *takes a few more steps forward.*) Is the great Vanan here yet?

BATA: No.

CROZ: Do any of you know if the old fool intends to come?

BATA: I don't really see why we should

know any more than you do. With the wind blowing the way it is, I should think it's pretty unlikely.

CROZ: In that case, since the President is absent, it is my duty, as senior judge of the division, to deputize for him. (*Half-turning to* MALGAI.) You: get out. What are you doing here?

MALGAI: I'm just going, sir. (*He points to the* STRANGER, *who has just risen.*) I only wanted to tell your worship that there was a gentleman here waiting to see you. (*He goes out.*)

CROZ: (*Turning to observe the newcomer.*) You wanted . . . to speak to me?

STRANGER: Yes, Justice Croz. I have a private communication for you.

CROZ: (*To the other judges.*) He said private.

(*The other judges, half-curious, half-worried, withdraw to the other half of the room.* CROZ *walks a few steps towards the back. The* STRANGER *follows, speaking to him in a very low voice.* CROZ *listens, asking questions from time to time: finally he leads the* STRANGER *with great deference to an imposing armchair; then he once more approaches his colleagues.*)

Dear colleagues. (*He pauses and thinks.*) I have to tell you . . . (*Breaking off.*) Damn it, Persius, you *have* gone green in the face! You look scared to death.

PERSIUS: You can spare me your little jests, Croz. You'd do much better to think about yourself.

CROZ: You mean if anyone ought to be scared to death, it's me, eh? But, my dear Persius, I'm already dying in any case, am I not? *Moribundus.* So obviously—

PERSIUS: *Moribundus,* yes, you've been *moribundus* for a long time. It's an old trick, Croz; we're used to it, by now.

CROZ: (*Grinning.*) Oh, such unkindness! Come, come. Well, dear colleagues, it appears that the Minister and the Lord High President are both very disturbed, very upset, poor dear things. Because of the lawcourts. The city is full of gossip. (*Satirically.*) Justice! Justice! *Justitia fondamentum regni.* (*He breaks off, coughing and gasping heavily.*)

BATA: Quite, my dear Croz, quite; the city is full, etc. etc. I don't quite see the point in coming here to tell *us* that; *we* can't shut the mouths of several million scandal-mongers. The only thing to do is to wait till they are tired of this subject and have found another. I don't see . . . (*He breaks off, under* CROZ's *stare.*)

CROZ: You very rarely do see. Anything. The Minister and the High President have issued orders for an inquiry.

(*A silence.*)

BATA: (*Faintly.*) An inquiry?

CROZ: I think that's what I said. (*Teasing.*) But come, come, bless my soul, we mustn't let it frighten us.

MAVERI: We are not frightened, as a matter of fact.

CROZ: Good, good. It's nothing very serious, just a little something among ourselves. A little look round, that's all, a few inquiries, clear things up . . . That's all.

BATA: (*Warmly.*) And naturally we all agree very heartily. We shall all be very glad to put our modest talents at the public disposal in order to . . . to investigate the matter and find out what's wrong.

(*Murmurs of assent.*)

CROZ: Perhaps I didn't make myself clear. It is not ourselves who have to do the investigating.

BATA: No?

CROZ: No. Others will be doing the investigating.

BATA: But what about us?

CROZ: Well, we, if I might so put it, are the ones who have to be investigated. Which is slightly different. (*A silence.*)

PERSIUS: (*Bitterly.*) I would like to know why respectable magistrates, after years and years of irreproachable service —I myself have been on the bench for twenty years—I'd like to know why we have to submit to—

CROZ: You are an ass, Persius! What about me? I'm on the eve of promotion. I've set great store by the thought of being buried with a President's cap on my head —always supposing of course that dear old brother Cust doesn't pop in ahead of me —eh, Cust? What do *you* think about all this nonsense? It *would* have to happen just now, of course, and endanger my promotion . . . My dear Persius, we are *all* respectable and irreproachable. I thought I'd made it quite, quite clear: all we have to do is to look into the matter, among ourselves. The magistrate who will carry out the inquiry is a friendly colleague of ours . . . (*He points to the* STRANGER, *who has risen.*) Councillor Erzi, from the Upper House; he himself was saying to me only a moment ago . . .

ERZI: (*With great courtesy.*) Yes, all we need is a certain amount of discussion, in strict confidence, as between friends. My only reason for coming was to exchange a few preliminary words with you . . . and to shake hands with you all.

BATA: (*Advancing with hand outstretched.*) But of course, of course. My dear Erzi, I am so glad to meet you.

PERSIUS: (*Following suit, together with the others.*) Welcome into our midst!

MAVERI: My dear Erzi! I've heard a good deal about you. Surely we've met before somewhere?

BATA: Yes, you can understand, my dear friend, that we're the first people, the very first, to want to see the whole thing . . .

PERSIUS: . . . floodlit!

BATA: In strict confidence—that was

your own expression—would you like to know my own humble opinion?

ERZI: That is what I'm here for.

BATA: (*Pompously, to the others.*) We have to be quite frank about all this. The time for circumlocution is over. My dear Erzi, we're far from trying to pretend that there hasn't been a considerable amount of confusion piling up in these courts.

CUST: It's slackness, more than anything else; people have been a bit too easy-going.

PERSIUS: A bit too casual, too broadminded perhaps. One can be too broadminded, you know.

BATA: One might go even further, I think, and admit that there's been a certain lack of moral earnestness, a certain tolerance towards rogues.

CUST: The law courts have become almost a rogues' paradise.

MAVERI: There are certain forms of tolerance I'm afraid I've always disapproved of.

PERSIUS: Oh, we all have. We've all disapproved of them.

BATA: One might put it like this, I think: it is as if in this immense ramification of corridors and offices and stairs and —and so forth—it's as if there were odd nooks and corners here and there which have never been properly lit; and piles of dirt and dust and what-not have accumulated in them. But who are the people scratching about in the middle of it all? Doormen, clerks, pen-pushers and other fusty old rubbish—

PERSIUS: The main trouble about this place is that out of every hole—

MAVERI: —an army of gnawing rats comes tumbling . . .

BATA: I'd be inclined to say myself that the whole thing has nothing to do with the magistrates at all.

ERZI: The Minister's opinion is that the staleness and poisonous air you speak of have actually produced something rather more: it might be called a poisonous plant. (*A silence.*)

BATA: I see. But think of ourselves for a moment: there are many hundreds of us here, all flapping our black gowns about the place and groaning out our prayers. It would be a little unnatural if so vast a monastery didn't harbor at least one or two wicked or negligent brethren.

ERZI: It is not about negligent brethren that the Minister is concerned. He is convinced that under one of the flapping gowns you speak of, securely hidden away, there must be somewhere a little red pustule of leprosy. Corruption.

BATA: Corruption?

ERZI: It is a leper we're looking for.

BATA: And why . . . why do you begin looking for your lepers in here, pray?

ERZI: You must regard that as an honor. Isn't this the division reserved for Major Causes?

CROZ: Hahaha! It's been a real pleasure to listen to you. What elegant conceits, what metaphors! I'm crazy about that sort of thing; I even try my hand at it myself sometimes. But the one you should really hear is Cust, he's an absolute artist. He's being very quiet today for some reason. I always think eloquence of expression adds so much to a magistrate—it's the sign of a highly developed brain, I think one can say. Well, perhaps you'll listen to a few of my own little similes? Do you know, my dear Erzi, what we poor devils really are?—we judges, in this division—yes, yes, I know, the division for Major Causes. But each of us, every single one, is a little, lonely, insecure rock on which from every direction tremendous waves keep breaking; frightful; great foaming mountains. And those waves are the implacable interests, the boundless wealth, the iron

blocks manipulated by dreadfully powerful men: genuine wild forces, whose blows —unhappily for us—are something savage, irresistible, ferocious . . .

ERZI: (*Completing.*) . . . a species of telluric phenomenon.

CROZ: Telluric: exactly. Telluric.

ERZI: And it's very difficult to teach that phenomenon good manners.

CROZ: You take the words right out of my mouth. I'd like to see how the Minister would get on in our place.

ERZI: The pity of it is that amidst these iron blocks a fair number of very fragile shells are also tossed about on the waters; and they very easily get dashed to pieces. Take the case, for example, the day before yesterday, of that prostitute in Panama Street: a little smoke and burnt paper were sufficient to send her to her Maker. Was it not this division that had decided in complete secrecy to raid the house in Panama Street and confiscate certain documents?

CROZ: Yes.

ERZI: But when the police arrived, the place had been blazing for a good ten minutes; so had the documents, and so, unfortunately, had a harmless caretaker. The papers are still screaming about it.

CROZ: Do you mean—?

ERZI: I mean that someone from here had warned the interested parties. (*Pause.*) That is only one case among many: but it sums up the situation. (*A silence.*)

CROZ: Someone from here? One of us?

ERZI: One of you.

CROZ: (*Laughing loudly.*) My dear friends. Just let's all take a close look at each other, shall we? You, for example, Bata: you have a look at me, while I of course have a look at you, eh? Can it be possible that not a tiny bead of sweat, not a single movement of the Adam's apple, not the slightest, smallest sign . . .

should betray our ailing comrade? Our leper I mean. It could be myself; it could be you, Maveri; you've gone quite white. Or you, Cust.

CUST: No, no, Croz. That's not quite the way things work. There's an error in psychology there. If it were anybody, it would be the innocent man—if he had any imagination: he'd be the one who started to sweat, etc. Feel. (*He holds out his hand.*)

CROZ: (*Touching it.*) Cold and clammy.

CUST: Yes. Once when I was a boy staying with friends, someone came and said a watch was missing. I . . . fainted.

CROZ: So you're the one with the imagination?

CUST: Obviously. And quite apart from that, I'd like to point out—simply in the interests of accuracy—that it isn't quite exact to say: one of us. It isn't true that *all* the men who took part in the decision you mentioned are here at this moment. Now, I don't want this to be taken as an insinuation, mind you. I am, after all, a referendary judge, and because of that I am always in very close contact with President Vanan; and no one knows better than I how completely above suspicion he is. I'm only saying this in order that we may maintain a certain precision, a certain strictness of method: President Vanan also took part in that decision. And he is not here at the moment.

CROZ: (*Pointing to* CUST, *and speaking to* ERZI.) Cust. A very fine brain. My great enemy, my rival as successor to Vanan. A most worthy character; and gnawed by the most infernal ambition. We've hated each other from the minute we met.

CUST: That isn't true as far as I am concerned.

CROZ: Old humbug. He's like one of those iron safes. Absolutely impregnable.

BATA: Well, since Vanan's name's been mentioned—and as colleague Erzi has in-

vited us to make a full and friendly disclosure . . . and also . . . out of a real wish for sincerity, mind you, and since all this will remain strictly among ourselves . . .

PERSIUS: (*Slightly hysterical.*) Get *on!* Don't you see we've all got to defend ourselves!

BATA: I consider it my duty to state . . . at all events, it seems to me an affectation to deny that the responsibility for the disorder here, the . . . uneasiness we were talking of earlier, does, unfortunately, lie largely—well, not largely perhaps but partly—with the great Vanan himself.

CROZ: (*To* ERZI.) You don't know the great Vanan?

ERZI: No.

CROZ: He has been a great man in his time; a very handsome one too. Very fond of the women. Well, well. It's horrible to grow old.

BATA: Like Cust, I would be very ashamed indeed to suggest that the great Vanan . . . had let himself be corrupted or bought up by Ludvi-Pol, or by anyone else for that matter. But he has great weaknesses: that I'm bound to say.

MAVERI: There are certain jobs he is no longer fitted for. He seems somehow . . . finished. That's the word, if the truth must be told.

MAVERI: One of those old wooden beams that if you go like that to them, your finger goes in.

BATA: Rotten.

CROZ: And terrific with the women, you understand? He himself must know where his strength's gone to, at any rate.

MAVERI: And it's still the same. Even now! One gathers that's the reason for his rapid disintegration, as you might call it. Poor old thing, it's very sad and terrible. He's been seen in the most frightful places.

BATA: In fact, when you talk to President Vanan, it's difficult to be sure if he really knows what he's saying and doing any longer. A thousand pities. A thousand pities.

MAVERI: These last few months, I almost think you could tell from the way he talks and moves about . . . well, he's in the final stages. It's become pathological by now.

CROZ: (*To* MAVERI.) It's simply this, my dear fellow: he keeps himself going with drink. (*He laughs and coughs.*)

BATA: Naturally, I must repeat that I'm not saying I . . . believe that Vanan himself is the one . . . the man . . .

PERSIUS: (*Suddenly and brutally.*) My dear colleagues, does this really seem to you the moment for delicacy? Do you understand or don't you, what a hell of a position we're in?

MAVERI: (*Supporting him.*) The whole city's waiting. It wants somebody's head.

PERSIUS: It's a matter of life and death. Do we want to ruin ourselves, just for Vanan's sweet sake? Don't you think it's about time we all spoke out?

ERZI: Well?

PERSIUS: Look: if there was one man in this place who was absolutely *made* to be swallowed up by Ludvi-Pol, it was Vanan. If there was one man . . .

CUST: (*Interrupting.*) One man. And why only one man? There's not the slightest evidence to show that our leper stands alone. We might all be infected. We might all have sold our souls to the devil, that is, to Ludvi-Pol.

CROZ: Perfect. Clever old Cust. (*To* ERZI.) Logic goes to old Cust's head at times, like drink. He's gleaming with sweat!

(*He breaks off. Some one has knocked on the door leading to the corridor. They all turn. A gloomy-looking stranger, possibly a* POLICE OFFICER, *comes in, and goes and speaks privately to* ERZI. ERZI *listens to him, then signs to him to wait, and stands for a moment, lost in thought.*)

ERZI: It's very unfortunate Vanan isn't here. Do you know where he could be found?

CUST: As a matter of fact, it's been rather difficult lately to know where you will or won't find Vanan. His habits have become rather uncertain.

ERZI: You've been very close to him?

CUST: Yes.

ERZI: Would you say that what we've heard about Vanan in here this morning is more or less the truth?

CUST: (*After a silence.*) You put me in rather an embarrassing position; Vanan and I were fond of each other. There has perhaps been a certain amount of exaggeration.

ERZI: Go on.

CUST: The scale of human duties has become a little confused in Vanan's mind. He's been sentencing people far too long. That can be rather dangerous after a time.

ERZI: Is there anything else?

CUST: (*After a silence, looking down.*) Yes.

ERZI: Go on.

CUST: Vanan did know Ludvi-Pol. They had dealings. (*A silence.*) It's painful, for me, to speak of it. I think . . . I had the impression that Ludvi-Pol had passed a certain sum of money to President Vanan. (*His voice is low and calm.*) But look, Erzi, if what you said is true, surely Ludvi-Pol himself is the one who could give you the name you're after— or names, as the case may be. Don't you think he'd talk?

ERZI: No. I don't.

BATA: Yes, but surely Ludvi-Pol's papers would talk!

CROZ: (*Laughing.*) Do you think he's such a fool as to have put these things down on paper?

CUST: No, but perhaps under prolonged expert interrogation—

ERZI: No. We shan't get anything out of Ludvi-Pol.

CUST: Why not?

ERZI: Because he's dead. (*A silence.*) His body was discovered by accident in the early hours of this morning; do any of you know where?

CROZ: Where?

ERZI: Here. In this building, in a place where Ludvi-Pol had no reason whatever to be, least of all at night. He's lying there now.

CUST: So he was another fragile shell.

ERZI: It was suicide.

CUST: Are they sure of that?

ERZI: Yes.

CUST: (*Almost imperceptibly excited.*) Forgive me, but that too could be a put-up job. The person you're looking for had a great interest in seeing that Ludvi-Pol kept his mouth shut, hadn't he? That person must be feeling very relieved at this moment. In any case, this Ludvi-Pol was a very contemptible creature, his death sentence is hardly likely to arouse much protest in the tribunal of any human soul I can think of. Or . . . look: the very things put there purposely to suggest murder, even those could be the results of a put-up job. For what purpose? To put you off the trail. To implicate some innocent person. There are so many possibilities, one can go on multiplying them as one chooses . . . always supposing we attribute a certain amount of subtlety to the man you're looking for. I advise you not to disregard any of those threads.

ERZI: Suicide. (*Pause.*) Are there many people in the building at night?

CUST: Oh, you can see quite a number of windows lit up till a very late hour. Industrious officials, all anxious to get on, losing their sleep over their papers. I myself, as a matter of fact, was here very late last night. (*As though recalling something.*) In fact . . . (*He breaks off.*)

ERZI: Go on.

CUST: (*Lower.*) When I leave, I always have to go along the corridor that goes past the great Vanan's door. I may as well tell you the truth. As the corridor was in darkness . . . I saw a line of light under the door. I heard—(*He breaks off.*)

(MALGAI *enters excitedly: he clearly realizes what the situation is.*)

MALGAI: President Vanan.

(MALGAI *withdraws immediately. After a few moments* VANAN *appears; he is an old man, very tall and erect; his face is angry and inflamed, his hair like a mop of white cotton-wool; his tones are slightly stentorian. Sometimes he mutters to himself. He comes in, and looks round him.*)

VANAN: Quite. Quite . . . of course. Good morning to you all, my dear . . . friends. Here we are. (*To* BATA, *who is the nearest to him.*) Good morning, Bata; of course, yes . . . Give me a what-is-it, a match. (*His words drop into a great silence; everyone has risen.*)

BATA: (*Backing away.*) I don't think I have any.

VANAN: What's the matter? What's the matter? Sit down. You could . . . surely, surely have waited for me too? Eh? Eh? Cust, I'm talking to you. Absolutely. Good morning, Erzi, I'm glad to see you. (*Shouting.*) Sit down! I'm perfectly aware of what's going on. You are here too, my clever Croz.

CROZ: (*Shrugging his shoulders.*) Of course. What do you expect?

VANAN: Good. All of us. Absolutely. . . .

(*They are now all seated; only* VANAN *is standing.*)

ERZI: (*With great courtesy.*) Mr. President, we were just waiting for you. There is a little information we need, if you would be so very kind as to give it to us.

VANAN: Absolutely. I know perfectly well what's going on. Fantastic, isn't it? Absolutely disgraceful.

ERZI: Mr. President, I have no doubt that you are acquainted with a person who has in recent years been at the center of the biggest concerns in the city, and who has consequently also been involved here in a number of very important law suits. I mean Ludvi-Pol. (*A silence.*)

VANAN: (*Muttering.*) No . . . not that man . . . no, certainly not. Never. Listen, Erzi; I knew him.

ERZI: You have, however, judged many cases in which he was involved.

VANAN: But . . . my dear Erzi, how . . . how can you possibly ask . . . (*Suddenly roaring.*) me, *me,* questions like this. It's fantastic . . . absolutely fantastic.

ERZI: (*With extreme politeness.*) There was nothing in my question that could possibly offend you.

VANAN: Eh? What? That man . . .

ERZI: Yes. It would appear that you know him. That has been confirmed by several people here. (*A silence.*)

VANAN: Private. Private. An absolutely private matter. Absolutely. (*Dropping his voice slightly.*) In the lift. In the lift, Erzi, that's all! (*He laughs.*) In the lift in this building, that's all. What happens? A gentleman recognizes me and speaks to me. An acquaintance from long long ago, lost sight of. Boys . . . boys together, the family . . . ages ago, ages ago. In the lift. Ridiculous that I should have to . . . talk about that.

ERZI: (*Gently.*) You received a sum of money from Ludvi-Pol? (*A silence.*)

VANAN: (*His voice seems to diminish and he looks round him uncertainly.*) Croz . . . but why . . . why am I being asked all this? What's going on? Cust, you, say something. And the rest of you, you all know me, what do you think you're doing? (*A silence.*)

ERZI: (*Quietly.*) Certainly, we all know you, Mr. President. You can speak with perfect frankness.

VANAN: Quite, quite, my dear Erzi, quite. There's no reason for me to hide anything . . . it's simple. The whole thing is absolutely . . . simple. It seems that Ludvi-Pol was slightly in debt to us, to my family I mean . . . nothing important, old liabilities, I'd quite forgotten them. But he . . . he remembered. Perfectly. He was very determined . . . to pay them back. That's the truth, that's the truth, Erzi. Absolutely . . . ridiculous, isn't it? He remembered it all perfectly.

ERZI: And did you remember?

VANAN: Well, actually I . . . yes, vaguely.

ERZI: Was it a large amount? Was it at a time when you happened to be in need?

VANAN: (*Overcome with a kind of anguish.*) I don't . . . I don't . . . why . . . Cust! It's all so unexpected, so sudden. Ludvi-Pol himself will surely explain all this to you, won't he? You'll only have to ask him, won't you? He will tell you everything.

ERZI: Were you in this building last night?

VANAN: I? In this building? (*Roaring.*) But whatever do you . . . what does this mean . . . ?

ERZI: In your office, Mr. President: last night: were you alone?

VANAN: Absolutely. Absolutely. Alone. Absolutely.

ERZI: Cust.

CUST: (*Slowly approaching.*) Yes. (*Affectionately, with regret.*) I had to tell him, Vanan. Last night . . . possibly you don't remember now . . .

VANAN: (*With some fury.*) I? I don't remember? Shameful! Ridiculous! Absolutely grotesque! I don't remember, don't I? (*He breaks off; there is a moment of absolute silence; suddenly shouting and almost weeping.*) Do you think I don't understand what . . . what you're all trying to do? You're trying to drag me down . . . trying to accuse me . . . aren't you? I understand perfectly! You blackguards! You filthy little pigmies! I'll crush you! I'll show you! I'll bring . . . I'll bring the whole court down! I'll tell them who's the guilty man, I'll tell them in the minutest detail! They don't know me yet. They don't know who Vanan is! I'll tear them to pieces, the whole lot of them. And after that . . . after . . . (*He stands there for a moment with his arm raised, breathing heavily: and then, as though his memory had suddenly given way, he drops slowly across the table, his face in his hands. A silence.*)

ERZI: (*Politely, rising.*) Gentlemen, thank you all very much; I shan't need to take up any more of your time today. Though I shall have to ask for a little of yours, Croz, in a short while; and I also hope that you will all help me in the course of this inquiry. At the moment I am being waited for elsewhere. (*Thoughtfully, he turns to the police official who is still waiting.*) You. It's about time they removed Ludvi-Pol's body. I don't suppose they will be able to get it out of the building unnoticed. It's probably too late for that now. All the same, try to keep it covered up, if you possibly can, so that we shan't have to see his face in all the newspapers tomorrow, streaked with blood, with his eyes closed. He was a greatly respected man in his time. The

city has all the rest of him to trample on now; let's leave his body for the worms alone—to whom all faces are the same. (*To the others.*) Good morning.

(*He goes out, followed by the official.* BATA, MAVERI, *and* PERSIUS, *one after another, go out cautiously and almost on tiptoe, so as not to attract the attention of* VANAN.)

(CROZ *and* CUST *are standing at some distance from him.*)

CROZ: (*Observing his colleague.*) What's the matter, Cust?

CUST: (*Looking at him before speaking.*) This is going to require a certain amount of courage.

CROZ: What do you mean?

CUST: (*Drawing him away from* VANAN, *with a wan smile, and whispering.*) Croz, have you ever been out hunting?

CROZ: No.

CUST: Neither have I, but I've often been told about it. Do you know what it is the hunter always dreads most?

CROZ: No.

CUST: Finishing off the wounded quarry. Dying animals go on struggling; you have to take pity on them. Everyone'd be so very obliged to them, if only they'd die by themselves. But no, they struggle and fight for life; it's almost a point of honor with them. They almost make the hunter feel angry with them, because they actually in the end force one to . . . (*Dropping his voice still lower.*) smash their skulls in. It's horrible, isn't it? But it's something that has to be faced.

CROZ: (*Looking at* VANAN.) Yes, yes, of course. The fool is going to ruin himself completely if he goes on like this. All those infantile lies! We shall have to . . . use a little persuasion.

· CUST: It may not be difficult. A man who's just had a heavy blow on the head often behaves strangely docile. We are all of us fragile, but old men are like glass.

VANAN: (*Has risen: his words are threatening, but his voice has completely changed.*) Croz, Cust. Eh? What do you say about all this? Why don't you say something, you filthy traitors! (CUST *and* CROZ *look at him in silence.*) What are you thinking? Tell me what to do . . . don't stand there looking at me . . .

CUST: (*Quietly.*) My dear Vanan, do you know who it is *you* must talk to, now? Yourself.

VANAN: Myself?

CUST: Yes. You must explain to yourself the reason for all the lies you've been telling.

VANAN: Lies?

CUST: Lies, Vanan. What was the reason for them?

VANAN: Because . . . my God, actually . . . Cust, I was so confused . . .

CUST: Why were you confused? M'm? Reflect on that, my dear Vanan, and then you'll see for yourself the best way to go about things. Reflect on it, at great length.

VANAN: But oh, my God, I'm . . . an old man now.

CUST: Why ever did you deny that you talked to Ludvi-Pol last night?

VANAN: Cust, I swear to you . . . that man had come simply to plead with me . . . he thought I could still save him . . . he was a fool, a madman . . .

CUST: But why did he come to you? First he asked something from you; and then he asked something else, from death. You were the last door but one he knocked at. Why?

VANAN: (*Shouting.*) I don't know, Cust! I don't know!

CUST: And why are you so frightened, even now? (*Very quietly.*) Oh no, Vanan, it's all too evident that your conscience is not untroubled. There is a doubt, in your conscience. They're saying that in this fine building of ours there is something rotten. But if you reflect on what you have been doing in here, yesterday, and every other day of your life, are you certain, quite certain, that you will be saved? What I advise you to do, my dear Vanan, is to make a long and minute examination of your conscience. Explore yourself, scrutinize yourself, go to bed with your doubt, carry it about with you by day. And only when one of the two, either you or it, has won, only then, and not before, must you come back here.

VANAN: Cust, what do you mean?

CUST: But of course, Vanan. You wouldn't want to insist on remaining here, in the courts, struggling, threatening, telling more bungling lies.

VANAN: You mean I ought to go away? Now?

CUST: For a few days.

VANAN: Never, never, never. I won't move from here, I'll defy them.

CUST: Good. And let them be even more vindictive against you in their inquiries, and lay more traps for you to fall into.

VANAN: No, Cust, I can't do it. To go away now would be . . .

CUST: . . . to put the matter in the hands of a very great doctor: time. Besides, would you really have the strength to face, day after day, the looks of contempt, the rudeness, the innuendoes? The very porters, the very walls are cruel to anyone who has fallen.

VANAN: My God.

CUST: Just be clever; let your enemies have a little rope. The important thing is simply to get through these next few days of suspicion and anger, and noise. Admit to some little thing or other, so as to give the fools, who are shouting so loudly, the illusion of victory. Throw a piece of flesh to the wolves who are following you . . .

VANAN: My God.

CUST: And very soon they'll all be thinking of something else; what you should do now is . . . (*He pauses.*)

VANAN: What?

CUST: My belief is that you ought to send the Investigating Councillor a note today; without saying too much, without giving your hand away; just telling him simply that in view of what has happened you don't feel that you ought, for the present—for the present—to remain in the building. For the present. Instead . . . (*He pauses again.*)

VANAN: . . . instead . . .

CUST: Very quietly, very very quietly, just stay at home and think. Reflect. And in the meantime do you know what you can do as well? On your own account, silently. You can write.

VANAN: Write what?

CUST: A full statement, in which you explain everything. Just pass the time doing that. For the present.

VANAN: For the present. . . .

CUST: The important thing is the little note; and you must hurry: the note must arrive before they can decide anything disagreeable. It will restrain them. Write it now, straight away. (*Pointing to a desk.*) There.

VANAN: Cust, I don't want . . . Croz, what do you think?

CUST: Listen, Vanan, I've given you a piece of advice. I've probably gone too far in doing so.

VANAN: (*Suddenly pleading.*) But, of course, I know, I am grateful, you must forgive me. And you too, Croz. Actually . . . you must understand my . . . (*He is gradually approaching the desk.*) Yes, Cust, there's a good deal of sense in what you say. A full . . . precise statement, absolutely! Absolutely. And now, a note: yes, I must write it now. You know, Cust: you've been the only . . . (*almost weeping.*) I've no friends: I've always been too proud. And now they'll all . . . be delighted, they all want to humiliate me. They've all become suddenly . . . wicked, treacherous . . . (*He is fumbling at the desk; suddenly he breaks off, and listens intently; runs to the door, listens; and turns back to the other two men, his eyes widening in real fear.*) She's talking to the porter! My God! Look; the only person I have in the world will be here in a minute! I beg you by whatever you hold most dear . . . (*Trying to control himself.*) Listen: it's my daughter. You don't know her. There's always been just the two of us; her mother died. She thinks I'm almost a king in here, she wouldn't understand anything of what's happened. I beg you, I beseech you not to let her suspect anything: pretend nothing has happened. It's a great favor. (*Changing his tone, speaking towards the door, which has just opened.*) Yes, Elena. Come in, my dear. I'm glad you stopped in, we can go home together. (*A radiant young girl, and at the moment looking rather surprised, is in the doorway. She comes shyly into the room.*) (*Breathlessly, to his two colleagues.*) This is my daughter. Elena. Fancy, she's never been here before. (ELENA *smiles at the two judges.*) (*Stammering, and fumbling about on the desk.*) Elena, these are two very clever . . . friends of mine who . . . are very fond of me, in spite of the fact that your father is the most exacting president there could possibly be. Yes, certainly . . . I'm an absolute . . . tyrant. Absolutely, quite, quite. (*Fumbling confusedly on the desk.*) Forgive me, Elena, I'm coming at once, I just have to finish a . . . a note; I'll finish it at once, my dear Cust. Tell me, Elena: I wonder whether you heard me in the corridor? I'm always shouting, I get angry over nothing, because . . . because everything falls on my shoulders, do you understand? The President. I'm the President. It's an honor, but it's also . . . a terrible responsibility.

(*He is already scribbling; there is a silence.* ELENA, *like someone in very great awe, smiles again at the two judges, who look at her attentively.*)

(VANAN *has finished. He goes over in silence to* CUST, *and places the letter in his hand, and then goes over to his daughter and lifts his hand, vaguely touching her hair, as if he wished to smoothe it.* ELENA *takes his hand and kisses it.*)

(VANAN *looks at the two judges with a flicker of sudden pride; slips his daughter's arm beneath his own, nods good-by, and goes out, very upright, in silence.*)

(CROZ *and* CUST *stand there for a moment as though lost in thought.* CROZ *gives a long glance at his companion, and then goes out, leaning heavily on his cane, without speaking.*)

(CUST, *after his departure, goes slowly across to a desk, sits at it, and suddenly seems overcome by a genuine prostration; he remains for a little while thus: with his head in his hands.*)

(MALGAI *enters and begins to put the room in order.*)

MALGAI: (*At the door.*) Please sir, may I . . . ?

CUST: (*Without raising his head.*) Yes.

MALGAI: (*As he tidies up.*) That was the President's daughter, wasn't it, sir?

CUST: (*As before.*) Yes.

MALGAI: A pretty girl. She's quite grown up . . . quite a young lady.

CUST: (*As before.*) Yes. (*He looks up.*) She reminded me of something.

MALGAI: Sir, you're not looking very well.

CUST: I'm just tired, that's all. I feel rather upset. (*He pretends to unfold a roll of documents, and begins to hum to himself; thinking, quietly.*) My Cod, how horrible everything is. What a wasted life. Judge Cust. (*He hums again, and thinks idly.*) Yes, the girl reminded me of something. There was something about her. (*Lost in thought, as he goes on.*) Attilio, do you know who Vanan's daughter looked like? She looked like the figure on a box, a tin box we once had at home when I was a boy; a woman with flowing hair . . . and a crown . . . She was lifting a glass, it was an advertisement for something. I used to be tremendously fond of her. Tremendously. She looked like Vanan's daughter.

MALGAI: (*As he goes out.*) Ah, Mr. Cust, sir . . . When I was a boy, *I* used to . . . (*He smiles.*) Oh, dear, the things that went through one's mind! Well, well . . . (*He goes.*)

CUST: (*Almost singing the word.*) Tremendously. Tremendously. (*He begins to hum again; then, thinking.*) I might very well have had a daughter like that. "Elena, let's go out for a little shall we? Dear Elena". Judge Cust and his daughter . . . (*Hums.*) Or else my wife. "Come on, Elena, let's go home, shall we?" Judge Cust and his wife . . . (*Hums.*) Or my mother perhaps. I am a tiny little frog. She gives me milk. A young beloved mother, very young. (*He rises slowly to his feet.* ERZI *and* CROZ *have come in, and are walking across the room.* CUST *stares at them fixedly; just as they are about to go out, he calls:*) Councillor Erzi!

(ERZI *and* CROZ *stop.*)

CUST: How's it going?

ERZI: What?

CUST: The inquiry.

ERZI: Are you interested in it?

CUST: Can't stop thinking about it.

ERZI: (*Dropping his voice a little.*) Cust, was there something you wanted to say to me?

CUST: I? I only wanted to tell you that . . . if I can help you at all . . . in any humble way . . . I'd of course be very pleased.

ERZI: Have you had any ideas?

CUST: Any ideas? Any ideas. (*He looks at* ERZI *for a moment, and then hands* VANAN's *letter to him.*) All the same, it would be a good thing, wouldn't it if President Vanan were innocent, and the leper was somebody else.

ERZI: (*Has glanced at the letter, and now turns and stares at* CUST.) Do you think so?

CUST: (*Sighs.*) I'm just thinking. I wonder if it wouldn't after all be a good thing to abandon the inquiry . . .

ERZI: And who's suggested that we intend to abandon it? No. It will be pursued. Right to the end. And you will help me.

(*He shakes* CUST's *hand warmly, and goes out with* CROZ.)

(CUST *stands looking after him.*)

CURTAIN

ACT TWO

Several days have passed. On one side of the stage, bored and impersonal, stands the gloomy police officer. BATA *and* PERSIUS, *wearing hats and overcoats, are wandering furtively about, rather as if they were spying. They meet, rapidly whisper something together, and part again with assumed indifference, as the door from the corridor opens.*

CUST *enters slowly.* BATA *and* PERSIUS, *torn between curiosity and the fear of* compromising *themselves by starting a conversation, make cautious nods of greeting towards him: prudence prevails however; and nodding once more to* CUST, *they both slip towards the door; here they throw a further long glance at him; and disappear.*

CUST *has followed them with his eyes. He hesitates; at last he removes his hat and overcoat, and approaches the police officer.*

CUST: I am Judge Cust. Councillor Erzi has sent for me. I don't know what he wants. Would you mind telling him I'm here?

(*The officer nods and goes out. After a few moments a door opens and* ERZI *enters.*)

ERZI: Ah thank you, my dear Cust, thank you; how good of you to come. Sit down. Well, now. It's always a pleasure to talk with a colleague like yourself. You've no idea, I suppose, why I asked you if you'd mind coming?

CUST: No.

ERZI: (*After a pause.*) Did it really never occur to you to wonder?

CUST: No.

ERZI: Well . . . you did, after all, make me a promise. Yes, I asked you to help me in my investigation. I was greatly impressed by the acuteness of some of your observations. So I've always been expecting to see you. But you've been in very seldom, and then only fleetingly. I've been rather surprised at that.

CUST: I never thought you'd seriously need me.

ERZI: I needed someone who'd been breathing the air of this place for a long time. Besides, you're expecting a promotion which will be almost the goal of your whole career. It is in your own interest that this mess should be cleared up.

CUST: I'm not the only one with such an interest.

ERZI: Quite so. But Judge Croz will also be here in a short time. So will some of the others. (*A short pause; he smiles.*) My dear Cust, this evening I am expected to present my conclusions. The whole city is holding its breath. But before I go, as I shall do shortly, up to the office of the Lord High Chancellor, I wanted to call a few friends together again in here, and test the evidence once more.

CUST: I thought that the inquiry had already uncovered a great many facts and implicated a great number of people.

ERZI: Yes. But in the end everything must center on one particular fact. There must have been a beginning somewhere.

CUST: Has the inquiry broken down on that point?

ERZI: I'm not at all satisfied in my mind.

CUST: You had your eye on Vanan, or so I thought?

ERZI: Yes. Everything would seem to point to Vanan . . . if it were not that one authoritative voice had spoken in his favor.

(CUST *does not break the silence.*)

ERZI: Yours. It was you who told me that Vanan might in fact be innocent. Your observation showed me two things: first, that you had your own opinions, and secondly, that I must regard you yourself as above suspicion. Though in theory I might have suspected you also.

CUST: Yes.

ERZI: But I rather imagine that a guilty person would take great care not to call an investigator back off a false trail . . . and run the risk of having him at his own heels.

CUST: Unless he did so in order to *make* himself above suspicion.

ERZI: Quite so.

CUST: (*Slowly.*) You have in fact sent for me in order to know what I really think of this matter.

ERZI: Precisely.

CUST: I think that if your leper really exists, and if it's not Vanan, then you're going to find it difficult to catch him.

ERZI: Not impossible, however. And why should it be difficult?

CUST: Because the thread of facts, which might have led you to him, has been snapped. Ludvi-Pol is dead: the mouth that could have talked has been shut.

ERZI: Then you think that, at this very moment, somewhere in one of the many rooms in this vast building, there is a person in whom by now, all fear has ceased.

CUST: (*Thoughtfully.*) The rooms in this place are very quiet ones. Unhealthy-looking men sit in them; they have the faces of men who rarely see the sun. Over a period of many years, they have listened in silence to thousands of lies; they have examined human actions of the most extraordinary subtlety and wickedness. Their experience is immense. The people who have faced them across the table have seen merely a few polite, rather tired gentlemen. But in reality, especially among those who achieve very high office, there are wrestlers, dear colleagues; despite the fact that their hardened veins burst so easily. As a rule they find it difficult to sleep at night. And as a result of that . . . (*He breaks off.*)

ERZI: Well?

CUST: As a result they have a great deal of time to brood over their thoughts. They're capable of listening very attentively; they're tough; and they are extremely careful.

ERZI: It would be difficult to catch them out, in that case.

CUST: Yes. And one of them is the man you're looking for.

ERZI: The leper.

CUST: Today that man is on the heights. The day you succeed in unmasking him, he will stand for a moment dumbfounded; millions of eyes will be on him; and then he will hurtle down into an abyss of darkness.

ERZI: And then?

CUST: Then he will begin to defend himself, dear colleague. I believe that his situation must give him a strange intoxicating feeling of liberty.

ERZI: (*Looking hard at him.*) I imagine that one evening, at a very late hour, this man, this judge we're looking for, lifted his gaze from his desk. The person who had come in was very polite, the visit was a perfectly legitimate one. Then the conversation drifted, important friendships, secret powers, attractive enticements flickered about it . . . (CROZ *appears at the door of the clerk's office and stands listening, unseen by the others.*) (*Continuing without interruption.*) . . . The cautious visitor was trying to grope his way towards something already waiting there in the judge's mind: something called ambition; or greed perhaps; or envy; or hate. And at what exact point did that perfectly legitimate cordiality, those vague promises, become something more? When did that subtle bond between them become a leash, held in a master's hand?

CUST: (*Sweating slightly.*) Yes: I think it's a very likely reconstruction.

ERZI: (*With a barely perceptible increase of urgency.*) That is how this judge of ours came to place an acute and powerful intelligence at the disposal of a master, and in the service of injustice. He falsified decisions, he betrayed secrets, and he changed human destinies. He spread in here a trouble which rapidly defiled the entire Courts of Justice; he drove the iron wheel of the law over many innocent men and women. Even a murderer can sometimes regard himself as an executioner. But our man was well aware that he was falsifying the sacred scales of justice. For the sake of what? Why?

CROZ: (*From the back, interrupting unexpectedly.*) Probably because he'd begun to have his doubts.

ERZI: (*Turning.*) About what?

CROZ: Oh, about the sacred scales and so forth. (*He laughs, coughs, and goes on.*) The devil—Ludvi-Pol I mean—had come to get him that night, but that was probably just what our man had wanted, wasn't it, Cust! A judge is just like a priest in these matters: after officiating all his life in front of the holy altar, he conceives a terrible hatred of it and a great wish to see the devil himself appear in front of him for a change.

ERZI: (*Staring now at* CROZ.) But hadn't so many years of being there made him wise, so many years of being outside the game?

CROZ: (*Bursts out laughing.*) Outside the game? But one's never outside the game, my dear Erzi! My dear good fellow, just think for a minute of one of those nasty black insects, that sting. You excite one of them: and it stings. You cripple it: and it stings. You cut it in two: and it stings. You transfix it and smash its head in: and its sting goes on stinging, stinging, stinging. Just for nothing. That's what life is.

CUST: (*Pointing a finger towards* CROZ.) A spite which amuses even the dying quarry. Doesn't it Croz?

ERZI: (*Suddenly turning to* CUST.) But then, Cust, if the thread of facts is broken off, and if the person is so sure of himself, and so determined and cautious, why do you only say it will be *difficult* to find him, and not impossible? After all, that's what you said. What can possibly betray him?

CUST: (*Speaking first with his eyes*

lowered, and eventually lifting them towards his questioner.) This: that men are rather fragile; the very things that they themselves construct, their thoughts . . . their laws . . . their crimes . . . lie too heavy on their backs.

ERZI: (*Slightly urging him on.*) You mean that the man who was guilty of this crime doesn't sleep very easily.

CUST: Yes.

ERZI: Why?

CUST: Because he thinks about it too much.

ERZI: Guilt?

CUST: No; he's beyond that.

ERZI: Why then?

CUST: (*Smiling and staring at him.*) Because he doesn't want his little red spot to be discovered.

ERZI: Well?

CUST: (*A little uneasily.*) Well, with extraordinary subtlety and patience, he calculates; he imagines that the slightest break in his voice, the quickest glance, may have left here and there traces, imperceptible signs . . .

ERZI: . . . which someone may find, and follow up . . .

CUST: Yes, and which he, with supreme caution, takes care to baffle and disperse.

ERZI: In what way?

CUST: He hastens to meet every tiny possible suspicion, even before it's born; sometimes indeed he even prompts the suspicion; and then he stares hard at it, and baffles it, makes it unsure of itself, dazed, destroyed by its own vagueness.

CROZ: (*With a loud laugh.*) It's a big job, isn't it, Cust?

CUST: It is. If one's to discover the man, the secret is to *be* him.

ERZI: What do you mean?

CUST: . . . to feel that one *is* the man.

(*His breathing thickens slightly.*) To feel the same chill here on the scalp, the same heavy pounding, not quite in the heart, but lower, almost in the belly. Boom . . . boom . . . boom . . . the same trembling at the knees . . . the same weariness. I hope you see what I mean?

ERZI: Perfectly. (*Very quietly.*) Then what exactly are his feelings, when he hears that we are at his heels? Fear, wouldn't you say?

CUST: You're wrong.

ERZI: Doesn't he know he's being pursued?

CUST: He's not a fool.

ERZI: You mean it doesn't alarm him?

CUST: Certainly not.

ERZI: Well?

CUST: He manages to control himself.

ERZI: What does he do?

CUST: We pretend to be him; he pretends to be us. He assumes we have a quite supernatural foresight. He dare not make a mistake.

CROZ: (*Satirically.*) It really is a big job.

CUST: (*Pointing a finger at* CROZ, *harshly and aggressively.*) Above all, he has to keep beginning over and over again.

ERZI: Why?

CROZ: (*Staring at* CUST *in his turn.*) Because our eyes are always on him, our suspicions are always pursuing him . . .

CUST: (*Counterattacking.*) . . . and he goes on arranging and constructing defenses ever more subtle and ingenious. (*Laughing, rather harshly.*) Today, for example, his hand . . . It occurred to me, watching your hand, Croz, lying idly there on the table . . . What I mean is that his hand, or even one finger of his hand, at the precise moment that someone utters the name of Ludvi-Pol . . . at that moment one finger of his hand . . . (*He is still pointing at* CROZ's *hand.*) causes a tiny slackening of control; he is affected: for barely a second . . .

CROZ: (*Nervously and jestingly moving his hand.*) Like that?

CUST: Like that. And what a mistake to make. Just because someone was staring at it . . . as we are staring at yours. And suppose someone had noticed that coincidence? And had thought about it? Was that imperceptible movement a confession? Yes, it's *that* that the guilty man thinks about all night long. And by daybreak: he has made up his mind.

ERZI: What to do?

CUST: An experiment. He will go back and face the other person . . . and name Ludvi-Pol again! And he'll put his hand there again, in the same position . . . just as Croz has done! And he'll repeat that imperceptible movement! But what matters this time is that the color of his cheeks, the sweat of his forehead, the sound of his voice, everything shall be beyond question. His hand will feel itself scorched by our look. He'd love to withdraw it . . .

CROZ: You describe it with great accuracy.

CUST: But he has to hold on. The moment has come . . . his heart turns to marble . . . Like this . . . (*He holds his breath for a moment, and then shakes himself and laughs.*) And then everything's all right, he can breathe again!

CROZ: A bit tired?

CUST: (*With a wan smile.*) Almost exhausted.

CROZ: Can I move my hand, now? These moments are rather overpowering.

ERZI: (*Pointing his finger at* CUST.) But it would be incautious of him to rest for a moment, you said so yourself. . . .

CROZ: (*Also urgently.*) There's not a moment that may not bring him some fresh danger . . .

CUST: (*Suddenly, hoarsely, looking down.*) I believe the real dangers are inside himself.

ERZI: How?

CUST: (*Painfully, and as though bewildered.*) He is at the end of his tether. He longs to run away . . . To run away . . . To be dead and buried. That's the most complete flight of all. But then . . .

ERZI: Go on.

CUST: (*Almost to himself.*) Who would be left, to keep the thing snug and warm, the crime I mean, the danger, who would watch over it . . . ? Who would *live* it?

CROZ: (*Bending over him.*) Do you know what I think, Cust, really? I believe his real wish, his most terrible need, is to talk about it. The whole thing. To talk about it. Am I right?

CUST: (*Bewildered and lost in thought.*) Perhaps. He is alone. Everyone is a long way away from him. Alone. And so . . .

ERZI: (*Returning to a previous question, almost cruelly.*) Guilt!

CUST: (*As before.*) No. Astonishment. He is amazed. Amazed to see himself so busy, thinking and doing such strange, wild, ridiculous things . . . but he's forced on to them by the chain of consequences.

ERZI: And doesn't he feel a certain alarm?

CUST: (*Whispering.*) Yes . . . he has the feeling one sometimes has in dreams: when one whispers to oneself: "But this isn't true! It's not true! It's not true! . . . I shall wake up in a minute." (*He breaks off. Someone has knocked at the door leading to the corridor. They all turn. The door opens. The* POLICE OFFICIAL *appears in the doorway; he looks at* ERZI *with a slight lift of the eyebrows and immediately withdraws.*) (*Coming up to the surface again, and laughing cheerfully to* ERZI.) There are times when I even fear you suspect him. (*He points to* CROZ.) . . . or me!

ERZI: (*Also laughing.*) Oh please, please! I'm just looking for help. Well, Cust, since you've penetrated so well into the psychology of our criminal, what would you say, now, are the moves which he expects us to make? What is the point that worries him, in the circle of his defense.

CUST: (*Is still looking at the doorway where the* OFFICIAL *appeared; he thinks for a moment; then he turns and points to the archives; almost shouting.*) The papers! That's where I advise you to attack him!

ERZI: Explain what you mean exactly.

CUST: (*Almost mildly.*) We're dealing with a judge, aren't we? Very well then; think of the vast number of words he uses to sustain the arguments in his statements, in pronouncing sentence, in discussions. All those words are now slumbering in there. The archives. Everyone of them was a weight thrown into the scales you spoke of: but a weight that had been falsified. The records in there, taken singly, page by page, would tell you nothing. But if you were to consider them all together, however tough and clever he had been, don't you feel there must be something there that is bound to betray him? The insistent recurrence of such and such an ambiguity or quibble: the flavor of corruption. That will be the flavor that will distinguish that judge's words from those of all the others. That is the one single thread. (*He points once more.*) The papers.

ERZI: My dear Cust, did you know that the record clerk was already outside in the corridor? It's just as though you'd been reading my thoughts. But you have gone deep down into them, thrown light on them. We are here to obey you, in a sense. But not only because of that, Cust. Your guilty man hasn't thought of everything.

CROZ: (*Raising his voice slightly.*) Are you there, Malgai? Come in.

(*The door from the corridor opens and* MALGAI *appears. He crosses and opens the door of the archives, and goes inside.*)

ERZI: He calls it his graveyard. Well, we shall exhume from it whatever may be needed to put our man into our hands. (*Confidentially.*) It seems, among other things, that Ludvi-Pol himself was in the habit of suggesting certain specific and characteristic arguments in his own favor. We shall discover them all in there, shan't we? But with another signature attached to them. Eh? What do you think, Cust?

CROZ: Do you think our leper will be able to escape us?

CUST: It won't be easy. (*Suddenly, almost frightened, pointing towards the corridor.*) But who's that who's come as well? There was someone else besides the record clerk . . . I thought I heard . . .

ERZI: It's another of the people I needed to have here. (*Turning towards the corridor.*) Come in, come in, Vanan. We were expecting you.

(VANAN *enters. They look at him in surprise. He is extraordinarily wasted, and even shrunk in size. His daughter accompanies him, and almost pushes him forward as though he were a naughty child. She makes him advance to the middle of the room.*)

CROZ: Compassionate Antigone, gentle Cordelia, your father is among friends now, and doesn't need you any more.

(ELENA *is about to speak.*)

ERZI: (*Preventing her.*) You may leave us. You would not be of any help to him.

(ELENA *strokes her father's arm, and goes out.*)

CROZ: (*With cruel gaiety as soon as the door is shut.*) By God, Vanan, I believe you've actually shrunk. What's happened to you? I never thought you were so soft.

VANAN: Eh . . .

CROZ: You've crumpled right up, Vanan. It would be damned funny if you went before I did, wouldn't it? Now, you've got to listen to something. Our colleague Erzi, as you no doubt know, has a number of things to say to you.

ERZI: (*In severe tones.*) Mr. President Vanan! The High Council had allowed you a deferment; that deferment is up today. You have been summoned here today to make your final statement. You promised to prepare your defense.

VANAN: (*Uncertainly.*) I . . . yes . . . yes, sir.

ERZI: Have you done so? (*A silence.*)

CROZ: (*Mutters.*) You even seem to have lost the power of speech.

ERZI: A number of very grave charges are being made against you. You declared that you could disprove and demolish them. How?

(*A silence.*)

CROZ: He's lost his tongue.

ERZI: (*His voice becoming steadily more stern as he speaks.*) Above all, you declared that if you were to reconsider certain remarks made by Ludvi-Pol, you would find yourself in a position to reveal the real criminal. Well? Vanan, who is it? (*A silence.*) Tell us the name, Vanan! (*A silence; he turns away and resumes his seat.*) Either from you, or in some other way, we shall know that name today. (*To the others.*) But perhaps this silence is itself an answer. Vanan, am I to assume that you are acknowledging yourself guilty? Is it true then? Is it you who are responsible for the fraud that has poisoned this bench, this whole building, and the city itself?

CUST: (*Hoarsely.*) Do speak, Vanan; speak out.

VANAN: (*Stammering, pleading, and oddly false in tone.*) I must . . . express my thanks.

ERZI: (*Surprised.*) What?

VANAN: (*As before.*) I have to say . . . that actually . . . the Administration has treated me . . . with very great kindness . . . (*Agitated.*) so that I have nothing to complain of.

ERZI: (*Surprised.*) What are you talking about, Vanan?

VANAN: (*As before.*) As an old . . . magistrate, I feel . . . it's my duty to express my . . . to kiss . . . the generous hand . . .

ERZI: (*Suddenly shouting.*) What do you mean, Vanan!

VANAN: (*Rather frightened.*) No, don't do that . . . Of course . . . I'm very old, and . . . sick now, as you know.

ERZI: (*Quickly.*) Vanan, are you admitting that you are guilty?

VANAN: (*Looks at him suspiciously; suddenly in a false oratorical voice.*) I am innocent, sir! Innocent and falsely accused. Nailed to the cross . . . like our innocent Savior . . . Gentlemen, these gray hairs have been . . . trampled on . . .

ERZI: Vanan, who is the guilty man?

VANAN: (*As before.*) Oh, yes, sir, yes. There is, there *is* a guilty man. I swear before . . . before God's throne that someone is guilty! And I . . . and I can unmask him . . . The wicked shall be hurled to the dust . . . (*Suddenly becoming once more pitiful and pleading.*) I am innocent, sir, innocent. . . .

ERZI: (*Sadly.*) Vanan, what has happened to you? You don't seem like the same man.

VANAN: (*In the tones of a beggar.*) Sir . . . you must intercede . . . for this poor unfortunate judge . . . I don't deserve such . . . severity. (*With sincerity, almost whispering.*) I only want . . . a little quiet. Nothing else.

(*A silence.*)

ERZI: (*Thoughtfully.*) My dear Croz, although the whole thing is really quite clear, it is rather disturbing when one thinks how fragile and delicate the human organism is. Man is far more perishable than even the most trivial object shaped by his own hands. Our colleague is indeed much changed.

CROZ: (*Giggling.*) He'll be even more changed before long.

ERZI: But those cunning papers which he—and the others—blackened with their hurrying pens, those, we shall now find, though they're dead and buried, will be more alive than he is. (*Raising his voice, to* VANAN.) They will tell us the things which you wouldn't or couldn't tell us. You will wait for us here. (*To the others.*) Shall we go?

(ERZI *goes across to the archives and enters.* CROZ *follows him.* CUST *and* VANAN *remain behind.*)

VANAN: (*Uneasily, his voice and attitude changing somewhat.*) What are they going to do? Why . . . did they tell me to wait for them? I hate those two, I don't trust them. Cust . . . (*He sees* CUST's *face.*) Cust! For God's sake, what's the matter with you?

CUST: (*Approaching him.*) Listen, Vanan. I am here to help you, I want you to trust me! It rather looks to me as if you're not being sincere in all this. Or am I wrong? Eh? (*He wipes his brow.*) Listen, Vanan, is it really true that you . . . have been reconsidering . . . certain remarks made by poor Ludvi-Pol . . . Is it true that you have actually discovered the man . . . we're looking for?

VANAN: (*Moans.*) I don't remember anything any more . . .

CUST: (*Dropping his voice.*) But I remember advising you to write a detailed, exact statement. . . .

VANAN: I . . . I . . . what?

CUST: (*Harshly.*) A statement.

VANAN: (*Moans.*) No, no . . .

CUST: (*Urgently.*) Where is it?

VANAN: But I . . .

CUST: Have you written it?

VANAN: No . . . No . . . I couldn't do it. I only want . . . I don't want them to hurt me.

(*A silence.*)

CUST: (*With sudden fierceness.*) My God, it's almost comic to think you can let yourself be buried so willingly. It's unnatural. (*Urgently and whispering.*) What's happened, Vanan? What is it? Tell me.

VANAN: (*Suddenly whispering.*) Cust, I'll tell you the truth. I'm tired.

CUST: What of?

VANAN: The whole thing. You told me to think about it.

CUST: Well?

VANAN: People were cross with me, because I always kept saying the same things.

CUST: Well?

VANAN: Well, actually . . . I began to think about it by myself, at night.

CUST: Good. Well?

VANAN: The trouble was that I was alone; everyone believed that things had happened . . . that other way; and so— Cust, have you ever been bathing in a river, and suddenly seen the water all running the other way? You stand there, still, alone, by yourself, in the middle of the flowing water . . . and you feel a sort of giddiness . . . It was like that; I began to . . .

CUST: Yes?

VANAN: I began to feel weighed down, Cust, disheartened. There were times when I spoke out loud, all by myself, boldly, saying I was innocent . . . but even my own voice hadn't any conviction in it any longer . . . (*Suddenly*.) Do you know what it was? (*Whispering*.) I almost stopped believing in it myself.

CUST: In what?

VANAN: I stopped believing in it. I admit there may have been some little things, when I've been taking evidence, that I may have modified a little . . . Perhaps I've been responsible for a certain amount of confusion . . . I don't know: I may even have been a bit at fault myself; they all say so . . . (*Suddenly pointing towards the corridor*.) You know, Cust. She's my principal torment.

CUST: Who?

VANAN: (*Still pointing*.) My daughter. It's she who drives me on.

CUST: What do you mean?

VANAN: Oh, yes, yes. She's become so naughty. She never leaves me in peace. Sometimes I pretend to be asleep, or feel unwell. But she has no pity, none at all.

CUST: Your daughter?

VANAN: Yes, yes.

CUST: What does she want you to do?

VANAN: She wants me . . . to . . . to write . . . to accuse somebody. She knows I'm innocent, so she wants me to make them listen to me . . . But I'm old, Cust, I'm tired . . . And now everyone here is so rude and insolent to me the whole time. She can't understand that. She can't see that to insist on speaking out only means getting into worse trouble!

CUST: Was it she who brought you here?

VANAN: It was, yes. (*He laughs*.) You can't think how furious she must have been when they sent her away. She's out there now, waiting for me. But do you know what I'm going to do? I shall go out that way, through the clerk's office. (*Suddenly pushing* CUST *aside, with a loud cry and a strange unexpected energy*.) I hate all this! I hate you too, Cust. I

could kill you. (*Moving almost solemnly towards the office door*.) Let me go away. I don't want to think about these things any more. (ELENA *slips in through the corridor door. She makes a sign to* CUST *not to say anything*.) (*In a completely different voice, stopping*.) Listen, Cust, I know I keep going about shouting that I am innocent, like Our Lord on the Cross; but suppose that was just a bit of hypocrisy? and suppose the Lord chastised me? (*Vaguely*.) A man needs peace, he can't stand against the whole world . . . sometimes I tell my daughter that I'm coming to the courts, but I actually go to a little public garden I know in the town, and just sit there a little. That's where I go. Goodbye, my dear Cust. Goodbye.

(*He moves towards the door of the clerk's office: there he nods goodbye to* CUST, *and disappears;* CUST *and* ELENA *remain alone*.)

ELENA: I'm his daughter.

CUST: I know.

ELENA: (*In distress*.) He hasn't anyone else in the world. Neither have I. Don't you think it's sad he should run away from me like that? And silly that I should run after him?

CUST: It's never easy to understand what goes on inside us.

ELENA: Are you in charge of the inquiry?

CUST: Is there something you want to say?

ELENA: Yes, I came specially.

CUST: Well, you can speak. Is it about the inquiry?

ELENA: Yes. It's important, and private.

CUST: You'll have to be quick then. A decision has to be reached this evening.

ELENA: Sir, what my father told you wasn't the truth. I know he wasn't being sincere.

CUST: (*Cautiously*.) When is a man

being truly sincere? It's always difficult to be quite sure.

ELENA: Forgive me, sir. The earliest thing I can remember is when I used to sit on my father's knee. His hair wasn't gray in those days. He used to sit with his eyes closed, and I used to pretend I was drawing his face; I used to touch his eyes with my finger, like that, his nose, his mouth . . . it was one of our games; but we had so many games. I can't describe the happiness and delight we both had in those days! When I hear anyone talking of the people they love, I know that no one can ever be as we were, father and I. Whenever anyone said I looked like him I used to feel my cheeks go scarlet with pride. I would have refused to go to heaven, if my father wasn't to be there too. (*She is silent for a moment; then, without saying anything, she takes from her bag an envelope and shows it to him.*)

CUST: What is that?

ELENA: It's his defense, sir. The statement. They've only to read it, and I know my father will be acquitted. (*A silence.*)

CUST: But only a few moments ago your father said. . . .

ELENA: I know. He refuses to present it. I brought it myself, without telling him.

CUST: But he's definitely denied having written it.

ELENA: But he's spent night after night on it . . . I helped him.

CUST: Then why should he deny it now?

ELENA: (*Sadly and anxiously.*) Because he's so bewildered and frightened. Someone has put the most dreadful doubts and fears into him; it's almost like an illness . . . He's like someone who has fallen down . . . and doesn't want to get up again; he just wants to shut his eyes.

CUST: Do you know the contents of this statement?

ELENA: Yes, of course. Father has remembered a thousand details . . . his innocence is quite plain. It throws light on everything.

CUST: And does this light help us to find who the other man is? The real culprit, I mean.

ELENA: Yes, sir, of course it does. As you read it, page by page, bit by bit, you can see who the real culprit is, you can guess.

CUST: Can you recall the name? Is it someone called Croz?

ELENA: (*Uncertainly.*) No, that isn't the name. (*She puts the statement into* CUST's *hand.*)

CUST: Good. (*He fingers the statement for a moment: suddenly he hums for a moment to himself.*) My dear child. Elena your name is, isn't it? Sit down. The friendship that binds me to your father . . . and also something that really shines in you yourself and . . . genuinely moves me . . . (*He breaks off.*) When I first saw you, I said to myself: this is true innocence; the radiance of justice herself entering into this sad place . . . (*Resuming.*) Well, all that, I was saying, compels me to make a request of you. You don't imagine, do you, that what you feel is really anything more than a mere hope? Or that the investigating magistrate (*Holding up the document.*) is likely to find anything more than that in here?

ELENA: I am certain, sir.

CUST: You will admit that the opinion of a judge may differ from that of a daughter?

ELENA: When you have read it you will run to my father and embrace him. You'll punish everyone who doubted him. You'll be so indignant; there's not a soul on earth who could be indifferent.

CUST: But your father, who is after all not inexperienced in these matters, must have had a reason for keeping silent about this document.

ELENA: But I've explained . . .

CUST: Yes, but you are probably not aware of all he said in here just now. He expressed a fear that any further light thrown on the facts might damage himself.

ELENA: Yes, exactly, he doesn't understand, it's what I was telling you.

CUST: He declares that the treatment given him by the Administration has been extremely indulgent; and that to insist might provoke great severity. Your father expressed his gratitude to us all.

ELENA: Sir, I have read that even people condemned to death—even when they've been innocent—at the last moment, they've begged forgiveness just as though they were guilty. I know that can happen. My father is a very tired man; but he is innocent.

CUST: Very well. (*He hums for a moment between his teeth, throws the statement down on the table, and goes on.*) Very well. You force me to this, my dear child. You are being very stubborn. Just now, while I was listening to you . . . (*He casts a glance towards the archives.*) I know time is very short and we haven't time to dawdle over all this . . . nevertheless, while I was listening to you, there were a lot of things I couldn't help thinking: rather silly things. For example: I'm old enough to be your father. Everything desirable that passes near us we would like in some way to make our own. (*Suddenly, in an almost anguished outburst.*) And I made you my daughter, I stole you from Vanan! I would have held my breath so as not to sully you in any way. I tell you that in a way I have known you ever since I was a boy, but that's too long to tell about now. There is a very simple word which to me expresses what you seem like: loyal. Loyal. But everyone of

us runs on, tied to the indifferent ribbon of time; and that produces an infinite number of mistaken meetings, wrong relationships. One could have been father, brother, husband, son, receiving and giving . . . something. Instead . . . you don't even realize how absurd it is that I, at such a moment, should waste so much time telling you this. However. I wanted to tell you . . . (*With exaggerated anger, to force himself to stop talking.*) . . . a few moments ago, in here, your father explicity confessed himself guilty.

(*A silence.*)

ELENA: (*Almost to herself.*) I can't believe it.

CUST: You mean you don't want to believe it. Didn't you say your father avoided you? What does that mean? It means that it's you in particular he wants to hide something from.

ELENA: (*Lost in her own thoughts.*) There will have been a reason. I will believe anything, but not that he could have disgraced himself.

(*A silence.*)

CUST: (*Rather harshly.*) What a cruel word. Disgraced. Sad that you should use it, since it's your own father we're talking about. An inhuman word. (*Almost pleading.*) Can't you believe that one may make mistakes . . . which one only notices . . . after one's made them, and it's too late to turn back? One mistake is enough: the first one.

ELENA: (*After reflecting for a moment.*) If I were to think that at some given moment—and that moment must come sooner or later, mustn't it, to people who commit these evil things—if I were to think of my father, at some given moment, doing something furtive, and secret, and looking round to see that no one was watching; or sitting there listening to a man whispering secret, wicked orders to him, and my father whispering back, hurriedly consenting . . . My father! My father, doing that! My father! (*She almost laughs.*)

CUST: (*Agitated, pleading.*) Don't you think that everyone in the world, even your father, may at some time or other, need a little pity?

ELENA: But my father couldn't, couldn't possibly do anything he'd have to be ashamed or embarrassed about! You should see my father when he's really angry and outraged! There is nothing in my father but nobility and goodness and pride. People who disgrace themselves in such filthy ways have to be made of very different stuff from my father. You can tell at a glance when people are capable of such treachery: you feel a kind of contempt for them the minute you see them.

CUST: Yes, hideous toads leap from their mouths, and go hopping about these rooms. (*He hums for a moment.*) How cruel you are, my little angel. But it's only your age. The blank blue snow of childhood, smitten by the first incandescent ray of youth. (*With a gust of anger.*) Intoxicating dazzle of light! It leaves one melancholy, humiliated; oh, it's not your fault; you shine, literally, in the midst of this hell of ours. You remind one of the pure crystals of which, as you've perhaps been taught at school, inorganic matter is composed. Do you mean to hand in this statement?

ELENA: (*A little disturbed.*) Yes.

CUST: Good. (*With a touch of harshness in his voice.*) I was saying that we were all crystals like you, once, my dear child; that's why it makes one sad to look at you. It seems that life comes into existence at a later stage, born on the icy geometric forms of the inorganic, like a kind of rash, a malignant growth . . . yes, a leprosy indeed. And on that day your voice will have lost this resonant light, and you won't talk any more about disgrace.

ELENA: My father . . .

CUST: (*Interrupting.*) Your father. Why not let us be quite frank about him? He's a successful man, he's one of those who have got a great deal out of life. Are we to believe that life simply *gave* him what he got? Did he get it for nothing? Was it a gift from life? A birthday present? Did it cost him nothing? Not even cleverness? Cleverness: a name by which many kinds of villainy get past. It is unlikely that the statement refers to those.

ELENA: But my father . . .

CUST: Is after all rather like the unfortunate rest of us, isn't he? The only consolation is we're all made of the same stuff, my dear. Haven't you ever noticed . . . how shall I put it, haven't you ever caught a look on your father's face . . . something in his voice—yes, his voice would be enough to show you—something that worried you a little? That voice, so familiar to you, so dear to you: but did you never hear that voice talking to one of your father's superiors, someone high up: the Minister perhaps; and being very polite, and excited, and eager? And then suddenly did you never hear the same voice, sharp and impatient, speaking to a beggar? Well? Did that never happen? It happens with all of us. And then again . . . didn't you ever hear him pretending to be kind and gentle, from above, with the old man at the gate . . . well? Look at me: of course you remember. You're already a little tarnished, my fair crystal. Such a daily heap of hypocrisy and wickedness in the inflections of one single voice! After all that, shall we really be so very surprised if these pages (*He waves the document in the air.*) turn out to be a skillful selection of things which are true in themselves, but have been cunningly prised out of the whole. But if you really want to present it—

ELENA: (*At a loss.*) I'd like . . .

CUST: And we haven't even got to the

real thing yet, have we? We haven't mentioned the words, have we?—only the voice! Do you believe that these actions, just because no law book condemns them, are any less vile than those that you've called vile? Evil actions, hypocrisies, betrayals. Everywhere! Even here, in our own thoughts, which we falsify—yes, even those! As we formulate them inside us . . . not as they first tremble in our conscience, but as soon as certain cunning poisonous calculations occur to us; even in some of our highest impulses whose mysterious purity we contrive to cheat and twist and sully. (*Greatly agitated, but still with an attempt at sarcasm.*) Think, my dear, of the housewife who has carefully stored away her beautiful jars of jam for the winter: it's like that; one day we also decide to open our nice little boxes of fine ideas, and what do we find inside . . . (*He throws the statement on to the table.*) A swarming heap of maggots! And I can think of nothing, nothing on earth, that escapes that fate! (*He breaks off and turns round, as* MALGAI *enters.*) Have you found anything, Malgai?

MALGAI: Not yet; we're still working. (*He takes up a paper from the table and returns to the archives.*)

CUST: (*Between his teeth.*) Good, so am I. (*He wipes his brow and goes on.*) No, my dear. I know of nothing that escapes. A single opaque mess asking one thing alone: to live. To live.

ELENA: But my father . . .

CUST: (*Shouting.*) Your father was a man, and he was a man here in this ditch! And let me tell you that there was nothing on earth a man could do that he didn't know of!

ELENA: (*Impetuously.*) But I am sure—

CUST: Of what? Sure of what?

ELENA: Whenever there's been any sort of injustice or mistake I've always thought

of my father; I used to think of him here, in this building, in his ermine gown, looking very stern; and I used to feel calm again at once.

CUST: Well, you were wrong, my dear! Look at me! You know I'm not lying!

ELENA: (*With a cry, and moving forward as though to retrieve the statement.*) You don't know my father! You're not his friend!

CUST: (*Violently, breathing heavily, and seizing the statement again.*) My God! How stubborn you are! You only want to create havoc here! I want to tell you something. Perhaps it's not even connected with all this; I don't know. But once when I was only a boy, I remember an afternoon of atrocious, suffocating heat. It was during the siesta; everyone was asleep, soaked in sweat, naked. I must have heard a whisper somewhere in the house, perhaps that was it; or perhaps it was some vicious instinct calling me. I got up, and crept barefoot, furtively, through the shadowy house, towards that whisper, and at last, through a half-open door . . . What a silly disgusting commonplace story! Through the half-open door, that white-faced child saw a man and a woman . . . a man and a woman turned into animals by the stifling heat . . . unrecognizable faces, horrible gestures, choking, appalling words . . . It was my father and mother. My father, and my mother. Quite obvious, after all; what of it? Silly to make a tragedy of it; a door not closed properly, a nervous boy. (*Suddenly.*) But no, they weren't my father and mother any more! They were something confused, black, blind, insane! Before that moment I'd never really known them, never known my father and mother; nor myself; nor anyone else. I was horribly shocked. There always comes a day when a door opens a little way and we look through. And that day has come for you too, now, my dear. Look! Look at your father, for

God's sake, look at him for the first time; and look at yourself too, my dear child! What do you think, do you think that this sweet flower of your body will never be sullied, that it too won't one day be filled with desire and frenzy, do you think that you'll never damage it, never contaminate it, your beautiful little body— and your voice as well, your angel's breath, your very mind? (*Still excited, but suddenly quiet.*) And did you really not know that the great Vanan was sick? Sick, sick, poor devil, that was what was making such a farcical muddle of everything he said. Life is very long, you know, it's very rare that towards the end a venerable white head is much more than to cover over a heap of nastiness; and nasty filthy sicknesses too, those are the things that make age weigh so heavily upon us. That wasn't written in the statement, I'm sure of it. Sad matters, aren't they? You know that I'm telling you the truth, the absolute truth, don't you? As a rule you blush very quickly. I've noticed. But now your color is slowly draining away from your cheeks. You are saying goodbye to the enchantment of youth. You are becoming a woman; it's a small disturbance, it has to come; like the first cigarette, we feel discomfort here. Yes, so it was I who didn't know the great Vanan! If you only realized how little *you* knew about him! And about the others! And about yourself. That is why you were unjust. You never even knew . . . (*With a sudden cry.*) that your father hates you! He hates you, yes, he said so in here! (*With a change of tone.*) You didn't even know about the slimy love affairs in which poor Vanan has got himself mixed up. The court itself, this very office, has had to look into it. No, that wasn't in the statement either. Slimy intrigues: the loves of old men. It's a sad and terrible thing, my poor angel; the loves of old men, horrible, unspeakable, tormenting! We all come to it. That's how we're made.

They are things he never spoke to you about, aren't they? The man you used to kiss when he came back home at night! Suppose *you* look through the open door as well; it's a thing you have to get used to. You know it's the truth I'm telling you, don't you? Very well: you didn't even know that on the day when they first accused him, the great Vanan wrote a letter! And confessed! Yes, he confessed, my dear. He confessed right from the start. Do you want me to repeat the exact words of that letter! (*Striking his forehead.*) They're engraved here. (*Beginning.*) "My dear Lord Chief Justice . . . an aged magistrate writes to beg of you your extreme kindness . . ."

ELENA: (*Signing to him not to go on.*) No. (*After a few moments, in a whisper.*) Poor father. (*A pause.*) And poor me.

(*A silence.*)

CUST: Do you want your statement back? (*He holds it out to her.*)

ELENA: (*Shaking her head.*) It won't be any use now. (*She goes towards the door; and stops.*)

CUST: You'd better be quick, and go; no one has seen you.

ELENA: (*Takes a few steps forward; whispers.*) I'm embarrassed, because now when I meet my father . . . I shan't know what to say to him. I'm afraid that when he looks at me, he'll see that I know. Poor father. I don't want to meet him. (*She moves still nearer to the door; and repeats, almost to herself.*) I don't want to meet him. (*She goes out.*)

(*Perturbed,* CUST *stands looking at the door through which she has departed; suddenly, he begins feverishly unwrapping the statement; a few pages fall to the floor, quickly he picks them up. He breaks off in order to listen for any noise from the archives. He looks once more at the door through which the girl has disappeared.*)

CUST: After all, she was no more than a child. Her gentleness will be enough to . . . She is too gentle almost . . . Tomorrow the color will have returned to her cheeks; and she will have forgotten. (*A pause.*) But I . . . Oh God, how tired I am! Tired to death. (*He covers his face with his hands; suddenly he hears steps approaching; he throws the statement down on the table, turns, and waits. The door of the archives opens, and* ERZI *comes out, followed by* CROZ.) (*Loudly, almost shouting.*) Well, dear friends, has any good come of your labors?

CROZ: (*With a loud laugh.*) Haha. You're very cheerful, Cust. You've already guessed.

CUST: (*As before.*) Haven't you found anything?

ERZI: (*Casually laying a hand upon the statement.*) We find that in none of the suits have the documents survived.

CROZ: (*Grinning.*) Cust! One of us has removed them.

CUST: (*Excited and suspicious.*) Removed them? And then what?

ERZI: (*Removing his hand, and moving away.*) Destroyed them.

CUST: Destroyed them? How? (*He laughs and almost shouts, excitedly, harshly.*) How! How! (*He gradually gets nearer the statement, takes it up, gesticulates with it, and then without disguising what he is doing, drops it into a basket.*) But, my dear friends, would it really have been as easy as all that? Do you think the criminal would have found it easy, or even possible, to burn or destroy, here, such a great number of documents?

ERZI: He could have . . .

CUST: . . . taken them away bit by bit, hidden about himself, do you think? That man, who doesn't want, (*Almost shouting.*) DOES NOT WANT to be found out, do you imagine he'd have gambled

his whole position here, with the risk, however remote and theoretical, of being found with the papers on him in some accident or other, a fall, or a faint . . . ! My dear friends, you can't have the slightest idea what he must be really like! Why the very thought of it would have given him a fit!

ERZI: (*Interrupting him almost with a cry.*) Cust. Where are those papers?

CUST: (*Calmly, pointing to the archives.*) Still in there, in my opinion. But hidden away under mountains and mountains of other documents and papers. The man had patience, so we must have patience too . . . (*He breaks off.*) Did you hear that?

ERZI: What?

CUST: A noise. Not a noise exactly. Down there, somewhere in the building. It sounded to me like . . . (*Breaking off again.*) Yes, there must be something wrong. There's someone running up the corridor.

MALGAI: (*Comes running out of the archives and hurries out of the door to the corridor.*) They say there's been an accident. (*He disappears.*)

BATA: (*Comes running in from the corridor, crosses the room towards the clerk's office.*) There's been an accident! Why are people always so careless? They go up and down, up and down, God knows what they're looking for. The gate up at the top must have been opened. Didn't you hear the shout? Yes, as she fell. A loud scream. (*He disappears.*)

(ERZI *runs out into the corridor.*)

CROZ: (*Following him.*) This building: horrible things happening the whole time, blood on the ground, accidents. And it's no worse than they deserve, most of the people who come here. If you ask me . . . (*He disappears.*)

(CUST *is alone; he has stood perfectly still throughout; hurried footsteps and voices are heard outside.*)

A VOICE: (*Outside the room.*) Let's have some light! Put the lights on!

ANOTHER: Call somebody! Tell somebody to come!

ANOTHER: Where's the porter? Porter!

MALGAI: (*Re-entering, breathless.*) It was there, down at the bottom of the elevator shaft. It's so dark everywhere in this damned place, especially the stairs, and the passages. (*He is hastily clearing a divan of the documents on it.*)

CUST: (*Without turning, almost tonelessly.*) Is she dead?

MALGAI: They don't think so, not yet. They say it's the daughter—

CUST: (*Interrupts him with a gesture, turning round in sudden terror.*) What are you doing?

MALGAI: I'm getting this couch ready...

CUST: (*Horrified.*) Here? Why . . . No. No. (*He childishly points towards the clerk's office.*) In there . . .

ERZI: (*Rushing back in: to* MALGAI.) Yes, in there, that'll be better. We'll take her in there. Call somebody! Do call somebody! Telephone. (*He runs out again.*)

MALGAI: But who am I to call? There's no one there at this hour; everything's shut up. I ought to be at home too . . .

CUST: (*Stopping him.*) Malgai, did you hear her cry out . . . ?

MALGAI: Yes, a loud cry—

CUST: (*His teeth almost chattering.*) What . . . what do you think?

MALGAI: About what?

CUST: Do you think it's . . . an accident?

MALGAI: I think she must have tripped, people never look where they're going. She tried to dart back, but it was too late. (*He breaks off, and turns toward the corridor.*) Here she is.

(*A low murmur of voices is heard, and the scrape of footsteps approaching: finally the door on the corridor is thrown open wide. A big man enters carrying the girl in his arms, apparently unharmed and as though asleep, her hair flowing over her shoulders. A number of people follow. The man crosses the room, and disappears into the clerk's office: the door remains open. The others, except for* CUST, *follow him, talking in low tones, as though in church.*)

A VOICE: . . . yes, some strands of hair . . . in the iron work . . .

ANOTHER: . . . there was oil . . . there were traces of oil from the elevator shaft . . . They ought to . . .

ANOTHER: . . . clean it, of course, clean it . . .

ERZI: (*Crossing the room with* MALGAI.) Anyway, send for somebody . . . send for a woman. Warn them . . . that they must send a car. And her father. Send for him . . . Make some excuse . . . Don't tell him . . .

CUST: (*They have all gone into the clerk's office.* CUST *remains alone; he approaches the door of the office; stares at it: suddenly in a hushed voice, with an extraordinary note of pleading.*) Elena. (*A pause.*) Elena. Don't die. Try to live. (*A silence.*) Elena . . .

(*He breaks off, as* MALGAI *hurries back in.*)

CUST: How is she, Malgai?

MALGAI: I don't think there's very much hope for her.

CUST: (*With terror, almost with fury.*) Do you mean this girl is going to die?

MALGAI: It's a terrible accident, sir.

CUST: (*Stammering.*) But that girl . . . she was in here a few moments ago . . . blushing, at a mere nothing . . . she was so young . . . I want to tell her . . . (*He breaks off.*)

MALGAI: (*Alarmed.*) What's the matter, sir?

CUST: (*Stands looking at one of his*

hands in real terror; suddenly with a suffocated cry.) Malgai! I have her blood here on my hands! I've not touched her, Malgai! I've not touched her! (*He rubs his hand hysterically.*)

MALGAI: But . . . but there's nothing odd about that, sir. I touched her myself. You might easily have touched me, you might have brushed by me. Or you might have touched the others, there's nothing strange about that. (*He breaks off.*)

CROZ: (*Rushes in from the corridor, in great distress.*) Oh my God, Cust; Her father's here! They sent for him. Who's going to tell him, what shall we do? Oh how dreadful it is, what a terrible mess, the whole thing is . . .

CUST: (*With a fierce wild movement, runs to the door, throws it open and cries.*) Come in, Vanan! Come in. Quickly!

VANAN: (*Letting himself be dragged in, suspicious and whimpering.*) But what more do you want of me? What is it? Leave me alone! Leave me in peace, why can't you?

CUST: (*Shouting.*) You'll never be at peace any more, Vanan! (*Louder still.*) Never, never at peace, Vanan! You must do something! Something terrible! Your daughter. Your beautiful . . . dear Elena. (*Almost to himself alone.*) She's dead. She's dead.

CURTAIN

ACT THREE

Late in the evening; a single lamp is burning. MALGAI *is just coming from out of the archives. He puts on his hat and overcoat in preparation for leaving.* CUST *appears at the corridor door.*

MALGAI: (*Noticing him.*) Good evening, sir. Did you want something?

(CUST *does not reply.*)

MALGAI: I'm really off duty now, but . . . never mind. We are always here when anybody wants us.

CUST: (*Absently.*) No, you go along, Malgai. There's something I want to do, I shall be staying for a little while.

MALGAI: Ah yes, sir. You're another one who wears himself out, sir, working after hours!

CUST: Yes, I'm another. Are the archives open?

MALGAI: Yes sir, they're open. Mr. Justice Croz wanted to—

CUST: I'll see that they're locked up afterwards. Good night.

MALGAI: (*Surprised.*) Then what shall I . . . very well, sir, very well. (*He goes out, hesitatingly.*)

(CUST *waits until* MALGAI's *footsteps have died away; then he goes to the door on tiptoe and turns the key; immediately afterwards he goes into the archives, and returns with an armful of documents which he throws on a table and begins to examine; very soon, however, something seems to distract him, and he stands there lost in thought; suddenly he starts: all the lamps have gone on.* CROZ *has risen slowly from a large armchair whose back has hidden him from sight; he has switched on the lights; now he gives way to a long burst of laughter mingled with coughing.* CUST *has turned round quickly; then he slowly returns to his previous attitude.*)

CROZ: (*Frequently pausing for breath.*) Once upon a time there was a little mouse. And there was a trap. Instead of cheese, there were certain well-known papers hidden under mountains and mountains of other papers . . .

CUST: (*Absently.*) What do you mean?

CROZ: You're losing your grip, Cust! For example, you just turned the key in the door there: excellent, but what about the other doors? A bit of a surprise, wasn't it, Cust, to find old Croz here?

CUST: (*As before.*) We heard bad news about your health.

CROZ: Yes, I hardly managed to get up here, as a matter of fact. But if I've got to die, I wanted to die here. Besides, I know that spite is almost as good as oxygen. (*With a change of tone.*) Cust, it's all fixed for tonight, isn't it? The sentence on the guilty man; and the naming of the new president. (*He points towards the ceiling.*) The old men are already taking their seats up there. Cust, which of us two is going to walk off with it?

CUST: (*As before.*) Do you think the Upper Council will definitely eliminate Vanan?

CROZ: Self-possessed, aren't you? You even indulge in the luxury of thinking about Vanan! . . . (*Sarcastically.*) Oh, he'll be sentenced all right . . . (*He pauses for breath.*) . . . and you or I will get the nomination. But you're not looking very well either, Cust. In fact, quite the opposite.

CUST: (*In a monotone.*) It's just that my thoughts keep going over and over things which are already beyond the possibility of being changed.

CROZ: You must look after yourself.

CUST: I shall have to. Look at my hand: it costs me a great effort to stop trying to wipe it, though it's perfectly clean already. Like that, you see? (*He wipes his hand.*) I have done that so often that just here the skin has changed. I don't do it quite so much now.

CROZ: Cust, you've always interested me, you know. You've given me the creeps before now, often. You are very tough, aren't you? Stubborn. But now we're on the last lap.

CUST: (*In a staccato monotone.*) Yes, I'm very stubborn. And Vanan's daughter showed that she too was pretty stub-

born. She hasn't spoken since that day. They say she won't last until tomorrow morning.

CROZ: Cust, what are you doing in here?

CUST: Most of all, it was the cry she uttered as she fell which shocked me. I have tried to analyze it, these last few days; tried to reconstruct it.

CROZ: (*Louder.*) Cust, what are you doing here?

CUST: (*Quietly, and as though lost in thought.*) You can see; I am looking for something. It wasn't so much a fall into an elevator shaft—I keep getting the idea of her being sucked down into a funnel. Slowly at first, then quickly, then down, vertically, swallowed up. I think that cry expressed other things, besides fear. But what other things? A kind of reproach. But most of all—incredulity; surprise.

CROZ: Cust, you keep on talking to me about that girl. Has she some connection with our problem?

CUST: (*As before.*) No real connection. What annoys me most of all is the fact of the interruption. That girl still had little round cheeks, almost like a baby's; and in fact she was very young: when you looked at her, it was like looking at a beautiful fresh leaf moving gently on the branch: one caught a hint of seasons, enchanting hours yet to come, long, long days drenched in sun . . . And where is all that now? Broken off. It's very strange. I don't think any logic in the whole world can explain that.

CROZ: Cust, I don't know if you've understood. This is the epilogue, Cust, the auditing. You've waited for the right moment to take me into your confidence.

CUST: Perhaps I've never really talked to anyone. Sometimes one begins to need to. Perhaps you'd understand me better than anyone else.

CROZ: Undoubtedly. I've always understood you. In a way, you've kept me company. I should have been bored without you. Cust, today you've made your first mistake.

CUST: (*Still in the same indifferent, slightly surprised tones.*) Possibly. What was it?

CROZ: You were wrong to come here tonight! Those famous papers, eh? A feeling of fright lest they should still exist in there, subtle, slight, evil: they've drawn you here, like a rope. Right at the last moment, when everything was over, when the old men up aloft were actually dipping their pens into the ink, you had to stumble over this little pebble. (*Shouting.*) Cust, what are you doing here? What are you looking for?

CUST: (*Almost wearily.*) The criminal.

CROZ: Well, help me then, because I'm looking for him too. And what is it that drives you on?

CUST: The idea that from tonight onwards he may begin to be calm again, that his footstep from tonight onwards may once more begin to be assured and authoritative in this place; as may his voice. I feel a sort of revulsion and stupefaction at the thought. It's like that girl's cry: I can't find a place for it anywhere in the world.

CROZ: Cust, you're a liar! You've sent the record clerk away by a trick! You've come here at this time of night, in secret! You've fallen into the trap; I have found you out!

CUST: (*In a monotone.*) Croz. You too are here in secret. It's I who've found you out.

CROZ: Oh, is it really? Well, tell me then, (*Pointing to the documents.*) have you found nothing in those things there?

CUST: Nothing.

CROZ: (*Gives a long laugh, and finds difficulty in getting his breath back*). Nothing! Nothing! A fine result after all

the risks you've taken. (*Mockingly.*) Do you know what I'm afraid of? That it's useless to go on looking any more; and that even in there (*Pointing to the archives.*) everything's vanished.

CUST: Nothing left. That too is strange.

CROZ: Why is it strange? Suppose the papers kept on going in through that door there, and never came out; suppose all the scoundrels in the city had to sign a piece of paper for every penny they ever stole, every lie they ever told; and suppose all the papers stayed in there: by this time there'd be nothing else left on the surface of the earth but papers; and the sea of papers would go on growing and growing till it reached the moon. Haha. Fortunately (*Pointing towards the door of the archives.*) so much goes in, and so much comes out. As in everything else. Here's a graveyard that's even more of a graveyard than that: it's called the pulping-mill. (*In satirically mysterious tones.*) Our friend has taken advantage of that. There's nothing left.

CUST: (*In a monotone.*) Not a single trace. At this moment that girl too is perhaps gone without trace. Nothing. It's that that's strange.

CROZ: Nothing? No trace? (*He taps himself on the forehead.*) What about this? You don't count what's inside here? The papers have gone to the pulping-mill, but Croz will have to be sent there as well, because Croz knows who the criminal is. (*Shouting.*) He knows, he knows! Stay where you are, Cust. Don't you dare come near me. I know you're not a man of action, but you've good cause to send me to the pulping-mill too, haven't you? (*He goes over and unlocks the door.*) We don't quite know yet how this interview is going to finish. (*He pauses for breath.*) What a comfort it would be, wouldn't it, with me here, *moribundus*, almost at death's door, how very nice, when you come to think of it, if just one little vein, here inside me somewhere, were to burst and take your trouble away, now, here, at once, before Old Croz could get out of here and begin to chatter, eh?

CUST: (*In a monotone.*) It's you whose real interest is that *I* don't get out of here; because the criminal, and I've known it for some time, is you, Croz. Possibly some of the others as well. But you, quite certainly. Not me.

CROZ: Cust, I've always admired you. That was really why I always hated you: and you have quite seriously shortened my life, did you know? You're made of steel. Good God, you're not tired yet: what are you still frightened of? It's done now; there's nothing left inside there. Even if I wanted to accuse you, now, my words would be no more than words. A rival's spite, to try and undermine you. Your words against me would be the same. You needn't hold your breath, Cust. You can speak. I know how much you want to; you're dying to.

CUST: (*Rubbing his hand.*) But I'm not guilty. It's you.

CROZ: (*Shouting.*) Yes! Yes! I too! I've also been a cheat! Bah. I've never even taken much trouble to hide it. I'd go on being one. Yes, it would have been worth it, wouldn't it, being honest among our dear fellow-citizens—a lot of filthy traitors in exactly the same way, but above all stupid, and villainous, all of them. And how they multiply! Not a drop of cleanliness in one of them; how disgusting! You too: you were quite right, Cust. They must be stamped out underfoot. Cust! I've spoken! You speak too!

CUST: (*In a monotone.*) But I am not the criminal.

CROZ: Bah. (*He spits towards him: and stands there panting.*) What a swine you are. And you're a fool as well. It's stupid to care so much. (*He breathes heavily*

again.) Who can tell how many men, century after century, must have stood . . . like us two, glaring at each other, quarrelling . . . their foreheads covered in sweat . . . and what a silly fuss to make of anything. It was all a lot of nonsense . . . because . . . (*He grips the table and sits down slowly in a strange way; and mutters.*) Damnation. (*He stays there gasping for breath.*)

CUST: (*Without moving.*) Do you feel bad?

CROZ: (*Almost speechless.*) Yes.

CUST: You've upset yourself. Do you want a drink of water?

CROZ: (*Does not answer; after a moment.*) That'd be very nice. (*He gasps.*) Cust. You've always had the most outrageous luck. (*He slips to the floor.*)

CUST: (*Without moving.*) Croz! (*Silence.*) Croz! (*Silence.*) Come on! (*Seeing that the other is trying to speak.*) What is it, do you want to tell me something?

CROZ: (*In a whisper.*) I'm going, Cust.

CUST: Going? (*Calmly.*) Ah, one can never tell that.

CROZ: (*As before.*) It's all over. (*He collapses onto the floor.*)

CUST: (*After observing him for a moment.*) By God, Croz, I'm almost afraid you're right. Croz! Can you hear me? Where are you in pain? (*A silence.*) It's been the same with me these last few days: did you know? I've felt as if there were something at my back, I've felt like a boy going along a dark corridor and whistling. Mustn't turn round, must go straight on, Croz, stick it out. (*A silence.*) Is it your heart? I don't want to frighten you, but this time it does really look like it, doesn't it? These have been hard days for me too, Croz. I've tried to sleep as much as I possibly could. Even a man condemned to death is like a free man, when he's asleep. Sleep is the same for everyone. And let us hope death will be the same, Croz. You are going to sleep for a very long time now, I think. (*A silence.*) Listen, if it's really true that you're going, that it's all over, and there's no more danger, then . . . I may tell you . . . it's true, I *have* been a lucky man. Yes, Croz, I was the man we were all looking for, and I really needed, *needed,* to say so to somebody. I couldn't bear it any longer. *I* was the leper. You were looking for me, weren't you? But I'm still hopeful. I think I'm quite safe still. It's been a big job. I'd been frightened that I might not be able to carry it through, frightened I might suddenly begin to shout. We take far too much upon ourselves. Do you know, Croz, I've kept having the same dream over and over again, all these nights. I dreamt about a child, a boy. I've never had any children. And what an ugly child this was of mine! Naked, with an enormous belly, an evil face, and horrible, quick, crooked little legs, leaping about like a frog, yes, just like a frog; I would see it hiding in the record clerk's trolley, or disappearing among the bookshelves and the papers, in the most ridiculous places, and I would be after it . . . always after it . . . trying to grab hold of it; sometimes I managed to cut it, with a knife . . . cut it up in a hundred pieces . . . but every piece began to grow again with those little legs . . . and to leap about with me after it, I couldn't catch it. I was soaked in sweat, I had too many things to look out for, here, there, everywhere; it was too much, yes, it was too much! Nobody else could have borne it, I'm sure of that. (*In wild desperation.*) That girl's cry, Croz! I *studied* it! I pored over it! It's difficult to understand what she meant, one can make all sorts of guesses. "Aaaaah!" Like that, she cried! "Aaaaah!" The idea I've formed of it . . . is that it had somehow scratched something, made a scratch on

a piece of glass. No, not quite, not on a glass . . . it was one of those scratches from which small drops of blood issue. Every now and then, a little drop. It all seems finished; but you look again; and there is another drop of blood. Yes, a scratch. Blood. They all believe it was an accident . . . But I . . . I'm mystified. I can't see . . . (*He breaks off.*)

CROZ: (*Raises his head, gets up slowly from the ground; in an ordinary voice, quietly.*) To see ourselves clearly is a great privilege, Cust. You want to set too many things in order. (*Suddenly, wildly, and harshly, he begins to shout.*) Help! I'm dying! Help me, help me! Porter, porter! Hurry! (*He gasps for a moment.*) Quickly someone! Porter! Porter! (*He begins to beat his stick on the table.*) Help, help, help, help!

MALGAI: (*Running in.*) What's the matter?

CROZ: It's me, I'm feeling bad, I am dying. Send for the Investigator, first . . . Councillor Erzi . . . tell him to come here at once. Then call the judges. All of them. Fetch as many people as you can, and Vanan as well, of course. Warn them . . . that I'm here, at the point of death, in the company of . . . him, my colleague Cust, look at him; tell them to hurry if they want . . . to find me alive. Hurry up, you fool. (MALGAI *runs out.*) (*Worn out by his efforts, speaks more slowly, breathing with difficulty.*) My poor Cust, I wish I could say that all this had only been . . . a charade for your benefit. Unfortunately . . . it's only too true . . . that I'm about to die; what a bloody disgrace. (*He pants slightly.*) My dear friend, the popular superstition about the words of the dying, strengthens . . . my credit. Strengthens it a great deal. I shall tell the truth; they will believe me; and you, at the very last minute, will have slipped up. You've spoken, you've told me. I could save you too, my dear fellow, I've always . . . liked a good joke . . . in that case I'd be the one who nominated you as president, I'd be the one who put the ermine gown on the back of the great leper; this filthy shell would have a snail inside worthy of it. A juicy sight! But I could never bring myself to help *you*, Cust. I don't like you. You're conceited. I want to punish you. (*He gasps for breath.*) The point of death makes me very powerful. I don't believe I have any duties. (*He gasps.*) I believe that things develop . . . according to a purely vegetable law. And it's not without . . . its comic side. I believe that if we . . . decided to think it was disgraceful to wear gray . . . (*He laughs.*) ha-ha, to wear gray stocking . . . anyone who actually had worn gray stockings . . . ha-ha-ha, would feel terrible guilt and shame. That's all it is. I don't believe that anything remains of us. We'd be in a real mess if . . . if anything could really be distilled from such a load of nonsense.

(BATA *arrives, in haste, accompanied by* MAVERI.)

BATA: Croz, how are you?

CROZ: Much as you'd expect a man to be, who knows he'll be dead . . . in about ten minutes. Just stay over there, my dear fellow, there's something I have to say . . . to my colleague. (*To* CUST, *privately.*) All these judges . . . they've always turned my stomach. A lot of them are very upright and very worthy . . . and they'll live for a long time . . . They are made of wood. As for the rest . . . come a bit closer, Cust. They administer justice! Ha-ha-ha (*He laughs.*) Which means they express their opinion that certain actions are just, and certain others are not. Just as one sausage is hung on to another sausage, this opinion is hung on to the law books . . . beautifully bound of course . . . and these law books are

hung on to other law books—and statutes and tables . . . older still. The trouble is, my dear fellow . . . (*He breaks off, and says to* PERSIUS, *who has just arrived.*) What's he doing?

PERSIUS: Who?

CROZ: Erzi. Silly old tortoise.

PERSIUS: They've sent for him. Everybody's on their way here.

CROZ: (*Turning to* CUST.) . . . the trouble is that the main hook is missing, the original clasp . . . and without that . . . the whole string of sausages falls to the ground! But where, and how, and when! Who was it who decided one thing was right and another wasn't? We know perfectly well that things . . . are what they are, all equal. That's why we judges are all hypocrites, all of us stuffed with stale rancid sausage-meat. That's what the real corruption in these courts is, the whole place stinks terribly of it; I can't wait to be free of it. (*He breathes with difficulty: he points to the group of judges and winks.*) They all pretend. They don't really believe it, those chaps, they don't really believe in the resurrection after death, nor even in Lord Free-will; don't you see? (*He emits a soft scandalized whistle; suddenly thoughtful.*) And as a matter of fact, what reason on earth is there to expect that at some point in this chain, something autonomous will break out? The soul, I mean. I am speaking of the soul. But anyway, all that . . . is rapidly ceasing . . . to concern me. Naturally. (*He remains for a moment with drooping head.*) What about Erzi?

MALGAI: (*Coming in.*) He's coming up from the offices.

CROZ: Good. Come here, Malgai. And you, Persius. (*The two men obey.*) Take hold of me firmly. You on that side, like that. You on this. That's right. (*He has made the two men take him firmly by the arms and lift him up.*) Now let's go and meet him. I've a number of disclosures to make to him. (*With a touch of pride.*) I don't want . . . to wait for him and death . . . in here . . . bent double . . . like a rat that . . . somebody's trampled on.

(*Supported by the two men, indeed almost carried by them,* CROZ *slowly crosses the room and goes out.* CUST, BATA *and* MAVERI *stand looking at each other.*)

BATA: (*Excitedly to* CUST.) Poor Croz, the whole of his life, he's been nothing but an old tin of poison. What does he want to talk to Erzi about? Revelations at the point of death! What sort? Against whom?

MAVERI: (*Distressed.*) Do you know anything about it, Cust? What was he saying to you just now?

CUST: (*In a monotone.*) I ought in duty to warn everyone that our poor friend is no longer himself; I'm afraid he's raving . . . (*He breaks off.*)

MALGAI: (*Appearing at the door, excited and jubilant.*) Croz is talking to Erzi! Big things! He has said—and he is dictating to the secretary also—that he, Croz, in solemn declaration, testifies that President Vanan . . .

BATA: (*Taking the words out of his mouth.*) . . . is innocent!

MALGAI: . . . and that if he manages to live another five minutes, he intends to reveal . . .

BATA: . . . the name of the real criminal!

MALGAI: Exactly! (*He rushes out again.*)

CUST: (*As before.*) Unfortunately the trust we can put in Croz's words is only relative. This crisis has produced a genuine disorder in him, and . . . (*He turns.*)

(VANAN *is entering, bent and terrified: a* NURSE *leads him in.* BATA *rushes up to him, making an overwhelming fuss of him.*)

BATA: Vanan! Vanan! Please allow someone who has never had a moment's doubt of you and your . . .

MAVERI: (*In competition with* BATA.) . . . your absolute integrity, which now shines again in such a sudden, unexpected, even marvellous . . .

NURSE: (*Stepping between the two judges and* VANAN, *who has timidly drawn back.*) Forgive me, he has to be treated and spoken to very gently. I always have to be with him.

CUST: (*Who has stood staring at the* NURSE, *quietly, but in a voice slightly louder than necessary, almost solemnly.*) You have left Elena? (*Something in his voice makes the others turn and look at him.*)

NURSE: Didn't you know, sir? The poor child has no need of me or anyone else now.

CUST: (*In the same tones.*) Is she dead?

NURSE: Two days ago, sir. What am I saying? Three. Her sufferings are over.

(*A silence.*)

CUST: (*As before.*) What a very small coffin, she will have needed. They told me she was much changed.

NURSE: Just like a tiny little bird, sir. She weighed nothing at all.

CUST: She didn't say anything further?

NURSE: Nor even heard anything. Nor even looked at anything.

CUST: Did she complain at all?

NURSE: No, poor little thing. Only towards the end, she kept doing this with her poor little hand: as though to try and push something from her, or drive it away, a fly or something.

CUST: Was anyone at her side, when that gesture ceased?

NURSE: (*Dropping her voice.*) You will hardly believe it, sir, but poor Mr. Vanan refused to go and see her again. He made the excuse that he was suffering too much. (*She shakes her head.*) At the end he made even stranger and more childish excuses. It isn't his fault.

CUST: (*Thoughtfully, while they all look at him in some amazement.*) So no one will ever again meet the young girl I saw at that door. She stood there a little out of breath, as though after a race . . . No one ever said anything more to her, she never listened to anyone. (*To the woman almost threateningly.*) You: why didn't you make her listen to you, while there was time? Now no one will ever be able to do that. (*Almost to himself.*) I talked to her, I passed long nights with her, begging her not to die, all night through; but she didn't believe in me anymore.

NURSE: But that's not true, sir; you never once came.

CUST: (*In a monotone, quietly, turning to* VANAN.) Vanan, I fear your daughter did not attribute enough importance to her own life. She ought to have been persuaded that in her there was . . . (*He pauses with his arm upraised.*)

PERSIUS: (*Bursting in, greatly agitated.*) At this very moment Croz is revealing the criminal's name! They even sent *me* away. It appears it really is one of us!

CUST: (*Who has listened without turning, goes on after a moment, in a louder voice.*) . . . that in her there was something which does not exist and will never again exist at any other point of eternity . . . (*Suddenly, almost with fury.*) Something immenser than the immensest star . . .

VANAN: (*Retreating a little, to the woman.*) Take me away, I don't want to see that man.

CUST: (*In amazed tones*). Vanan, her cry split the crystal of the heavens in two, and was heard far, far away. You cannot

have forgotten, for you were her father. It is your duty . . .

VANAN: (*In a distant, almost childish voice*). But it was all so long ago, and our Lord knows what He does. (*Fervently.*) I hope, hope, hope for heaven, and I don't want to know anything more. (*He makes the sign of the cross several times.*) Our Lord be praised forever. (*He mumbles a prayer; suddenly with a strange obstinacy and almost overbearingly.*) My daughter died when she was a little girl. It was years ago.

CUST: (*Bewildered.*) What do you mean, Vanan?

VANAN: (*With the same childish obstinacy and distrust.*) Yes, yes, my daughter died when she was a little girl. The Lord willed it so . . .

CUST: Vanan . . . (*He breaks off; they have all turned to the door.*)

MALGAI: (*Has entered in haste, breathlessly.*) We know the criminal's name!

BATA: Come on, out with it, Malgai!

MALGAI: (*Excitedly, enjoying the delay.*) I can imagine the outcry there's going to be!

MAVERI: Come on!

PERSIUS: What about Croz?

BATA: Is he dead?

MALGAI: No one will ever hear that fiendish old voice again. Even *I* couldn't tell you the impudent things the old devil invented before he was willing to give the real name of the criminal! He kept coughing, and winking the whole time. He kept letting out the most dreadful curses; he even pretended in the end to make Councillor Erzi play at guess-who, trying the names of this man and that! And suddenly Croz said: (*Imitating him.*) "No. It isn't any of them. The criminal's name is . . ."

ERZI: (*Who has already entered.*) His name *was* . . . Croz. (*Advancing with a certain detachment.*) Yes, gentlemen, your colleague Croz has disclosed at the point of death that the person responsible for the corruption in these courts was himself, and no one else; that Vanan is innocent; and that all the other judges are likewise innocent, mainly, he observed, because they hadn't the brains to be anything else; and that the best of the lot and the most deserving of being nominated for the Presidency . . . was you, Cust. He spoke of you in very respectful terms . . . though also, of course, satirically and sharply, as is his wont. He asked me to say to you . . . Wait a moment . . . (*He tries to remember.*) "That every man has to scratch his own scabs by himself."

BATA: Very fine. Anything else?

ERZI: He coughed, he blew a little, and he said: (*Imitating him.*) "Well, well, you've been a hell of a bore, Erzi." And died.

BATA: (*Violently.*) And that filthy blackguard dared to pass judgment on his own colleagues!

MAVERI: Not only that, he still contrived to be smart and impudent right to the end.

BATA: Erzi, I'm not blaming you. But my God, dying or not, Croz ought to have been compelled—(*He points to the great doors at the back which have so far remained closed throughout the play.*)—to go out through there, through those doors; to drag himself at his last gasp up the great staircase and to knock at the door of the Lord High Chancellor, and humble himself there under the forms of law.

PERSIUS: And he could have died after that, if he wanted to!

BATA: And where, where, I should like to know are we to have any restitution for the offense against justice . . . ?

ERZI: (*Almost smiling, absently.*) But it's Time, my dear friends, it is Time that repairs all insults, and obliterates all scars. And besides, in this case, since Nature has looked after Croz already, the only thing that remains for us to do is to compensate Vanan for our unjust suspicions by conferring some high distinction on him . . . and also to nominate a new President. And I have a fancy that at this minute the High Council is nominating . . . you, Cust. The news should be here any minute now. I congratulate you, Vanan. And you, Cust.

CUST: (*Staring before him with wide-open eyes.*) The Council will nominate me President of this Court?

ERZI: (*Lightly and genially.*) It's highly probable. The desk behind which, from now onwards, you will cultivate your penetrating thoughts will be very imposing and monumental.

CUST: Have you finished your inquiries?

ERZI: Their goal has been reached, and besides things are hurrying on, everything is moving forward. The stone drops to the bottom, the water becomes calm once more. Croz is dead, Ludvi-Pol is dead. And they're not the only ones. The town is already turning to other things. . . .

CUST: (*Almost to himself, pointing to the archives.*) . . . Every trace of the crime gone . . .

ERZI: (*Good-humoredly, jesting.*) . . . Our good Vanan is at peace with God, the tempest calmed . . . in a few moments workmen will lower a number of levers and the lights will be extinguished; and while dawn quickens over life's enchanting lake, now once more blue and peaceful, we shall go home to bed, certain that the affairs of this court . . . (*Turning to* CUST.) . . . are once more in good hands.

BATA: (*Precipitating himself towards* CUST *with hand outstretched.*) Let me say, my dear Cust, that we're all proud and honored by this nomination. I am sure there can be no doubt about it! Are you glad?

CUST: (*Absently, nodding.*) Very glad.

BATA: You'll be able to have a holiday now, won't you?

CUST: Yes, I could do with one. A holiday.

BATA: Well, goodbye for the present, my dear fellow. (*He goes out.*)

MAVERI: (*Promptly.*) What is it, are you still a bit worried? No, no, don't worry, the nomination's certain. Well, so long. (*He goes out.*)

PERSIUS: (*Promptly.*) Today you will reach the goal for which you have spent the best years of your life.

CUST: Yes, my whole life has been directed towards this moment.

PERSIUS: (*Watching him.*) You will wait here for the news?

CUST: (*Absently.*) Yes. Yes.

PERSIUS: Goodbye then. Till tomorrow. (*He goes out after colleagues.*)

CUST: (*Suddenly.*) The stone dropping to the bottom . . . the lake becoming calm again . . . My God, Erzi! That image of yours . . .

ERZI: Is it that that's worrying you?

CUST: It's not that I'm worried . . . but I should like . . . (*With sudden anguish.*) . . . to be able to understand; otherwise . . . It's difficult to rest. (*Suddenly pleading.*) And God knows I have need of that . . .

MALGAI: (*Coming forward in his turn.*) You're a bit exhausted, sir. A little rest and you'll be back in your old form again, quite recovered, Mr. . . . President! We can say that now, can't we? (*He goes out.*)

CUST: (*In a low voice.*) But I *am* recovered. (*He raises his hand, and rubs it with the familiar gesture.*) Look, for some

days past I've kept wanting to do this. *I* have. I like it, it keeps me company. But now I'm beginning to forget to. Hours go by and I forget to do it. (*To* ERZI, *breathing heavily.*) No, it's not that I'm worried, but certainly . . . there is something . . . that doesn't . . . (*With a cry.*) doesn't fit, do you understand? (*Suddenly turning round.*) Vanan! It's you who frighten me. When I look at you I feel that underneath this building, underneath you and me, a black gulf is opening!

ERZI: (*His voice unexpectedly loud and severe.*) What's the matter, Cust? What's the matter?

CUST: (*Frantically.*) Vanan, the matter is the blood-stained face of your daughter! I can't find a single explanation on earth for that.

VANAN: My daughter died when she was a little girl . . . my daughter died when she was a little girl . . . it's so very long ago now . . .

CUST: (*As before.*) Vanan, suppose she . . . wanted to die . . . ? Suppose that was the terrible thing that happened? Suppose she threw herself down?

VANAN: (*Muttering.*) You liar. You reptile. My poor Elena died when she was a little girl.

CUST: (*With a cry.*) Vanan, I fear . . . that when she shouted . . . she was asking something! Is it possible that no one heard? That no one answered? That that has not been inscribed on any register? That such an enormous question should remain unsolved?

ERZI: (*Suddenly, with sombre intensity.*) Cust, I don't think that a man should be more stubborn than his little powers allow him to be! Administration: that is a human fact, its task is to smooth things out, not to dig things up, and turn them upside down! Nature: she heals her wounds so rapidly that perhaps the real truth is something else: that she is unaware of them. (*Dropping his voice.*) And after all, if we want to talk about God . . .

VANAN: (*Suddenly interrupting, and then slowly making his way to the door.*) . . . God is so good. He forgives. He forgets. And we too shall forget, in His blessedness. (*He goes out, supported by the* NURSE.)

ERZI: You are left alone to think about these things, Cust. You alone.

CUST: (*Almost to himself.*) I alone. I alone. I alone. And when I too shall have turned my back and gone away . . .

ERZI: . . . what was done and what was left undone will all be the same.

(*The* POLICE OFFICIAL *enters and hands* ERZI *a paper.* ERZI *looks at it.*)

(*With a cry.*) Cust! The Council . . . has nominated you! You've won. (*Approaching him, with sombre pity.*) Poor Cust, you've almost changed in appearance during these last few days. In a short time you will have forgotten, exactly as Vanan has. The season granted to us is so brief, don't disturb it with your cries! Don't be stubborn. (*He points upwards.*) The Lord High Chancellor himself is happy that matters have been mended. He is very old; he is probably napping at the moment on his table. Pointless to go and disturb him. (*Moving towards the*

door.) Good-by, Cust, let the world roll on. That is mankind's job.

(*He goes out followed by the* OFFICIAL. *A silence.* MALGAI *reappears and begins putting out the lights one by one, preparing to close the place up and go away.*)

MALGAI: (*Moved by curiosity, and with rough kindliness.*) You are all alone, Mr. President. Aren't you going home?

CUST: Yes. I shall go now as well. (*He goes slowly towards the corridor entrance; and suddenly stops. The room is almost dark.*)

MALGAI: (*Worried.*) What's the matter? What are you waiting for?

CUST: (*His teeth are chattering slightly: he turns back.*) Because there is no argument on earth that would let me shut my eyes in peace tonight. I shall have to wake the Lord High Chancellor. I must confess the truth to him.

MALGAI: Shall I come with you, Mr. President?

CUST: No. I'm a bit frightened. But I know there is no one who can help me.

(*He makes his way to the door which leads to the office of the Lord High Chancellor, and which has hitherto remained unopened. He throws the door open. Beyond it a long staircase is revealed going upwards;* CUST *begins to make his way up the stairs, very slowly, as* CURTAIN)

SELECT BIBLIOGRAPHY

BOOKS: CRITICAL STUDIES

Abel, Lionel. *Metatheatre: A New View of Dramatic Form.* New York, 1963.

Barrett, William. *Irrational Man.* New York, 1958

Bowers, Fredson Thayer. *Elizabethan Revenge Tragedy, 1587-1642.* Princeton, 1940.

Bradbrook, M. C. *Themes and Conventions of Elizabethan Tragedy.* Cambridge, 1935.

Bradley, A. C. *Shakespearean Tragedy.* New York, 1955.

Brustein, Robert. *The Theatre of Revolt: An Approach to the Modern Drama.* Boston, 1962.

Else, Gerald F. *Aristotle's Poetics: The Argument.* Cambridge, Mass., 1957.

Esslin, Martin. *The Theatre of the Absurd.* Garden City, New York, 1961.

Fergusson, Francis. *The Human Image in Dramatic Literature.* New York, 1957

————. *The Idea of a Theater.* Princeton, 1949; New York, 1953.

Freedman, Morris. *The Moral Impulse. Modern Drama from Ibsen to the Present.* Carbondale and Edwardsville, 1967.

Henn, T. R. *The Harvest of Tragedy.* New York, 1966.

Jaspers, Karl. *Tragedy is Not Enough.* Boston, 1952.

Kerr, Walter. *Tragedy and Comedy.* New York, 1967.

Kitto, H. D. F. *Greek Tragedy: A Literary Study.* Garden City, New York, 1954.

Leech, Clifford. *Shakespeare's Tragedies and Other Studies in Seventeenth-Century Drama.* London, 1950.

Lucas, F. L. *Tragedy. Serious Drama in Relation to Aristotle's Poetics.* Rev. ed. New York, 1962.

Mandel, Oscar. *A Definition of Tragedy.* New York, 1961.

Muller, Herbert. *The Spirit of Tragedy.* New York, 1956.

Myers, Henry A. *Tragedy: A View of Life.* Ithaca, New York, 1956.

Niebuhr, Reinhold. *Beyond Tragedy.* New York, 1938.

Prior, Moody. *The Language of Tragedy.* New York, 1947.

Raphael, D. D. *The Paradox of Tragedy.* Bloomington, Indiana, 1960.

Scott, Nathan. *The Tragic Vision and the Christian Faith.* New York, 1957.

Sewall, Richard B. *The Vision of Tragedy.* New Haven and London, 1962.

Spingarn, J. E. *A History of Literary Criticism in the Renaissance.* 2nd ed. New York, 1930.

Steiner, George. *The Death of Tragedy.* New York, 1963

Unamuno, Miguel de. *The Tragic Sense of Life.* New York, 1954.

Weisinger, Herbert. *Tragedy and the Paradox of the Fortunate Fall.* East Lansing, Mich., 1953.

Wheelwright, Philip. *The Burning Fountain.* Bloomington, Ind., 1954.

COLLECTIONS OF CRITICAL ESSAYS

Aristotle's Poetics and English Literature, ed. Elder Olson. Chicago, 1965.

Essays in the Modern Drama, ed. Morris Freedman. Boston, 1964.

Modern Drama, ed. Travis Bogard and William I. Oliver. Berkeley, 1965.

Moderns on Tragedy, ed. and with an Introduction by Lionel Abel. New York, 1967.

Tragedy: Modern Essays in Criticism, ed. Laurence Michel and Richard B. Sewall. Englewood Cliffs, N. J., 1963.

Tragic Themes in Western Literature, ed. and with an Introduction by Cleanth Brooks. New Haven and London, 1955.

Tragedy: Vision and Form, ed. Robert W. Corrigan. San Francisco, 1965.

COLLECTIONS OF PLAYS (with critical introductions, notes, and essays).

Elizabethan and Jacobean Tragedy: An Anthology, ed. Robert Ornstein and Hazelton Spencer, Boston, 1964.

The Idea of Tragedy, ed. Carl Benson and Taylor Littleton. Glenview, Illinois, 1966.

Masters of Modern Drama, ed. and with an Introduction by Haskell M. Block and Robert G. Shedd. New York, 1962.

The Modern Theatre, ed. Robert W. Corrigan. New York, 1964.

Ten Greek Plays in Contemporary Translations, ed. and with an Introduction by L. R. Lind. Boston, 1957.

Tragedy: Plays, Theory, and Criticism, ed. Richard Levin. New York, 1960; alternate edition, 1965.